Library of
Davidson College

THE PRESIDENTIAL CONSTITUTION OF NIGERIA

Dedicated to
Chief F.R.A. Williams

B.O. NWABUEZE

THE PRESIDENTIAL CONSTITUTION OF NIGERIA

ST. MARTIN'S PRESS · NEW YORK

© 1982 B. O. Nwabueze
All rights reserved.   For information, write:
St Martin's Press, Inc., 175 Fifth Avenue, New York, NY 10010
Printed in Great Britain
First published in the United States of America in 1982
ISBN 0-312-64032-3
Library of Congress Catalog Card no. 82-47637

PREFACE

The adoption by Nigeria of a presidential system of government, on the model of the American, is an important milestone in the constitutional history of the country. It was an act of great courage. It involved abandoning the heritage of the Westminster system. By it the country took, as it were, a leap from the known to the unknown. The aim of this book is both to supply the necessary knowledge of the 1979 Constitution and its workings, and to provide insight into the general principles of the presidential system of government as contained in it. The supremacy of the law of the Constitution, the division of powers between two autonomous tiers of government, the executive presidency, separation of powers, participatory democracy, the constitutional guarantee of rights, judicial enforcement of constitutional limitations, and the responsibility of government for the wellbeing of the people — all these are analysed in great detail in the book.

These general principles of presidentialism, originating in the Constitution of the United States of America, have been adopted with substantial modifications designed to suit the circumstances of Nigeria. The central principle of presidentialism is that of an executive of one man in whom the entire executive authority is vested. Under the Nigerian Constitution 1979, that principle is substantially modified by constitutional limitations imposed on the president's executive power in favour of other functionaries of government. Not only is the president's executive power limited by the powers vested in other independent executive bodies, but the exercise of such powers as are left with him is restrained by the Constitution in a variety of ways. Restraints on the exercise of presidential power, aimed at minimising arbitrariness and abuse by the president, are a much more conspicuous feature of the presidency under the Nigerian Constitution than they are under the American. The presidency under the Nigerian Constitution has been described in the text as a consultative one because of the obligation laid on the president to consult with various executive bodies in the exercise of his powers — a national defence council on the defence of the sovereignty and territorial integrity of the federation; a national economic council on economic affairs; a national population commission on population problems; a council of state on the census, prerogative of mercy, award of national honours, and, when so requested, the maintenance of public order and any other matters; and an executive council on the determination of general policy, co-ordination of activities of government and the discharge of his functions generally other than those functions with respect to which he is to seek the advice or act on the recommendation of some other body or person. The

Nigerian Constitution differs from the American in numerous other important respects. These differences are discussed in detail in the book.

The twenty-nine chapters of the book can be grouped into six parts. There is the general part dealing with topics of a general nature — the nature of the Constitution and its rationale, federalism and the division of powers. Then there is the part dealing with the executive — the nature of the executive presidency, executive power and its extent, limitations on the president's executive power in favour of other executive functionaries and agencies, constitutional restraints on the exercise of executive power by the president, the relation of executive power to legislative and judicial power, the role of the president in legislation, and election and tenure of the president. The national assembly — its composition, proceedings and functions and the limits of its powers — form another part. The judicature, covering four chapters, forms another separate part wherein are discussed the organisation of judicial power and of courts, constitutional safeguards for the independence of the judiciary, principles of judicial review of the constitutionality of legislative and executive acts, constitutional remedies for justiciable violations of the Constitution, and the place of judicial review in democratic government. Fundamental rights, as guaranteed in the Constitution, occupy a prominent place in the book, covering seven chapters. The detailed discussion of the subject is altogether appropriate to its importance in a democracy. The two chapters on public service and citizenship, together with the concluding chapter on the subject of a national ethic, do not fit into any broad categorisation.

This, then, is the general scheme of the book. It attempts a fairly comprehensive coverage — from an analysis of the nature and general principles of the Constitution to a discussion of the organs of government, and their relationship *inter se* and with the individual.

The message of the book is in the final chapter. Democracy does not consist mainly of constitutional prescriptions about government and limitations on its power. It is constituted more by national habits, traditions and conventions which condition the attitudes of both the rulers and the governed within a polity, and therefore delimit the parameters of permissible political behaviour. It is this — the creation of a national ethic, more than the formal specifications of the Constitution with its nicely balanced structures and powers — that determines its success or failure. The 1979 Constitution of Nigeria is a fine document, suitably adapted to the peculiarities of the Nigerian history and character, but it has to be operated by individuals.

The discussion of the executive and legislature focuses on the federal government. The state governments are organised on much the same principles. The omission of discussion of the executive and legislative organs of the state governments is intended to avoid repetitiveness which would have burdened the book without adding any extra illumination. Except for one or two important differences, such as the unicameral character of the state legislatures, and the complete emptiness of the position of deputy governor compared with that of the vice-president, what is said in the book on the federal executive and legislature applies, *mutatis mutandis*, to the state executive and legislature.

Since the book was printed, the supreme court of Nigeria has handed down its decision in the celebrated Revenue Allocation Case (1981), which confirms the position taken in the text (pp. 217–19) that a money bill cannot be 'passed' by a joint committee of the national assembly any more than a non-money bill can. There must be reference back to the assembly in the one case as in the other. The decision also rejects the view established in certain decisions of the U.S. supreme court that the courts cannot go behind a duly authenticated and enrolled statute to enquire whether it was passed in the manner and form prescribed by the Constitution (pp. 288–92). Happily, too, the decision endorses the view expressed in the text (pp. 334–5) that the doctrine of waiver should have no application in the field of constitutional law. The judgment of the supreme court in the case constitutes a momentous landmark in the judicial history of Nigeria.

I wish now to acknowledge the generous assistance of my colleague, Felix Akpe, in correcting the proofs with the keen and scrupulous eye of a purist, which he is. Again I have derived enormous assistance from the collaboration of my friend and publisher, Christopher Hurst, another purist and perfectionist. The responsibility for any mistakes is solely mine. To my Secretary, Mr Fakola, who typed the entire manuscript with his usual patience and efficiency, I owe more than I can acknowledge. My wife has endured my silences and neglect.

Lagos BEN O. NWABUEZE
October 1981

CONTENTS

Preface *page* v

Chapters

1. NATURE OF THE CONSTITUTION

1. Source of the Constitution's authority — 1
2. The Constitution as law as well as a political charter: The question of its justiciability. — 7
3. Relation of the Constitution to the legislature: supremacy of the Constitution — 12
   (i) *Manner and form for ordinary law-making* — 12
   (ii) *Amendment of the Constitution* — 13
   (iii) *Supremacy of the Constitution and the sovereignty of the legislature.* — 16

2. THE RATIONALE OF THE 1979 CONSTITUTION FOR NIGERIA

1. The Constitution and the fundamental objectives of the nation — 18
2. Factors and ideas underlying the organisation of government and its powers and responsibilities under the Constitution — 20
   (i) *The need for principle and probity in government and politics* — 20
   (ii) *The centrality of man's humanity* — 24
   (iii) *National unity and stability* — 25
   (iv) *Need for effective government* — 27
   (v) *Need for economic development* — 29
   (vi) *Need for limitations on government* — 30

3. FEDERALISM

1. Governments rather than geographical entities or peoples as the basis of the federal arrangement — 37
2. Separateness and independence of each government — 39
3. The question of equality as between the regional governments — 42
4. Number of regional governments between whom a federal arrangement can meaningfully exist — 44
5. Techniques for the division of powers — 45

6.	Underlying objectives of the federal arrangement	46
7.	Constitutional forms	48

4. DIVISION OF POWERS UNDER THE CONSTITUTION

1.	Scheme of division	53
	(i) *Existing laws*	55
	(ii) *Federal capital territory*	56
2.	Extent of federal powers	57
	(i) *Public order and public safety*	57
	(ii) *Local government*	58
	(iii) *Economic activities*	61
	(iv) *Public revenue: its sources, collection, allocation and expenditure*	64
	(v) *Emergency*	68
	(vi) *Incidental and supplementary powers*	70

5. THE EXECUTIVE PRESIDENCY

1.	The president as representing the state	76
2.	The president as chief executive of the government	84

6. EXECUTIVE POWER AND ITS EXTENT

1.	Constitutional bases of the president's executive power	88
2.	Execution of the laws made by the national assembly	89
3.	Execution and maintenance of the Constitution	90
	(i) *Execution of the government and its functions*	91
	(ii) *Protection of the instrumentalities of government and of its property*	93
	(iii) *Preservation of the government and the nation*	95
4.	Extra-constitutional determinants of presidential power	102

7. LIMITATIONS ON THE PRESIDENT'S EXECUTIVE POWER IN FAVOUR OF OTHER EXECUTIVE FUNCTIONARIES AND AGENCIES

1.	Relation to the vice-president	111
2.	Relation to ministers individually and collectively as a council	114
3.	Relation to the ministries or departments and their staff	120
4.	Relation to the police force and the Nigerian security organisation	125

5.	Relation to the armed forces	128
6.	Relation to other executive bodies established by the Constitution	129
7.	Establishment of public offices outside the civil service, police and armed forces and appointments thereto.	132

8. CONSTITUTIONAL RESTRAINTS ON THE EXERCISE OF EXECUTIVE POWER BY THE PRESIDENT — 136

1. Checks and balances — 137
   - (i) *Approval for presidential action* — 137
   - (ii) *Inquisition into the president's administration* — 141
   - (iii) *Impeachment* — 141
2. Obligation to consult or to seek advice from various bodies — 144
3. Other constitutional restraints on the exercise of power by the president — 151
   - (i) *Proclamation of an emergency* — 151
   - (ii) *Appointments* — 152
   - (iii) *Conduct of government generally* — 153

9. RELATION OF EXECUTIVE TO LEGISLATURE AND JUDICATURE

1. Separateness and independence of the executive — 156
   - (i) *Independence of the president as regards his election and tenure of office* — 157
   - (ii) *Constitutional vesting of executive power in the president* — 158
   - (iii) *Independence of the executive in relation to the courts* — 163
2. Limits of the independence of the executive — 163

10. THE ROLE OF THE PRESIDENT IN LEGISLATION

1. Exclusion of the president in the vesting of legislative power — 168
   - (i) *Regulations relating to citizenship* — 170
   - (ii) *Adaptive legislation* — 171
2. Delegated legislation — 173
3. Emergency legislation by the president under the doctrine of state necessity — 180
4. Initiation of proposals for legislation — 183
5. The enacting process — 187

11. ELECTION AND TENURE OF OFFICE OF THE PRESIDENT

1. Election — 190
   (i) Qualifications and disqualifications — 190
   (ii) Method of election — 190
   (iii) Criterion for territorial acceptability — 193
2. Tenure — 201

12. THE NATIONAL ASSEMBLY

1. A bicameral assembly and relations between the two houses — 205
2. Membership — 207
   (i) Election of members — 208
   (ii) Disqualifications — 210
   (iii) Tenure — 211
   (iv) Determination of questions as to membership — 212
3. Life and sittings of the national assembly — 212
4. Proceedings of the houses — 214
   (i) Presiding at sittings — 214
   (ii) Clerk and other staff of the national assembly — 215
   (iii) Quorum — 216
   (iv) Language — 216
   (v) Voting — 216
   (vi) Procedure for making law — 217
   (vii) The committee system — 221
5. Powers, privileges and immunities of the national assembly and its members — 223
   (i) Privilege of freedom of speech, debate and proceedings — 223
   (ii) Immunity from process — 224
   (iii) Right of each house to regulate its own constitution — 225
   (iv) Contempt — 226
   (v) Punishment for contempts — 228

13. FUNCTIONS OF THE NATIONAL ASSEMBLY

1. Classification of functions — 232
2. Matters that may be determined by resolution or simple approval — 233
3. Legislation — 235
   (i) Extent of the legislative power of the national assembly — 235

	(ii)	Enactment of legislative proposals into law or their rejection	236
	(iii)	Role and importance of legislation in modern government	239
4.		The general critical and scrutinising function	243

14. LIMITS OF THE LEGISLATIVE POWER

1.	Constitutional guarantee of rights	250
2.	Separation of judicial from legislative power	255
	(i) *Legislation directed against named persons or associations*	256
	(ii) *Vesting of judicial power in persons or authorities other than the court*	262
3.	Preclusion of the vesting of non-judicial functions in the courts	264
4.	The prohibition of retrospective criminal legislation	271
5.	The prohibition of ouster of the court's jurisdiction	273

15. PRESUMPTION OF CONSTITUTIONALITY OF LEGISLATION

1.	Nature of the presumption	281
2.	Application of the presumption	284
3.	Presumption of the regularity of legislative process	288

16. THE JUDICATURE

1.	Organisation of judicial power and of courts	294
	(i) *Extent of federal judicial power*	294
	(ii) *Federal courts*	295
	(iii) *Jurisdiction of state courts to exercise federal judicial power*	299
	(iv) *Jurisdiction of federal courts to exercise state judicial power*	300
	(v) *Composition of the courts*	300
2.	Constitutional safeguards for the independence of the judiciary	301
	(i) *Appointment*	302
	(ii) *Removal*	306
	(iii) *Appointment, dismissal and disciplinary control of magistrates, judges and members of area courts and customary courts*	307
	(iv) *Other constitutional guarantees of judicial independence*	307

17. JUDICIAL REVIEW OF THE CONSTITUTIONALITY OF LEGISLATIVE AND EXECUTIVE ACTS

1. Dimensions of judicial review — 309
2. Jurisdiction of the court to review the constitutionality of legislative and executive acts — 310
3. Conditions for the exercise of the jurisdiction — 314
   (i) *Lack of initiative* — 314
   (ii) *Adversary litigation between individual parties as the context of the court's role in government* — 314
   (iii) *The nature of litigants' interest required for invocation of the court's intervention in constitutional cases* — 316
4. A policy of avoidance — 332

18. CONSTITUTIONAL REMEDIES FOR JUSTICIABLE VIOLATIONS OF THE CONSTITUTION

1. The constitutional basis of the right to relief for justiciable violations of the Constitution — 342
   (i) *Declaratory relief* — 344
   (ii) *Injunction* — 351
2. Constitutional remedies for the enforcement of the bill of rights — 353
3. Constitutional remedies relating to elections and membership of legislative houses — 356

19. JUDICIAL REVIEW AND DEMOCRATIC GOVERNMENT

1. The checking function of judicial review — 363
2. The legitimating function of judicial review — 369

20. PUBLIC SERVICE

1. Public service defined — 374
2. Structure of the public service — 378
   (i) *Civil service* — 379
   (ii) *Constitutional commissions* — 380
   (iii) *The disciplined forces* — 380
   (iv) *Statutory corporations* — 381
3. Obligations and duties of public service — 382
4. Restrictions, disqualifications and disabilities — 383
   (i) *Political neutrality* — 383

(ii) Ban on private business or receipt of multiple emolument	388
(iii) Prohibition of corruption	389
(iv) Declaration of assets	390
(v) Disqualification with respect to elective offices	391
5. Sanctions and enforcement procedures	391
(i) Investigatory or inquisitorial proceedings	391
(ii) Trials	394
(iii) Punishments, disciplinary penalties and remedial actions	394

21. CITIZENSHIP

1. The categories of citizenship	397
(i) Citizens by birth	397
(ii) Citizens by registration	399
(iii) Citizens by naturalisation	400
2. Loss of citizenship	400
3. Status of citizens and aliens distinguished	401
(i) Entry	402
(ii) Restriction on residence, movement, etc.	402
(iii) Deportation	404
(iv) Extradition	404
(v) Diplomatic immunity	405

22. RIGHT TO LIFE AND DIGNITY OF THE HUMAN PERSON

1. The constitutional guarantee	409
2. Constitutionality of the death penalty	411

23. PERSONAL LIBERTY

1. The constitutional guarantee	420
2. Arrest	422
3. Detention	425
(i) Detention in connection with the commission of a criminal offence	425
(ii) Preventive detention	426
(iii) Detention pursuant to conviction and sentence by a court for a criminal offence	429

24. CONSTITUTIONAL SAFEGUARDS FOR TRIAL IN CRIMINAL CASES

1. Trial must be for an existing offence defined in written law — 431
2. Prompt notification of charge — 433
3. An accused person must be given adequate time and facilities for the preparation of his defence — 433
4. A person charged with a criminal offence must be tried within a reasonable time — 436
5. Trial must be in public — 438
6. Accused is presumed innocent until proved guilty — 439
7. Accused must be given a fair hearing at the trial — 441
8. Accused must not be compelled to give evidence at the trial — 442
9. Court must keep record of proceedings and furnish a copy of judgment to accused — 444
10. A person convicted or acquitted of or pardoned for an offence shall not be tried again for the same offence — 444

25. FREEDOM FROM DISCRIMINATION

1. The constitutional guarantee — 452
2. Equality as a fundamental objective and principle of state policy — 455

26. FREEDOM OF SPEECH AND THE PRESS

1. The preferred position of speech and the press — 457
2. Press freedom defined — 460
3. Guarantee of freedom of speech and press in the Constitution — 465
4. Freedom of expression and the state's regulatory authority — 467
   (i) *Freedom from censorship* — 468
   (ii) *Freedom from subsequent proscription or ban of publication or distribution* — 471
   (iii) *Freedom from unreasonable punishment for what is said or published* — 473
5. Nigerian courts and the enforcement of the constitutional guarantee of freedom of speech and the press — 478

Contents

27. **FREEDOM OF ASSOCIATION**
    1. The constitutional guarantee — 483
    2. Rights secured by the constitutional guarantee — 484
    3. State control of freedom of association and assembly — 489
        (i) *Membership and participation* — 490
        (ii) *Licensing and registration of associations* — 495
        (iii) *Public meetings and processions in streets or other public places* — 496
    4. State control of political parties — 501
    5. State control of trade unions — 505

28. **FREEDOM OF PRIVATE ENTERPRISE**
    1. Freedom of private enterprise defined — 517
    2. Extent of freedom of private enterprise under the Constitution — 518
        (i) *Freedom of private enterprise under the bill of rights* — 519
        (ii) *Freedom of private enterprise and the directive principles of state policy* — 530
        (iii) *The non-justiciability of the fundamental objectives and directive principles* — 534

29. **PROSPECTS FOR THE FUTURE: A NATIONAL ETHIC** — 539

    Index — 551

1
NATURE OF THE CONSTITUTION

The nature of a constitution is determined essentially by the source of its authority, i.e. whether or not it is an original act of people, and, secondly, by the justiciability of its provisions, i.e. whether it is a law enforceable in the court or merely a political charter of government unamenable to judicial enforcement.

1. *Source of the Constitution's authority*

A constitution is an act of the people if it is made by them either directly in a referendum or through a convention or constituent assembly popularly elected for this specific purpose, subject or not to formal ratification by the people in a referendum. The making of a constitution in this context refers to the act by which its substantive content, particularly the system of government, and the relations of governmental structures *inter se* and with the individual, is determined and adopted, rather than the formal act of promulgation. If the substantive content of a constitution is freely agreed and adopted by the people either in a referendum or through a constituent assembly popularly elected for the purpose, then it is their act, although promulgation may, in the interest of formalism and regularity, have been done by an existing state authority. Promulgation in this context is a purely formal act, which should not detract from the popular will.

But adoption in a referendum or by a constituent assembly, in order to be a genuine reflection of the popular will, needs to be preceded, at the drafting stage or after, by serious discussion on as wide a platform as possible of the constitutional proposals. Since a constituent assembly can reflect the popular will only in an approximate sense, it is necessary that its mandate in this respect should be specifically conferred through an election specially organised for that purpose and at which the people are made clearly to understand that they are voting to authorise the adoption on their behalf of a constitution. Whatever its symbolic advantage may be, any process by which an existing legislative assembly, without prior popular mandate, resolves itself into a constituent assembly for the purpose of enacting a constitution is not a genuine reflection of the popular will simply because its mandate is limited to law-making according to the existing constitution. Such a process is both hypocritical and disingenuous. The position is no different from what it would be if the assembly in its normal capacity just assumed the power without going through the meaningless formality of first resolving itself into a constituent assembly, on the ground that thereby 'the dignity and importance of the proceedings would be enhanced'.[1]

In the light of this, whether Nigeria's new Constitution is an original act of the people or an act of the federal military government is very much a matter for argument. The Constitution was not adopted by the people in a referendum. There has been a constituent assembly established by a decree in 1977, with 230 members, of whom twenty were appointed by the federal military government and seven were the chairman of the constitution drafting committee and the chairmen of its six sub-committees.[2] (There were a chairman and a deputy chairman appointed by the government but without a vote either original or casting.) The remaining 203 members were elected, not directly by the people but by the local councils acting as electoral colleges. Clearly a constituent assembly elected in this way could not claim to have the mandate of the people to adopt a constitution on their behalf. The local government councils had no such mandate themselves and could not confer it on the constituent assembly which, being at one remove from the people, is indeed, as regards reflecting the popular will, in a position inferior to that of a national assembly which constitutes itself into a constituent assembly without a prior popular mandate. Besides, the composition of the local government councils had not been fully democratic. Election in many cases was by indirect method or by selection by village or family heads, while in some places traditional members were brought in by nomination.

There is next the question of the legal power, as distinct from the popular mandate, of the constituent assembly established in 1977 to adopt the Constitution. Its constituent statute defined its role as being to 'deliberate upon the draft Constitution of the Federal Republic of Nigeria drawn up by the Constitution Drafting Committee appointed by the Federal Military Government'.[3] There would seem to be implied in this provision a suggestion that the assembly had no power to decide the substantive content of the Constitution, or, if it had, that its decisions would only be by way of recommendation, which might be accepted or rejected by the federal military government. The assembly was certainly not a mere deliberative body, with no power to take decisions on the form and content of the Constitution. The draft Constitution was presented to it in the form of a bill, and its proceedings on it were, by the terms of the governing statute, to be conducted in accordance with prescribed regulations which clearly required that it should take decisions on the form and content of the Constitution following a procedure of first and second readings and detailed consideration in a committee of the whole assembly.[4] And the procedure left the assembly pretty ample scope for meaningful choice. The proposals contained in the draft constitution bill presented to it, being those of a committee of forty-nine independent people chosen for their specialist knowledge or background, did not carry the somewhat inhibiting force of government proposals. More important, the procedure did not preclude departure from these proposals. An amendment seeking to replace the presidential system proposed in the draft bill with a parliamentary system of cabinet government was in fact vigorously urged upon the assembly in two different forms and lost.[5]

But the really critical point, which nearly created a stalemate between the assembly and the federal military government, was whether the decisions of the assembly were to have finality or be open to change by the supreme military council. The threatened stalemate was averted by a verbal assurance of non-interference by the federal military government with the decisions of the assembly. This assurance was however not kept, and the government, in enacting the decisions of the assembly into law, made a considerable number of amendments to them. The mere fact of a substantive amendment, as distinct from a purely formal one, seems, irrespective of its nature or importance, to have further eroded the basis of the Constitution as an original act of the people. And, while the form and structures of the government have remained as they were approved by the constituent assembly, the changes resulting from the amendments are in many cases of far-reaching significance. Such are the amendments radically limiting the guarantee of property rights; abolishing the quota system in the composition of the officer corps of the armed forces; attenuating the procedure for the removal of judges; removing the disqualification imposed on candidates for the first election who had been found guilty of corruption, unjust enrichment or abuse of office by a tribunal of enquiry since October 1960; incorporating into the Constitution the provisions of the decrees of the military government on land use, public complaints, national security organisation, and the national youth corp service; prohibiting designated public officers from having foreign accounts, and so on.

There is a conceptual argument as to whether the people, acting either in a referendum or through a constituent assembly specially elected for the purpose, are legally competent to adopt a constitution and bestow validity upon it as law. The argument is that law-making is a function *only* of a political community, and not of the people in their mass; and that only a people organised as a political community can enact law through the machinery of the state. On this hypothesis, while the power of the people in their mass to constitute themselves into a political community is admitted, any such constituent act by which a constitution is established is purely a *political* act, giving the constitution only a political existence, as distinct from a legal one. If it is intended that the constitution should also be a law, then it is for the resultant political creation, the state, to enact it as such through its regular procedure for law-making.

The argument smacks of excessive formalism. If the state is a creation of the people by means of a constitution, and derives its power of law-making from them, it may be wondered why the people who constitute and grant this power cannot act directly, in a referendum or otherwise, to give the constitution the character and force of law. After all, the constitution, being the starting-point of a country's legal order, its 'lawness' should not depend upon its enactment through the law-making mechanism of the state, but rather upon its recognition as such by the people to be governed by it.

The United States Constitution, as a law 'ordained and established' by the people, is said to have broken with 'the dominant tradition',[6] which is sought to be reconciled by asserting that 'the agency by which constitutions are nowadays drawn up, namely constitutional conventions, had become such usual phenomena as to have been substantially assimilated to the machinery of organised government, so that one looking back to the State conventions that had in 1787 ratified the Constitution found it natural to regard them as organs of existing political societies, rather than as directly representative of the individuals back of these societies.'[7]

It is today generally accepted that the American Constitution 'obtains its entire force and efficacy, not from the fact that it was ratified by a pre-existent political community or communities — for it was not — but from the fact that it was established by the people to be governed by it.'[8] There can be no doubt that today a referendum or plebiscite is a legally accepted way of adopting a constitution, although adherence to formalism still sometimes requires that, after adoption by the people, the constitution should be *formally* promulgated by a pre-existing state authority, usually the Head of State.

Need for a Constitution to be adopted by the people. The need for a constitution to be adopted by the people lies, first, in its bearing on the legitimacy of the constitution. A constitution is no less a constitution because it is an act of a colonial power or of the local legislature, but its moral authority, that is to say its legitimacy, is another matter. The legitimacy of a constitution is concerned with how to make it command the loyalty, obedience and confidence of the people. It cannot be disputed that a major cause of the collapse of constitutional government in many of the new states has been the general lack of respect for the constitution among the populace and even among the politicians themselves. The state itself is an alien, if also a beneficial creation; its existence is characterised by a certain artificiality in the eyes of the people, and it is remote from their lives and thought. The constitution embodies ideas that are not part of the native cultural heritage of the people, ideas originating in Roman law and Greek philosophy, but which by a process of assimilation have become a common heritage of the whole of Europe but certainly not of Africa. It is not of course suggested as a condition for the legitimacy of a system of government that it must be the product of a traditional culture and philosophy; if that were so, no modern system of government could ever have legitimacy in most of the emergent countries whose traditional cultural systems have yielded little that is relevant to the organisation of the central government of a modern complex society. Yet the alien character of the system of government instituted by the constitutions of the new states and of the ideas underlying it made it necessary that something should have been done to legitimise them in the eyes of the people. What this means is that a constitution should be generally understood by the people and be acceptable to them. A constitution cannot hope to command the loyalty, respect and confidence of the people otherwise. And to achieve this understanding and acceptance, a constitution needs to be put through a process of popularisation, with a view to generating public interest in it and an attitude that everybody has a stake in it, that it is the common property of all. The people must be made to identify themselves with the constitution. Without this sense of identification, of attachment and involvement, a constitution would always remain remote and artificial, with less real existence than the paper on which it is written.

If the final act of adoption is that of the people, that may conceivably enhance the constitution's legitimacy by fostering among the people a feeling that the constitution is their own, and not an imposition by the government, and that they thus have a stake, a responsibility, in observing its rules. It would serve to give meaning and reality to the phrase 'We the people . . . do hereby make, enact and give to ourselves the following Constitution', which, since the adoption of the American Constitution in 1787, has become a familiar feature of modern republican constitutions.

Adoption of the constitution is also important as providing a rationale for the constitution's supremacy which does not rest merely on its logical priority in time, but on the superior authority of the people as the source and donor of all political power in the state. A constitution enacted by a pre-existing local legislature may be accorded supremacy, but its supremacy must rest, not on the superior authority of the legislature that enacted it over the one taking office under it, but simply on the fact that the constitution is logically prior to the organs of governments. If the government and its organs are created by the constitution, then logically they can have only such powers as are granted to them by the instrument from which they derive their existence. But a supremacy resting wholly upon the logical priority of the constitution is much too tenuous to bestow upon it maximum efficiency and respect. This accounts to some extent for the lack of respect for the constitution in the emergent states. Theory apart, a legislative assembly which enacted a constitution is not likely to treat its own creation as being above it. There would naturally be a greater inclination on its part to disregard the constitutional limitations than would be the case if it had been an original act of the people. On the part of the people too, the idea of a constitution enacted by the legislative assembly being supreme over its creator is hardly intelligible. To them, the constitution is on exactly the same level as any other law enacted by the legislature, and is entitled to no greater or special respect. And because of the general ignorance about its provisions and the lack of interest in them, its role as the basis for ordered social life is insufficiently appreciated, with the result that it is not generally considered as entitled to any greater obedience than other laws. It is the recognition of the constitution as a *superior* law that compels the greater obedience which people are prepared to give to it.

Lastly, insistence on the constitution being adopted by the people will serve to explode the misconception common among African leaders that the power to govern embraces power to enact a new constitution. As previously stated, a government has no more than a limited mandate to govern according to the constitution under which it took office. When a frame of government has been established, and a group of rulers is elected to govern under it, the right to change the system under a new constitution remains always with the people, just like the right to choose the rulers. It is a usurpation for any government to assume to exercise that right, without specific mandate from the people.

In the case of Nigeria, this usurpation or denial has gone on for a long time. Throughout the colonial period constituent power was the exclusive preserve of the suzerain power, jealously guarded to emphasise the force of its imperium, and so as to enable it to dictate the pace of constitutional advance. The independence constitution was the product of a final exercise of the power by the departing colonial authority. The adoption of a republican constitution in 1963 was decided upon entirely by the prime minister and the regional premiers who, meeting for just one day, agreed among themselves that a republican constitution should reproduce the 1960 imperial constitution with such amendments as would conform it to a republican status. That their meeting attracted public notice at all was due to its controversial decision to incorporate into the new constitution provisions for the preventive detention of persons without trial. Public discussion was confined to just this issue. Thereafter parliament proceeded to enact the proposals as agreed among the premiers, and, as was usual in that body, there was hardly any discussion of them.

The coup of 1966 was yet another act of usurpation of the people's constituent power, since its effect was to destroy the existing constitution, and to replace it with a new one, based on the authority of the coup-makers. The return to civilian rule in 1979 was thus an opportunity for the people of Nigeria to exercise for the first time their birthright to adopt a constitution for themselves. Lamentably, however, the opportunity was all but spoilt by the method adopted by the federal military government in constituting the constituent assembly and by its arrogation of the supreme power to amend in many significant respects the decisions of the assembly.

2. *The Constitution as law as well as a political charter: the question of its justiciability*

A constitution is a mode of organising a state and its government. It is, in other words, a body of fundamental principles according to which a state is organised. This emphasises its character as essentially a political act; its authority and sanction are primarily political. This was its original meaning and function. Even today this approach to the purpose and function of a constitution still has its adherents. There are many countries in the world, perhaps a majority, that still consider the appropriate function of a constitution to be that of a political charter of government, consisting largely of declarations of objectives or directive principles of government and a description of the organs of government in terms that import no enforceable legal restraints.

Such a constitution has no more than a political existence; its provisions are political, not legal, serving merely to exhort, to direct and inspire governmental action, and to bestow upon them the stamp of legitimacy. As Dicey wrote of the Constitution of the French third republic, 'the restrictions it placed on the action of the legislature are not in reality laws, since they are not rules which in the last resort will be enforced by the courts. Their true character is that of maxims of political morality, which derive whatever strength they possess from being formally inscribed in the constitution, and from the resulting support of public opinion.'[9] That has remained a feature of subsequent Constitutions of France and those of her former African dependencies.

The Soviet Union is yet another modern example of this kind of constitution. Although it has 146 articles which, somewhat in the fashion of the democratic constitutions of some Western countries, contain a guarantee of individual rights as well as procedures for the exercise of governmental functions, indeed a full paraphernalia of a seemingly regularised system of restraints, yet the language and tone of its provisions and the context of the entire document make it clear that no legally enforceable code of fundamental law is thereby established, and that the only authority the constitution is intended to have as well as its sanction is political, with no room at all for judicial enforcement. The so-called guarantee of rights in the constitution of the Soviet Union means no more than a declaration of objectives, a statement of what it is hoped the state will do for its citizens. No procedure for the enforcement of the rights either by the ordinary courts or otherwise is provided for.

The United States is said to have broken new ground in its attitude to the authority and function of a constitution. The notions of a constitution as law enforceable by the court, and of government under law, acquired a new, stirring dimension with the establishment of the U.S. Constitution in 1787. The idea was born and popularised of a constitution as a formal document having the force of law, by which a society organises a government for itself, defines and limits its power, and prescribes the relations of its various organs *inter se* and with the citizen. In contrast with the language and tone of the Soviet Constitution, the U.S. Constitution 'reads like law, its language is the spare legal language of command and prohibition, indistinguishable at most points in texture and tone from the language of ordinary statute law, it neither argues nor exhorts, but lays down, as law lays down, what is to be.' In the breadth and sweep of its language and in its avoidance of prolixity and technicality, however, it differs markedly from an ordinary statute.

The origin of this notion of the constitution as law lies, as James Thayer has said, in American colonial experience. The American colonies were governed under written charters of government, issued by the crown and enforceable by the courts with ultimate appeal to the privy council. 'These charters were in the strict sense written *law*: as their restraints upon the colonial legislatures were enforced by the English courts of last resort, so might they be enforced through the colonial courts, by disregarding as null what went counter to them.'[10] With independence, and the replacement of the English sovereign and his organised enforcement agencies by the people as sovereign, the 'old methods and old conceptions were followed.'[11]

Clearly the American notion of a constitution as law is an innovating and distinctive achievement. But the achievement of the U.S. Constitution of 1787 lies also in its fidelity to the basic nature of a constitution as a charter of government, different from a code of criminal, property or contract law; also in its recognition that, to provide a workable and flexible framework of government, its provisions though framed as legal commands should not all be of a justiciable character. A constitution operating as law and imposing judicially enforceable restraints upon government should not abandon its other function as a source of legitimacy for those political concepts and governmental powers and relations that are, by their very nature, non-justiciable. Nor should it renounce its role in the affirmation of fundamental objectives and ideals or directive principles of government which serve to inform and inspire governmental actions along desirable lines. It is in this combination of judicially enforceable restraints and the legitimation of needed non-justiciable governmental powers and relations that the singular achievement of the U.S. Constitution lies.

Perhaps the most conspicuous example of the latter is the provision that the 'United States shall guarantee to every state in the Union a Republican Form of Government, and shall protect each of them against invasion; and on the application of the legislature, or of the Executive (when the legislature cannot be convened) against domestic violence.'[12] This provision clearly imposes a duty on the federal government, but it is a duty of a peculiarly political nature. Involving as it must the employment of military force, the duty of protection of the states from invasion or domestic violence surely is of a nature that cannot be judicially enforced. Since it too envisages the possible use of military force, an inference that is supported by its appearance in the same clause as the duty of protection, the guarantee of a republican form of government is also not intended to be justiciable.[13] These powers are essential to the preservation of the integrity of the union and its republican character. Their inclusion in the Constitution legalises and legitimates their exercise by the federal government. Yet, giving them legal character in order to legitimate their exercise should not also attract the sanction of judicial enforcement. That would be to carry much farther than is warranted the notion of a constitution as law; it would deprive a constitution of its basic nature as a charter of government and reduce it to the same level as an ordinary statute.

The long and short of this is that, desirable as is the notion of a constitution as law, that should not be its only function or purpose. A constitution having the force of law should be flexible enough to accommodate needed 'political' commands, using 'political' in the sense of legal but non-justiciable commands. It is the apparent complete denial of the essentially political nature of certain governmental powers and relations, in favour of a thoroughgoing definition in justiciable terms, that perhaps constitutes the major fault of the Commonwealth African constitutions. Governmental structures, functions, procedures and relations are spelt out to the minutest detail in ordinary statutory language, with its implication of judicial enforcement. No doubt, part of the reason for this lies in the origin of these constitutions as orders-in-council of the British government in the case of the independence constitutions, or acts of parliament in the case of the post-independence constitutions. But whatever the cause and the justification, the assimilation of these constitutions to the form of an ordinary statute has led to the omission from them of matters which, by their nature, may be considered not fit for, or not susceptible to, judicial enforcement. The constitution, thus reduced to a dreary, technical statutory document, is made the worse for such omission, losing its other function as a charter for the affirmation of fundamental objectives or directive principles of government, and as a source of inspiration for enlightened governmental action. In a few cases, notably India and Pakistan, the latter defect is partly made good by the inclusion in the constitution of directive principles of state policy, explicitly stated, in conformity with the rigid statutory character of the instrument, not to be amenable to judicial sanction. In some others, e.g. Zambia and Tanzania, the preamble, being outside the enacted portion of a statute, is pressed into service and is used to affirm fundamental objectives.

The rigid statutory character of the Commonwealth African constitutions had also resulted in another feature which does not match easily or naturally with the idea of a constitution, viz. the express exclusion from judicial review of certain provisions. There is, for example, the obligation of a constitutional head of state to act only as advised by the cabinet or individual ministers thereof, an obligation which in Britain and the older Commonwealth countries is sanctioned, not by judicially enforceable rules, but by non-justiciable constitutional conventions. By making it a *statutory* rule of law, the independence constitutions of Commonwealth Africa (Zambia and Botswana excepted) had been forced to exclude it from the jurisdiction of the courts. But for the rigid statutory character of these constitutions, this would not have been necessary, since this is an aspect of governmental relations which, by its nature, should not be susceptible to judicial inquiry and scrutiny. For it is not to be supposed that in a constitution appropriately framed as a flexible charter of government the courts would assume to inquire into this by bringing the head of state and the cabinet before them to answer questions on their confidential exchanges and conversations in the course of their official dealings as the executive of the country. Not only the problem of proof but also the confidentiality of such exchanges and conversations is therefore involved. And the courts do recognise the public interest in the confidentiality of such conversations, and have extended to them the protection of privilege.[14] In the context of a statutory constitution the privilege will probably be overborne by the justiciable character of its provisions (i.e. in the absence of exclusionary provisions).

The republican Constitution of Ghana, 1960, must be considered an exception to this Commonwealth African tradition. It followed quite closely the broad non-technical language of the U.S. Constitution, and it contained in article 13 certain fundamental principles and objectives of the government to which a president was required to declare adherence on his assumption of office. The article was not explicitly withdrawn from judicial enforcement, yet the Ghanaian court of appeal has held its provisions not to 'create legal obligations enforceable by a court of law. The declarations, however, impose on every President a moral obligation, and provide a political yardstick by which the conduct of the Head of State can be measured by the electorate. The people's remedy for any departure from the principles of the declaration is through the use of the ballot box, and not through the courts.'[15]

Herein therefore lies a basic difference between the Commonwealth African constitutions (Ghana's 1960 Constitution excepted) and that of the United States. From the character of the former as a statute in form as well as in origin it follows that violations of them are necessarily justiciable just as are violations of other statutes or laws. On the other hand, as Justice Frankfurter said, the U.S. Constitution 'has many commands that are not enforceable by courts because they clearly fall outside the conditions and purposes that circumscribe judicial action.'[16] They are called 'political questions' in the United States, because, though legal, the duty they impose is peculiarly political in nature, and their observance depends upon 'the fidelity of the executive and legislative action and, ultimately, on the vigilance of the people in exercising their political rights'.[17] There is no inconsistency in a command being legal and yet not judicially enforceable. Judicial enforcement is not an inexorable criterion of 'lawness'. A provision in a constitution or statute is no less legal because it is not judicially enforceable.

The 1979 Nigerian Constitution shares the same character as the American. It is law, but one which in certain of its aspects is not justiciable either because judicial enforcement is expressly excluded (such are the fundamental objectives and directive principles of state policy) or because they are just not fit for judicial action.[18]

3. Relation of the Constitution to the legislature: supremacy of the Constitution

The Constitution is not only law; it is the supreme law of the land. Its supremacy expresses the relation between it and the law-making organ of the state. It is the relation of a superior to an inferior authority. The Constitution is supreme over the legislature because it controls the legislature in the latter's law-making function. The implication of the supremacy of the Constitution is that the sovereignty of the legislature is not the highest norm of the legal order in Nigeria as it is in the United Kingdom.

The supremacy of the Constitution implies two forms of control of law-making by the legislature.

(i) Manner and form for ordinary law-making

The first form of control flows from the fact that it is the Constitution that establishes the legislature, and prescribes its composition, quorum and the method of arriving at decisions by simple or special majorities. Such a provision in a written constitution having the force of law binds the legislature, and disregard of it will invalidate any purported exercise of the legislative power. This form of control precludes any question of the legislature being supreme over the constitution, even when, as in New Zealand, it has power to amend the constitution by the same simple majority needed for ordinary law-making.

It is argued that a legislature which has power to amend the constitution in the way it makes ordinary law is sovereign in the fullest sense of the word, and that the concept of the sovereignty of the legislature implies that any act purporting to have been passed by it is valid and effective, irrespective of any defect in procedure; because, if a legislature is sovereign, a mere defect in procedure cannot operate to invalidate an act passed by it. The courts are bound to accept and act upon the official copy of the act, and cannot go outside it to ascertain whether it was passed in the manner and form prescribed by the constitution. On this view of sovereignty, a sovereign legislature operating under a written constitution is clearly above the constitution just like one operating under an unwritten constitution.

In an appeal in 1965 from Ceylon (now Sri Lanka),[19] the judicial committee of the privy council rightly rejected this argument, holding that under a written constitution which prescribes a procedure for law-making, the courts are not only entitled to go outside the official copy of the act in order to enquire into the question of procedure, but have a duty to declare the act invalid if in fact it was passed without due form. For where a legislature is given power subject to certain manner and form, *whether it be a simple or special majority*, that power does not exist unless and until the manner and form is complied with. The supremacy of the constitution demands that the court should hold void any exercise of power which does not comply with the prescribed manner and form. (Proof of non-compliance with a prescribed manner and form is in practice very difficult, but that is a different issue which will be considered in chapter 15.)

Herein lies the significant difference between a legislature operating under a written constitution, but with power to amend it by a simple majority and parliament in the United Kingdom. For since 'in the constitution of the United Kingdom there is no governing instrument which prescribes the law-making powers and the forms which are essential to these powers',[20] the courts are bound to take the validity of every act of parliament for granted, and there can be no question of non-compliance with any constitutionally prescribed procedure. 'There is no such doctrine as the unconstitutionality of legislation by parliament.'[21] The United Kingdom parliament is therefore not only sovereign but supreme, by which is meant that there is no law to which it is subject as regards either the content of its power or the procedure for exercising it. It is this supremacy that really excludes the supremacy of the constitution.

(ii) *Amendment of the Constitution*

The efficacy of the constitution's supremacy requires something more than the control of the forms of ordinary law-making. If every act of the legislature passed with due form is to operate *pro tanto* as an amendment of the Constitution in the event of inconsistency between them, then the constitution cannot be an effective control on the legislature. It is not even necessary that the act should be expressed to be an amendment of the constitution,[22] unless the constitution requires amendments to be made expressly, as in Ghana (1960) and in West Germany (1949). The danger of implied amendment is that it can be slipped through unnoticed among a mass of other provisions in a statute dealing with, say, land or some such subject. There would be none of the publicity and public comment that an express amendment usually attracts.

Clearly constitutionalism would be better secured if the amendment of the constitution is made to require more than the procedure for ordinary law-making. But how rigid or entrenched should the amending procedure be? Should it go beyond a special legislative majority and require popular approval at a referendum for the amendment of the more fundamental provisions, as did the independence constitutions of Ghana (1957), Kenya (1963), Zambia (1964), the Gambia (1965) and Botswana (1966)? Should some of these more fundamental provisions be made altogether unalterable? For example, the West German basic law, 1949, forbids any alteration of the territorial units of the federation, of the right of the *Länder* to participate in legislation, of the guarantee of human rights, and of the status of the German Federal Republic as 'a democratic and social federal state';[23] in France under the fifth republic (1958), the republican form of government is not subject to amendment;[24] while in Sri Lanka the guarantee of freedom of religion is unalterable.[25]

A high degree of entrenchment may be justified on the ground that a constitution is supposed to be a permanent charter, which is to endure for ages to come and not to be lightly altered to meet the temporary expediency of party politics. If the procedure for its amendment is not sufficiently rigid, and the temptation to alter it in accordance with the fancy or interest of the party in power is succumbed to too readily, the constitution loses its sanctity and authority as the bedrock of constitutionalism.

In the context of Africa, with the prevalence of one-party states or of nationalist parties commanding overwhelming support, a special legislative majority alone is not enough to secure the longevity of the constitution, since a special majority can be obtained as easily as a simple majority. There is, of course, no suggestion of the requirement for a special majority being entirely without effect in Africa, for if an amendment is so subversive of the spirit of the constitution or of the liberties of the individual, many government legislators may feel outraged to the point of rebelling against it and withholding their votes.

This is not to say that a constitution should be made unduly rigid, since that might invite its overthrow by revolutionary means when a genuine need for change arises and cannot be effected by constitutional amendment. The constitution should be able to respond to the needs of a developing country for change. Referring to the Cyprus Constitution, 1960, which made some forty-eight articles incorporated from the Zurich agreement completely unalterable, Justice Vassiliades has remarked upon what he calls 'the sin of ignoring time and human nature in the making of our constitution'. 'Time moves on continuously,' he says; 'man is, by nature, a creature of evolution and change, as time moves on. The constitution was, basically, made fixed and immovable. . . . As time and man moved on, while the constitution remained fixed, the inevitable crack came — perhaps a good deal sooner than some people may have thought — with grave and far-reaching consequence.'[26] Experience in Australia, where a referendum is necessary for every constitutional amendment, has also shown that, because of the natural conservatism of the public, popular approval is difficult to obtain, with the result that desirable constitutional change may be frustrated. Thus, of the more than twenty amendments submitted to the people in Australia before 1961, only four were approved, and only two of the four were important.[27] The problem of the amending power in a developing country is therefore that of reconciling the two conflicting needs of not making the constitution too easy to amend and thus be used as an instrument in the struggle for power while at the same time not making amendment too difficult or impossible, so that the constitution cannot respond to changing conditions in the country.

A federal set-up provides a way of avoiding the undesirable fetters of both a referendum procedure and an absolute ban on certain amendments without making a special majority in one legislature the sole requirement for constitutional amendment. Under such a set-up, a special majority in the central legislature can be coupled with ratification by the legislative houses of a prescribed number of states in the federation. If the number of states required to ratify an amendment represents a large majority of the states — say two-thirds or three-quarters — then this may operate to check hasty or politically-motivated amendments without frustrating genuine changes widely desired by the various political groups. The merits of this over the referendum procedure are borne out by the American experience. For although both methods of amendment are permitted by the U.S. Constitution — the procedure requires a proposal by two-thirds majority of Congress and ratification by the legislatures or by popular conventions in three-quarters of the states[28] — ratification by popular convention had been used only once out of a total of twenty-four amendments to date. (Congress decides which method of ratification is to be adopted in any particular case.)

In similar fashion, the 1979 Nigerian Constitution requires for its amendment a two-thirds majority of *all* the members of each house of the central legislature (four-fifths for the amendment of the amending procedure itself, the procedure for the creation of states or the bill of rights) and the approval of the houses of assembly of at least two-thirds of the states (s. 9). A referendum is required only where an amendment is for the purpose of creating a new state. A proposal for the creation of a new state may be initiated by two-thirds of the members in the senate, house of representatives, house of assembly and local government councils elected from the area of the proposed state, and thereafter approved by two-thirds of the people of the area at a referendum, by the houses of assembly of a majority of the states and by a two-thirds majority of each house of the central legislature. Only when these approvals have been obtained may the national assembly enact a law to give effect to the proposal (s. 8). However, the approval of a simple majority of each house of the central legislature and of the appropriate House of Assembly suffices to enable the national assembly to pass a law for adjusting the boundary of a state, but as with the creation of a new state the request for a boundary adjustment must be supported by two-thirds of the members in the senate, house of representatives, house of assembly and local government councils elected from the area to be affected by the boundary adjustment.

(iii) *Supremacy of the Constitution and the sovereignty of the legislature*

While, as has been shown, it precludes the supremacy of the legislature, the supremacy of the constitution does not preclude the sovereignty of the legislature where constitutional amendment rests entirely with the legislature, albeit acting with a special majority of its members. The judicial committee of the privy council has rightly held that no question of sovereignty arises in this kind of situation. For, as it observed:

> A parliament does not cease to be sovereign whenever its component members fail to produce among themselves a requisite majority, e.g. when in the case of ordinary legislation the voting is evenly divided or when in the case of legislation to amend the constitution there is only a bare majority if the constitution requires something more. . . . The limitation thus imposed on some lesser majority of members does not limit the sovereign powers of parliament itself which can always, whenever it chooses, pass the amendment with the requisite majority.[29]

Where, however, constitutional amendment requires approval by a body outside the legislature, for example the electorate at a referendum, then the sovereignty of the legislature would seem to be precluded. A sovereign legislature is that which has power, whether by a simple or special majority of its members, to make any and every kind of law, including a law that amends the constitution. Any other view of the matter makes nonsense of the idea of sovereignty; illimitability is indeed of the very essence of sovereignty.

But sovereignty can be divided between two or more legislatures within the same country, as under a federal structure. Under such an arrangement, no single legislature is sovereign unless it possesses the power to amend the constitution by the votes of its members alone, but together they hold the sovereignty of the country provided that nothing outside them is required for any constitutional amendment. The sovereign legislature in a federal set-up may therefore be defined as the federal and state legislative houses sitting separately. It follows that, because the amendment of the new Nigerian Constitution for the purpose of creating a new state requires approval by a section of the electorate at a referendum, which is not established by the Constitution as a legislative body, the federal and state legislatures, whether singly or in combination, are not sovereign.

REFERENCES

1. Bennion, *Constitutional Law of Ghana* (1962), 82.
2. Constituent Assembly Decree 1977.
3. s. 1.
4. s. 4.
5. Proceedings of the Constituent Assembly, Official Report, vol. II, cols. 1943−55; cols. 1981−8.
6. Edward S. Corwin, *The Doctrine of Judicial Review* (1963), 105.
7. Corwin, loc. cit.
8. Corwin, op. cit., 100.
9. Dicey, *The Law of the Constitution*, 3rd ed.
10. Thayer, 'The Origin and Scope of the American Doctrine of Constitutional Law', *Harv. L. Rev.* 7 (1893), 129.
11. Thayer, op. cit., 131.
12. art. IV, s. 4.
13. See Herbert Wechsler, 'Toward Neutral Principles of Constitutional Law', in *Selected Essays on Constitutional Law*, ed. Assn. of American Law Schools (1963), pp. 463, 468, reprinted from *Harv. L. Rev.* 73 (1959), 1; Frankfurter, 'John Marshall and the Judicial Function', *Harv. L. Rev.* 69 (1955), 217, 227.
14. *United States* v. *Burr*, 25 F. Cas. 2, 37 per Marshall C.J; *United States* v. *Nixon*, 41 L. Ed. 2d 1039.
15. *Re Akoto* (1961), G.L.R. 523, 535, per Korsah C.J.
16. Per Justice Frankfurter in *Colegrove* v. *Green*, 328 U.S. 549, 556.
17. Per Justice Frankfurter, loc. cit.
18. For a detailed discussion of the application of these criteria and of the whole doctrine of the 'political question', see Nwabueze, *Judicialism in Commonwealth Africa* (1977), 26−43.
19. *The Bribery Commissioners* v. *Renasinghe* [1965] A.C. 172.
20. *The Bribery Commissioners* v. *Renasinghe*, ibid. at 198; see Dicey, *The Law of the Constitution*, 10th edn., Introduction by E.C.S. Wade, xl.
21. Dicey op. cit. p. lxxix.
22. *McCawley* v. *The King* [1920] A.C. 691 (P.C.); *The Bribery Commissioners* v. *Renasinghe*, ibid. at 198; *Kariappar* v. *Wijesinha* [1967] A.C. 717 (P.C.)
23. art. 79(3).
24. art. 89.
25. s. 29(2).
26. *Att.-Gen. of the Republic* v. *Mustafa Ibrahim and Others* (1964) 1 Cyprus L. Rep., 195, 208.
27. Latham, in *Essays on the Australian Constitution* (1961), 1.
28. art. V.
29. *The Bribery Commissioners* v. *Renasinghe* ibid. at 200; also *Harris* v. *Donges* (1952) 1 T.L.R. 1245; *Minister of Interior* v. *Harris* S.A.L.R. (1952) 769.

2
THE RATIONALE OF THE 1979 CONSTITUTION FOR NIGERIA

1. *The Constitution and the fundamental objectives of the nation*

The idea of a constitution is one that is familiar to all of us in our various capacities as members of clubs, trade or professional associations, village or town unions, and so on. Every such association is governed by a constitution which sets out the aims and objectives of the association and how its affairs are to be conducted and managed. It is the same idea that is applied to the association of all the people living within a given geographical area.

In this wider context, a constitution is the means by which a people organise itself into a political community and defines the aims and objectives of its association, the conditions of membership, the rights and obligations of membership, the organs and powers necessary for the conduct of the affairs of the association and the duties and responsibilities of those organs to the individual members. That is what the idea of a constitution for a nation is about. It is the same simple idea to which our membership of clubs and trade or professional associations has familiarised us. Admittedly, the infinitely larger number of people involved in the association of a nation and its wider purposes call for a form of organisation and for a structure of power, rights and relationships that gives to a national constitution a complexity which makes it appear as if it is something different in nature and character from the constitutions of other associations.

It is unheard of for the constitution of a club, trade or professional association, or village or town union not to state the aims and objectives of the association. That is the axiomatic starting point. A statement of objectives is necessary because it focuses attention on the reasons for the existence of the association. It is perhaps one of those great distortions in ideas that something so basic to the idea of a constitution should be regarded as out of place in a national constitution. It is not really that a statement of objectives is taken for granted in a national constitution. On the contrary, it is strenuously argued that such a statement is undesirable because a national constitution is not a place for lofty but empty declarations of objectives, but that its proper concern is with the serious business of organising a state and government and powers. This argument is a distortion of the simple idea of a constitution. A national constitution should organise a government for the nation but it should also define the ideals of the national association and the organising ideas of the people, for a nation without an organising idea is not worthy of the name. As Wole Soyinka has rightly said, there is no other definition of a nation than a unit of humanity bound together by a common ideology. And there is no more appropriate and effective medium for proclaiming and affirming a nation's ideals and organising ideas than the basic instrument of its association. A national constitution should not be simply a code of legally enforceable rules and regulations about powers and institutional structures.

The need for a statement of ideals and objectives is all the greater in a new nation in search of identity and direction, and of integrating principles to counter the heterogeneity of the society and the cleavage between the various social groups. If the ideals and objectives are enshrined in the constitution, then this would make them appear less of a political slogan and invest them with the quality of constitutional, albeit non-justiciable norms, thereby making it easier for political leaders and all public functionaries to establish and show the desired identification with them.

The fundamental objectives stated in the 1979 Constitution for Nigeria are therefore in the best tradition of the idea of a constitution, especially a constitution for an emerging nation. The Constitution proclaims freedom, equality, justice, participatory democracy and social justice as the ideals upon which the nation is founded, and declares, by way of amplification, that the welfare of the people shall be the primary purpose of government; that government shall be responsible and accountable to the people; that every citizen shall have equality of rights, obligations and opportunities before the law; that the sanctity of the human person shall be recognised and human dignity shall be maintained and enhanced; that governmental actions shall be humane; that human exploitation in any form whatsoever shall be prevented; and that the independence, impartiality, integrity and easy accessibility of the courts shall be secured and maintained.

Free enterprise, combined with state monopoly of the 'major sectors of the economy', is proclaimed as the principle for the nation's economic life. The major sectors are defined as the economic activities being operated exclusively by the federal government or its agencies immediately before the coming into force of the Constitution, but the national assembly may by resolution add to or subtract from the list of such activities. Free enterprise is to be regulated by government so as to ensure (*a*) the promotion of a planned and balanced economic development; (*b*) that the material resources of the community are harnessed and distributed to the greatest degree possible to serve the common good; and (c) that the economic system is not operated in such manner as to permit the concentration of wealth or the means of production and exchange in the hands of a few individuals or a group.

Unity and faith, peace and progress are proclaimed the national motto, and discipline, self-reliance and patriotism the national ethic. This is of course a mere expression of sentiment, yet sentiment expressed in a solemn constitutional form has especial appeal. The question is whether these declarations correctly reflect the ideals and objectives of the Nigerian nation. It is important that the ideals and values to be enshrined in the constitution of a nation should be the truly fundamental ones widely shared in the community, and not the sectional objectives of a group or the particular social and economic policies of a ruling party. The ideals of freedom, equality, justice, participatory democracy and social justice are indisputably the organising ideas in Nigeria's political and social life. It may be said too that the principle of a socialist-oriented control of free enterprise mixed with state ownership of certain sectors of the economy correctly interprets the economic orientation and attitude of the nation at the present time. By enshrining this in the Constitution the direction in which the nation is to go in its economic life is thus made clear for all to see, and uncertainty and controversy are removed. These ideals and objectives are not of course invested with the quality of immutable, unchanging truths by the mere fact of their inclusion in the Constitution. All values are relative to time and place, and every society should attempt to formulate the values that are relevant to its time and place; embodying them in the national constitution does not entitle them to any more immutability than the form of government instituted in the constitution.

2. *Factors and ideas underlying the organisation of government and its powers and responsibilities under the Constitution*

A national constitution should organise a government, not in a theoretical context, but in the context of the circumstances of the country concerned, including its history, social structure, material resources, and the character of its people. It is these that should determine what forms the organisation should take and what objects it should try to achieve. The organisation of government and its powers under the new Constitution are conditioned by the following objects.

(i) *The need for principle and probity in government and politics*
The government of the first Nigerian republic and its politics were dominated by personal and ethnic interest and by expedient

accommodation of conflict between these interests. Governmental actions and political activities were utterly unprincipled. Expediency, rather than principle, was the all-pervading consideration. The wielders of power were motivated, first, by a personal desire for the wealth, prestige and influence that go with state power, and secondly, by a desire to secure for their friends, relations and ethnic group as large a share of the 'national cake' as possible in the form of jobs, scholarships, contracts and other forms of government patronage. The interest of the national community, its needs for principled policies of political action, of social security for the people, and of planned and integrated development, seldom entered into the calculation. Political activity was marked by coercion, perversion, thuggery and other forms of violence. Politicians jumped from the bandwagon of one political party to another according to the changing fortunes of the parties, and the parties entered into alliances as their selfish interests dictated. And when the pursuit of conflicting interests exploded into an inevitable crisis, an expedient accommodation was soon worked out, which allowed the nation an uneasy breathing space until the next round of crisis. Crises came in a cycle. Such were the government and politics of the first republic.

This state of affairs resulted in part from the failure of the Constitution to spell out principles of state policy to be observed by successive governments. Our 1963 Constitution, like its predecessors, spoke only in terms of power and of rights. It granted a full amplitude of powers to the government, power to make laws and to execute them. Power, by definition, is discretionary; he to whom it is given is under no duty to exercise it if he does not want to. The legislature is under no duty to exercise its power to make law on any matter, nor is the executive obliged to execute the law when it is made. Thus, although it had ample power to do so, the government under the 1963 Constitution was not obliged to provide adequate medical, educational and other social amenities for the welfare of the people.

Admittedly power, particularly political power, implies responsibility. However, the responsibility of political power is a purely political concept, which presupposes that those who wield the power are responsive to the needs and welfare of the people and fully accountable to them. It is that responsiveness and accountability that the 1963 Constitution failed adequately to sanction.

Of course the 1963 Constitution did not grant governmental powers without limitations; it did implement the concept of limited government, of constitutional democracy. Perhaps the most important of these limitations upon governmental power is the fundamental rights guaranteed in the Constitution. These rights do certainly imply an obligation on the part of the government not to contravene them. Yet the obligation is only a *negative* one, its effect is simply to limit the government by obliging it not to exercise its power so as to violate or interfere with the guaranteed rights. A constitutional guarantee of rights imposes no duty on the government *positively* to do anything to promote the material wellbeing of the people. Herein lies the difference between *constitutional limitations* and *constitutional duties*: the former refers to the limitations placed by the constitution on the powers of government in the interest of individual freedom and democracy generally, the latter to the duties imposed by the constitution on the government positively to secure and promote the wellbeing of the people.

Until the second decade of this century, constitution-makers had been pre-occupied largely with constitutional limitations. In a society built upon *laissez-faire* and economic individualism, as most societies were before the twentieth century, the securing to the individual of social and economic amenities is regarded as none of the state's business. But the economic and social consequences of the two world wars have compelled among some countries a change of attitude towards the duties of the state to the individual, with the result that increasing concern is now being shown for his claim to social and economic amenities. Throughout the world today the question is agitated as to how this claim could be more effectively secured against the state. The constitution is seen by many as perhaps the most appropriate means of doing so, as witness the Constitutions of Cyprus, India, Pakistan, the Soviet Union, the French-speaking African countries, and the Social Charter of the European Economic Community.

Nigeria's experience in the First Republic not only emphasises the need for principles of government but also suggests that they should be openly avowed and enshrined in the constitution. Spelling them out in the constitution invests such principles with the quality of a constitutional *directive* to the organs of the state to inform and guide their actions by reference to the declared principles. It also serves as a reminder to them that their position is one of trust involving powers as well as duties.

In recognition of this, the 1979 Constitution of Nigeria lays upon the government the duty to provide adequate facilities for, and encourage free mobility of, people, goods and services throughout the country; to secure full residence rights for every citizen in all parts of the country; and to direct its policy towards ensuring for all Nigerians suitable and adequate shelter, food, medical and health facilities, and facilities for leisure and for social, religious and cultural life, and free education at all levels. On the economic side, it is required to direct its policy towards ensuring that all citizens have the opportunity for securing adequate means of livelihood and suitable employment; that for all Nigerians there should be a minimum living wage, unemployment benefits, old age care and pensions, just and humane conditions of work, and equal pay for equal work without discrimination on account of sex; that the health, safety and welfare of all persons in employment be safeguarded and not endangered or abused; that children, young persons and the aged be protected against any exploitation whatever, and against moral and material neglect; that provision be made for public assistance in deserving cases or other conditions of need; that the national economy be controlled in such a way as to secure the maximum welfare, freedom and happiness of every citizen on the basis of social justice and equality of status and opportunity; that the material resources of the community be harnessed and distributed as best as possible to serve the common good; that the economic system should not be operated in such a way as to permit the concentration of wealth or the means of production and exchange in the hands of few individuals or of a group; and that planned and balanced economic development be promoted.

All organs of government and all persons or authorities exercising executive, legislative or judicial functions are required, as a matter of constitutional duty, to conform to, observe and apply these principles. Regrettably, however, the Constitution provides no machinery for ensuring such compliance, and expressly excludes the use of the courts for the purpose, even to the limited extent of a mere declaration by a court that the government is or is not complying with the principles. This exclusion is predicated on the danger of a confrontation between the court and the political organs and on the alleged incompetence of lawyers to decide such matters. The danger of confrontation hardly justifies the complete exclusion of judicial intervention, and judges are no less competent than politicians to assess the performance of a government. However, the National Assembly is given power to provide for a machinery to promote and enforce the directive principles of the Constitution.

Political parties also are required to conform their aims and objects and programmes to the declared principles and to the fundamental objectives and ideals of the nation. The use of organised coercion or any other form of organised violence for political purposes is prohibited.

A code of conduct is established aimed at ensuring that the administration of government would no longer be abused for the amassing of personal wealth or for sheer personal aggrandisement. To this end, a government functionary is prohibited from doing, in abuse of his office, any arbitrary act prejudicial to the rights of any other person, and from accepting any property or benefit for the discharge or non-discharge of his duties. The acceptance of benefit by the president, or vice president, a governor or his deputy, ministers, permanent secretaries or heads of public corporations, university or other parastatal organisation from a company, contractor, businessman or their nominee or agent is prohibited, even when such benefit is unrelated to the discharge or non-discharge of their duties, so is the acceptance by them of a loan which is not from the government or its agencies, a bank, building society or other financial institution. A check on corrupt acquisitions by public officers is to be maintained through a system of declaration and verification of assets at the time of first appointment, at intervals of four years during tenure and at the end of the appointment.

(ii) *The centrality of man's humanity*
It has been suggested that a national constitution should not proceed from the premise that there is an inherent opposition between the state and its members, for an association cannot really be in opposition to its members. An association is an instrument created by its members for the pursuit of purposes beneficial to themselves, and the state is no different in this respect from other associations. To guarantee rights in a national constitution, it is argued, is to postulate a conflict between the state and its members, the effect of which would be to alienate from the state the loyalty of the members.

While it is true that a state is organised to serve the welfare of its members and cater for their needs for order, social security and a decent life, yet the exercise of state power for these purposes must necessarily impinge on those rights which are a fundamental attribute of the members' humanity, the right to breathe, to speak, to feel, to think and to move about. Once a human being is brought into relationship with other human beings and with an organisation for the pursuit and promotion of their common security, peace, progress and general wellbeing, conflict is necessarily created between the fundamental attributes of his humanity and the powers that may be exercised over him and society for the attainment of communal welfare.

In organising a government, therefore, a national constitution should recognise that man is first and foremost a *human* being and only secondly a *social* being, that his individuality comes before his social instincts, and that the attributes of his humanity are more basic and fundamental to his existence than the material benefits of social life. The latter are meaningless to him if he is no longer able to breathe, think or feel. The material conditions of a good, decent life are meant to complement his humanity, to enable him fully to realise his human personality. It would be a contradiction if the pursuit of social security and social wellbeing were to override man's humanity. Neither of course should override the other. It is important however that the opposition between them should be recognised, and efforts made to balance them. This balancing is one of the most difficult aspects of constitution-making.

Recognising the centrality of man's humanity, the Nigerian Constitution guarantees the right to life, to the dignity of the human person, personal liberty, freedom of thought, conscience and religion, freedom of expression and freedom of movement, but it does so subject to reasonably justifiable restriction which the state may by law impose in the interest of defence, public safety, public order, public morality or public health or for the purpose of protecting the rights and freedoms of others. However, life may only be taken as an act of war, and personal liberty may only be restricted in these interests during an emergency. In the event of such a restriction being imposed, an aggrieved person may apply to the court to determine whether the restriction is reasonably justifiable in the specified interests.

It is believed that the balance thus struck would allow ample scope for the enjoyment of human rights and for the exercise of state power if the courts interpret it with insight and understanding, bearing in mind that liberty is the rule and restriction an exception.

(iii) *National unity and stability*
The idea of national unity runs right through the Constitution. It begins with an affirmation in the preamble of the resolve of the people of Nigeria 'to live in unity and harmony as one indivisible and indissoluble Sovereign Nation . . . and to provide for a Constitution for the purpose of . . . consolidating the unity of our people'. Proclaiming unity as part of the motto of the republic, the Constitution enjoins on the state, as a fundamental objective, actively to encourage national integration and 'to foster a feeling of belonging and of involvement among the various peoples of the country, to the end that loyalty to the Nation shall override sectional loyalties'.

With this objective of consolidating the unity of the country, state power is divided between a federal government and nineteen state governments in a manner carefully designed to forge unity out of diversity. The concept of the federal character of the country is made a guiding principle for the composition of the federal government and its agencies. It is provided that 'the composition of the Federal Government or any of its agencies and the conduct of their affairs shall be carried out in such manner as to recognise the federal character of Nigeria and the need to promote national unity and to command national loyalty'. Accordingly, the predominance in the government or in its agencies of persons from a few states, or from a few ethnic or other sectional groups shall be avoided. Further, the composition of a state government, a local government council or any of the agencies of such government or council, and the conduct of their affairs, shall be carried out in such manner as to recognise the diversity of the peoples within their area of authority and the need to promote a sense of belonging and loyalty among all the peoples of Nigeria (s. 14[3] and [4]).

The concept of the federal character of Nigeria is defined as referring to 'the distinctive desire of the peoples of Nigeria to promote national unity, foster national loyalty and give every citizen of Nigeria a sense of belonging to the nation' (s. 277). In furtherance of this concept, each state in the Federation is, by the Constitution, given representation in the federal cabinet and in some of the more sensitive federal commissions. With regard to the armed forces, it is provided that 'the composition of the officer corps and other ranks shall reflect the federal character of Nigeria' (s. 197); the National Assembly is required to set up a body to ensure this (s. 199).

An executive presidency is established for the country with the idea, among other things, that it should serve as a focal point of loyalty in the nation. The method for the election of the president is designed deliberately to ensure national solidarity, by requiring not only a majority (or the highest number) of the popular votes but also at least one-quarter of the votes in each of at least two-thirds of all the states in the federation. This requirement applies even in the case of a sole candidate. The idea is to ensure that no one is to become the president of the country on the votes from one section of the country, whether north or south. A presidential candidate is thus compelled to identify himself with nearly every part of the country and by so doing to make himself a national figure and leader, concerned with the interest of the nation as a whole. It is of course recognised that this requirement may be difficult to satisfy, yet its rigour would serve to compel political parties to sink some of their differences and come together for the common benefit of themselves and the nation.

The same principles are also ordained for the election of the governor of a state: he must win the highest number of the popular votes and at least one-quarter of the votes in each of at least two-thirds of all the local government areas in the state.

The executive presidency and governorship are predicated also on the need for stability in the nation, the necessity to avoid the clashes of personalities and of interests, the conflict of authority and the unnecessary complexity and uncertainty in government relations which are attendant upon the system of separation between a titular head of state and an executive head of government. The history of the first republic is replete with these clashes and conflicts and with their destabilising effects. The dismissal of the premier of Western Nigeria by the governor in 1962 and the refusal of the premier to accept his dismissal plunged the region into an emergency which consumed the passion and energies of the people; and the flames lit by it grew into a mighty conflagration in the arson, pillage, murder and other violence which followed in the wake of the election fraud of 1965 by which the same premier sought to maintain himself in power against the clear verdict of the people of Western Nigeria. The disagreement between the president and the prime minister of Nigeria over the conduct of the 1964 federal elections rocked the federation and eventually precipitated a military coup. Not only stability but also national unity suffered in all these conflicts and clashes. For any clash between the head of state and the premier necessarily divides the country into factions, based either on tribe or purely on party interests or both. The experience of the country with the system of separation underlines the need for a single national leader, who would symbolise the state and rally the people around himself in loyalty to the nation.

The need for national integration and stability also underlies the provisions of the Constitution relating to political parties. No association can function as a political party unless, among other things, (*a*) its name, emblem or motto has no ethnic or religious connotation and does not give the appearance that its activities are confined to a part only of the geographical area of Nigeria; and (*b*) membership is open to all Nigerians irrespective of religion, place of origin or ethnic affiliation. Furthermore, the executive committee or other governing body of every political party must reflect the federal character of Nigeria in the sense that its members must be drawn from not less than two-thirds of the states; and its programme, aims and objectives must conform to the fundamental objectives and ideals of the nation (ss. 202, 203 and 204).

(iv) *Need for effective government*
'Energy in the executive', Alexander Hamilton has said, 'is a leading character in the definition of good government. [. . .] That unity is conducive to energy will not be disputed. Decision, activity, secrecy, and dispatch will generally characterise the proceedings of one man, in a much more eminent degree, than the proceedings of any greater number; and in proportion as the number is increased, these qualities will be diminished.'[1] This is not, of course, to deny the virtue of collective discussion and consultation in bringing the views and experiences of different people to bear upon a problem or upon the determination of policy. Yet it is essential to effective leadership in government that there should be a single individual in the capacity of a chief executive who can decide and act promptly when despatch is

demanded, and who can impose his will when differences of opinion among cabinet members threaten to paralyse the government. Blackstone has rightly said that many wills (where the executive power is placed in many hands and therefore subject to many wills) 'if disunited and drawing different ways, create weakness in a government; and to unite those several wills, and reduce them to one, is a work of more time and delay than the exigencies of state will afford.'[2]

Another demerit of the plural executive stressed by Alexander Hamilton is that it undermines responsibility. It does so in two ways: first, through the weakened authority of the prime minister to enforce collective responsibility and, secondly, by making it difficult to determine on whom the blame or punishment for misconduct should fall. One of the factors that has discredited cabinet government in the developing countries of the Commonwealth was the inability of the prime minister to control the actions of ministers and enforce the requirements of collective responsibility. In Pakistan until 1958, when parliamentary government was finally abrogated, the situation was near-chaotic, with ministers openly disagreeing with each other and with cabinet decisions and the prime minister unable to enforce discipline and the unity of the government. The federal government of Nigeria before the army take-over in 1966 exhibited much the same record of irresponsibility and indiscipline among ministers, and an inability on the part of the prime minister to control them, although this inability in his case was attributable both to the attitude of independence bred in ministers by the system of a plural executive itself and to the unique circumstance that he was only the deputy leader of his party owing allegiance to the party leader outside the federal government, to whom the other party members in the federal cabinet also owed allegiance.

Therefore, as Carl Friedrich has observed, it is 'precisely the need for vigorous and if necessary decisive action, unhampered by the need to consider parliamentary majorities, which has made constitution-makers in recent years look with increasing interest at the American presidency as a paradigm of how to organise effective executive government. Especially in the newly developing countries, in Africa and Asia, the efforts of British advisers to set up parliamentary systems have been crowned with anything but success, when their advice was accepted. In one after another of these states, a shaky parliamentary democracy has been superseded by some kind of military rule, and it may well be questioned whether these countries would not have been better off with some properly modified presidential system.'[3]

Nigeria's Presidential Constitution is designed to implement this need through 'the creation of an office of President which contains a manifest potential for leadership and which functions as a centre of activity and initiative within the political system — one, that is, which is able to supply a positive source of direction *vis-à-vis* the course of governmental affairs'.[4]

(v) *Need for economic development*
Economic development is a paramount need of the country. Subject to the centrality of man's humanity discussed above, the primary need of a developing nation is to combat ignorance, disease and poverty by securing to the people the minimum basic requirements for their existence — food and clothing, water, housing, education, medical and health facilities, and so on. This is a need that calls for effective leadership, a leadership that would be able to mobilise the nation and its resources, and to provide purposeful direction for its people. But total mobilisation of the nation towards the task of economic development requires that the leader should be endowed with the powers of the state as well as with its symbolic authority. The organisation of executive government around a single individual in the name of president is well designed therefore to serve the country's need for a leadership able to mobilise its people and resources towards economic development.

The federal arrangement also is envisaged as serving more than the need for forging unity out of ethnic diversity. The increase in the number of states in 1967 from four to twelve had virtually removed the threat to the unity of the country posed by the struggle between three (later four) large regions for the control of the federal government, by the strong separatist pool of regionalism, and by the acrimonious cleavage between major and minority ethnic groups within the large regions. The latest increase from twelve to nineteen states in 1975 has largely served the different purpose of creating new centres for development, equipped with the central powers of a state government. The excessive centralism of the military administration in terms of the concentration of power and resources in the federal military government inhibited the realisation of the full advantages for development of these revolutionary changes. The new Constitution for a civilian government would enable the state governments to come into their own as centres for development with a will and an authority of their own, rather than as mere appendages of the federal government. It is also hoped that a new revenue allocation formula would be found which would secure to the state governments adequate independent revenue for the implementation of development within their respective territories.

The capacity of the creation of new states to facilitate development is of course not unlimited. A point is reached when further use of the device becomes counter-productive. It is believed that that point has now been reached. The creation of more states *now*, while it might serve political interests, would operate as a drag on development by stretching the resources of the country to a point where meaningful application of them for development becomes frustrated, and by diverting resources needed for development to the payment and maintenance of an unduly proliferated apparatus of state government. The country's resources, as they are at present, cannot take such an increased financial burden of new governmental structures. The Technical Committee on Revenue Allocation has observed that 'the increased size of government budgets in both capital and recurrent expenditures was largely the result of the creation of seven additional states in 1976, accounting for a 99 per cent increase in those budgets in 1977–8. The lesson of this should be clear in handling demands for additional creation of States.'[5] It would be reckless not to heed this lesson.

Development of the local communities should be pursued through the new local government system whose structures are much less expensive than those of a state government. The benefit of the local government reform of the military administration is preserved by the new Constitution, which guarantees to the local communities administrative machinery and financial resources needed for their development. The Constitution guarantees 'the system of local government by democratically elected local government councils', and requires the government of each state to 'ensure their existence under a law which provides for the establishment, structure, composition, finance and functions of such councils' (s. 7[1]).

(vi) *Need for limitations on government*
If the country's need for economic development demands effective leadership by an executive president, the character of the people is equally intolerant of arbitrary or autocratic rule. The Nigerian is intensely individualistic and resentful of any arbitrary or autocratic impositions upon his freedom of action. He accepts the necessity for effective government provided that the arbitrariness of power is curbed by placing adequate limitations and restraints upon it.

In line with the character of the people, the new Constitution makes the limiting and restraining of governmental power one of its central concerns. Limitation on government is indeed perhaps the most conspicuous feature of the Constitution, running right through it with the unyielding tenacity of an ideal — from the constitutional definition of citizenship and the guarantee of rights to the institution of popular elections, at four yearly intervals, as the basis of all governmental powers, the division of powers between a federal and nineteen state governments, the separation of legislative, executive and judicial functions and of the personnel and procedure for their exercise, the limitation of the formal extent of legislative and executive power and the limiting of the president to two terms of office. The exercise of presidential power, within these limits, is restrained and moderated by various checks and balances — the requirement of legislative approval for certain of his acts or appointments, the necessity for him to consult or obtain the advice of various independent executive bodies before taking certain actions, the sanction of removal from office for abuse of power, etc. These limitations and restraints operate with an overriding force by virtue of the supremacy of the Constitution and its nullifying effect on all governmental acts that are incompatible with its provisions. The courts are empowered to review governmental acts for their conformity to the Constitution, and to pronounce invalid such of them as are contrary to its provisions.

Popular election imposes a limitation upon government because it places ultimate control of government in the hands of the people by enabling them to decide who should govern. Their decision is not of course confined to personalities. It involves also a choice of policies, of a political programme for the government of the community. An election is an opportunity for the people to express their needs, and to turn out a government whose performance fails adequately to provide for them. For this reason, its periodicity is important. It is necessary that the choice of rulers and policies should take place at frequent intervals, if elections are to be effective as a means of control of the government by the people. This is because the outlook of the people concerning government and their own needs changes with time. The issues upon which the government won an election may have ceased to be relevant after, say, five years, while on the other hand the people may have developed a new outlook diametrically opposed to that upon which their earlier decision had been based. If government is to be representative of the changing outlook and needs of the people, it is necessary therefore that the people should be able at reasonably frequent intervals to give practical expression to their changing wishes concerning government. Nigeria's new Constitution fixes the periodicity of elections at four-yearly intervals.

Control through the medium of popular elections is exercised by the majority. It is not an individualised control. The vote of the lone individual that makes up this majority has no significant effect in this mechanism of control while the vote of the individual in the minority is altogether without effect. Indeed the control operates against the latter. But democracy, as a system of limitation upon government, regards not only the majority but also the lone individual, whether he is with the majority or minority. It places a premium as much on popular as on individual participation. Control of the government by the individual operates, first, through the right, guaranteed to him by the Constitution, freely to comment on the government's conduct of public affairs, and to disseminate his comments with a view to influencing public opinion; and secondly, through his right in appropriate cases to initiate action in court when the limitations and other safeguards of the Constitution are being transgressed by the government. A constitutional guarantee of rights and judicial enforcement of the limitations of the Constitution have a special value in limiting government because they enable the lone individual to intervene personally to check governmental arbitrariness. A government of the people by the people is not fully democratic unless the instrument constituting it guarantees and protects the basic rights of the individual, particularly his freedom to comment on public affairs, and enables him, unhindered by the majority, to intervene personally where his guaranteed right or other limitations on governmental powers are being violated.

Concentration of governmental powers in the hands of one individual is the very definition of dictatorship, and absolute power is by its very nature arbitrary, capricious and despotic. The executive function of government — the maintenance of peace, order, the security of the state, the provision of social welfare, etc. — has an inherent tendency towards arbitrariness. Its arbitrariness is greatly accentuated and legitimised where the function of law-making is also reposed in the same hands. For it is not just that the repository of the combined power can pass tyrannical laws and then execute them tyrannically; he can also act arbitrarily in flagrant disregard of the limits of his power and then proceed to legalise his action by retrospective legislation. Government in such a situation is not conducted according to pre-determined rules; it is a government not of laws but of will, a government according to the whims and caprices of the ruler.

Limited government demands therefore that the organisation of government should be based on some concept of structure, whereby the functions of law-making, execution and adjudication are vested in separate agencies, operating with separate personnel and procedure. 'We are not prepared', writes Vile, 'to accept that government can become, on the ground of "efficiency", or for any other reason, a single undifferentiated monolithic structure, nor can we assume that government can be allowed to become simply an accidental agglomeration of purely pragmatic relationships.'[6] And as he rightly observes, 'the diffusion of authority among different centres of decision-making is the antithesis of totalitarianism or absolutism.'[7] By separating the function of execution from that of law-making, by insisting that every executive action must, in so far at any rate as it affects an individual, have the authority of some law, and by prescribing a different procedure for law-making, the arbitrariness of executive action can be effectively checked.

The idea of procedure has in itself an important limiting role. Where a procedure, separate from that involved in execution, is laid down for law-making, and must be complied with in order for the government to secure the necessary authority for measures which it contemplates taking, then regularity in the conduct of affairs is ensured. The opportunity for critical discussion and persuasion afforded by this separate procedure further assures regularity and minimises arbitrariness. And regularity in the conduct of public affairs enables the individual to know in advance how he stands with the government, and how far the latter can go in interfering with the course of his life and activities.

Not even the sternest critics of the doctrine of separation of powers deny its necessity as regards the judicial function. For the rule of law as an element of constitutionalism depends more upon how and by what procedure it is interpreted and enforced. The limitations which the law imposes on executive and legislative action cannot have much meaning or efficacy unless there is a separate procedure comprising a separate agency and personnel for an authoritative interpretation and enforcement of those limitations. The necessity for a procedure to interpret the law with finality is underlined by the fact that both the executive and the legislature have also to interpret the law in the course of carrying out their primary functions. An administrator will first have to interpret the law before applying it in his task of execution or administration, and so will the legislature have to determine the limits of its law-making powers. If, then, it is accepted that an act of the legislature contrary to the constitution is void, who is to exercise the function of declaring it so? The legislature in enacting the act may be said to have already given its interpretation of the limits of its powers under the constitution; in other words, it has by implication declared that the act is within the constitution, for otherwise it would not have passed it, except as a deliberate attempt to violate the constitution. If, therefore, the legislature were to have the last word on the meaning of the constitution with respect to its own powers, the position will have been reached that every legislative act will have automatically to be accepted as within the constitution and valid. This would certainly make nonsense of the whole purpose of a constitutional limitation of government from the point of view at least of the relationship between the government and the individual. For the legislature's interpretation of its powers would naturally be coloured by self-interest, which would operate to make its interpretation biased in favour of itself. There is thus clearly an incontrovertible necessity for a procedure separate, in terms both of structure and personnel, from — and independent of — that for execution and legislation, which would enable the administrator's or the legislature's view of what the law means to be reviewed with finality.

This separate procedure is normally provided by the ordinary courts. The unique virtue of the separate procedure of the courts is that, being unaffected by the self-interest and consequent bias of the legislature or the executive in upholding their action, it can be expected to apply to the interpretation of the constitution or a statute an impartiality of mind which inhibits any inclination to vary the law to suit the whims or personal interests of either the judge or a party to a dispute, thus ensuring 'that stability and predictability of the rules which is the core of constitutionalism'. While admittedly judges may not be entirely devoid of self-interest in the subject-matter of a legislative act — for no human procedure is ever completely neutral — yet this impartiality serves at once as a safeguard against the possible danger of arbitrariness on the part of the judges in the discharge of their interpretative function, and is reinforced for this purpose by the doctrine of precedent and the tradition of judicial self-restraint. Furthermore, the process by which the courts exercise their function — affording, as it does, ample opportunity for full argument by the parties or their lawyers on the possible interpretations of the law in the context of the facts before the court — ensures that the court's decision would reflect the reasonable or accepted view of the meaning of the law.

Properly conceived, the nature of the legislative function requires the laws should be made for the generality of the population. This at once implies that the making of laws is or should be a separate function from that of applying the law to the determination of the rights of individuals in given situations. The latter function requires a different kind of procedure from that of legislation, a procedure which would ensure that the individual is to be condemned only by an impartial tribunal and only after he has had adequate opportunity to defend himself against his adversary. Legislation is manifestly ill-suited for this function. If therefore the legislature were to be able to make laws to pronounce a named individual guilty of an offence and to punish him by, say, imprisonment, or to confiscate his property or to deprive him of other rights enjoyed by other citizens, the door is left wide open for arbitrariness and for victimisation. The best guarantee against arbitrariness in the exercise of the legislative function is to require legislation to be made for the generality of the population, and not separately for each individual and for each situation. Generality of application ensures that individuals will be treated equally and uniformly in accordance with the general law. Once admit *ad hominem* laws as a general principle of legislation, and there will be an end to liberty. Herein lies perhaps an even more compelling necessity for separating the judicial from the legislative function. 'There is no liberty yet,' writes Montesquieu, 'if the power to judge is not separated from the legislative and executive power.' The U.S. supreme court has put the point equally strongly in disallowing, as unconstitutional, a congressional act which barred permanently from government employment certain named American citizens believed to have engaged in subversive activities against the United States. It declared:

> Those who wrote our Constitution well knew the danger in special legislative acts which take away the life, liberty, or property of particular named persons, because the legislature thinks them guilty of conduct which deserves punishment. They intended to safeguard the people of this country from punishment without trial by duly constituted courts. . . . And even the courts to which this important function was entrusted, were commanded to stay their hands until and unless certain tested safeguards were observed. . . . When our Constitution and Bill of Rights were written, our ancestors had ample reason to know that legislative trials and punishments were too dangerous to liberty to exist in the nation of free men they envisioned. And so they proscribed bills of attainder.[8]

The separation of the procedure or agency for the authoritative interpretation of the law may therefore with justification be characterised as the most significant feature of modern government from the legal point of view. It was the establishment of judicial restraint upon the executive agencies of government that marked the beginning of the era of constitutionalism. There is yet another way in which the evolution of the judicial power as a restraint upon the executive power has contributed to the development of constitutional government. Judicial review of administrative activities has introduced into government standards of judicial behaviour, such as those of openness, fairness, reasonableness, and the more specific requirements of natural justice, namely that a party affected by an administrative determination of a quasi-judicial nature should be given adequate notice and opportunity of being heard, and that the agency or tribunal giving such determination should be disinterested and unbiased. Constitutionalism, it has been truly said, 'is the application of judicial methods to basic problems of government; administrative justice, extending this application, attempts to extend the judicial methods to the wider sphere of activities which government is handling today.'[9]

REFERENCES

1. *Federalist*, no. 70.
2. 1 Bl., Comm., 250.
3. Carl J. Friedrich, *The Impact of American Constitutionalism Abroad* (1966), 39.
4. R.A. Young, 'Zambia's Independence Constitution', unpublished paper.
5. Report (1978), 27.
6. M.J.C. Vile, *Constitutionalism and the Separation of Powers* (1967), 10.
7. ibid., 15.
8. *U.S.* v. *Lovett*, 328 U.S. 303 at 318 (1945).
9. Carl J. Friedrich, *Constitutional Government and Democracy*, revised edn. (1950), 117.

3
FEDERALISM

Federalism is an arrangement whereby powers of government within a country are shared between a national, country-wide government and a number of regionalised (i.e. territorially localised) governments in such a way that each exists as a government separately and independently from the others operating directly on persons and property within its territorial area, with a will of its own and its own apparatus for the conduct of its affairs, and with an authority in some matters exclusive of all the others. Seven different principles and issues are involved in this definition.

1. *Governments rather than geographical entities or peoples as the basis of the federal arrangement*

Federalism is essentially an arrangement between governments, a constitutional device by which powers within a country are shared among two tiers of government, rather than among geographical entities comprising different peoples. The relationships created by the arrangement are between governments, not between peoples in different geographical locations. From a legal standpoint therefore the federal state with its territory and people is one and indivisible. The federation, declares the 1979 Nigerian Constitution, 'is one indivisible and indissoluble sovereign State to be known by the name of the Federal Republic of Nigeria' (s. 2[1]). The federation is the only territorial entity recognised by law, and its people form one nation. The territorial divisions, known as states, exist simply for the purpose of delimiting the areas within which each regional government is to exercise the powers assigned to it. But their existence does not imply that power is shared between them as geographical divisions with distinct legal identity, on the one hand, and the federation on the other or between their different peoples and the nation. Federalism implies no such dichotomy or antithesis between the nation and the people living in the different geographical locations of the country. The supreme court of the United States underscored the point when it said that 'the people of the United States are an integral, and not a composite mass, and their unity and identity, in this view of the subject, are not affected by their segregation by state lines for the purposes of state government and local administration.'[1] A state government cannot sue the federal government to enforce against it the rights of the inhabitants of the state.²

The point is central in any definition of the nature of federalism. It expresses the difference between a federal state and a confederacy of states. A federal government does not, like a confederate organisation, derive its authority by delegation from the regional governments, but exists independently of them. Within the area of competence assigned to it by the constitution, it has independent and direct authority over the territory, the people and property in each region; it is as such a part of the government of the people, and so entitled to their allegiance.³ The language of 'the territory and people of a state' is often apt to create an erroneous impression that the authority of the regional government over the territory and people within its jurisdictional boundaries is superior to or exclusive of that of the federal government. So far from that being the case, the title or authority of the state government in relation to the territory and people within the state is of the same quality and nature as that of the federal government. Given thus the equal right of both, within their respective spheres of competence, to exercise governmental authority over the property, people and territory in the component geographical units of the federal state and to claim the allegiance of the people, there can be no question of a regional government having the right to interfere with the presence of the federal government in the region as by taking over any of its undertakings or assets or by ousting it completely therefrom. To attempt to do the latter is tantamount to secession. An act of secession by a regional government is clearly inconsistent with the provision of the Nigerian Constitution investing the federal government with an authority exercisable, within its constitutional limits, directly over the territory and people of the whole country or any part thereof. In the case of Nigeria, indeed, encroachment by a regional government upon the federal sphere of power is positively prohibited by the provision that the executive authority of a state government 'shall be so exercised as not to impede or prejudice the exercise of the executive powers of the federation or to endanger the continuance of federal government in Nigeria' (s. 5[2]). In the event of a state government contravening this prohibition, the president can use force against the state so impeding or prejudicing the exercise of his executive powers or so endangering the continuance of federal government. As the U.S. supreme court held in sustaining a similar action by the president of that country: 'The entire strength of the nation may be used to enforce in any part of the land the full and free exercise of all national powers and the security of all rights entrusted by the Constitution to its care. The strong arm of the national government may be put forth to brush away all obstructions. . . . If the emergency arises, the army of the nation, and all its militia, are at the service of the nation to compel obedience to its laws.'[4]

The words of the court in another case are also worth noting:

> We hold it to be an incontrovertible principle, that the government of the United States may, by means of physical force, exercised through its official agents, execute on every foot of American soil the powers and functions that belong to it. This necessarily involves the power to command obedience to its laws, and hence the power to keep the peace to that extent. This power to enforce its laws and to execute its functions in all places does not derogate from the power of the state to execute its laws at the same time and in the same places. The one does not exclude the other, except where both cannot be executed at the same time. In that case, the words of the Constitution itself show which is to yield.[5]

The national government, said Chief Justice Marshall of the same court, can in executing its functions under the U.S. Constitution, 'legitimately control all individuals *or governments* within the American territory. [. . .] The States are constituent parts of the United States. They are members of one great empire — for some purposes sovereign, for some purposes subordinate.'[6]

If a state government is not merely impeding or interfering with the exercise of the president's executive power in the state, but is attempting to terminate it completely by armed insurrection or rebellion, then the president is bound to accept the challenge and to try to suppress it, and, although a war cannot formally be declared against a region within a federal state, to engage the regional government concerned in open war if organised armed resistance if offered. In prosecuting such war he may blockade the region and capture as 'enemy property' the property of any person, whether neutral or rebel, residing within the rebellious region.[7] Insurrection or organised rebellion by a state government or group of state governments is unconstitutional because it is a unilateral attempt to oust the authority of the national government from a part or parts of the country.

2. *Separateness and independence of each government*

The autonomy of each government, which necessarily presupposes its separate existence and its independence from the control of the other governments, is essential to the federal arrangement. The autonomy of each government requires not just the legal and physical existence of an apparatus of government — a legislative assembly, governor, courts, ministries and departments, etc. (Separateness need not extend to the entire governmental machinery; certain agencies may be common, e.g. the police and the courts, and the executive of one government may be empowered to execute some of the laws of the other.) But more than the separate existence of an apparatus of government, autonomy requires that each government must exist, not as an appendage of another government, but as an autonomous entity in the sense of being able to exercise its own will in the conduct of its affairs, free from direction by another government. An arrangement, such as existed in Nigeria under the military regime, which legally obliges one government to accept direction from another on the conduct of its affairs is not federalism in the true sense of the word.

There is also no autonomy where, as under Nigeria's 1951 Constitution, the national government is able legally to override the regional governments in all matters. While certain matters may be common or concurrent to both the national and regional governments, and while either one may be permitted to override the other in such concurrent matters, there must be certain matters over which each can operate to the exclusion of the other and without interference or competition from it. And the exclusive area must be substantial enough to give meaning and reality to the autonomous existence of each government. There is equally no autonomy where, as happened under the 1960 Constitution, the national government can legally remove the representative organs of a regional government and take over, albeit temporarily, the administration of the government itself. Such a takeover is antithetical to federalism conceived as a device for enabling each group in a plural society to look after its own internal affairs free from outside interference and as an instrument of constitutionalism in limiting the powers of the centre so as to prevent it from becoming an instrument of total domination.

Autonomy also implies that neither the national government nor the regional ones can confer functions or impose duties on the functionaries of the other without the consent of its chief executive. This particular implication of the principle of autonomy was expressly enshrined in the 1963 Constitution in the provision forbidding not only the president but also the national legislature from entrusting functions or imposing duties on the functionaries of a regional government without the consent of the regional governor; a similar prohibition was also imposed on the regional governors and legislatures (see ss. 99 and 100). While these provisions are not repeated in the 1979 Constitution, the same result follows as a necessary implication of the principle of the autonomy and independence of each of the two tiers of government under the thoroughgoing federal system instituted by the Constitution. In the absence of constitutional authorisation, therefore, it is a contradiction of this principle for the national government to lay duties on the officers of a state government or to confer functions on them without the consent of the chief executive of the state, and vice versa.

Even without a legal power to direct or override, the power-sharing arrangement should not place such a preponderance of power in the hands of either the national or the regional government as to make it so powerful that it is able to bend the will of the other to its own. The sharing should be so weighted as to maintain a fair balance between the national and the regional governments. Federalism presupposes that the national and regional governments should stand to each other in a relation of meaningful independence resting upon a balanced division of powers and resources. Each must have powers and resources sufficient to support the structure of a functioning government able to stand on its own against the other.

Autonomy carries with it therefore some notion of equality, but it is equality of status as a government. Each government has, by virtue of its independent existence, an equal status with the others, and so entitled to an equal say, though not necessarily equal weight, in the common councils of the federal state. In the nature of things the notion of equality between the national and regional governments can extend no further than this. The national government is necessarily bigger than a regional government in terms of the territorial area over which its powers are exercised. Its powers are exercised over the whole country while those of a regional government are confined to only a part of it. Secondly, while, as has been said earlier, a fair balance should be maintained between the powers assigned to each, they cannot be so weighted as to be equal. Matters within their respective competence must necessarily differ in their relative importance, and equality is not determined by how numerous or few are the matters assigned to it. Nor can the resources available to each be made equal. Federalism accommodates a certain amount of inequality in powers and resources between the national and regional governments, so long as any preponderance in favour of one is not such as to reduce the other relatively to virtual impotence.

The conception of federalism as implying a dualism between two equal and competing sovereignties therefore gives a misleading picture. From the standpoint of the relations of the federal state to foreign governments and their citizens, in all the ramifications of such relations, including the making of war and the conduct of peaceful diplomacy, sovereignty in a federal state is one and indivisible, and reposes entirely in the national government. For this purpose the federal state exists as but one undivided political entity, with one, not dual, sovereignty.

Viewed in terms of powers of internal government, sovereignty in a federal state may be said to be shared between the national and regional governments, but that creates no dualism as such. The relations in a federal arrangement, like in all other human associations, must of necessity recognise the inescapable need for leadership and direction in the union. There must be a dominant centre of authority to provide the necessary leadership and direction. Given that the economy of the country is a single, integrated one, and that events and activities in one state must inevitably have an impact in other states of the federation, a federal system must inevitably accommodate a dominant centre of authority, with power to regulate the impact of state actions in the national economy and society, and to provide leadership and direction generally. That role necessarily belongs to the national government, implying the predominance of the national government over the regional governments even in terms of powers of internal government — which at once precludes the notion of duality or equality of powers.

It follows, therefore, that the concept underlying the federal arrangement is more appropriately described as that of national federalism rather than of dual federalism. The notion of equality of powers implied in the concept of dual federalism is apt to foster the attitude that the national and regional governments are jealous rivals engaged in perpetual competition and confrontation, with each trying to frustrate the other. Such an attitude would be unfortunate. For in a federal relationship the national and regional governments are conceived, not as rivals, but as 'mutually complementary parts of a single governmental mechanism', and should therefore co-operate with each other in order to promote the welfare of the nation through their combined powers. This is the concept of co-operative federalism which in the United States has enabled the national legislature, aided by supplementary state legislation, to enact legislation to deal with the social and economic effects of the depression that held the American nation in its grips in the 1930s. It has also manifested itself in the system of federal subventions to the state governments. But co-operative federalism does demand an attitude on the part of the regional governments which, recognising the national government as the dominant centre of power and money in the federal union, is prepared to accept its leadership and direction in dealing with the social and economic problems of the nation.

3. *The question of equality as between the regional governments*

From the premise that the federal relationship is between the national government on the one hand and the regional governments on the other, and not between it and each regional government separately, the powers of the regional governments and their relations to the national government should be exactly the same. No regional government should have more or less powers than the others or be accorded a special position in the national government. Otherwise the regional governments cannot interact among themselves and with the national government as equal partners. The lodging of greater powers in one regional government would tend to produce in it an attitude of superiority and arrogance towards the others, and thus destroy the equilibrium which should exist between them.

The supposedly federal constitution of Uganda of 1962 was a departure from the rule, but it was a departure that demonstrated the justification for the rule. There were in the arrangement the national government and five regional governments. Powers were shared between them under two different schemes, one applying between the national government and the regional government in Buganda, the largest of the regions, and another between the national government and the other four regional governments. The schemes differed not only in the methods used but also in the quantum and importance of matters assigned to the regional government in Buganda and to the others. Within Buganda there were two legislative lists, one exclusive to the regional legislature and the other exclusive to the national legislature, while the residue belonged to both. But in the other regions, there was only one list exclusive to the regional governments, with the residue belonging exclusively to the national government. More significantly, the matters assigned to the other regional governments were so few and unimportant as to bear no comparison whatever with the exclusive powers of the Buganda regional government, not to speak of its combined powers in respect of the exclusive and residual (concurrent) matters.

Moreover, the Buganda regional government was accorded a special position in the national government in that the members from Buganda in the national legislature were elected, not directly to represent individual constituencies, as was the case in the other regions, but by the regional assembly. The Buganda regional government was also granted special and incomparably more favourable financial relations with the national government. As was to be expected, its overwhelming power and financial resources compared with the other regional governments infused it with an arrogance that made it always wish to impose its will on the other governments, both national and regional. It was enabled to exert considerable influence in the national government because the members elected by it to the national assembly regarded themselves as its delegates, voting and acting as it directed them. When the inevitable crisis erupted, the Constitution had to be overthrown in 1966 by a coup staged from within the government by the prime minister himself.

As regards the areas and populations over which the regional governments exercise their powers, equality is not constitutionally required. Yet any inequality that exists must not be such as to create a great imbalance. Such a situation of imbalance was exemplified before 1967 in Nigeria, where the Northern region was larger than the rest of the regions put together, encompassing 75 per cent of the land area and 60 per cent of the population of the country. Of the danger of this kind of imbalance, John Stuart Mill has said that if there should be 'any one state so much more powerful than the rest as to be capable of vying in strength with many of them combined . . . it will insist on being master of the joint deliberations: if there be two, they will be irresistible when they agree; and whenever they differ everything will be decided by a struggle for ascendancy between the rivals.' There must therefore, as Sir Kenneth Wheare has said, be 'some sort of reasonable balance' between the units in area, population and wealth, which will 'insure that all the units can maintain their independence within the sphere allotted to them and that no one can dominate the others.'[8]

The truth of this was amply borne out in Nigeria before the military intervention in January 1966. The Northern regional government was able, by reason of its disproportionate size in area and population, to dominate the national government, almost turning it into an extension of itself, and dictating the actions and policies to be pursued, which ultimately precipitated, as in Uganda, the overthrow of the Constitution in a military coup.

4. *Number of regional governments between whom a federal arrangement can meaningfully exist*

If federalism is to be meaningful at all and be effective in achieving its objectives, a certain minimum number of constituent units would seem to be necessary. It can easily be perceived that to form a federation of two units, as was the case in Pakistan after 1955, is to pitch them against each other in a continual battle for ascendancy. A federation of three regions is much the same thing. Federalism thrives upon a multiplicity of interest-groups reacting upon one another to produce an equilibrium. A multiplicity of units creates a feeling of inter-dependence, which in turn encourages co-operation and mutual tolerance. A union of fifty states, as in the United States of America, must inevitably force upon each state an awareness of its relative insignificance *vis-à-vis* the whole, and the futility of a policy of separatism, which in such circumstances would be like the act of an individual ostracising himself from his society and thereby denying himself the comradeship and co-operation of communal life. In Nigeria before 1967 the three states structure had created an attitude of self-sufficiency, of separatism and of intolerance among the regions. There was not enough scope for that interplay of interests upon which a lasting equilibrium could be based. The influence of numbers in promoting a communal outlook and in preventing the victimisation of a member was lacking. Two regional governments agreeing could gang up against the third to make life uncomfortable for it, as was indeed the situation produced in relation to the Western region by the North-East coalition from 1959 to 1964. Pitched thus against the combined strength of the two regional governments, the third (the Western regional government) became an object of victimisation by the coalition. Such acts of victimisation could not but alienate from the federal state the loyalty of the regional government and its supporters. How could they be expected in the circumstances to feel a sense of belonging? It is needless to say that such ganging up, flagrantly and unquestionably violating the spirit and purpose of federalism, would have been inconceivable in a federation composed of a multiplicity of units. The interplay of a multiplicity of interest-groups would have imposed sufficient equilibrium in the system to ensure against that.

5. *Techniques for the division of powers*

The technique for the division of powers is that of enumerated powers and residual powers. The enumeration may be made under one list of matters exclusive to either the national or regional governments, or there may be two or even three lists, one for the central government exclusively, one exclusive to the regional governments and another concurrent to both; in addition certain specific matters may be assigned to either one or the other or to both concurrently in other provisions of the constitution (i.e. outside the legislative lists). The division of executive powers follows the legislative, though the executive of one government may, in respect of some matters, be empowered to execute the laws made by the legislature of another, as in Kenya under its Independence Constitution of 1963.

Having only one list of matters exclusive to either the national or regional governments and leaving the residue to the other has the advantage of simplicity, and eliminates the uncertainty and conflict which necessarily result from a second (i.e. concurrent) list; a third list inevitably adds to such uncertainty and conflict.[9]

Yet the technique of concurrent powers has undoubted advantages, which, it may be said, outweigh the disadvantages of conflict and uncertainty. Its advantages have been cogently articulated by Watts:

First, [a concurrent] list enhances flexibility. In a new federation it permits the central government to postpone exercising its authority in a field until such time as the matter has assumed national importance, while not preventing any region which is forward-looking from going ahead and legislating in the meantime on its own account. Secondly, it provides a means whereby, in certain spheres, especially the social services, the central government may legislate to secure a basic national uniformity and to guide regional legislation, while leaving with the regional legislatures the initiative for details and for adaptation to local circumstances. Thirdly, a concurrent subject allows the general government to step into what is normally a regional field of activity, in order to provide remedies for particularly backward regions or for difficulties arising from regional legislation which affects other regions. Fourthly, concurrent lists may facilitate 'comparative federalism', by encouraging co-operative rather than independent action in these fields. Fifthly, such a list may reduce the necessity for complicated, minute subdivisions of individual functions assigned exclusively to one government or another.[10]

Where there is a list of matters concurrent to both the national and regional governments, the national government almost invariably prevails in the event of conflict. The power to override has given rise to a doctrine which attributes to a concurrent power a potentially exclusive effect; the reasoning is that where the government with the overriding power has enacted comprehensive and exhaustive legislation on a concurrent matter, then, the field having been completely covered, the other government is *ipso facto* excluded from entering it in the first place. The doctrine is of doubtful constitutional validity. The constitutional provision speaks of a conflict or inconsistency between the laws of the two governments. It follows that legislation on a concurrent matter must first be made by both governments before any question of inconsistency between them can arise. Only then can a comparison be made to see if one has conflicted with the other. Furthermore, inconsistency connotes contrariety or incompatibility. It is not enough that two laws make different provisions on the same matter; the difference must involve some contrariety or incompatibility; the different provisions must be at variance, they must run counter to one another. Thirdly, it is difficult to conceive of legislation on any matter which will be so exhaustive and comprehensive that no room whatever is left for further regulation not at variance with its provisions. The power of pre-emption implied in the doctrine of covering the field is fundamentally subversive of the purpose and spirit of concurrent power.

6. *Underlying objectives of the federal arrangement*

Federalism is predicted upon the existence of a society composed of various geographically segregated groups divided by wide, fundamental differences of race, religion, language, culture or economics. Its purpose is to enable each group, free from interference or control by the others, to govern itself in matters of local concern, leaving matters of common interest to be managed centrally, and those which are of both local and national concern to be administered concurrently. By this, the differing interests and circumstances of the component groups are accommodated while at the same time securing the peace and stability of the country and its survival against the forces of division and conflict inherent in the heterogeneous nature of the society. With the decentralisation of powers to the regional governments and the consequent reduction in the powers exercisable centrally, the national government cannot become an instrument of total domination, so that the question of who controls it can be expected to excite less conflict and bitterness than if all powers are concentrated at the centre.

The attainment of these two seemingly conflicting objectives of national unity and regional autonomy involves therefore two factors: first, the extent and nature of the central powers; and secondly, the number of component units and their sizes in both absolute and relative terms. A federation of a few regions, as has been previously observed, tends to encourage ganging-up and conflict while large regions tend to attract large powers. If the regions are small, it would be futile to give them powers which they cannot handle because of the smallness of their territory, population and resources.

Within the national government, the intensity of conflict varies according to the scope and importance of powers assigned to it, and the bearing which they have upon life and development in the regions. If the central powers are few or unimportant from the point of view of the internal affairs of the regions, conflict will be minimised. But undue regional autonomy will tend to glorify the regions at the expense of the nation. If, as was the case in Nigeria before 1967, the regions are so powerful as almost to submerge the centre, or to cause the inhabitants to think of government in terms exclusively or mainly of the regional governments, then it will be hard for them to develop any loyalty to the nation, let alone one which would transcend loyalty to the region. This might appear to be a vicious circle; yet regional autonomy and a strong central government are not really mutually exclusive objects. It is perfectly possible to strike a balance between them; the centre can be made strong enough to act as a focus of national loyalty and consciousness, and yet prevented from interfering in matters which can, without detriment to other regions, be left within the competence of a region. If the federal system can be structured to guarantee against control of the centre by any one group, then it is desirable, in the interest of national unity, that the centre should be as strong as possible in order to be able to give effective leadership and direction to the country. In an emergent state therefore, federalism should be so structured as to favour unity against regional autonomy.

However, the approach should be based not upon a confrontational dualism, but upon the need for co-operation and comity.[11] As a safeguard against abuse by the national government in the exercise of powers in matters of both local and national concern, the principle of co-operation and comity should be written into the constitution, by requiring the national government to consult with the regional governments upon any proposed exercise of a concurrent power, and by instituting machinery for such consultation.

The main charge against federalism is that it recognises and crystallises group differences, thereby making it impossible for people to rise above tribal loyalty to a higher order where tribe, language, religion and geographical origin have no political significance, giving place to a common nationality as the highest loyalty. This is not entirely true. All that can be said with certainty is that federalism provides a local institutional base for an appeal to tribal or group sentiment. But what really creates the necessity for such an appeal is not federalism but the struggle for political power, and the fear of domination. The differences and mutual antagonism between the groups create divergent interests, which make it difficult for them to come together under one party. Each group naturally wants its own party to champion its interests against those of the other groups. Reconciliation within a single party might be possible if the differences and disparity in the level of economic development are not so great and fundamental, but where they are, 'a single party supported equally by all the tribes is an impossible dream.'[12] 'Any idea', writes Arthur Lewis, 'that one can make different peoples into a nation by suppressing the religious or tribal or regional or other affiliations to which they themselves attach the highest political significance is simply a non-starter. National loyalty cannot immediately supplant tribal loyalty; it has to be built on top of tribal loyalty by creating a system in which all the tribes feel that there is room for self-expression.'[13]

7. Constitutional forms

The issue here is as to the constitutional forms necessary and appropriate in a federal system, whether the autonomy of the component governments requires that they should each have their separate constitutions. A government presupposes a constitution by which it is organised and its powers defined. It follows that under federalism independent governments should strictly imply independent constitutions. This is implicit in the definition of federalism by the judicial committee of the privy council. 'The natural and literal interpretation of the word [i.e. federal]', said the committee, 'confines its application to cases in which these States, while agreeing on a measure of delegation, yet in the main continue to preserve their original constitutions.'[14] The constitutions of the governments of the federating states pre-date that of the federation, and continue to exist and operate with their original authority after the formation of the union. That is the constitutional form which modern federalism has taken in its birthplace, the United States. The same constitutional form was followed when the states in Australia federated in 1900.

Apart from this 'natural and literal' meaning, the judicial committee of the privy council acknowledges that federalism is also applied in another, if loose, sense, but even this loose application of the system is equally predicated upon the separateness and independence of the constitutions of the constituent governments. This occurs when, as in Canada, the federating states surrender their original constitutions and accept new ones — where, in the words of the judicial committee, 'self-contained States agree to delegate their powers to a common government with a view to entirely new constitutions even of the States themselves.'[15]

The application of the federal system in Nigeria and in many later federations has shown that a federation could be formed by a state hitherto under a unitary government, devolving part of its powers to two or more independent state governments. Noting the uniqueness of this application of the federal concept, the drafting committee on the review of the Nigerian Constitution in 1951 observed:

The federal governments of U.S.A., Canada, and Australia have been built on the basis of separate states surrending to a federal government some of their powers for the benefit of all. The reverse process on which we are engaged — that of the creation of a federal government by devolution — is a political experiment for which . . . there is no precedent to guide us and we are very conscious of the dangers inherent in such an experiment.[16]

In a federation formed by devolution from a unitary state, a separate constitution for each of the constituent states is no longer a logical necessity. Thus, when the federal system was established in Nigeria in 1951–4, new independent regional governments were organised and powers devolved upon them by a common constitution with no differentiation of any kind. The same sections of the one, single constitution established the organs of both the federal and regional governments and defined their powers.

Independence in 1960 brought new constitutional forms. Separate constitutions were established for the federal and for each of the regional governments in separate schedules annexed to the independence order-in-council. Though separate and independent of one another, the several constitutions derived from a common authority, namely the Independence Order made by the British government. A common source of authority which is not that of the federal government is not inconsistent with the federal principle.

But the independence of the state governments (and consequently the federal principle) would be violated if their constitutions were established for them by the federal government. That was the issue that confronted the making of the republican constitution in 1963. Since the imperial constitution of 1960 had to be done away with on the transition to a republican status, and there being no intention to use any other body than the existing established legislatures for the adoption of a republican constitution, the only constitutional form consistent with the federal principle in the circumstances was for each government to enact its own constitution. There was however an initial legal hurdle arising from the fact that only the federal parliament had power to repeal the imperial constitution and the act of the British parliament, the Nigeria Independence Act 1960, which constituted Nigeria an independent state. In pursuance of its power in that respect,[17] the federal parliament enacted the Constitution of the Federation Act 1963, which repealed and replaced the Nigeria Independence Act and the order-in-council insofar as they applied to the federation, and delegated a like authority to the regional legislatures;[18] whereupon each region enacted its own Constitution Law repealing and replacing the Independence Act and the order-in-council in their application to it.[19] (When the Mid-Western region was created in 1964, its Constitution was enacted by the federal parliament in pursuance of power conferred on it in the Constitution of the federation, but that was after approval at referendum in the area of the state and by the prescribed number of states.)

The new Constitution (1979) has reverted to the 1951–4 form of organising the federal and state governments under one, single constitutional instrument. In the original draft of the Constitution prepared by the constitution drafting committee, as under the 1951–4 form, agencies of the federal and state governments and their powers were dealt with in the same sections. As finally enacted, however, the Constitution segregates in separate parts of the same chapters, provisions relating to the federal and state governments, except that miscellaneous and transitional provisions common to both tiers of government are dealt with together in the same sections, as are the division of powers, fundamental objectives and directive principles, citizenship and fundamental rights.

The federal principle is not violated by the form of the new Constitution, even if the Constitution be regarded as having been made by the federal military government. For, unlike the pre-republican federal government, the federal military government was an absolute, supreme legislature, unlimited by the federal principle; the state governments were merely its agents, with no independent existence or power.

There is just one problem, which results from inadvertent drafting. It is provided that, subject to other provisions of the Constitution, the executive authority of the federal government, and likewise the executive authority of a state government, shall 'extend to the execution and maintenance of this *Constitution*', with the proviso that a state government should exercise its executive authority so as not to impede or prejudice the exercise of the executive authority of the federal government or to endanger the continuance of federal government in Nigeria (s. 5). This proviso may be said to limit a state government to the execution of provisions of the Constitution relating to that government, but the federal government is not, on a literal interpretation of the provision, similarly limited. To empower the president to execute the constitutions of the state governments amounts, in quite a significant way, to a denial of the independence of the state governments. (The nature and extent of executive power implied in the execution of the constitution is discussed in chapter 6.) Consistently with the federal principle, the executive authority of the federal government should extend only to the execution of the provisions of the Constitution with a federal or national application, not to those applying exclusively within a state. That seems clearly to have been the intention, and the provision should be so interpreted.

REFERENCES

1. *White* v. *Hart*, 13 Wall. 646 at 650 (1872).
2. *Massachusetts* v. *Melon*, 262 U.S. 447, 485–6 (1923); see ch. 17 below for discussion of this principle.
3. Cf *Re Debs*, 158 U.S. 564 (1894) where the supreme court said that the national government, within the limits of its powers, 'has all the attributes of sovereignty, and, in the exercise of those enumerated powers, acts directly upon the citizen, and not through the intermediate agency of the state' at 578. Also *Lane County* v. *Oregon*, 74 U.S. 71, at p. 76, where Chief Justice Chase observed that the people, through the Constitution, 'established a more perfect union by substituting a national government, acting, with ample power, directly upon the citizens, instead of the confederate government which acted, with powers greatly restricted, only upon the states'. See further per Chief Justice Marshall in *McCulloch* v. *Maryland*, 17 U.S. 316, 405.
4. *Re Debs*, op. cit. at 582.
5. *Ex parte Siebold*, 100 U.S. 371, 395.
6. *Cohens* v. *Virginia*, 19 U.S. 264, 413.

7. The *Prize Cases* 2 Black (67 U.S.) 635 (1863).
8. Wheare, *Federal Government*, 4th edn, 50−1. The quotation from Mill is from *Representative Government* (Everyman edn., 367−8).
9. loc. cit.
10. Watts, *New Federations: Experiments in the Commonwealth* (1966), 174−5.
11. See McWhinney, *Comparative Federalism*, 2nd edn., particularly ch. vii.
12. Arthur Lewis, *Politics in West Africa*, 1965, 50.
13. ibid., 68.
14. *Att.-Gen.* v. *Colonial Sugar Refining Co. Ltd.* [1914] A.C. 237 at p. 253. The use of the word 'delegate' is inappropriate in the context.
15. ibid.
16. Committee's Report (1951), 3.
17. Nigeria (Constitution) Order-in-Council, 1960, s. 18; Nigeria Independence Act, 1960, First Sch. para. 2.
18. Constitution of the Federation 1963, s. 154.
19. Constitution of Western Nigeria, s. 76, and corresponding provisions in the Constitutions of Northern and Eastern Nigeria.

4
DIVISION OF POWERS UNDER THE CONSTITUTION

1. *Scheme of division*

The federal arrangement under our Constitution assigns to the national government power over specified matters, leaving to the state governments the residue of matters not so specified. The specification of matters within the competence of the national government is done partly by specific provisions in the body of the Constitution and partly by enumeration under two lists scheduled to the Constitution (2nd Schedule) — one exclusive to the national government and the other concurrent to it and the state governments, called exclusive and concurrent legislative lists respectively.

The exclusive list has sixty-five specified matters, but the matters provided for in the body of the Constitution are incorporated by reference in the list as the sixty-sixth item; the last item on the list (67) relates to matters incidental or supplementary to any matter mentioned elsewhere in the list. The scope of incidental and supplemental matters is defined in part III of the lists. The incorporation as an item in the list of exclusive federal matters provided for in the body of the Constitution is intended to get round the decision of the judicial committee of the privy council that the extended scope given to incidental or supplementary matters in part III applies only to matters mentioned in the list, but not to those in the body of the Constitution.[1]

The concurrent list, which has twelve matters, is somewhat innovative in its approach, since, apart from enumerating the twelve matters, it also defines the respective extent of federal and state power in respect of those matters, with the aim of reducing possible conflict, especially through the application of the doctrine of covering the field. The result is that a concurrent matter no longer necessarily implies that both the federal and state governments are competent to act over its entire field. In respect of some matters in the list, their competence is respectively restricted to some aspects only of a so-called concurrent matter, making such aspects exclusive to the one or the other. With respect to scientific and technological research, for example, the function of the federal government is merely to regulate and co-ordinate; it does not include power to establish or run research institutes. On the other hand, the federal government has competence over the whole field of university, technological and professional education, including the establishment of institutions for the purpose, while the state governments may only establish institutions for university, professional or technological education. Electric power is dealt with in the same way, with the general power being lodged in the federal government, while a state government is restricted to the generation, transmission and distribution of electricity to areas within the state not covered by a national grid system.

Some matters in the list, e.g. trigonometrical, cadastral and topographical surveys, and archives, remain strictly concurrent in the sense, as the word is ordinarily understood, that both the federal and state governments can act over their entire fields. To the extent that a matter is truly concurrent, the federal government prevails over a state government in the event of inconsistency between a federal and a state law.

As noted earlier, any matter not included in the exclusive or concurrent list or which is not mentioned in the body of the Constitution, belongs exclusively to the state governments (s. 4[7]). Such matters are called residual matters. It needs hardly be said that the extent and importance of residual matters depend largely on the coverage of the enumerated matters. The enumerated matters may be so extensive as to leave little in residue or, while not so extensive in their coverage, they may be so important as to determine the balance of power in the federation. In our case, the residual matters are by no means insignificant. While their exact content is difficult to identify, they certainly include religion, primary and secondary education (excluding educational standards which are a matter exclusively for the federal government), local government (with certain exceptions), land tenure, agriculture, housing, chieftaincy and indigenous customs, and social relations generally including contracts, torts and general civil relations among the inhabitants of a state. There is no doubt that these are the matters that affect the ordinary man in his daily life. He is thus apt to think of government in terms mainly of the state government. Yet it does not follow that the lodging of residual powers in the state governments necessarily makes them stronger than the federal government. One has to study the nature and scope of the matters assigned to the latter in order to be able to form an intelligent opinion as to where the balance of power lies in the federation.

It is perhaps necessary to state that the scheme of division just described applies to both legislative and executive powers. Although the enumeration of matters is specifically for purposes of the exercise of legislative power, the division of executive power follows upon the same principle. Laws made by each tier of government are executed and administered by its own executive authorities. The executive power of the federal government is accordingly defined to extend to all matters within federal legislative competence; the executive power of a state government is similarly defined. But executive power seems to be wider than legislative power, for it extends also to the maintenance and execution of the Constitution. The power to protect, preserve and defend the Constitution clearly goes beyond what may be considered the appropriate realm of legislative action. Throughout this chapter, unless the context indicates otherwise, the term federal government or state government is used to refer to government as an entity comprising three organs, and not to the executive government alone.

(i) *Existing Laws*

The scheme of division applies not only to the making of law in the future but also to laws in existence at the commencement of the Constitution. Such laws are deemed to be an act of the national assembly or a law of a state house of assembly to the extent that they relate to a matter within the competence of the national assembly or a state house of assembly, as the case may be (s. 274[1]). The provision presents no difficulty in respect of an existing law dealing with a matter which is either of exclusively federal or state concern; such of its provisions as relate to exclusively federal matters will be deemed to be federal enactments while those relating to exclusively state matters will be deemed to be state enactments. An existing law may thus consist partly of federal enactments and partly of state enactments.

But where the subject-matter of an existing law is within the concurrent competence of both the federal and state legislatures, then all its provisions will, in accordance with the constitutional provision, be deemed to be federal as well as state enactments. But they will have to be applied as state enactments by the state courts. In its application as a state enactment, the law is within the competence of the executive of the state to execute and administer; it is also within the power of the state legislature to amend, but if such amendment is inconsistent with the law as it was originally enacted, then the latter in its character as a federal enactment will prevail. This is a departure from the arrangement under the 1960 Constitution whereby an existing law on a concurrent matter was deemed to have been enacted by the regional legislatures, except in so far as the governor-general may have otherwise declared. (By the Concurrent Legislation [Designation as Federal Ordinances] Order, 1959, nineteen ordinances were so declared.)

It is important to emphasise that, contrary to the impression created in the judgment of the Lagos State high court in a case in 1980,[2] the effect of the provision in the new Constitution as it relates to an existing law on a concurrent matter, is not to make such law an exclusively federal enactment. The laws in question in the case, s. 20 of the Local Government Edict 1976 of Lagos State and the Local Government

Electoral Regulations made thereunder, relate to matters — registration of voters and the procedure regulating elections to a local government council — which are made concurrent to both federal and state legislatures by the Constitution (item E, concurrent legislative list). The court held that these enactments became federal enactments by virtue of the provision of the Constitution relating to existing laws. While this is true, they do not thereby cease to be state enactments, and it is as state enactments, rather than as federal enactments, that they should have been applied by the Lagos State high court.

An existing law is defined, significantly, to mean any law, including 'any rule of law or any enactment whatsoever which is in force immediately' before the coming into force of the Constitution or which, having been passed or made before the commencement date, comes into force after that date (s. 274[4]). What this means is that the rules of the common law and equity which have been received in the country as well as those of customary law and Islamic law are now to be deemed to be either Acts of the national assembly or Laws of the state house of assembly, as the case may be. As a *form* of law, they become, notionally at least, converted to — and acquire the character of — statute law. In the result, there is now only one stream of law in the country, namely statute law. The common law, equity, customary law and Islamic law have relevance only as *sources* of law. This result may have important consequences for the jurisdiction of customary and area courts and for other purposes too. The English statutes of general application which have been imported into the country along with the common law and equity also operate today as either Acts of the national assembly or Laws of the state house of assembly.

(ii) *Federal capital territory*

The Constitution establishes a federal capital with clearly defined territory, and vests in the federal government the ownership of all lands therein and all powers of government (ss. 261 and 262). Within the federal territory, therefore, the federal government is the sole governmental authority with undivided powers, consisting of a combination of all federal and state powers under the federal scheme of division. Thus the legislative and executive powers exercisable within a state by its house of assembly and governor enure, with suitable modifications and adaptations, respectively to the national assembly and the president of the republic as the legislative and executive authorities for the federal captial territory; similarly, the judicial power of a state enures to the courts of the federal capital territory (s. 263). In its application to the federal capital territory, the Constitution is accordingly to be construed as if

(a) references to the governor, deputy governor and the executive council of a state were reference to the president, vice-president and the executive council of the federation respectively;
(b) references to the chief judge and judges of the state high court were references to the chief judge and judges of the high court of the federal capital territory; and
(c) references to persons, offices and authorities of a state were references to the persons, offices and authorities of the federation with like status, designations and powers respectively; and in particular, as if references to the attorney-general, commissioners and the director of audit of a state were references to the attorney-general, ministers and auditor-general of the federation with like status, designations and powers (s. 264).

It may be mentioned in parenthesis that for purposes of election to the national assembly the federal capital territory counts as one senatorial district and one federal constituency from which one member is to be elected to each of the two houses (s. 264).

2. *Extent of federal powers*

The powers of the federal government are indicated in the exclusive and concurrent lists and the relevant provisions in the body of the Constitution. Yet the extent of federal powers cannot be fully appreciated by merely looking at the lists without an explanatory note on the significance of some of the matters included therein.

(i) *Public order and public safety*

The maintenance of public order and safety is the primary duty of any government. It is therefore significant that the instruments of law and order — the police and the armed forces — are centralised. But the function of law and order involves much more than police action in preventing disturbances of the public peace. It embraces the whole field of the regulation of human behaviour — the prohibition of antisocial behaviour, the creation of criminal offences generally, and the imposition of penalty therefor. This is the main concern of the function of law and order. Significantly, the Constitution places this vital function within the concurrent authority of both the federal and state government by empowering the national assembly to legislate 'with respect to the maintenance and securing of public safety and public order and providing, maintaining and securing of such supplies and services' as it may designate to be essential supplies and services, but without prejudice to the power of a state house of assembly to legislate on those matters (s. 11[1] and [2]). The federal legislature is thus empowered to create offences. It can, for example, legislate on sedition, particularly sedition against the government of the federation. It follows that, except for offences relating to matters within exclusive federal or state competence, the criminal code operates both as a federal and state law under the provisions of the Constitution relating to existing law (s. 274[1]).

Public safety demands more than the maintenance of law and order and the protection of the members of the community from danger. It extends to the preservation of the state itself and its Constitution together with the governments, both federal and state, established by the Constitution. The power of the national assembly to make laws with respect to the maintenance and securing of public safety will thus enable it to make any laws necessary for the preservation of the republic and its Constitution against acts endangering their safety, whether the acts be those of a foreign country or those of a constituent government in the federation or of individuals. A state government is expressly enjoined by the Constitution to exercise its executive authority so as not to impede or prejudice the exercise of the executive powers of the federation or to endanger the continuance of federal government in Nigeria (s. 5[1]). Any contravention of this prohibition may be checked by means not only of appropriate executive action by the president but also by appropriate legislation enacted by the national assembly in pursuance of its power to make laws with respect to the maintaining and securing of public safety. Under the 1963 Constitution the power of the federal legislature to act in this way was reinforced by a specific provision, which authorised it to make laws for any state outside the legislative lists to an extent necessary to secure compliance with the prohibition.[3] This provision is omitted from the new Constitution, but its omission does not affect the competence of the national assembly to act under its general power to maintain and secure public safety.

(ii) *Local government*

Except for certain aspects of it shortly to be mentioned, local government is not specified in the body of the Constitution or in the legislative lists as being within federal competence. It is therefore a residual matter, and as such lies within the exclusive competence of the state governments. The authority of a state government over local government derives thus from the fact that it is a residual matter, and not, as is commonly supposed,[4] from the provision of the Constitution requiring every state government to ensure the existence of democratically elected local government councils under a Law which provides for their establishment, structure, composition, finance and functions (s. 7[1]). That provision is not a grant of power. It assumes that a state government has power over local government under some other provision of the Constitution. Its purpose is, by imposing a mandatory directive on how this power is to be exercised, to restrict it. With the restriction implied in this mandatory directive, a state government cannot, as hitherto, conduct local government as it pleases; it is bound to conduct it through local government councils democratically elected under a Law that provides for their establishment, structure etc. The concern is to ensure that a state government will not abuse its power, by, for example, using its own appointed agents to conduct the business of local government. The effect of the provision is thus to take away from a state government the discretion normally implied in a power. Instead, it obliges a state government not only to enact the necessary legislation to provide for the establishment, structure, composition, functions and finances of local government councils, but, more importantly, to ensure the existence of democratically elected local government councils under such law. Whether the duty thus cast upon a state government can be compelled raises an interesting question into which it is not necessary to go here.

But the really significant point for our present purposes is not the basis of a state government's authority over local government, but rather the fact that its authority is not exclusive in respect of every aspect of the matter. In this, our Constitution marks an innovation from the normal pattern of the distribution of powers under federalism. For local government, being an example *par excellence* of a matter of local concern, is universally recognised to be the exclusive responsibility of the state governments in accordance with the underlying principle of federalism which requires that, within the framework of a central government, matters of local concern should be managed by regionalised governmental units free from interference by the central government. Federal government involvement in local government is thus a contradiction of the very idea of federalism. The innovation of our Constitution has come as a concession to the extreme demand that local government should be established in the Constitution as a third tier of government, with powers and resources derived directly from the Constitution in exactly the same way as the federal and state governments.

The compromise adopted by the Constitution is to make it obligatory on a state government to ensure the existence of democratically elected local government councils, to prescribe criteria for delimiting the areas of authority of such councils, and the minimum functions to be assigned to them under state laws and to guarantee to them direct allocation of funds from federal revenue. As regards allocation of federal revenue, the national assembly is required, as a matter of duty, to make provisions for statutory allocation of public revenue to local government councils (s. 7[6][*a*]). A state house of assembly is under a similar duty (s. 7[6][*b*]).

Registration of voters and the procedure relating to elections to a local government council are another area of federal government involvement in local government under the Constitution (item E, concurrent legislative list). These may be legislated upon by the national assembly, but this is without prejudice to the authority of a state house of assembly to legislate on local government elections generally, including the narrow aspects relating to registration of voters and the procedure for elections. But while a state house of assembly may, concurrently with the national assembly, legislate on the registration of voters, it is the responsibility of the federal electoral commission, to the exclusion of the state electoral commission, to compile a register of voters and to ensure that it is prepared and maintained in such form as to facilitate its use for the purpose of elections to local government councils (3rd Sch., para. 6). The role of the state electoral commission as regards the compilation of a register of voters is merely to advise the federal electoral commission in so far as the register is applicable to local government elections in the state. On the other hand, the state electoral commission has the exclusive responsibility for organising, undertaking and supervising all local government elections within the state, under federal or state law.

It is contended that the creation of local government areas is also the responsibility of the national assembly. The reasoning behind this contention is that since the area of each state is defined in the Constitution by reference to named local areas which happen to be the same as the existing local government areas, the creation of local government areas will necessarily involve a constitutional amendment by means of legislation enacted by the national assembly, with the approving resolution of the houses of assembly of not less than two-thirds of all the states. The argument is untenable. The first point to notice is that the areas named in the Constitution as forming the area of each state are not explicitly stated to be local government areas. Nowhere in the Constitution are they referred to as local government areas. It just happens that they correspond to the names of existing local government areas. But some of them, e.g. Abakaliki, Onitsha or Enugu in Anambra state, are also the names of existing towns. It follows that the areas named could be references either to existing local government areas, existing towns or simply local communities comprising a group of towns. They are perhaps better regarded simply as local communities. But whether they are regarded as local communities or as local government areas, the important point is that their designation in the Constitution carries no implication as to the number of local government *councils* that may exist within each of them. The area of a state, as defined by reference to the named localities, would not have been increased or decreased by the establishment of two or more local government *councils* within each of the named areas.

Furthermore, the boundaries of each named area are not defined in the Constitution so as to identify its territorial extent and thereby to preclude the transfer of any part of it to another area by a law made by the state legislature. So long as all the named areas remain in existence, the extent of the land area comprised in each of them has no constitutional significance; the Constitution is not amended or violated in any way by the transfer of any part of the territory of some areas to others.

This lack of a constitutional delimitation of boundaries affects not only the component areas but the state itself. The territorial area of a state can only be defined in a legally meaningful way by delimiting its boundaries by reference either to identifiable boundary marks or by a detailed survey description showing the longitudes and latitudes. That was how the areas of the regions were defined in the 1960 and 1963 Constitutions. The area of the federal capital territory is also defined by the same method in the new Constitution (1st Sch., Part II). The definition of the area of each state by reference to named localities is perhaps aimed at brevity and simplicity, but it fails completely to provide a precise constitutional delimitation of the boundaries of the states.

(iii) *Economic activities*

The federal government has exclusive responsibility in respect of the entire field of trade and commerce, not just inter-state and international trade and commerce as under the 1963 Constitution. The clause (item 61) assigning trade and commerce to the federal government also particularised the following —

(*a*) trade and commerce between Nigeria and other countries including import of commodities into and export of commodities from Nigeria, and trade and commerce between the states;
(*b*) establishment of a purchasing authority with power to acquire for export or sale in world markets such agricultural produce as may be designated by the national assembly;
(*c*) inspection of produce to be exported from Nigeria and the enforcement of grades and standards of quality in respect of produce so inspected;
(*d*) establishment of a body to prescribe and enforce standards of goods and commodities offered for sale;
(*e*) control of the prices of goods and commodities designated by the national assembly as essential goods or commodities; and
(*f*) registration of business names.

By its power over trade and commerce within each state, the federal government is put in a position to control industrial and economic activities throughout the country, resulting in a marked predominance of federal over state power, since the authority to regulate economic activities is today the mainstay of governmental power in a federation. The federal government in the United States has been able to achieve something approaching this overriding authority through a purposeful application of its power to regulate inter-state commerce. For example, it has by virtue of it been able to impose an embargo on child labour,[5] to enforce minimum working hours and wages in the states. As Bernard Schwartz has so pertinently commented:

If wheat production intended by the farmer solely for his domestic consumption can be regulated by Congress because of its possible effect upon inter-state commerce however indirect it may be, there are, in practice, no restrictions upon federal regulation of even so-called purely local commerce. And, if this is true, the American system is clearly no longer one of dual federalism. The American Union today is not based upon a division of sovereignty between governmental equals. It is, instead, characterised by the predominance of federal over state power. There is no longer an exclusive area of state authority over commerce within which federal authority cannot be exerted.[6]

This new development in the American federalism has been justified on the ground that

active intervention by the state in social and economic affairs, such as is felt to be necessary at the present time, can, as a practical matter, normally best be carried on upon a national, rather than a purely local, scale. Business in America is today nation-wide in scope, and regulation limited to state boundaries would prove futile to cope with most economic abuses. In addition, the uniformity needed for effective regulation could hardly be secured by individual regulatory laws on the part of each of the 48 American states.[7]

The implications of the exclusive power which the federal government has under these provisions to control economic activities within the states would appear not to be fully appreciated by the draftsman in framing the specification in item H of the concurrent legislative list relating to industrial, commercial or agricultural development. It is there provided that the national assembly may make laws with respect to

(a) the health, safety and welfare of persons employed to work in factories, offices or other premises or in inter-state transportation and commerce including the training, supervision and qualification of such persons;
(b) the regulation of ownership and control of business enterprises throughout the federation for the purpose of promoting, encouraging or facilitating such ownership and control by citizens of Nigeria;
(c) the establishment of research centres for agricultural studies; and
(d) the establishment of institutions and bodies for the promotion or financing of industrial, commercial or agricultural projects.

The federal government already possesses, under the trade and commerce clause, exclusive power over all the matters enumerated in item H of the concurrent list, so that their enumeration here is unnecessary. Secondly, their enumeration here suggests that the power of the federal government in respect of industrial, commercial or agricultural development is limited to the matters so specified, whereas under the trade and commerce clause the power embraces much more than that. Clearly the stipulations of item H of the concurrent list must be read subject to those of the trade and commerce clause in the exclusive list.

Item H of the concurrent list further provides that 'subject to the provisions of this Constitution a House of Assembly may make laws for that State with respect to industrial, commercial or agricultural development of the State', and that 'nothing in the foregoing paragraphs of this item shall be construed as precluding a House of Assembly from making Laws with respect to any of the matters referred to in the foregoing paragraphs.' It is necessary to emphasise that whatever power is conferred on a state government by this provision is expressly made subject to the exclusive power of the federal government under the trade and commerce clause.

The federal control of industrial and economic activities in Nigeria which is derived from the allocation of trade and commerce to the federal government is complemented by its exclusive power in respect of bankruptcy and insolvency (item 5); banks, banking, bills of exchange and promissory notes (item 6); borrowing of money within or outside Nigeria for the purposes of the federation or of any state (item 7); commercial and industrial monopolies, combines and trusts (item 11); control of capital issues (item 12); copyright (item 13); currency, coinage and legal tender (item 14); designation of securities in which trust funds may be invested (item 20); exchange control (item 24); incorporation, regulation and winding up of bodies corporate, other than co-operative societies, local government councils and bodies corporate established directly by any Law enacted by a state house of assembly (item 31); insurance (item 32); labour, including trade unions, industrial relations, conditions, safety and welfare of labour, industrial disputes, national minimum wage and industrial arbitrations (item 33); maritime shipping (item 35); patents, trade marks, trade or business names, industrial designs and merchandise marks (item 42); professional occupations as may be designated by the national assembly (item 48); the declaration of economic activities to be managed and operated exclusively by the government, and the establishment and regulation of authorities to promote and enforce the observance of the fundamental objectives and directive principles (s. 16[4] and item 59); and weights and measures (item 64).

A factor of controlling significance in economic activities is transport and communications. These again come largely under federal regulation — posts, telegraphs and telephones (item 45); railways (item 54); construction, alteration and maintenance of such roads as may be declared by the national assembly to be federal trunk roads (item 9); traffic on federal trunk roads (item 62); wireless, broadcasting and television other than broadcasting and television provided by the government of a state; allocation of wave-lengths for wireless, broadcasting and television transmission (item 65); aviation, including airports, safety of aircraft and carriage of passengers and goods by air (item 3); maritime shipping and navigation, including (*a*) shipping and navigation on tidal waters; (*b*) shipping and navigation on the River Niger and its affluents and on any such other inland waterway as may be designated by the national assembly to be an international waterway or to be an inter-state waterway; (*c*) lighthouses, lightships, beacons and other provisions for the safety of shipping and navigation; (*d*) such ports as may be declared by the national assembly to be federal ports (including the constitution and powers of port authorities for federal ports) (item 35). As Professor Cole observed, 'the ties provided by the main transportation routes, now under the jurisdiction of the federal authorities, accentuate the growing economic inter-dependence of the regions.'[6]

(iv) *Public revenue: its sources, collection, allocation and expenditure*

Control over sources of revenue. The main sources of public revenue are placed under the control of the federal government — export duties (item 22); mines and minerals, including oilfields, oil mining and natural gas (item 37); and stamp duties (item 57); taxation of incomes, profits and capital gains (item 58). The entire property in — and control of — all minerals, mineral oils and natural gas in, under or upon any land in Nigeria and its territorial waters are vested in the federal government to be managed in such manner as the national assembly may prescribe (s. 40[3]).

Collection of revenue. The national assembly may authorise a state government to collect tax or duty or to administer a law relating to capital gains, incomes or profits of persons other than companies, and stamp duties (item D concurrent list).

Allocation of revenue. Legislation by the national assembly has acquired an additional role because of the fact that, with one exception presently to be mentioned, no formula for revenue allocation between the Federation and the States is provided for in the 1979

Constitution as was done in the 1963 Constitution (ss. 136–42). The matter is left to be prescribed by the national assembly (s. 149[2]). Pending legislation on the matter by the national assembly, the system of revenue allocation in force for the 1978/9 financial year is continued in force by the Constitution, with the proviso that where functions have been transferred under the Constitution from the federal government to the state government or from the latter to local government councils, the appropriations in respect of such functions shall also be transferred to the state governments or local government councils, as the case may be (s. 272). No obligation is placed on the national assembly to prescribe a new revenue allocation formula either at all or within any given time. It has the same discretion to enact or not to enact the necessary legislation as it has in respect of its law-making power generally.

The revenue over which the national assembly is given power to prescribe the terms and manner for its distribution is defined in s. 149(1) of the Constitution to embrace *all* revenues collected by the federal government, except the proceeds from the personal income tax of the personnel of the armed forces, the Nigeria police force, the ministry of external affairs and residents of the federal capital territory. The federal government is required to maintain a special account, to be called 'the Federation Account', into which shall be paid *all* revenues collected by it (except those mentioned above). The amount which is to be distributed according to a formula prescribed by the national assembly is not the total sum collected by the federal government and paid into the Federation Account, but only so much as stands to the credit of the account after deducting any revenue collected by the federal government from capital gains tax, personal income tax (other than those mentioned above) and stamp duty, which the Constitution directs shall be distributed among the states on the basis of derivation, or be treated as part of the consolidated fund of the state where it is collected by a state government (s. 150).

Subject to this, the national assembly has a discretion as the 'terms and manner' on or in which the revenue shall be shared (*a*) among the federal, state and local governments; (*b*) among the states *inter se* in respect of their own share; and (*c*) among the states for the benefit of their respective local government councils in respect of the local government share (s. 149[2], [3] and [4]). The national assembly has therefore a free hand to determine what proportions of the revenue are to go to the federal, state and local governments, from which it follows that no state or local government has a right to any definite or fixed proportion of it; accordingly they cannot legally complain of the allocation to them being too small.

Yet the power of the national assembly to legislate with respect to revenue allocation is by no means absolute. Its power is in fact restricted in three ways. First, the assembly is not free to give all the revenue to the federal government. Each tier of government, federal, state and local, has a right to a share by virtue of the stipulation in the Constitution that the revenue 'shall be distributed among' them; only the proportions and other terms and manner of distribution are within the power of the national assembly to prescribe.

Secondly, while the national assembly decides what share of the revenue is to go to local government, and what proportion of the local government share is to go to the group of local government councils in a state taken as a body, the state government has a right to have allocated to it in the first place the proportion due to its local government councils as a body, though the allocation is only made to it in trust for purposes of distribution to its local government councils individually. Having received the share of its local government councils as a body, it is for the state house of assembly to prescribe by law the terms and manner for sharing it among its local government councils individually (s. 149[7]). The national assembly has no right to by-pass the state government and authorise allocation direct to individual local government councils within a state of the share due to them as a body from the federation account. And while it can prescribe the terms and manner for apportioning the local government share among the States, it cannot prescribe the terms and manner of distribution by a State to its individual local government councils. A stipulation that the share due to the group of local government councils within a state shall be distributed 'promptly' to the individual local government councils is usurpation of the powers of the state.

It is true that under part II of the second schedule to the Constitution (the concurrent legislative list), the national assembly is empowered to make law for 'the division of public revenue (a) between the Federation and the States, (b) among the States of the Federation, (c) between the States and local government councils, (d) among the local government councils in the States'. However, this provision is expressed to be subject to other provisions of the Constitution. In so far as the provision may be said to empower the national assembly to authorise allocation from the federation account direct to individual local government councils within a state, and to prescribe the terms and manner of such allocation, it conflicts with s. 149 of the Constitution, and is therefore to that extent inoperative. The wording in part II of the second schedule is also repeated in s. 272, but the latter section confers no power as such on the national assembly to allocate revenue; it merely provides that, pending allocation under s. 149 and part II of the second schedule, the pre-existing system of revenue allocation shall continue.

The wording in part II of the second schedule has another source of confusion. It suggests that the initial sharing of the revenue in the federation account is to be between the federation and the states, and that what is to be shared between the states and local government councils is the share due to the states from that initial apportionment between them and the federation. On the contrary, s. 149(2) makes it clear that the initial apportionment shall be between the Federation, the States and the local government councils.

The third qualification is that the power given to the national assembly is to prescribe the 'terms and manner' for the sharing of the revenue in the federation account. It is not a power to prescribe the application or use of the revenue after it has been shared out. In other words the words 'terms and manner' in s. 149(2), (3) and (4) relate to the sharing or apportionment or distribution of revenue, not to its application or use by the beneficiaries. After it has been apportioned, the money represented by the various shares belongs to the respective beneficiaries who are free to apply and administer it as they like without anyone else's dictation or control. The national assembly is thus not competent to stipulate that part of the share apportioned to a state shall be administered by the federal government for a prescribed purpose, e.g. developmental.

There is yet another power given to the national assembly with respect to revenue allocation, which it is necessary to mention. The assembly is empowered to prescribe what proportion of the total revenue of a state is to be paid by the state government to its local governments, and the terms and manner for making the payment (s. 149[6]). The allocation from the federation account to the local government councils as a body together with the allocation from the state government is paid into a special account, to be called 'State Joint Local Government Account' (s. 149[5]). While the national assembly is empowered under s. 149(6) to prescribe not only the proportion of a state's total revenue to be paid by it to its local government councils but also the 'terms and manner' for making the payment, s. 149(7) provides that both the allocation from this source and from the federation account 'shall be distributed among the local government councils of that State on such terms and in such manner as may be prescribed by the House of Assembly of the State'. This suggests that the 'terms and manner' for the distribution of the allocation from the state government are concurrent to both the national assembly and the state house of assembly, so that in the event of conflict the prescription made by the national assembly prevails.

Expenditure. The spending power of the federal government is not limited to matters within its competence. It can by legislation make grants or loans to a state government or other authority or body for any purpose, notwithstanding that it relates to a matter outside its competence; it can also by legislation impose charges upon the consolidated revenue fund or upon the revenue and assets of the federation for any such purpose (item A). It seems that this will enable the federal government to spend money directly in a state on any project it considers desirable, such as housing or agriculture. Being richer than any of the states, the ability of the federation generally to make loans and grants to the former increases its power and standing in relation to them. It is pertinent to note that this power has been much used in the United States by the practice of the federal government granting subventions to the states for various purposes, as for example, old-age assistance, payment of unemployment benefits, aid to dependent children, maternal and child welfare, public health, assistance to the blind, and the establishment of colleges. This practice, which has rather fittingly been described as 'co-operative federalism', has become such a prominent feature of American federalism that up to 15 per cent of the revenue of the states is estimated to come from this source.[9] But federal bounties are not given with no strings attached; on the contrary, the federal government has used them as a means to control the activities and policies of the states in these matters. The result has been to alter the balance of power within the federation significantly in favour of the federal government.

Federal aid has been extended only at the price of ever-increasing control by Washington over state legislation and administration. 'It cannot be denied that all federal grants for administrative expenses drive stakes of important federal control into state administration. . . . The old adage that he who pays the piper calls the tune contains an element of truth in relation to grant-in-aid services'.[10]

(v) *Emergency*
The proclamation of a state of emergency is the exclusive prerogative of the federal government, though if the proclamation is not to be in force throughout the country but in parts of it only, then it cannot be made unless it is requested by the governor(s) of the state(s) so affected, with the approval of a resolution supported by two-thirds majority of the house(s) of assembly of the state(s) (s. 265[4]). But should the governor, after such resolution has been passed, fail within a reasonable time to make the request, the President may issue a proclamation of emergency within the state (s. 265[5]). Unlike its predecessor, the new Constitution prescribes the situation which must exist as an objective fact to justify the proclamation of an emergency.

The federal government does not possess under the new Constitution the same amplitude of emergency powers as it had under the

1963 Constitution. The proclamation of a state of emergency does not necessarily confer upon it power to legislate generally for Nigeria or any part of it outside the legislative lists for the purpose of maintaining or securing peace, order and good government during the period of the emergency. It can assume such power only in two situations. First is when the federation is at war (s. 11[3]). Even so, it can make only such laws for the peace, order and good government of the federation or any part thereof during such war period as may appear to it to be necessary or expedient for the defence of the federation. The other situation is when, by reason of the circumstances prevailing in a state, the state house of assembly is unable to perform its functions in the sense of being unable to hold a meeting and transact business. In such event, the national assembly may make such laws for the peace, order and good government of that state on matters within exclusive state competence as may appear to it to be necessary or expedient until such time as the state assembly is able to resume its functions (s. 11[4]).

The departure from the wide emergency powers given to the federal government under the 1960–3 Constitutions is aimed at guarding against the kind of abuse that occurred in 1962 when the federal government, on the strength of disturbances in the West regional house of assembly, declared an emergency in the region, suspended the regional governor, premier, ministers, the president, speaker and members of the regional houses of chiefs and assembly, and appointed an emergency administrator charged with the function of administering the government of the region and equipped with all necessary powers, including power to make all such orders as appeared to him necessary or expedient for the purpose of maintaining and securing peace, order and good government.

Apart from its power to legislate generally for the peace, order and good government of Nigeria or any part of it in the two situations mentioned above, only the national assembly can by law authorise derogations from the rights to life and personal liberty as emergency measures, provided that in the case of personal liberty any measures taken in pursuance of such legal authorisation are reasonably justifiable for the purpose of dealing with the situation that exists during that period of emergency, and that in the case of the right to life only death resulting from an act of war can be authorised (s. 41[2]). No state legislature has the power to authorise measures derogating from these two rights even during an emergency. And no legislature, both federal and state, can, during an emergency, authorise derogations from the right to dignity of the human person and the right to fair hearing.

An emergency increases the demands of defence, public safety, public order, public morality and public health, and consequently justifies greater interference by both the federal and state governments with the rights to privacy, freedom of thought, conscience and religion, freedom of expression and the press, peaceful assembly and association, and freedom of movement for the purpose of maintaining and securing the public interest in safety, order or health. Considering that public order and public security are concurrent to both the federal and state government (s. 11), the federal government is put in a position to assume a predominant role in the regulation of these rights during an emergency.

(vi) *Incidental and supplementary powers*
It is a well-established principle of Nigerian law, which now has statutory force,[11] that every grant of power includes by implication all such powers as are reasonably incidental thereto and not expressly excluded.[12] The exclusive list concludes with a recital of this rule which it extends so as to include supplementary powers as well. Part III of the legislative lists, which is concerned almost entirely with amplifying incidental and supplementary powers, provides that any references to them include, without prejudice to their generality (*a*) offences; (*b*) the jurisdiction, powers, practice and procedure of courts of law; (*c*) the acquisition and tenure of land.

Part III of the legislative lists is therefore of considerable importance because it seems to enlarge the matters enumerated in the exclusive list beyond what might be implied as being reasonably incidental or supplementary to them, for, as the Privy Council pointed out in *Balewa* v. *Doherty*,[13] it is arguable that the creation of offences and the compulsory acquisition of land are subjects too important in themselves to be implied as incidents.[14] It is therefore necessary to consider these matters in some detail.

Creation of offences. As we have observed, the general regulation of conduct under penalty within each region is to a large extent concurrent to both federal and state governments. The power of the federal legislature under part III to create offences in relation to matters included in the exclusive list is thus additional to its general power. The extent of this supplemental power is illustrated by the decision in *Balewa* v. *Doherty*. By the Commissions and Tribunals of Enquiry Act 1961, the prime minister of the federation was empowered to set up a commission of enquiry into:
(*a*) any matter or thing within or affecting the general welfare of the federal territory; or
(*b*) any matter or thing within federal competence anywhere within the federation, in respect of which in his opinion, an inquiry would be for the public welfare; or

(c) the conduct of any chief; or
(d) the management of any department of the public service.[15]

A commission of inquiry appointed under the Act was endowed with power to summon witnesses to attend to give evidence or to produce documents, to examine them on oath, and to issue a warrant to compel the attendance of any person summoned who failed to attend without satisfactory excuse.[16] In regard to the federal territory both the appointment of a commission and the conferment of compulsive powers upon it (with the correlative duty on the subject) are within the powers of the federal legislature whose powers in the federal territory are unlimited. Outside the federal territory, however, it has no general regulatory authority over the conduct of chiefs and none at all over the management of the public service of a region, from which it follows that it could not lawfully authorise the appointment of a commission to enquire into them, so that no question of compelling persons in the region to appear as witnesses before such commission could arise at all. The purported imposition of such duty in the regions by the 1961 Act was therefore *ultra vires* the powers of the federal legislature and void.

As far as the Act authorised the appointment of a commission to enquire into matters within federal competence anywhere in the country, it was *prima facie intra vires*, but it was argued that the equipment of such a commission with power to compel the attendance of persons as witnesses was not so *intra vires*; compulsive powers, it was contended, could never be regarded as an incidental or supplementary matter. This argument found acceptance with the federal supreme court,[17] but was rejected by the privy council on appeal. In the opinion of the privy council, whether the incidental power conferred by part III of the legislative lists to appoint a tribunal of enquiry into matters included in the lists comprehended power to compel the attendance of witnesses depended upon the meaning of 'tribunal of enquiry' as used in part III. The Privy Council held that a tribunal of enquiry in the context of that part meant a body with compulsive powers, because a tribunal of enquiry, as it was understood in Nigerian law at the time the constitution was framed, meant a tribunal capable of having compulsive powers. But, granted that part III contemplated a tribunal with compulsive powers, the power to authorise the appointment of such a tribunal was attached not to all matters within federal competence but only to those enumerated in the lists. In so far, therefore, as the 1961 Act purported to authorise the appointment of commission of enquiry with compulsive powers into all matters within federal competence it went beyond the federal legislature's constitutional powers. In other words, it was not within the power of that legislature to impose upon persons in the regions the duty to appear as witnesses before a commission enquiring into federal matters which are not included in the legislative lists. The privy council declined to sever the part of the provision that was *ultra vires* in order to save the rest; the entire provision was accordingly held to be void.[18] (Following upon this, the 1963 Constitution, and now the 1979 Constitution, has an item which incorporates in the list matters on which the federal legislature is given power to make law in the body of the Constitution.)

Indeed, even if the offending part of the provision could be severed, what would be left was still *ultra vires* and void. For the power to compel the attendance of witnesses before a commission enquiring into matters specified in the legislative lists was only an incidental and not a main power. As such it could be assumed only in relation to actual legislation in being or in the process of enactment or to a function of the federal government actually being discharged. Unless there was such a legislation in being or in the process of enactment, one could not meaningfully talk of powers incidental to its subject-matter, for the idea of an incidental power implies that there must be some connection between it and the main power to which it is sought to be attached.

> Some connection must be shown between the two matters and when shown, it must be examined to see whether the one is sufficiently close to the other to be called incidental or supplementary to it. Now, one cannot talk sensibly of an offence being incidental or supplementary to banks or banking, or to railways (Item 37) or to trunk roads (Item 39). But if there has been legislation about trunk roads, one can ask oneself whether the creation of the particular offence can properly be called an incidental or supplementary part of that legislation. . . . There must be actual legislation in being . . ., only then can the connection between the two matters be examined to see whether it is sufficiently close. It can . . . readily be appreciated that a statute authorising the Prime Minister to create any offence in relation to any subject on the legislative lists would be too wide; it would enable him to remodel the criminal law.[19]

Exactly the same conclusion was reached by the privy council in the earlier Australian case of *Attorney-General for Commonwealth of Australia* v. *Colonial Sugar Refining Co. Ltd.*,[20] where the Royal Commissions Acts 1902–12, enacted by the parliament of the Commonwealth of Australia, authorised the setting up of commissions of enquiry into all matters of federal competence irrespective of whether there had been actual legislation on them. The privy council held that

> until the Commonwealth Parliament has entrusted a Royal Commission with the statutory duty to inquire into a specific subject legislation as to which has been by the Federal Constitution of Australia assigned to the Commonwealth Parliament, that Parliament cannot confer such powers as the Acts in question

contain on the footing that they are incidental to inquiries which it may some day direct.

(As a result of this decision, the tribunal of enquiry was made a main and independent item in the legislative lists under the 1963 Constitution, but the new Constitution has reverted it to an incidental or supplemental matter.)

It may be mentioned that the power of the federal legislature to create offences with respect to matters in the exclusive list could operate as a factor limiting the residual powers of the state legislatures to legislate generally for the peace, order and good government of their states. Thus, in *Akwale v. R.*,[21] the accused was charged under a section of the Northern Region Penal Code 1959, which makes it a criminal breach of trust, punishable with up to fourteen years' imprisonment, for a person entrusted with property or with any dominion over property in the way of his business, as (*inter alia*) a banker, dishonestly to misappropriate it or to dispose of it unlawfully or wilfully to suffer any other person to do so.[22] It was argued that since the exclusive power of parliament in respect of banks and banking includes as an incident exclusive power to create offences in relation to banks and banking, the above provisions of the Northern Region penal code constituted an encroachment on the exclusive field of the federal parliament and as such were unconstitutional and void. The supreme court held that the provisions in question were within the powers of the Northern region legislature to enact, as being substantially for the peace, order and good government of the region; they were not an enactment 'in respect of' banks and banking. It was emphasised that in deciding whether a statute exceeded the power of the legislature which enacted it the court should have regard to its 'true nature and character,[23] [and] if, on the view of the statute as a whole, you find that the substance of the legislation is within the express powers, then it is not invalidated if incidentally it affects matters outside the authorised field.'[24]

This does not, however, mean that a legislature with limited powers can, under the guise of dealing with one matter, encroach upon fields forbidden to it.

The jurisdiction, powers, practice and procedure of courts of law.
Power to establish a court reasonably implies an incidental power to prescribe its jurisdiction, powers, practice and procedure. With regard to matters mentioned in the exclusive legislative list, this is expressly stated to be so. Again it must be borne in mind that the power is only an incidental power, and cannot therefore be exercised generally in regard to all matters enumerated in the list but only with respect to the subject-matter of an actual piece of legislation.[25] If it

were otherwise, the federal legislature could authorise a court to apply regional laws on concurrent matters upon which it has itself not yet legislated. It should further be explained that it is not competent for the federal legislature by virtue only of its incidental power in this respect to confer jurisdiction on courts established for a state by the constitution or by its legislature.

The acquisition and tenure of land. Again, the control of land within a state is a residual matter falling primarily under the general regulatory authority of the state legislature. However, the federal legislature may legislate with respect to the acquisition and tenure of land within a state as an incident to its power to legislate on matters included in the legislative lists. But since its power so to do is only an incidental one it cannot authorise the acquisition of land for any matter in the legislative lists upon which it has not actually legislated. In delivering the opinion of the privy council in *Balewa* v. *Doherty* Lord Devlin observed: 'It can be seen that a statute authorising the Prime Minister to acquire compulsorily any land that might be needed if there were in future to be legislation on any subject in the legislative lists would be too wide; it would be tantamount to giving him power to nationalise the land.'[26]

It will be recalled that in *Balewa* v. *Doherty* the privy council thought that compulsory acquisition of land is too important a matter to be regarded as an incidental power in the absence of express provision making it so (such as that in part III). With respect, this view seems unduly generalised. Whether the power of compulsory acquisition of land can be implied in a grant of power should depend on the nature and purpose of that power. For example, the federal legislature had power under the 1963 Constitution to establish courts in the states. Now, power to establish a court would seem reasonably to imply an incidental power compulsorily to acquire land for that purpose. The same may also apply to the power to establish and regulate an authority with power to administer trusts or to carry out censorship of cinematograph films in the states.

REFERENCES

1. *Doherty* v. *Balewa* (1961), 1 All N.L.R. 604.
2. *Lawal* v. *The Lagos State Electoral Commission*, Suit No. ID/93/80 of 24/3/80, High Court, Ikeja.
3. s. 71.
4. *Balogun* v. *Att.-Gen. of Lagos State*, Suit No. ID/114/80 of 17 March 1980, High Court, Ikeja.
5. *United States* v. *Darby*, 312 U.S. 100 (1941), overruling *Hammer* v. *Dagenhart*, 247 U.S. 251 (1918).
6. Bernard Schwartz, *American Constitutional Law* (1955), 170.
7. Schwartz, op. cit., 48.
8. *Constitutional Problems of Federalism in Nigeria* (1960), 5.
9. Schwartz, op. cit., 177.
10. Schwartz, op. cit., 178.
11. s. 10(2) Interpretation Act, 1964, which is applied to the interpretation of the Constitution, s. 277(4).
12. See *Att.-Gen.* v. *Great Eastern Railway* (1880), 5 App. Cas. 473.
13. [1963] 1 W.L.R. 949 at 961.
14. Some of the matters in the list seem however necessarily to imply a power to create offences in relation to them, e.g. control of capital issues, copyright, currency, coinage, exchange control etc.
15. s. 3(1).
16. s. 8(*c*) and (*d*).
17. *Doherty* v. *Balewa* (1961), 1 All N.L.R. 604.
18. This prompted the enactment of a statute in the Western and Eastern Regions that a law or ordinance in excess of powers conferred by the Constitution on the legislature shall be construed as valid to the extent to which its provisions are not in excess of the power: see Interpretation (Amendment) Law 1964 (W.R.); Revised Edition Law of Interpretation (Amendment) Law 1964 (E.R.) amending the Interpretation Ordinance, Cap. 167.
19. [1963] 1 W.L.R. at 961 per Lord Devlin, delivering the judgment of the Privy Council.
20. [1911] A.C. 237.
21. 1963 N.N.L.R. 105.
22. s. 315; see also s. 311.
23. See *Russell* v. *R.* (1882), L.R. 7 App. Cas. 827 (P.C.).
24. Per Lord Atkin in *Gallagher* v. *Lyon* [1937] A.C. 863 at 869.
25. *Balewa* v. *Doherty*, ibid.
26. [1963] 1 W.L.R. at 961.

5
THE EXECUTIVE PRESIDENCY

In Nigeria the office of president pertains not to the government alone, but to the entire state which, besides the government, also embraces the territory and people inhabiting it. Unlike a minister whose office relates only to the government, as is shown by his designation as minister of the government, the president is referred to in the Constitution as the president of the federation (ss. 122[1], 260 & 263 and 5th Sch., Part II) or as the president of the Federal Republic of Nigeria (s. 277 & 6th Sch.). He presides therefore over the entire state and its government.

1. *The president as representing the state*

In relation to the state, the presidency connotes headship. The title of head of state is expressly conferred on him by the Constitution (s. 122[2]). The position of head of state has been aptly described as follows:

As a State is an abstraction from the fact that a multitude of individuals live in a country under a sovereign government, every State must have a Head as its highest organ, which represents it, within and without its borders, in the totality of its relations. . . . The Head of a State, as its chief organ and representative in the totality of its international relations, acts for his State in its international intercourse, with the consequence that all his legally relevant international acts are considered to be acts of his State.[1]

The Constitution acknowledges the president's representative status by vesting in him and the government of the federation all property, right, privilege, liability or obligation of the federation, and making it exercisable or enforceable by or against them (s. 276). The vesting of the property, right or liability of the federation in the president and government of the federation must be considered joint and several, subject to the exception that the ownership and control of minerals, mineral oils and natural gas and the ownership of land in the federal capital territory are vested exclusively in the government of the federation (ss. 40[3] & 261[2]).

By virtue of his headship of the state and of being its representative in the totality of its relations, the president is endowed with all the symbolism and dignity of the state. 'I deny', said a U.S. attorney-general, 'that there is a particle less dignity belonging to the office of President than to the office of King of Great Britain or of any other potentate on the face of the earth. He represents the majesty of the law and of the people as fully and as essentially, and with the same dignity, as does any absolute monarch or the head of any independent government in the world.'²

However, the president's headship of the state has to be viewed and appreciated in the context of Nigeria as a republican state. After proclaiming the state a republic by the name of the federal republic of Nigeria (s. 2[1]), the Constitution goes on to affirm that 'sovereignty belongs to the people of Nigeria from whom government through this Constitution derives all its power and authority' (s. 14[2][*a*]), that the state is 'based on the principles of democracy and social justice' (s. 14[1]), and that 'the state social order is founded on ideas of Freedom, Equality and Justice' (s. 17[1]).

The republican character of the state makes the president's relation to it quite unlike that of the British sovereign to the state. The latter does not merely represent, but personifies, the state in a real, as distinct from a symbolic, sense. The king is invested with the title of sovereignty (he is the sovereign), implying *dominium* or ownership. The government is his, his majesty's government. Allegiance is owed to him personally, and public functionaries are required to swear that they will be 'faithful and bear true allegiance' to him, and will 'well and truly serve' him. He is indeed the state, a fact which is acknowledged in the national anthem (*God save the King*), in the reference to state land as crown land, and in various other ways.

Because of the personal identification with the state which the title of sovereignty implies, the monarch as sovereign attracts greater pre-eminence in society. He is set apart from the rest of the community; as between him and them the relationship is one of sovereign lord and liege, a relationship that demands from the subject not only allegiance and obeisance but also a reverence that borders on obsequiousness. The monarch is 'fawned on in public and carped at in private'. He is 'his majesty', which again expresses his claim to be the state. His style of living is equally majestic, since grace, pomp and splendour are indispensable to the dignity of a personal sovereign. On state occasions, he is adorned with the full insignia of state and attended by uniformed guards. His person is inviolable. He can no more be made personally amenable to the process of the law than the state itself can. He is the fountain of justice. The courts are his courts, and administer justice in his name. It follows that it would be a manifest absurdity if he were to be triable by his own court. What this means is that he is above the law. 'The king can do no wrong' is a well-recognised maxim of law, which expresses the fact that his misdeeds are not cognisable by the courts. The only redress against an erring king is to force him to abdicate or to have him impeached and dethroned, but not to put him on trial in his own courts.

By comparison, the president of the federal republic of Nigeria is not the state, and does not personify it except perhaps in a symbolic sense only. The government is not his, neither is he the government. Allegiance is owed, not to him, but to the sovereign people who make up the federal republic of Nigeria. A public functionary swears, not that he will well and truly serve the president, but that he will 'discharge my duties to the best of my ability, faithfully and in accordance with the Constitution of the Federal Republic of Nigeria and the law, and always in the interest of the sovereignty, integrity, solidarity, well-being and prosperity of the Federal Republic of Nigeria' (6th Sch.). The president himself is required, as a condition of assuming the functions of his office, solemnly to swear that he will be 'faithful and bear true allegiance to the Federal Republic of Nigeria' (6th Sch.). (The president's oath of office is considered in chapter 8.) He is not 'majesty' but simply 'excellency', as befits one who represents the state.

In the balanced words of Lord Bryce writing on the American presidency:

The President is simply the first citizen of a free nation, depending for his dignity on no title, no official dress, no insignia of state. . . . To a European observer, weary of the slavish obsequiousness and lip-deep adulation with which the members of the reigning families are treated on the eastern side of the Atlantic, fawned on in public and carped at in private, the social relations of an American President to his people are eminently refreshing. There is a great respect for the office, and a corresponding respect for the man as the holder of the office, if he has done nothing to degrade it. There is no servility, no fictitious self-abasement on the part of the citizens, but a simple and hearty deference to one who represents the majesty of the nation. . . . He is followed about and fêted, and in every way treated as the first man in the company; but the spirit of equality which rules the country has sunk too deep into every American nature for him to be expected to be addressed with bated and whispering reverence. He has no military guard, no chamberlains or grooms-in-waiting; his everyday life is simple; . . . he is surrounded by no such pomp and enforces no such etiquette as that which belongs to the governors even of second-class English colonies, not to speak of the Viceroys of India and Ireland.[3]

This picture of the social relations of an American president to his people does not exactly fit the presidency in the context of Nigeria as a developing African country. Equality expresses, by and large, the economic standing of a person in relation to another. But it is not so much economic power as the general economic condition that truly determines equality in society. Equality is basically an attitude of mind, which in turn is a product of social conditions. In comparison with the peasant farmer or urban labourer in Africa, the factory worker in Britain or the United States has a fairly good income and good living, medical, water, transport, electric and educational facilities. These amenities have improved his conditions of life to an extent where the gap between him and the upper wealthy classes has become narrowed. He can therefore afford to regard the latter with an attitude, if not of equality, then certainly not of inferiority. To him the president or prime minister is just another member of the community like himself, elevated no doubt by the power and perquisites of his office, but not basically different from himself. The march of economic progress, which has almost obliterated the distinction between the haves and the have-nots, has sobered the arrogance of power, so that the president or prime minister does not now feel himself different from the rest of the community. Equally sobering is the realisation that his tenure of the office is temporary, and that sooner or later he will have to relinquish it and resume the life of an ordinary citizen.

On the other hand, the poverty and ignorance of the masses in Africa create in them a different kind of attitude. A modern, well-furnished house excites wonder, and a car even more so; its owner is regarded with equal curiosity, as though he were a being from another planet. His world is indeed different from theirs, because of the fantastic gap in their respective standards of living. Now, if we remember that the president represents the highest point in magnificent living in the society, the contrast between him and the masses becomes glaring, excluding at once any attitude of equality on either side. In these circumstances it can only border upon the ridiculous to speak at all of equality between them. The masses, sunk deep in poverty and never having experienced anything better or more elevating than life in a thatched hut, barren of any kind of furnishing, not to mention other modern comforts, can hardly be expected to develop any attitude of equality with the president. If anything, he is to them like a demigod who occasionally comes down from his high pedestal to visit them during a tour of inspection or what is sometimes called a meet-the-people tour, in the course of which he addresses huge crowds, and tells them nice, seductive things about what the government plans to do for them in the next planning period — promises which as often as not remain unfulfilled. Such meetings are an occasion for adulation and the display of slavish obsequiousness. The president is hailed, fêted and entertained with traditional dances, and showered with gifts.

Splendour is indeed a feature of the life style of African presidents. 'Personifying the state', writes Arthur Lewis, 'they dress themselves up in uniforms, build themselves palaces, bring all other traffic to a standstill when they drive, hold fancy parades and generally demand to be treated like Egyptian pharaohs.'[4]

One should not be understood to be condemning ceremony of all kinds or as suggesting that the president should move with the traffic on a busy street. Ceremony may indeed have a useful role in the life of a nation, provided that it is limited to appropriate state occasions and not made to attend the everyday life of the president. It gives expression to a nation's past and culture, and in Africa there is a special need for salvaging African traditional forms of ceremony from years of neglect and suppression under colonialism. It was this desire for cultural revival, a desire to demonstrate that the African has a past, that lay behind the elaborate and somewhat extravagant pomp and pageantry that marked ceremonial occasions in Ghana under Nkrumah. It was a desire to recreate in the institutions of the present the glory and splendour of ancient African kingdoms, like that of ancient Ghana, whose king was said, when holding audience, to sit 'in a pavilion around which stand his horses caparisoned in cloth of gold; behind him stand the pages holding shields and god-mounted sword. . . .'[5] This is a desire in which every African should feel a special pride. George Washington too tried to create ceremony and pomp for the new American nation. For the state opening of congress he drove to Capitol Hill in 'his coach and six, with outriders and footmen in livery'.[6] As it happened, however, his taste for ceremony and pomp on state occasions was not shared by his successors. And so, as Lord Bryce wrote, 'after oscillating between the ceremonious state of George Washington . . . and the ostentatious plainness of Citizen Jefferson, who rode up alone and hitched his horse to the post at the gate, the President has settled down into an attitude between that of the mayor of a great English town on a public occasion, and that of a European cabinet minister on a political tour.'[7] Yet, granted the need for ceremony, a desire for African cultural revival might be only a cover for indulging personal vanity and a desire to assume the style and attributes of a king. 'The adulation of ancient monarchs might overspill and help to create modern equivalents. Ancient kings and modern presidents are then forced to share royal characteristics.'[8] Some of the African presidents, Nkrumah in particular, cannot be acquitted of this charge.

The equality that characterises the relations of an American president to his people is carried to the point of making him amenable to the process of the courts just like any other citizen. The constitution, it is argued, grants him no immunity from suit, so that any concession of it would amount to placing him above the Constitution and thereby violating the cornerstone of American constitutionalism that the government is one of laws, and not of men. 'Under our system of government', said Chief Justice Bartley in granting a *mandamus* against a state governor, 'no officer is placed above the restraining authority, which is truly said to be universal in its behests, all paying it homage, the least as feeling its care, and the greatest as not being exempt from its power.'[9] These observations, it is argued, should apply with equal, if not greater, force to the president of the United States. The argument was indeed accepted by Chief Justice Marshall when he sustained an application for a *subpoena duces tecum* against President Jefferson. Rejecting the president's contention that he could not be drawn from the discharge of his duties at the seat of government and made to attend the court sitting at Richmond, the chief justice drew a distinction between the president and the king of England, and held that all officers in the United States were subordinate to the law and must obey its mandate. In 1973 an action was allowed against President Nixon personally.[10]

Unlike the American constitution, ours grants to an incumbent president, vice-president, governor and deputy governor immunity from court action, both civil and criminal, arrest or imprisonment in pursuance of a court process, and from any court process requiring or compelling their appearance (s. 267[1]). The immunity prevails only during their period of office. A civil action against the president, vice-president, governor or deputy governor in his official capacity as well as a civil or criminal action in which he is only a nominal party, is not affected by the immunity (s. 267[2]).

It seems that the procedural immunity from suit and from court process granted to an incumbent president, vice-president, governor or deputy governor can be defended. The protection is essentially for the office, not of the individual incumbent as such. It is the majesty and dignity of the nation that is at stake. To drag an incumbent president to court and expose him to the process of examination and cross-examination cannot but degrade the office. The interest of the nation in the preservation of the integrity of its highest office should outweigh any objections to the immunity. After all, members of the national assembly are also granted some immunity from legal process for the very same reason that it is necessary for the protection of their office and for the unhindered discharge of its functions.

But it is necessary to emphasise that the protection is against suit and compulsory process. It does not extend to liability. The Constitution does not say that an incumbent president, vice-president, governor or deputy governor shall, during their tenure of office, be immune from civil and criminal liability for their acts; only that 'no civil or criminal proceedings shall be instituted or continued' against them during that period. The institution of proceedings or their continuation is a procedural matter, which presupposes the existence of a cause of action, i.e. an antecedent liability for the violation of a right or criminal prohibition. A president, vice-president, governor or deputy governor who, before or during his tenure of office, commits a criminal offence, a tort or breach of contract is as fully liable therefor as any other person. The office affords him no immunity from liability for acts done during his tenure any more than it wipes out liability for acts done before. The only effect of the immunity is to suspend enforcement of the liability by civil or criminal proceedings until the time when the office is vacated. Equally any such proceedings already instituted and pending at the time of assumption of office are suspended. But since liability is not affected, the incumbent becomes amenable to civil or criminal action after he ceases to hold office. The Constitution confirms this by providing that the period covered by his tenure of office shall be discounted in calculating the period prescribed by law for instituting civil actions.

The immunity from civil or criminal process has also only a procedural significance. The fact that legal process cannot be issued for the arrest or imprisonment of an incumbent president, vice-president, governor or deputy governor, or to compel his appearance before any tribunal or body does not imply that he is unanswerable for his actions, nor does it take away his competence as a witness. It leaves unaffected his obligation to answer for his acts or omissions and his competence as a witness. Thus, while he cannot be compelled to appear before any tribunal or body, he is not precluded from volunteering to do so. His freedom to volunteer appearance is not taken away by the fact that he cannot waive his immunity from suit or from compulsory process. If the position were that he is unanswerable for his acts or incompetent as a witness, then impeachment before the national assembly for gross misconduct committed in office, and his appearance to defend himself at an impeachment trial, would have been a manifest contradiction. His answerability for his official acts is affirmed not only by the impeachment procedure but also by the fact that he may be sued in his official capacity in civil proceedings and even be compelled to appear (s. 267[2]).

In the light of the purely procedural effect of the immunity, the ruling by the crude oil tribunal of inquiry that the official acts of a head of state are clothed with immunity under the Constitution is misconceived. 'It is thus our view', said the majority of the tribunal, 'that the evidence now required of him being matters affecting his performance in office as Head of State at that time, such matters being clothed with the immunity he had at that time, it would be odd indeed if we could now as it were remove this immunity retroactively as it were, in order to compel him to testify.'[11] This view assumes, quite wrongly, that merely because a head of state cannot, during his tenure of office, be compelled by process to testify, he is not answerable for his acts both official and private. Admittedly, a president who is immune from liability or answerability for acts done while in office cannot be made to answer for them after leaving office. But the Constitution grants him no such immunity. No act of the president is clothed with immunity whether during or after his tenure of office. On the contrary, he is fully answerable for them both during and after his tenure of office. The only protection is against the coercion of legal suit or legal process while he is in office. But the protection from suit and compulsory process ends when the office ceases. This point is important for a proper understanding of the nature and character of the presidency instituted by the Constitution.

It is also important to emphasise that the need for protecting the president from suit or legal process does not mean that he should also be protected by law from insult or abuse beyond the protection afforded by the ordinary law of libel and sedition. Such a protection was conferred in Ghana and Zambia by an amendment to the criminal code in 1961 and 1965 respectively. It was made an offence to publish by writing, word of mouth or in any other manner any defamatory or insulting matter concerning the president with intent to bring him into hatred, ridicule or contempt.[12] The justification for this is questionable. The Ghanaian minister of justice, Mr. Ofori Atta, had defended the provision on the ground that the 'Head of State of Ghana is a sacred person, irrespective of the party to which he belongs.'[13] Ideally, a head of state should be above politics in order that his embodiment of the state and its majesty should attract maximum respect. But an apolitical head of state is possible, if at all, only if he is a titular head; such a head can be above partisan politics because he exercises no political function and belongs to no political party. An executive head of state is in a different position because the exercise of executive powers necessarily invites criticism. Moreover, an executive president is not just the chief functionary of the government; he is to a large extent the government itself. And to ban criticism of him is unduly to inhibit criticism of government. Where an executive president is a partisan leading a political party in a two- or multi-party system, as in Ghana or Zambia in 1961 and 1965, the protection becomes even more objectionable. Such a system necessarily implies political competition. The president should not be a partisan in politics and at the same time refuse to accept its price. Verbal attacks, sometimes of a very derogatory kind, are inseparable from political competition. Within reason it is legitimate for politicians to try to discredit each other as part of the effort to enhance their own standing and undermine that of opponents. The leader of the opposition in Kenya, Mr. Ngala, put the point aptly when he said that, as a political head, the president is 'a person who throws mud at other fellow-politicians and mud can be thrown at him and he can have political fights with other leaders.'[14]

This should not, of course, be turned into a licence for vulgar insult against the head of state, though the danger in prohibiting vulgar insult which is not an offence by the ordinary law of libel or sedition lies in the difficulty of drawing the line between it and permissible criticism. Nor does the use so far made of the prohibition in Ghana and Zambia lead one to believe that the law was aimed against vulgar abuse only. In Ghana a man who, in a conversation with a friend, said that Nkrumah's doctorate degree was an honorary one was prosecuted under the law; the prosecution was later withdrawn and the man detained instead.[15] The vituperation against President Kaunda of Zambia by the opposition M.P., Liso, was singularly vulgar, and his conviction under the provision was probably merited. However, there was nothing vulgar in the other cases in respect of which prosecution had been threatened but not proceeded with; the criticisms might have been incautious and indiscreet but they were by no means vulgar.

2. *The president as chief executive of the government*

The government of the federation is organised around the president. With certain exceptions and restrictions, the Constitution invests him with the entire executive power of the federation and, what is more significant, makes it exercisable by him in his discretion as a personal ruler, uninhibited by the artificial separation between nominal and real authority, whereby powers legally vested in one person can only constitutionally be exercised by others. Unlike his predecessor under the constitution of the first republic, the president under the new Constitution is no figurehead who takes no executive decisions or actions except through or as advised by others, and who therefore bears no personal responsibility whatever for government. On the contrary, he is an executive president in every sense of the term, required to bring his judgment to bear upon every issue presented for decision and upon the content of all advice offered, and to accept personal responsibility for decisions and actions of government.

He differs not only from the ceremonial president of the first republic, but also from the prime minister as head of government of that republic. Again, subject to certain exceptions and restrictions, the authority for the government of the federation belongs to him alone and is not shared with anyone else, whereas the executive authority in the first republic was shared among a cabinet of ministers of whom the prime minister, though the leader, was strictly only the first among equals. The executive president as a single individual combines the effective powers of the cabinet, the head of government and the individual ministers with the symbolic authority of the head of state in the First Republic. It is this *singleness* of authority that marks the characteristic attribute of the executive presidency, distinguishing it from other arrangements, in which the executive power is held and exercised concurrently by a plurality of persons of co-ordinate authority, such as the Roman triumvirate, the collegiate executive of the Swiss system or the cabinet system of the Westminster type practised in the First Republic. The singleness of the authority for government equally rules out the idea of a national or coalition government. There can constitutionally be no question of the executive authority being shared between the president and the leaders of political parties, whether his own or others.

However, this attribute of a single authority does not require that the president should administer the government alone and unaided. He is by the express terms of the Constitution permitted to act either directly or through the vice-president and ministers or officers in the public service of the federation (s. 5[1][a]). Even without such an express provision, the U.S. supreme court has ruled that, although 'the President's duty in general requires his superintendence of the administration, yet this duty cannot require of him to become the administrative officer of every department and bureau, or to perform in person the numerous details incident to services which, nevertheless, he is, in a correct sense, by the Constitution and laws required and expected to perform. This cannot be; first, because, if it were practicable, its effect would be to absorb the duties and responsibilities of the various departments of the government in the personal action of one chief executive officer. It cannot be, for the stronger reason, that it is impracticable — nay, impossible.'[16] Expediency and practicability demands therefore that the president should be free to act through others. 'There can be no doubt', the U.S. supreme court has observed in another case, 'that the president, in the exercise of his executive power under the Constitution, may act through the head of the appropriate executive department. The heads of the departments are his authorised assistants in the performance of his executive duties, and their official acts, promulgated in the regular course of business, are presumptively his acts.'[17] No express delegation is necessary except in cases where he is required to exercise a personal judgment; even then a general delegation suffices.[18]

Is the position, then, that the president is the government? It is claimed for the president of the United States that he is. The designation chief executive is objected to because, in the words of a leading authority on the American Constitution, William Anderson, 'the Constitution does not say that the President is "chief executive". That would imply that there are other executives, of lesser power, associated with him. This vesting clause places the entire executive power of the United States in the hands of one man. It does so by constitutional provision, beyond the power of Congress or the Courts to take away.'[19]

Nigeria's Constitution, while vesting the executive power in the president, does in terms say that he is chief executive. It certainly contemplates the government as an entity different from, and wider than, the president. The separation or differentiation of the two is manifested in the reference to 'the President and Government of the Federation' (s. 276), while the wider coverage of the government is evident from the establishment by the Constitution of other executive authorities and functionaries besides the president — a vice-president, an attorney-general, other ministers, an auditor-general, a police force, armed forces, an executive council, ministries or departments and other executive bodies. But the question is whether all these bodies and functionaries are merely instruments and assistants of the president, lacking any independent functions of their own and acting as mere agents for the exercise on the president's behalf and subject to his control of powers vested in him, so as to make their acts presumptively his acts. If so, then he is, to all intents and purposes, the government of the federation. If, on the other hand, any of the bodies or functionaries possesses any executive functions which, though of less account than the president's, are nevertheless independent of his control, he is certainly not the government but is only the chief executive of the government.

Thus whether the president is the government or, as the Constitution says, only the chief executive cannot be answered by *a priori* generalisation, but by an analysis of the constitutional provisions establishing these bodies and functionaries and defining their functions. In this connection it is worth emphasising that the vesting of executive power in the president as well as the exercise of it is expressly made subject to other provisions of the Constitution. The relevant provisions must therefore be analysed to see what independence, if any, any of the bodies or functionaries enjoys from the president as regards either their existence or their functions or both. This is the subject of a later chapter (chapter 7).

REFERENCES

1. Oppenheim, *International Law*, 8th edn., ed. Lauterpacht, vol. 1, 757.
2. Quoted in *Mississippi* v. *Johnson* (1867), 4 Wall 475.
3. Bryce, *The American Commonwealth*, ed. Hacker, vol. 1 (1959), 25−6.
4. Arthur Lewis, *Politics in West Africa* (1965), 31.
5. Stephen Dzirasa, *Political Thought of Dr. Kwame Nkrumah* 19−20.
6. Bryce, op. cit., 26.
7. loc. cit.
8. Ali Mazrui, 'Nkrumah: the Leninist Czar', *Transition*, 26 (1966), 16.
9. *State of Ohio* v. *Salmon P. Chase*, Governor, 5 Ohio St. 529.
10. See *United States* v. *Nixon* (1973), 41 L. Ed. 2d 1039.
11. *National Concord*, 14 June 1980. The majority relied on a case in which the supreme court held that a civil action cannot lie against a state governor and that his immunity from suit cannot be waived: see *Rotimi* v. *McGregor* (1974) 11 S.C. 133. But the decision lends no support to their ruling.
12. s. 183A Ghana; s. 69 Zambia.
13. Nat. Ass. Deb., 1961.
14. House of Reps. Deb., 27 Oct. 1964, col. 3910.
15. H.L. Bretton, *The Rise and Fall of Kwame Nkrumah* (1966), 58.
16. *Williams* v. *United States* (1843), 1 How. 290 at 297.
17. *Runkle* v. *United States* (1886), 122 U.S. 543 at 547, and the host of other decisions there cited.
18. See *Williams* v. *United States*, ibid.
19. William Anderson, National Government.

6
EXECUTIVE POWER AND ITS EXTENT

1. *Constitutional bases of the president's executive power*

Executive power is difficult of precise delineation. Its limits are obscure. By the terms of the Constitution, the executive power of the federation shall, subject to other provisions, '(*a*) be vested in the president, and (*b*) shall extend to the execution and maintenance of the Constitution, all laws made by the National Assembly and to all matters with respect to which the National Assembly has for the time being power to make laws' (s. 5[1]). This is a simple enough declaration, but its apparent simplicity only serves to mask complex constitutional issues that have divided both judicial and academic opinion.

To begin with, is the clause a grant to the president of the whole of the executive power of the federation as defined in the second part of the provision? Two opposing views are held upon the question. It is asserted upon one view that the vesting clause is not a grant of power, but simply an amplication of the designation or title, chief executive, and that the powers of the president are limited to those specifically granted to him either in the Constitution or other laws. 'The true view of executive function', wrote William Taft, President of the United States in 1909–13, 'is . . . that the President can exercise no power which cannot fairly and reasonably be traced to some *specific* grant of power or justly implied and included within such express grant as proper and necessary to its exercise. Such specific grant must be either in the Constitution or in an act of Congress passed in pursuance thereof.'[1] It is argued that the clause vesting executive power in the president is not such a *specific* provision, and cannot therefore operate as a grant of power. Thus the United States Constitution, after declaring that the executive power shall be vested in the president, goes on to give him specific powers, such as supreme command of the army, and the power to reprieve offences, to take care that the laws be faithfully executed, and with the concurrence of the senate to make treaties and appoint public servants. It is from these specific grants, and not from the general executive power clause, that the president derives whatever executive power he has under the Constitution. For if the general executive power clause were a grant of power, the specific enumerations in the subsequent clauses would be a mere surplusage, serving no purpose except perhaps as an emphasis. Thus Mr. Webster, in a senate debate in February 1835, said the following:

It is true that the Constitution declares that the executive power shall be vested in the President; but the first question which arises is, What is executive power? What is the degree, and what are the limitations? Executive power is not a thing so well known, and so accurately defined, as that the written Constitution of a limited government can be supposed to have conferred it in the lump. . . . I think it perfectly plain and manifest that, although the framers of the Constitution meant to confer executive power on the President, yet they meant to define and limit that power, and to confer no more than they did thus define and limit. When they say it shall be vested in a President, they mean that one magistrate, to be called a President, shall hold the executive authority; but they mean, further, that he shall hold this authority according to the grants and limitations of the Constitution itself.[2]

The other school of thought holds that the clause vesting executive power in the president 'constitutes a grant of all the executive powers of which the Government is capable'.[3]

The U.S. supreme court is divided between these two views. In 1926 a majority of six, in an opinion written by the same former President Taft, then chief justice, held that 'the vesting of the executive power in the President' was 'essentially a grant of power to execute the laws'.[4] In 1951 the court, again by a majority of six, adopted much of the reasoning of the minority in the 1926 case but without directly expressing an opinion on the point. But one of the Justices, in a separate concurring judgment, commented as follows on the government's claim that the vesting clause is a grant of all the executive powers of which the government is capable:

If that be true, it is difficult to see why the forefathers bothered to add several specific items, including some trifling ones. The example of such unlimited executive power that must have most impressed the forefathers was the prerogative exercised by George III, and the description of its evils in the Declaration of Independence leads me to doubt that they were creating their new Executive in his image. Continental European examples were no more appealing. And if we seek instruction from our own times, we can match it only from the executive powers in those governments we disparagingly describe as totalitarian. I cannot accept the view that this clause is a grant in bulk of all conceivable executive power but regard it as an allocation to the presidential office of the generic powers thereafter stated.[5]

It seems clearly more in accord with a commonsense interpretation of the clause to regard it as a grant of power subject to the limitations and restrictions in other provisions of the Constitution. So regarded, the extent of the powers thereby granted, as defined in the second leg of the clause, needs to be amplified.

2. *Execution of the laws made by the national assembly*

The type of action which the president can take under a law enacted by the national assembly depends on the provisions of the law. The law may require the execution of some public work, or police action to enforce its provisions, or it may be just pure administration involving no execution or enforcement action at all. The president can do no more than is authorised to him by the law.

Laws enacted by the legislature are the predominant source of presidential power, since there is hardly any law that does not call for one kind of action or the other. For example, the postal laws need to be executed by building post offices, printing stamps and generally by operating postal services; and the education laws by building schools, enforcing standards, conducting examinations etc. For anything like an adequate picture of the extent of powers available to the president in the administration of government one has therefore to consult the statute book.

Such executive action as is called for under the laws is the constitutional prerogative of the president by virtue of the vesting of the executive power in him. The passing of a law requiring execution calls the power into existence without any specific authorisation to that effect in the law itself. Once the legislature enacts a law authorising, say, the provision of medical and health facilities, then — whether the law specifically vests him with the power to do so or not — the president can, by right of the vesting of executive power in him by the Constitution, execute the law by building hospitals and organising medical and health facilities provided of course an appropriation has been made therefor by the legislature.

Execution of the laws involves more than taking the specific actions required by particular statutes. The laws must be viewed not only individually but also as a mass forming a system. It is in this sense that one speaks of the duty to maintain law and order in society. As Chief Justice Vinson of the U.S. supreme court says, 'unlike an administrative commission confined to the enforcement of the statute under which it is created, or the head of a department when administering a particular statute, the President is a constitutional officer charged with taking care that a "mass of legislation" be executed.'[6]

3. *Execution and maintenance of the Constitution*

Execution and maintenance of the Constitution are the core of presidential power. A tremendous amount of power, of an undefined extent and potency, can be derived from it. By the explicit grant of the power, the presidency under our Constitution is made considerably more powerful than its American counterpart. Maintenance of the Constitution (as distinct from its execution) invests the presidential office with the power, which has been unsuccessfully claimed for the American president via his oath of office, to preserve, protect and defend it. That is precisely what maintenance connotes.

The power is of vast potentiality and potency because what is to be executed and maintained is not just abstract concepts on parchment. The Constitution in this connection must be viewed as a living charter by which a government with a full amplitude of instrumentalities, powers and rights is created for the administration of public affairs. And the government established by the Constitution presupposes a community of people of differing individual interests but bound together by a common desire for the stability and security of the society as a nation. The execution and maintenance of the Constitution implies therefore a power and a duty in the president to execute the business of government in all its ramifications, to protect the instrumentalities established by the Constitution for the purpose as well as government property, and to preserve the government and the nation by ensuring their stability, security and safety.

(i) *Execution of the government and its functions*

Execution of the government and its functions is covered mostly by specific grants of power — power to establish ministries, departments and offices, to appoint and remove ministers and top civil servants and to assign functions to them (ss. 138–9); to formulate policy (s. 136); to maintain order, and to that end to direct and control the operational use of the police force (ss. 195–6); to suppress insurrection, using as occasion may dictate the armed forces (ss. 197–8); to initiate and execute social welfare and economic development projects (s. 140 and 3rd Sch.); to manage the finances of the country (ss. 74–7); to conduct relations with other countries (ss. 122[1] and 136[2]); etc.

Apart from functions specifically granted by the Constitution, the extent of the powers exercisable by the president in the execution of the government is unclear. Is he thereby empowered, without specific authorisation by statute enacted by the legislature, to do all things, perform all functions, that he deems necessary or beneficial in the interest of the nation so long as such things or functions are not positively prohibited by law? Opinion on this is sharply divided. According to one school of thought, to which President Theodore Roosevelt of the United States gave classic expression in his famous 'stewardship theory' of presidential power, the executive power was limited only by specific restrictions and prohibitions appearing in the Constitution or imposed by congress under its constitutional powers, and the president has not only the right but the duty to 'do anything that the needs of the nation demanded unless such action was forbidden by the Constitution or by the laws.'[7]

The other school of thought strenuously denies such a general power, castigating the claim for it as mere political dialectic, not to be countenanced by a court in deciding a constitutional case.[8] It maintains that executive power is limited to the execution of the specific grants of the Constitution and of laws made by the legislature.

It seems that a power, explicitly conferred by the Constitution, to execute the government may well be said to imply an authority to do anything necessary for the purpose, provided only that it is not forbidden by the Constitution or other law. The 1979 Nigerian Constitution goes further to support this view by providing that the executive power shall extend not only to laws made by the national assembly, but also to all matters within its legislative competence. The implication of this provision is that, without legislative authorisation, the president can act in these matters to the extent that they admit of executive action in advance of legislation.

It is also necessary to consider the power to execute the government in the light of the duties imposed on the government under the directive principles to provide adequate medical and health facilities, adequate educational facilities at all levels, suitable and adequate shelter, food, a national minimum wage, employment opportunities, old age care, and unemployment and sickness benefits; to promote a planned and balanced economic development; to control the national economy in such a manner as to secure the maximum welfare, freedom and happiness of every citizen on the basis of social justice and equality of status and opportunity (ss. 16–18). These are the central concern of the modern welfare state. These directives must therefore necessarily enhance and enlarge the power of the president to execute the government.

However, this is not to say, as some advocates of this school of thought have done, that the vesting of executive power in the president 'confers upon him all the power which, in any age of the world and under any form of government, has been vested in the chief executive functionary, whether King or Czar, emperor or dictator'.[9] Surely there is a vast difference in powers between an absolute monarch or dictator and a president under a Constitution which denies legislative power to him, vesting it in an independent assembly, and which prohibits interference by the executive with the fundamental rights of the individual. In the exercise of his constitutional power to execute the government, the president under the Nigerian Constitution, unlike an absolute monarch or dictator, can neither make law nor interfere with individual rights without authorisation by a law enacted by the legislature within the limits allowed by the Constitution. The general principle of Nigerian law is that, in the absence of legal authorisation, the executive has no inherent power to interfere with private rights — except again in cases of imperative state necessity. The point assumed the character of a great constitutional issue in 1931 in a case involving the then traditional ruler of Lagos, Eshugbayi Eleko, who was deported from Lagos to another part of the country by the colonial governor of Nigeria. There was no law authorising the deportation, but the governor claimed that as the executive of the country he had an inherent power, independent of legislative authorisation, to act as he did. The judicial committee of the privy council emphatically rejected this claim, even in the context of a colonial constitution which reposed in the governor plenary law-making power. In a judgment that has become a great constitutional landmark, it said that the executive 'can only act in pursuance of the powers given to him by law. In accordance with British jurisprudence no member of the Executive can interfere with the liberty or property of a British subject except on the condition that he can support the legality of his action before a court of justice.'[10]

This principle, which is a fundamental presupposition of our constitutional system, was recently applied in the now celebrated private school case in Lagos state. The state government had, in a circular letter, informed proprietors of private primary and secondary schools in the state that their schools would not be allowed to operate with effect from 1 September 1980, and that only public schools managed and controlled by the government would be permitted. Now, under the general law, a parent has a right, whether or not it is also protected by the Constitution, to direct the upbringing of his children, and to decide whether to have them educated in a private or a public school. The interference with this right involved in the abolition of private schools could only be sanctioned by legislation validly enacted by the state legislature. As however the purported abolition was not backed by any law, it was illegal.[11] Happily, the state attorney-general himself admitted that the state governor lacked power to carry out the abolition without legislative authorisation.[12]

It follows that, since most executive acts impinge directly or indirectly on the rights of individuals, this operates to limit quite severely what the President can do without statutory authorisation.

(ii) *Protection of the instrumentalities of government and of its property*

The protection of the instrumentalities of the government as well as its properties is the next power implied in the execution and maintenance of the Constitution. The extent of this power, whether it enables the president to interfere with individual rights, was in issue in a case before the U.S. supreme court in 1890. A justice of that court, while on circuit in California, was threatened with assault and murder by a person against whom he had given judgment. To protect him against the threatened attack, a marshal of the United States was, on the instruction of the U.S. attorney-general, assigned to act as bodyguard to the justice. While the justice was at a railway station in the course of travelling from one circuit court to another, he was attacked by the author of the threats, whereupon the marshal shot and killed the attacker. The question before the supreme court was whether the attorney-general, on behalf of the president, had power to assign a marshal to act as bodyguard to a justice of the supreme court travelling on circuit, so as to constitute the killing of the attacker an act done in pursuance of a law of the United States, which would entitle the marshal to be released on a writ of *habeas corpus* from the custody of the authorities of the state of California. There was no statute or any specific provision of the Constitution enabling the president to protect judges, but it was argued that the action was justified by his power to execute the Constitution, because the assignment of the marshal was made in discharge of an obligation fairly and properly inferable from that instrument, namely the preservation of the Constitution against a person seeking to interfere with the discharge of his duty by a member of one of its agencies.

The argument was accepted by the majority of the court which held that the power to execute the laws extended to all the rights, duties and obligations growing out of the Constitution and to all the protection implied by the nature of the government under the Constitution. And the protection of the judges was essential to the existence of the government, since it would be a great reproach to the system of government of the United States if there was to be found within the domain of its powers no means of protecting the judges in the conscientious and faithful discharge of their duties from the malice and hatred of those upon whom their judgments might operate unfavourably.

A minority of two, while admitting that the president's executive power extended to the execution of the law of the Constitution, held that the Constitution established no law specifically requiring the protection of judges in their official capacity against murderous attacks. On the contrary, the Constitution vests in congress the power 'to make all laws which shall be necessary and proper for carrying into execution [its own powers] and all other powers vested by this Constitution in the government of the United States, or in any department or officer thereof.'[13] Accordingly, in the absence of any enactment by congress providing for protection as being necessary and proper for carrying the judicial power into execution, the president could not assign a marshal to act as a bodyguard to a judge and to follow him in his journey while in circuit. 'The protection needed and to be given must proceed, not from the President, but primarily from Congress';[14] and 'the right claimed must be traced to legislation of Congress, else it cannot exist.'[15]

(iii) *Preservation of the government and the nation*
Self-preservation is acknowledged by all a paramount duty of every government and every state. 'To preserve its independence and give security against foreign aggression and encroachment', the supreme court of the United States has said, 'is the highest duty of every nation, and to attain these ends nearly all other considerations are to be subordinated.'[16] But how much power is the president constitutionally permitted to exercise for this purpose in the absence of legislation by the national assembly authorising specific actions to deal with an extraordinary situation? More specifically, can he make law or interfere with individual rights?

The 1979 Nigerian Constitution empowers the president to proclaim an emergency in certain clearly defined circumstances (s. 265), but grants him in terms no special emergency powers. Only the national assembly is empowered to interfere, by legislation and within the limits set by the Constitution, with the rights of the individual in the interest of defence, public order or public safety; even so, interference with the right to life and personal liberty in these interests is permitted only during a period of emergency proclaimed in accordance with the constitutional stipulations; moreover, with the authority of an enabling legislation by the national assembly only executive measures reasonably justifiable for dealing with the situation actually existing during the particular period of emergency can be taken in derogation of the two rights (i.e. life and personal liberty). The national assembly is not even permitted, in normal as well as in emergency periods, to legislate so as to authorise interference with or derogation from the rights to the dignity of the human person (except for forced labour during an emergency) or the right to fair hearing.

Granted that no special emergency powers are expressly granted to him by the Constitution, the question still remains however whether a president, enjoined and mandated by the same Constitution to preserve the government and the nation, is altogether without power, in the absence of statutory authorisation, to deal with an extraordinary situation threatening or endangering public order, public security or public safety, especially when the situation does not admit of the delay that would be involved in securing the passage by the assembly of the necessary legislation. The Constitution could not reasonably have intended such helplessness in an organ conceived, in the words of the brief of the U.S. government in a celebrated case in 1951,[17] as the 'watchful eye, the active hand, the overseeing dynamic force' of the nation. His duty to preserve the government and the nation must clearly imply a certain measure of power to act in such a situation until the legislature intervenes with appropriate legislation.

The extent of powers that can be exerted must depend, however, on the actual situation, its nature, imminence and seriousness, whether it is an industrial action affecting essential supplies and services, widespread rioting, insurrection, armed rebellion, aggression from outside or other public danger.

There is, happily, in the constitutional jurisprudence of many countries, particularly the United States, a wealth of cases in which the independent power of the president in relation to the various types and gradations of emergency situations has been adjudicated upon, and its scope and limits expounded without of course dispelling completely the obscurity surrounding the subject. The decision of the U.S. supreme court in 1951 in a case arising out of a threatened nation-wide strike in the steel industry is perhaps a good starting point.[18] The strike call had occurred at a time of national emergency formally proclaimed by the president because of a full-scale war in Korea in which the United States was involved. On the premise that, steel being an indispensable component of substantially all of the weapons and materials needed for the war, a work stoppage in the steel industry would immediately jeopardise and imperil national defence, and endanger the armed forces fighting in the theatre of war in Korea, the president, without express statutory authorisation, but solely on his own independent authority under the Constitution to preserve the security and safety of the nation, ordered the steel factories to be seized and operated by government agents in order to avert a national catastrophe. But he immediately sent a message to congress informing it of his action, and inviting it to approve or revoke it as it thought fit. In an action by the owners of the factories challenging the constitutionality of the seizure and praying that they be returned to them, the U.S. supreme court, by a majority of six to three, held that, without express statutory authorisation, the president had, in the particular circumstances of the case, no independent power under the Constitution to take possession of the steel mills and operate them by his agents, on the ground that seizure of private property requires legislative authorisation by congress, to which alone the Constitution has entrusted the law-making power in both good and bad times.

It rejected the argument of the president based on his authority as commander-in-chief, saying that 'even though "theatre of war" be an expanding concept, we cannot with faithfulness to our constitutional system hold that the Commander-in-Chief of the Armed Forces has the ultimate power as such to take possession of private property in order to keep labour dispute from stopping production.'[19] 'No doctrine that the court would promulgate', said Mr. Justice Jackson in a separate concurring judgment, 'would seem to me more sinister and alarming than that a president . . . can vastly enlarge his mastery over the internal affairs of the country by his own commitment of the Nation's armed forces to some foreign venture. [. . .] The Constitution did not contemplate that the title Commander-in-Chief of the Army and Navy will constitute him also Commander-in-Chief of the country, its industries and its inhabitants.'[20]

It is, however, a well-recognised doctrine of law that in an emergency imperilling public security, the safety of the state and nation is the supreme law — *salus populi est suprema lex*. The safety of the nation is necessary to the very existence of the Constitution itself, and must therefore override some of its prohibitions and limitations in a situation of grave danger to it. As President Lincoln aptly asked, 'is it possible to lose the nation and yet preserve the Constitution?'[21] By this supreme law of necessity, the organs of the state are entitled, in the face of such a grave danger, to take all appropriate actions, even in deviation from the express provisions of the constitution, in order to safeguard law and order and preserve the state and society. The doctrine does not operate from outside the law, but is implied in it as an integral part thereof. It is 'implicit in the constitution of every civilised community'.[22] This is so because 'no constitution can anticipate all the different forms of phenomena which may beset a nation.'[23] Thus the doctrine has been held to be incorporated into the written constitutions of Pakistan (1947), Cyprus (1960), Nigeria (1963), Rhodesia (1965), Italy, Greece and the United States; and that, as so incorporated, it operates to qualify, though not to abolish, the concept of the inviolability of the constitution's supremacy and consequently of the limitations which it imposes upon governmental power. Its application is subject to the following conditions:

(*a*) There must exist an imperative necessity arising from an imminent and extreme danger affecting the safety of the state or society;

(*b*) action taken to meet the exigency must be inevitable in the sense of being the only remedy;

(*c*) it must be proportionate to the necessity, i.e. it must be reasonably warranted by the danger which it was intended to avert;

(*d*) it must be of a temporary character limited to the duration of the exceptional circumstances or until the legislature is able to enact the necessary legislation to authorise it.

Thus, the commandeering, without statutory authorisation, of three private steamboats into the service of the government to meet an imperative military necessity during the civil war in the United States was sustained as lawful and as not constituting a trespass (subject of course to the payment of compensation) on the ground that in cases of extreme necessity in time of war or of immediate and impending public danger, the president has power under the Constitution to impress private property into the public service or even to destroy it without the consent of the owner.[24] It has also been held that the president has a power under the U.S. Constitution to institute a blockade of ports in the possession of persons in armed rebellion against the government, and to capture on the seas as 'enemy property' the property of any person, whether neutral or rebel, residing within the rebellious regions.[25]

The mere existence of a war involving the territory of the country is not by itself alone such a situation of grave and extreme danger to public safety to justify the exercise of such powers by the president. Interference with individual rights in time of war without statutory authorisation is justified only if it is necessary in connection with military operations, as where 'property taken is imperatively needed in time of war to construct defences for the preservation of a military post at the moment of an impending attack by the enemy, or for food or medicine for a sick and famishing army utterly destitute and without other means of such supplies, or to transport troops, munitions of war, or clothing to reinforce or supply an army.'[26] If the interference is necessitated by some other kind of public danger than war, such danger must be 'immediate, imminent and impending, and the emergency in the public service must be extreme and imperative, and such as will not admit of delay or a resort to any other source of supply.'[27]

The extent of the power which the executive can, without statutory authorisation, assume over individual rights in times of grave emergency was again in issue in the series of cases involving Japanese living on the west coast of the United States during the second world war. The United States had gone to war with Japan on 8 December 1941, following the Japanese attack on Pearl Harbor the previous day. The existence of a state of belligerence between the two countries and the likelihood of a further Japanese attack created a necessity for safeguarding the west coast. Espionage and sabotage were particularly feared, a danger which was aggravated by the presence on the west coast of some 112,000 persons of Japanese origin of whom about 70,000 were American citizens by birth. The protective measures which the military authorities, with the approval of the executive and the legislature, instituted to combat the danger were, first, to impose a night curfew on all Japanese on the west coast, and eventually, when a curfew was thought inadequate, to have them segregated at various so-called assembly or relocation centres, which they were not to leave without military permission. These centres were a kind of concentration camp. Neither the curfew nor the segregation order differentiated between various classes of Japanese; both citizens and aliens, the loyal and the disloyal, were alike incarcerated. Unquestionably these orders were an invasion of the constitutional rights of the Japanese Americans, and the question was whether this was legally justified by the danger against which it was meant to be a protection. The supreme court sustained the validity of the curfew order on the ground that it was necessary 'to meet the threat of sabotage and espionage which would substantially affect the war effort and might reasonably be expected to aid a threatened enemy invasion'.[28] For the same reason, too, the court upheld the validity of the segregation order.[29]

Although the decisions were based upon the war power expressly vested in the president by the Constitution, the premise was clearly the doctrine that the 'state must have every facility and the widest latitude in defending itself against destruction.'[30] While affirming the inviolability of the individual's civil liberties, the court nevertheless conceded that 'pressing public *necessity* may sometimes justify the existence of such restrictions' on them.[31] The decisions in these cases have provoked much criticism,[32] particularly as regards the segregation order, which could hardly have been warranted by the exigency of the occasion. The curfew alone, it has been argued, would have met the danger adequately, especially in view of the fact that the danger of further attack seemed to have receded in the interval of five months between Pearl Harbor and the proclamation of the orders. And even if the segregation order was considered really necessary, an effort should have been made to separate the loyal from the disloyal Japanese, and to confine the order to the latter.[33] It seemed that the action of the military authorities was dictated more by the pressure of racial prejudice exerted by certain groups on the west coast. However that may be, the cases do give recognition to the doctrine of necessity as a legal justification for action otherwise contrary to the express provisions of the constitution, but which is necessary to save the nation from destruction.

The right of the individual not to be deprived of his liberty or life in pursuance of the judgment of a military court is more jealously guarded. The U.S. supreme court has rejected the argument that in time of war state necessity justifies the assumption by a military commander of absolute power to suspend all civil rights and their remedies, and to subject civilians as well as soldiers to the rule of his will. In pursuance of this alleged power, one Milligan had been tried, convicted and sentenced to death by a military commission, with the approval of the president, for alleged conspiracy against the government in giving aid and comfort to the rebels while in the loyal state of Indiana, whose citizen and resident he had been for twenty years. The court held unanimously that the trial, conviction and sentence were illegal as being unauthorised by the Constitution and the laws. The majority rested its decision on the ground that trial of civilians by a military court cannot be authorised, whether by the president or congress, except when, as a result of military operations, the ordinary courts have ceased to function or can no longer function. But so long as they continue to function, then, notwithstanding the existence of war, the independent and impartial administration of the law by them with the assistance of an impartial jury cannot be suspended or superseded, not even by the authority of an act of congress. The court observed:

Martial law cannot arise from a threatened invasion. The necessity must be actual and present; the invasion real, such as effectually closes the courts and deposes the civil administration. . . . If, in foreign invasion or civil war, the courts are actually closed, and it is impossible to administer criminal justice according to law, then, on the theatre of actual military operations where war really prevails, there is a necessity to furnish a substitute for the civil authority, thus overthrown, to preserve the safety of the army and society; and as no power is left but the military, it is allowed to govern by martial rule until the laws can have their free course. As necessity creates the rule, so it limits its duration; for if this government is continued after the courts are reinstated, it is a gross usurpation of power. Martial law can never exist where the courts are open, and in the proper and unobstructed exercise of their jurisdiction.[34]

The implication of the view taken by the majority is that since congress could not have authorised the trial of Milligan by the military tribunal, it could not indemnify the tribunal's members from the legal consequences of the illegal trial. A minority of the court took the view that only the power of the president to declare martial law was limited in the way suggested. As far as congress was concerned, however, it was competent, by virtue of its power to provide for the government of the national forces, to declare war and to provide for its prosecution, to authorise martial law in districts where the threat of invasion was such as to justify it. The fact that the ordinary courts are open might have been sufficient reason for its not exercising the power, but could not affect its existence.

The 'open court' rule of the majority was substantially affirmed by the court in 1945 in a series of cases arising out of the second world war.[35] After the surprise Japanese air attack on Pearl Harbor, the governor of Hawaii (the island group in which Pearl Harbor lay), with the approval of the president, placed the territory under martial law and handed over the entire administration to the military authorities. The military government then closed down all the civil courts and established military tribunals in their place. The two appellants in this case were respectively convicted of embezzlement and assault by the military tribunals seven months and two-and-a-half years after the attack on Pearl Harbor, at a time when any threat of further attack or invasion had completely disappeared. The court held that, in view of the fact that the Constitution has the same force and effect in Hawaii as in other parts of the United States, the provision of the territory's organic act authorising the governor, with the approval of the president, to declare martial law 'in case of rebellion or invasion or imminent danger thereof, when the public safety requires it' did not include power to supplant civilian laws and courts by military orders and tribunals where conditions were not such as to prevent the enforcement of the laws by the civilian courts; the provision was only intended to authorise the military to act vigorously for the maintenance of an orderly civil government and for the defence of the Territory against actual or threatened rebellion or invasion. The court reiterated what it had said in the earlier case of *ex parte Milligan*[36] that 'civil liberty and this kind of martial law cannot endure together; the antagonism is irreconcilable; and, in the conflict, one or the other must perish.'[37] It rejected the argument that, however adequate the 'open court' rule might have been in 1864, it was distinctly unsuited to modern warfare conditions where all the territories of a warring nation might be in combat zones or imminently threatened by long-range attack even while civil courts were operating. The trials were accordingly declared illegal as an unjustified interference with the constitutional guarantee of a fair trial. 'Those who founded this nation', said Justice Murphy, 'knew full well that the arbitrary power of conviction and punishment for pretended offences is the hallmark of despotism. [. . .] From time immemorial despots have used real or imagined threats to the public welfare as an excuse for needlessly abrogating human rights. That excuse is no less unworthy of our traditions when used in this day of atomic warfare or at a future time when other types of warfare may be devised. [. . .] There must be some overpowering factor that makes a recognition of those rights incompatible with the public safety before we should consent to their temporary suspension.'[38]

The fact that martial law has been *validly* declared does not therefore by itself confer unlimited power on the executive. It may enable it to do no more than to effect summary arrests and detentions and the forcible entry and searching of private houses. Thus, when a revolutionary group, dissatisfied with the old charter government of the state of Rhode Island, established a new constitution and government, and raised an army which attempted by force to seize possession of the state arsenal, the supreme court held that the legislature of the old government was, in the circumstances, entitled to declare martial law, and to use extraordinary powers of arbitrary arrest and detention and the forcible entry into private houses of persons reasonably believed to be engaged in the insurrection, in order to maintain itself and overcome the unlawful and armed opposition.[39] The decision, as the court explained in the subsequent cases,[40] did no more than approve the specific action taken in that case, namely forcible entry into the plaintiff's house for the purpose of effecting his arrest. But it did not decide that every lawful declaration of martial law, by the fact of having been lawfully made, authorises any conceivable kind of power. The extent of power it justifies depends upon the gravity of the situation, and in particular upon whether the civil authorities have been incapacitated by military operations.[41]

A decision in 1972 of the Pakistan supreme court follows on the same principle. The court held that the martial law declared in March 1959 did not justify the military in assuming complete power to govern by military decrees and ordinances, and that the military regime so established from 1959 to 1971 was illegal, with the consequence that all the laws made by that regime were void except to the extent that any of them might be saved under the doctrine of necessity.[42]

4. *Extra-constitutional determinants of presidential power*

The Constitution is only one of the sources of presidential power, though no doubt a supremely important one. The reality of power depends on other factors besides its formal structure as defined in the Constitution. Two such factors of overwhelming importance are the character of the individual president and the circumstances of the country concerned, including social, economic and political forces, conditions and events.[43] It may be said that the circumstances of Africa favour an authoritarian presidency. To begin with, there is the relative impotence of extra-constitutional sanctions against the abuse of power. The social values of the advanced democracies enshrine a national ethic which defines the limits of permissible action by the wielders of power. This national ethic is sanctified in deeply entrenched conventions operating as part of the rules of the game of politics. Thus, although an action may be well within the powers of the president under the constitution, still he cannot do it if it violates the moral sense of the nation, for he would risk calling down upon himself the wrath of public censure. The force of public opinion is sufficiently developed to act as a watchdog of the nation's ethic, and no action that seriously violates this ethic can hope to escape public condemnation. More than any constitutional restraints, perhaps, it is the ethic of the nation, its sense of right and wrong, and the capacity of the people to defend it, which provides the ultimate bulwark against tyranny.

Julius Nyerere of Tanzania has underscored the point: 'When the nation does not have the ethic which will enable the government to say: "We cannot do this, that is un-Tanganyikan" — or the people to say: "That we cannot tolerate, that is un-Tanganyikan" — if the people do not have that kind of ethic, it does not matter what kind of constitution you frame. They can always be victims of tyranny.'[44] Africa is yet to develop a strong moral sense in public affairs. Standards of public morality have not become deeply rooted, nor are they effectively articulated and enforced, partly because the instruments of public opinion are controlled by the very people who have to be checked. Because of this, an African president can get away with a lot of things which an American president dare not venture.

The traditional African attitude towards power is not of much assistance either. Tradition has inculcated in the people a certain deference towards authority. The chief's authority is sanctioned in religion, and it is a sacrilege to flout it, except in cases of blatant and systematic oppression when the whole community might rise in revolt to destool, banish or even kill a tyrannical chief. Thus, while customary sanctions against extreme cases of abuse of power exist, there is also considerable toleration of arbitrariness by the chief. This attitude towards authority tends to be transferred to the modern political leader. The vast majority of the population, which of course is still illiterate and custom-bound, is not disposed to question the leader's authority, and indeed disapproves of those who are inclined to do so.

In a sense, therefore, the presidency in Africa is regarded by many in the light of the attitudes inculcated in them towards chiefly authority, and its power as the projection of chiefly authority into the national sphere. The president, in effect, is the *chief* of the new nation, and as such entitled to the authority and respect due by tradition to a chief. This has not rested entirely on attitudes carried over from tradition. In places there has indeed been a conscious attempt to implant the attitude in the minds of the people, by, for example, publicly investing the president with the attributes of a chief. Thus, when he attended public rallies in Ghana, Nkrumah used to assume the style of a chief. He sat upon a 'chiefly throne under a resplendent umbrella, symbol of traditional rule', and he took 'chiefly titles meaningful to all major tribal units in Ghana: *Osagyefo, Katamanto, Kasapieko, Nufeno*, etc.'[45] His opening of parliament was also done in chiefly style. His approach was 'heralded by the beating of *fantomforom* [traditional drums]. He was received by eight linguists representing the various Regions and each carrying a distinctive stick. A libation was poured and the president then entered the chamber to the sound of *mmenson* [the seven traditional horns]'.[46] Although this is explicable in part by Nkrumah's aspiration for the revival of the African cultural heritage, the political significance is obvious. It was intended to harness to the presidency the authority of tradition and the legitimacy which it confers. By aligning the presidency with the institution of chieftaincy in the public imagination, it is hoped to inspire public acceptance of the office and respect for its authority.

Similarly relevant to the reality of presidential power in Africa is the African's conception of authority. Authority in African traditional society is conceived as being personal, mystical and pervasive.[47] The chief is a personal ruler, and his office pervades all the other relations in the community, for he is both legislator, executive, judge, priest, medium, father, and so on. These characteristics are reflected in the modern African presidency. The presidency in Africa is indeed clothed with a considerable amount of mystique which bestows upon it an authority transcending that of an ordinary head of state. An attribute of mystique is charisma. No leader around whom such a fantastic myth is built can fail to arouse a charismatic appeal among the people.

These factors — tradition, mystique and charisma — are sources of power which are not easily accessible to a president in America and Europe. It has been said of the American presidency that its essential dimension today is how to 'generate sufficient authority for presidential action to match the needs of the nation'.[48] No modern American president, with the possible exception of Franklin D. Roosevelt, has been able to harness to the presidency a deep, widely-felt loyalty based upon charisma. This means that the authority of the American presidency in modern times is in no way comparable to that of its counterpart in Africa.

The circumstance of underdevelopment is yet another source of presidential power in Africa. It is usual for Americans to classify their presidents as either 'strong' or 'weak'. The strong president, writes Hirschfield, is one 'who regards government as the appropriate instrument for achieving progressive change in society and the presidency as the vital generating force in government. [. . .] His principal concern is not the administration of an inherited office, but the use of that office to bring about change in . . . society.'[49] Every African president is a strong president in this sense, for the condition of underdevelopment now prevailing on the continent makes imperative an interventionist policy based on socialism. Just as the economic depression of the early 1930s called forth Franklin Roosevelt's New Deal measure, which was perhaps the highest point presidential power has attained in peace-time in America, so also does the poverty of African societies aggregate power to the presidency. Given this poverty, and the illiteracy which contributed to it, the challenge and burden of development must rest first and foremost upon the state, since it alone has anything like the type of resources needed for development programmes in industry, commerce and agriculture. The nationalist struggle is an on-going struggle. Its political objective having been won, the next phase is in the economic field. The economic dependence of the new state upon the old colonial business interests must be brought to an end by nationalisation or by the state taking over majority shareholdings. Every African nationalist leader is therefore willy-nilly a socialist.

Nation-building is an objective to which all are committed. But it is a task that calls for total mobilisation of the nation if any impact is to be made upon it. An African president is therefore necessarily cast in the role of popular leader. This again makes him a 'strong' president in another sense of the American conception of the term. In this second sense, American presidents have been rated as strong or weak according to their ability to mobilise the nation. 'The greatest Presidents have all ranked high on this scale, whatever their skills as administrators or legislative managers. All have made themselves national symbols; in so doing they have given substance and purpose to the nation itself.'[50] But the popular leadership required of an African president is of a much more personal and spiritual kind, for he has to be at once leader, guide and teacher. The leader of a predominantly illiterate, poverty-stricken community has not only to lead, but to guide as well. He has to provide the light so that people may see the road in the first place, and then guide and direct them along that road to the ultimate destination of prosperity and progress. He may be likened to one who leads a blind man. The leader of a blind man has to establish an intimate personal identification with him. So it is with the leader of a new nation. Having got the people on the difficult road to development, it is his duty 'to propose, to explain, and to persuade',[51] to preach to them the need for hard work, for self-reliance, and for integrity in order to maximise national productivity. Preaching has to be accompanied by example; as, for example, the leader working with the farmers in the field.

Not the least of an African president's leadership role is that of a showman. Whatever progress has been achieved needs to be advertised to the people in order to keep up national morale and enthusiasm. The president has therefore to perform the formal opening of completed public projects, and to launch 'events' that advertise the national effort, like agricultural and commercial shows and trade fairs. All this is part of the total mobilisation of the nation. It gives to presidential power in Africa a reality that is usually lacking in advanced countries. The inadequacy of the American presidency in providing this kind of leadership is often a source of disillusionment among Americans. But the inadequacy results, not from the personality of American presidents but from the nature of American society as compared with the African.

The African president's role of popular leadership is of course greatly facilitated by the virtual state monopoly of the media of mass information, perhaps the most crucial source of power in modern government. The radio and television are always state-owned, as are the most influential newspapers, and a large part of the news items in all three media is taken up by news about the president, his speeches and other activities. The president is always in the news, perhaps inevitably so, since the functions of government in Africa are all-pervading. Either he is laying the foundation stone of, or opening, a new factory, a new school or a new hospital, or he is touring different parts of the country, and preaching the need for unity, hard work or self-reliance. His being constantly in the news immensely enhances his legitimacy and authority. But the monopoly of the information media is significant also in determining popular consent in government. Whoever has it is put in a position where he can mobilise public opinion and the nation in support of himself and his policies and actions. Such a person can, literally, get away with murder, for murder can be made to wear the appearance of a virtue or be represented as serving the best interests of the nation.

There is yet another respect in which the poverty of African societies is a source of power for the president. In a developing country where there is mass unemployment, where the state is the principal employer of labour and almost the sole provider of social amenities, and where a personal ambition for power and wealth and influence rather than principle determines political affiliations and alliances, power to dispense patronage is a very potent weapon in the hands of the president, enabling him to gain and maintain the loyalty of the people at various levels of society. Water installed in one area, industry sited in another, a school or hospital built in yet another may capture for the president the support and loyalty of the inhabitants of those areas. Scholarships, roads, government contracts, jobs — all these are crucial sources of power in Africa. Moreover, loyalty of the type secured by patronage can often border on subservience. It produces an attitude of dependence, a willingness to accept without question the wishes and dictates of the person dispensing the patronage. Patronage has therefore been one of the crucial means by which African leaders have secured the subordination of the legislature, the bureaucracy, the police and even the army.

Then there is the fact of the newness of the state, the heterogeneity of its society and the tensions of modernisation. The new state requires a legitimising force. The problem of legitimacy is peculiar to a new state, and is complicated by three factors. An artificial creation of colonialism, the state in Africa has no roots in the traditions or thoughts of the people. Their attitude towards it was that it was an instrument of the white man for the subjugation and exploitation of Africans. To the subject people, therefore, the state was not 'ours' but 'theirs', the white man's state. Such an attitude must be eradicated if the state is to be able to fulfil its purpose. And this requires the fostering among the people of a feeling of identity with the state. The second complicating factor is that the concept of state is a mere abstraction totally incomprehensible to the simple mind of a peasant. It needs therefore some visible, physical object to symbolise it in the eyes of the people, and no other subject can be more readily comprehensible for this purpose than the personality of the president. The president thus assumes a symbolic role as the embodiment of the state. Third is the fact that the state in Africa has an artificial and heterogeneous social composition, embracing a large variety of peoples of differing origin, culture, language and character. This heterogeneous collection needs to be integrated into a unity, infused with a sense of common destiny and common national aspirations. It is the role of the president as leader to serve as the focal point of unity around which this heterogeneous mass can be knit together.

This integrating role of an African president involves the exercise of power — power to prevent the inevitable cleavages of tribalism from destroying the state. Tribal conflicts create a condition of instability, which is made worse by the tensions of rapid change from a traditional to a modern economy. In the view of the African leaders the state of affairs is comparable to a state of emergency, and a state of emergency, even in the most advanced democracies, demands actions of an authoritarian type to preserve the peace and integrity of the state. The experience of the United States illustrates the great potency of a situation of emergency as a source of presidential power, for it is during such periods that the presidency has attained its zenith of power, as is 'illustrated by Lincoln's "dictatorial" regime during the Civil War, by Wilson's highly-centralised World War administration, and by Franklin Roosevelt's executive-dominated government during the emergencies of domestic depression and global conflict'.[52]

The preservation of the state against the insecurity inherent in tribal cleavage and the tensions of rapid social change is perhaps the greatest source of presidential power in Africa. Tribalism may also operate in other ways to put greater power in the hands of the president. For in the clash of interests between various tribes and their leaders, an atribal president may become a kind of counterpoise holding the balance of power in the state.

Then there is the personality of the president. For, as Hirschfield has pointed out, 'while circumstances, and particularly crisis conditions, can make vast authority available to the president', yet they cannot by themselves 'guarantee an appropriate response. . . .

Only he can make the decision to use it.'[53]

Finally comes the political system. Of the influence of this, Justice Jackson has aptly observed that 'party loyalties and interests, sometimes more binding than law, extend his [i.e. the president's] effective control into branches of government other than his own and he often may win, as a political leader, what he cannot command under the Constitution.'[54] In Nigeria, without the 'accord' between the president's party and the party with the third largest support in the national assembly, the president would have been without the majority needed to get his ministers approved and an effective administration established, able to get its measures through the assembly. The administration in Kaduna state was all but paralysed because of the antagonism between the governor and the majority party in the state house of assembly which has made it impossible for him to get the necessary approval for the appointment of commissioners.

REFERENCES

1. William Taft, quoted in E.S. Corwin, *The President: Office and Powers*, 4th edn. (1957), 63.
2. Quoted in Justice McReynolds' dissenting judgment in *Myers* v. *United States*, 272 U.S. 52 at 229–30.
3. Brief of the U.S. Govt. in *Youngstown Sheet & Tube Co.* v. *Sawyer*, 343 U.S. 579, at 640.
4. *Myers* v. *United States*, ibid., at 117.
5. Per Justice Jackson in *Youngstown Sheet & Tube Co.* v. *Sawyer*, ibid. at 640–1; see also the concurring opinion of Justice Douglas at 632.
6. *Youngstown Sheet & Tube Co.* v. *Sawyer*, ibid. at 702.
7. Theodore Roosevelt, *Autobiography*, 388–9; referred with apparent approval in some of the judgments in the *Youngstown* Case, ibid.
8. See the judgment of Justice Jackson in the *Youngstown* case.
9. See *Kendall* v. *United States* (1838), 12 Pet 524.
10. *Eshugbayi Eleko* v. *Govt. of Nigeria* [1930], A.C. 662.
11. *Archbishop Okogie* v. *The Att.-Gen. of Lagos State*, Suit No. D/17M/80 of 18 July 1980, decided by Agoro J.
12. ibid.
13. art. 1, s. 8.
14. *Cunningham* v. *Neagle*, 135 U.S. 1, at 83 (1890).
15. ibid. at 90.
16. *Chae Chan Ping* v. *United States*, 130 U.S. 581.
17. *Youngstown Sheet & Tube Co.* v. *Sawyer*, ibid. at 691–2.
18. *Youngstown Sheet & Tube Co.* v. *Sawyer*, ibid.
19. ibid. at 587, per Justice Black delivering the opinion of the court.
20. at 642–4.

21. Quoted with approval by Justice Clark in the *Youngstown* case at 661.
22. *Federation of Pakistan* v. *Shah* (1955), reported in Jannings, *Constitutional Problems in Pakistan* (1957), 353, 357 — per Muhammed Munir C.J. See also the Brief of the U.S. Govt. in the *Youngstown* case, ibid.
23. *Lakanmi* v. *The Att.-Gen. (West)* SC58/69 of 24 April 1970 (Nigeria) — per Ademola C.J.
24. *United States* v. *Russell*, 13 Wall (80 U.S.) 623.
25. *The Prize Cases* (1863), 2 Black (67 U.S.) 635.
26. *United States* v. *Russell*, ibid. at 627.
27. ibid. at 629.
28. *Hirabayashi* v. *United States* and *Yasui* v. *United States* (1943), 320 U.S. 81 and 115.
29. *Korematsu* v. *United States*, 323 U.S. 214.
30. Eugene Rostow, 'The Japanese American Cases — a Disaster', 54 *Yale L.J.* (1945), 489–505.
31. *Korematsu* v. *United States*, ibid. at 216 — per Justice Black delivering the opinion of the court.
32. Rostow, op. cit.; Nanette Dembitz, 'Racial Discrimination and the Military Judgment: the supreme court's Korematsu and Endo Decisions', 45 *Columbia L.R.* 175 (1945).
33. In *ex parte Endo* (1944), 323 U.S. 283, the supreme court held that a loyal Japanese was entitled to be released unconditionally from a relocation centre.
34. *Ex parte Milligan*, 4 Wall 2 at 127.
35. *Duncan* v. *Kahanamoku*, 327 U.S. 304.
36. 4 Wall 2 at 124.
37. 327 U.S. 304 at 324.
38. ibid. at 325, 330.
39. *Lurther* v. *Borden* (1849), 7 How 1.
40. *Ex parte Milligan*, ibid.
41. Contrast the dissenting judgment of Justice Woodbury where the learned justice wrongly assumed that every declaration of martial law authorises not only summary arrests and detentions and the forcible entry into private houses, but also arbitrary trials by court-martials. 'By it', he said, 'every citizen, instead of reposing under the shield of known and fixed laws as to liberty, property, and life, exists with a rope round his neck, subject to being hung up by a military despot at the next lamp post, under the sentence of some drumhead court-martial.' *Lurther* v. *Borden*, 7 How 1, at 62.
42. *Malik Ghulan Jilami and Alter Gauhar* v. *The Province of Sind and Others*, Cr. Appeals nos. 19 and K2 of 20 April 1972.
43. See R.S. Hirschfield, 'The Reality of Presidential Power', XXI *Parliamentary Affairs*, (1967/8), 375.
44. Nat. Ass. Deb., 1962, col. 1104.
45. H.L. Bretton, *The Rise and Fall of Kwame Nkrumah* (1966), 80.
46. Bennion, *Constitutional Law of Ghana* (1962), 110.
47. Alvin A. Wolfe, 'African Conceptions of Authority', unpublished paper (1965); cited by K.W. Grundy and M. Weinstein, 'The Political Uses of Imagination', *Transition* 31 (1966), 5.

48. Grant McConnell, *The Modern Presidency* (1967), 15.
49. Hirschfield, op. cit., 379–80.
50. Grant McConnell, op. cit., 15.
51. Julius K. Nyerere, *Ujamaa — Essays on Socialism* (1968), 90.
52. Hirschfield, op. cit. 382.
53. ibid., 381.
54. *Youngstown Sheet & Tube Co.* v. *Sawyer*, ibid. at 654.

7

LIMITATIONS ON THE PRESIDENT'S EXECUTIVE POWER IN FAVOUR OF OTHER EXECUTIVE FUNCTIONARIES AND AGENCIES

As noted in chapter 5, the Constitution establishes other executive functionaries and agencies besides the president — a vice-president, ministers, an executive council, ministries and departments, police force, armed forces, etc. The question it is proposed to discuss here is the relation of the president to these functionaries and agencies, and in particular the extent to which the executive power vested in him is limited by the Constitution in favour of these others.

1. *Relation to the vice-president*

The office of vice-president owes its existence not to the president, but to the Constitution by which it is directly established (s. 130). A candidate for the office is nominated in the first place by the president but ascension to it is by election by the people directly. He and the presidential candidate are voted for together on one ticket at one and the same election. The relevant provision of the Constitution stipulates that 'a candidate for an election to the office of President shall not be deemed to be validly nominated unless he nominates another candidate as his associate for his running for the office of President, who is to occupy the office of Vice-President; and that candidate shall be deemed to have been duly elected to the office of Vice-President if the candidate for an election to the office of President who nominated him as such associate is duly elected as President' (s. 131[1]). The same qualification and disqualifications for election are prescribed for him as for the president (s. 131[2]). The president is however to nominate and, with the approval of each house of the national assembly, appoint a new vice-president to fill a vacancy occurring in between general elections either by death, resignation or otherwise (s. 134[3]). The president has no discretion whether or not to fill such a vacancy. It is mandatory on him to do so. The Constitution does not envisage that he is to govern without a vice-president.

The tenure of office of the vice-president, whether elected by the people or appointed by the president to fill a vacancy, is governed by the Constitution, and is not at the will and pleasure of the president. His tenure is co-terminous with that of the president, and cannot be prematurely determined by the latter before the normal effluxion of the time prescribed by the Constitution, which is four years or the residue of the term for which a new vice-president is appointed. Apart from death or resignation, his tenure, like the president's, can only be prematurely determined by impeachment by the national assembly (s. 132) or by compulsory retirement on the ground of incapacity according to a procedure laid down by the Constitution (s. 133).

It may be argued that a vice-president appointed by the president to fill a vacancy should be removable by him at will. It is a rule of interpretation, enacted in the Interpretation Act 1964, which is made applicable to the interpretation of the Constitution (s. 277[4]), that power to appoint imports a power to revoke the appointment. But this rule is overborne where there is a contrary intention to be gathered either from express provision or from necessary implication. Thus, where a provision in a constitution manifests a clear intention to be all-embracing on the conditions of tenure of the holder of a particular office, the rule has been held inapplicable.[1] In the case of the vice-president the constitutional provisions relating to tenure of office of the president are by the express terms of the Constitution made applicable to him as if references to the president were references to the vice-president (s. 131[?]). These provisions are clearly all-embracing and exclusive on the tenure of office of both the president and the vice-president. The vice-president cannot therefore be removed from office in any other way, any more than the president can, nor can he be prevented by the president from performing his constitutional functions, such as attendance at meetings of the executive council. The reported action of the governor of Kano State stopping his deputy governor from attending meetings of the executive council, as well as stopping his salary, is unconstitutional.

The vice-presidency is thus clearly an office existing by the Constitution independently of the president. But it is an office without any separate and independent executive powers of its own. The only constitutional functions of the vice-president are not separate to him but are derived from his membership of certain executive bodies established by the Constitution. He is by the Constitution the chairman of the national economic council, and deputy chairman of the council of state, the national defence council and the national security council. As deputy chairman of the three latter bodies he takes second place to the president who is himself chairman, though his designation as deputy chairman gives him the right to preside at meetings of those bodies in the absence of the president. Thus, it is only in relation to the national economic council that he comes fully into his own as chairman. Yet neither the national economic council nor any of the other three councils has any independent executive powers. Their role is merely to advise the president, with no power to bind him by their advice.

The next role of the vice-president is as a member of the executive council of the federation. The constitutional position of the executive council in the government of the federation and its relation to the president is considered below, but it is an accurate summary of its role to say that it is essentially an instrument of the president, with little independent constitutional power of its own. For the exercise of its one and only truly independent constitutional function, namely to initiate the procedure for vacating the presidential or vice-presidential office on the ground of incapacity, the vice-president as well as the president is, quite appropriately, discounted in the membership of the executive council. For this purpose, the executive council is defined as 'the body of Ministers of the Government of the Federation, howsoever called, established by the President and charged with such responsibilities for the functions of government as the President may direct' (s. 133[5]).

Apart from his advisory role as a member of the executive bodies mentioned above, the vice-president has and can have only such executive functions as the president may choose to delegate to him. And for the exercise of such delegated functions, he is just as much a delegate or agent as a minister exercising functions assigned to him by the president. It is a further mark of the emptiness of the office from a constitutional standpoint that he is not even designated by the Constitution to act for the president during the latter's absence on leave or abroad. A proposal by the writer so to designate him was lost in the constituent assembly, the argument being that an acting president should not be imposed on the president if he does not want to have one. The president has thus a discretion to appoint or not to appoint an acting president during any period of absence. Without a constitutional provision empowering him in that respect, there can be no question of the vice-president stepping in automatically to act for the president in his absence. Only his appointment as such by the president will provide the necessary legal authority for him to exercise the powers of the president in the latter's absence. The title vice-president (or deputy governor) implies by itself alone no constitutional authority to exercise the president's powers without a valid delegation by the president himself. Informally, he can hold the fort and look after the government, but the exercise of power so as to affect legal relations requires formal appointment or delegation. However, where the president is disposed to appoint anyone at all, it is a matter for argument whether he can constitutionally by-pass the vice-president in favour of someone else, as the governor of Kano state did when he appointed his commissioner for agriculture to act for him during his absence on leave. It would be difficult to maintain that such an action on the part of the president is a violation of the letter of the Constitution, though clearly its spirit envisages the vice-president as the person to be appointed.

Of course the vice-president succeeds to the presidency in the event of a vacancy occurring by death, resignation or removal in accordance with the provisions of the Constitution (s. 134[1]). His succession is automatic, and he has no choice in the matter, except to resign immediately thereafter if he is really so deeply reluctant to succeed. But succession to the presidency brings no powers to the vice-president as such, since by it an incumbent vice-president ceases to be such.

2. *Relation to ministers individually and collectively as a council*

The office of minister is clearly implied in the Constitution, but it is left to the president to establish particular ministerial offices and, as a necessary incident, to dis-establish them. The wording of the relevant constitutional provision shows that the Constitution establishes no offices of ministers directly, except for the office of the attorney-general (s. 138[1]). The provision says that 'there shall be such offices of Ministers of the Government of the Federation as may be established by the President' (s. 135[1]). The clear implication of this is that the president has the prerogative to determine what ministerial offices to establish, but he is constitutionally obliged to establish some. He is not free not to have ministers at all. The exercise of the power requires no formal act, and can even be done informally by presidential memorandum, but usually a gazette notice is used.

The establishment of ministerial offices is a significant power in the hands of the president as a source of patronage. By it he can create as many ministerial positions as he likes simply to make more juicy jobs available for the boys, although the needs of the country may not justify it. It is for this reason that in some countries, including the United States, ministerial offices are created only by law enacted by the legislature, while in some others the number that can be created by the legislature or by the president is fixed by the Constitution.

Appointment of ministers is also made by the president, though with the prior approval of the senate (s. 135[2]). Candidates are first nominated by the president, then presented to the senate for confirmation and thereafter formally appointed by the president. The requirement of senate confirmation does not make ministerial appointments the joint responsibility of the president and the senate. The responsibility belongs exclusively to the president, subject to a check exercised by the senate to ensure the integrity and probity of persons to be appointed ministers. The nature of the senate's checking role is explained in a later chapter (see chapter 8 below).

The Constitution is silent on the ministers' tenure of office. It follows that, by the general rule of interpretation referred to above, the president can, as an incident of his power to appoint them, revoke their appointment at will.

The assignment to ministers of specific functions of government, including in particular the administration of any department of government, is in the discretion of the president (s. 136[1]). Although he is constitutionally obliged to have ministers, he is not bound to assign specific functions of government to them. He is constitutionally within his right to keep all the departments under his direct responsibility and use the ministers for general duties as ministers without portfolio; or he could, while assigning specific departments to them, hive off to his own office vital aspects of the functions of those departments, as was done by President Nkrumah in Ghana. (It is arguable that this may not be in consonance with the provision requiring the conduct of government to reflect the federal character of the country.)

In respect of any part of the president's executive power which is assigned to a minister, the minister's authority is constitutionally a delegated one, and its exercise is subject to control by the president. He is there only in the role of a subordinate to assist the president in the exercise of an executive power that belongs to him alone. The minister is not a co-beneficiary with the president of the executive power, and although he exercises initiative and personal discretion within his department, he does so only as a delegate. The appointment of a minister to be in charge of a department does not imply an abdication by the president of his power in and over that department. Constitutionally he always remains free to act directly in the department even without prior consultation with the minister, and he may also overrule a decision or action taken by the minister within the department.

The *actual*, as distinct from the strictly constitutional, relation of the president to the minister is of course another matter. This would depend on the extent of the president's direct ministerial responsibility, the extent of the control or direction which he actually exercises over the ministers within their respective departments, and the role which he allows to the cabinet in the co-ordination of the activities of the various departments and in the determination of policy affecting the government as distinct from purely departmental policy which, subject or not to presidential direction, is determined within each ministry by the responsible minister. It is these three factors that condition the *actual* relations of the president to his ministers individually. The powers of a minister depend upon the degree of autonomy he enjoys within his ministry, while his standing in relation to the president depends on the extent and nature of the latter's direct ministerial responsibilities and the role allowed to the cabinet. A concentration of direct ministerial responsibilities in the hands of the president, coupled with his specific powers under the Constitution and the statutes, will create such an imbalance between him and the ministers as cannot but diminish the status of the latter. Such a concentration is bound to emphasise the ministers' inferiority and subordination to the president.

This is exemplified by the experience in Ghana under President Nkrumah. The ministers there were deprived of initiative and autonomy following the transfer to the president's office of the vital functions of their ministries. Since the functions so transferred must impinge on the work of the ministries, very little scope was left for independent action by the ministers. They could hardly initiate policy entirely on their own. By their nature and importance, the functions transferred to the president were bound to be the factors controlling policy, which meant therefore that the president was to be the source of initiative in departmental policy as well as in general policy. Without the power to initiate policy for his ministry, a minister can be little more than an administrator concerned in the main to ensure that policy decided elsewhere is properly executed. In the result, the ministries in Nkrumah's Ghana were reduced to mere 'hollow shells'.[2]

The attorney-general stands out as the only minister invested by the Constitution with a separate, independent function. This relates to public prosecutions (s. 160). He is empowered
(*a*) to institute and undertake criminal proceedings against any person before any court of law in Nigeria, other than a court-martial, in respect of any offence created by or under any act of the national assembly;
(*b*) to take over and continue any such criminal proceedings that may have been instituted by any other authority or person; and
(*c*) to discontinue at any stage before judgment is delivered any such criminal proceedings instituted or undertaken by him or any other authority or person.

The provision in the 1963 Constitution insulating public prosecutions from the direction or control of any other person or authority than the attorney-general (s. 104[6]) is inappropriate in a presidential system, and is rightly omitted from the 1979 Constitution. The latter only requires him to have regard to the public interest, the interests of justice and the need to prevent abuse of legal process (s. 160[3]). It seems that, subject to the above-stated considerations, the president can direct the attorney-general with regard to public prosecutions.

The president's relation to the ministers collectively as a body is equally crucial to his overall position in the government and in the determination of the question whether he is the government or not. The Constitution does not, like its predecessor, establish a council of ministers in explicit terms, but it clearly does so indirectly. First, it refers explicitly to the executive council of the federation (see ss. 133 and 264), defining it as 'the body of Ministers of the Government of the Federation' (s. 133[5]), and by that name entrusts to it the function of declaring, by a resolution passed by two-thirds majority of all its members, that the president or vice-president is, on ground of ill-health, incapable of discharging the functions of his office (s. 133[1]). Such a declaration, if verified and confirmed by a medical panel of five practitioners appointed by the president of the senate, operates to vacate the office of the president or vice-president from the date of the publication in the gazette of the report of the medical panel. A function that enables the ministers collectively as a body to initiate the removal of the president from office, albeit only on the ground of mental or physical incapacity, is indeed a crucial power that gives to the council of ministers a significant standing as an organ of government independent of the president.

Secondly, the president is constitutionally required 'to hold regular meetings with the Vice-President and *all* the Ministers of the Government of the Federation for the purposes of

(*a*) determining the general direction of domestic and foreign policies of the Government of the Federation;

(*b*) co-ordinating the activities of the President, the Vice-President and Ministers of the Government of the Federation in the discharge of their executive responsibilities; and

(*c*) advising the President generally in the discharge of his executive functions other than those functions with respect to which he is required by this Constitution to seek the advice or act on the recommendation of any other person or body' (s. 136[2]).

Now, a council of ministers is nothing but an assembly or meeting of ministers held regularly. That is also its dictionary meaning. This provision has therefore the effect of establishing a council of ministers, though in a somewhat oblique fashion. It is perhaps pertinent to emphasise that by the strict stipulations of the Constitution every minister is entitled to be in the council. The constitutional direction to the president is to hold regular meetings with the vice-president and *all* ministers. The practice whereby some ministers are given cabinet rank while others are not, is strictly contrary to the Constitution.

The high court of Bendel state has held, rejecting a contrary argument, that an executive council is established and exists by virtue of the provision requiring the president to hold regular meetings with his vice-president and ministers, and by the vesting of power in it in regard to the removal of a president incapacitated by ill-health.[3] The point arose in connection with the power vested in the executive council under the existing Local Government Edict 1976 to suspend any local government council found not to have discharged its function in a manner conducive to the welfare of the inhabitants of the area of its authority as a whole, and to replace it by a committee of management, and, after due inquiry into the affairs of the council, either to re-instate the chairman and members or to declare their seats vacant, and order an election. After the hand-over by the military to elected civilian governments but before commissioners had been appointed in the state, the state governor, purporting to act in pursuance of power under this provision, suspended all the local government councils and removed their chairmen and members, replacing them with committees of management made up entirely of his party's supporters. It was asserted in justification for his action that, the governor being the sole repository of all executive power in the state under the new Constitution, and as no provision was made for an executive council, all powers vested in the executive council under any existing law enured to, and might be exercised by, the governor alone, as he did in this case.

Rejecting this argument, the court held that while the Local Government Edict 1976 remained in force, only the executive council could, in the circumstances and manner prescribed in the edict, lawfully order the suspension of a local government council and the removal of its members and their replacement by a committee of management, and that as commissioners had not been appointed so as to enable an executive council to be constituted in accordance with the provisions of the new Constitution, the suspension of the local government councils and the removal of their members by the governor was unconstitutional, unlawful and void. (The removal of the members was also declared unlawful on the further ground that, even assuming the governor to have possessed the powers of the executive council, the seats of members could not be declared vacant without first holding an enquiry into the affairs of the councils. The appointment of management committees to replace the suspended councils was declared unconstitutional as derogating from the constitutional guarantee [s. 7] of a system of local government by democratically elected local government councils and the duty enjoined on the state government to ensure the existence of such councils.)

That an executive council exists by the Constitution has also been affirmed by the federal court of appeal. Given that an executive council is established by the Constitution, the appeal court, by a majority of four to one, held that, since the Local Government Law of Kaduna state vests the appointment of a commission of enquiry into a local government, not in the governor, but in the executive council, the appointment by the governor of a commission of enquiry into the affairs of the Kaduna local government at a time when there was no executive council was null and void.[4] Justice Coker, in minority, took the view that the legislature could not take away an executive function from the governor or vest it in him and others jointly; and that, as the appointment of a commission of enquiry in pursuance of a statutory authorisation is an executive function, the vesting of it in the executive council by the Local Government Law of Kaduna State is unconstitutional and void. This aspect of the matter is considered in chapter 9 below.

The next question is as to the exact position of the executive council in relation to the determination of general policy and the coordination of government activities under the constitutional provisions quoted above (s. 136[2]). Is the position that, by these provisions, the determination of general policy and the co-ordination of government activities are vested in the president in council as a distinct organ of government? Or are they vested in the president personally, but subject to a constitutional direction that he is to exercise them, acting not alone in the solitude of his office or bedroom, but in council with the vice-president and ministers? The difference between these two alternative interpretations has important constitutional implication.

In the case from Kaduna state referred to above, the federal court of appeal held the determination of general policy and the co-ordination of government activities to be the collective responsibility of the president, the vice-president and the ministers, and that the president cannot therefore override the council in such matters. As Justice Ademola puts it, speaking for a majority of the court (a majority of 4−1) 'this is cabinet government as super-imposed on presidentialism. . . . The built-in of a cabinet or an executive council around the operation of a presidential system in Nigeria could not make occurrence of the famous story possible about Abraham Lincoln consulting his cabinet and announcing, "noes, 7 — ayes, 1. The ayes have it." ' In his own separate, concurring judgment, the appeal court president, Justice Nasir, also said that the constitutional provisions under consideration are 'intended to incorporate in the Constitution a cabinet system of government in a modified form with a view to making it much more difficult for the governor to assume the role of a dictator'.

It seems that the decision of the federal court of appeal over-stretches the provisions of the Constitution. Policy and the co-ordination of government activities are indisputably part of the executive power vested in the president by the Constitution. The provisions under consideration (s. 136[2]) do not divest him of these functions in favour of the president in council; all they do, and are intended to do, is to direct how those functions are to be exercised. They require him (the president) to exercise them, not alone in the solitude of his office or bedroom, but in council with the vice-president and ministers. The president is constitutionally enjoined to determine general policy and to perform his co-ordinating role at a meeting with the vice-president and the ministers. The aim is to bring the collective views of the president, vice-president and ministers to bear upon such matters, but without depriving the president, as the sole repository of the power, of his authority to override the views of the rest of the council if and when he thinks fit. Having submitted a question on these matters to the deliberation of the council, the president is within his constitutional right to refuse to accept the views of the rest of the council. He can act exactly as Lincoln did in the story above.

It follows that the role of the executive council is largely deliberative and advisory, whether it be in respect of the determination of general policy and the co-ordination of government activities or in relation to the discharge by the president of his other executive functions. Whether the advice of the executive council is required in every case of the exercise by the president of his other executive functions as in the case of the determination of general policy and the co-ordination of government activities, the value of the council's advice in restraining and moderating the president's executive actions, and the constitutional consequences of failure to seek necessary advice are issues which will be considered in the next chapter.

This, then, sums up the constitutional relation of the president to the executive council. It shows the council as essentially an instrument of the president's, except for the function of initiating the removal of a president who would not resign when he has become incapable of discharging the duties of his office because of ill-health, and except as any particular functions may be validly conferred on the executive council by the legislature.

3. *Relation to the ministries or departments and their staff*

The Constitution implies that the administrative machinery for the government of the federation should be organised into ministries and departments, with divisions and sections. The implication arises from references made to ministries (s. 264), to the assignment to a minister of responsibility for a department of government (s. 136), to the permanent secretary or other chief executive in any ministry or department of government (s. 157[1][*d*]), to the ministry or department of government charged with responsibility for external affairs (s. 149[1]), to the head of a division in a ministry (3rd Sch., para. 4[2]), and to staff of a ministry or department of the government (s. 277[1]).

In the absence of a provision in the Constitution establishing the ministries and departments and offices in them or expressly authorising the president to do so, the question arises whether a power in the president to establish them may reasonably be implied as a necessary incident of the constitutional vesting of executive power in him. As regards the power to appoint executive officers, a majority of the U.S. supreme court has held that this is implied in the president's power to execute the laws.[9] The reasoning of the Court is that the president could not execute the laws alone and unaided, and since therefore he must need have the assistance of subordinates of various types and grades, he should as part of his executive power be able to appoint such subordinates. The power to appoint attracted as a necessary incident the power of removal, for otherwise the president might be saddled, to the prejudice of his administration, with subordinates who could not be removed, notwithstanding that they were disloyal, incompetent or otherwise unfit. The minority of the court based their dissent on the ground that the removal power was not a necessary incident either of the general executive power or of the power to take care to see that the laws be faithfully executed, and was therefore not vested in the president by virtue of the grant of these powers. The majority must surely be right.

But, except in the case of non-established staff, the ministries or departments and offices in them must first be established before appointments to them can be made. It must therefore follow too that the establishment or disestablishment of ministries or departments and the creation or abolition of offices in them are equally the prerogative of the president by virtue of the executive power vested in him. Until they are disestablished, abolished or revoked, ministries or departments and offices in them, together with appointments to such offices existing at the commencement of the Constitution, are deemed to have been established or made under the Constitution (s. 275).

The establishment power assures to the president a potent source of control over the administrative machinery of the government. It enables him to determine the policy governing the entire civil service and its administration, particularly rules of conduct, terms and conditions of service, staff complements and gradings, salaries and allowances. Every staff member in the ministries and departments is bound by his directives in this respect, and it is within these directives and general orders that the civil service functions.

As stated earlier, the executive power vested in the president embraces as a necessary incident the appointment, promotion, removal and disciplinary control of the staff in the ministries and departments.[5] These incidents of the power are however limited by the Constitution. For this purpose civil servants fall into two categories. The president can appoint and remove only the secretary to the government, the head of the federal civil service, an ambassador, a high commissioner or other principal representative of Nigeria abroad, the permanent secretary or other chief executive in any ministry or department, and any member on his personal staff (s. 157[1] and [2]). This category of civil servants (with the exception of the last) may be regarded as the representatives of the government in the ministries and departments, making it impolitic that their appointment and removal should be withdrawn from the control of the president. The strategic importance of their positions makes them so much part of the government that loyalty must be a pre-eminent consideration in their appointment. If they are ill-disposed towards the government, this may affect not only the advice they give to it but also the way they conduct the affairs of their ministries and departments.

The auditor-general belongs to this category, but the president's power to appoint and remove him is restricted because of the nature of his work as a watchdog of the nation's finances. He is to be appointed on the recommendation of the federal civil service commission and with the confirmation of the senate whilst his removal can be effected only when requested by the senate by a two-thirds majority of its members on the ground of mental or physical incapacity or misconduct (ss. 80[1] and 81[1]).

The appointment, promotion, removal and disciplinary control of all other civil servants are vested in the federal civil service commission, though the commission is required to consult the head of the civil service before exercising its powers in this behalf in relation to such heads of divisions of ministries or departments as may be designated by the president (s. 140 and 3rd Sch., para. 4). The object of vesting in a constitutional commission the appointment and disciplinary control of civil servants (other than those mentioned above) is to ensure that merit rather than political considerations should be the criterion for appointment and promotion, that dismissals and disciplinary control are not to be used as an instrument of political victimisation, and that the political neutrality of the civil service, that cornerstone of our inherited civil service system, would not be jeopardised. The device is also part of the total scheme of institutional safeguards for political and ethnic minorities.

Now, a president with the executive power of the country, yet lacking power to appoint or remove his executive officers, is like a contradiction in terms, a situation unrecognised in the United States where a law by congress fettering the president's power to remove a civil servant by requiring the consent of the senate was held void as an unconstitutional encroachment on the president's executive power.[6] To deny him this power is indeed to cut off a critical part of the apparatus for executing the business of government. If a government is to be able to govern effectively it must be free to choose those who are to work for and with it, and to fire them if they prove incompetent or disloyal.

Not only is the president divested of these powers in favour of the commission, but the latter is guaranteed independence from the direction or control of the president or any other authority or person in the exercise of its powers (s. 145[1]). (The delegation of functions to any of its members or to any officer in the civil service and the making of rules regulating its procedure require the approval of the president — ss. 147 and 156.) Its members are given immunity from removal except when removal is requested by the senate by two-thirds majority of its members on the ground of inability or misconduct (s. 144[1]). Their salaries and allowances are to be determined, not by the president, but by the national assembly, and are made a direct charge on the consolidated revenue fund while their conditions of service generally (including salaries but not allowances) cannot be altered to their disadvantage after appointment (s. 78). Only as regards the appointment of its members does the president have control, that being his prerogative, subject however to confirmation by the senate (s. 141[1]). Insulated against the influence of the removal power the commission enjoys real and effective independence from the president, such as to impart to the appointment and removal powers lodged in it effective and meaningful immunity from presidential control.

The power of the president to regulate, by general orders and rules, the conduct of civil servants, and of the civil service commission to exercise disciplinary control over them, is subject to a constitutionally-prescribed code of conduct, observance of which is made mandatory on every public officer, including the president. The implementation of the code is vested, not in the president or the civil service commission, but in other bodies, the code of conduct bureau and the code of conduct tribunal.

The bureau, composed of nine members, is charged with responsibility concerning declarations of assets by public officers. It receives such declarations, processes them to ensure conformance with the requirements of the code, receives complaints about non-compliance and, where it considers it necessary so to do, refers them to the code of conduct tribunal (5th Sch., para. 15). In the exercise of its functions, the bureau is responsible to the national assembly. Its staff (but not the members) are appointed and controlled as regards discipline by the senate. The members of the bureau are appointed by the president with the approval of the senate, but they have the same tenure as civil servants, which means that their removal and disciplinary control is a matter for the civil service commission.

On a reference from the bureau, a complaint is heard by the code of conduct tribunal of three members which, if it finds the public officer concerned guilty, shall, subject to an appeal to the federal court of appeal, impose any of the following punishments: vacation of office, disqualification from the holding of any public office for not more than ten years, seizure and forfeiture to the state of any property acquired in abuse or corruption of office, and such other punishment as may be prescribed by the national assembly (5th Sch., paras. 17–20). The members of the tribunal are appointed by the president on the recommendation of the judicial service commission, but he can only remove them upon an address by each house of the national assembly supported by two-thirds majority of its members requesting removal on the ground of inability or misconduct or the contravention of the code of conduct. The tribunal is given power to appoint its own staff and to exercise disciplinary control over them; for the rest, their tenure is the same as that of civil servants.

Yet another independent mechanism instituted by the Constitution for controlling the conduct of civil servants is the public complaints commission which, as a safeguard against injustice, is given power to investigate the administrative action of any ministry or department or of any staff thereof, and to recommend appropriate remedial action, which may be re-consideration of the matter, modification or cancellation of the offending administrative act or the giving of full reasons for it (s. 274[5] and Decree no. 31 of 1975). The commission is independent of the president as regards the appointment and removal of its members and staff while its immunity from the direction or control of any other person or authority is also guaranteed.

The establishment of these bodies and the power given to them over civil servants does not alter significantly the constitutional relation of the president to them (i.e. civil servants). They, like the political heads of the ministries and departments, the ministers, are merely delegates, appointed to act for him and in his name; their acts are presumptively his acts, and they are subject to his direction or control in the performance of their duties. If they should refuse to carry out the president's lawful directives or prove otherwise disloyal or unfit, he can request the civil service commission to discipline or remove them, provided that disciplinary action or removal would be lawful under the general orders or other regulations governing the civil service. However, excepting those employed in his own office or in a ministry or department under his direct responsibility, in practice the president is not expected, and normally does not, by-pass the minister in order to give directives directly to civil servants within a ministry. His control over them is exercised remotely through the minister and permanent secretary and through his power to determine, by means of general orders and regulations, the policy governing the entire civil service and its administration.

The auditor-general is an exception to what is said above. The audit of the public accounts of the federation and of all its offices, courts and authorities, including all persons and bodies established by law and entrusted with the collection and administration of public moneys and assets, and the certification of payments in respect of revenue allocation are vested in him (ss. 79, 149–55). For an audit exercise, he is to have access to all books, records, returns and other documents relating to the public accounts. The report of his audit is submitted straight to the national assembly, and not to the president. He is independent of the direction or control of both or any other authority in the exercise of his functions, audit as well as certification of payments (s. 79).

4. *Relation to the police force and the Nigerian security organisation*

The maintenance of law and order and the preservation of national security are basic to the government of any political community. Two organs, the Nigeria police force and the Nigerian security organisation, are established by the Constitution for their exercise (ss. 141 and 274[5]). (The establishment of any other police force is prohibited — s. 141[1].) The relation of the two organs to the president is therefore important in evaluating his place in the government of the country.

The command of the entire police force is vested in an inspector-general assisted by a commissioner who, subject to the authority of the inspector-general, has the command of any contingents of the force stationed in a state (s. 195). Command implies supreme authority and control as regards not only operational use but also organisation, administration, equipment and staffing. However, the full implication of vesting the command of the police force in the inspector-general is limited by the Constitution, although only some of the limitations are in favour of the president. First, the organisation and administration of the force are to be prescribed by law, which means that the national assembly is constitutionally competent to confer the two functions away from the president and independently of his control. The president does not therefore have the *constitutional* power possessed by the government of the First Republic over the organisation and administration of the police force.[7] A police council (composed of the prime minister or a federal minister nominated by him, as chairman, the regional premiers or ministers nominated by them and the chairman of the police service commission), was of course established, charged with the general supervision of the organisation and administration of the police force. In other words, the council did not control the organisation and administration of the force, it merely supervised, and even then it was concerned only with general, not detailed or day-to-day, supervision, which only enabled it to make recommendations to the federal government. The latter was free to accept or reject its recommendations, though where it acted contrary to such recommendation, the matter had to be reported to parliament with reasons for the action. These provisions are not repeated in the new Constitution, which simply provides that the police force is to be organised and administered as the national assembly may by law prescribe.

Secondly the members of the police force are to have only such powers as may be conferred upon them by law (s. 194[2][b]). Neither the inspector-general nor the president can therefore lawfully order the police to act outside or beyond the powers conferred on them by law.

Thirdly, the appointment, removal and disciplinary control of members of the force (other than the inspector-general) are vested in a police service commission, consisting of a chairman and such number of other members, not being less than seven nor more than nine, as may be prescribed by an act of the national assembly (s. 140 and 3rd Sch., paras. 17 and 18). The members of the commission are secured against removal by the president except on the prayer of a two-thirds majority of the senate for reasons of inability or misconduct (s. 144). Their salaries and allowances, which are to be prescribed by the national assembly and not by the president, are made a charge upon the consolidated revenue fund and not to be altered to their prejudice after appointments (s. 78).

The president is not however without a considerable measure of constitutional control over the police force. He appoints the members of the police service commission, subject to confirmation by the senate (s. 141[1]); the making of rules regulating its procedure and the delegation of functions to any of its members or to any member of the police force require the approval of the president (ss. 147[1] and 196[1]). From the non-inclusion of the commission in the provision insulating certain executive bodies, e.g. the civil service commission, from the direction or control of any other authority or person in the exercise of their power of appointment and disciplinary control (s. 145), it is arguable that the intention was that the president is to have power to direct the police service commission in the appointment and disciplinary control of members of the force. The non-inclusion is more likely to have been an oversight, since otherwise it might seem somewhat pointless to have vested the power in the commission instead of leaving it where it belongs i.e. with the president.

The president also appoints and removes the inspector-general in consultation with the police service commission. But the main control which the president has over the police force is his power to direct the inspector-general on the use of the police for maintaining and securing public safety and public order; any direction which he gives for this purpose must be carried out by the inspector-general, provided of course it is something within the powers conferred upon the police by law (s. 195[3]). The inspector-general is not bound to comply with an unlawful direction of the president on the maintenance of public safety and public order. A state governor can also, for the same purpose, direct the commissioner of police in his state, but the latter is entitled to postpone action to await the directions of the president (s. 195[4]).

Furthermore, as earlier stated, the vesting by the Constitution of public prosecutions in the attorney-general enables him, and the president through him, to direct the police on that important aspect of law and order. Also the power vested in the president to pardon offenders impinges on the functions of the police, since it is not a condition for its exercise that the offender should have been convicted or sentenced or even charged before a court. Any one 'concerned' with an offence may be pardoned by the president (s. 161[1]).

The Nigerian security organisation, established in 1976, was given a constitutional basis by the incorporation of the establishing decree as part of the Constitution with the same force and authority as other provisions of the Constitution and amendable only by the same procedure (s. 274[5]). It is designed as an instrument to be employed by the president for the preservation of the security of the country. Its structure, including the designation and appointment of its principal officers, its administration, operation and other incidental matters are to be regulated by the president by means of an instrument, which is to have the same effect as a decree (Decree no. 16 of 1976).

To advise the president on public security, including matters relating to any organisation or agency established by law for ensuring national security, the Constitution establishes a national security council composed of the president as chairman, the vice-president as deputy chairman, the chief of defence staff, federal ministers for internal affairs, defence and external affairs, head of the Nigerian security organisation, the inspector-general of police, and such other persons as the president may in his unrestricted discretion appoint

(s. 140 and 3rd Sch. paras. 15 and 16). Any member so appointed by the president may also be removed by him. As its composition shows, the council is, like the Nigerian security organisation, an instrument of the president.

5. *Relation to the armed forces*

The president is designated by the Constitution the commander-in-chief of the armed forces of the federation (s. 198[1]). His power of supreme command is explicitly stated to *include* the control of operational use and the appointment of the chief of defence staff, and the heads of the army, navy, air force and such other branches of the armed forces as may be established by an act of the national assembly (s. 198[1] and [2]). It must also include, by implication, the removal of these service chiefs. The appointment, promotion and disciplinary control of other members of the armed forces are, however, to be regulated by the national assembly by law (s. 198[4][*b*]), which may therefore lodge them elsewhere than in the president. Even the president's power as commander-in-chief is subject to regulation by a law enacted by the national assembly (s. 198[4][*a*]), although this only enables the assembly to regulate the manner of its exercise but not to take it away completely.

The exact location of the power to establish, equip and maintain an armed force for the country is left rather vague. It is provided that 'the federation shall, subject to any Act of the National Assembly made in that behalf, establish, equip and maintain an Army, a Navy, an Air Force and such other branches of the armed forces of the Federation as may be considered adequate and effective' for the defence of Nigeria from external aggression, the maintenance of its territorial integrity, the suppression of insurrection, the aid of the civil authorities to restore order when called upon to do so by the president, and the performance of such other functions as may be prescribed by an act of the national assembly (s. 197[1]). The phrase 'subject to any act of the national assembly' is apt to suggest that the federation in the context of the provision is not intended to refer to the national assembly. Clearly too the president is not the federation, and neither is the government. On the other hand, the later references to the national assembly 'giving effect to the functions specified' in the provision above, and to 'such other branches of the armed forces as may be established by an act of the national assembly' provide a strong, if not conclusive, indication that the power to establish, equip and maintain an armed force belongs to the national assembly. The president cannot therefore raise an armed force except on the authority of a law enacted by the national assembly. This is in keeping with the inherited British principle, won after a long-drawn-out contest between king and parliament.

A national defence council is established to advise the president on matters relating to the defence of the sovereignty and territorial integrity of the country (s. 140 and 3rd Sch. paras. 9 and 10). It is composed of the president as chairman, the vice-president as deputy chairman, the minister of defence, the chief of defence staff, the heads of the army, navy and air force, and such other members as the president may appoint. The council is thus clearly an instrument of the president.

6. *Relation to other executive bodies established by the Constitution*

Two vital and sensitive functions, elections and census, which should normally form part of the power of the president to execute the Constitution and the laws, are lodged in executive bodies established directly by the Constitution (s. 140).

There is the electoral commission, which is composed of one member from each state (one of whom is to be appointed chairman) and not more than five other members appointed on their merits. It is charged with functions relating to the organisation and conduct of presidential and gubernatorial elections as well as elections to both the federal and state legislative houses; registration of political parties, and the examination and audit of their accounts; the registration of voters and the maintenance and revision of the register of voters, and ensuring that the register of voters is prepared and maintained in such form as to facilitate its use for the purpose of elections to local government councils (3rd Sch. para. 6).

Then there is the national population commission, comprising a chairman and one member from each state. It has responsibility for periodical enumeration of population through sample surveys, censuses or otherwise, the establishment and maintenance of machinery for continuous and universal registration of births and deaths throughout the federation, and the provision of information and data on population for the purpose of facilitating economic and development planning (3rd Sch. para. 14).

For the purposes of their functions, both commissions have power to appoint and remove staff who, though not civil servants, are members of the public service of the federation in the wider sense as defined in the Constitution (s. 277[1]).

The chairman and members of each commission are appointed by the president with the confirmation of the senate; they enjoy, however, the same protection as members of the civil service commission as regards removal, salaries, allowances and conditions of service generally (ss. 78, 140 and 144). More important in assuring their independence is the extent to which they are insulated from presidential control and direction in the exercise of their functions.

The provision relating to the electoral commission merely states that it shall not be subject to the direction or control of any other authority or person in exercising its power of appointment and disciplinary control of its staff. The implication seems to be that immunity from control does not apply in respect of the rest of its functions. Is the intention then that an incumbent president can direct or control the commission in the conduct of presidential, gubernatorial and legislative elections and in the registration of voters? The purpose of vesting these powers in a commission, away from the president to whom they should normally belong, is to enable them to be exercised independently of his control in order to avoid undue political influence. This purpose would have been defeated if their exercise by the commission could be controlled by the president. The provision of the Constitution that 'the registration of voters and the conduct of elections shall be subject to the direction and supervision of the Federal Electoral Commission' (s. 72) is emphatic enough to rule out a power in the president to control the exercise of these functions by the commission.

The Constitution specifically provides that the national population commission cannot be directed or controlled by the president or by any other person or authority as regards the conduct of a census, including the acceptance or revision of the census return submitted by any of its officers, the compilation of its report on a census, and the appointment or training of its staff involved in the conduct of a census. But while the commission is insulated from presidential control in the conduct of a census, its report on it is not conclusive on the president or the country. The commission through its chairman is required to submit its report to the president who may accept or reject it (s. 193). The decision to accept or reject does not however lie in the president's personal discretion, *he must act as advised by the council of state*, although any advice to reject can only be on the ground of inaccuracy of the census or perverseness of the report. Upon the rejection of its report, all the members of the commission vacate their offices (s. 144[3]). If the census is accepted, it must then be laid before each house of the national assembly.

This therefore constitutes the council of state, rather than the president, the effective constitutional authority for the acceptance or rejection of a census report, making its relation to the president a matter of considerable importance. The council is a high-powered body. It consists of the president as chairman, the vice-president as deputy chairman, all former presidents and all former heads of government of the federation, all former chief justices of Nigeria who are Nigerian citizens, the president of the senate, the speaker of the house of representatives, all state governors, the federal attorney-general, and one person from each state appointed by the state's council of chiefs from among themselves. With the exception of the attorney-general, therefore, all the members are independent of the president. They are secured against removal except by the same rigorous process prescribed for members of the civil service commission, viz. address by a two-thirds majority of the senate praying removal on the ground of inability or misconduct.

One other function in respect of which the council of state, by virtue of being able to bind the president by its advice, is the real, effective authority, concerns the grant of pardon to persons offending against naval, military or air force law or convicted or sentenced by a court-martial (s. 161[3]).

Aside from these two functions, the council of state is purely an advisory body. It advises the president on the exercise of his functions relating to census and the grant of pardon generally, award of national honours, federal electoral commission, the federal judicial service commission and the national population commission (including the appointment of their members) and, when so requested, the maintenance of public order and any other matters (3rd Sch., para. 2).

Finally, the Constitution establishes a national economic council to advise the president on matters relating to the economic affairs of the country, particularly measures necessary for the co-ordination of the economic planning efforts or economic programmes of the various governments of the federation (3rd Sch., paras. 11 and 12). Its members are the vice-president as chairman, the governor of each state, and the governor of the central bank. Although its members (with the exception of the governor of the central bank) are independent of the president, the council has no independent executive function, being, as already stated, merely advisory to him.

All these bodies have power by rules or otherwise to regulate their procedure and to confer powers and impose duties on any officer or authority for the purpose of discharging their functions, but this has to be approved by the president (s. 147[1]).

7. Establishment of public offices outside the civil service, police and armed forces and appointments thereto

The public controversy over the appointment by the president of presidential liaison officers to the states raises an important constitutional issue concerning the extent of his power to constitute offices outside the civil service, the police and the armed forces, and to make appointments thereto. The president is certainly entitled, as an incident of the executive power vested in him, to constitute executive offices in the public service and to make appointments to them, since it is impossible for him to discharge his vast executive responsibilities singlehanded. But this undoubted incident of his office has to be taken in the context of the limitations and restrictions put on it by the Constitution.

The functions of the civil service in advising the government on policy, and in the execution of such policy and in the administration of the laws, are viewed by the Constitution as much too critical and sensitive for the appointment, removal and disciplinary control of its members to be left solely in the hands of a politician president; accordingly appointment, removal and disciplinary control in the civil service are insulated from political control and influence, and vested in an independent agency, the civil service commission, free from direction or control by the president. The president may constitute offices in the civil service, but having done so he must leave to the civil service commission appointments to the offices so constituted and the removal and disciplinary control of the incumbents. While this policy is open to criticism as a contradiction of the notion of an executive presidency, yet it would be a perversion of constitutional safeguards to try to get round it by transferring to public functionaries not appointed by the civil service commission the functions of the civil service in the administration of government services. The establishment of secretariats of the federal government in the states to undertake the execution or implementation of its projects and services there, and the appointment of resident liaison officers to superintend or oversee such activities may be a commendable policy, yet the Constitution does clearly require that the administration of federal government services, whether directly from the capital or by officers resident within the states, should be by civil servants appointed by the civil service commission.

The Constitution does of course, as an exception to the general policy, empower the president to make, without reference to the civil service commission, an appointment to any office on his personal staff. But the appointment must be within the civil service, and must be restricted to civil servants to be attached to the president personally, as distinct from the office. In cases of personal service involving close personal contact or interaction, it is right and proper that personal likes and dislikes should be respected, and that anyone to whom personal service is to be rendered should be allowed to choose whom to appoint. It would be utterly wrong to inflict upon him the services of someone he intensely dislikes as a person or for any other reason. But an office on the personal staff of the president cannot, in any proper sense of the phrase, be construed to include a presidential liaison officer. It would be an abuse of language so to construe it, and even if it could properly be so construed, still the administration of federal government services within a state cannot, consistent with constitutional safeguards, be transferred to officers on the personal staff of the president. In any case, the appointment of the presidential liaison officers was announced to have been made outside the civil service; its constitutionality must therefore be considered on that basis.

Considered as a public officer outside the civil service, a presidential liaison officer cannot, as has been observed, be appointed to assume within a state the functions of the civil service in the administration of federal government services. The Constitution no doubt recognises the imperative need for the superintendence at a political level of the administration of government services. Hence it empowers the president to appoint ministers. But the appointment of ministers is not left by the Constitution in the absolute discretion of the president. It prescribes qualifications for them, and requires presidential nominations for ministerial appointments to be approved by the senate. While the Constitution does not specifically limit the number of ministers the president can appoint, the requirement of senate approval can be used to supplement the control on numbers necessarily implied in the practice of government over the years and its needs. As is the practice in some countries, e.g. Zambia and the regions in Nigeria before 1966, a government is perfectly competent to decide to appoint resident ministers to co-ordinate and superintend its services in the constituent regions or provinces of the state. But if the presidential liaison officers are conceived in the role of resident ministers, then they must satisfy the constitutional requirements regarding qualifications and the approval of their nomination by the senate. The constitutional restrictions on the appointment of ministers would have been stultified if they could be circumvented by a mere change of designation where the functions to be performed are essentially those of a minister.

Apart from ministers, the Constitution does empower the president to appoint another category of executive public functionaries outside the civil service, viz special advisers. The office of special adviser is certainly not required by the compelling necessity that makes the office of minister imperative in the government of a modern state, and the proposal to create it in the Constitution was heavily criticised in the constituent assembly on the grounds, *inter alia*, that it would have a demoralising effect on civil servants, and that it might be abused to provide jobs at public expense for the president's supporters without subjecting such appointments to the qualifications and other safeguards prescribed by the Constitution in the case of ministers.[8] The proposal was allowed to pass eventually only on the following rationalisation proffered in the assembly by Chief Jerome Udoji: 'What is intended is not a political appointment but a professional assignment. Government in these days have become big business. It has become a complicated business, [and] big business requires big expertise. Therefore the idea here is for the President or the Governor to be able to appoint specialists. That is why they call them special advisers. They are not civil servants, they are not Ministers, they are specialists to do specialised jobs.'[9]

But the proposal was accepted and implemented in the Constitution only subject to the condition that the number of special advisers and their remuneration and allowances must be prescribed by law or by resolution of both houses of the national assembly (s. 139[2]).

The inference fairly to be drawn from these constitutional restrictions on the appointment of ministers and special advisers is that the Constitution does not intend that the president should have power to appoint other categories of executive public functionaries outside the civil service the police and armed forces. Ministers, special advisers and presidential liaison officers all fall within the same class — they are special assistants to the chief executive. To what end does the Constitution require ministers to have certain qualifications and to be approved by the senate, and the number and emoluments of special advisers to be prescribed by the national assembly if, by using a different designation — presidential liaison officer or any other — the president is to be free to appoint any number of special assistants that he likes? Constitutional restrictions cease to have meaning if they can thus be by-passed.

REFERENCES

1. *Molapo* v. *Seeiso*, High Court of Lesotho (1966), 166.
2. See H.L. Bretton, *The Rise and Fall of Kwame Nkrumah* (1968), 183.
3. *Jideonwo* v. *Governor, Bendel State of Nigeria*, Suit No. B/292/79 of 28 February 1980, High Court, Benin.
4. *Lawal Kagoma* v. *The Governor of Kaduna State & Others*, FCA/K/97/80 of 16 January 1981.
5. *Myers* v. *United States*, 272 U.S. 52.

6. ibid.
7. 1963 Constitution, ss. 107 and 108.
8. Constituent Assembly Debates, 23 January 1978, cols. 2422–5.
9. ibid., col. 2426.

8
CONSTITUTIONAL RESTRAINTS ON THE EXERCISE OF EXECUTIVE POWER BY THE PRESIDENT

An executive presidency is apt to create in our minds the image of dictatorship. We immediately think of the record of presidential tyranny in various parts of the world. In our own continent, presidential tyranny has a frightful reality that has, deservedly, earned for the system the rather pejorative appellation 'African presidentialism'. Yet it is important for a proper understanding of the nature of the executive presidency in Nigeria to free our minds of the distortions of preconceived impressions, and to consider it in the context of the complex structure of relationships and restraints in which it is set under the Constitution.

The Nigerian Constitution of 1979 has not accepted President Nyerere's idea that there should be no constitutional brake on the momentum of presidential action for the reason that the needs of a developing African country are not for a brake to social change but rather for accelerators powerful enough to overcome the inertia bred of poverty. We need accelerators certainly, but we need brakes too in order to ensure that the president does not get carried away by the intoxicating influence of power. Quite appropriately, therefore, the Constitution erects here and there checks and restrictions on the exercise of presidential power, aimed at creating a fair balance between effective government and liberty. Checks and restrictions are indeed a conspicuous feature of the presidency as instituted by the Constitution.

It is appropriate to emphasise again the distinction between the vesting of power and its actual exercise. The vesting of power may have no more than a nominal significance. What is overwhelmingly important is how the power is to be exercised — by whom and in what manner it may be exercised. Nigerians have become accustomed to this distinction through experience of the system of government in the first republic which vested executive power in the president but made it exercisable by, or as advised by, ministers, led by a premier. Although the presidential system established by the 1979 Constitution avoids this kind of separation as a general pattern, in three instances — the acceptance or rejection of a census report, the grant of pardon to persons concerned with offences against naval, military or air force law, and the appointment of justices of the supreme court and the president of the federal court of appeal — the power, though vested in the president, is exercisable by him only as advised by certain bodies established by the Constitution. Apart from these three instances, the restraints of the Constitution leave the exercise of executive power with the president while imposing checks and restrictions on the manner in which it is to be exercised. Such checks and restrictions constitute a serious qualification upon the power. Thus the formal extent of power is one thing: its effective use and, consequently, its reality, is another.

The restraints will now be considered.

1. *Checks and balances*

'Checks and balances' is a concept in the relationship between the executive and the legislature whereby the political organs with a view to the balancing of powers are enabled to check one other in the exercise of their respective functions. Checks by the national assembly over the president's exercise of executive power take three forms — approval for presidential action, inquisition into the president's administration and impeachment of the president and vice-president.

(i) *Approval for presidential action*

The Constitution makes certain powers of the president exercisable with the approval of either both houses of the national assembly or the senate alone, the approval being a condition either precedent or subsequent to the validity of the action in question. Where approval is a condition precedent, it must first be obtained before the act can validly be done. In the other case, the president is empowered first to take action, but the act lapses unless it is approved.

The prior approval of both houses of the national assembly is required for the appointment of a new vice-president in the event of a vacancy occurring in the office (s. 134[3]). The procedure is that a nomination is first made by the president followed by a formal appointment after the approval of each house has been obtained. The removal of a member of the code of conduct tribunal by the president also requires the prior approval of each house, supported by two-thirds majority of its members on the ground of inability or misconduct (5th Sch., para. 19[3]). Other instances of the exercise of power by the president requiring the prior approval of both houses are the declaration of war between Nigeria and another country (approving resolution of both houses sitting jointly) (s. 5[3][*b*]), and determination of the number of special advisers and their remuneration and allowances (s. 139[2]).

In one case the approval of each house is required not before but after the president has acted; this concerns the proclamation of an emergency. Such a proclamation lapses unless, within two days of its publication in the gazette or ten days when the national assembly is not in session, it is approved by each house by resolution supported by two-thirds of all its members (s. 265[6]). If the proclamation of a state of emergency is not to have effect throughout the federation but only within the territory of a state, then it cannot lawfully be made unless it is first requested by the state governor with the approving resolution of the state assembly supported again by two-thirds of its members (s. 265[5]). However, should the governor fail to make the request within a reasonable time after the resolution of the state assembly, the president may proclaim a state of emergency in the state.

The approval required in all other cases is that of the senate only. The deployment of any members of the armed forces on combat duty outside the country must be approved by the senate in advance (s. 5[3][b]). The appointment of various categories of public officers requires the prior or subsequent approval of the senate. Three formulas are employed. In the case of ministers, the president first makes nominations which, if confirmed by the senate, are then finalised by formal appointment by the president (s. 135[2]). The senate must make a response to the nominations within twenty-one days of receiving them or else the appointments will be deemed to have been made (s. 135[6]). It seems that this provision is satisfied if a nomination, without being confirmed or rejected, is merely returned for more information. For the second category of officers, ambassadors, high commissioners or other principal representatives of the country abroad, it is provided that their appointment by the president shall not take effect unless it is confirmed by the senate (s. 157[4]). The appointment is first made by the president but its effect is postponed pending the senate's approval. The third formula permits an appointment to be made in the first place by the president with immediate effect, subject to subsequent confirmation by the senate. It lapses in the event of the senate's rejection. This relates to appointed members of the civil service commission, electoral commission, judicial service commission, national population commission and police service commission (s. 141[1]), the auditor-general (s. 80[1]), the chief justice of Nigeria (s. 211[1]), justices of the supreme court (s. 211[2]), president of the federal court of appeal (s. 218[1]), and members of the code of conduct bureau (5th Sch., para. 16[2]).

It is provided that where 'any authority or person has power to make, recommend or approve an appointment to an office, such power shall be construed as including power to make, recommend or approve a person for such appointment, whether on promotion or otherwise, or to act in any such office' (s. 277[2]). The power given to the president to appoint an acting auditor-general (s. 80[2]) is thus subject to senate approval like the substantive appointment itself. The provision does not however apply to the appointment of a person to act as chief justice of Nigeria or president of the federal court of appeal, not only because the appointment is stated to lie in the president's discretion, but also because of the specific provision that, without the approval of the senate, it shall cease to have effect after three months (ss. 211[4] and [5] and 218[4] and [5]).

The president's power to remove the chief justice of Nigeria, the auditor-general, the chairman and members of the civil service commission, the council of state, electoral commission, judicial service commission, national population commission and the police service commission is also checked by the requirement of senate approval. Again different wording is employed in the three cases, but the effect of the provision relating to the chief justice and the chairmen and members of the named executive bodies is that the approval of the senate is only a condition for removal; the president cannot remove without it, but he is not obliged to do so simply because senate has asked for it (ss. 256[1] and 144). The provision relating to the auditor-general says that he '*shall* be removed from office by the president upon an address by the senate praying for his removal' (s. 81[2]). The implication is that the president is bound to remove him upon such address. In all these cases the address of the senate praying removal must be supported by a two-thirds majority of its members and be based on the ground of inability to discharge the functions of the office (whether arising from infirmity of mind or body) or misconduct.

The requirement of approval by the national assembly or the senate of certain acts of the president tends sometimes to be misunderstood. Its effect is not to subordinate the president to the national assembly or the senate, for it neither divests him of discretion in the exercise of the power in question nor makes the function a joint responsibility. The fact that an appointment can only be validly made with the approval of the senate does not make the appointment the joint responsibility of the president and the senate. As the U.S. supreme court has held, the approval of the senate does not make an appointment;[1] this still remains an act of the president, and is also a voluntary act.[2] Alexander Hamilton puts the matter quite lucidly in *The Federalist*:

> It will be the office of the president to *nominate*, and with the advice and consent of the senate to *appoint*. There will of course be no exertion of choice on the part of the senate. They may defeat one choice of the executive, and oblige him to make another; but they cannot themselves *choose* — they can only ratify or reject the choice of the president. They might even entertain a preference to some other persons at the very moment they were assenting to the one proposed; because there might be no positive ground for opposition to

him; and they could not be sure, if they withheld their assent, that the subsequent nomination would fall upon their own favourite, or upon any other person in their estimation more meritorious than the one rejected.[3]

The requirement of approval for the exercise of the removal power has more serious consequence for the president. 'A veto by the Senate . . . upon removal', said the U.S. supreme court, 'is a much greater limitation upon the executive branch and a much more serious blending of the legislative with the executive than a rejection of a proposed appointment.'[4] If a proposed appointment is vetoed by the senate, this would not frustrate completely the president's discretion in respect of the appointment nor greatly embarrass the work of his administration. He can nominate another person of his choice, and he has a wide field from which to choose. A veto upon removal, on the other hand, will, whenever it is exercised, completely frustrate the president's discretion.

It is said, in criticism of a check by the senate on ministerial appointments through the approval device, that the president's election is a mandate for him to govern, and to choose his principal assistants. He has full responsibility for his choice, and that responsibility he owes to the electorate that gave him the mandate. Accordingly, his ability to create a working administration as speedily as possible should not be fettered by the interposition of senate approval. 'Among all the modern fallacies that have obscured the true teachings of constitutional history', says Professor McIlwain, 'few are worse than the . . . indiscriminate use of the phrase "checks and balances".'[5] He maintains that the only restraints necessary for constitutionalism are the ancient legal restraint of a guarantee of civil liberties enforceable by an independent court and the modern concept of the full responsibility of government to the whole mass of the governed.

The criticism misses the point about the purpose which senate approval is intended to serve. The conferment by the electorate of a mandate to govern in no way implies that the public should no longer be concerned about the way the mandate is exercised. It is of the essence of constitutional democracy that the light of public scrutiny should at all times be focussed on the exercise of executive power by the president. And for this purpose the senate is the 'public eye' for ensuring that the appointment of the president's principal assistants conforms to the standards of integrity, competence and national interest required for the efficient management of the nation's affairs. Apart from scrutiny of the character and suitability of the persons for ministerial appointments, the check also enables the senate to ensure that it complies with constitutional provisions prescribing qualifications and disqualifications for such appointments, and that, as directed by the Constitution, it reflects the federal character of the country. The president may well lose sight of these in a desire to favour friends or to satisfy pressure from party leaders. There is of course nothing in the Constitution to prevent the president from re-submitting a name earlier rejected or the senate from reversing an earlier rejection if it is satisfied, on the basis of fresh information, that the earlier decision had been wrong, but a reversal is not to be lightly made if the senate is to retain credibility with the public.

(ii) *Inquisition into the president's administration*
Each house of the national assembly is empowered by resolution to 'direct or cause to be directed' an investigation into the conduct of affairs of any person, authority, ministry or government department in so far as the conduct relates to the execution or administration of laws enacted by the national assembly or the disbursement or administration of funds appropriated by it, and the investigation is for the purpose of enabling the assembly to make laws or to correct defects in existing laws or to expose corruption, inefficiency or waste in the execution or administration of laws or in the disbursement or administration of funds (s. 82). A resolution by either the senate or the house of representatives (concurrence of both houses is not required) can direct an investigation by the house itself, by a committee of the house or, where there is concurrence of the two houses, a joint committee, or by an outside body such as the public complaints commission. The houses or a committee are given certain compulsive powers for carrying out an investigation (s. 83).

An inquisition by the national assembly into the president's administration of the government, within the scope and for the purpose defined by the Constitution, is one of the innovations by the 1979 Constitution for keeping the government in check. The knowledge that such an inquisition can be instituted at any time cannot but have a restraining influence on governmental action.

(iii) *Impeachment*
An impeachment of the president or vice-president may be initiated by notice to the president of the senate, signed by not less than one-third of the members of the national assembly, stating with detailed particulars that the president or vice-president is guilty of a grave violation of the Constitution or of other gross misconduct in the performance of his functions (s. 132). The notice must be served on the president and on each member of the national assembly within seven days. Each house is then required, within fourteen days of the notice, to resolve by motion, supported by two-thirds majority of *all* its members, whether or not the allegation is to be investigated. No debate is allowed on the motion at this stage.

If the motion is carried in both houses, an investigation must begin within seven days, and is to be conducted by a committee of seven persons of proven integrity appointed, with the prior approval of the senate, by its president from outside the public service, the legislative houses and the political parties. The powers of the committee and its procedure in conducting the investigation will be prescribed by the national assembly by law. But the president or vice-president is constitutionally entitled to defend himself in person and to be represented by legal practitioners of his choice. The committee must submit its report to each house within three months of its appointment.

A finding by the committee in favour of the president or vice-president concludes the matter, but a finding of guilty has to go to each house for adoption or rejection within fourteen days of the submission of the committee's report, by means of a resolution which must be supported by not less than two-thirds of *all* its members. Upon adoption by each house but not otherwise, the president or vice-president stands removed from office.

The procedure for the removal of the president or vice-president by impeachment has been made extremely rigid in order to emphasise the gravity of the matter and to discourage a handful of disaffected members from embarking upon it for frivolous or purely partisan reasons. The interposition of a committee appointed from outside the houses is intended to ensure that the scales of justice are held even between the president or vice-president and the national assembly. Unfortunately, no machinery is provided for checking abuse or perversion of the process, the proceedings or determination of the committee or of the national assembly or any matter relating thereto being immuned from judicial inquiry (s. 132[10]).

It is important again that the true role of impeachment by the national assembly as a mere check should be appreciated. The power of impeachment is not meant to give to the national assembly a control over the president's tenure or administration of the government. Impeachment, it has been aptly said, 'is not an "inquest of office", a political process for turning out a president whom a majority of the house and two-thirds of the Senate simply cannot abide. It is certainly not, nor was it ever intended to be, an extraordinary device for registering a vote of no confidence.'[6] If it were, then it would upset the balance of the scheme of government under the Constitution, and destroy the independence of the executive, replacing it with the principle of executive responsibility to the legislature which characterises the parliamentary executive of the Westminster type. It is little wonder that, throughout the history of the American government, it has only once been called into use, and on that sole occasion the attempt failed. (The second occasion when its use was imminent was averted by the resignation of the president, Richard Nixon.) That failure has served to re-affirm the intention behind its inclusion in the Constitution — that it is not to be a legislative censure device against the president's conduct of the government.

The impeachment of President Andrew Johnson in 1868 — the single occasion of the use of the power in the United States — was a disreputable perversion of power for a purely sectional and partisan motive.[7] The ground of the impeachment was that the president had violated the Tenure of Office Act 1867 by removing his secretary of state without the consent of the senate as was required by the act (senate approval for removal is not a constitutional requirement in the United States). His offence is certainly not covered in the grounds for impeachment specified in the Constitution, viz treason, bribery or other high crimes or misdemeanors. It was at worst only an improper exercise of a power which, under the Constitution, belonged to him. Even its impropriety depended upon the constitutionality of the act of congress itself, and in the view of the president and his advisers the act was a manifest contravention of the Constitution. It was upon this view of the act that he acted in removing the secretary of state, a view which half a century later the supreme court affirmed when it declared the act unconstitutional and void.[8] In view of the court's decision one may perhaps reflect what a great injury would have been done to the president and the entire American governmental system had the impeachment succeeded (it failed by only one vote). The main, unavowed reason for the impeachment had to do with the politics of the immediate post-civil war period. President Johnson, who had succeeded Lincoln on the latter's assassination, was a southerner, and was alleged not to be co-operating in the execution of the repressive reconstruction laws passed by congress against the southern states after the war.

In Nigeria, barely twenty months after the inauguration of the 1979 Constitution, the impeachment power was already being invoked, as a weapon in the stalemated confrontation between the governor and house of assembly of Kaduna State. Talks of impeachment had been in the air for some months, but it was on 7 May 1981 that the process was actually initiated by a notice signed by sixty-nine members of the state assembly alleging certain violations of the Constitution by the governor. The violations alleged were, *inter alia*, the removal of the state director of audit without the consent of the house, the appointment of a single individual to the offices of secretary to the government and head of the civil service, the establishment of certain executive boards and the appointment of members thereto without an enabling law passed by the assembly, the expenditure of public money without legislative authorisation, and disregard of established procedure for the withdrawal of public money. A seven-man committee of investigation had since been appointed and sworn in. On his part, the governor had initiated two court actions, one for an injunction to stop the impeachment on the ground that it was an abuse of the Constitution, and the other challenging the qualifications of members of the investigation committee. These proceedings were a source of anxiety in the nation, and the hope of many people was that somehow the matter should not be pursued to its logical conclusion.

The situation that gave rise to the invocation of the impeachment procedure in Kaduna state was hardly one contemplated by that procedure. The impression was strong that it was being invoked for purely partisan reasons to redress the political anomaly created by the marginal and contested victory of a Peoples Redemption Party (PRP) gubernatorial candidate in what, judging from the results of the elections to the state assembly, was obviously a stronghold of the National Party of Nigeria (NPN). The dismissal of the petition against the governor's election seemed to have aggravated the feeling of disappointed expectations on the part of the NPN majority in the state assembly, and immediately set both parties upon a path of confrontation marked by extreme intransigence, non-co-operation and recrimination on both sides, with the assembly turning down, in abuse of its power, successive lists of commissioners presented to it by the governor. In a situation of prolonged stalemate between the two primary organs of the state, it was perhaps to be expected that violations of the Constitution by both sides might occur here and there; but the violations alleged by the assembly against the governor, assuming them to be well-founded, were not of the gravity contemplated by the Constitution as warranting the impeachment of the chief executive of a state government.

2. *Obligation to consult or to seek advice from various bodies*

Consultation with or advice by various executive bodies is a conspicuous device instituted by the Constitution for restraining presidential action. The presidency under the Nigerian Constitution may well be described without impropriety as a consultative one. The council of state must be consulted by the president in the appointment of the chairman and members of the electoral commission, judicial service commission and national population commission (s. 141[3]) and in the grant of a pardon (s. 161[2]), while the police service commission must be consulted in the appointment or removal of the inspector-general of police (s. 196[2]). The provision in each of these cases, that the 'president *shall* consult' the appropriate body, clearly imposes a peremptory obligation on him to consult. Any appointment or removal made without the necessary consultation is unconstitutional and void.

Consultation goes beyond merely giving information or announcing a decision already taken. It implies that an opportunity must be given to the person or body consulted to exercise an opinion, to criticise any proposal brought forward by the president and to offer an advice; and that the opinion, criticism or advice so offered should genuinely be taken into consideration by the president in arriving at a decision. Having done that, the president is free to decide as seems best to him, whether in accordance with or contrary to the advice. No obligation is cast on him to accept it.

The president is required to act on the advice of the judicial service commission in the appointment of justices of the supreme court and the president of the federal court of appeal (ss. 211[2] and 218[1]), and on its recommendation in the appointment of justices of the federal court of appeal, chief judge and judges of the federal high court (ss. 218[2] and 229[1]). Whatever the reason might be for the different phraseology used, even in the same section, the provisions seem to differ in their implication. The phrase 'acting on advice' has acquired a definite legal connotation as implying that the advice is binding and must be complied with. The change from 'acting on advice' to 'acting on recommendation', especially in the very section that also requires the appointment of the president of the court to be on the advice of the commission, suggests an intention to avoid the binding implication of the former phrase. Unquestionably acting on recommendation implies an obligation to consult as defined above, but while the president is not bound to accept a particular recommendation, he cannot go outside it. He may refuse to appoint the person recommended but he cannot appoint someone else not recommended or considered at all. Furthermore, if a person is considered by the commission which recommends that he should not be appointed, the president cannot rightly be said to be acting on the recommendation of the commission in appointing him.

As we have seen, the Constitution sets up certain executive bodies to advise the president on a variety of matters — the national defence council on the defence of the sovereignty and territorial integrity of the federation; the national economic council on economic affairs; the national population commission on population problems; the council of state on the census, the prerogative of mercy and the award of national honours, and on matters relating to other executive bodies electoral commission, judicial service commission and national population commission and, when so requested, on the maintenance of public order and any other matter (s. 140 and 3rd Sch.); and the executive council on the discharge of his functions generally other than those functions with respect to which he is required to seek the advice or act on the recommendation of any other person or body (s. 136[2][*c*]).

The question is whether an obligation to seek the advice of these bodies in the exercise of these functions is thereby imposed on the president. Clearly an obligation to consult is implied. This is shown by the reference to 'functions with respect to which he is required by this Constitution to seek the advice or act on the recommendation of any person or body' (s. 136[2][*c*]). It is also borne out by the distinction drawn by the Constitution between matters which the council of state can advise on without being so requested and those on which it can advise only when so requested (3rd Sch., para. 2). However, the subject-matter for which advice is required will determine whether advice must be obtained before any kind of decision or action can be undertaken. The grant of a pardon, the award of national honours, appointments or removals are specific enough to make it reasonable to require their exercise to be preceded in every case by consultation with the appropriate body. But it would be unreasonable and most inexpedient to suggest that the president cannot take any decision on, say, economic affairs or public security without first consulting the national economic council or, as the case may be, the national security council, and obtaining its advice.

The point is also relevant in relation to the advisory functions of the executive council. The Constitution enjoins the president to 'hold regular meetings with the vice-president and all ministers of the government of the Federation for the purposes of
(*a*) determining the general direction of domestic and foreign policies of the government of the Federation;
(*b*) co-ordinating the activities of the president, the vice-president and the ministers of the government of the Federation in the discharge of their executive responsibilities; and
(*c*) advising the president generally in the discharge of his executive functions other than those functions with respect to which he is required by this Constitution to seek the advice or act on the recommendation of any other person or body' (s. 136[2]).

As regards the determination of general policy and the co-ordination of government activities, this provision may, as noted in the last chapter, be interpreted either as constituting the president, vice-president and ministers collectively as the repository of these functions or as not in any way affecting the president's authority as the sole repository of the functions but merely casting upon him an obligation to exercise them at a meeting with the vice-president and ministers. However this may be, the provision does cast upon the president, at the very minimum, an obligation to consult, and obtain the advice of, the executive council every time these two functions are to be exercised.

With regard to the function of the executive council to advise the president generally in the discharge of his other executive functions, the provision leaves it unclear whether the advice of the council must be sought whenever the president is to exercise executive functions other than the determination of policy, the co-ordination of government activities and such other functions as require the advice of some other person or body. In the view of the federal court of appeal, the executive council's advice is necessary in every case. The point arose in the context of the stalemate between the governor and the house of assembly of Kaduna State, whereby the latter refused to approve all the various lists of nominees for the offices of commissioners presented by the governor — with the result that eighteen months after the inauguration of a new civilian administration, Kaduna State was still without commissioners and an executive council, with the governor therefore having to carry on the political administration of the State alone.

It was in this setting that the governor instituted an inquiry into the Kaduna local government, basing his action on two different sources of power. One such source was the Commission of Inquiry Law of the State, empowering him personally as governor to appoint a commission of inquiry into the conduct of any officer in the State's public service, or of any chief or the management of any department of the public service or of any local institution, or into any matter in respect of which, in his opinion, an inquiry would be for the public welfare.

The federal court of appeal held, by a majority of 4−1, that the governor could not validly exercise his power to institute an inquiry under the Commission of Inquiry Law without the benefit of the advice of an executive council, and as there was no such body in Kaduna State, 'the conclusion is inescapable that [his] purported exercise of power under s. 2 of the Commission of Inquiry Law Cap. 25 is invalid.'[9]

The implication of this is that, without an executive council, the political administration of the government by the president (or governor) alone is, to a large extent, unconstitutional. By making it mandatory for the president to establish offices of ministers and, with the approval of the senate, to appoint persons to such offices, and by casting upon him the obligation to hold regular meetings with the vice-president and ministers for the purpose of advising him on the exercise of his executive functions, the Constitution clearly manifests an intention that the president is not to govern without the restraining and moderating influence of the collective advice of an executive council. Clearly, therefore, in a situation where the president refuses or neglects to establish ministerial offices and to appoint persons to them or where, having appointed ministers, he refuses or neglects to hold regular meetings with them for the purpose of getting their advice on his executive actions, the administration of government by him in these circumstances would be a violation of both the spirit and letters of the Constitution, no matter how benevolent or liberal his actions may be. 'I am of the view', said the learned president of the federal court of appeal, 'that if the governor . . . refuses to hold these regular meetings, he constitutes himself as a dictator and this will be in my view not only contrary to the spirit of the Constitution but is clearly a breach of the specific provisions of this section.'

However, it is a different matter to say that the Constitution contemplates or requires that every executive action of the president must be backed by the advice of the executive council. That would involve the president having meetings with the vice-president and ministers every day or even several times a day. What the provision seems to require is, first, that all major or important executive actions must be submitted to the deliberation and advice of the executive council. Clearly government would be impossible if every minor or unimportant executive action had first to be referred to the executive council for its advice; that could not have been the intention of the Constitution, nor do the words used compel such a conclusion with its clearly paralysing effect on government.

The provision requires in the second place that the president's meetings with the vice-president and ministers should be both regular and frequent. The word regular connotes constancy in time, and not as and when it suits the president's whim. In the context it also implies a notion of frequency in time. A meeting once every fortnight or every month, although satisfying the idea of constancy in time, would not be in conformity with the spirit of the provision.

The frequency of the meetings is important. If, say, they took place once every week, it would be reasonable to presume in favour of the president that his executive actions proceeded upon the advice of the executive council. And the presumption is buttressed by the confidentiality accorded to conversations or communications between the president and his assistants, which, given frequent and regular meetings, would preclude the courts from enquiring whether the advice of the executive council was obtained in any particular case or not.

In the particular case from Kaduna State, the appointment of a commission of inquiry into the affairs of a local government is certainly a matter of considerable gravity requiring that the advice of an executive council should have been obtained upon it. Yet the fact that the absence of an executive council in the State was due, not to a refusal or neglect on the part of the governor to appoint commissioners, but to a persistent rejection of all his nominees by the house of assembly in clear abuse of their power, was a material circumstance to have been taken into account by the court. Does the situation created by this stalemate not amount to a grave exigency justifying the application of the doctrine of necessity? (The doctrine of state necessity is discussed in chapter 6.)

The special place of the council of state in the machinery of consultation and advice deserves emphasis. As stated earlier, apart from the specific cases relating to the census, the prerogative of mercy, the award of national honours etc., when its advice must be sought by the president, it is also to advise the president whenever requested to do so on the maintenance of public order and on any other matter. The council is composed of the president as chairman, the vice-president as deputy chairman, all former presidents, all former chief justices of Nigeria who are citizens of Nigeria, the president of the senate, the speaker of the house of representatives, all state governors, the federal attorney-general and a member of each state council of chiefs appointed by that council.

As President Shehu Shagari said in a speech inaugurating the council on 22 November 1979, the composition of the council marks it out as a unique body, characterised by non-partisanship, by the bringing together of the past and present leadership of the country in the pursuit of a common solution to the nation's problems, by the presence of leaders with rich experience in modern government in both political, judicial and administrative fields which can be brought to bear upon the problems of the present, and by the mingling of that kind of experience with experience in the traditional system represented by the traditional chiefs. The council is thus well equipped to provide wise, balanced, non-partisan advice to the president on sensitive matters affecting the political stability, progress and welfare of the country, such as census and the maintenance of public order clearly are. As the 'highest advisory body' in the country, the president said, the council has a unique responsibility for the success or failure of the nation. He assured the council members that any advice honestly and frankly given in the interest of the welfare of the country would be welcomed, however sensitive.

Consultation with a council has obvious democratic virtue. First, as has truly been said, the interaction of many minds 'is usually more illuminating than the intuition of one. In a meeting representing different departments and diverse points of view, there is a greater likelihood of hearing alternatives, of exposing errors, and of challenging assumptions.'[10] Perhaps even more important is what has been described as the 'increased public confidence inspired by order and regularity and the increased *esprit de corps* of the participants'.[11] Modern government challenges the capacity of a single mind to deal with its many and complex problems. Crisis increases the intensity of this challenge, and modern government faces an ever-recurrent series of crises.

Secondly, collective consultation is likely to have more restraining effect on the president than an individual one. It is less easy to ride roughshod over a determined opposition from a council than from an individual, and a president who does that faces a heavier responsibility in the event of failure or mistake; and where ministers are concerned he may also provoke the resignation of some and a consequent undermining of the unity of his administration as well as a possible loss of public support and confidence. There can be no doubt therefore that an obligation to consult a council does operate to fetter the discretion of the president in the exercise of his powers.

In this respect the American Constitution is markedly different from the Nigerian one. For no such obligation to consult with a council, not even a council of ministers, is imposed by it on the president. While it clearly recognises the office of minister, or departmental head as it is called, as a collective body they (the ministers) have no existence whatever in the Constitution. The reference to writing in the provision empowering the president to require the written opinion of a departmental head suggests that the Constitution never contemplated a collective opinion or advice. However, collective consultation has developed informally in response to the demands and pressures of modern government. Before 1793 there was nothing that could be called a cabinet. Although the first president, George Washington, occasionally called into collective consultation his departmental heads, of whom there were then only four, the meetings did not assume such frequency and regularity as to stamp them with an institutionalised character as an established machinery of government. It was the diplomatic crisis of that year, arising out of the question whether or not America should adopt a position of neutrality in the war between England and France, that gave the cabinet formal birth by impelling the president to meet his secretaries almost every day over the issue, the culmination being the meeting at which the decision was taken to proclaim American neutrality in the war.

But the point that deserves to be noticed about the cabinet in the United States is that, after nearly two centuries of existence as a definite institution of government, it has acquired no constitutional status by convention. There is no conventional obligation upon the president to consult it at regular intervals. How often he convenes the cabinet is a matter entirely within his discretion, and the practice has varied as between individual presidents. Some hold meetings of the cabinet fairly regularly; others, distrustful of meetings, consult their cabinet at infrequent intervals, preferring informal consultations with various types of advisers.

The authoritarianism of President Lincoln, and his predilection for personal government with only occasional cabinet meetings now and again, was due to a large extent to the failure of the Constitution to provide for a cabinet. It seemed to have vindicated those critics who at the time of the Constitution's adoption decried this omission as an open invitation to 'despotism', 'caprice, the intrigues of favourites and mistresses, etc.'[12] According to Kenneth Kaunda, the establishment of a cabinet in the Commonwealth African presidential constitutions was in order to ensure that, by subjecting him to the advice and influence of a cabinet, the president 'would not be able to assume dictatorial powers'.[13]

3. *Other constitutional restraints on the exercise of power by the president*

The Constitution restrains the exercise of power by the president in respect of the following matters:

(i) *Proclamation of an emergency*

The Constitution of the First Republic defined a period of emergency to mean any period during which the federation was at war or there was in force a resolution by parliament declaring that a state of public emergency exists or that democratic institutions in Nigeria were threatened with subversion (s. 70). What was to constitute a state of emergency was left undefined. A declaration by parliament was all that was required, no matter that the situation in the country was quite peaceful. Parliament was thus able to declare an emergency in the western region of the country merely on the strength of a single, isolated event within the chamber of the regional house of assembly, although no disturbances or threat of them occurred anywhere else in the region. In its ordinary meaning, emergency presupposes some event, usually of a violent nature, endangering or threatening public order or public safety. The danger or threat must be an imminent one, and the event giving rise to it must involve a considerable section of the public, since only so can public order or public safety be said to be in jeopardy.

Our new Constitution has rectified the anomaly of the past, by stipulating what kind of situation is to constitute an emergency justifying a proclamation by the president. It provides that the president shall have power to proclaim a state of emergency *only* when
(*a*) the federation is at war or in imminent danger of invasion or involvement in a state of war;

(b) there is actual breakdown of public order and public safety in the federation or any part of it or a clear and present danger of such breakdown requiring extraordinary measures to deal with it;
(c) there is an occurrence of imminent danger or the occurrence of any disaster or natural calamity, affecting the community or a section of it; or
(d) there is any other public danger which clearly constitutes a threat to the existence of the federation (s. 265[3]).

A proclamation made when none of these situations actually exists is void and may be so declared by the court.

(ii) *Appointments*
The federal character of the country is accorded constitutional recognition as a principle which must be reflected in the composition of the government and its agencies, with the aim of 'ensuring that there shall be no predominance of persons from a few states or from a few ethnic or other sectional groups in that government or in any of its agencies' (s. 14[3]). More specifically, the appointment of ministers (s. 135[3]), the secretary to the government, the head of the civil service, ambassadors, high commissioners or other principal representatives of Nigeria abroad, permanent secretaries or other chief executives in any ministries or government departments and officers in the personal staff of the president (s. 157[5]) must have regard to the federal character of the country and the need to promote national unity. The composition of the officer corps and other ranks of the armed forces must also reflect the federal character (s. 197[2]), and the national assembly is to establish a body to ensure this (s. 199).

Certain appointments are made the subject of still more specific constitutional requirements. At least one minister must be appointed from each state from amongst its indigenes (s. 135[3]). Nor is the president free to appoint as a minister any one he likes: he must be a person qualified for election as a member of the house of representatives (s. 135[5]). Members of executive bodies established by the Constitution must be similarly qualified and, in addition, must not have been removed as a member of such body for misconduct within the preceding ten years (s. 143[1]); and except for ex officio members they are permitted only two terms of five years each (ss. 142[1] and 143[3]). Only persons who, in the opinion of the president, are of unquestionable integrity and sound political judgment can be appointed to the civil service commission (3rd Sch., para. 3). The head of the civil service must be appointed from among members of the civil service of the federation or of a state (s. 157[3]).

The attorney-general, in addition to being qualified for election as a member of the house of representatives, must be qualified as a legal practitioner with at least ten years post-qualification experience (s. 138[2]), while judges must have a post-qualification standing ranging from not less than fifteen years for justices of the supreme court, to twelve years for justices of the federal court of appeal to ten years for judges of the high court (ss. 211[3], 218[3] and 229[2]).

These requirements are designed to guide and control the discretion of the president in making public appointments.

(iii) *Conduct of government generally*
The federal character principle applies not only to appointments, but also to the conduct of the affairs of government. It follows that assignment of responsibilities to ministers should be done in such a way as to avoid the concentration of the strategic or important ministries in the hands of persons from a few states or a few ethnic or other sectional groups. It seems also that this requirement would preclude such an undue concentration of ministerial responsibilities in the president as occurred in Ghana under President Nkrumah (see chapter 7).

The Constitution directs that governmental actions shall be humane (s. 17[2][c]). Perhaps the greatest restraint on presidential action is the constitutional prohibition of abuse of power, with the sanction of removal from office. Proclaiming the eradication of corrupt practices and abuse of power a fundamental objective of the nation, the Constitution prohibits in a code of conduct abuse of power either for the amassing of wealth or for sheer personal aggrandisement, as where a president proclaims a state of emergency and incarcerates people when no situation of emergency in fact exists, or where he accepts a benefit or loan from a company, contractor, businessman or their nominee, the presumption being that such benefit or loan will influence him in the discharge or non-discharge of his functions. Receipt of such benefit or loan may be inferred from the fact that his assets after four years in office exceed what he declared on assumption of office by more than may be fairly attributable to approved income, gift or loan.

Apart from court proceedings to challenge his action in appropriate cases, a president who abuses his power faces removal from office either by impeachment in the manner described above, or where the abuse of power is a breach of the code of conduct as the two examples above certainly are, by trial before the code of conduct tribunal which, if it finds him guilty, shall decree his office vacated, disqualify him from the holding of public office for fifteen years and order the seizure and forfeiture to the state of any property acquired in abuse or corruption of office. That the president should be amenable to the jurisdiction of the code of conduct tribunal in just the same way as any other public officer is an innovative device by the Constitution to curb the pretensions of the office and bring it down to our common humanity.[14]

It is appropriate here to mention the restraint implied in the president's oath of office. A person elected president cannot lawfully begin to perform the functions of the office until he has taken and subscribed the oath of allegiance and the oath of office (s. 129[1]). By the oath of office the president solemnly swears:

As President of the Federal Republic of Nigeria, I will discharge my duties to the best of my ability, faithfully and in accordance with the Constitution of the Federal Republic of Nigeria and the laws, and always in the interest of the sovereignty, integrity, solidarity, well-being and prosperity of the Federal Republic of Nigeria; that I will strive to preserve the Fundamental Objectives and Directive Principles of State Policy contained in the Constitution of the Federal Republic of Nigeria; that I will not allow my personal interest to influence my official conduct or my official decisions; that I will to the best of my ability preserve, protect and defend the Constitution of the Federal Republic of Nigeria; that I will abide by the Code of Conduct contained in the Fifth Schedule to the Constitution of the Federal Republic of Nigeria; that in all circumstances, I will do right to all manner of people, according to law, without fear or favour, affection or ill-will; that I will not directly or indirectly communicate or reveal to any person any matter which shall be brought under my consideration or shall become known to me as President of the Federal Republic of Nigeria, except as may be required for the due discharge of my duties as President; and that I will devote myself to the service and well-being of the people of Nigeria (6th Sch.).

An oath does certainly create a legal obligation, though one, it seems, not legally enforceable except where the act done in violation of it is a criminal offence under the law relating, e.g. to treason, official secrets or perjury. Even then liability to the sanction flows, not from the oath, but from the law creating the offence. Apart from imposing a non-justiciable legal obligation, an oath is intended to put in bonds the conscience of the person taking it.

REFERENCES

1. *Myers* v. *United States*, 272 U.S. 52 (1926).
2. *Marbury* v. *Madison*, 1 Cranch 137, 155 (1803).
3. *Federalist* No. 66.
4. *Myers* v. *United States*, 272 U.S. 52, 121 (1926).
5. *Constitutionalism: Ancient and Modern*, revised edn. (1947), 141.
6. Clinton Rossiter, *The American Presidency*, 2nd edn. (1960), 52–3.
7. For a full account, see Koenig, *The Chief Executive*, revised edn. (1969), 64–6; Corwin, *The President: Office and Powers*, 4th edn. (1957), 64–6.
8. *Myers* v. *United States*, ibid.
9. *Lawal Kagoma* v. *The Governor of Kaduna State & others*,

FCA/K/97/80 of 16 January 1981.
10. Theodore C. Sorensen, Decision-Making in the White House (1963), 59.
11. ibid.
12. Koenig, op. cit., 20.
13. Colin Legum (ed.), Zambia, *Independence and Beyond: the Speeches of Kenneth Kaunda* (1966), 83–4.
14. It is arguable that when the Constitution says that 'the president or vice-president may be removed from office in accordance with the provisions of this section' (s. 132), removal in any other way is thereby precluded.

9
RELATION OF THE EXECUTIVE TO THE LEGISLATURE AND JUDICATURE

The relation between the executive, the legislature and the judicature is characterised by the fact that each is established by the 1979 Constitution as a separate organ of government, distinct from, and independent of, the others in terms of its personnel and powers. The concept that underlies the relationship is thus one of a somewhat rigid separation.

The rationale for such a rigid separation has already been explained in detail in chapter 2 above. In the words of Justice Brandeis of the United States supreme court, the aim is 'not to promote efficiency but to preclude the exercise of arbitrary power. The purpose was, not to avoid friction, but, by means of the inevitable friction incident to the distribution of the governmental powers among three different departments, to save the people from autocracy.'[1]

The rigidity of the separation is, quite appropriately, moderated by a system of checks and balances, whereby both the president and the national assembly are enabled to check one another in the performance of their respective functions, as, for example, by the requirement of the approval of the national assembly or the senate for certain presidential acts or appointments, and the requirement of the president's assent to legislation passed by the assembly. Such checks do not contradict the principle of separation, since their effect is not to subordinate the one checked to the authority of the one exercising the check. The exercise of a check neither divests the president or the national assembly of discretion in the exercise of functions vested respectively in them nor does it make such functions a joint responsibility. And, far from being contradictory to the doctrine of the separation of powers, its purpose is to make the separation a more effective instrument of constitutionalism. The system rests on an open recognition that particular functions belong primarily to a given organ while at the same time superimposing a power of limited interference by another organ in order to ensure that the former does not exercise its acknowledged functions in an arbitrary and despotic manner.

1. *Separateness and independence of the executive*

The separateness of the executive is secured, first, by the fact that the president, as chief executive, owes neither his election nor his tenure of

Relation of the Executive to the Legislature and Judicature

office to the legislature, and, secondly, by the constitutional vesting of executive power in him.

(i) *Independence of the president as regards his election and tenure of office*

The president is elected by the people in direct, popular elections conducted throughout the country. His constituency is the nation as a whole. His right to govern is thus derived from the people by the votes at the elections. Accordingly, it is to them and to no one else that he is answerable for his conduct of the government.

He may of course be criticised by the national assembly, but he owes to the assembly no obligation to justify his actions. He may, if he chooses, give an explanation in an address or policy statement or message to the assembly, and his ministers may be required by either house to come and explain the activities of their ministries, but his accountability to the assembly does not extend beyond this. The national assembly may deny him approval for his demands or for his legislative proposals, but it cannot remove him or his ministers by means of a censure or no-confidence motion.

Once elected he holds his office for four years unless before that time has elapsed he dies, resigns or is removed for grave violation of the Constitution or for abuse of power, gross misconduct or incapacity in accordance with a procedure laid down by the Constitution. The procedure for removal by impeachment in the national assembly is not intended as a weapon in the hands of the assembly for censuring or getting rid of a president of whose policies or actions two-thirds of its members disapprove on partisan grounds; it is not a legislative censure device against the president's conduct of government.

All this is in marked contrast to the system of government in the first republic. Government under that system (i.e. the system in the first republic) is the rule of the legislature, hence it is called parliamentary government. What justifies this appellation is the fact that the right to govern flows through the legislature to the executive. There is only one popular election — that for members of the legislature. No separate popular election is held for the executive. Thus the only popular mandate for the government is that conferred by the votes that elected the members of parliament. Since that mandate is the only authority for government, the authority belongs to parliament. However, because government by the entire membership of parliament is not practicable or desirable under modern conditions, parliament then delegates its authority to one or more of its members. This delegation may be revoked at any time by means of a vote of no confidence. An independent executive is thus a contradiction of the parliamentary system.

Furthermore, neither the president nor his ministers are or can be members of the national assembly. A member of the assembly who becomes the president, the vice-president or a minister automatically vacates his seat; conversely the president, vice-president or a minister is disqualified from election to the assembly.

Membership of the national assembly by the president or his ministers may carry the implication that the assembly can remove them by means of a censure motion. For it may be argued that if membership is a qualification for being president or minister, then the confidence of the assembly should be an implied condition of tenure; accordingly the assembly should have a right to censure and remove them. The real rationale for the exclusion of the president and his ministers from the national assembly is not so much that it might subordinate them to the assembly as a concern to avoid concentration of powers in the hands of the executive with the danger of tyranny to which that is prone.

(ii) *Constitutional vesting of executive power in the president*
The constitutional vesting of executive power in the president secures the separateness and independence of the executive because the legislature is thereby constitutionally precluded from taking over the executive power or transferring it to other persons or authorities who are independent of the president or who are not amenable to control by him. In this connection it is important to emphasise that the president's executive power extends not only to the execution and maintenance of the Constitution, but also to the execution of the laws made by the legislature. It follows that once the legislature enacts a law, the right of the president to execute it flows inexorably from the Constitution and independently of that law. It does not need to be specifically conferred by the law in question. More importantly, the legislature cannot, in making the law, divest the president of the right to execute it and transfer it either to itself or to some other body or person who is independent of the president.

The vesting of executive power in the president is not subject to the proviso which appeared in the 1963 Constitution to the effect that 'nothing in this section [i.e. the vesting clause] shall prevent Parliament from conferring functions on persons or authorities other than the President' (s. 84[2]). By this proviso the legislature was thus competent under the 1963 Constitution to dispose in any manner it pleased of the power to execute its laws, and could therefore authorise any particular enactment to be executed by other persons or authorities who were independent of the president. The omission of this proviso from the 1979 Constitution is therefore significant in strengthening the separateness of the executive and its independence from the legislature.

Actually, the draft of the 1979 Constitution as approved by the constituent assembly had made the president's executive power, not just the *exercise* of it by him, subject to any law made by the national assembly. It states that 'subject to the provisions of this Constitution and of any law made by the National Assembly, the executive powers of the Federation shall be vested in the President.' The reference to 'any law made by the National Assembly' was removed from the Constitution as it was finally enacted into law by the supreme military council. It is easy to see that such a power in the legislature may enable it to subvert and revolutionalise the system of executive government instituted by the Constitution, by so dividing and sharing the executive power as to convert the government into one of plural executive.

However, while the president's *right or title* to the executive power cannot be taken away by the legislature, the latter can regulate his *exercise* of it. This follows from the provision that 'the executive powers of the Federation shall be vested in the President, and may, subject as aforesaid and *to the provisions of any law made by the National Assembly*, be exercised by him either directly or through the Vice-President and Ministers of the Government of the Federation or officers in the public service of the Federation' (s. 5[1][*a*]). What this means is that, while the legislature cannot take away the president's right to execute its laws, e.g. by transferring it to itself or to some other independent person or authority, it can quite competently regulate the manner in which or the conditions on which its laws are to be executed by him. The extent of the power of the legislature to regulate the president's *exercise* of executive power is considered more fully below.

The unconstitutionality of any act of the legislature which interferes with the right of the president to execute the Constitution and the laws made by it is illustrated by certain decisions of the U.S. supreme court. A law enacted by the congress of the United States which had the effect of negating the general pardon granted by the president to the insurgents at the end of the American civil war was declared invalid as a usurpation of the prerogative of mercy vested in the president by the Constitution. It was not, the court held, within the constitutional power of congress to inflict punishment beyond the reach of executive clemency.[2]

A law interfering with the right of the president to execute the laws enacted by the legislature has also been held unconstitutional and void. By an act of congress, postmasters of the first, second and third grades were to be appointed for a fixed term of four years subject to earlier removal by the president with the consent of the senate. Myers, a first-class postmaster, was removed from his office by the president without the consent of the senate, and he sued for arrears of salary on the ground of wrongful dismissal. The U.S. supreme court by a majority held the part of the act making the senate a party to the removal power to be void as an unconstitutional interference with the president's power to execute the laws, on the ground that, since he could not execute the laws alone, there was implied in the grant a power to appoint assistants. The power to appoint attracted as a necessary incident the power of removal, for otherwise the president might be saddled, to the prejudice of his administration, with assistants who could not be removed, notwithstanding that they were disloyal, incompetent or otherwise unfit. As part of the executive power granted to him, the appointing and removal power could only be limited or controlled by the Constitution or by congress in accordance with the Constitution. As regards the appointing power, the Constitution contains express limitation (namely, concurrence of the senate), but it neither restricts the removal power nor authorises congress to do so. Congress's attempt to restrict it without constitutional authority was therefore, in the view of the majority, void as an unconstitutional interference with the president's executive power. The minority of the court based their dissent on the ground that the removal power was not a necessary incident either of the general executive power or of the power to take care to see that the laws be faithfully executed, and was therefore not vested in the president by virtue of the grant of these powers.[3] The court took the opportunity in this case to pronounce invalid the Tenure of Office Act of 1867 which made the consent of the senate necessary for the removal of a minister by the president. It will be recalled that the stated reason for the abortive impeachment of President Andrew Johnson was that he removed his secretary of state without the consent of the senate as required by the 1867 act. The impeachment failed by just one vote.

The question also arose in the Kaduna State in relation to a law authorising the institution of a commission of inquiry while at the same time vesting in the executive council the power to appoint a commission of inquiry. In a minority judgment in the federal court of appeal, Mr. Justice Coker held the appointment of a commission of inquiry in pursuance of statutory power to be an executive function belonging to the governor by the terms of the Constitution, and the provision of the law vesting it in the executive council to be unconstitutional and void.[4] For this conclusion he drew support from the fact that the 1979 Constitution omitted the provision which appeared in the 1963 Constitution, empowering the legislature to confer functions on persons or authorities other than the governor, and from the fact that under the 1979 Constitution (as under the 1963 one) the governor's executive power extends to all laws made by the legislature. 'Any other construction', he said, 'which does not prevent the State house of assembly from conferring executive functions on persons or authorities as was done in s. 33(2) of the 1963 Constitution will be in gross contradiction of the very essence of the separation of powers of the three arms of the government as envisaged in the present Constitution.'

The learned judge is certainly right in his statement of the principle, but his application of it in this case is misconceived. The principle does not prevent the legislature from vesting executive functions arising under its laws in persons or authorities who are subject to the direction or control of the president, or at any rate are not independent of him. The executive council is clearly not independent of the president. If it were otherwise, it would mean that the legislature cannot confer functions on individual ministers or other subordinate executive functionaries. The ministers are after all agents of the president, and their lawful official acts are presumptively his acts.

The constitutional inability of the legislature to confer executive functions on other persons or authorities who are independent of the president raises a troublesome question in view of the widely prevalent practice of modern governments of creating by legislation more or less independent agencies for the exercise of certain administration functions. The U.S. Supreme Court has got round the difficulty by drawing a distinction between the executive power strictly so-called and functions which, though associated by governmental practice with the executive branch, do not really involve execution, i.e. purely administrative functions of a quasi-judicial or quasi-legislative nature.

For example, the Federal Trade Commission Act 1914 created a commission charged with responsibility for the prevention of unfair methods of competition in commerce. The commission is empowered to prefer and try charges of unfair competition, to issue a 'cease and desist' order against any person, partnership or corporation found after due hearing of using unfair methods of competition. If the order is disobeyed, the commission may apply to the appropriate circuit court of appeal for its enforcement, subject to the right of the person against whom the order is made to apply to the circuit court of appeal for a review of the order. The commission also has wide powers of investigation in respect of certain matters; when it investigates any matter it must report to congress with recommendations. Its members are appointed for a fixed term of years by the president by and with the advice and consent of the senate, and may be removed by him for inefficiency, neglect of duty or malfeasance in office. Humphrey, a member of the commission, was removed by the president before the expiration of his normal term, not for any of the causes specified in the act, but because he and the president entertained divergent views with respect to matters of policy. Humphrey then sued for arrears of salary for wrongful dismissal. For the president it was argued that the provision of the act prescribing the grounds upon which a member of the commission may be removed was unconstitutional as being an interference with the president's executive power.

In its opinion on the case, the supreme court defined the status of the commission to be that of an agency created by statute to carry out the policy not of individual presidents but of the law; accordingly it is to be independent of executive authority and direction, whether it be that of the president or any regular executive department. Its functions, the court held, are purely administrative, and do not involve the exercise of 'executive power'. 'In administering the provisions of the statute in respect of "unfair methods of competition" — that is to say filling in and administering the details embodied by the general standard — the commission acts in part quasi-legislatively and in part quasi-judicially. [. . .] To the extent that it exercises any executive function — as distinguished from executive power, in the constitutional sense — it does so in the discharge and effectuation of its quasi-legislative powers.' Since they are not comprehended in the president's executive power, therefore, the functions of the commission and the tenure of its members are unquestionably within the power of congress to prescribe. 'The authority of congress', the supreme court declared, 'in creating quasi-legislative or quasi-judicial agencies, to require them to act in discharge of their duties independently of executive control, cannot well be doubted; and that authority includes, as an appropriate incident, power to fix the period during which they shall continue, and to forbid their removal except for cause in the meantime.'[5]

The power of the legislature to confer away from the president administrative functions of a quasi-judicial or quasi-legislative nature is undoubtedly a serious qualification on the president's executive power. As the committee on administrative management in the United States observed in 1937:

The multiplication of these agencies [i.e. the independent commissions] cannot fail to obstruct the effective overall management of the Executive Branch almost in geometric ratio to their number. At the present rate we shall have 40 to 50 of them within a decade. Every bit of executive and administrative authority which they enjoy means a relative weakening of the President, in whom, according to the Constitution, 'the executive Power shall be vested'. As they grow in number his stature is bound to diminish. He will no longer be in reality the Executive, but only one of many executives, threading his way around obstacles which he has no power to overcome.

(iii) *Independence of the executive in relation to the courts*

The separation of the executive from the judicature means that the courts cannot, any more than the legislature can, control the president as to when, if at all, to exercise his powers or, so long as he keeps within the limits set on his powers by the Constitution or other law, as to how he exercises them. The unwisdom, undesirability or inexpediency of his act done within the law cannot be questioned by the courts. However much the public welfare may require that certain acts be done, whether it be the provision of water, roads, medical, health or educational services, etc., the courts cannot compel their execution by the president. To presume to compel or restrain the exercise by the president of his executive power would be, in the words of Chief Justice Marshall, 'an absurd and excessive extravagance' on the part of the courts.[6]

The president's discretion to exercise or not to exercise his executive power is of course fettered by his obligation to observe and implement the fundamental objectives and directive principles of state policy declared in the Constitution. However, the implementation or otherwise of the objectives and principles is deliberately removed from judicial control, and presidential independence from the courts thereby preserved.

It is necessary to draw a distinction between a discretionary power and a ministerial duty. While the functions of the executive under the Constitution are largely discretionary, the law may cast upon individual officers specific duties of a purely ministerial character, that is to say, peremptory duties in which nothing is left to discretion. In regard to such a duty, the officer concerned is amenable to the law. The court can compel its performance, as the U.S. supreme court did when it compelled the secretary of state to exercise his statutory duty to deliver to the plaintiff Marbury a commission, which had been duly signed by the president, appointing him to the office of justice of the peace;[7] and the postmaster-general to perform his duty under a statute requiring him to credit a plaintiff with a sum which the solicitor of the treasury had certified to be due to him.[8] The court can also restrain the exercise of a ministerial duty in violation of the law.

2. *Limits of the independence of the executive*

The separateness of executive power does not however imply that the legislative power is completely excluded from its area of operation. On the contrary, their operation is 'partly interacting, not wholly disjointed',[9] or, in the apter words of Justice Holmes, 'the great ordinances of the constitution do not establish and divide fields of black and white.'[10]

To begin with, the vesting of executive power in the president is expressly made subject to the provisions of the Constitution. And certain aspects of specific executive functions are, by the Constitution, subjected to the regulatory authority of the legislature. While the national assembly cannot say that the president is no longer commander-in-chief, or that he is not to direct their operational use or appoint the service chiefs as authorised to him by specific provisions of the Constitution, it is empowered to regulate by law the powers of the president as commander-in-chief and his power in regard to the appointment, promotion and disciplinary control of members of the armed forces (s. 198[4]). And, as Justice Jackson of the U.S. supreme court said, 'while congress cannot deprive the president of the command of the army and navy, only congress can provide him an army or navy to command.'[11] The president cannot be deprived of his power to direct the operational use of the police force for maintaining and securing public safety and public order, yet the police can exercise for this and other purposes only such powers as the national assembly may by law confer upon them; and the organisation and administration of the police force are to be prescribed by an act of the national assembly (s. 195[2]).

The conduct of foreign relations, a peculiarly executive function, is subject to an even greater legislative control. While the Nigerian president has power, unfettered by any requirement of senate approval, as in the United States, to make treaties with other countries, no treaty concluded by him shall have the force of law in Nigeria except to the extent to which it has been enacted into law by the national assembly (s. 12[1]). A treaty has no self-implementing operation under the 1979 Nigerian Constitution, as it has under the U.S. Constitution, which means that the Nigerian president is denied a potent source of power available to his American counterpart to legislate for the nation by means of treaties and thereby to override laws made by the legislatures of the states, since the Constitution, acts of congress and treaties made by the president with the concurrence of the senate are, by express constitutional provision, declared the supreme law of the land.[12] This power has been the cause of much concern in the United States, and provoked many proposals for the amendment of the Constitution.[13] Nor, under the Nigerian Constitution, is the power of the national assembly with regard to external affairs limited to the implementation of treaties. It embraces the entire field of the subject-matter (item 25, exclusive legislative list), with the consequence that the national assembly can always by legislation nullify or override any presidential action on the matter, so far at any rate as concerns the people and authorities of the country, although it would scarcely want to conduct foreign relations by legislation since their delicacy and confidentiality make legislation unsuited for their conduct. Even in the United States, treaties are, notwithstanding their self-executing operation, subject to the overriding authority of congress, and their operation within the country can by legislation be controlled[14] or completely abrogated.[15]

If the power to execute the laws includes as a necessary incident power to appoint and remove assistants, it must also by the same reasoning include the determination of the salaries and allowances of such assistants, other conditions of service, grading, staff complements, etc. But the national assembly is empowered to legislate generally on public service of the federation (item 52, exclusive legislative list), and in particular on pensions, gratuities and other like benefits payable out of the consolidated revenue fund or any other public funds of the federation (item 43, exclusive legislative list). It follows that the control of the civil service as part of the public service is a concurrent matter for both the president and the national assembly. While the assembly cannot, by legislation, make appointments in the civil service or order the removal of named officers,[16] it can prescribe conditions for appointments and removals, salaries and allowances, pensions and other conditions of service in the civil service;[17] any regulation made by it in that connection overrides the orders of the president. Indeed, its power to prescribe by law the salaries and allowances of certain designated public functionaries is exclusive, and not merely concurrent. The designated functionaries are the president, the vice-president, the federal auditor-general and the chairmen and members of the federal civil service commission, the federal electoral commission, the federal judicial service commission, the police service commission and the national population commission; others in the list whose salaries and allowances are in any event beyond the power of the president to fix are the chief justice of Nigeria, justices of the supreme court, the president and justices of the federal court of appeal, and the chief judge and judges of the federal high court (s. 78[1] and [4]).

Apart from these specific cases of the conjunction of executive and legislative power, there is the general provision that the *exercise* of executive power by the president, either directly or through the vice president and ministers or officers in the public service, shall be subject to the provisions of any law made by the national assembly (s. 5[1][a]). The application of this provision seems to require that a distinction should be made between the vesting of the general executive power and the specific grant to the president of particular functions, such as the appointment of ministers, the prerogative of mercy, the grant of certificate of naturalisation etc. In regard to the former, the provision has ample scope of operation because of the absence of specifications in the Constitution. There is therefore ample scope for legislation to control or restrict the president's exercise of the general executive power, e.g. his power to protect the agencies and property of the government and to preserve the state and the nation. With regard to the specific grants, the scope of application of the provision would depend on the extent to which a function is spelt out in the Constitution. In the case of appointment and removal of ministers, for example, the Constitution prescribes their qualification, but not their tenure or their maximum number. It is possible to interpret the provision as enabling the national assembly to prescribe both the tenure and the maximum number of ministers and to prescribe other things concerning them not inconsistent with the Constitution.

The U.S. Constitution has no provision exactly corresponding to this. The nearest is the provision empowering congress to 'make all laws which shall be necessary and proper for carrying into execution [its own] powers, and all other powers vested by this Constitution in the Government of the United States, or in any Department or Officer thereof.'[18] This cannot have the effect of subjecting executive power to the regulatory control of the legislative power in the way which the provision in the Nigerian Constitution apparently seeks to do.

REFERENCES

1. *Myers* v. *United States*, 272 U.S. 52, 293.
2. Ex parte Garland, 4 Wall 333.
3. *Myers* v. *United States* (1926), 272 U.S. 52.
4. *Lawal Kagoma* v. *Governor of Kaduna State*, FCA/K/97/80 of 16 January 1981.
5. *Humphrey* v. *United States* (1934), 295 U.S. 602.
6. *Marbury* v. *Madison* (1803), 1 Cranch 137, 170.
7. *Marbury* v. *Madison*, ibid.
8. *Kendall* v. *United States*, 12 Pet 527.
9. Per Justice Frankfurter in *Youngstown Sheet & Tube Co.* v. *Sawyer*, 343 U.S. 579 at 610.
10. *Springer* v. *Philippine Islands*, 277 U.S. 209.
11. *Youngstown Sheet & Tube Co.* v. *Sawyer*, ibid. at 644.
12. art. VI; see *Hauestein* v. *Lynham* (1880), 100 U.S. 483; *Geofroy* v. *Riggs (1890), 133 U.S. 258; Fairfax's Devisee* v. *Hunter's Lessee* (1813), 7 Cranch 608.
13. See Arthur Sutherland Jr., 'Restricting the Treaty Power', 65 *Harv. L. Rev.*, (1952) 1305.
14. *La Abra Silver Mining Co.* v. *United States* (1899), 175 U.S. 423.
15. *Chae Chan Ping* v. *United States* (1889), 130 U.S. 581; *Mose* v. *United States* (1951), 341 U.S. 41.
16. *United States* v. *Lovett* (1945), 328 U.S. 303, holding invalid a law by

the U.S. congress which barred certain named individuals from employment in the public service because of certain subversive activities in which they are alleged to have been involved.

17. See *United Public Workers* v. *Mitchell* (1947), 330 U.S. 75.
18. art. 1, s. 8.

10
THE ROLE OF THE PRESIDENT IN LEGISLATION

1. *Exclusion of the president in the vesting of legislative power*

Nigeria's 1979 Constitution abandons the concept, prevalent in the Commonwealth, of a legislature, called parliament, consisting of the head of the executive and an assembly together. The assembly has vested in it alone, and not jointly with the president, the legislative power of the federal government, and is mandated to exercise it for the purpose of making law for the peace, order and good government of the federation or any part of it (s. 4[1] & [2]).

The exclusion of the president from the vesting of the legislative power is a logical consequence of the doctrine of the separation of powers upon which the whole governmental system is built. In part too it is a reflection of the republican character of the state. The device of making the head of the executive a constituent part of parliament was in origin an attempt to reconcile monarchy with popular sovereignty. The monarch is the sovereign, and the cardinal essence of sovereignty in the legal sense is the power to make law. Time was indeed when the monarch, as sovereign, possessed and exercised an unfettered power of law-making. But then he had to bow to the forces of representative democracy, and to concede legislative power to the people's representatives in parliament. Yet while monarchy remains the framework of government, the monarch's title of sovereignty must needs be given cognisance in the distribution of power to the representative organs of government. The device of making him a constituent part of the legislature seeks therefore to accommodate his title of sovereignty with the popular sovereignty of the people which the assembly represents. Such a device should have no place in a republic; it has none indeed in the first modern republic, the United States of America. The American Constitution vests legislative power in congress alone, i.e. the senate and the house of representatives. Undoubtedly, the framers' preoccupation with the doctrine of separation of powers greatly influenced the provision, but the principles of republicanism were also a crucial factor.

The fact that the president is not a constituent part of the legislature has constitutional significance. Where he is such, his assent or concurrence is integral to the exercise of legislative power. It is not extraneous to the legislative power, something brought from outside to qualify the exercise of a power self-contained by itself. By the inherent logic of making him a constituent part of the legislature, no bill passed by the assembly can become law without his assent. His concurrence cannot be dispensed with. This means that, in the event of conflict between him and the assembly, the bill is killed completely by the president withholding his assent from it, unless the constitution obliges him to assent to it against his will. Alternatively, he may be given the choice of either assenting or dissolving parliament.

Where, however, an assembly alone is the legislature, with power to make law, then unless the Constitution otherwise provides, a bill becomes law directly it is passed by the assembly. A constitutional requirement of presidential assent would in this case be something extraneous to the power of the assembly to make laws. It operates not from within the power as an integral part thereof, but as a qualification upon it. It operates by way of veto in the strict sense of the word, to block the effectuation of the decision of an otherwise competent authority, since a veto implies that the power of decision-taking is elsewhere than in the person exercising the veto. A member of a body may be enabled to veto the decision of that body, but that is because the decision-taking power is for all practical purposes in the majority.

The presidential veto is designed as part of the system of checks and balances, whereby, in order to guard against abuse, both the legislature and the executive are enabled to check each other in the exercise of their respective functions but without depriving either of final discretion over such functions or making them a joint responsibility. That this is the true significance of the requirement of presidential assent to legislation passed by the assembly is shown by the fact that whereas, as previously stated, in British constitutional theory and practice the concurrence of the monarch to legislation, being an integral part of the legislative power, cannot be dispensed with under any circumstances, under the Nigerian Constitution a bill passed by the national assembly becomes law without the president's assent if he fails to assent within thirty days of its being presented to him and the bill is again passed with two-thirds majority (s. 54[5] & s. 55[4]). Thus, while the president can check it, the final discretion in the exercise of the legislative power still lies with the national assembly as the repository of the power. The form of the enacting words used in the United States — 'Be it enacted by the Senate and House of Representatives of the United States of America in Congress assembled' — shows quite clearly that presidential assent is not integral to the legislative power. The enacting words in the federation of Nigeria are to similar effect: 'Be it enacted by the National Assembly of the Federation of Nigeria and by the authority of the same'. A formula such as that adopted by the Lagos state house of assembly, that says that law is enacted by the assembly with the assent of the chief executive, completely misconceives the role and significance of requiring his assent to legislation.

However, although the legislative power is vested in the assembly alone, rather than in it and the president together as two component parts of the legislature, the president is by the Constitution given power to make law in two types of cases. The power is a strictly limited one, and is in no way comparable to the system in France and some of the French-speaking African countries where the constitution reserves certain matters for rule-making by the executive to the exclusion of the legislative assembly. Under such a system as obtains in France and some of her former dependencies, the executive is a second legislature in respect of the matters within its exclusive rule-making power under the constitution.

The two cases in which the president is empowered by our Constitution to make law are:

(i) *Regulations relating to citizenship*
The president is empowered by the Constitution to make regulations 'prescribing all matters which are required or permitted to be prescribed or which are necessary or convenient to be prescribed for carrying out or giving effect to the provisions of this Chapter, and for granting special immigrant status with full residential rights to non-Nigerian spouses of citizens of Nigeria who do not wish to acquire Nigerian citizenship' (s. 29[1]). Regulations made by the president under this chapter may thus prescribe what is acceptable evidence of good character or of intention to be domiciled in Nigeria as required for registration as a citizen, the form and manner of application for naturalisation, the conduct of an inquiry into allegations of disloyalty or trading with the enemy made against a person who is a citizen by registration or naturalisation, etc. Any such regulation must be laid before the national assembly (s. 29[2]).

When the president makes regulations under these provisions, he is exercising *original* legislative power, i.e. power conferred directly by the Constitution, as contra-distinguished from one delegated to him by the national assembly. The regulations derive their authority and force directly from the Constitution.

But the national assembly is also empowered by the Constitution to make laws on citizenship, naturalisation and aliens (Item 10, exclusive legislative list). A question of interpretation arises as to whether the president's regulation-making power is exclusive of the national assembly, or whether, if they are concurrent, it overrides legislation by the assembly in the event of conflict. The purpose of the president's regulation-making power suggests that it is intended to be exclusive. It is intended to be an implementing legislation only, one to give effect to the citizenship provisions of the Constitution. If a matter is required to be prescribed and is prescribed by the president by regulation, it is as if the implementing regulation is incorporated into the Constitution as part thereof. The power of the national assembly to legislate on any matter included in the legislative list is given to it subject to the specific stipulations of the Constitution.

(ii) *Adaptive legislation*

A change of constitution creates a necessity for adapting existing laws to the new constitution. Such adaptation is an exercise of legislative power by way of amendment of existing laws in order to bring them into conformity with the new constitution, and so facilitate an orderly transition to the new order. In the Commonwealth it has become the invariable practice to give this power to the head of state, i.e. the executive. This is both expedient and desirable. For not only are the necessary adaptations often extensive, involving the whole body of existing legislation, but they are also very minute, like changing names, titles and designations, substituting appropriate functionaries, etc; also they require prompt action such as the process of a legislative assembly would not admit of.

In accordance with this practice, the 1979 Constitution empowers the president (or the governor in a state) to make, by order, 'such changes *in the text* of any existing law as [he] considers necessary or expedient to bring that law into conformity with the provisions of this Constitution' (s. 274[2] & [3]).

Adaptive legislation has a restricted scope, being limited to clerical or verbal changes. It is not intended to authorise changes of substance or policy in the law, as a case in Pakistan in 1963 illustrates. The 1962 constitution of the country empowered the president to 'direct by order that the provisions of the constitution shall have effect subject to such adaptations . . . as he may deem necessary and expedient'.[1] Under the Pakistan constitution, a member of the national assembly vacated his seat if he was appointed a minister. The president found this inexpedient in the case of two members of the assembly whom he wanted to appoint as ministers; accordingly, he used his adaptive power to amend the provision, which then made it possible for the two members to retain their seats after being appointed ministers. The amendment was held to be *ultra vires*, as being outside the scope of adaptation, since otherwise the president would have been enabled to alter fundamental provisions of the Constitution 'without resorting to the special and massive machinery of amendment'.[2]

In Nigeria too a controversy has arisen as to whether the adaptive provisions in the 1979 Constitution authorise amendments to the local government law, which will abolish councils composed entirely of hereditary chiefs as well as councils chosen through a mixture of indirect election and nomination, in order to bring the law into conformity with the provision of the Constitution guaranteeing 'the system of local government by democratically elected local government councils' (s. 7[1]), and with the duty imposed on the government of a state to 'ensure that every person who is entitled to vote or be voted for at an election to the House of Assembly shall have the right to vote or be voted for at an election to a local government council' (s. 7[4]). In purported exercise of their adaptive power, some state governors have either repealed the provision of the law establishing the chiefs' councils or dissolved all the local government councils and appointed management committees in their place.

Now, the reference to textual changes in the enabling provision in the 1979 Constitution is an indication that repeal is outside its ambit. To make changes in the text of a law, i.e. in its wording, presupposes that the law continues in force with all its provisions. If the law or any of its substantive provisions is abrogated, the text will not be there to be changed to bring it into conformity with the Constitution. Secondly, the dissolution of a council can in no way be regarded as a textual change in the law. The changes necessary to bring the local government law into conformity with the provisions of the Constitution quoted above require an amendment of such a substantive character as cannot be made by means of the power of adaptive legislation, otherwise the president or governor would have been constituted into a full-blown legislature with power to amend any existing law that he considers not in conformity with the Constitution.

It seems that there has been a tendency to confuse two different provisions appearing in the same section of the Constitution.[3] One relates to the power given to the president (or the governor in a state) to make changes in the text of an existing law necessary to bring it into conformity with the Constitution (s. 274[2]). The other stipulates that 'an existing law shall have effect with such *modifications* as may be necessary to bring it into conformity with the provisions of this Constitution.' (s. 274[1]), with a further stipulation that 'modification' includes 'addition, alteration, omission or repeal' (s. 274[4][c]). The latter provision is a direction addressed, not to the executive, but to the courts as to how to interpret existing laws. Only a court can, in the exercise of its interpretative jurisdiction, say that an existing law has been impliedly repealed by the Constitution. The president or governor has no power to do that or to *modify* an existing law by repeal or by adding or omitting anything of substance. His power is limited to the making of *textual* changes, which, as previously stated, presuppose the continued existence of the law.

Adaptive law-making is by its nature a power of limited duration, and is usually made by the explicit provisions of the constitution to expire within twelve months, sometimes longer. (It is three years under Nigeria's 1963 Constitution.[4]) The 1979 Constitution makes the power exercisable 'at any time' with no express limitation as to time, but the intention clearly is not that it should become a permanent and continuing power. A time limit is implied from the fact that the provision conferring it appears under a part of the Constitution headed 'transitional provisions'. A power designed to facilitate the transition from an old to a new constitution must, by its transitory character, be of a temporary, short duration. It would be an abuse of language if a transitional provision were to be given a permanent application.

Whatever its duration, the president's adaptive power neither excludes[5] nor overrides the power of the legislative assembly to amend the existing law so as to make both its text and substance conform to the provisions of the Constitution. The legislative power of the assembly covers necessary adaptations in existing laws, and any adaptive law so made by it overrides an adaptive order by the president or governor in the event of conflict between them. The adaptation of existing laws to the Constitution is thus not a matter in respect of which the president can legislate to the exclusion of the assembly, while the power of the latter to override him in the matter preserves to it the status and authority of a supreme legislature.

2. *Delegated legislation*

With the very limited scope of the president's original legislative power under the Constitution, it may rightly be said that the assembly is the supreme legislature for the country, and that, lacking by and large an independent authority to make law, the executive can legislate only by delegation from the assembly. But delegation of legislative power to the executive raises the question of its constitutionality in the context of the separation of powers under the Constitution, and the limits of permissible delegation, assuming its constitutionality. It is possible to justify a certain amount of subsidiary legislation by the executive by reference to the power of the president to execute the laws, since a law can be implemented or carried into effect by means of detailed regulations.

On the issue of constitutionality, the earlier attitude of the courts in the United States was that the constitutional vesting of legislative power in the legislature implied that only it, and nobody else, could lawfully exercise the power, and that accordingly delegation was constitutionally prohibited. 'That Congress cannot delegate legislative power to the President', said the supreme court of the country in 1892, 'is a principle necessarily recognised as vital to the integrity and maintenance of the system of government ordained by the Constitution.'[6]

This view was eventually abandoned. The constitutionality of delegation within proper limits has ever since been unquestioned.[7]

The acceptance of the constitutionality of delegated legislation rests on the absolute necessity for it if the government of a modern state is to be carried on. Modern government consists increasingly in the regulation of social and economic activities; it is simply impracticable to make all the necessary regulations by law enacted in every case by the legislative assembly, with its procedure of debates spread over various stages. Delegated legislation by the executive comes in handy to supply a quick and informed method of regulation within the broad provisions laid down by the assembly. By a combination of both types of regulation, the attainment of the overall purpose of government, which is the welfare of the people, is facilitated. Delegated legislation is thus aptly described as the 'handmaiden of regulation'.[8] Without it government as a complex of processes for the effective management of social life might be wellnigh impossible. In complementing regulation by the assembly, delegated legislation plays an invaluable and indispensable role in the legislative machinery of government.

And, though this is beside the constitutional issue, delegated legislation has acknowledged advantages — greater knowledge of what will work; increased speed enabling urgency to be met; more flexibility; greater suitability in cases of great technicality or cases requiring a course of continuous supervision; need for local variation, etc.[9]

Yet, indispensable as delegated legislation is in modern government, it is equally unquestioned that the power to delegate is not without limits under a system of separated powers. 'In every case in which the question has been raised, the Court has recognised that there are limits of delegation which there is no constitutional authority to transcend.'[10] The judicial attitude on the necessity of delegation and its limits is stated thus:

Undoubtedly legislation must often be adapted to complex conditions involving a host of details with which the national legislature cannot deal directly. The Constitution has never been regarded as denying to the Congress the necessary resources of flexibility and practicality, which will enable it to perform its function in laying down policies and establishing standards, while leaving to selected instrumentalities the making of subordinate rules within prescribed limits and the determination of facts to which the policy as declared by the legislature is to apply. Without capacity to give authorisation of that sort we should have the anomaly of a legislative power which in many circumstances calling for its exercise would be but a futility. But the constant recognition of the necessity and validity of such provisions, and the wide range of administrative authority which has been developed by means of them, cannot be allowed to obscure the limitations of the authority to delegate, if our constitutional system is to be maintained.[11]

The unequivocal nature of this statement of the law is an emphatic rejection of the argument that delegation is necessarily valid in every case because the legislature's ever-present power of control and revocation makes delegation a logical impossibility.[12]

The difficulty, however, has been to define the limits with anything approaching precision. The distinction between abdication and delegation is perhaps a convenient starting point. Abdication implies the surrender by the legislature of its law-making power, in whole or part, to another body, as by authorising a body outside itself, e.g. the electorate or the executive — to make any law it pleases or to legislate on an area — e.g. regulation of industry — covering an undefined variety of matters. The transfer of the power of general law-making, i.e. power not limited to a single, particularised matter, is clearly forbidden by the separation of powers. Such a transfer of power is 'unknown to our law and is utterly inconsistent with the constitutional prerogatives and duties of the legislative.'[13] Congress, said the U.S. supreme court, 'is not permitted to abdicate or to transfer to others the essential legislative functions with which it is thus vested' by the Constitution.[14]

An illustrative case is that involving a power given to the president of the United States by statute to make codes of 'fair competition' for any industry or trade in the country where such code will tend to effectuate the policy of the statute.[15] The authority given to the president was thus not confined to any single, defined enterprise, but embraced the entire field of industry and trade. Not only was it not confined to one particular industrial or commercial enterprise, there was also no limitation as to the kind of activity, conduct or relations to be regulated. Its scope is indicated by the fact that the code made for the live poultry industry dealt with such things as working hours, age of employment, wages, collective bargaining, trade practices constituting unfair methods of competition, and machinery for the protection of consumers, competitors, employees and others. Neither in the statement of policy nor in any other part of it did the statute provide a definition of 'fair competition' which would serve as a measure for delimiting the scope of a code. Far from limiting the meaning, fair competition was given an extended meaning in the statute so as to embrace whatever might be considered wise or beneficial for the welfare of any industry or trade. This clearly amounted to a power of general law-making. Holding the delegation unconstitutional and void in a unanimous decision, the U.S. supreme court observed that a code of fair competition, given the absence of limitation as to subject matter and the absence of any statutory measure of fair competition, 'becomes as wide as the field of industrial regulation. If that conception shall prevail, anything that Congress may do within the limits of the commerce clause for the betterment of business may be done by the President . . . by calling it a code. This is delegation running riot. No such plenitude of power is susceptible of transfer.'[16] As Justice Cardozo said, 'what is fair, as thus conceived, is not something to be contrasted with what is unfair or fraudulent or tricky.'

Even when delegation relates to a single subject-matter, which is sufficiently particularised and defined by the enabling statute, it is still not valid unless the statute lays down an intelligible standard or measure reasonably adequate to guide and control the exercise of the discretion being delegated. Thus a statutory grant of power to the president to prohibit the transportation in interstate and foreign commerce of petroleum and petroleum products produced in excess of the amount permitted by state law was held an unconstitutional delegation, on the ground that, though it related to a single, defined subject-matter, namely the transportation in interstate and foreign commerce of excess production of petroleum and petroleum products, the statute had left the president free to impose prohibition or not as he liked without laying down any intelligible standard or principle to control the exercise of the discretion.[17] It declared no policy on prohibition, whether it considered transportation of excess production as injurious to the national interest or as involving unfair competition, and it laid down no conditions or circumstances in which prohibition might be imposed.

In contrast, the delegation of power to fix maximum prices of commodities as a temporary wartime measure was upheld, because it was limited by the statutory requirement that such prices must be generally fair and equitable, and be based so far as practicable on prices prevailing in a stated base period and on such other relevant factors as general increases or decreases in costs of production, distribution and transportation, and general increases or decreases in profits earned by sellers of the commodity during the period subsequent to a prescribed date; the statute also prescribed that the power was to be exercised only when prices had risen or threaten to rise to an extent or in a manner inconsistent with the purposes of the statute, which were declared to be the prevention of inflation and its enumerated consequences.[18] These, the court held, were adequate standards to control the delegated discretion as regards both the occasion for its exercise and as to the particular prices to be fixed.[19] It is noteworthy that one of the justices considered the delegation unconstitutional as not setting any really meaningful limits as to whether, and, if so, when, the price of any commodity shall be regulated; in his view the delegation amounted to the grant of a commission 'to take any action with respect to prices which he believes will preserve what he deems a sound economy during the emergency'.[20]

The test of permissible delegation laid down in the American decisions admittedly lacks precision. A commentator has thus pointedly remarked that 'the question still remains, however, "what is a standard". How much of a standard has been set up . . . that rates be "just and reasonable" . . . and that . . . rules be consistent with the public interest?'[21] And in many cases where delegation is upheld, it is questionable whether what is accepted as a 'standard' imports any really intelligible principle or yardstick. The impression is thus created that the application by the courts of the doctrine of limited delegation is often arbitrary. Yet the imprecision of the test does not negate the principle of limitation. The reason for a limitation is clear. For unless the enabling statute lays down a standard to guide the exercise of the delegated power, then the concept of limited government which underlies the separation of powers may be subverted, especially where this results in vital decisions of policy being given force of law binding on the country without being put through the process of discussion prescribed in the Constitution for law-making, with the object that legislation should have as wide a basis in popular consent as possible.

In a decision handed down on 17 March 1980, Justice Balogun of the high court of Lagos state held unconstitutional and void the delegation to the state governor under the Local Government Law 1980 of power to delimit the areas of authority of local government councils in the state, on the ground that, 'this being a very important subject . . . it was not within the contemplation of the makers of the Constitution that the state assembly will delegate to the governor the power to define the area of authority of a local government area without the house of assembly setting out the standards which an area of authority of a local government area must conform with.'[22] While the absence of 'standards of action' renders delegation unconstitutional, the American decisions discussed above make it clear that the standards need not be set out in the statute itself if they can be gathered from the legislative programme of which the particular statute is part or from other relevant sources. The Constitution being such a relevant source, its provisions should be read into the Local Government Law, so far as they are relevant. And it sets out adequate standards to govern the creation of local government areas either by the house of assembly or by the governor in pursuance of a delegated power. The relevant provision (s. 7[2]) states:

The person authorised by law to prescribe the area over which a local government council may exercise authority shall

(a) define such area as clearly as practicable; and

(b) ensure, to the extent to which it is reasonably justifiable, that in defining such area regard is paid to

(i) the common interest of the community in the area,
(ii) traditional association of the community, and
(iii) administrative convenience.

Judged by the standards held sufficient in the American cases, these standards are more than adequate.

Furthermore, the Constitution clearly contemplates that the power of defining local government areas may be delegated, as is borne out by the reference to 'the person authorised by law to prescribe the area over which a local government council may exercise authority'. The state assembly is hardly a person, and it makes little sense that the assembly should by law authorise itself to prescribe local government areas.

Emergency increases the need for delegation, but it does not remove the limitation on the power to delegate. It gives to the legislature no greater power to delegate than it ordinarily possesses. Rejecting the argument that it does, the U.S. supreme court has said that 'extraordinary conditions may call for extraordinary remedies', but they 'do not create or enlarge constitutional power.'[23] The delegation under the Emergency Powers Act, 1961, has therefore to be judged according to the same principles as applied in other cases. The act empowers the president in council to make 'such regulations as appear to him necessary or expedient for the purpose of maintaining and securing peace, order and good government in Nigeria or any part thereof.' Furthermore, the president in council may amend, suspend or modify a law on any subject whatever enacted by any legislature in the country; also any regulation made by him has 'effect notwithstanding any thing inconsistent therewith contained in any law; any provision of a law which is inconsistent with any such regulation . . . shall . . . to the extent of such inconsistency have no effect so long as such regulation . . . remains in force.'[24]

This amounts clearly to abdication or the transfer of the power of general law-making, and, since the term 'peace, order and good government of Nigeria' covers the whole field of the powers possessed by the legislature itself, the delegation here goes far beyond that which, notwithstanding that it was also designed to deal with a grave national emergency, was held unconstitutional as an abdication in the American case discussed above. (The decision of the supreme court of Nigeria holding the delegation valid[25] is unsupportable in the context of the 1979 Constitution, even assuming it to be justified by the parliamentary system under which it was rendered.) The Constitution contemplates that the national assembly should be the effective legislature as much during an emergency as in normal times. The necessity for the assembly to lay down the main provisions of legislation touching on any aspect of the peace, order and good government of the country which may then be supplemented by executive regulations where necessary, is no less in an emergency than in normal times. However much it may be necessary that the executive should have adequate powers to deal effectively with an emergency, it is clearly incompatible with the rather rigid separation of legislative and executive powers under the Constitution to delegate to the executive during such a period almost the full amplitude of powers possessed by the legislature. The words of Justice Douglas of the U.S. supreme court in a case arising out of a declared emergency are quite apt here:

> There can be no doubt that the emergency which caused the President to seize these steel plants was one that bore heavily on the country. But the emergency did not create power; it merely marked an occasion when power should be exercised. And the fact that it was necessary that measures be taken to keep steel in production does not mean that the President, rather than the Congress, had the constitutional authority to act. [. . .] The President can act more quickly than the Congress. The President with the armed services at his disposal can move with force as well as with speed. [. . .] Legislative power, by contrast, is slower to exercise. There must be delay while the ponderous machinery of committees, hearings, and debates is put into motion. That takes time; and while the Congress slowly moves into action, the emergency may take its toll in wages, consumer goods, war production, the standard of living of the people, and perhaps even lives. Legislative action may indeed often be cumbersome, time-consuming, and apparently inefficient. But . . . "the doctrine of the separation of powers was adopted by the Convention of 1787, not to promote efficiency but to preclude the exercise of arbitrary power. The purpose was, not to avoid friction, but, by means of the inevitable friction incident to the distribution of the governmental powers among three departments, to save the people from autocracy." '[26]

It is important that delegated legislation should not only be strictly confined within its proper limits but also be strictly controlled by the legislature through such means as the affirmative procedure whereby subsidiary legislation may be required to be laid in draft before the legislative houses and is not to come into operation until they have resolved affirmatively that it should do so; or the procedure of requiring in the enabling act that copies of a subsidiary legislation shall be laid before the legislative houses which may resolve to annul it.[27] Then there is the procedure whereby a select committee scrutinises statutory instruments either in draft or after they have been made, and draws the attention of the house to any objectionable provision such as a provision making the legislation unchallengable in the courts or giving it retrospective effect where the parent statute confers no express authority to that effect.

3. *Emergency legislation by the president under the doctrine of state necessity*

We have seen in chapter 6 that in a grave emergency imperilling the life of the nation, the president can, by the imperative necessity of saving the state and society from ruin, interfere with individual rights without specific statutory authorisation. The question is whether such a necessity would also justify the exercise of legislative power where the legislature is not in existence or is temporarily put out of action.

With regard to the English common law, the view has been expressed by Chitty that the King as head of state 'is the first person in the nation . . . being superior to both Houses in dignity and the only branch of the Legislature that has a separate existence, and is capable of performing any act at a time when the parliament is not in being.'[28] This view was expressed in 1820, but does it still represent the position prevailing in English law today? Glanville Williams thinks not. 'The prerogative of necessity,' he writes, 'is now in disuse, because it is covered by and therefore superseded by statutes.'[29] Elaborating on this, he says:

The King cannot acquire new prerogatives by reference to state necessity. . . . However necessary the behaviour, the Government must today invoke the aid of Parliament if the behaviour involves breaking the letter of the law. It can act under the doctrine of necessity only to the same extent as a private person. Parliament's alleged failure to give adequate powers cannot be an excuse for conduct, because the necessity of powers claimed is for Parliament to decide, not for the judges over the head of Parliament. The question is not whether it is necessary to do the act but whether it is necessary to do it without the sanction of Parliament.[30]

On the other hand, in Greece, Italy, France and West Germany it seems to be generally accepted among writers on constitutional law that the doctrine may justify the exercise of legislative power by the executive. 'Jurisprudence', declares a French authority, 'was thus led to appreciate that there was a hierarchy in the juridical rules and that the executive authorities were behaving more in conformity with the spirit of constitutional institutions by a temporary encroachment on legislative prerogatives than by limiting themselves to a narrow conventionality or by remaining inactive when such inactivity imperils public order.'[31] In Greece the courts have in many cases since 1945 upheld the exercise by the executive of legislative power in times of emergency by reference to the doctrine.[32]

Its most remarkable application for this purpose has been in Pakistan in 1955. The country acceded to independence in 1947 with a constituent assembly which was empowered by the Independence Act to legislate both generally and in particular for the purpose of enacting a constitution. In the course of seven years while it was trying to adopt a constitution, the assembly, conceiving itself as possessing the sovereign power of the state on behalf of the people of Pakistan, passed some forty-four constitutional laws which it put into force without submitting them for the governor-general's assent as the Independence Act required (ordinary enactments were duly submitted for the governor-general's assent). These purported enactments were thus clearly invalid and were declared so by the court.[33] The governor-general then dissolved the assembly, basing his action on the ground that it had proved itself incapable of accomplishing the task set for it by the Independence Act; that it had become unrepresentative and had lost the confidence of the people, as the resolutions of the various representative bodies in the country made clear; and that it had become an illegal legislature by purporting to exclude the governor-general from the process of law-making.

After dissolving the assembly, the governor-general issued an ordinance declaring a state of emergency and purporting, by virtue of his emergency powers under an act of 1935, to validate with retrospective effect most of the void constitutional enactments of the dissolved assembly. The validation of these enactments, so far as it purported to be based upon the governor-general's emergency powers under the 1935 act, was pronounced invalid by the court as going beyond the provisions of the act.[34]

Thereafter the governor-general summoned a new constituent assembly for the purpose of making provision as to the constitution for Pakistan. He next proceeded by proclamation to re-validate the enactments which the court had earlier declared he had no power to validate. But whereas the earlier attempt at validation was based upon the governor-general's emergency powers under the 1935 act, the basis of the new proclamation was the doctrine of state necessity. It was stated that the invalidation of the enactments having rendered unlawful all acts — executive, administrative and judicial — done under them, the constitutional and administrative machinery had broken down, thereby threatening the state with imminent collapse; the validation of the enactments was therefore necessary in order to preserve the state and society and maintain the *status quo* until the new constituent assembly had met and enacted the necessary validating laws. The proclamation was made subject to the opinion of the federal court. The governor-general now asked for the court's opinion whether, there being no legislature in existence competent to validate the void constitutional enactments of the dissolved assembly, 'there is any provision in the constitution *or any rule of law* applicable to the situation by which the governor-general can by order or otherwise declare that all orders made, decisions taken, and other acts done under those laws shall be valid and enforceable, and those laws . . . shall be treated as part of the law of the land until the question of their validation is determined by the new constituent convention.'[35]

Among the questions referred for the court's opinion was whether the assembly had been validly dissolved. For if it had not, then the whole premise for the exercise of the power of validation claimed by the governor-general would not arise. It would suffice to say simply that the court unanimously accepted that under the circumstances the governor-general had power to dissolve the assembly and that the power had been validly exercised. Upon the crucial question concerning the governor-general's power to validate by proclamation the void constitutional enactments, the court was sharply divided, three for and two against. In the leading judgment delivered by Chief Justice Muhammad Munir, who went into a far-ranging examination of the doctrine of civil or state necessity, the majority affirmed the doctrine to be 'implicit in the constitution of every civilised community'.[36] On the premise stated in the Special Reference, namely that in consequence of the dissolution of the assembly and the invalidation of all the constitutional laws enacted by it during a period of seven years, the constitutional and administrative machinery of the state had broken down, so that the state itself stood in imminent danger of collapse, and since the measures proposed by the governor-general for dealing with the situation were only temporary until the new constituent assembly had met to decide the matter finally, they (the majority) held that the retrospective validation of the laws by the governor-general was legally justified as a temporary measure by the exigency of the situation. In coming to this conclusion they relied on the statement of the law by Chitty quoted above, but were nevertheless at pains to emphasise that the application of the doctrine in this case in no way implies that during an emergency the head of state steps into the position of the legislature as the sovereign legislative authority. On the contrary, legal sovereignty remains with whatever authority the constitution has invested it, and no transfer of it is or can be effected by the principle of imminent state necessity; all it does is to enable the executive to exercise legislative power temporarily on behalf of the incapacitated legislative authority, in order to save the state or society from ruin, but subject to the ultimate authority of the legislature, when it recovers from its incapacity, to ratify or annul what the executive had done on its behalf. As Chief Justice Muhammad Munir said, the law of civil necessity 'in no way interferes with, or affects, the sovereignty of the legislature.'[37]

The minority maintained that the common law of civil necessity is confined to cases where, in times of war or other national disaster, the executive might interfere with private rights, but that it has never been extended to changes in constitutional law; and that so to extend it would be wholly repugnant to the 1935 act which prescribed the circumstances and the limits within which the governor-general might exercise legislative powers. Insofar as Chitty's statement of the law, relied upon by the majority, implied that the executive could exercise the legislative powers of parliament when that body is not in existence, that relates to 'periods when, and to territories where, the power of the King was, in fact, supreme and undisputed. The records of these affairs are hardly the kind of scripture which one could reasonably expect to be quoted in a proceeding which is essentially one in the enforcement and maintenance of representative institutions.'[38] Once admit that the doctrine of necessity may justify executive encroachment upon the legsilative field, and one may not then quarrel with its application in Pakistan's situation, since what was done involved no separate legislative initiative on the part of the governor-general, but merely a confirmation of legislation already passed by the legislature.

As stated in chapter 6, the kind of situation that may justify the exercise of this power is not just any emergency. The emergency must be such as, by its imminence and extreme danger, so imperils the safety of the government and nation as to make the assumption of legislative power by the president an imperative necessity. And of course the legislature must have been temporarily put out of action.

4. *Initiation of proposals for legislation*

The right to initiate proposals for legislation is admittedly an integral part of the law-making power, but does it follow too that the legislative initiative, with all the policy implications of modern legislation, is the exclusive prerogative of the national assembly?

In a recent press statement on the matter of remuneration of public officers, the national assembly said that 'both the President and the National Economic Council under the chairmanship of the Vice-President have *proposed* their own alternative remuneration figures, *even though the matter was beyond their competence* [author's emphasis].' And further that 'it is equally essential to impress it upon the President that neither the Executive nor any of its agencies like the National Economic Council will be permitted to undertake to discharge the constitutional responsibilities of the National Assembly as defined and clearly stated in the Nigerian Constitution.' All federal law-making, and not just the making of a law to prescribe the salaries and allowances of members of the national assembly and the few designated public officers, is beyond the competence of the president, but to deny to the president, as the statements quoted above seem clearly to do, the right to initiate proposals for legislation on any matter within the legislative competence of the national assembly (including salaries and allowances) is another matter.

In the United States the matter is covered by express constitutional provision empowering the president from time to time to 'recommend to [the congress] such measures as he shall judge necessary and expedient'.[39] The 1979 Constitution of Nigeria has no such explicit stipulation on the point. Yet by vesting in the president in council with his vice-president and ministers responsibility for policy in respect of all matters within the legislative competence of the national assembly (s. 5[1] and s. 136[2]), the Constitution manifests a clear intention that the president is to be the main organ for the initiation of legislation.

Even had the Constitution been completely silent on the matter, the realities of modern government make it impracticable to regard the legislative initiative as belonging exclusively to the legislature as an integral part of the legislative power. In a recent report, the Study of Parliament Group in Britain has sought to dispel the popular misconception on this point. 'Legislation today', the Group affirms, 'is pre-eminently a function of government. It is largely by means of legislation that administrations implement party programmes, react to the need for basic changes in the economic, social and political structure of the country, and bring the law into conformity with current standards of what is acceptable or tolerable. That being so, it is misleading to regard the legislative process as something in principle separable from government, still less to see it as beginning and ending in parliament.'[40]

This statement underlines the change that has taken place in the character and content of modern legislation. In the days before the emergence of the positive welfare state, the matters that needed to be regulated by legislation were few and simple — domestic relations, land, criminal offences, etc. These were easily within the initiative of individual legislators. The concern of the government was mainly with foreign relations, the maintenance of law and order, and execution generally. Modern government has an infinitely wider concern, involving active intervention in the life of society with a view to improving its quality. This, as has just been observed, requires legislation, and legislation with high policy content. But policy is essentially an executive function. It is implicit in the right to govern, a fact which the 1979 Constitution recognises in the provision vesting the responsibility for policy in the president in council with his vice-president and ministers (s. 136[2]).

There is another reason why high policy legislation must be a function of the executive. Much of it is of an extremely complex and technical nature, with wide-ranging ramifications, which at once put it beyond the capacity of an individual legislator to manage or even to comprehend. The dimension of the issues with which it deals may be beyond his vision; they may be issues arising in the administration of the departments or other institutions of state and about which only someone inside the government can have knowledge and experience; such are questions of fiscal policy, social reform, economic development and even pure administration. Their complexity and technical nature require special expertise. Thus we find that because of this, the introduction of such legislation in the legislature is usually preceded by a long and protracted period of gestation during which it is put through an elaborate process of consultation and discussion among various interested groups — the government party, the sponsoring department, the cabinet and its committees, and other interested sections of the community, such as trade unions, trade associations, etc. When at last the polity aspects have been thrashed out, then comes the drafting stage. Even this may be a complex and complicated matter.

These, then, are some of the factors which have necessitated that the legislative initiative should be largely in the hands of the executive, rather than of the legislature. In Britain the reality of the matter has been recognised since at least the middle of the eighteenth century. Most bills in Britain, estimated at 85 per cent, are government bills.[41] In Commonwealth Africa executive monopoly of the legislative initiative is complete, to an extent that most legislators simply take it for granted that the initiation of legislation is the exclusive prerogative of the government, and that they themselves have no role in the matter at all. With only one private member's bill introduced in 1966, the Kenyan parliament stands out as the only parliament in Commonwealth Africa in which a private member's bill has ever been introduced — and passed. (Under Nigeria's presidential system introduced under the 1979 Constitution, five private member's bills have in a period of six months been introduced in the national assembly.)

In the United States, however, congress regards itself as the main organ for the initiation of legislation by reason of the separation of powers in the Constitution. Congress (or rather, its leaders) exercises the final discretion as to which bills should be introduced. It is these leaders who determine and control the business of congress; no government ministers are in congress anyway. Naturally these legislative leaders are quite jealous of their own and their colleagues' right of initiative, which has therefore a far wider scope than in Britain. And there exist in congress facilities to assist members in the preparation and drafting of bills; of which the committee system, with the legislative expertise which it has developed, is perhaps the most helpful. For those reasons private members' bills account for a substantial proportion, estimated at half or perhaps even more,[42] of all bills introduced in the congress.

Yet even in the United States, congress is coming increasingly to yield legislative leadership to the executive, because of the latter's superior resources and capacity for action. The process has been accentuated by the budgetary reform of 1921, which entrusted to the president the responsibility for the preparation of an annual budget to be presented to congress, thereby enabling him to 'work out a general and integrated plan of government programmes and operations, which hitherto had been lacking'.[43] The present position is summed up thus by McConnell:

The relationship between the President and Congress is considerably different from that formally drawn in the great scheme of the constitution. The separation of powers between these two branches has not indeed been removed; a vast gap separates the two. Nevertheless, the increasing complexities of modern political life have required an increasing role for the President, and the presidency has become increasingly institutionalised. Correlatively the legislative branch has become less and less capable of mastering the daily flow of events of which policy is so largely composed; it is compelled to leave much to the executive branch. If present trends were to be projected into the future, we could envision a government system in which the President with the whole executive branch under his effective control governs, and Congress checks and criticises. Already, this picture accords with what happens in some areas of policy, military and foreign affairs for example.[44]

In Nigeria the preparation of the budget (i.e. estimates of revenues and expenditure) is vested in the president or governor by the Constitution itself (ss. 75[1] and 113[1]). Although this is not explicitly stated, the implication is that an appropriation bill can only be initiated by the executive. The Constitution provides that the heads of expenditure contained in the estimates prepared by the president (other than expenditure charged upon the consolidated revenue fund by the Constitution which includes the salaries and allowances prescribed by the national assembly for the public officers designated in s. 78) shall be included in a bill, to be known as an appropriation bill, providing for the issue from the consolidated revenue fund of the sums necessary to meet the expenditure and the appropriation of those sums for the purposes specified therein. If, in respect of any financial year, it is found that the amount appropriated by the appropriation act for any purpose is insufficient, or that a need has arisen for expenditure for a purpose for which no amount has been appropriated by the act, a supplementary estimate (again to be prepared by the president) showing the sums required shall be laid before the legislature and the heads of any such expenditure shall be included in a supplementary appropriation bill. It seems clear from the fact that an appropriation bill or supplementary bill is to contain only the heads of expenditure in the estimates prepared by the president that its initiation is the prerogative of the president exclusively of the national assembly.

There is very good reason for lodging exclusively in the president the right to initiate financial legislation. Orderly government requires that only those who administer the government, and therefore have an intimate connection with it, should propose national expenditure, and how the money needed for it can be raised; there would certainly be financial chaos if every member were to be free to propose expenditure, since members would then be competing among themselves to secure as much of the public funds as possible for the constituencies or interests which they represent. Desirable as it may be that only the executive should propose expenditure, its effect is undoubtedly to increase the dominance of the executive over policy. For finance and policy are intricately interwoven. Finance is the lever that links all activities of government, from which it follows that the organ controlling it is also given an overview of the entire functions of government, including policy.

5. *The enacting process*

The 1979 Constitution denies to the president the right, possessed by the prime minister under the parliamentary system, to lead the business of the assembly (either personally or through a minister designated by himself), and consequently denies him the control conferred by such leadership. Under the parliamentary system, the business of the assembly is controlled effectively by the leader of the house and the other ministers who, as members of the assembly, are able, by virtue of the authority of their office, to assume a position of leadership in the house. They determine whether and, if so, how much of the assembly's time is to be allotted to private members' business. Furthermore, since a majority in the assembly is not an inherent feature of the presidential system as it is of the parliamentary, the choice of a speaker is not the government's prerogative, so that it is not constitutionally assured of the enormous powers available to the speaker to control the business of the assembly. The president is thus entirely dependent on the political process for whatever influence he can exert on the enacting process.

REFERENCES

1. art. 224(3).
2. *Hague* v. *Chowdhury*, *Times* Law Report, 22 November 1963.
3. See, e.g., Ovie-Whiskey C.J. in *Jideonwo & others* v. *Governor, Bendel State of Nigeria & others*, Suit No. B/292/79 delivered 28 February 1980 at the High Court, Benin.
4. s. 156(2).
5. So held by Mohammed C.J. in *Mohammed* v. *Att.-Gen. of Kaduna State & another* reported in the *New Nigerian Newspaper* of 21, 22 and 23 April 1980.
6. *Field* v. *Clark* (1892), 143 U.S. 649, 692.
7. *Buttfield* v. *Stranaham* (1904), 192 U.S. 470; *United States* v. *Grimaud* (1911), 220 U.S. 506.
8. Jaffe, 'An Essay on Delegation of Legislative Power', 47 *Columbia L.R.* 359, 561 (1947).
9. Jaffe, op. cit., n. 10.
10. *Panama Refining Co.* v. *Ryan*, 293 U.S. 388, 430 (1935), where most of the U.S. decisions on the matter are reviewed.
11. *Panama Refining Co.* v. *Ryan*, ibid. at p. 421; repeated in *Schechter Poultry Corp.* v. *United States*, 295 U.S. 495 at 530.
12. So argued on behalf of the government in *Currin* v. *Wallace*, 306 U.S. 1 (1939).
13. *Schechter Poultry Corp.* v. *United States*, ibid., 537.
14. loc. cit.
15. *Schechter Poultry Corp.* v. *United States*, ibid.
16. ibid., 553.
17. *Panama Refining Co.* v. *Ryan*, *ibid*. The doctrine of limitation on the delegation of legislative power is applied in West Germany, Austria, Italy and many other European countries; see the comparative treatment of the subject in Jacoby, 'Delegation of Powers and Judicial Review', 36 *Columbia L.R.* (1936), 871.
18. *Yakus* v. *United States* (1944), 321 U.S. 414.
19. For other decisions to same effect, see *Sunshine Anthracite Coal* v. *Adkins*, 310 U.S. 381 (power to fix just and reasonable rates); *New York Cent. Securities Corp.* v. *United States*, 287 U.S. 12 (power to approve consolidations of railroads in the 'public interest'); *National Broadcasting Co.* v. *United States* 319 U.S. 225 (power to regulate radio stations engaged in chain broadcasting 'as public interest, convenience or necessity requires'); *Federal Trade Commission* v. *Keppel & Bros.* 291 U.S. 304 (power to prohibit unfair methods of competition not defined or forbidden by the common law); *Mulford* v. *Smith*, 307 U.S. 48 (power to allot marketing quotas among states and producers on the basis of a variety of stated economic factors); *Hampton Jr. & Co.* v. *United States*, 276 U.S. 394 (power to adjust tariffs to meet differences in cost of production taking into consideration a variety of stated economic factors).
20. Per Justice Roberts, ibid., 451.
21. Weeks, 'Legislative Power versus Delegated Legislative Power', 25 *Geo.*

L.J. 314, 335 (1937).
22. *Balogun* v. *Att.-Gen. of Lagos State*, Suit No. ID/114/80 of 17 March 1980.
23. *Schechter Poultry Corp.* v. *United States*, 295 U.S. 495 at 528 (1935).
24. s. 6.
25. *Williams* v. *Majekodunmi* (1962) 1 All N.L.R. 328, particularly 336; *Williams* v. *Majekodunmi* (No. 3) (1962) 1 All N.L.R. 413, 420−1.
26. *Youngstown Sheet & Tube Co.* v. *Sawyer*, 343 U.S. 579 at 629; quoting Justice Brandeis in *Myers* v. *United States*, 272 U.S. 52, 293.
27. Wade and Phillips, *Constitutional Law*, 6th edn. (1960), 581−2.
28. Chitty, *Prerogatives of the Crown*, 1820 ed., 68.
29. Glanville Williams, 'The Defence of Necessity', 6 *Current Legal Problems* (1953), 216, 231.
30. ibid., 229.
31. Conseiller R. Odient, Contentieux Administratif, 1961, vol. 1, 137−8, quoted in *Att.-Gen. of the Republic* v. *Mustafa Ibrahim and Others* (1964) Cyprus Law Reports, 195 at 272 — per Josephides J. (Cyprus) discussed in Nwabueze, *Constitutionalism in the Emergent States* (1973), 188−96.
32. See *Att.-Gen. of the Republic* v. *Mustafa Ibrahim and Others*, ibid. at 235 and 261.
33. *Federation of Pakistan* v. *Khan* (1955), reported in Jennings, *Constitutional Problems in Pakistan* (1957), 77.
34. *Usif Patel and Two Others* v. *The Crown* (1955), reported in Jennings, op. cit., 241.
35. *The Special Reference by the Governor-General of Pakistan*, reported in Jennings, op. cit., 259.
36. See *Federation of Pakistan* v. *Shah*, (1955), reported in Jennings, op. cit., 353, 357.
37. *Federation of Pakistan* v. *Shah*, Jennings, op. cit., 357.
38. The Special Reference Case, Jennings, op. cit., 342 — per Cornelius J.
39. art. 2, s. 3.
40. *Parl. Affairs* (1969), vol. xxii, 210.
41. K.C. Wheare, *Legislatures*, 2nd edn. (1968), 102.
42. K.C. Wheare, op. cit., 103.
43. Grant McConnell, *The Modern Presidency* (1967), 34.
44. op. cit., 50−1.

11
ELECTION AND TENURE OF OFFICE OF THE PRESIDENT

1. *Election*

(i) *Qualifications and disqualifications*

The presidency is more than just an office, the highest in the nation. Its holder is the embodiment of the state and its majesty. His personality, credentials and moral character are therefore of the greatest concern to the nation so is the method of his election.

The first requirement in his credentials is that he should be of competent and mature understanding if he is to be able to grapple with the very complex task of governing Nigeria. Hence the Constitution prescribes a minimum qualifying age of thirty-five years, and a mind that is free of any infirmity (ss. 123 & 128).

The president is constitutionally required to be a Nigerian citizen, not by registration or naturalisation, but by birth, and not to be at the same time a citizen of another country by a voluntary act or to have made a declaration of allegiance to another country. Considering that citizenship by birth is conferred on any person either of whose parents is a Nigerian citizen, this requirement falls short of what should be necessary for a president. In the context of Africa where nationality as a concept based on birth in a particular country is not yet fully accepted, the president should belong to Nigeria as a full-blooded indigene, with a genealogy deeply rooted in the soil of the country, so that he may be seen to identify fully with it in interest, loyalty and patriotic feelings.

With regard to his moral character, he must not be an undischarged bankrupt, and must not have been convicted and sentenced for an offence involving dishonesty or been found guilty of a contravention of the code of conduct during the period of ten years before the date of the presidential election. Of course if a person is under a current sentence of imprisonment for homicide or for an offence involving dishonesty, whether before or after the election, he cannot be president.

(ii) *Method of election*

The personality of the president, and his credentials in so far as they are not specifically prescribed in the Constitution, are to be determined by the people at a presidential election. In such election, every Nigerian citizen who has attained the age of eighteen years and is registered as a voter is entitled to vote. For this purpose the whole country is regarded as one constituency, from which it follows that the president represents the nation as a single entity, not as an aggregate of separate constituencies with different interests. It may be said that his election provides a greater representation for the nation than the sum of the different interests represented by members of the national assembly.

It is the concern of the Constitution that this representation should have as much reality as possible. For this reason, no one can be returned as president unopposed. A sole, unopposed presidential candidate must nevertheless submit himself to popular approval, which is to be determined by a majority of Yes votes over No votes at the election, failing which, fresh nominations must be ordered (s. 125). To minimise a situation of uncontested election, the Constitution provides that where, by reason of disqualification, withdrawal, incapacitation, disappearance or death, only one of two or more candidates nominated for election remains as the sole candidate after the close of nomination, the federal electoral commission shall extend the time for nomination (s. 124). The provision has the additional object of deterring the practice, so rampant in the First Republic, of nominated candidates withdrawing on a price or disappearing or being abducted.

The actual election of the president, contested or uncontested, combines two great principles — the principle of popular approval and that of territorial spread (ss. 125 & 126). What this means is that the popular votes needed for the election of the president must be spread in a prescribed proportion across the frontiers of as many states as possible. The intention is that popular votes alone, even when they amount to a majority of the votes cast at the election, should not enable a person to rule Nigeria as president if those votes are drawn almost entirely from a section of the country and not spread territorially across the frontiers of most of the states in the federation. Undoubtedly, by the combination of the two principles, victory at the election is made difficult, but it is made deliberately so, in the hope of fostering truly national parties and encouraging coalition, alliance or accord among them.

The idea of combining the two principles in this way is predicated upon the heterogeneous nature of the Nigerian society, which is reflected in its territorial division into states. It is not intended by the principle of territorial spread that the election of the president should necessarily provide representation for the states as states, but that he should be a national rather than a tribal figure, with a measure of public acceptability in most of the states. The requirement is also designed in part to compel a presidential candidate to carry his election campaign into each state and thereby gain acquaintance with its people and problems.

The Constitution fixes the degree of public acceptability required of the president within a state at 25 per cent of the popular votes cast in that state while the number of states in which this must be obtained is fixed at two-thirds of all the states.

Popular approval is determined by a majority of the votes cast in the elections throughout the country. To get elected as president, therefore, a candidate must obtain a majority of the votes cast, and the votes cast for him must be spread across at least two-thirds of all the states in the proportion of not less than 25 per cent per state. Since, however, a majority of the votes may be too difficult to obtain where there are more than two candidates, the candidate with the highest number of votes is taken as having secured popular approval, and will be declared the winner if the votes cast for him are also spread territorially across two-thirds of all the states in the proportion of not less than 25 per cent per state.

The real risk in requiring the votes for a candidate to be spread territorially across two-thirds of all the states in the proportion of not less than one-quarter of the total votes in the state is that no candidate may get elected, even after a series of successive elections, since it is possible that a candidate with a majority or the highest number of votes may not achieve the necessary geographical spread. The Constitution, as originally enacted, sought to get round this possibility of indefinite successive elections, with the risk of disruption of the life of the community, by providing that in the event that no candidate is able to obtain a majority or the highest number of votes with the necessary geographical spread, the federal and state legislative houses, sitting separately, will, by a combined simple majority vote of their respective members present and voting, elect a president from among the candidates in the first election, but where there were more than two such candidates, only the candidate with the highest number of votes and the one with a majority of votes in the highest number of states shall qualify for the election. The election must be held in all the federal and state legislative houses on the same day and at the same time.

Clearly election of the president by the legislative houses is an aberration of the principle underlying the presidential executive, which is that his mandate of office is to be conferred through direct election by the people. It is also liable to the risk that, being a small body relative to the national electorate, the members of the legislative houses can be bought over or swayed by corrupt, partisan or other perverse influences. Between the evil of election by the legislative houses and that of the disruption of two or more popular elections, the latter may be less pernicious, provided that the number of such successive popular elections is limited to not more than three.

By a post-election constitutional amendment, the outgoing military regime on 28 September 1979 did away with election by the legislative houses, replacing it with a maximum of two run-off elections. At the first of such run-off elections victory is, as in the first election, to be determined by a majority of the votes, spread territorially across two-thirds of all the states in the proportion of not less than one-quarter of the votes cast in each of those states.[1] The run-off election can be contested by two candidates only, i.e. the two candidates in a two-sided contest in the first election, or, where there were more than two candidates in the first election, it can be contested by the candidate with the highest number of votes and the one among the remaining candidates who has a majority of votes in the highest number of states — i.e. where there are more than one such candidate, then the one among them with the highest total number of votes. If neither of the two candidates is elected at the first run-off election, then there will be a second run-off election between them at which the one having the majority of votes becomes the winner without any regard to the geographical spread of the votes.

(iii) *Criterion for territorial acceptability*

The requirement of the Constitution that votes must be spread territorially across two-thirds of all the states in the proportion of not less than one-quarter of the votes cast in each of those states raises two interpretative issues. First, given the present nineteen-state structure of the federation, what is two-thirds of nineteen states? If the answer is $12\frac{2}{3}$ states, how is one-quarter of the votes in two-thirds of the thirteenth state to be determined?

The view that two-thirds of nineteen states is $12\frac{2}{3}$ states was first adumberated by the legal adviser of one of the political parties contesting the 1979 presidential election, the National Party of Nigeria (N.P.N.), who further argued that one-sixth of the votes in the thirteenth state was all that the Constitution required. In announcing the result of the election, the federal electoral commission, the authority responsible for the election, accepted this view and used it to decide the winner, on the ground that it accords with the ordinary meaning of the expression, in the absence of any contrary indications in the Electoral Decree, 1977. The commission was upheld by the special election tribunal set up to hear and determine petitions against the election, and on appeal by the supreme court by a majority of five to two.[2]

In the opinion of the majority of the supreme court, delivered by Chief Justice Fatayi-Williams, the reason stated by the federal electoral commission for accepting this view of the matter provides 'unassailable justification' for it. For 'not only is the meaning of the general words used ... plain enough, there is also no reason for doubting the intention of the Federal Military Government' which, in enacting the provision, 'must be deemed to know that two-thirds of nineteen states will be $12\frac{2}{3}$ states. If the number thirteen which is the number nearest to two-thirds of a state had been intended, the Federal Military Government would have said so in clear terms. In any case, as between thirteen states and $12\frac{2}{3}$, considering all the circumstances, $12\frac{2}{3}$ appears to us to be the intention of the Federal Military Government in the context' of the provision.

The interpretation of statutes should be guided not so much by what the law-makers may or may not have intended as by the purpose which the provision in question is designed to serve. The words should be interpreted in the light of the underlying purpose and rationale of the provision. Interpretation of statutes is not an exercise in semantics, the ascertainment of the literal meaning of words. It should be guided and informed by the purpose of the provision being interpreted. Herein lies the cardinal defect in the judgments of both the tribunal and the majority of the supreme court. Dominated as they were by an obsessive concern with the intention of the law-makers and the ordinary, literal meaning of the words, the learned judges omitted completely to address their minds to the purpose of the provision they were interpreting, although the point had been vigorously urged upon them by counsel.

The underlying purpose of the requirement of territorial spread is that a majority or the highest number of votes is not to be regarded as a conclusive index of acceptability throughout the country, because it can be obtained from only a part of the country. The emphasis is not on the votes as such (otherwise the majority or the highest number of votes obtained from one part only of the country should have sufficed), but on their spread within the territorial area of each of at least two-thirds of the states. What this means is that a candidate should be acceptable in a state taken as one whole, undivided territorial entity, whatever its population or the size of its electorate may be relatively to other states. He is required to carry the entire state, not a two-thirds part of it. He is, by the constitutionally prescribed measure (i.e. one-quarter of the votes), either acceptable in a state taken as one whole, undivided territorial entity or he is not. There can be nothing like acceptability in a two-thirds part of the geographical area of the state. While the territory of a state may be divisible for many purposes, acceptability within it is not. It is conceived by the Constitution, not in relation to a fraction of a state, but in relation to a state as one whole, undivided geographical entity. Since it is agreed on all sides that twelve states are less than the Constitution requires and that a thirteenth state is indicated, a candidate, in order to be elected, must satisfy the acceptability test in the twelve states equally as in the thirteenth state by securing one-quarter of the votes cast in them. He does not and cannot satisfy it by winning one-sixth of the votes cast in the thirteenth state any more than he can do so by winning one-sixth of the votes cast in the twelve states. Any other view of the matter would be a distortion of the purpose of the requirement of territorial spread as conceived in the Constitution.

It is a canon of interpretation, acknowledged by the majority of the supreme court, that an enactment should be viewed in its entirety and interpreted so that, in the interest of consistency, the same expression is given the same meaning throughout, unless the context otherwise requires. The expression 'two-thirds of all the states' in the provision relating to the election of the president should not therefore be interpreted in isolation from the other contexts in which it appears in the Constitution. For example, an amendment of the Constitution must, among other things, be approved by 'resolution of the houses of assembly of not less than two-thirds of the states' (s. 9). If two-thirds of nineteen states is $12\frac{2}{3}$ states, is the approving resolution of the house of assembly in the thirteenth state to be determined by a majority of two-thirds of the members? That would be simply preposterous. And what is meant by 'a majority of all the houses of assembly in the federation' required for the ratification of a bill for an act of the national assembly for implementing a treaty (s. 12[3]), or 'a simple majority of all the states of the federation supported by a simple majority of members of the house of assembly' required for the creation of a new state (s. 8[1][*c*])?

There is also a practical reason against accepting the view that two-thirds of nineteen states in $12\frac{2}{3}$ states. For while this is true in a literal sense, it is hardly practicable, particularly in the circumstances of this case, to demarcate two-thirds of the thirteenth state for purposes of apportioning the votes. This would have required dividing the state into three equal parts — a most complex exercise indeed which, as testified in evidence before the tribunal, would have involved a great number of permutations. But the fact fatal to the application of this view in the present case is that no demarcation had been done for the purpose of the 1979 election, so that the returning officer could not, as a practical matter, have been able to ascertain the votes cast in two-thirds part of the thirteenth state (i.e. Kano state in this case). In the persuasive words of Justice Eso, 'once it is accepted that

(*a*) the word 'state', as used in the sub-section, means a physical territorial area;

(b) the legislator of the Electoral Decree was aware there are nineteen states in the federation before making the decree;
(c) there is no provision for the division of a state into units of three or multiples of three in the Decree or in any other enactment;
(d) it is impracticable and absurd to use the permutations and combinations of the local government areas to get units of three or multiples of three;
(e) the FEDECO [federal electoral commission] itself, conscious of its responsibility, never divided states into units of three or multiples of three; and
(f) the decree requires that the extent of geographical spread of the votes received by the candidate should be measured by the quantum of physical states,

the obvious thing the FEDECO and the returning officer should do, and my unhesitating answer to the question, what should they do, is to interpret the words 'in each of at least two-thirds of nineteen states' to mean in each of at least thirteen states.

It is to escape from the impracticability of this view that both the tribunal and the supreme court accepted the submission that the dominant factor in the provision is votes, drawing from that the conclusion that 'two-thirds state would be synonymous with two-thirds of the total votes cast in that state.' The fallacy of this conclusion can be demonstrated in at least two ways. First, in determining territorial spread, a two-thirds part of a state must be given the same meaning for the purposes of both presidential and gubernatorial elections. Suppose then that the provision for the election of a governor, instead of requiring the votes to be spread across at least two-thirds of all the local government areas in the state, had required them to be spread across at least two-thirds part of the state. To interpret a two-thirds part of the state as synonymous with two-thirds of the total votes cast in that state would make the principle of territorial spread completely otiose, since one-quarter of two-thirds of the total votes would certainly have been covered by a majority of the votes (where only two candidates contested) and even by the highest number of votes in an election contested by five candidates.

Secondly, as Justice Eso observed most pertinently, 'if the tribunal is right, and two-thirds state is synonymous with two-thirds of the votes cast in the state, then it would be correct to obtain the $12\frac{2}{3}$ states by taking two-thirds of all the votes cast in *each of the nineteen states*. [. . .] If the tribunal is right, and two-thirds votes cast in each of the nineteen states are taken as the basis, a candidate, to qualify, must have his twenty-five per cent of the two-thirds votes scored in *every one of the nineteen states*. If he scores less than twenty-five per cent in any one state in such circumstances, he fails.' This point seems unanswerable.

It follows, therefore, that if, for the purpose of determining acceptability in the thirteenth state, the state is to be regarded, not in its entirety as one undivided entity, but only as to a two-thirds part, then the constitutional provision requires that the votes should be spread territorially in the two-thirds part of the state in the prescribed percentage. It must be ascertained what the total votes cast in the two-thirds part of the state were, and whether the candidate's share of those votes amounted to one-quarter. Only thus can it be said that the votes of the candidate have been spread across the territorial area of $12\frac{2}{3}$ states in the prescribed percentage. Once the territorial area of acceptability is determined, whether it be thirteen or $12\frac{2}{3}$ states, the criterion for acceptability prescribed by the Constitution (i.e. one-quarter of the votes in a state) must be applied in the same way to a whole state as to a fraction of it. It is a distortion to say, as was done by the federal electoral commission and affirmed by the tribunal and the supreme court, that the criterion is satisfied by a candidate scoring one-sixth of the votes cast in the thirteenth state. One-sixth of the votes is not the measure prescribed by the Constitution for a candidate's acceptability in any part of the country. To so hold is to do great violence to the underlying purpose of the constitutional requirement. Nor is it a justification for so holding that the polling areas have not been so delimited as to enable the votes in a two-thirds part of the territorial area of a state to be ascertained. In the view which it took of the constitutional requirement, the federal electoral commission should have taken steps before the election to demarcate two-thirds of the area of each state.

Clearly therefore the only votes relevant in determining a candidate's acceptability in a two-thirds part of a state are the total votes cast in that part and the candidate's share of those votes. The votes cast for him in the whole area of the state cannot be used to determine whether he achieved one-quarter of the votes cast in a two-thirds part of the state. To do that would be yet another distortion. Accordingly, the decision (clearly wrong) to equate a two-thirds part of a state with two-thirds of the total votes cast in the state should have necessitated that the votes scored by the candidate should be correspondingly scaled down by one-third before determining whether the ratio they bear to two-thirds of the total votes is up to one-quarter. To the majority of the supreme court, however, 'it is fallacious to talk of scaling down the votes cast for [the candidate].'

The majority of the supreme court also erred in holding that a candidate who scores one-sixth of the votes cast in the thirteenth state has nevertheless *substantially* complied with the criterion for acceptability (i.e. one-quarter of the votes) prescribed by the Constitution. The principle of substantial compliance is enacted in s. 111(1) of the Electoral Decree 1977 as follows: An election shall not be invalidated by reason of non-compliance with Part II of this Decree if it appears to the Tribunal having cognisance of the question that the election was conducted substantially in accordance with the provisions of the said Part II and that the non-compliance did not affect the result of the election.

It seems clear that substantial compliance suffices only in respect of those provisions of Part II that relate to the actual conduct of an election, to the way in which an election is conducted. For example, a complaint that polling in a particular polling station did not start at the stipulated time because of the absence of polling clerks, that polling was extended beyond the time prescribed by law, insufficiency of ballot papers in a polling station, etc., is not necessarily to invalidate an election if it was otherwise conducted in substantial compliance with the procedure prescribed in Part II for the election. The complaint must relate to procedure at the election. But Part II, though entitled 'Procedure at Elections', deals with other matters besides, such as qualification and disqualification for election (ss. 72 & 73) and the number of votes required by law for a candidate to be elected. These are not matters of procedure at all; they have nothing to do with the conduct of an election, and have to be satisfied in their precise terms, not just substantially. A candidate is either qualified or not qualified, he cannot be substantially qualified; and he either gets the prescribed number of votes or he does not.

Thus while non-compliance with the provisions of Part II is a ground for an election petition under the decree, it is made a separate ground for such petition that (a) the person whose election is questioned was, at the time of the election, not qualified to be elected; and (b) the respondent was, at the time of the election, not duly elected by a majority of lawful votes at the election. Both of these two grounds relate to matters covered in Part II, and yet are made grounds of petition separate from non-compliance with the provisions of Part II. The reference to 'a majority of lawful votes' was a lapse on the part of the draftsman who apparently forgot to amend that reference to reflect the newly-incorporated provisions for the election of the president and governor. That ground should have read instead that 'the respondent was, at the time of the election, not duly elected by the prescribed percentage of the lawful votes cast at the election.'

The error in drafting proved a serious handicap to the petitioner in this case, as he was thereby obliged to aver, in terms of the decree, that 'Alhaji Shehu Shagari was at the time of the election not duly elected by a majority of lawful votes at the election.' A majority of votes being irrelevant in a five-cornered contest, the election tribunal rightly held that this averment is not a proper ground for an election petition in this case.

The petition was doomed to failure from its inception because of the defective drafting of the decree. The petitioner had made two prayers, but neither of them was within the power of the tribunal to grant under the decree. He had prayed

(*a*) that the tribunal should determine that the said Alhaji Shehu Shagari . . . was not duly elected or returned and that his election or return was void;
(*b*) that Alhaji Ahmadu Kurfi, the Chief Electoral Officer of the Federation, and Mr. F.I.O. Menkiti, the Returning Officer at the Presidential Election . . . be ordered to arrange for an election to be held in accordance with the provisions of Section 34A(3) of the Electoral (Amendment) Decree (Decree no. 32 of 1979) [i.e. election in the federal and state legislative houses].

The power of the tribunal, as defined in s. 124(2) of the decree, is simply to 'determine what person was duly returned or whether the election was void, as the case may be, and [to] certify its determination to the Electoral Commission', upon which 'the election shall stand confirmed or a fresh election shall be held on a date to be appointed by the Electoral Commission' (see also s. 134). The tribunal and the supreme court on appeal have therefore no power to determine that Alhaji Shehu Shagari had not been duly returned. They could only invalidate the *whole* election (not just Alhaji Shehu's return) or otherwise declare one candidate to have been duly returned. If they invalidated the whole election, then a fresh *general* election would have to be held.

The tribunal and the supreme court on appeal could not order the chief electoral officer of the federation and the presidential returning officer to hold an election in the federal and state legislative houses, because their power is merely to order a fresh general election, which presupposes that the whole election would first have to be invalidated. But the petitioner wanted neither the invalidation of the whole election nor a fresh general election. Even assuming that the tribunal could have ordered an election in the federal and state legislative houses, the chief electoral officer of the federation and the presidential returning officer had no power to hold such election. The electoral commission, which was the body vested with power to hold an election in the federal and state legislative houses, was not a party to the petition, and could not have been made so anyway, since under the decree only the successful candidate, the federal chief electoral officer and the presidential returning officer can be made respondents in a petition relating to the election of the president. Furthermore, the power of the electoral commission to hold an electoral college must be exercised within seven days of the preceding general election, and this had long since passed.

The petitioner thus found himself in an agonising dilemma, which left him almost without a remedy except, as the supreme court observed, a declaration by the tribunal on the meaning of the provisions. Section 124(2) of the decree has been lifted from the Electoral Act of 1962 without any attempt on the part of the draftsman to adapt it to meet the peculiar requirements of a presidential election under the new Constitution.

The petitioner did not attack the presidential election itself but only the electoral commission's declaration or return of Aihaji Shehu Shagari as having been duly elected president. No grounds were therefore averred and no evidence was led for invalidating the election. The petitioner certainly did not want that, since it might have robbed him of his precious position as the first runner-up and of the prospect that he might emerge the winner in an election between him and Alhaji Shehu Shagari in the electoral college. Invalidation of the whole election would have upset the programme for the hand-over to civilians, and this is something which hardly anyone could have wanted.

Whether it was right or wrong from a legal standpoint, the electoral commission's declaration of Alhaji Shehu Shagari created in the country a situation of which a judicial tribunal, particularly a court of last resort, cannot but take cognisance. The situation created by the declaration had put it out of the power of the electoral commission to hold an electoral college, since the power to do that had to be exercised within seven days of the preceding general election. The seven days having long since passed, it would have been irresponsible for the tribunal to have invalidated Alhaji Shehu Shagari's return (assuming even that the tribunal had had power to do so), knowing that an election in the federal and state legislative houses (the electoral college) between the petitioner and Alhaji Shehu Shagari was no longer possible. The nation would have been plunged into an intolerable impasse. A judicial tribunal called upon to decide such a grave issue should take account of national expediency, and to ask itself whether the country should be thrown into such an impasse and the inevitable chaos that would follow merely because Alhaji Shehu Shagari's votes in the thirteenth state (i.e. Kano state) fell short of the prescribed percentage by 0.5 per cent votes. In cases of great constitutional or political gravity affecting the peace and stability of the nation, while legalism should be the dominant principle for deciding them, the court is also entitled to take into account other factors, such as the ethical presuppositions and moral sensibilities of the society, the attitude of the public in the matter as manifested in the people's expressed sentiments and actions, the social consequences of a decision, and national expediency generally — or what is best for the common good of the community and other social facts. These are what is generally referred to as the public policy elements of constitutional adjudication, which have played a significant role in the constitutional decisions of the supreme court of the United States, sometimes as inarticulate major premise and sometimes as openly avowed principles of judicial action.[3] In the light of these considerations, the decision reached by the majority of the supreme court seems justified, though for different reasons.

2. Tenure

The Constitution limits the presidential term of office to four years, although this may be extended from time to time for a period not exceeding six months at a time by a resolution of the national assembly if the federation is at war involving its territory and the president considers that it is not practicable to hold elections (s. 127). The four-year period is calculated from the date of swearing-in, but an incumbent president does not vacate office until his successor is actually sworn in.

The number of terms a person can hold office as president under the 1979 Constitution is limited to two terms, which need not be consecutive. Once a person has been elected to the office at any two previous elections, he is for ever barred from holding the office again. This limitation constitutes perhaps one of the most remarkable characteristics of the presidency under the Constitution. It is a recognition of the dangerous tendency of indefinite eligibility to personalise government, to elevate the president into a cult and an institution, and the office into an inheritance. A president who has held office for twenty years is a different kind of functionary from one who is limited to a maximum of two terms of four years each. His authority is bound to be greater, for after twenty years in office he is apt to become an institution himself, attracting loyalties of a personal nature. His authority tends to be all-pervading. A cult of personality is built up around him, generating belief in his infallibility and indispensability.

This propensity to personalise rule and to perpetuate it indefinitely is a disastrous factor in the politics of African countries. It has undermined the quality of democracy on the continent, and exposed government to disaffection and acts of subversion, often culminating in its forcible overthrow by the military, with all the attendant instability, and the disruption in the country's normal democratic evolution. It also deprives the country of the benefit of change in leadership, for change may prevent or check sterility and complacency by enabling a fresh vitality and a fresh approach to be brought to bear upon the problems of government. 'An untried president', it has been aptly said, 'may be better than a tired one; a fresh approach better than a stale one.'[4] The cult of indispensability is an empty myth; in the government of a nation, even a developing nation, there is really no such thing as an indispensable man. To accept that there is, as Corwin has said, 'is next door to despairing of the country'.[5]

In limiting the president to two terms of four years each, the Constitution departs from the prevailing African tradition of indefinite eligibility, which is rationalised on the grounds that such a limitation would stifle zeal and make the president indifferent to his duty; that a president, knowing he would be barred from the office for ever after, might be tempted to exploit for personal advantage the opportunities of the office while they lasted; that an ambitious president might be tempted to try to prolong his term by perverse means; that it would deprive the country of the advantage of the president's previous experience in the office; and that it would lead to a lack of continuity in policy, and consequently to instability in administration.[6] It is also argued that the development crisis and the clash of cultures which African countries are going through create a kind of emergency that calls for continuity in leadership.

The advantages of indefinite eligibility, such as they are, are far outweighed by its dangers. These dangers have been recognised in the United States from the very inception of the presidency there. To be sure, until 1951 the American Constitution imposed no restriction on the eligibility of a president to seek re-election indefinitely. At the time of the Constitution's adoption, most Americans wished indeed that George Washington, the first president, would remain president indefinitely, so profound was the confidence and love he inspired in them. As a matter of general political principle, quite apart from the personality of Washington, the question of indefinite eligibility had provoked a disagreement of views. Washington himself and Alexander Hamilton favoured it, while Jefferson opposed it. Washington did, however, retire after two terms, much against the wishes and expectations of his countrymen. His example was followed by Jefferson, also against appeals from eight state legislatures that he should continue in office. 'If', he argued, 'some termination to the services of the Chief Magistrate be not fixed by the Constitution, or supplied by practice, his office, normally four years, will in fact become for life, and history shows how easily that degenerates into an inheritance.'[7] Since then the tradition has stuck that no person should be president for more than two terms. Until 1940, this tradition had been consistently observed except when, taking advantage of the uncertainty as to whether two terms meant two consecutive terms, Theodore Roosevelt sought (but failed) to be elected in 1912 for a third term some years after his first two consecutive terms. Tradition was finally breached when Franklin Roosevelt was re-elected for a third consecutive term in 1940 and for a fourth in 1944. But this was in a period of grave emergency, that of the second world war. It is such emergencies that present the strongest argument in favour of indefinite eligibility, and when they occur the prestige and authority of the president's personality might be invaluable in saving the life of the nation. This was the consideration underlying the break with tradition of Franklin Roosevelt's third and fourth consecutive re-elections. Roosevelt himself professed a desire to adhere to the tradition, and to relinquish office in 1941 to a successor, if only he could do so with an assurance that 'I am at the same time turning over to him as president a nation intact, a nation at peace, a nation prosperous, a nation clear in its knowledge of what powers it has to serve its own citizens, a nation that is in a position to use those powers to the full in order to move forward steadily to meet the modern needs of humanity — a nation which has thus proved that the democratic form and methods of national government can and will succeed.'[8]

These are words which might be used by any African president to justify his rule in perpetuity, and it might even be more cogent and compelling in his case. As Corwin points out, this is just the 'indispensable man' argument. In a temporary emergency like a war it might perhaps be condoned, but in the context of the sort of emergency created by the development crisis in the emergent states it is a positive evil. For since the development crisis is a continuing 'emergency', the argument is tantamount to making the presidency a life appointment. In any case, the Americans, after the Roosevelt experience, had to amend their Constitution in 1951 to give force of law to the tradition limiting the presidential office to two full elective terms or one full elective term plus more than half of another term inherited from a previous president.[9]

Apart from the normal expiration of his term, the president's tenure may be terminated sooner by death, resignation or removal from office in accordance with the provisions of the Constitution. Resignation would play a much smaller role in terminating the president's tenure than it does in the parliamentary system. This is because the president is not constitutionally obliged to resign because he does not enjoy the confidence of the national assembly or because his legislative or financial measures are thrown out by the assembly. But a president involved in public scandal may be forced to resign because of mounting pressure from the national assembly and the public at large. His resignation has to be by notice in writing addressed to the president of the senate, and takes effect from the date it is received (s. 261).

As noted in chapter 8, the president may be removed from office on being found guilty by the code of conduct tribunal for breach of the code of conduct or upon impeachment in the national assembly for grave violation of the Constitution or other gross misconduct. In addition, an ailing and incapacitated president who refuses to resign may be removed from office. The procedure on impeachment and for removal on ground of incapacity has been discussed in chapter 8, and need not be repeated here.

REFERENCES

1. Constitution of the Federal Republic of Nigeria (Amendment) Decree, 1979.
2. *Chief Obafemi Awolowo* v. *Alhaji Shehu Shagari & others*, Suit No. SET/1/1979 delivered 10 September 1979; and Suit No. SC.62/1979 delivered 26 September 1979 — unreported.
3. For a full discussion, see Nwabueze, *Judicialism in Commonwealth Africa* (1977), chapters 2 and 6.
4. E.S. Corwin, *The President: Office and Powers*, 4th edn, 37.
5. Corwin, loc. cit.
6. See Alexander Hamilton in *The Federalist*.
7. Quoted from Corwin, op. cit., 332.
8. Quoted from Corwin, op. cit., 336.
9. XXII Amendment.

12
THE NATIONAL ASSEMBLY

1. *A bicameral assembly and relations between the two houses*

The national assembly is a bicameral body. It consists of two houses, the senate and the house of representatives.

For the exercise — whether by means of legislation, resolution or otherwise — of any power or function conferred on the national assembly by the Constitution, the two houses rank equally. As regards a power exercisable by resolution, a motion has to be proposed and passed in each house. A resolution on a matter by one house alone does not make it a decision of the national assembly unless and until it is adopted by the other house. If a motion passed in one house is lost or held up in the other, the matter lapses.

In the case of legislation, a bill on any matter within the legislative competence of the national assembly may originate in either house and, subject to the procedure for resolving disagreement over a money bill, its passage requires the separate concurrence of both; neither can override the other on any matter. The house of representatives has no such right exclusively to originate a money bill as in the United States, or to pass it over the head of the senate after a period of delay as under the parliamentary system.

In the result therefore a bill passed by one house but not by the other lapses completely. Also an amendment proposed by one must be agreed by the other, or the bill lapses in its entirety. This means that in a conflict in which each house is unwilling to yield ground to the other, the bill is killed completely. An exception is made, however, in the case of a money bill because of the imperative need for ensuring that money is appropriated for carrying on the administration of government and its services. It is provided therefore that where a money bill passed by one house is not passed by the other within two months of the commencement of the financial year, the conflict should be resolved by a joint finance committee, drawn equally from both houses, and failing that, by a joint sitting of both houses presided over by the president of the senate. The joint session may pass the bill or reject it by a majority of the members present and voting, provided again that there is present a quorum (i.e. one-third of the total combined membership of the two houses).

While the joint finance committee may be able to resolve a conflict, it cannot itself pass the bill. The passing of a bill is the function exclusively of the legislative houses, and cannot be delegated to a committee, whether the joint finance committee in the case of a money bill or any other committee. As for the passing of a bill into law (or the passing of a resolution on any matter which the national assembly is authorised to determine by resolution), a committee can only make recommendations. If therefore a disagreement over a money bill is successfully resolved by the joint finance committee, this would operate by way of recommendation to the houses, which will then meet in separate sittings to pass the bill in accordance with the settlement reached by the joint finance committee. (A money bill is one which appropriates money from the public funds of the federation or state, or which relates to the raising of revenue.)

The basis for the equality between the two houses is the fact that both houses are elected directly by the people. Given that the states have equal representation in the senate, irrespective of population, the parity of power between it and the house of representatives may appear to water down somewhat the popular basis of representative democracy. Equal representation of the states in the senate is predicated upon another constitutional principle of similarly great importance in a federation, namely the equality of the states *inter se*. The smallest state is equal to the most populous in terms of its constitutional existence as a government. And since the senate is meant essentially to provide representation for the states as states, it is right and proper that parity should be applied not only as regards representation in the senate, but also as between the senate and house of representatives in the exercise of powers conferred on the national assembly by the Constitution.

Yet, by vesting certain powers exclusively in the senate or its president, the Constitution does clearly intend that the senate should have primacy over the house of representatives. Power vested in the senate to the exclusion of the house of representatives relate to the confirmation or approval of the appointment by the president of specified state functionaries, namely the auditor-general, ministers, ambassadors, high commissioners or other principal representatives of Nigeria abroad, the chief justice of Nigeria, justices of the supreme court, the president of the federal court of appeal, the chairman and members (other than *ex-officio* members) of the civil service commission, electoral commission, judicial service commission, national population commission, police service commission, and the code of conduct bureau; the appointment by its president of a committee to investigate allegation of misconduct against the president of the republic; and the removal from office of the auditor-general, the chief justice of Nigeria, and the chairman and members of the civil service commission, council of state, electoral commission, judicial service commission, national population commission and police service commission. The senate is given the power to appoint, not merely to approve the appointment of, members of staff of the code of conduct bureau. The deployment of any members of the armed forces on combat duty outside the country also requires the prior approval of the senate.

The president of the senate has the exclusive right to receive the notice of any allegation of misconduct against the president or vice-president of the republic and to cause it to be served on the president or vice-president and on each member of the national assembly; on a resolution by each house that the allegation should be investigated, to appoint, with the approval of the senate, an investigation committee of seven members who in his opinion are persons of high integrity; to appoint a medical panel of five medical practitioners of eminence to verify a declaration by the members of the executive council that the president or vice-president is, owing to ill-health, incapable of discharging the functions of his office; to preside at joint meetings of the two houses; to arrange and convene a meeting of the joint finance committee to try to resolve disagreement between the two houses over a money bill; to receive notice of resignation of the president of the republic (the notice must be addressed to him); and most important of all, to succeed to the presidency for three months (during which an election must be held) in the event of a vacancy in the office occurring at a time when there is no vice-president. As the second in the line of succession to the presidency, the president of the senate ranks in precedence immediately after the vice-president but before every one else.

The Constitution seems clearly to envisage the senate as an 'upper' house of elder statesmen who are to serve as the eye of the public in ensuring that the appointment and removal of certain public functionaries by the president are made with the national interest in view, and not from purely personal, sectional or partisan considerations. It therefore prescribes for senators an upper age qualification — not less than thirty years as against a minimum of twenty-one years for members of the house of representatives. The functions vested exclusively in the senate or its president are by no means 'marginal', as one member of the house of representatives has described them. Whether of course they justify giving to senators a higher salary than members of the house of representatives is another matter.

2. *Membership*

The senate consists of ninety-five members, five from each state. (There will be an additional member from the federal capital territory when the section relating to federal capital territory comes into force.) The house of representatives has 450 members. Though not a civil servant, a member is a public officer as defined in the Constitution (s. 277[1] and 5th Sch.).

(i) *Election of members*

Membership of both houses of the national assembly is by direct, popular election. Subject to disqualifications mentioned below, any Nigerian citizen who has attained the age of thirty years in the case of the senate or twenty-one years in the case of the house of representatives may be elected. The franchise is open to every Nigerian citizen who has been registered as a voter; registration is equally free to every Nigerian citizen who has attained the age of eighteen years and is resident in the country at the time of registration. The franchise is thus universal and equal.

The elections are organised on the principle that members of the national assembly represent distinct geographical areas, called constituencies, delimited on the basis of equality of population. The constituencies thus correspond in number to the total membership of the house, and must each have a population as 'nearly equal to the population quota as is reasonably practicable'. The population quota is arrived at

(*a*) by dividing the population of the country by 450 in the case of the house of representatives, provided that no constituency shall fall within more than one state;

(*b*) by dividing the population of a state by five in the case of the senate;

(*c*) by dividing the population of a state by the number of seats in the state house of assembly.

Within a state there are thus three sets of constituencies respectively for the house of representatives, senate and state house of assembly, with different geographical boundaries.

The delimitation of constituencies, which is vested in an independent constitutional commission, the federal electoral commission, is therefore governed largely by principle which is justiciable in the courts. No doubt, the fact that the principle is not one of absolute equality, but rather one of as near equality as is reasonably practicable, imports a certain amount of discretion in the federal electoral commission. Yet the discretion must be exercised within the governing context of the principle of equality of representation. Its use so as to apportion to any states greater representation in the house of representatives than their population would entitle them or to perpetrate discrimination in representation between different ethnic groups or between urban and rural communities within a state can be nullified by the courts. The discretion exercisable by the federal electoral commission is even less than it was under the old Constitution which, in addition to the inevitable inequalities reasonably attributable to the practicalities of constituency delimitation, specifically provided that 'the number of inhabitants of a constituency may be greater or less than the population quota in order to take account of means of communication, geographical features, the distribution of different communities and the boundaries of the territories' (s. 51[2]). These exceptions are omitted from the 1979 Constitution and cannot now be used to justify inequality of representation between constituencies.

In the United States, the supreme court has, after an initial false step, affirmed the justiciability of the principle of equality of representation. The false step was exemplified in a case where certain voters in Illinois complained that under the Illinois Apportionment Act their electoral district was nine times as populous as certain other electoral districts in the state with the result that the effectiveness of their votes was reduced, and that this was a wilful discrimination against them, amounting to a violation of the fourteenth amendment guarantee of equal protection of the law and the guarantee of the privileges or immunities of citizens against abridgment by state law: among these privileges was the right to vote guaranteed by article 1, which, it was asserted, was abridged unless their vote was given approximately equal weight to that of other citizens.[1] The supreme court, by a majority of four to three refused to entertain the complaint of malapportionment on the ground, as stated by Justice Frankfurter, that 'there is not — as there has never been — a standard by which the place of equality as a factor in apportionment can be measured.'

This decision was overruled by the court sixteen years later in a case where the disparity between rural and urban constituencies in Tennessee ranged from 2,340 to 33,990.[2] In a series of subsequent cases, the supreme court ruled as unconstitutional, malapportionment under various state laws.[3] As the court observed: 'Construed in its historical context, the command of art. 1, s. 2, that Representatives be chosen "by the People of the several States" means that as nearly as is practicable one man's vote in a congressional election is to be worth as much as another.'[4]

In Nigeria the federal electoral commission has responsibility not only for the registration of voters and the delimitation of constituencies, but also for the actual conduct of the elections, acting of course in accordance with the electoral laws enacted by the national assembly. The Constitution however requires that the date to be appointed by the commission for elections shall not be 'earlier than 60 days before and not later than the date on which the House stands dissolved, or where the election is to fill a vacancy occurring more than 3 months before such date not later than one month after the vacancy occurred' (s. 70).

(ii) *Disqualifications*
The disqualifications are primarily a bar to election, not to membership directly. Election constitutes a person a member as soon as the returns of his election have been made, even before he formally takes his seat by subscribing to the prescribed oaths. A disqualifying event occurring after an election does not therefore bar membership in the first instance, though it operates automatically to vacate it, because of the provision that a member shall vacate his seat if circumstances arise that, had he not been a member, would cause him to be disqualified. That membership predates the taking of the oath is clearly implied in the provision that 'every member . . . shall, before taking his seat, take and subscribe the Oath of Allegiance and the oath of membership prescribed in the Sixth Schedule to this Constitution but a member may before taking the oaths take part in the election' of a president or speaker of the legislative house. A person who declines, neglects or omits to take the required oath becomes disqualified from entering upon his office, or, if he has already entered, he will be deemed to have vacated it from the date of refusal, without prejudice, however, to acts already done.[5]

Disqualification attaches to the following persons:
(*a*) a person who has voluntarily acquired the citizenship of another country or, except as may be permitted by the national assembly, has made a declaration of allegiance to such a country;
(*b*) a person adjudged to be a lunatic or otherwise declared to be of unsound mind under any law in force in any part of Nigeria;
(*c*) a person under a sentence of death or imprisonment for more than six months for an offence involving dishonesty where such sentence is imposed by a court of law in Nigeria;
(*d*) a person who, within a period of less than ten years before the date of an election to a legislative house, has been convicted and sentenced for an offence involving dishonesty or has been found guilty of a contravention of the code of conduct;
(*e*) a person who has been adjudged or otherwise declared bankrupt under any law in force in Nigeria and has not been discharged; or
(*f*) a person employed in the public service of the federation or of any state.

Of these grounds of disqualification, the last is the most important. Public service is defined as service of the federation or state in any capacity in respect of the government, and includes, among others, staff (but not a member) of a statutory corporation, an educational institution established or financed principally by the government, or a company or enterprise in which the government or its agency owns the controlling share or interest. Thus ministers and other office-holders are barred. The disqualification of ministers is reinforced by the provision vacating the seat of a member upon his appointment as a minister.

This removes yet another instrument of executive control of the legislature, for under the parliamentary system it is not unknown for as many as half or more of the membership of the legislature to be persons holding government appointments of one kind or another. Such a preponderance in a legislature of government office-holders clearly destroys its independence. The partial fusion of personnel of the legislature and the executive which the Westminster system entails can only be defended if the proportion of government office-holders to the total membership of the legislature is kept low. Where it is as much as half, the position becomes quite indefensible, since the assembly would then have become an extension of the executive, and would thus be incapable of fulfilling the role of watchdog of the nation's liberties against the pretensions of power on the part of the executive.

Under our new Constitution, not only are ministers barred from election and membership, a minister has no right of attendance except when invited to explain to the house the conduct of his ministry or when the affairs of the ministry are under discussion. The president's right of attendance is likewise limited to formal occasions for the purpose of delivering an address on national affairs or making important statement of government policy (s. 63).

(iii) *Tenure*

A member of a legislative house is elected for the normal life of the national assembly which is four years.

A member vacates his seat not only upon the dissolution of the legislature or his own demise but also if:

(*a*) he becomes a member of another legislative house;

(*b*) any other circumstances arise that, if he were not a member, would cause him to be disqualified for election as a member;

(*c*) he ceases to be a citizen of Nigeria;

(*d*) he becomes president, vice-president, governor, deputy governor or a minister or commissioner of the government of the federation or state, as the case may be;

(*e*) he becomes a member of a commission or other body established by this Constitution or by any other law;

(*f*) without just cause certified as such by the president or speaker, he is absent from meetings of the house of which he is a member for a period amounting in the aggregate to more than one-third of the total number of days during which the house meets in any one year; or

(g) being a person whose election was sponsored by a political party, he becomes a member of another political party before the expiration of the period for which the house was elected, provided that his membership of the latter political party is not as a result of a division in the political party of which he was previously a member or of a merger between the party that sponsored him and two or more other political parties or factions; or

(h) he resigns by notice in writing addressed to the president of the senate (in the case of members of the senate) and to the speaker of the house of representatives (in the case of member of the house).

A member elected as an independent is prohibited from joining or declaring himself a member of a political party until the next general election (s. 37[b]). The consequence of a breach of this prohibition, e.g. whether membership of the house has to be given up as the price of membership of the political party, is nowhere stated, but it seems more reasonable to say that membership of the house would not be thereby affected.

(iv) *Determination of questions as to membership*

Determination of the question as to whether a person has been validly elected as a member of a legislative house or whether his seat has become vacant is vested in the high court of the state (or the high court of the federal capital territory) where the senatorial district, federal constituency or state constituency of that member or person is located (s. 237).

The national assembly or a state house of assembly, as the case may be, is required to make provisions as to

(a) persons who may apply to the competent high court for the determination of the validity of a person's election or the tenure of his membership;

(b) circumstances and manner in which, and the conditions upon such application may be made; and

(c) powers, practice and procedure of the competent high court in relation to such application.

3. *Life and sittings of the national assembly*

The life of the national assembly is by the Constitution fixed at four years calculated from the date of the first sitting. At the expiration of the four years each house stands dissolved. Although dissolution follows automatically on the expiry of the prescribed period, it may nevertheless be given formal promulgation by the president issuing a proclamation of dissolution (s. 60 as amended by the Constitution of the Federal Republic of Nigeria [Amendment] Decree no. 104 of

1979). It is important to emphasise however that, since dissolution takes effect due to the passage of time and not by virtue of the proclamation, non-issuance of a proclamation by the president will not stop dissolution taking place directly and automatically on the expiration of the four-year period. The point is important since the president is not bound, and consequently cannot be compelled, to issue a proclamation of dissolution. The issuing of a proclamation is a matter of power (which is discretionary), not a duty which he can be compelled to perform. The president has, however, no power to dissolve the assembly before the expiration of its normal life.

If the federation is at war in which the territory of Nigeria is physically involved, and the president considers that it is not practicable to hold elections, the national assembly may by resolution extend the four-year period for successive periods of six months at a time (s. 60[2]). An extension of the normal life of the national assembly therefore requires the concurrence of both the president and the national assembly as well as the objective factor, justiciable by the court, of a war involving the territory of Nigeria. Whether the opinion of the president that such a war situation makes the holding of an election impracticable can be reviewed in a court of law is a question of some difficulty. The situation created by a war involves an appraisal of the scope of present military operations, the danger they present for the country and the anticipated future development of the war. These are military matters which no court can undertake to enquire into. It seems therefore that, demonstrable bad faith apart, the subjective opinion of the president is conclusive.

Each house of the national assembly must sit for not less than 181 days in a year (s. 59). Each year of 181 sitting days forms a session. There are four meetings in a session, and each meeting covers a number of sitting days. The first session after a general election is convened by the president by a proclamation fixing the date, time and place for the sitting (s. 60[3] as amended by the Constitution of the Federal Republic of Nigeria [Amendment] Decree no. 104 of 1979). No other power is given to the president to summon a sitting of either house, not even, as in the United States, on an extraordinary occasion to consider a matter of urgent national importance. Each house decides for itself when to adjourn its sittings during a session and when to bring a session to an end, and when to resume sitting again after an adjournment and when to begin a new session. Under the standing orders, however, whenever the house is in adjournment, the president of the senate or speaker of the house of representatives shall summon a sitting if so requested by the executive council.

4. Proceedings of the houses

The proceedings of each house are regulated by the rules made by it, subject to the provisions of the Constitution (s. 56). Until each house does so, the standing orders of the former senate are made applicable to the proceedings of the senate, and those of the former house of representatives to the proceedings of the house of representatives and the state houses of assembly (s. 270).

Provisions are, however, made in the Constitution itself with respect to the following:

(i) *Presiding at sittings*

A president and deputy president are established for the senate, and a speaker and deputy speaker for the house of representatives (s. 46[1]). They are to be elected by the members of the respective houses from among themselves. The first business of each house after a general election is to elect these functionaries, and a member may take part in each election even before taking and subscribing to the oath (s. 48[1]).

With the support of a two-thirds majority of its members, each house can remove its president or speaker or his deputy. Apart from removal by the house, the president or speaker or his deputy vacates his office if he ceases to be a member of the house otherwise than by reason of a dissolution or when the house first sits after any dissolution (s. 46[2]). The president or speaker wishing to resign shall address his notice of resignation to the clerk of the national assembly (s. 266[6]).

The president of the senate or the deputy president in his absence presides at any sitting of the senate, while a sitting of the house of representatives is presided over by the speaker or the deputy speaker in his absence (s. 49[1]). In the absence of both the president or speaker and his deputy, the house elects one of its members to preside for the occasion (s. 49[3]). The president of the senate or in his absence the speaker of the house of representatives presides at a joint sitting of both houses (s. 49[2]).

The president or the speaker or anyone else presiding at a sitting of the house has wide powers to rule on the meaning and requirements of the Constitution insofar as they are relevant to the proceedings of the house, what majorities are required for various actions, whether a quorum is present, whether a matter proposed for decision has been carried, whether the house is competent to adopt a certain measure, whether the absence of a member is for a just cause or not, etc; to interpret the standing orders, to rule on the relevance of a member's contribution and on other points of order, to ensure orderly debate, and generally to enforce order and discipline in the house.

To challenge or flout the president's or speaker's authority is to invite the risk of reprimand, exclusion or suspension. A partisan and dictatorial president or speaker may get impatient of criticism of the government or condone unnecessary interruptions of a critical speech.

Thus the most important quality required of a president or speaker is impartiality. It is his paramount duty to hold the balance evenly between the competing elements in the house, and to 'ensure that the voice of the minority is always given a fair hearing.'[6] He is there to guard the dignity and independence of the house, and not to reflect the wishes of the majority or to carry out its directives on the conduct of business or the interpretation of relevant points of law. Should the government try to invade the autonomy of the assembly, he should not allow his loyalty to it as his sponsors to the office to override his duty to the house. His duty as chairman demands that he should apply his own independent judgment in resolving points of dispute in the house, with the assistance where necessary of independent expert advice, and not merely act on the opinion of the attorney-general, however learned.

However, a government-nominated president or speaker can hardly be completely independent of it. No doubt much would depend on the character and outlook of the individual concerned. While most chairmen of legislative houses in Commonwealth Africa have been remarkably impartial, quite a number have displayed over-zealousness in their support of the government, and have thereby undermined opposition members' freedom of criticism. Nor is it unknown for the government to direct the chairman on what ruling to give. Given the separation of executive and legislative power under the 1979 Constitution, the possibility of a legislative majority controlled by a party opposed to the president removes this form of control, since the speaker or president would then be a nominee, not of the government, but of the 'opposition' majority party.

(ii) *Clerk and other staff of the national assembly*

The office of clerk is established as the head of the national assembly secretariat, which comprises such other staff as may be prescribed by an act of the national assembly (s. 47). He and the other staff are to be appointed in the manner to be prescribed in such act. Until an act is passed, the clerk and other staff of the national assembly shall be appointed by the federal civil service commission in consultation with the president of the senate or speaker of the house of representatives, as appropriate (s. 269). In view of the provision requiring the president and speaker and their deputies to take and subscribe to the oath of allegiance and oath of membership before the clerk (s. 48[2]), which implies that the appointment of a clerk must initially predate the election and swearing in of the president and speaker and their deputies, the consultation required by s. 269 is not possible, except in the case of an appointment to fill a vacancy occurring after a swearing-in. Moreover, a person who, immediately before 1 October 1979, held office as clerk by virtue of any other Constitution or law in force at the time is deemed to be duly appointed to that office by virtue of the new Constitution or by the authority by whom his appointment falls to be made under the Constitution (s. 275[2]).

The clerk has the responsibility for keeping minutes of the proceedings of each house, and for the custody of the votes, records, bills and other documents laid before the house. It is also his duty to prepare the order paper showing the business of the house for each day, and to distribute it to members. As earlier noted, he administers the oath to the president and speaker and their deputies (s. 48[2]), and any notice of resignation by them has to be addressed to him (s. 266[6]).

(iii) *Quorum*
The quorum for each house is one-third of all its members (s. 50[1]). The absence of a quorum does not however prevent the house from transacting business unless and until objection is raised. If the person presiding then ascertains that a quorum is not present, he must adjourn.

(iv) *Language*
English and, 'when adequate arrangements have been made for their use', Hausa, Ibo and Yoruba are the permitted languages of business in the national assembly (s. 51).

(v) *Voting*
The normal way of taking decisions in the house is by a simple majority of the members present and voting (s. 52[1] and [2]). The person presiding has no vote except in the event of an equality of votes. A simple majority of a quorum can therefore pass any measure.[7] What this means is that a majority of thirty-two (one-third of the senate) i.e. seventeen or a majority of 150 (one-third of the house of representatives) i.e. seventy-six can take any decision on behalf of the respective houses.

A special majority, two-thirds or four-fifths, either of the members or of *all* the members, is required for certain purposes. As a quorum constitutes a house with full power to transact business, two-thirds of the members means a two-thirds majority of a quorum or of the members present and voting provided a quorum is present, and not of all members, unless the latter is specifically prescribed.[8]

Only four matters require a four-fifths majority of *all* the members, namely alteration of the provisions relating to fundamental rights, alteration of the procedure laid down by the Constitution for the amendment of its provisions, for the creation of new states, or the alteration of boundaries between existing states (s. 9[3]). Two-thirds majority of *all* the members is required for a resolution ordering investigation into allegation of misconduct by the president or vice-president or adopting a recommendation for his removal by an investigation panel (s. 132[4] and [9]) or approving a proclamation of a state of emergency by the president (s. 265[6]). The creation of a new state, the removal of the president of the senate or speaker of the house of representatives or the deputy of either by the appropriate house, a prayer by the senate for the removal of the auditor-general, the chief justice of Nigeria, the chairman and members of the code of conduct tribunal, the federal civil service commission, the council of state, the federal electoral commission, the federal judicial service commission, the national population commission and police service commission require a two-thirds majority of the members of the appropriate house. A bill can become law without the president's assent only if it is passed again by two-thirds majority of each house, or of both houses sitting jointly in the case of a money bill passed initially at a joint sitting.

(vi) *Procedure for making law*
Only the broad outline of the procedure for law-making is prescribed in the Constitution. A legislative proposal is required to be presented to the assembly in the form of a bill. This has a significant bearing on the reality and effectiveness of the enacting function of the national assembly. For it enables the proposal to be considered from the point of view both of its substance and the implications of the actual words used.

A bill may originate in either house, but not in both concurrently. In whichever house it originates it must be passed by both separately, first by the house in which it originates, whence it then goes to the other house. The concurrence of each house cannot be dispensed with, nor is a joint sitting to resolve disagreement allowed except in the case of a money bill, i.e. a bill which appropriates money from the public funds or which relates to the raising of revenue. A disagreement over a money bill which continues two months after the beginning of a financial year must, within fourteen days from the expiry of the two months be referred by the president of the senate to a joint finance committee composed of an equal number of members from both houses, who will 'examine the bill with a view to resolving the differences between the two houses'. If the committee is unable to resolve the disagreement, the matter is to be decided at a joint sitting of the two houses.

The use of the word 'resolve' introduces an element of ambiguity in the procedure relating to a money bill. It seems to envisage the joint finance committee as a body which, in the detached and intimate atmosphere of a small group, may be expected to reach a negotiated settlement based on unanimity or consensus, or at the very least a settlement agreed to by a majority on both sides of the dispute. One cannot in any proper sense of the word talk of differences having been resolved between two parties unless what is proposed has the agreement of the two sides. Differences are not resolved where the casting vote of the chairman of the committee is allowed to override the united opposition of the members representing one side to the dispute. In default of a settlement supported by at least a majority on both sides, the differences must be regarded as unresolved.

But assuming the differences to have been resolved in any sense in which the words may be interpreted, the crucial question is whether the bill may, on the strength of that, be regarded as having been passed by the national assembly, and be sent direct to the president for his assent, or whether it needs still to be referred back to the two houses for formal adoption or endorsement. Is the joint finance committee, in a situation of conflict between the two houses, invested by the Constitution with the power of the national assembly to pass a money bill into law? It is necessary to emphasise that if the joint finance committee has any power at all to pass a money bill in the circumstances of a conflict, then it has it by virtue of direct grant by the Constitution, and not by way of delegation from the national assembly. The point under discussion is therefore not affected by the fact that the national assembly cannot delegate power to pass a bill to a committee (s. 58[4]).

The absence of any explicit constitutional provision on this question means that the ambiguity and uncertainty thereby created has to be resolved by inferences from the words actually used. The provision that the bill is to be referred to a joint meeting of the national assembly in the event that the joint finance committee is not able to resolve the conflict supports the inference that where the committee is successful in resolving the conflict, its decision cannot be reversed by the full assembly. It seems that the assembly is not free not to accept or confirm the committee's decision. But does it also support the further inference that a reference back to the assembly for endorsement, albeit as a matter of formality, is dispensed with? This depends on what inference can reasonably be drawn from the provision in s. 54(1) of the Constitution that 'the power of the national assembly to make laws shall be exercised by bills passed by both the senate and the house of representatives and, except as otherwise provided by subsection (5) of this section, assented to by the president.' In more emphatic terms, s. 54(2) provides that 'a bill may originate in either the senate or the house of representatives and shall not become law unless it has been passed and, except as otherwise provided by this section and section 55 of this Constitution, assented to *in accordance with the provisions of this section* [author's emphasis]'. The meaning of 'passed' is thus fixed by the Constitution; the passing of a bill must be in accordance with s. 54, meaning that it must have the approval, even if only formal, of both the senate and house of representatives. The approval of the two houses is not expressed to be subject to any exception. The exceptions provided for in the section relate only to the assent of the president. It is noteworthy that presidential assent is made subject to the contrary provisions in ss. 54 and 55 enabling such assent to be dispensed with in the circumstances therein specified; the inclusion of s. 55 (which provides for the procedure in the case of a money bill) in this exception is highly significant. If the intention is that the approval of both houses is dispensed with where a conflict between them over a money bill is resolved by the joint finance committee, then an exception would have been made just as in the case of presidential assent. The fact that the approval of the two houses is not expressed as being subject to the provision of s. 55 empowering the joint finance committee to resolve differences between the houses is conclusive that no bill, including a money bill, can become law unless it has been passed by the two houses in separate or joint sittings. But, as earlier stated, where differences over a money bill have been resolved by the joint finance committee, the approval of the two houses, though still legally required, becomes a formality; no discretion is left in the houses to reject the decision of the committee.

This conclusion is supported not only by the clear and necessary implication of the words used by the Constitution but also by the democratic ideal that informs the entire governmental system instituted by the Constitution. When it is realised that the joint finance committee's resolution of a conflict between the houses may follow along a line which represents, not the views of either house, but a compromise position, then it amounts to a negation of democracy to give finality to the decision of the committee without even the appearance of approval by the houses. (At the time of writing there is before the supreme court a series of actions instituted by each of nine state governments on this question as it concerns the Revenue Allocation Act 1981, which received the presidential assent after the joint finance committee had finished with it, but without reference back to the houses of the national assembly.)

A money bill is defined as a bill which appropriates money from the public funds, or which authorises the payment, issue or withdrawal of money from such funds; also as a bill for the imposition of or increase in any tax, duty or fee or a reduction, withdrawal or cancellation thereof (s. 55[1]). A bill for the sharing of money between the federal, state and local governments is a money bill within this definition, since, although it does not appropriate money for specific government services, it authorises payment from public funds to the various governments in the federation.

After a bill is passed by both houses with or without amendments, it is presented to the president for his assent, which must be signified in either the affirmative or the negative within thirty days. In the latter event the bill may still become law without the president's assent if it is again passed by each house by two-thirds majority. The president's veto over a money bill passed initially at a joint sitting can only be overborne at another joint sitting with a two-thirds majority. The wording of s. 54(3) suggests that it is a condition of the validity of presidential assent that the bill must be passed by the two houses.

How a bill is to be passed in a legislative house is not spelt out in the Constitution beyond what is stated above. This is left to be prescribed by each house by means of standing orders. As stated earlier, until standing orders have been so adopted, proceedings are to be governed in the case of the senate by the standing orders of the former senate, and in the case of the other legislative house by the standing orders of the former house of representatives.

The important consideration in the procedure is that it should allow opportunity for discussion, which should be ample under the 1979 Constitution, not only because of the absence of government control of the business of the house but also because of the constitutional requirement of a minimum of 181 days sitting in a year.

The first step in the procedure under the standing orders is to obtain leave of the house for the bill to be presented, though leave is normally dispensed with in the case of government bills. The bill is then published in the official gazette and distributed to members for study. It is next presented to the house by its short title being read aloud by the clerk of the house. This constitutes a first reading. Thereafter the bill is printed and distributed to members. Then comes the second reading during which the general merits and principles of the bill but not its details may be criticised and its second reading may be opposed. If the bill succeeds in being read a second time, it is next committed to a committee of the whole house, unless the house resolves to commit it instead to a standing committee or a select committee to be designated by the president or speaker. In the committee the details but not the principles of the bill are discussed and amendments may be proposed to the clauses, each clause being specifically voted upon and adopted with approved amendments, if any. Thereafter the bill is reported back to the house, and ordered to be read a third time either at once or on a future day. Any member may, on the order for the third reading, move that the bill be recommitted to a committee in order that further amendments might be proposed. On the motion for the third reading opposition to the principles and merits of the bill may be renewed with a view to defeating its third reading, but no further amendments may be moved, except with the permission of the president or speaker, for purely verbal corrections or oversights.

After the third reading a printed copy of the bill signed by the clerk and endorsed by the president or speaker is forwarded to the clerk of the other house for its concurrence; in the other house the bill is subjected to exactly the same process as that just described. If the bill is passed by the other house without amendments the originating house is informed accordingly, but if amendments are proposed the bill together with such amendments is sent back to the originating house. When the amendments have been agreed, four copies of the bill are printed by the government printer and sent to the clerk of the house who, after making sure that they correspond with the original bill, authenticates them with the words: 'This printed impression has been carefully compared by me with the Bill which has passed the Legislative Houses and found by me to be a true and correctly printed copy of the said Bill.' The authenticated copies are then submitted to the president for his assent which is recorded as follows in each of the four copies: 'Assented to this . . . day of . . . .' followed by the president's name. The president's assent transforms the bill into law, though it takes effect only as from the date it is published in the gazette, unless its operation is suspended. The four authenticated copies on which the assent is given become the original copies of the law and are sealed with the public seal of the federation, one copy being deposited with the clerk of the house. A transcript of the law, authenticated under the public seal of the federation and by the signature of the president, is transmitted to the chief justice for enrolment in the supreme court.

It is necessary next to publish the law in the gazette from the impression of one of the original copies kept by the clerk.

(vii) *The committee system*

The committee system is given express recognition in the Constitution. Each house is authorised to appoint committees of its members for such special or general purposes as in its opinion would be better regulated and managed by means of a committee, and to determine their composition, quorum, and terms of reference which may relate to any of the functions of the house (s. 58). Whilst, however, a committee may make recommendations to the house appointing it on a matter presented for legislation or which is required by the Constitution to be determined by resolution, it cannot itself pass a bill into law or pass the required resolution (s. 58[4]). The appointment of joint committees by both houses is also authorised on the same basis (s. 58[3]).

There are two committees whose appointment is made mandatory by the Constitution. One is the joint finance committee composed of equal number of members appointed by each house, with responsibility to try to resolve any disagreement between the two houses over a money bill. The joint finance committee must be convened by the president of the senate within 14 days if a money bill passed by one house is not passed by the other house within two months from the commencement of a financial year (s. 55[2]). The other is the public accounts committee to whom each house must refer for consideration the report of the auditor-general on the public accounts of the federation (s. 79[3]).

In addition to the public accounts committee, the senate has set up twenty-one other standing committees on appropriation and finance, defence, foreign relations, trade and industry, petroleum and energy, labour, internal affairs, federal capital, transport and aviation, housing, urban development and local government, communications, education, science and technology, public works, the judiciary, public service, veterinary and social welfare, banking and currency, water and mineral resources, mines and power, and public petitions.

The committee system is of especial value in enabling a bill or any other matter coming before the house for decision to be examined more closely and in less formal atmosphere by a small group of members with a special interest and experience in its subject-matter.

The importance of the committee system will be considerably enhanced because of a provision under the 1979 Constitution: in order that it should be enabled to make law on any matter within federal legislative competence, to correct any defects in existing laws, or to expose corruption, inefficiency or waste in the execution of laws within federal legislative competence or in the disbursement or administration of funds appropriated by it, each house is empowered to direct an investigation into any matter or thing within federal legislative competence or into the conduct of affairs of any person, authority, ministry or government department charged with responsibility for executing or administering federal laws or disbursing or administering moneys appropriated by the national assembly (s. 82). It seems clear that investigations under these provisions will be conducted through committees.

There is also the procedure whereby, under the standing orders, a bill affecting some particular person or association is referred to a select committee or whereby the house can refer any other bill or matter to a select committee for investigation and report. The sponsors of such a bill have to justify its provisions before the committee by means of oral or written evidence. Those to be prejudicially affected by the bill if passed into law may also be allowed to appear before the committee either in person or by counsel. If, upon the evidence before it, the committee considers the enactment of the bill into law to be inexpedient, it will report accordingly to the house, otherwise it will proceed to consider it clause by clause proposing such amendments as it thinks fit, and thereafter reporting the bill back to the house.

5. *Powers, privileges and immunities of the national assembly and its members*

The national assembly is empowered by the Constitution to make law with respect to its own powers and the privileges and immunities of its members (item 46, 2nd Sch., part I). The existing federal law on the matter, the Legislative Houses (Powers and Privileges) Act,[9] operates therefore as an act of the national assembly by virtue of a stipulation to that effect in the Constitution (s. 274[1]).

The word 'privilege' has a special meaning in this connection. Erskine May defines it as follows:

> Parliamentary privilege is the sum of the peculiar rights enjoyed by each House collectively . . . and by members of each House individually, without which they could not discharge their functions and which exceed those possessed by other bodies or individuals. . . . The distinctive mark of a privilege is its ancillary character . . . they are enjoyed by individual members, because the House cannot perform its functions without unimpeded use of the services of its Members; and by the House for the protection of its Members and the vindication of its own authority and dignity.[10]

Deriving from statute and not from any inherent authority possessed by the national assembly, the powers, privileges and immunities of the assembly are part of the general and public law of the federation or state, of which the courts are bound to take judicial notice.[11]

The privileges of the house and its members are of different types as follows.

(i) *Privilege of freedom of speech, debate and proceedings*

Of the privileges enjoyed by the legislature that of freedom of speech, debates and proceedings is probably the most fundamental to the proper discharge of its functions because

> speech is the element which gives life and power of action to [a deliberative] body, as air does to the natural body. And the free and fearless discussion of every plan and purpose, which is essential to wise legislation, would be impossible if members were subjected to the restraints imposed by law with respect to private reputation.[12]

Thus, each member of a legislative house is protected against civil or criminal proceedings in respect of any speech, report, petition, bill, resolution, motion or question made or introduced by him in the house or its committee.[13] Implicit in freedom of speech is the right which is also expressly conferred by the Constitution, of each House to regulate its internal proceedings,[14] to judge of their lawfulness and to enforce the due observance by the members of its rules of procedure. A member is therefore immune from liability not only for words spoken or written by him but also for acts done during any proceedings in the House, other than criminal acts, since the commission of crimes other than by speech cannot form part of the lawful proceedings of the house.[15] As we have seen, it is the president or the speaker who directs the proceedings of the house, and the effective discharge of his duties requires that he should be specially protected. Accordingly, it is provided that neither he nor any officer of the house 'shall be subject to the jurisdiction of any court in respect of the exercise of any power conferred upon or vested in him by or under this law, the Constitution or Standing Orders.'[16] So also 'no person shall be liable in damages or otherwise for any act done under the authority of the House and within its legal powers.'[17]

To ensure against the possibility of disorderly interruption of debates by strangers, the president or speaker of the house is empowered to order any non-member permitted to be in the house to withdraw and to order his forcible removal if he does not comply.[18]

A publisher of any reports, papers, minutes, votes or proceedings of the house is also, like the member who uttered, introduced or recorded them, immune from liability for them, if in any suit against him on account of the publication he produces before the court a certificate signed by the president or speaker to the effect that the publication was authorised by the house.[19] A person who *bona fide* and without malice publishes an extract from authorised reports of parliamentary proceedings is also protected against liability on that account.[20] Furthermore, evidence of debates or other proceedings of the House or its committee given without its permission by any member or officer thereof is not admissible in any court.[21]

Witnesses appearing before any committee of the house are, like its members and like witnesses before a court of law, immune from liability for any evidence given by them, such evidence being also privileged against disclosure in any judicial proceedings.[22]

(ii) *Immunity from process*

While the house is sitting no civil process can be served or executed within its precincts and a criminal process may be served or executed only if the leave of the house is first obtained.[23] During any sitting of the house, therefore, a member is, within the precincts of the house, protected against arrest in pursuance of a civil or criminal process unless in the case of a criminal process the house waives its privilege.[24] Immunity from civil process attaches also to a member in the Western states not only while he is in attendance at the house but also while proceeding to or returning from it, and in the Eastern states during forty days before and after a session.[25] It is an offence for any stranger to hinder or obstruct a member coming to, going from or being within the chamber or the precincts of the house.[26] If the definition of a stranger includes a police constable, as it apparently does, it means that a member of a legislative house is also immune from criminal process while proceeding to or returning from the house, and that ought indeed to be so.

Where a member is arrested or detained upon the warrant or order of a court or is sentenced to a term of imprisonment, the court shall as soon as practicable inform the president or speaker accordingly.[27]

(iii) *Right of each house to regulate its own constitution*
Under this head comes the privilege of each house to remove a suspended member and to decide whether the seat of any member has become vacant by reason of events occurring after his election or selection. A suspended member who is found within the chamber or precincts of the house may be forcibly removed from them by an officer of the house, and no action for assault can lie on account of such forcible removal. The right of the house to determine whether the seat of a member has become vacant seems, however, to have been doubted. As we have seen, jurisdiction over such questions and over election petitions is vested in the competent high court.[28] It seems however that the jurisdiction of the court to determine whether the seat of a member has become vacant is not exclusive, and that any legislative house in the Eastern and Western states is competent to pronounce upon it. This is because it is provided in both groups of states that 'the House and the members thereof shall hold, enjoy and exercise, in addition, the privileges, immunities and powers as are for the time being held, enjoyed and exercised by the Commons House of Parliament of the United Kingdom of Great Britain and Northern Ireland and by the members thereof, so far as the same are not inconsistent with the Constitution Order or this Law.'[29]

The British house of commons has an undoubted power to determine the legal disqualification of persons returned thereto as members. In the northern states and at the centre no power is either directly or indirectly conferred on the legislative houses for this purpose and it has been argued that they lack it. In *Obi* v. *Waziri*,[30] the speaker of the house of representatives had declared Obi's seat vacant on the ground that he had resigned it, and had ordered him to withdraw and vacate it. Obi denied having resigned his seat, and applied to the high court of Lagos for a declaration that the speaker was not competent to declare his seat vacant and for an injunction restraining the speaker, his servant and agents from illegally preventing or interfering with the plaintiff's right to take his seat in the house. The court declined to decide the question on the ground that the high court of the eastern region from where the plaintiff was elected and not the high court of Lagos was the competent court to decide it.[31] It appears, however, that the speaker is quite competent to do what he had done in this case. He has power to order strangers to be removed from the house. Now, power to remove a stranger implies power to decide whether a person is or has become a stranger. With regard to resignation indeed, it is now provided that a resignation takes effect from the time it is received by the president or speaker. It would be inconvenient, perhaps even absurd, to suggest that on the resignation of a member the speaker should first invite the court to pronounce on the validity of the resignation before ordering the exclusion of the member from the house. Although a resignation may be alleged to be ineffective, it seems that the speaker is entitled in the first instance to act on the basis that it is valid and declare the member's seat vacant, leaving it to the member to establish the invalidity of this resignation in the court.

(iv) *Contempt*

It may be stated generally that any act or omission which obstructs or impedes either House of Parliament in the performance of its functions or which obstructs or impedes any member or officer of such House in the discharge of his duty, or which has a tendency, directly or indirectly, to produce such results may be treated as a contempt even though there is no precedent of the offence.[32]

Every breach of privilege amounts therefore to a contempt, though not every contempt involves a breach of privilege.[33] The Legislative Houses (Powers and Privileges) Law of the Western and Northern states contains a schedule specifying acts and omissions which amount to contempt,[34] namely

1. assaulting, insulting or wilfully obstructing any member coming to or going from a house or on account of his conduct in a house, or endeavouring to compel any member by force, insult or menace to declare himself in favour of or against any proposition or matter depending or expected to be brought before the house or any committee;
2. making any oral or written threats to a member or challenging a member to fight on account of his conduct in the house or committee;

3. tampering with, deterring, threatening, beguiling or in any way unduly influencing any witness in regard to evidence to be given by him before a house;
4. presenting to a house any false, untrue, fabricated or falsified document with intent to deceive that house;
5. wilfully publishing any false or perverted report of any debate or proceedings of a house or wilfully misrepresenting any speech made by a member in a house;
6. wilfully publishing any report of any debate or proceedings of a house conducted behind closed doors or the publication of which has been prohibited by that house;
7. publishing any defamatory statement reflecting on the proceedings or character of a house;
8. publishing any defamatory statement concerning any member in respect of his conduct as a member;
9. the offering to or acceptance by any member or officer of a house of a bribe to influence him in his conduct as such member or officer, or the offering to or acceptance by any member or officer of a House of any fee, compensation, gift or reward for or in respect of the promotion of or opposition to any bill, resolution, matter, rule, or thing, submitted to or intended to be submitted to a House;[35]
10. molesting any officer of a house on his way to or from that house or on account of his conduct as such officer;
11. molesting any witness on account of evidence given by him before a house;
12. destroying any document which a person has been ordered to produce before a house;
13. printing a copy of any law or of any report, paper, minute, notes or proceedings of a house, which purports to have been printed by the government printer or by or under the authority of a house but which in fact has not been so printed, or tendering in evidence any such copy as aforesaid;
14. wilfully disobeying any order or resolution of a house or of the president or speaker duly made under the law;
15. wilfully disobeying any order for attendance or for production of papers, books, records, or documents made by a house or any committee duly authorised in that behalf;
16. refusing to be examined before or to answer any lawful and relevant question put by a house or any committee;
17. assaulting, insulting or wilfully interfering with any member in the chamber or precincts of a house, or an officer in the execution of his duty;
18. creating or joining in any disturbance in the chamber or precincts of a house while that house is sitting, knowing or having reasonable

grounds to believe that proceedings of that house will be interrupted thereby;
19. disrespectful conduct in the precincts of a house;
20. publishing any proceedings of a committee of a house before they are reported to that house;
21. abetting any of the foregoing acts or omissions.

(v) *Punishment of contempts*

Every contempt of a legislative house constitutes an offence, punishable by a £200 fine or two years' imprisonment[36] and since parliamentary privilege is part of the general law, such offences are cognisable in the courts, the high court in the Western and Northern states, and magistrates' courts and high court in the Eastern states. Only the attorney-general can start proceedings for contempt of a legislative house, and then only upon information given by the president or speaker (in the Eastern states) or upon the request of the house in the Western and Northern states.[37]

Not being a court like the parliament of the United Kingdom, the power of a legislative house in Nigeria to punish for contempts of itself is limited both as to the contempts it can punish and as regards the punishment it can impose. In the Western and Northern states[38] only the contempts listed 14–21 above are punishable by a house, provided that in a case referred to him, the attorney-general has reported that there is sufficient evidence to warrant action being taken by the house, and the starting of proceedings in the high court completely excludes the house's jurisdiction. The house can reprimand an offender at the bar or order him to be removed from its precincts; in addition or in the alternative an offender who is not a member may be forbidden from entering the house or its precincts for six months, and a member-offender may be suspended for any period not extending beyond the last day of the meeting next following that in which the order of suspension is passed, or of the session in which the order is passed, whichever shall first occur.[39] A person ordered to come before the House for reprimand or whose removal has been ordered or whose entry has been prohibited may be arrested without warrant by the serjeant-at-arms on the order of the speaker or president at any place within the precincts of the house, using such reasonable force as may be necessary. So also a person creating or joining in any disturbance in the house or its precincts while it is sitting may be arrested without warrant on the order of the president or speaker, and may be kept in the custody of an officer of the house for the duration of the sitting pending the determination by the house of what sanction is to be applied.[40]

In the Eastern states,[41] all contempts are punishable by a house by suspension (which applies only to members) and reprimand. The period of suspension is not to exceed five days for a first offence and twelve days for a second offence while for further offences the suspension lasts until the house resolves to terminate it. But suspension or reprimand by the house is additional to and not in substitution for the fine or imprisonment that may, after trial and conviction, be awarded by the courts. Only contempts committed by a member can be punished by a federal house by reprimand or suspension for a period limited as in the Western and Northern states.[42]

REFERENCES

1. *Colegrove* v. *Green*, 328 U.S. 549.
2. *Baker* v. *Carr*, 369 U.S. 186.
3. *Gray* v. *Saunders* (1963), 373 U.S. 368; *Wesberry* v. *Sanders*, 376 U.S. 1; *Reynolds* v. *Sims* (1964), 377 U.S. 533; *Wmca Inc.* v. *Lomenzo* (1964), 377 U.S. 633; *Lucas* v. *Forty-Fourth Gen. Assembly* (1964), 377 U.S. 703; *Maryland Committee for Fair Representation* v. *Tawes* (1964), 377 U.S. 656; *Davis* v. *Man* (1964), 377 U.S. 678; *Roman* v. *Sincock* (1964), 377 U.S. 695; *Hill* v. *Davis* (1964), 378 U.S. 565; *Meyers* v. *Thigpen* (1953), 376 U.S. 902; *Pinney* v. *Butterworth* (1964), 378 U.S. 569; *William* v. *Moss* (1964), 378 U.S. 558; *Germano* v. *Kerner* (1964), 375 U.S 991; *Hearne* v. *Smylie* (1964), 378 U.S. 563; *Marshall* v. *Hare* (1964), 378 U.S. 561.
4. *Wesberry* v. *Sanders*, 376 U.S. 1, 7.
5. Oaths Act, 1963, s. 4.
6. Speaker, Kenya House of Reps., Debates Vol. 1, 7 June 1963, col. 2.
7. *United States* v. *Ballin* (1892), 144 U.S. 1.
8. *Missouri Pac. Ry. Co.* v. *Kansas* (1919), 248 U.S. 276.
9. Cap. 102, Laws of the Fedn., 1958 edn. The existing state laws on the matter are the Legislative Houses (Powers and Privileges) Law, cap 63, Laws of Western Nigeria, 1959; Legislative Houses Law, 1959 Eastern Region; Legislative Houses (Powers and Privileges) Law, 1962 Northern Region.
10. *The Law, Privileges, Proceedings and Usage of Parliament* (17th edn. 1964), 42–3.
11. See W.R. Law, s. 10 and E.R. Law, s. 20. Cf. position in England where there has been an age-old controversy whether the *lex et consuetudo Parliamenti*, of which parliamentary privilege is comprised, is a 'particular' law or part of the general law of the land: May, op. cit., 150–74.
12. Quoted from Schwartz, *American Constitutional Law* (1955), 57.
13. Legislative Houses (Powers and Privileges) Act (Federation), s. 3, and State Laws.
14. s. 56.
15. See May, op. cit., 64–6.
16. Legislative Houses (Powers and Privileges) Act (Federation), s. 30; see also provision in State Laws.
17. W.R. Law, s. 7, and E.R. Law, s. 15.

18. Federal Act, ss. 14 and 18, and corresponding provisions in the State Laws.
19. ibid., s. 26; also State Laws.
20. ibid., s. 27; also State Laws.
21. ibid., s. 23; also State Laws.
22. ibid., s. 8; also State Laws.
23. ibid., s. 31; also State Laws. The Federal Act prohibits only the serving or execution of civil process but see s. 16, which makes it an offence for a stranger to hinder or obstruct a member being within the chamber or the precincts of the house.
24. See particularly E.R. Law, s. 18.
25. W.R. Law, s. 5; E.R. Law, s. 19.
26. Federal Act s. 16; also state Laws.
27. ibid., s. 29; also State Laws.
28. Cf. position in the United States where election petitions are removed from the courts and vested in the congress. An American commentator has remarked about the American system that it 'causes injustice to individuals, sometimes defeats the will of the people, and tends to multiply contests. It also imposes a heavy burden upon the committee concerned, takes the time of the House, and costs about 4,000 dollars per contest.' Galloway, *Congress at the Crossroads* (1926), 23, quoted from Schwartz, *American Constitutional Law*, 55. The system is said to defeat the will of the people because 'all too often contests over seats in the Congress have been awarded to the candidates of the dominant party.' Schwartz, loc. cit.
29. E.R. Law, s. 21, as amended by the Revised Edition (Laws of E. Nigeria) (Amendment) Law 1964; W.R. Law, s. 8.
30. (1961) 1 All N.L.R. 371.
31. The plaintiff has argued that his case did not involve a question as to whether his seat had become vacant, but as to the competence of the speaker to declare it so. The court held that the latter question is inseparable from the former.
32. May, op. cit., 109.
33. May, op. cit., 43; Hood Phillips, *Constitutional Law* (1952), 141. A libel on the house is a contempt, though no privilege is thereby breached.
34. In the Eastern states and at the centre, acts and omissions amounting to contempts are largely the same though they are differently defined.
35. As the British house of commons resolved in 1947, 'it is inconsistent with the dignity of the House, with the duty of a member to his constituents, and with the maintenance of the privilege of freedom of speech, for any member of this House to enter into any contractual agreement with an outside body, controlling or limiting the member's complete independence and freedom of action in Parliament or stipulating that he shall act in any way as the representative of such outside body in regard to any matters to be transacted in Parliament; the duty of a member being to his constituents and to the country as a whole, rather than to any particular section thereof.' Quoted from May, op. cit., 52. The passing of this resolution was connected with the case of a member who had a contractual relationship with a trade union from which he received financial payments.

36. In the Eastern states contempts committed by members are punished less severely; apart from two cases carrying up to £200 fine or two years' imprisonment, the punishment is £25 fine.

37. The procedure in the Western and Northern states is as follows. Upon the complaint of a member to the president or speaker that an offence has been committed, the president or speaker refers the matter for investigation to the attorney-general, who has to report to the president or speaker whether there is sufficient evidence to warrant application being made to the court. After considering the attorney-general's report the house may then by order request him to commence proceedings.

38. W.R. Law, ss. 29–32; N.R. Law, ss. 26–30.

39. A suspended member gets no salary for the period during which he is suspended; this is so throughout the country, see Federal Act, s. 21(3), and see State Laws.

40. W.R. Law, s. 23, and N.R. Law, s. 20(1); Police officers on duty in the house are required to assist in the apprehension and detention of disorderly persons.

41. ss. 38–42.

42. Federal Act, s. 21(2). As in the Western and Northern states, an officer of the house in the Eastern states and at the centre is empowered without warrant to arrest any person engaged in disorderly behaviour in the house. See Federal Act, s. 17, and E.R. Law, s. 35.

13
FUNCTIONS OF THE NATIONAL ASSEMBLY

1. *Classification of functions*

The principal function of the national assembly, and one from which it takes its distinctive character and place in the governmental structure, is that of law-making. Indeed, the appellation, 'legislature' is apt to create the impression that law-making is its only function. But the impression is misleading. The national assembly has another function which, although it involves no exercise of power as such, is of a much more general and continuous nature, i.e. the critical and scrutinising function. Moreover, not every exercise of power by the assembly involves law-making. The assembly has vested in it by the Constitution various other powers exercisable, not by legislation, but by resolution or simply by approval without a substantive motion. The functions of the national assembly are thus of three types:

(a) those involving the exercise, by resolution or by simple approval, of constitutional power;
(b) legislation;
(c) the general function of criticism and scrutiny of the administration of government.

It is certainly not for nothing that the Constitution draws a distinction between resolution or simple approval and legislation, as methods for the exercise of constitutional power, prescribing legislation as the normal method by which the national assembly can make its will binding on the community as a whole. Resolution or simple approval without a substantive motion is unlike legislation both in effect and in the process for making it. As a method for exercising constitutional power, it is simply a decision on an individual case; it lacks a generality of application to persons and things, which is the hallmark of a law. Although a resolution or simple approval has, like a contract, a binding legal effect of which the courts and the community must take cognisance, yet its effect is confined, on the whole, to the individual case determined by it. It is a decision that legislates nothing and therefore creates no general law. Legislation is often an expression of policy, embodying some important societal value, whereas a resolution or simple approval is generally conditional upon personal, sectional or partisan sentiment.

For this reason a resolution usually involves no such elaborate process as characterises legislation — careful study based on facts, consultation with various interests, formal presentation in the form of a bill, prolonged debate on the merits and demerits of the matter and clause-by-clause examination in committee. All it needs is a substantive motion by a member, seconded by another. Indeed a motion involving no exercise of constitutional power need have no factual basis at all apart from the 'strong feeling that something needs to be done about a given issue. And in taking a position on a motion, facts are far less important than eloquence. Bills, on the other hand, quite often mean a lot of drudgery, of poring over statistics, of hard work and patience.'[1] Even the formality of a substantive motion proposed by one member and seconded by another is dispensed with where all that is required is just the approval of the assembly or one of its houses. And while legislation requires the president's assent, a resolution does not.

2. *Matters that may be determined by resolution or simple approval*

The following are the matters that may be decided or sanctioned by the national assembly by resolution: presidential declaration of war with another country (approving resolution at a joint session required: s. 5[3][*a*]), proposal for the creation of a new state (two-thirds majority: s. 8[1][*d*]), declaration of economic activities to be managed and operated exclusively by the federal government (s. 16[4]), removal of the president of the senate or speaker of the house of representatives (resolution of the appropriate house: s. 46[2][*c*]), extension of the life of the national assembly or of the president's tenure of office beyond four years because of a war involving the territory of Nigeria and which in the president's opinion makes it impossible to hold elections (ss. 60[2] and 127[3]), directing investigation in aid of legislation or for the purpose of exposing corruption, inefficiency or waste in the execution or administration of its laws or in the disbursement or administration of funds appropriated by the assembly (s. 82), ordering investigation into allegation of gross misconduct by the president or vice-president (two-thirds of all members: s. 132[3] and [4]), acceptance or rejection of a report by an investigating committee finding the president or vice-president guilty of gross misconduct (two-thirds of all members: s. 132[9]), prescribing the number of special advisers and their remuneration and allowances (s. 139[2]), approval of a proclamation of a state of emergency made by the president (two-thirds of all members: s. 265[6]), and extension of such a proclamation beyond six months (two-thirds of all members).

It is provided that where in the legislative lists scheduled to the Constitution (Sch. 2) 'the National Assembly is required to designate any matter or thing or to make any declaration, it may do so either by an Act of the National Assembly or by a resolution passed by both Houses of the National Assembly.' The assembly's power in this respect relates to the declaration of any roads as federal trunk roads; designation of any internal waterway (other than the River Niger and its affluents) as an international or inter-state waterway; declaration of ports as federal ports; designation of occupations as professional occupations and of parks as national parks; declaration of ancient and historical monuments and records and archeological sites and remains as of national significance or importance; designation of any agricultural produce as an export commodity; designation of goods or commodities as essential goods or commodities for purposes of price control; declaration of sources of water as sources affecting more than one state; designation of antiquities and monuments as national antiquities or monuments; and designation of any professional education as within federal legislative competence.

The matters that require the sanction or approval of the national assembly or of the senate alone but without the formality of a resolution following on a substantive motion are the deployment of any members of the armed forces on combat duty outside Nigeria (senate alone: s. 5[3][b]); proposal for the (state) boundary adjustment (s. 8[2][b]), alteration of senatorial districts or federal constituencies by the electoral commission following upon a change in the number of states in the federation or upon a census pursuant to an act of the national assembly (s. 68), appointment of a vice-president in the event of vacancy (s. 134[3]), revocation of a proclamation of emergency (s. 265[6][d]), appointment and removal of specified state functionaries.

It will have been noticed that the functions enumerated above are mostly of an executive nature. The intention is, by involving the national assembly in the executive field, to enable it to exercise a check and moderation on the actions of the executive. They enable the assembly, for example, to ensure that the appointment and removal of important public functionaries are not abused for purely personal, sectional or partisan motives, that the country should not needlessly be dragged to war on the whims of a reckless president, that the deprivations and repressions of a state of emergency are not inflicted on the people by the president unless justified by the exigencies actually existing in the country, that the country's affairs and its resources are not mismanaged through corruption, inefficiency or waste, and that in the last resort the nation is rid of a president who flagrantly violates the Constitution or grossly misconducts himself in other ways.

3. Legislation

(i) *Extent of the legislative power of the national assembly*

The national assembly is the repository of the entire legislative power of the federal government, which is defined to extend to sixty-five matters listed in part I of the second schedule to the Constitution, to the twelve matters listed in part II of the said schedule to the extent therein stated, and to the matters over which it is given legislative competence in the body of the Constitution (s. 4). The nature of these matters and their importance in the government of the country as a whole have been considered in chapter 4. While the state assemblies are excluded from the sixty-five matters listed in part I of the second schedule, the rest of the matters mentioned above are either exclusive to the national assembly or concurrent between it and the state assemblies depending on the terms in which power over them is granted by the Constitution. Provided the national assembly has acted within the limits of its powers under the Constitution, its laws prevail over those of the state assemblies in the event of conflict (s. 4[5]).

The lack of consistency in the language of the provisions in the body of the Constitution granting powers to the national assembly is apt to be a source of confusion as to whether legislation is required for the exercise of some of the powers. Where the language used explicitly empowers the assembly to make law on the matter in question or to provide for it by law, no difficulty arises. Confusion may however arise because, whereas for certain matters it is stipulated that they are to be 'prescribed by an act of the national assembly', (ss. 47, 71[1], 74[4] and 194[2][*a*]), the provision in certain other cases stipulates only that they are to be 'prescribed by the national assembly' without making it explicit that legislation is required. Clearly the provision that certain designated public officers shall be paid 'such salaries and allowances as may be prescribed by the national assembly' (s. 78[1]) or that 'the federation may make grants to a state to supplement the revenue of that state in such sum . . . as may be prescribed by the national assembly' (s. 151) may reasonably be read as involving nothing more than merely determining, by resolution or by a simple vote without a substantive motion, the amounts to be paid or granted. One has to read the provision together with the definition in s. 277(1) to know that the assembly can prescribe something only by means of legislation. Admittedly the context of some of the provisions may also make it clear that legislation is required, e.g. the provision empowering the national assembly to prescribe the procedure of a committee investigating allegation of misconduct against the president (s. 132[7]); terms and manner for the allocation of revenue (s. 149), terms and conditions of which declarations of assets by public officers may be inspected (5th Sch., para. 15[1][b]), or how minerals, mineral oils and natural gas may be managed (s. 40[3]).

(ii) *Enactment of legislative proposals into law or their rejection*
It has been shown in chapter 10 that, although the initiation of legislative proposals is a part of the legislative power and comes therefore within the right of the national assembly and its members, it is essentially a function for the executive as the organ primarily responsible for government and for policy. But while the legislative initiative is an important aspect of the law-making process, it does not really entail the exercise of power. Legislative power is exercised by the passing into law, with or without amendments, of a legislative proposal, however it may have originated, or by its rejection.

The power to pass or reject a legislative proposal is not so important for its own sake. Its importance lies more in the opportunity it affords to the assembly for a thorough scrutiny and criticism of the proposals in question, especially when they originate from the government. The fact that a legislative proposal is passed, with or without amendments, should not obscure the impact on the government of the debate that preceded the final vote. It is the critical quality and effectiveness of such debate that determines the character of a legislative body. Its independence depends not only on the separation of powers in the Constitution but perhaps even more on the effect of its critical function in producing in the government an attitude of responsibility and restraint and a feeling that the reaction of the assembly has to be reckoned with in the framing of legislative proposals.

A legislature able to offer strong and effective opposition to the executive is better secured under a constitution that separates the legislative and executive agencies and functions. Separation implies a certain degree of opposition between the two organs, each anxious to assert and guard its independence. The entire legislative assembly is thus in a sense in opposition to the executive. In asserting and guarding their independence, the legislative houses are helped by their freedom from the dominating presence of ministers. More important is the possibility, inherent in the separation, that the legislative and executive agencies may be under the control of different parties. A legislative majority is not a necessary condition of the presidential system as it is of the parliamentary. Indeed a majority in the legislature controlled by a party in opposition to the president is by no means an infrequent phenomenon under the former system.

An opposition majority in the legislature, when it does occur, affords the greatest opportunity for the effective control of the government by the legislature. It creates a situation which is almost the reverse of that under the parliamentary system. The business of the legislature is controlled by the leaders of the opposition party almost as completely and effectively as it is controlled by the government under the parliamentary system. Its members dominate the speeches and use them to subject government proposals to severe scrutiny and criticism. Every government measure, including indeed its financial proposals, faces the risk of the sanction of rejection. It is as if the government of the country is transferred from the executive branch to the legislature. No government, faced with an opposition majority in the legislature, can afford to bring before it arbitrary or otherwise objectionable proposals, knowing that they would almost certainly be thrown out, to its own discredit.

Herein lies the cardinal merit of the system from the point of view of the control of the government by the legislature. But that merit is also its greatest disadvantage. An opposition majority in the legislature tends to lose sight of the fact that its main function is to scrutinise and criticise, and that rejection of government measures is not to be done lightly or for its own sake. Rejection is an ultimate sanction to be applied only when a government measure is fundamentally objectionable as being, for example, unreasonable, arbitrary, tyrannical or otherwise destructive of constitutional safeguards.

Independence of the legislature does not mean freedom, at the whim and pleasure of its members, to reject government measures. The government of a modern state cannot be run effectively in the assembly; even if all the expert advice and information available to the cabinet were to be laid before the assembly, its numbers alone make it singularly unsuited to undertake the determination and formulation of policy. It is a function that requires the mental concentration of an individual or a small committee of men whose members can analyse and co-ordinate the various aspects of the policy in an atmosphere of detachment, free from the emotion and heat of parliamentary debate. It would be difficult to have effective government if legislators were to be free always to substitute their own policy for that of the government, and would lead to chaos if every government measure which might have occupied the time, mind and skill of ministers and their expert advisers for many months were to be rejected capriciously by the legislators who in all probability have had only a few days to reflect upon its purport, if they are in any position at all to appreciate it.

As experience in the United States bears out, the tendency of an opposition majority in the legislature to show off its power by rejecting government measure at will and indiscriminately has often resulted in relations between the two organs being marked by antipathy and antagonism instead of by regular healthy co-operation which is what governmental effectiveness demands. What co-operation there is, is of a somewhat 'intermittent and haphazard' type, rather than 'regular and predictable'.[2] Now and again, the antagonism precipitates a stalemate which paralyses the government, leaving the nation without a clear, co-ordinated leadership. Even without such a breakdown, the policy that results from such a system of executive-legislature antagonism is seldom an integral whole, but rather a patchwork, with vital pieces cut off by a congress jealously asserting its power, regardless of the true needs of the nation.

This danger is likely to be greater in Nigeria because of the prevalent Nigerian attitude towards politics as a kind of feud between opposing groups. In the developed democracies, rivalry and antagonism between the parties are moderated by a better appreciation of the responsibilities of power. When, however, political rivalry goes beyond ordinary competition and assumes the character of a feud, then an attitude to power is engendered which demands that no quarter of any sort should be given to the enemy. An opposition party may then want to use its majority in the legislature to throw out every government measure in the hope of forcing the president to resign. Already this was happening in Kaduna state, where the state governor had been at loggerheads with the state house of assembly which was controlled by a party different from, and opposed to, his own; both sides adopted an attitude of confrontation and non-co-operation, to the extent that the assembly rejected every measure submitted to it by the governor, including every successive list of nominees for ministerial appointment. In the result the governor had had to administer the executive government of the state without the assistance and advice of commissioners required by the Constitution while the state as a whole had been thrown into a situation of complete impasse. (The constitutional implication of the situation in Kaduna State is discussed in chapters 7 and 8 above.)

Yet in spite of this danger, an opposition majority in the national assembly (or in one at least of its houses) as well as in the state assemblies is healthy for Nigeria in its new experiment in constitutional government. It would provide a most effective safeguard against the tendency of presidential rule towards arbitrariness and autocracy. The danger of a capricious use of its power by an opposition majority in the legislature is admittedly a serious one, but the opposition of power by power may produce a *modus vivendi* that would enable the government of the country to be carried on effectively without the arbitrariness and autocracy of presidential power. However, legislators need to be educated to appreciate that healthy co-operation between the two organs of government is needed, and that the legislative power of the state entrusted to them is not to be used for capricious political motives.

It is not intended to suggest by what has been said above that the critical function of the legislature is the responsibility of opposition legislators alone, and that government members are completely absolved from it. They, as much as the opposition legislators, owe it to their electors to be alert to any government measures that encroach on the liberties of the people. Their ability to criticise and attack the government is of course greatly handicapped under the parliamentary system because of the dependence of executive tenure on the confidence of the legislature and the obligation of the government to resign when that confidence is lost. In this respect again, the separation of the executive and legislative agencies under the scheme of the 1979 Constitution has great merit. The president is not constitutionally obliged to resign because his legislative or other measures are rejected by the legislature. His supporters in the legislature should therefore feel less inhibited in criticising and attacking his measures. No doubt, there is need to preserve the unity and credibility of the party among its supporters outside the legislature, but self-criticism is a mark of maturity; it should not be regarded as necessarily reflecting discredit on the government.

Here again the African's attitude towards politics as a feud may not allow the advantage of the new system to be fully realised. Its effect may be, as in the past, to induce the president's party to require its members in the legislature not to deviate, by word or vote, from the party line, and to do nothing that might open even the smallest hole in the party defences. This is an attitude that needs to be abandoned or at least considerably relaxed. A government party legislator should be free within limits to speak against a measure and to abstain from voting or even to vote against where his conscience is sufficiently offended. Government members in the legislature should appreciate that they too, together with the opposition members, have a responsibility to scrutinise and criticise government measures.

(iii) *Role and importance of legislation in modern government*

Legislation occupies a place of paramount importance in modern government as providing the necessary authority for governmental action. Almost every activity of government requires the authority of some enabling law. Whether it is the provision of social welfare, economic and industrial development, social reform, land tenure, maintenance of law and order, etc., government can hardly act without a law to back up its action.

The necessity for legislation as a basis for governmental action stems partly from the principle that, under our inherited conception of law and government, the executive has no inherent power over the citizen. Even on the view, which is strenuously disputed, that the executive can sometimes act on its own inherent authority without specific authorisation by some law,[3] it is universally accepted that the executive cannot so act if the act would prejudicially affect the right or interest of an individual.[4]

What this means is that, since most executive acts operate on individuals in one way or another, an executive which does not control the law-making process has very limited capacity for arbitrariness or despotism. Without such control, he cannot get through the necessary law to back up the assumption and exercise of arbitrary or dictatorial power, while any existing law conferring such power can be amended by the legislature on its own initiative. A legislature the majority of whose members are independent of executive control is therefore the greatest bulwark against tyranny on the part of the executive. This is the cardinal merit which the system of separated powers has over the parliamentary one. For whereas the latter necessarily implies a legislature dominated and controlled by the executive, the former makes it possible for the majority in the legislature to be controlled by a party different from, and opposed to, the president. It is only in such a situation that there may be said to exist true and complete independence in the legislature, such as would provide a truly effective bulwark against the tendency of executive power towards arbitrariness and despotism.

Even if the executive can undertake certain activities without specific legal authorisation, it will need money to do so. The raising of money by taxation and, with certain exceptions, its spending for the services of the government require legislative authorisation. All revenues or other moneys raised or received by the government, whether by taxation, loan or otherwise, must be paid into and form one consolidated revenue fund, unless payment into some other fund is authorised by the Constitution or by an act of the national assembly (s. 74[1]).

No withdrawals can be made from the consolidated revenue fund without legislative authorisation, except for expenditure charged on it directly by the Constitution. The legislative authorisation for expenditure cannot, as in the past, take the form of an act permanently charging particular items of expenditure on the consolidated revenue fund or some other fund; it can only be given year by year by an annual appropriation act, supplemented in the event of deficiency by a supplementary appropriation act (s. 74[2]).

The appropriation (or supplementary appropriation) act does two things: it both grants supply and appropriates it to specific services. An appropriation bill does not however provide the legislature with any insight into the services for which supply is sought to be appropriated, the reason being that the bill merely indicates the heads of expenditure without describing or explaining them in detail. This does not mean that the legislature just grants supply in ignorance of the nature of the requirements of the services. The details of these requirements are supplied by the estimates of revenue and expenditure, which the president is required to have prepared and laid before the legislature separately from the appropriation bill. The annual appropriation meeting is an opportunity for the legislature to discuss the financial and economic state of the country and the government's financial policy. If, in respect of any financial year, it is found that the amount appropriated by the appropriation act for any purpose is insufficient or that a need has arisen for expenditure for a purpose for which no amount has been appropriated by the act, a supplementary estimate showing the sums required shall be laid before the legislature and the heads of any such expenditure shall be included in a supplementary appropriation bill.

Even with the authority of the appropriation act, the issue of money from the consolidated revenue fund cannot be effected except in a manner prescribed by legislation enacted by the national assembly (s. 74[4]). Under the procedure prescribed by the existing legislation — which is deemed by the Constitution to be an act of the national assembly (s. 274) — no money can be issued from the consolidated revenue fund except with the warrant of the minister to whom responsibility for the management, supervision, control and direction of the expenditure and finances of the government is entrusted.[5] The minister is required to exercise his supervision in such manner as to ensure that full account is made to the legislature.[6]

The national assembly has a responsibility under the Constitution, not only to authorise appropriation and the withdrawal of money, but also to ensure that money so appropriated and withdrawn is properly spent on purposes for which it is appropriated. It exercises this responsibility through a public accounts committee. The accounts of all the various services must be audited by the auditor-general, and his report on them has to be laid before each house; the accounts together with the auditor-general's report have then to be examined and reported upon by the public accounts committee (s. 79[3]).

The present machinery for post-appropriation control by the national assembly has been rightly criticised as not being structured for maximum effectiveness, because the job of ensuring that funds are used for the purposes for which they are appropriated and as efficiently as possible requires that performance should be monitored as it proceeds, by a body outside the executive branch, made up of a mixture of accountants, high-calibre administrators, economists, lawyers, political analysts *et al.*[7] The aim should be to detect irregularities before they are carried too far. But audit as at present performed by the auditor-general's office is only a post-mortem inquest by figure-oriented accountants employed within the executive branch and so accountable to the president rather than to the national assembly. In the United States there is effective performance audit because it is performed by a body such as is described above, which is an agency of congress. It is suggested that the national assembly should establish a similar body.[8]

The rigid legislative control of expenditure of public money is relaxed only in three cases. The first relates to certain expenditure which, as already noted, is charged on the consolidated revenue fund directly by the Constitution and so requires no separate legislative authorisation. These are the salaries and allowances of specified constitutional office-holders, the pension or gratuity of the president and vice-president, the recurrent expenditure of judicial offices (other than the salaries and allowances of judges) and the share of federally-collected revenue due to a state under the prevailing system of revenue allocation (ss. 78 and 154).

Secondly, if the appropriation bill in respect of any financial year has not been passed into law by the beginning of the financial year, then to enable the service of the government to be carried on for a period not exceeding six months or until the coming into operation of the appropriation act, whichever is the earlier, the president may authorise the withdrawal from the consolidated revenue fund of money not exceeding the proportionate amount authorised by the appropriation act for the corresponding period in the immediately preceding financial year. No doubt, this is a serious aberration from the principle that all public expenditure must have legislative authorisation, yet it seems desirable that government should be allowed to go on for some time while an effort is made to resolve any differences that may arise between the executive and legislature concerning the management of public finance and the conduct of government generally. Furthermore, the fact that the amount authorised by the legislature in the previous year is made the measure of the amount that may be authorised by the president serves as a limitation upon the power.

The third relaxation results from the power given to the legislature to establish for specific purposes other public funds than the consolidated revenue fund, and to authorise payment into them of any part of public revenue raised or received by the federal government (s. 74[1]). One such fund specifically referred to in the Constitution is the contingencies fund. The legislature may authorise the president to make advances from the contingencies fund if he is satisfied that there has arisen an urgent and unforeseen need for expenditure for which no provision exists in the appropriation act and which cannot be postponed or cannot without serious injury to the public interest be postponed until a supplementary appropriation act providing for it can be passed into law, but a supplementary estimate and a supplementary appropriation bill must be presented as soon as possible to enable the amount so advanced to be replaced (s. 77). The actual withdrawal of money from the contingencies fund must, as in the case of withdrawal from the consolidated revenue fund, be authorised by the warrant of the responsible minister. In addition to the contingencies fund, ten other funds have been established by legislation,[9] the most important being the development fund. The development fund is made up of (*a*) loans raised by the government for development purposes; (*b*) development grants made to the government by other governments or bodies; and (*c*) sums from time to time authorised by law.

The difference between these funds and the consolidated revenue fund is that, while withdrawal from them requires statutory authorisation, the authorisation is not required by the Constitution to be given annually in the form of an annual appropriation or supplementary appropriation act (s. 74[3]). A standing authorisation suffices. A statute of 1958 which established these funds authorises withdrawal from them on the warrant of the minister of finance. The development fund is, however, treated differently. Estimates of receipts and expenditure in respect of it for each financial year must be laid before the house of representatives, and the proposals for all expenditure require the approval by resolution of the house. Expenditure for any item in excess of that approved or for an item which has not been approved at all cannot be incurred without the like approval, but to ensure that an existing project is not brought to a standstill for lack of funds, the president in council may, without the prior approval of the house, authorise, by warrant under the hand of the minister of finance, the issue from the fund of such money as may be necessary to carry on the project, provided that such issue does not result in the fund being exhausted and provided further that the approval of the house of representatives is obtained at its next meeting. Furthermore the warrant of the minister of finance for the withdrawal of money from the development fund cannot be issued without the authority of a resolution by the house of representatives.

4. *The general critical and scrutinising function*

As will have been observed, much of the critical and scrutinising function of the national assembly is exercised during the debate on matters presented to it for determination by legislation, resolution or by a simple approving vote. The function is of course not limited to these occasions. Any matter within the competence of the national assembly under the Constitution can be the subject of criticism and scrutiny although no bill or motion is presented on it for formal action. A member is free within the rules of debate prescribed by the standing orders to raise any such matter in debate at any time. The question, however, is whether the critical and scrutinising function extends beyond this. Can the national assembly criticise or scrutinise the exercise of functions within the exclusive competence of the executive or the judiciary, notwithstanding that it cannot competently pass a law on such matters? And can it debate matters within the exclusive competence of the states? In other words, do the separation of powers, the independence of the other organs of government and the federal system limit the debating competence of the assembly? The president of the senate, Senator Wayas, admonished members on one occasion not to mention the executive in their speeches, but gave up the point when objection was taken to it. Definite rulings on the matter have, however, been made in two Commonwealth African countries operating a modified form of the presidential system. The speaker of Kenya's national assembly ruled in 1967 that the assembly could not debate the conduct of the president except on a substantive motion of no confidence.[10] The ground for the ruling was not stated. It could not have been based on the ground that the express provision in the Constitution for a vote of no confidence in the government altogether excludes debate on the president's conduct except on the occasion of such a motion. The ground for the ruling would appear instead to be that it is unfair to discuss the president when he is not present in the assembly to defend himself. This is hardly justification for a ban on debate on the president's conduct. If it were, it should also bar debate on the conduct of every public functionary who is not present in the assembly.

A similar ruling was made by the speaker of the Zambian national assembly in 1969. In October that year, during a debate on an amendment to the constitution the speaker repeatedly reminded opposition members of the assembly of his ruling that the president should not be made the subject of debate. For, he said, 'a head of state is a head of state for everybody',[11] and is 'the nucleus of the pride of the nation, whether he be UNIP, Congress or otherwise'.[12] 'If', he continued, 'hon. members wish to attack each other politically, there are many official members here, ministers, to attack, rather than attacking a person who is not connected with the debates of this house.'[13] The particular amendment under debate was that which sought to abolish the Barotseland agreement. In opposing the abolition, an opposition member recalled President Kaunda's assurances to the chief and people of Barotseland on the eve of independence that the agreement would be respected, and how the president had turned round to denounce the agreement at a UNIP meeting in 1969. This drew from the speaker a warning that the member was violating his ruling not to involve the president's name in debate; upon which the member protested that the political activities of a president who is also the secretary-general of the ruling party ought not to be above discussion in parliament. The speaker then rose in anger and adjourned the house. The member was arraigned before the standing orders committee and found guilty of a most serious offence of a nature rendering him unfit to be a member of the house, and for which therefore a severe punishment was demanded. As, however, the offending member had only recently been discharged from hospital after an operation, the committee felt disposed to be lenient with him, and accordingly imposed only the requirement of an apology. Thus condemned, the member was ordered the following morning to stand at the bar of the house and 'register my sincere apology and say that I never intended to be disrespectful to his excellency the president. My loyalty to his excellency the president and government is unquestionable.'[14] In discharging the member after this apology, the speaker further warned that 'a time might arise in the future when I will not inconvenience the whole house by adjourning it, but I will be forced to mete out immediately some punishment to an hon. member who does not heed the ruling of the chair, like naming him.'[15] Was all this really warranted by what the member had said? The assurances given by the president in 1964 to the chief and people of Barotseland were most relevant to the debate on the proposal to abrogate the agreement, and it was legitimate, for the proper discharge of his duty to his constituents (the Barotse), that the member should criticise the president for denouncing what he had previously praised publicly and undertaken to respect.

It is submitted that the debating and critical function of the national assembly is not limited to the matters in respect of which it is given power by the Constitution to act either by legislation, resolution or otherwise. Freedom of speech, including freedom to comment on public affairs, is guaranteed to every person by the Constitution. Members of the national assembly should not cease to have the full benefit of this freedom when they are inside the chambers of their respective houses. If an ordinary citizen can criticise the conduct of any aspect of public affairs notwithstanding his lack of power to make laws, the limitations on the powers of the national assembly should not limit the right of the members to use its forum to discuss and criticise any matters relating to the administration of government both at the centre and in the states.

REFERENCES

1. Stanley Macebuh, *Daily Times*, 29 November 1979, 5.
2. Q.L. Quade, 'Presidential Leadership: Paralysed or Irresponsible', XVII *Parliamentary Affairs* (1963/4), 66.
3. See chapter 6, above.
4. See chapter 8, above.
5. Finance (Control and Management) Act 1958 (as amended), s. 3. Also Control and Management of Public Finances Law 1958 (Northern Region); Finance (Control and Management) Law 1959 (Eastern Region).
6. ibid., s. 3.
7. Josef Omorotionmwan, *Daily Times*, 26 June 1980, 3.
8. ibid.
9. Finance (Control and Management) Act 1958 (as amended).
10. Nat. Ass. Deb., vol. XII, part II, 6 July 1967, col. 1853; 19 July 1967, col. 2410.
11. Zambia Hansard No. 19, 7–17 October 1969, col. 135.
12. ibid., col. 155.
13. col. 135.
14. ibid., col. 143 (personal statement by the member for Mongu, Mr. Mumbuna).
15. ibid., col. 145.

14
LIMITS OF THE LEGISLATIVE POWER*

The legislative power of the national assembly is defined as power to make laws for the 'peace, order and good government of the federation or any part thereof' with respect to the matters within its assigned sphere of competence (s. 4). The phrase 'peace, order and good government' is not a delimitation of the purpose for which the power is given, in the sense that a law must be for peace, order or good government in order to be valid. The phrase is simply a legal formula for expressing the widest amplitude of legislative power exercisable by a sovereign legislature. A law cannot therefore be challenged on the ground that it is not for peace, order and good government.

Furthermore, the motives which prompted a legislation, whether they are for the public interest or not, are irrelevant to its validity. 'It has been held to be well settled', said Mr. Justice Uwaifo, 'that the motives of any legislative act do not affect its validity.'[1] In the words of Cooley:

The validity of legislation can never be made to depend on the motives which have secured its adoption, whether these be public or personal, honest or corrupt. . . . To make legislation depend upon motives would render all statute law uncertain, and the rule which should allow it could not logically stop short of permitting a similar inquiry into the motives of those who passed judgment. Therefore the courts do not permit a question of improper legislative motives to be raised, but they will in every instance assume that the motives were public and befitting the station.[2]

Given legislation on any subject-matter, for example, provision of water or drainage facilities, its sponsors, whether the government, a legislative committee or a single individual, are likely to be motivated by a variety of reasons for sponsoring it, which may be public or private (e.g. benefit to the public, a relative, a friend or themselves) or, more usually, a mixture of both. And the legislators who voted for it might also be expected to be motivated by a similar mixture of reasons. Such reasons of public or private benefit that induced the

*Delivered at a public lecture at the Nigerian Institute of International Affairs, Lagos, 19 February 1979. Apparently in response to the lecture, the federal military government on 28 September 1979, i.e. two days before the handover, repealed or amended many of the decrees considered in the text to be incompatible with the Constitution. It has been thought better to leave the text substantially as it was delivered, only indicating in the numbered references the decrees that have been so repealed or amended.

sponsors and other legislators to support the legislation are peripheral to its purpose. That purpose is determined largely by its subject-matter. Accordingly, if the purpose is proper, i.e. within the constitution, the motives or the reasons which induced the introduction and passage of the legislation are irrelevant. Motive in relation to legislation is often difficult to prove by evidence; this is partly because it is nearly always mixed, and partly because it tends to be a matter of imputation. This is not of course to say that legislative motive is altogether impossible of proof, because it would necessarily involve cross-examination of each individual legislator.[3] Assuming motive to be relevant in relation to a particular piece of legislation, cross-examination of each individual legislator may not be necessary to determine it. The decisive motive would not be that of every legislator but rather that of the initiators of the legislation, and this can be proved by evidence drawn from the circumstances that led to it. However this may be, motive being irrelevant, it follows that even when it can be proved by evidence, such evidence is equally irrelevant.[4]

It is not always that the purpose of a governmental act is manifestly proper. A purpose, ostensibly proper, may serve to disguise the real motivation, which may be unconstitutional. It is here that the application of the rule confronts a difficulty, owing to the inevitable confusion that arises in such a situation between purpose and motive. Any attempt to determine the real purpose gets inevitably entangled in a motive inquiry, and the line of demarcation tends to be blurred. This situation is well illustrated by the U.S. case of *Gomillion* v. *Lightfoot*.[5] The legislature of Alabama, in purported exercise of its undoubted power to determine the boundaries of its political subdivisions, altered the boundaries of the city of Tuskegee in a way that removed from the city 'all save only four or five of its four hundred Negro voters while not removing a single white voter or resident.' Was the real purpose of the act the ostensible one of fixing how far the city boundaries should desirably extend or was it to fence out the negro residents from the city so as to deprive them of their municipal vote? It seems obvious that the distinction between the ostensible and real purpose must involve some inquiry into motive. Yet to accept the ostensible purpose as conclusive in this sort of case is to condone discrimination in the name of the rule forbidding motive analysis. This is certainly not the kind of situation for which the rule was intended. Happily, the U.S. supreme court invalidated the Alabama law on the ground that it was discriminatory of the negro residents. An Oklahoma law requiring literacy as a qualification for the franchise but framed so as to disenfranchise only illiterate blacks but not illiterate whites was struck down for the same reason.[6]

While the legislative power cannot be impeached on the ground that an item of legislation is not for peace, order or good government or that it is ill-motivated, it is limited by the following factors — formal requirements for law-making, the division of legislative power between the federal and state legislatures, the separateness and independence of executive power, the incapacity of the legislature to abdicate its powers, the constitutional guarantee of rights, the separateness and independence of judicial power, the prohibition of retrospective criminal legislation, and the prohibition of ouster of the court's jurisdiction. The first four limiting factors have already been discussed in chapters 1 and 4 respectively. Here it is proposed to discuss the last four. (Legislation which does not offend against any of these factors may still be unconstitutional if it is otherwise inconsistent with the Constitution; this is illustrated in chapter 16 below.)

It is necessary to observe at this juncture that these limitations apply both to laws made after the coming into force of the Constitution on 1 October 1979 and to those existing before that. (The manner and form prescribed by the Constitution for law-making does not apply to existing laws.) Laws in force on 1 October 1979 are indeed specifically subjected to the overriding supremacy of the Constitution (s. 274[3]), and are deemed to be an enactment of that legislature, the national assembly or a state house of assembly, which, under the scheme of division, has competence over their subject-matter (s. 274[1]).

However, the operation of a law and any actions validly taken under it before 1 October 1979 cannot be challenged thereafter, unless such actions are of a continuing nature. Thus, a law that forfeited an individual's land to the state before 1 October 1979, cannot be challenged after that date on the ground that forfeiture is prohibited by the Constitution. This is because the act of extinguishment of the individual's title and its transfer to the state would have been completely accomplished before 1 October 1979, a forfeiture law being self-executing. If the law had instead attainted the individual of treason and ordered him to be imprisoned for life, the attachment of guilt for treason, being again completely accomplished, cannot be undone by the Constitution when it comes into force. Also the initial imprisonment will not be invalidated by the Constitution, just as the hanging of a person under a statute that specifically authorises it cannot be undone, but the continuation of the imprisonment from 1 October 1979 will be invalid if the authorising law is unconstitutional. The point being emphasised is that the Constitution does not apply retrospectively to invalidate actions already completely accomplished before 1 October 1979.

The limitations will now be considered in turn.

1. Constitutional guarantee of rights

The Nigerian Constitution guarantees to a person the right to life, dignity of the person, personal liberty, fair hearing, private and family life, the right to freedom of thought, conscience and religion, freedom of expression and the press, peaceful assembly and association, freedom of movement, and freedom from discrimination. However, the guarantee is not absolute. With the exception of the right to life, dignity of the human person, personal liberty, fair hearing and the right to freedom from discrimination, all the other rights are guaranteed subject to any law that may be made by the legislature imposing restrictions that are reasonably justifiable in a democratic society in the interest of defence, public safety, public order, public morality or public health or for the purpose of protecting the rights and freedoms of other persons.[7]

The limit set on the legislature's law-making power by the constitutional guarantee of rights depends, therefore, on what it may be thought is to be the kind of relationship that should exist between a regulatory legislation and public order, public safety etc., to make the legislation reasonably justifiable in a democratic society in those interests. The Constitution itself provides no guidance on what the relationship should be, whether any kind of relationship or connection, no matter how tenuous, unsubstantial, irrational, indirect or remote, is sufficient; whether the connection must be proximate, and if so how proximate; whether the danger to public order, public safety etc. should be clear and present or probable or merely likely. And there is the further question as to when a regulatory law that is substantially and rationally related to the specified interests may be said to be not reasonably justifiable in a democratic society? What is a democratic society, and what are the optimum standards of liberty required by it? By failing to provide guidance on these questions, the Constitution has thrown the burden on the courts.

The U.S. supreme court has established as a principle of the Constitution that, to be valid, an item of legislation that restricts a constitutionally guaranteed right must have a substantial and rational relation to the appropriate public interests, and must not be otherwise unreasonable, arbitrary or discriminatory;[8] and that where freedom of speech, the press, assembly and association is involved, the danger to the public interests must be shown to be clear and present, not merely likely or even probable. In a Zambian case where the question was whether the power given by the Exchange Control Regulations to customs officers to open and search without warrant postal packets reasonably suspected of containing articles or currency notes being imported into or exported out of the country in contravention of the

Regulations was "reasonably required" in the interest of public order and public safety, the high court held that, although exchange control has a bearing on public order and safety, the bearing is not sufficiently proximate and rational to make exchange control reasonably required in those interests.[9] The court observed:

> It could conceivably happen that complete financial anarchy might so weaken the economy that internal disaffection might be caused, leading to rioting and civil disturbance. So might widespread unemployment caused, say, by overpopulation. So might prolonged drought which disrupted agricultural production. One might think of many things which could, ultimately, affect the public safety. None of them would, however, have the quality of proximateness which would justify involving this exception. Nor do I think that exchange control is sufficiently proximate to public safety to warrant the present legislation being adopted in the interest of public safety.

On the standard of liberty required by a democratic society, Chief Justice Blagden, also of the high court of Zambia, has held that it is the standards of the democratic society existing in the particular country concerned that have to be used. 'We should look', he said, 'to the democratic society that exists in Zambia; and having found that these regulations are reasonably required in Zambia, I have no hesitation in finding that they are reasonably justifiable in the democratic society that exists here.'[10] The explanation was that democracy in a newly emergent nation like Zambia cannot be judged by the standards of the long-established democracies. This is beside the point. The question is not whether the measure in question is conformable with the highest standards of democracy which may exist only in the most advanced democracies; it is the standards of an average democracy that have to be used, and the standards of the particular country concerned may or may not come up to this average. No doubt it may be difficult to define the criteria for an average democracy, yet the difficulty should not oblige us to accept a position that would make the constitutional requirement otiose. Some objective yardstick must be applied if the provision is not to be mere decoration.

Chief Justice Blagden's reasoning has thus rightly been rejected by Justice Magnus in the case just referred to, on the ground that it would involve:

> adopting an axiom, namely that Zambia is a democratic society, and to proceed from there to the assumption that 'Zambia' must be equated with 'democratic society'. . . . I think it is necessary to adopt the objective test of what is reasonably justifiable, not in a particular democratic society, but in any democratic society. I accept the argument that some distinction should be made between a developed society and one which is still developing, but I think one must be able to say that there are certain minima which must be found in

any society, developed or otherwise, below which it cannot go and still be entitled to be considered as a democratic society.

He went on to adopt the definition of a democratic country by the U.S. supreme court as a 'free society in which government is based upon the consent of an informed citizenry and is dedicated to the protection of the rights of all, even the most despised minorities,'[11] 'a free government . . . that leaves the way wide open to favour, discuss, advocate, or incite causes and doctrines however obnoxious and antagonistic such views may be to the rest of us.'[12]

The power of the state (both federal and state) to regulate constitutionally guaranteed rights — police power as it is sometimes called — is narrower in Nigeria than in the United States. In the United States rights can be regulated or restricted in the interest of public welfare generally. As was said by the country's supreme court in 1905, 'there are, however, certain powers, existing in the sovereignty of each State in the Union, somewhat vaguely termed police powers, the exact description and limitation of which have not been attempted by the courts. Those powers, broadly stated and without, at present, any attempt at a more specific limitation, relate to the safety, health, morals, and general welfare of the public.'[13] In Nigeria, on the other hand, public welfare is specifically limited to defence, public safety, public order, public health, public morality and the protection of the rights and freedom of others. It does not extend to national unity, economic well-being, economic development or any other aspect of public welfare outside those specified. Economic well-being of the community, for example, is thus not a justification for the state to interfere with guaranteed rights as it is in the United States.

Nigeria's statute-book contains many legislative restrictions on constitutionally guaranteed rights, which cannot stand up to the test of substantial and rational proximateness, not to say of a clear and present danger. Such, for example, are the laws relating to sedition, the publication of false news likely to cause fear and alarm,[14] or that authorising the head of state to prohibit the circulation in the country or in any state of any newspaper if he is satisfied that its unrestricted circulation is or may be detrimental to the interest of the federation or of any state[15] or that making it an offence, punishable by imprisonment for two years, without the option of a fine, to publish or reproduce any false statement, rumour or report alleging corruption against a public officer. Happily, some others among the restrictive military decrees had been repealed in 1978 to allow a certain measure of the democratic processes necessary for the return to civil rule, e.g. laws authorising the imposition of a curfew whenever it was considered necessary in the interest of public safety and public order, or prohibiting the formation of new political parties after having dissolved all existing ones, or authorising the dispersing of any political procession.[16]

The constitutional guarantee of rights may also operate to invalidate legislation directed solely against the guaranteed right of a named individual(s), since such legislation may be arbitrary and discriminatory. Under the Constitution therefore, the forty-two *ad hominem* decrees soon to be discussed may be invalid in so far as they affect a guaranteed right.

Restriction of guaranteed rights in the interest of defence, public safety, public order, public morality or public health does not in normal times apply to the right to life, dignity of the human person, personal liberty, fair hearing and freedom from discrimination. These rights are guaranteed free of any restrictions that the legislature may want to impose in these specified interests. An individual is thus guaranteed against arbitrary detention or arbitrary killing merely on the ground that such detention or killing is in the interest of public security or public order. The demands of public security or public order provide no justification under the Constitution for the detention of an individual, much less for killing him, except to the extent that detention is necessary to prevent him from committing an offence against public security or public order.

Detention in the interest of public security or public order is constitutionally permitted only during an emergency declared in accordance with the provisions of the Constitution, but then it must be reasonably justifiable for the purpose of dealing with the situation created by the emergency. Except for death resulting from the use (to such extent and in such circumstances as are permitted by law) of such force as is reasonably necessary for the purpose of suppressing a riot, insurrection or mutiny, and except in respect of death resulting from acts of war, a law cannot validly authorise that an individual be deprived of his life in the interest of public security or public order, not even during a period of emergency.

Also a situation of emergency provides no justification for any restrictions on or derogations from the right to dignity of the human person, fair hearing and freedom from discrimination. Inhuman or degrading punishment or treatment is prohibited absolutely, and no exception is made, as under the 1963 Constitution, for punishment that was lawful and customary in any part of Nigeria on 1 November 1959. It seems that whipping or haddilashing, being clearly degrading, is now outlawed. Death by the firing squad, especially when it is carried out in the view of the public, is also degrading, and its prescription as a punishment for certain offences under various decrees of the federal military government may also be invalid. It is worthy of note in this connection that the federal military government has under various decrees considerably increased the offences punishable by death; such are offences relating to armed robbery, kidnapping, counterfeiting of the currency, disruption of the production and distribution of petroleum products and offences against public order. According to Amnesty International, 608 persons were under sentence of death in Nigeria in April 1977.[17]

The fact that the right of the individual to a fair hearing in civil and criminal cases by a court or other tribunal established by law and constituted in such manner as to secure its independence and impartiality cannot be taken away in the interest of public safety or public order, in normal times exactly as in periods of emergency, deserves also special notice. This guarantee incorporates into our Constitution the principle established by the U.S. supreme court that martial law or the trial of civilians by military tribunals is constitutionally justified only if the territory is involved in actual military operations making it impossible for the ordinary civil courts to function. 'If', said the court, 'in foreign invasion or civil war, the courts are actually closed, and it is impossible to administer criminal justice according to law, then, on the theatre of actual military operations where war really prevails, there is a necessity to furnish a substitute for the civil authority, thus overthrown, to preserve the safety of the army and society; and as no power is left but the military, it is allowed to govern by martial rule until the laws can have their free course. [. . .] Martial law can never exist where the courts are open, and in the proper and unobstructed exercise of their jurisdiction.'[18]

The decrees of the federal military government authorising the trial, conviction and sentencing of civilians by military tribunals, such as the Suppression of Disorder Decree 1966 (repealed in 1978) and the Treason and other Offences (Special Military Tribunal) Decree 1976, are clearly an infringement of this guarantee and invalid. So also are the various special tribunals established for the trial of offences relating to armed robbery, kidnapping, counterfeiting and the disruption of the production and distribution of petroleum products. As these tribunals contain in their membership military or police officers, who are clearly functionaries of the executive government, and since their decisions are in all cases subject to confirmation by the executive as regards either conviction or sentence or both, they are unquestionably not independent and impartial tribunals within the meaning of the constitutional provisions.[19]

2. Separation of judicial from legislative power

Unlike its predecessors, the 1979 Nigerian Constitution, in clear, unequivocal terms, separates judicial from legislative power by making an express vesting of it in the courts (s. 6). By this, it puts beyond doubt that the legislative power granted to the national assembly and the state assemblies, ample as it is, does not subsume judicial power. Certainly it is plausible to argue, as was done in a Sri Lankan case in 1967,[20] that a constitution which confers legislative power in its widest amplitude and merely creates superior courts or prescribes the method of appointing and removing judges, without an express vesting of judicial power in them, does not intend that judicial power shall exist as a limitation upon the legislative power. All that can necessarily be asserted from the actual provisions is that the legislature cannot abolish the courts or alter the method prescribed for the appointment and dismissal of judges except by a valid amendment of the constitution.

The limitation implied in the vesting of judicial power in the courts is that any legislation that usurps, infringes or otherwise interferes with that power is unconstitutional and invalid; it also precludes the legislature from vesting non-judicial functions in the courts. But we need to know what is judicial power in the constitutional sense to understand the true extent of this limitation. This is necessary because, in the nature of modern government, executive agencies of various kinds must and do in fact exercise compulsory power to inquire into and determine facts and even questions of law affecting the rights of individuals. The compulsory character of the power and the fact that opposing parties or questions of law may be involved, that private rights are affected, and that a party may be bound not to controvert the determination on the facts make it look very much like a judicial function, since these are distinctive, though not exclusive, characteristics of judicial power. What, then, are the attributes exclusive to judicial power?

It may be stated, without elaboration,[21] that the only functions exclusive to judicial power are the determination of the legal rights and liabilities of parties to a dispute through the application of the law, as authoritatively found by the court, to the facts of the dispute, and the fact that the determination results in an obligation or liability enforceable by a coercive process backed by the organised force of the state. Conviction for an offence and the imposition of punishment for it is thus exclusive to judicial power.

We need further to know what is a court in the constitutional sense. By the relevant clause of the Constitution, the judicial power is vested in six named courts (the supreme court of Nigeria, the federal court of appeal, the federal high court, the high court, the *sharia* court of appeal and the customary court of appeal of each state) and in 'such other courts' as may be established by the national assembly or the state house of assembly within their respective areas of legislative competence. When an agency, constituted by law for a special purpose outside the ordinary court system, is designated a court and vested with judicial power, it becomes a question whether it is a court within the meaning of the constitutional provision. Clearly, as Chief Justice Griffith of Australia has said, the constitutional limitation cannot be circumvented by 'designating a body, which is not in its essential character a court, by that name, or by calling the functions by another name.'[22]

The essential character of a court in the constitutional sense is determined not so much by the legal qualification of its members or by the method of their appointment and dismissal, as by its independence and impartiality and the procedure for its proceedings and determinations. The procedure of a court of law is characterised by the following attributes: (*a*) absence of bias, i.e. a court of law is required to be free of bias or even an appearance of bias, which means in practical terms that a judge should be independent of the disputants in the case, and should have no interest of his own in the subject matter of the dispute; (*b*) openness, i.e. its proceedings must be in public, unless the interest of justice or other public interest dictates otherwise; (*c*) presentation of their case by the parties to the dispute; (*d*) the ascertainment of the facts in issue by means of evidence given on oath or affirmation; (*e*) the submission of argument on the facts and on the law by or on behalf of the parties; (*f*) a binding decision which disposes of the whole matter by a finding upon the facts and an application to the facts so found of the law as interpretated by the court.

No matter that it is designated a court and that its procedure is the same as or similar to that of a court, an agency invested with judicial power is not a court in the constitutional sense if it is composed of an executive functionary, or if its members are subject to the direction or control of the executive in the discharge of their functions or if its decision is subject to confirmation by the president or other executive authority. The requirement of confirmation implies that the final decision is in reality that of the confirming authority, to whom therefore the tribunal is completely subordinated, losing thereby that independence which is the hallmark of a court of law.

Legislation may usurp or interfere with judicial power in several ways. Two ways which it usually takes may be noted here:

(i) *Legislation directed against named persons or associations*
Legislation is conceived as a system of rules with a generality and

uniformity of application for the regulation of the life and activities of the community as a whole, while judicial power is an individualised function, concerned with the application of law in the adjudication of specific cases. Singling out a person for individualised treatment by legislation may not only be arbitrary and discriminatory, it can easily lend itself to oppression, favouritism or other kinds of abuse. It becomes singularly oppressive when it inflicts punishment, forfeiture, disability or other disciplinary action on the individual affected without the benefit of trial by a judicial process.

Individualised legislation of this kind acquired great prominence in the country during the military regime which resorted to it as a corrective device to safeguard order in the country and to clean up the society of corruption and other forms of abuse. Perhaps another explanation for the frequent resort to this kind of legislation is that in its law-making function the military government is much like an executive issuing executive orders, a fact that is reflected in the form of its legislation: a legislative decree, like the decree of a court, seems quite apt for individualised application.

From the inception of the military government in January 1966 to January 1979, there have been some forty-two decrees (edicts of state governments excluded) directed against named persons or associations. The actions directed by the decrees fall into seven broad categories:

(a) *Arrest and detention of named persons*. There were altogether twenty decrees in this category, directing the arrest and detention of some eighty-seven individuals.[23] The release of these individuals from detention was initially effected by means of revocation decrees, but this was changed by a later decree which empowered the head of state to effect release by means of an order published in the gazette. One of the decrees merely validated and at the same time terminated the detention of a named person under an edict of a state government.

(b) *Dissolution of named associations*. Altogether 107 associations — eighty-one political parties and twenty-six tribal or cultural associations — were affected. A later decree forfeited to the state the assets of these associations, and directed that any cash in the bank forming part of such assets shall be paid into the consolidated revenue fund of the federation, but liabilities of the associations in respect of which a claim is lodged are to be discharged out of the forfeited assets.[24] In addition there is the decree that dissolved three named registered trading companies, and forfeited to the federal military government all properties belonging to the companies as well as all rights in them by whomsoever held and the properties of two named individuals associated with the companies.

(c) *Nullification of specified transactions*. A decree of 1971 nullified a contract by which a certain company sold to the Nigerian Ports Authority tug boats, and directed the refund of the purchase money. Such refund may be effected from any sum accruing to the vendors in respect of currency conversion or accruing to any person from a policy of insurance on the life of one Lawrence Etim (deceased) and from any money standing in any bank account to the credit of the vendors, the said Lawrence Etim, any individual or company having an interest in the vendor company or any company in which the vendors or Lawrence Etim have a controlling interest; other assets belonging to any of these persons could also be seized and sold, and the proceeds paid to the Nigerian Ports Authority on account of the refund.

(d) *Imposition of disability on named persons*. A decree of 1977 disqualified eleven named individuals from holding office in or belonging to any trade union or taking any other part whatsoever in any trade union including the management of property or any other affair of any trade union.

(e) *Vacation of office or annulment of the appointment of named individuals*. A decree of 1969 vacated retrospectively from 1967 the office of chief justice of the Mid-Western state held by a named individual and another annulled the appointment of a judge of the high court of the Northern states. The first decree recited in a preamble as the reason for the action that the individual incumbent had, by reason of absence, failed for a considerable period to discharge the duties of his office and that it had not proved possible to communicate with him; the decree then went on to appoint another person to the office, also from 1967.

(f) *Recovery of public property from named persons*. A sum of money in Barclays Bank standing to the credit of a Nigerian, and another sum to the credit of an alien, who had been deported from the country, were confiscated by decrees of 1968 and 1970 respectively, which also directed the money to be paid into the consolidated revenue fund of the federation. Another decree of 1970 sequestrated the assets of a certain army officer, Captain Din, or any person or company accused with him in certain criminal proceedings. The assets, if in the hands of the police, were to be sold and paid into the consolidated revenue fund, and if in the form of money in the bank, the bank was, on pain of a fine, to pay it into the consolidated revenue fund.

(g) *Forfeiture of assets of named persons.* This is the commonest and perhaps the most drastic, involving various kinds of assets, company shares, cash, bank credit balances, land including buildings and other fixtures (and in one case furniture) etc. In seven cases, the forfeiture decree was directed against a single individual or company. In another, the decree validates fifteen orders (scheduled thereto) made under various enactments of a state government, whereby twenty-six persons named in the decree had had their assets forfeited or were adjudged liable to make reparation. Apart from these, forfeiture of assets has normally been effected by means of an order made under the decree authorising it as a general kind of measure. It was on this basis that an order of 1977 forfeited ninety-nine landed properties and shares in seven companies belonging to eleven public officers (ten state governors and one commissioner).

The question is whether a law that is directed against a named person(s) is necessarily a usurpation or interference with the judicial power and so invalid under the Constitution. The question is one of considerable difficulty, and has provoked a conflict of judicial opinion. No doubt, the role of the courts in the application of law in the settlement of disputes would be seriously whittled down if *ad hominem* legislation were to be made the general practice. Yet a law that merely confers benefit on a named individual cannot possibly be said to interfere with judicial power. We may also agree with the judicial committee of the privy council that 'a lack of generality in criminal legislation need not, of itself, involve the judicial function, and their Lordships are not prepared to hold that every enactment in this field which can be described as *ad hominem* and *ex post facto* must inevitably usurp or infringe the judicial power.'[25]

However, a usurpation or interference clearly occurs where *ad hominem* legislation is in reality a disguise for a *judgment* whereby the legislature, without trial, finds a person guilty of a criminal offence and punishes him accordingly. As previously stated, the function of finding a person guilty of a breach of the criminal law and sentencing him for it is exclusively that of a court under the Constitution, and its exercise by means of legislation is unconstitutional and invalid.

The area of conflict concerns an *ad hominem* law which, although it makes no explicit judgment of guilt against a named person, nevertheless inflicts punishment, forfeiture, disability or other disciplinary action on him. In the view of the supreme court of Nigeria, the forfeiture of an individual's assets, at any rate in circumstances suggesting that it was being exacted because of the individual's involvement in corruption, which may or may not amount to a criminal offence, is a legislative exercise of judicial power and a usurpation.[26] What follows upon this courageous decision — its prompt reversal by the Federal Military Government (Supremacy and Enforcement of Powers) Decree 1970 — forms an important chapter in Nigerian legal history.

The view of the Nigerian supreme court on the issue of forfeiture seems to have the support of the supreme court of the United States. Upon an allegation that 'undue means' had been used to secure a statute which made a grant of large tracts of land belonging to the 'state of Georgia, a subsequent legislature of the state enacted another statute which revoked the earlier one and reverted the lands to the state. The supreme court of the U.S. held the later statute invalid, on the ground that it was repugnant to either the general principle of legislation or the prohibition by the Constitution of laws which impair the obligations of contract.[27] The words of Chief Justice Marshall, delivering the unanimous judgment of the court, are well worth noting. He said:

> To the legislature all legislative power is granted; but the question, whether the act of transferring the property of an individual to the public, be in the nature of the legislative power, is well worthy of serious reflection. It is the peculiar province of the legislature to prescribe general rules for the government of society; the application of those rules to individuals in society would seem to be the duty of other departments.

Sir William Blackstone, one of the greatest authorities on the law, has also written: 'Therefore a particular act of the legislature to confiscate the goods of Titius, or to attaint him of high treason, does not enter into the idea of a municipal law. [. . .] it is rather a sentence than a law.'[28] Though this passage had been quoted with approval by the judicial committee of the privy council in 1966,[29] in a case in 1967[30] the committee declined to express an opinion as to the circumstances in which a confiscating law may constitute a legislative exercise of judicial power, saying that in the sphere of constitutional law it is unwise to go beyond what is necessary for the determination of the case in hand.

As regards a statute which vacated the seats in parliament or a local authority of named persons who had been found guilty of bribery by a commission of inquiry, and disqualified them from being voters or candidates for parliament or a local authority for seven years, the judicial committee of the privy council has held in a Sri Lankan case that such a law is not an exercise of judicial power, but a legitimate exercise of the legislative power.[31] The grounds for this were: first, that the statute contained no declaration of guilt of bribery or of any other offence — parliament did not by the act make any finding of guilt against the persons named therein, that finding having been made by a commission of inquiry independently of the act: Secondly, the disabilities imposed by the act were not, in all the circumstances, punishment. They were intended, not really to punish, but to discipline and to 'keep public life clean for the public good'. In the opinion of the committee there is a difference between a disciplinary penalty and a punishment for an offence. The view that the statute has nothing to do with the guilt for bribery of the named individuals is correct only in a formal sense. Having assumed their guilt as something predetermined, the statute by implication accepted and confirmed it, and then proceeded on that basis to inflict the disabilities which it prescribed. The distinction between punishment for an offence and a disciplinary penalty is, in the circumstances of the case, too formalistic and rigid. The application of a constitution should not proceed on such unduly legalistic lines.

The United States supreme court was not disposed towards such excessive legalism when it held invalid an act of congress which permanently debarred from government employment certain named American citizens believed to have engaged in subversive activities against the United States, on the ground that a permanent bar on named individuals from government employment, without the safeguard of a trial, was in the nature of a bill of attainder which was prohibited by the Constitution.[32] Now, a bill of attainder is a legislative act which attaints a person of treason for which it condemns him to death. The act in question in this case made no declaration of guilt for subversion against the named individuals, and a permanent bar from government employment is not remotely like a death sentence. But in holding that, in the circumstances of an allegation of subversion, such a bar was in the nature of a bill of attainder, the court was concerned more with the spirit than the form of the constitutional prohibition. The words of the court invalidating the statute are worth quoting again. It said:

Those who wrote our Constitution well knew the danger in special legislative acts which take away the life, liberty, or property of particular named persons, because the legislature thinks them guilty of conduct which deserves punishment. They intended to safeguard the people of the country from punishment without trial by duly constituted courts. . . . And even the courts to which this important function was entrusted, were commanded to stay their hands until and unless certain tested safeguards were observed. [. . .] When our Constitution and Bill of Rights were written, our ancestors had ample reason to know that legislative trials and punishments were too dangerous to liberty to exist in the nation of free men they envisioned. And so they proscribed bills of attainder.[33]

The approach of the U.S. supreme court in the two cases mentioned above and of the Nigerian supreme court is to be preferred to that of the judicial committee of the privy council. On the authority of those decisions, legislation that forfeits the property of a named person or nullifies his contract as a punishment or penalty for some act, whether criminal or merely dishonest, is unconstitutional and invalid.

Of the decrees of the federal military government which dissolved certain named associations or ordered the arrest and detention of named individuals, it may be said that, being intended merely for the prevention of disorder, they involved no interference with the judicial power.

(ii) *Vesting of judicial power in persons or authorities other than the court*

Not only is the legislature not permitted to exercise judicial power directly itself, but also it cannot transfer it or any part of it to persons or authorities other than the courts. Thus a law authorising the president or other executive functionaries to exercise judicial power is invalid. Constitutional invalidity results inexorably from the fact that the function partakes of judicial power and that the agency entrusted with it is not a court in the constitutional sense.

The statute book of the military government contains some nine glaring cases of this kind of legislation. There is the case of the five tribunals which, under five different decrees, the head of the federal military government or the military governor of a state was empowered to establish for the trial of the offences of robbery with or without armed violence;[34] kidnapping for purposes of ritual or obtaining ransom; wounding of persons suspected of witchcraft, juju, sorcery, enchantment or conjuration;[35] counterfeiting of the currency and allied offences;[36] obstructing or preventing the production, procurement or distribution of petroleum products;[37] and corruption.[38]

The power given to the tribunals under these decrees is unquestionably judicial power, since it enabled them, after trial, to convict for the relevant offences, and to inflict punishment, which is death for most of the offences and long terms of imprisonment for others. While the procedure of the tribunals is similar to that of a court of law, it is equally unquestionable that they are not a court in the constitutional sense. With the exception of the chairman, who in four of the five tribunals was a high court judge, military or police officers accounted for all the rest of the membership in two of the tribunals and for at least half the membership in the remaining two. In the fifth, the chairman and all the other members must be military officers. The presence in the tribunals of functionaries of the executive, as military and police officers are, destroy the independence and, it may be, the impartiality of the tribunals and any claim which they might have to being described as a court in the constitutional sense.

Furthermore, although an appeal to the supreme court was allowed from three of the tribunals but not from the others, the decisions of all five were subject to confirmation by the head of the federal military government or governor as regards conviction and sentence in four, and as regards sentence only in one. As previously stated, the requirement of confirmation of a tribunal's decision by the executive destroys its independence.

The relevant provisions of the decrees were thus clearly incompatible with the vesting of judicial power in the courts by the Constitution. Under the Constitution, an individual is entitled not to be convicted or punished for a criminal offence except by a court after due trial. The decree of 28 September 1979, promulgated on the eve of the hand-over, has now abrogated two of the decrees establishing these tribunals,[39] and amended the provisions of two others by abolishing the tribunals and transferring their jurisdiction to the high court, and by repealing the provision relating to confirmation by the head of state or military governor of conviction and/or sentence.[40] But the provision authorising execution of the death sentence by the firing squad is not repealed. Nor has the decree creating offences in respect of petroleum products been repealed or even amended.

Another interfering legislation of this kind is that concerned with the trial of persons, both civilians and soldiers, involved in the abortive coup of 1975. Under the decree (Treason and other Offences [Special Tribunal] Decree 1976), trial of any offence committed during that coup attempt (treason, murder or other offences) is by a special military tribunal composed of a military chairman and not less than four other military or police officers. The tribunal is empowered to convict for any of these offences and to impose any penalty for it prescribed in the relevant law, but its sentence, though not conviction, is subject to confirmation by the head of the federal military government. The decree is more drastic than those discussed earlier in that it subjects civilians to trial by a military tribunal which, where a civilian acted in concert with a military man, is empowered to treat him like a person subject to service law. Again, in so far as the operation of the decree continues after the coming into force of the Constitution, it is, for reasons stated above, unconstitutional and invalid as an interference with judicial power.

The Treason and other Offences (Special Tribunal) Decree 1976 is an echo of an earlier decree of 1966, the Suppression of Disorder Decree, and is distinguishable from it only by the fact that the power conferred by it is limited to offences connected with a particular event while the 1966 Decree had a general application. The 1966 decree empowered the head of the federal military government to declare as a military area any part of the country appearing to him to be affected by widespread public disturbances, and to constitute for it a military tribunal, consisting of a military president and two, three or four other military members, with power, to the exclusion of all other courts in the country, to try a wide range of offences listed in the decree, and to convict and sentence anyone found guilty of them, subject only to confirmation of its sentence (though not conviction) by the head of the federal military government or a military governor. The decree had in a military area almost the effect of a declaration of martial law. Happily, no military area was ever declared under the decree, and it has since been repealed as part of the relaxation of autocratic military control preparatory to a return to civil rule.[37] But were it to continue in operation after the coming into force of the new Constitution, those of its provisions relating to the military tribunal would be unconstitutional and invalid.

The tribunal that attracted the widest publicity and provoked some members of the legal profession into making a public protest is the foreign exchange tribunal established under the Exchange Control (Anti-Sabotage) Decree of 1977. The decree creates certain offences relating to foreign exchange. The foreign exchange tribunal which was charged with the trial of these offences had the same type of composition (a high court judge as chairman and two other members of whom at least one was to be a military officer) as some of the tribunals discussed earlier, and much the same procedure and power to convict and impose the punishments of imprisonment or fine as prescribed in the decree, but subject again to the confirmation of the head of the federal military government as regards both conviction and sentence. No appeal was allowed from a decision of the tribunal. Like the other tribunals and for the same reasons, the foreign exchange tribunal is incompatible with the Constitution.[42]

(iii) *Preclusion of the vesting of non-judicial functions in the courts*
Three different schools of thought exist on the question whether the separation of judicial from legislative and executive power preclude the vesting of non-judicial functions in the courts. On the one hand, it is said:

Because of the distribution of the functions of government and of the manner in which the Constitution describes the tribunals to be invested with the judicial power by the Commonwealth (of Australia), and defines the judicial power to be invested in them, the parliament is restrained both from reposing any power essentially judicial in any other organ or body, and from reposing any other than that judicial power in such tribunals.[43]

Another school of thought holds that there is nothing in the vesting of judicial power in the judicature to preclude the conferment on it of non-judicial functions. Justice Higgins of the Australian high court argues:

> To say that Blackacre shall be vested in A (and A only) does not carry as a corollary that Whiteacre shall not be vested in A; to say that the judicial power of the Commonwealth shall be vested in the High Court (and other Federal Courts *and such other courts as Parliament invests with Federal* jurisdiction . . .) does not imply that no other jurisdiction or power shall be vested in the High Court or in the other courts. This is surely obvious, on the mere form of words. [. . .] The point is that the Constitution does not expressly forbid the vesting of other powers in this Court, and that there is no necessary implication to that effect.[44]

Between these two extreme positions there is a middle course championed by yet other judges. This admits the legitimacy of non-judicial functions being conferred on the court but only so long as such functions are not incompatible or inconsistent with judicial power. According to Chief Justice Latham:

> It is not possible to rely upon any doctrine of absolute separation of powers for the purpose of establishing a universal proposition that no court or person who discharges Federal judicial functions can lawfully discharge any other function which has been entrusted to him by statute. This proposition, however, does not involve the further proposition that any powers or duties of any description whatsoever, may be conferred or imposed upon Federal courts or Federal judges. If a power or duty were in its nature such as to be inconsistent with the co-existence of judicial power, it might well be held that a statutory provision purporting to confer or impose such a power or duty could not stand with the creation of the judicial tribunal or the appointment of a person to act as a member of it.[45]

The case in which the chief justice made these observations concerned an act which empowered a bankruptcy court to charge a bankrupt and try him summarily if, in any application for an order of discharge, it had reason to believe that the bankrupt had been guilty of an offence against the act. It was contended that the charging or prosecution of offenders against the criminal law is an executive, and not a judicial function, and that it was repugnant to the conception of judicial function for a court to act as both prosecutor and judge. The court, by a majority of three, rejected the contention, and affirmed the validity of the enactment, on the ground that the power given to the court to charge a bankrupt was not inconsistent with the co-existence of judicial power. A minority of two took the view that there was an inconsistency. The maxim *'nemo potest esse simul actor et judex'* (no one can be at once actor and judge), they said, 'does not express a mere caution against human frailty. It epitomizes part of the English notion of the judicial function. A long course of development produced a conception of the judicial process which placed the court in the position of a detached tribunal entertaining and determining civil and criminal pleas brought before it.'[46]

The power of the court to commit for contempt is a special exception, based on the necessity of keeping order and of preserving the court from actual interference in the discharge of its duties.[47] They concluded emphatically that 'the judicial power does not include the promotion, prosecution and proof of criminal charges by a court for its own determination.'[48]

In 1953 the high court of Australia had to decide the constitutionality of a statute which conferred upon a court of summary jurisdiction functions of an administrative nature.[49] The statute required preference to be given in matters of employment to servicemen of the two world wars. Where two servicemen competed for employment, the employer, in choosing between them, was to have regard to the respective length, locality and nature of their employment, their comparative qualifications, the qualification required for the job, and any other relevant matters. The choice of the employer might be challenged in an application to a court of summary jurisdiction, which would then make the choice anew having regard to the matters stipulated above. The high court held that the power given to the court by the act was a power of making an appointment in substitution for the appointment made by an employer, and that this was not a judicial function.

No antecedent rights exist in any of the persons concerned which the court of summary jurisdiction is called upon to ascertain, examine or enforce. There is no issue of fact submitted to it for decision. Its function appears to be entirely and to differ in no respect from the function of the employer himself in considering applications for employment which are affected by [the enactment].[50]

Accordingly the enactment was held unconstitutional and void. When the point arose again for decision in 1956–7, the question was whether arbitral functions could be conferred on a court. The high court was divided 4–3 against.[51] While of the opinion that functions essentially legislative or executive could not be conferred on a court, Justice Taylor, one of the minority, held that as arbitral functions did not bear an indelible legislative, executive or administrative imprint, and since, both in their nature and exercise, they presented a number of features in common with the judicial function, it was, in the absence of any clear provision or implication to the contrary in the Constitution, competent for parliament to confer them on the court. The test of legitimate union adopted by the second of the judges in the minority, Justice Williams, was that

The functions must not be functions which courts are not capable of performing

Limits of the Legislative Power 267

consistently with the judicial process. Purely administrative discretions governed by nothing but standards of convenience and general fairness could not be imposed upon them. Discretionary judgements are not beyond the pale but there must be some standards applicable to a set of facts not altogether undefined before a court can hear and determine a matter.

When the case went on appeal to the judicial committee of the privy council,[52] it ruled emphatically that the vesting of non-judicial functions in a court is contrary to the Constitution, and that it does not matter that the functions are not essentially legislative, executive or administrative in character, or do not bear an indelible imprint of that character or are not otherwise incompatible or inconsistent with judicial power. It denied that the functions of an individual arbitrator under the Australian Conciliation and Arbitration Act 'have any relevant similarity to judicial functions'.[53] On the contrary, it said, they are completely 'outside the realm of judicial power and [are] of a different order;'[54] they lack the essential attributes of judicial power, in that they are not concerned with a justiciable issue, *and import no power of enforcement*. Although the point was not specifically decided, it seems implicit in the decision and in certain observations of the judicial committee that even the function of giving an advisory opinion cannot validly be conferred upon a court by *ordinary statute*, in spite of its close similarity to a judicial function. For like an arbitral function, an advisory opinion is not concerned with a justiciable issue nor is it enforceable. The only exception the judicial committee was willing to concede was a function that can properly be regarded as forming an incident in the exercise of strictly judicial power, for example perhaps a preliminary investigation into a criminal charge by a magistrate. It has been held that the issue of a bankruptcy notice, though ministerial and not judicial in character, is incidental to the judicial power of a bankruptcy court, and can validly be conferred upon it.[55] It seems too that the making of rules of court, though legislative, can properly be regarded as incidental to the exercise of judicial power.

The rationale for the judicial committee's decision was that the vesting of non-judicial functions in the court would tend to 'sap its independence and impartiality',[56] and that if the function is one that is open to challenge by a citizen for inconsistency with the constitution or some other enabling law (as the executive or legislative function is), then the undesirable position of the courts having to review their own acts would result. To the argument that to bar the vesting of non-judicial functions in the courts would be to attach to the separation of judicial power a different significance and consequence from that attaching to the separation between legislative and executive power, the judicial committee answered that the delegation of legislative power by the legislature to the executive has a justification which it would be undesirable to apply to the courts. For in the exercise of delegated legislative power, the executive acts in a subordinate capacity, and remains 'at all times subject to the control of the legislature'.[57] To delegate functions to the courts and subject them to that kind of control would, in the view of the judicial committee, impair the independence of the courts, which is a much more important bulwark against tyranny than the independence of the executive from legislative control.

The United States supreme court, as far back as 1792 in *Hayburn's case*,[58] had come to a similar decision to the privy council's in 1957. An act of congress required the circuit courts of the United States to examine pension claims by disabled soldiers of the Revolution, to determine the amount of pension that would be equivalent to the disability suffered, and to certify their opinion to the secretary of war. Payment of a claim certified by the court might, on the grounds of a suspected imposition or mistake, be withheld by the secretary of war, and the claim might, upon the secretary's report to congress, be revised by the latter. The circuit courts for the districts of New York, Pennsylvania and North Carolina, which included all but one of the judges of the supreme court, declined to execute the act, on the ground that the duty it imposed on them was not a judicial one; that by reason of the separation of the three departments of government in the Constitution 'neither the Legislative nor the Executive branches can constitutionally assign to the judicial any duties, but such as are properly judicial, and to be performed in a judicial manner;' and that the suspensory and revisional power of the secretary of war and congress respectively was incompatible with the independence and separateness of the judicial power, inasmuch as, by the Constitution, neither the secretary of war, nor any other executive officer nor even the legislature were authorised to sit as a court of appeal on the judicial acts or opinions of the court. This opinion has subsequently been endorsed by the supreme court itself.[59]

These decisions were rendered and must, of course, be taken in the context of the Australian and U.S. Constitutions. The Constitution of Australia does more than vest judicial power in the courts. It also defines the original and appellate *jurisdiction* of the high court,[60] and subject to this, parliament is empowered to confer additional original jurisdiction on the high court and to regulate the jurisdiction of the inferior federal courts.[61] The word 'jurisdiction' used in these provisions is controlling; it means the administration of justice by the application of law.[62] A non-judicial function is thus not within its ambit. The U.S. Constitution is even clearer on this point, for apart from defining the original and appellate jurisdiction of the supreme court, it limits the judicial power which it vests in the courts to 'cases in law and equity'.[63] It seems that there is nothing in the Constitution of Nigeria to make the decisions inapplicable. Although legislative power is defined to extend to the jurisdiction or powers of courts of law,[64] the reference to powers is not intended to enlarge the scope of the functions that may be conferred on the courts. The word 'powers' here is not independent of jurisdiction; it merely refers to powers necessary for, or incidental to, the effective exercise of jurisdiction.

Is the prohibition against the vesting of non-judicial functions in a court applicable to individual judges or magistrates? There would seem to be no constitutional basis for applying such a prohibition to them. Judicial power is vested in the court, and not in judges as persons. It is true that a court can only exercise its power through the persons who compose it. Yet there is a significant difference between a judge in court and a judge outside it. A judge is the court only when he is sitting there. He is then invested with the full authority, power, dignity and independence of the court. He does not cease to be judge once he steps out of court, yet his position is vastly different and justifies the vesting of non-judicial functions in individual judges to be performed outside the court, a practice that has acquired almost the force of tradition, because of the qualities of integrity, impartiality and objectivity and the ability to analyse facts and weigh evidence which a judge is supposed to possess by virtue of his work. Thus judges are generally used to conduct public inquiries, to preside over industrial arbitration, to arbitrate in various other disputes of a public nature, to act as chief returning officer at elections, etc. Furthermore, the chief justice as head of the judiciary has necessarily to be invested with administrative functions, since the judicature, like any other department of state, needs to be administered — its accommodation, books, office equipment and stationery, its records, general financial needs, staff matters, etc., must be attended to.[65] Of course the administrative functions of the chief justice might still be justified as a necessary incident of the administration of justice even if the prohibition were held to apply to judges as individuals.

That the prohibition does not apply to judges as individuals seems to be recognised in several Australian cases. Thus in *Thornton's case*[66] the high court observed:

> It is to be noted that (the enactment) does not take any magistrate as a designated person or as a person who with his own consent . . . may be detached from the court to which he belongs and used for particular purposes. It is addressed to the court of summary jurisdiction as such. . . . All that matters here is that (the enactment) attempts to invest the . . . court of summary jurisdiction and not an individual, with a non-judicial power.[67]

There is happily an emphatic and affirmative decision of the United States supreme court on the point. In *Hayburn's case*, discussed above,[68] the circuit court of New York was prepared to construe the act as appointing judges of the court personally as commissioners to execute the provisions of the act, and that so construed they, as commissioners, were at liberty to accept or decline the office. And they proceeded in that capacity to execute the act. The judges of the circuit court of North Carolina expressed a similar willingness to act personally in the capacity of commissioners, but doubted whether they had the authority since 'the power appears to be given to the court only, and not to the judges of it.' Upon a reference of this specific question to the supreme court itself, it was decided that the power was given to the circuit court, and could not be construed as authorising its judges as individuals to act as commissioners.[69] However, this decision left unaffected the opinions of the justices of the court sitting in the circuit courts of New York and North Carolina that it would have been perfectly constitutional for them to have executed the act as individual commissioners had the power been given to them in that capacity.

In 1851 the supreme court unanimously affirmed the constitutional propriety of non-judicial functions being bestowed upon individual judges.[70] The function in this case was similar to that in *Hayburn's case*. In pursuance of a treaty with Spain after the war in Florida, an act of congress empowered the judges of the district court of Florida (ceded to the United States by Spain under the treaty) to adjudicate claims for injuries made by Spanish soldiers, and to report their findings to the secretary of the treasury, who, on being satisfied that the same was just and equitable, within the provisions of the treaty, should then pay the amounts adjudged to be due. The supreme court held the function not to be judicial.

It is nothing more than the power ordinarily given by law to a commissioner appointed to adjust claims to lands or money under a treaty; or special powers to inquire into or decide any other particular class of controversies in which the public or individuals may be concerned. A power of this description may constitutionally be conferred on a Secretary as well as on a commissioner.[71]

It makes no difference that a commissioner is designated by reference to his office as a judge.

British precedent supports judges performing essentially legislative and executive functions. Judges of the house of Lords, the highest court in the country, are, as peers, members of the upper house of the legislature, and as such participate in its work; they are also privy councillors, while the head of the judiciary, the lord chancellor, is a member of the cabinet.

In this connection the provision in Ghana's Constitution of 1969, vesting the judicial power not in the court but in the 'judiciary',[72] is significant.[73] The term 'judiciary' refers to judges as a body, and not to the institution, i.e. the courts, and the implication would seem to be that the prohibition applies to judges as well.

4. *The prohibition of retrospective criminal legislation*

Earlier we expressed the view, agreeing with the judicial committee of the privy council, that a retrospective legislation, otherwise called an *ex post facto* law, is not, by reason of being such alone, an interference with judicial power. But it does impinge quite seriously on judicial power where it is directed towards the reversal of a particular court decision. We may recall the retroactive constitutional amendment of 1963, which reversed the decision of the judicial committee upholding the validity of Chief Akintola's dismissal from the premiership of Western Nigeria, the effect being to maintain the chief in the office. If the court were to rule that an action of the president was done without legal authority or was in excess of his power under the enabling law, and the national assembly were to back up the action with a retrospective legislation, such use of the legislative power is oppressive and an abuse of power, but it cannot be an interference with the judicial power.

Retrospective legislation may be put to other oppressive uses. It may be used to take away accrued or vested rights, which may be rights arising under a contract or other transaction or rights arising from a public appointment, as where a public office is vacated retrospectively in order to disentitle its incumbent to the benefits of the office, or where an act of a public functionary, agency or individual, which was valid when done, is invalidated by a retrospective law. This is peculiarly so with a retrospective repeal statute, e.g. Income Tax (Rents) (Repeal etc.) Decree 1969, which repealed certain enactments with retrospective effect. A statute which alters retroactively the procedure for the exercise of power or function may also have that effect, for example Statutory Corporations Service Commission (Amendment) Decree which, with retrospective effect, made the approval of the federal executive council a condition for the exercise by a statutory corporation of its power to appoint a managing director for the corporation.

But the most oppressive use of retrospective legislation is to make a criminal offence of an act or omission that was not such when it took place. This may take either of two forms — by the usual method of back-dating the commencement of the criminal enactment or, without back-dating the commencement, by specifically making an offence acts done before that date as in the case of the Exchange

Control (Anti-Sabotage) Decree 1977, which made an offence acts done before its commencement (5 August 1977) but not earlier than 29 July 1975.

Retroactive legislation is thus an unmitigated evil. It is for this reason that it is prohibited absolutely by the Constitution of the United States (art. 1, ss. 9 and 10). The Nigerian Constitution does not go as far as that. It only prohibits the making of law which, 'in relation to any criminal offence whatsoever . . . shall have retrospective effect' (s. 4[9]).[74] A clause in the bill of rights, chapter IV of the Constitution, also provides that 'no person shall be held to be guilty of a criminal offence on account of any act or omission that did not, at the time it took place, constitute such an offence; and no penalty shall be imposed for any criminal offence heavier than the penalty in force at the time the offence was committed' (s. 33[8]). This latter provision is clearly apt to cover the situation in the Exchange Control (Anti-Sabotage) Decree 1977, but it is arguable whether it covers the case where the commencement of the law is backdated, which has the implication that the act or omission is deemed to have been an offence when it took place. But there is a clear difference between on the one hand, an act or omission *constituting* an offence, and on the other an act or omission being *deemed* to constitute an offence. It seems that the clause in the Bill of Rights, s. 33(8), is equally apt to cover the situation where the commencement of a criminal legislation is backdated. However that may be, the prohibition of retroactive criminal legislation in s. 4(9) clearly covers both situations.

There is another respect in which the prohibition in s. 4(9) may have a wider effect than that in s. 33(8). The former precludes a retrospective repeal of a criminal legislation. This could become important as disabling a political party in control of the legislature, by means of retrospective legislation, from relieving a supporter of liability for a criminal offence that he has committed or from relieving him of the effect of a conviction and sentence already awarded against him by a court of law.

The military government has a singularly bad record in this matter of retrospective legislation. Of the 522 decrees made by the federal military government between 16 January 1966 and 31 December 1978, 257, or nearly 50 per cent, have retrospective effect, with forty-six creating criminal offences. The period of retrospective operation was mostly less than a year, but in many cases it was more than a year, eight years being the longest, followed by six-and-a-half and five years.

5. *The prohibition of ouster of the court's jurisdiction*

The vesting of judicial power in the courts is not by itself a grant of jurisdiction to any individual judge or court. The two things need to be clearly distinguished. Judicial power in the sense in which it is vested in the courts by the Constitution refers to the general power of an organised political community to settle disputes among its members, and to try and punish those offending against it. The distribution or allocation of that power among individual courts or judges is a function of law-making either through the supreme law of the constitution or through ordinary law. It is the specific allocations of the general judicial power that bestow jurisdiction on individual courts. Jurisdiction relates therefore to the power of a particular court to hear and determine certain cases or classes of cases; as such it has to be specifically conferred by law (the constitution or ordinary law) quite apart from the general vesting of the judicial power in the judicature. The relation between judicial power and jurisdiction is thus that between the general and the particular; the former may be regarded as the unallocated whole embracing the separate jurisdictions and powers which under various enabling laws the courts exercise in the administration of justice. 'Without jurisdiction', said Chief Justice Chase for the U.S. supreme court, 'the court cannot proceed at all in any cause.'[75]

Normally, the constitution grants only the minimum of jurisdiction, leaving the rest to be prescribed by ordinary legislation. The situation is thus created that the legislature, by its control over the jurisdiction of the courts and consequently of judicial remedies, can effectively bar access to the courts to the individual for the determination of his rights against the government, in so far of course as jurisdiction in any particular case is not conferred by the Constitution. This is what is referred to as ouster of jurisdiction. Jurisdiction is ousted by means of a privative or exclusionary clause in a statute whereby finality, conclusiveness or unquestionability is conferred upon governmental acts done thereunder.

By the previous Nigerian Constitutions only a certain amount of original jurisdiction is conferred on the courts, viz. the specific jurisdiction granted for the determination of election petitions and for the enforcement of rights guaranteed by the Constitution. There is also the jurisdiction granted to the supreme court in respect of disputes between the federation and a state or between states in so far as such disputes involve any question (whether of law or fact) on which the existence or extent of a legal right depends. Being based in the Constitution, these jurisdictions are, as earlier stated, guaranteed against ouster by the legislature. Thus, while the general original jurisdiction of the high court was not specifically defined, the power of the legislature to oust it is somewhat confined.

Our new Constitution has not only confirmed these jurisdictions, but has gone further to spell out the general original jurisdiction of the high court. It grants to the high court 'unlimited jurisdiction to hear and determine any civil proceedings in which the existence or extent of a legal right, power, duty, liability, privilege, interest, obligation or claim is in issue or to hear and determine any criminal proceedings involving or relating to any penalty, forfeiture, punishment or other liability in respect of an offence committed by any person' (s. 236[1]). This seems effectively to bar ouster of the court's jurisdiction under any law.

As if to put the matter beyond any shadow of doubt the Constitution makes this further declaration in s. 4(8): 'The exercise of legislative powers by the National Assembly or by a House of Assembly shall be subject to the jurisdiction of courts of law and of judicial tribunals established by law; and accordingly, the National Assembly or a House of Assembly shall not enact any law that ousts or purports to oust the jurisdiction of a court of law or of a judicial tribunal established by law.' Although this declaration may appear somewhat superfluous, its inclusion should not surprise anyone familiar with the statute book of the military government, with its frightful record of forty-five decrees ousting the jurisdiction of the courts. This is the evil that prompted the constituent assembly to insert the declaration.

It is not only the fact of ouster but also the method and form of it that is frightful. It has taken a variety of forms and combination of forms, the aim being to ensure that all possible loopholes for the court's intervention are effectively plugged. The traditional formulas for conferring finality, conclusiveness or unquestionability on governmental acts are not completely watertight, because of the view taken by the courts that such a provision cannot, in itself, confer on governmental authorities power to determine, free from intervention by the courts, the limit of their powers under the law. In other words, examination by the court of the extent and limits of the authority's power under a law is not precluded by a clause providing that the act or decision of the authority shall be final or conclusive or shall not be questioned in any court of law.

To get round this, the decrees have designed new formulas which are used in combination to achieve comprehensiveness:

(*a*) Civil proceedings in respect of any act, matter or thing done or *purported to be done* under the decrees are barred; the words, 'purported to be done' are most significant indeed.

(b) If such proceedings have been or are instituted before or after the commencement of the decree, they shall abate, be discharged and made void.

(c) Any judgment, decision or order of any court given or made in relation to such proceedings shall have no effect or where appropriate be deemed never to have had effect.

(d) Specific remedies — *quo warranto, certiorari, mandamus*. prohibition, injunction or declaration — are barred.

(e) Rights guaranteed by the Constitution are excluded, with the additional stipulation that the question whether any of those rights has been or is being or would be contravened by anything done or purported to be done under the decree shall not be enquired into in any court of law.

(f) The persons acting under the decrees are relieved of liability for their acts.

Furthermore, the jurisdiction of the court is, either by express words or by implication, excluded whenever a special tribunal is established under various decrees for the trial of specified offences.

Executive or administrative acts of the military government are thus impenetrably shielded from judicial inquiry and review. As for its decrees, judicial review is anathema, an outrage. Thus when the supreme court, with a courage that is both noble and historic, dared to hold a decree invalid for unconstitutionality, the federal military government immediately responded with an assertion of its absolute supremacy in terms at once authoritative and imperious. The decree[76] is worth quoting *in extenso* in this connection:

WHEREAS the military revolution which took place on January 15 1966 and which was followed by another on July 29 1966, effectively abrogated the whole pre-existing legal order in Nigeria except what has been preserved under the Constitution (Suspension and Modification) Decree 1966 (1966 No. 1): AND WHEREAS each military revolution involved an abrupt political change which was not within the contemplation of the Constitution of the Federation 1963 (hereafter referred to as 'the Constitution of 1963'):

AND WHEREAS by the Constitution (Suspension and Modification) Decree (1966 No. 1) there was established a new government known as the 'Federal Military Government' with absolute powers to make laws for the peace, order and good government of Nigeria or any part thereof with respect to any matter whatsoever and, in exercise of the said powers, the said Federal Military Government permitted certain provisions of the said Constitution of 1963 to remain in operation as supplementary to the said Decree:

AND WHEREAS by section 6 of the said Constitution (Suspension and Modification) Decree 1966, no question as to the validity of any Decree or any Edict (in so far as by section 3[4] thereof the provisions of the Edict are not inconsistent with the provisions of a Decree) shall be entertained by any court of law in Nigeria:

AND WHEREAS by Schedule 2 of the said Constitution (Suspension and Modification) Decree 1966 the provisions of a Decree shall prevail over those of the unsuspended provisions of the said Constitution of 1963:

NOW THEREFORE THE FEDERAL MILITARY GOVERNMENT hereby decrees as follows:

1. — (1) The preamble hereto is hereby affirmed and declared as forming part of this Decree.

(2) It is hereby declared also that —

(a) for the efficacy and stability of the government of the Federation; and

(b) with a view to assuring the effective maintenance of the territorial integrity of Nigeria and the peace, order and good government of the Federation, any decision, whether made before or after the commencement of this Decree, by any court of law in the exercise or purported exercise of any powers under the Constitution or any enactment or law of the Federation or of any State which has purported to declare or shall hereafter purport to declare the invalidity of any Decree or of any Edict (in so far as the provisions of the Edict are not inconsistent with the provisions of a Decree) or the incompetence of any of the governments in the Federation to make the same is or shall be null and void and of no effect whatsoever as from the date of the making thereof.

That a military government, with a corrective and reforming mission, should be impatient with the judicial review of its measures, both legislative and executive, should not surprise us, since the two have different orientations. A military government is not a democracy, and, as Rupert Emerson has said, it is debasing the currency of political terminology to talk of 'military democracy'.[77] Its whole orientation is based upon command and unquestioning obedience, discipline and regimentation. Judicial review, on the other hand, is a distinctly democratic process; it is, in the words of Professor Charles Black, 'the people's institutionalised means of self-control',[78] the 'self-restraint of democracy'.[79]

The absolute supremacy of the decrees of the federal military government now yields to the overriding supremacy of the Constitution; like all other laws, they have validity only to the extent that they are in conformity with the Constitution (ss. 1[3] and 274[3]). Any privative or exclusionary clause in a decree which continues in operation after the coming into force of the Constitution is invalid. However, the Constitution makes one concession to the enactments of the military government. It is provided that the judicial power vested in the courts shall not 'extend to any action or proceedings relating to any existing law made on or after 15 January 1966 for determining any issue or question as to the competence of any authority or person to make any such law' (s. 6[6][d]). Furthermore, the Constitution entrenches four decrees by providing that their provisions are not to be invalidated by any inconsistency with its own provisions, and that they shall 'continue to apply and have full effect in accordance with their tenor and to the like extent as any other provisions forming part of this Constitution, and shall not be altered or repealed except in accordance with the provisions' for constitutional amendment (s. 274[5]). The four decrees so entrenched are the National Youth Service Corps Decree 1973; the Public Complaints Decree 1975; the Nigerian Security Organisation Decree 1976; and the Land Use Decree 1978.

REFERENCES

1. *Obayuwana* v. *The Governor of Bendel State & others*, Suit No. B/25/80 of 24/6/80. See also *Radio Corpn. Property Ltd.* v *Commonwealth* (1937) 59 C.L.R. 170 at 185; *Huddart Parker Ltd.* v. *Commonwealth* (1931) 44 C.L.R. 492 at 515, 516.
2. T.M. Cooley, *Principles of Constitutional Law* (2nd edn., 1891), 160–1. The rule was applied by Chief Justice Marshall in 1810. Dissenting in *United States* v. *Constantine*, 296 U.S. 287, 298–9 (1935), Justice Cardozo spoke of 'a wise and ancient doctrine that a court will not inquire into the motives of a legislative body'.
3. Bickel, *The Least Dangerous Branch* (1962), 215.
4. See *Latham C.J. in Elliot* v. *Commonwealth* (1935) 54 C.L.R. 657, 665–6.
5. (1960) 364 U.S. 339.
6. *Guinn* v. *United States*, 238 U.S. 347 (1915); *Lane* v. *Wilson*, 307 U.S. 268 (1939). For another illustrative case, see *Yick Wo* v. *Hopkins*, 118 U.S. 356 (1886).
7. See, e.g., *Lochner* v. *New York* (1905) 198 U.S. 45. For full discussion, see chapter 24 below.
8. *Schenck* v. *United States* (1919) 249 U.S. 47. For full discussion, see chapter 22 below.
9. *Patel* v. *Att.-Gen. of Zambia* (1968) S.J.Z. 1. Contrast *Kachasu* v. *Att.-Gen. for Zambia*, 1967/HP/273.
10. *Kachasu* v. *Att.-Gen. for Zambia*, 1967/HP/273.
11. *Speiser* v. *Randell* (1958) 357 U.S. 513.
12. *Yates* v. *United States*, 354 U.S. 298 (1958).
13. *Lochner* v. *New York*, 198 U.S. 45, 53 (1905).
14. For a discussion of the constitutionality of Nigerian law relating to sedition and the publication of false news likely to cause fear and alarm, see chapter 22 below.
15. Newspaper (Prohibition of Circulation) Decree 1967 — one of the decrees repealed on 28 September 1979 by the Constitution of the Federal Republic of Nigeria (Certain Consequential Repeals, etc.) Decree 1979.
16. Constitution of the Federal Republic of Nigeria (Certain Consequential

Repeals) Decree 1978.
17. Amnesty International Report 1978 (for the period 1 July, 1977 to 30 June 1978). See West Africa, 5 February, 1979, 195 and 197.
18. *Ex parte Milligan* (1864) 2 Wall 2; also *Duncan* v. *Kahanamoku*, 327 U.S. 304 (1945).
19. These tribunals were abolished and replaced by the high court under the decree of 28 September 1979.
20. *Liyange* v. *R* [1967] A.C. 259.
21. For full discussion, see Nwabueze, *Judicialism in Commonwealth Africa* (1977), chapter 1.
22. *Waterside Workers' Federation of Australia* v. *J.W. Alexander Ltd.* (1918) 25 C.L.R. 434, 442.
23. The only decree in this category which was still in force in September 1979 was among those repealed by the decree of 28 September 1979.
24. Repealed by the decree of 28 September 1979.
25. *Liyanage* v. *R*, ibid. at 289–90.
26. *Lakanmi* v. *Att.-Gen.* (West) S.C. 58/69 of 24 April 1970.
27. *Fletcher* v. *Peck* (1810) 8 Cranch 87.
28. *Commentaries* (4th edn) Vol. 1, 44.
29. *Liyanage* v. *R.*, ibid.
30. *Kariapper* v. *Wijesinha* [1967] 3 All E.R. 485.
31. ibid.
32. *United States* v. *Lovett* (1945) 320 U.S. 303.
33. at p. 318.
34. Robbery and Firearms (Special Provisions) Decree 1970.
35. Offences against the Person (Special Provisions) Decree 1974 – repealed by the decree of 28 September 1979.
36. Counterfeit Currency (Special Provisions) Decree 1974.
37. Petroleum Production and Distribution (Anti-Sabotage) Decree 1975.
38. Corrupt Practices Decree 1975 – repealed by the decree of 28 September 1979.
39. Offences against the Person (Special Provisions) Decree 1974; Corrupt Practices Decree 1975.
40. Robbery and Firearms (Special Provisions) Decree 1970; Counterfeit Currency (Special Provisions) Decree 1974.
41. See Constitution of the Federal Republic of Nigeria (Certain Consequential Repeals) Decree 1978.
42. The Exchange Control (Anti-Sabotage) Decree 1977 was repealed by the decree of 28 September 1979.
43. Per Justice Dixon in *Victorian Stevedoring and General Contracting Co. Pty. Ltd.* v. *Dignan* (1931), 46 C.L.R. 73, 97–8.
44. In *re Judiciary and Navigation Act* (1921), 29 C.L.R. 257, 271–2; later in his judgment he said: 'There is nothing in the separation of powers that necessarily involves that the High Court cannot be employed to aid the Executive – judicially, at all events' (276).
45. *The King* v. *Fed. Court of Bankruptcy; Ex parte Lowenstein* (1938), 59 C.L.R. 556.
46. ibid., 588.

47. Cf. the power of a judge to initiate disciplinary action against a lawyer for professional misconduct: *Att.-Gen. for The Gambia* v. *N'Jie* [1961] A.C. 617 (P.C.).
48. ibid., 589.
49. *Queen Victoria Memorial Hospital* v. *Thornton* (1953) 87 C.L.R. 144.
50. p. 151.
51. *Att.-Gen. for Australia* v. *R. & Boilermakers' Society of Australia* (1956) 94 C.L.R. 254.
52. [1957] A.C. 288; see also *R.* v. *Spicer, ex p. Australian Builders' Labourers Fedn.* (1957) 100 C.L.R. 277, where a statute conferring non-judicial powers on a court was declared invalid.
53. ibid., 319.
54. ibid., 310.
55. *Bond* v. *George A. Bond & Co. Ltd. and Bond's Industries Ltd.* (1930) 44 C.L.R. 11.
56. [1957] A.C. 288, 316. This reason has doubtful validity in relation to a function that is closely related to a judicial function, like the giving of an advisory opinion.
57. ibid., 315.
58. 2 Dall. 409 (1792), see n., 410–14.
59. *United States* v. *Ferreira* (1851) 13 How. 40; *United States* v. *Evans* (1909) 213 U.S. 297.
60. ss. 73 and 75.
61. ss. 76 and 77.
62. See *Ex parte McCardie* (1868) 7 Wall. 506: 'Jurisdiction is power to declare the law', 514.
63. art. III, s. 2.
64. 2nd sch., part III.
65. *Cf. Att.-Gen. of The Gambia* v. *N'Jie* [1961] A.C. 617, 630 (P.C.): 'Some of the powers of the Chief Justice are clearly judicial powers, as when he sits in court to decide civil or criminal cases. Others are equally clearly administrative powers, as when he directs the times at which the offices of the court shall be open, or appoints notaries public, or makes rules of court.'
66. (1957) 87 C.L.R. 144.
67. ibid., 152.
68. Above, 205.
69. *United States* v. *Yale Todd* (1794) unreported, but noted in some detail in a note in *United States* v. *Ferreira*, ibid.
70. *United States* v. *Ferreira*, ibid.
71. ibid., 48.
72. art. 102.
73. See James Read, 'Judicial Power and the Constitution of Ghana', *Review of Ghana Law* (1973) vol. III, no. 107, 120 n. 35; G. Sawer, *Australian Federalism in the Courts* (1967), 166.
74. See *The King* v. *Kidman & others* (1915) 20 C.L.R. 425 at 441–2 in relation to a similar provision in the Australian Constitution.
75. *Ex parte McCardie* (1868) 7 Wall. 506, 514.
76. Federal Military Government (Supremacy and Enforcement of Powers)

Decree 1970. Repealed by the decree of 28 September 1979.
  77. Rupert Emerson, *From Empire to Nation* (1962), 284.
  78. Charles Black, *The People and the Court* (1960), 107.
  79. ibid., 115.

15
PRESUMPTION OF CONSTITUTIONALITY OF LEGISLATION

1. *Nature of the presumption*

Legislation is an act of a competent authority of the state duly mandated by the Constitution. It is proper therefore that it should be presumed to be within the authority conferred by the Constitution until the contrary is proved. It is also desirable that the judiciary, as an unelected and oligarchic body, should approach its function of reviewing legislation for constitutionality with due respect for the judgment of the elected representatives of the people in the legislature, bearing in mind that the legislature is accountable to the people for a faithful discharge of the power entrusted to it.

Of course, before such a presumption can be made, a rational relationship must exist between a statute and the purpose of the power in pursuance of which it was enacted. If the statute cannot rationally be predicated upon the Constitution, if it is not rationally related to the interests for the regulation or protection of which the legislature is granted power by the Constitution, then it is unconstitutional. The court is, however, to presume the existence of facts supporting the rationality of the connection between the statute and the purpose of the power,[1] provided of course that they could rationally be supposed to exist.

The existence of facts supporting the legislative judgement is to be presumed, for regulatory legislation affecting ordinary commercial transactions is not to be pronounced unconstitutional unless in the light of facts made known or generally assumed it is of such a character as to preclude the assumption that it rests upon some rational basis within the knowledge and experience of the legislators.'[2]

The question of the nature of the presumption concerns more particularly the degree of proof required to disprove the presumed rationality of the connection between a statute and the purpose of the power enabling it, or, in Charles Black's phrase, 'the strength of the showing it takes to overcome it'.[3] Different degrees of proof are suggested by the various formulations of the presumption. Chief Justice Marshall of the U.S. supreme court has stated it thus:

The question whether a law be void for its repugnancy to the Constitution, is, at all times, a question of such delicacy, which ought seldom, if ever, to be decided in the affirmative in a doubtful case. . . . It is not on slight implication and vague conjecture that the legislature is to be pronounced to have transcended its powers, and its acts to be considered as void. The opposition between the constitution and the law should be such that the judge feels a clear and strong conviction of their incompatibility with each other.[4]

The judge's reference to his feeling 'a clear and strong conviction' suggests that more than the 'balance of probabilities' test applied in ordinary civil actions is required. It suggests the criminal case test of proof beyond reasonable doubt. This is borne out in subsequent cases. As Justice Isaacs of the high court of Australia has said:

Nullification of enactments and confusion of public business are not lightly to be introduced. Unless, therefore, it becomes clear beyond reasonable doubt that the legislation in question transgresses the limits laid down by the organic law of the Constitution, it must be allowed to stand as the true expression of the national will.[5]

And Justice Washington of the U.S. supreme court uses the same language.

It is but a decent respect due to the . . . legislative body by which any law is passed to presume in favour of its validity, until its violation of the constitution is proved beyond all reasonable doubt. This has always been the language of the court when that subject has called for its decision, and I know it expresses the honest sentiments of each and every member of this bench.[6]

What this means is that any reasonable doubt must be resolved in favour of the statute. The burden of proof on a challenger of a statute is thus very heavy indeed.

But James Thayer conceives of the presumption in terms that require an even higher degree of proof. He postulates that it is a settled principle of the courts in the United States not to disregard a statute unless 'those who have the right to make laws have not merely made a mistake, but have made a very clear one — so clear that it is not open to rational question.'[7] According to the formulations above, it is the subjective conviction of the judge that is relevant and conclusive as to whether the unconstitutionality of a statute has been proved beyond reasonable doubt. In Thayer's formulation, however, the judge's conviction is not conclusive. Whatever his feeling, if the matter is open to rational doubt in the minds of others, if the mistake is not very clear to every rational person, the statute must be allowed to stand. So conceived, the presumption becomes virtually irrefutable, since there must be few statutes of which the unconstitutionality would be so clear as not to admit of a rational doubt by someone.[8] The incidence of division among judges of an appellate court on the question of constitutionality bears this out. In the U.S. supreme court in particular, unanimity among the judges on the constitutionality or unconstitutionality of statutes is rather infrequent. A judge's dissent from a majority view holding a statute to be unconstitutional indicates conclusively the existence of a rational doubt. Thayer would thus make a minority, even a minority of one out of nine, prevail over the majority. The disregard of a statute for unconstitutionality would thus require unanimity among the judges. Thayer justifies this high degree of respect for the legislature thus:

> It must indeed be studiously remembered, in judicially applying such a test as this of what a legislature may reasonably think, that virtue, sense, and competent knowledge are always to be attributed to that body. The conduct of public affairs must always go forward upon conventions and assumptions of that sort. [. . .] And so in a court's revision of legislative acts, as in its revision of a jury's acts, it will always assume a duly instructed body; and the question is not merely what persons may rationally do who are such as we often see, in point of fact, in our legislative bodies, persons untaught it may be, indocile, thoughtless, reckless, incompetent, — but what those other persons, competent, well-instructed, sagacious, attentive, intent only on public ends, fit to represent a self-governing people, such as our theory of government assumes to be carrying on our public affairs, — what such persons may reasonably think or do, what is the permissible view for them.[9]

But insistence on unanimity would effectively exclude an appeal court, and consequently a trial court, from the function of reviewing statutes for unconstitutionality. It is not only the court's checking function that would thus be reduced to nothing; its legitimating role would also be destroyed,[10] for the latter has meaning only because of the former. 'If', says Charles Black, 'it became generally known that the Court . . . would . . . sustain any governmental act not shown to be unconstitutional beyond the possibility of rational doubt, then the Court's upholding of the measures of government would not even tend to establish the legitimacy of these measures.'[11]

Given its incompatibility with the actual practice of the courts, Thayer's claim that his test is settled by authority is in fact not warranted by the cases he cites as laying it down. As Charles Black has demonstrated by a close analysis, most of them were cases in which the court felt a strong conviction of the constitutionality of the statutes in question, so that no question arose of the court deferring to the judgment of the legislature against its own conviction of the statute's unconstitutionality. In the others the court held the statutes concerned unconstitutional, although in none of them could the unconstitutionality be said to be beyond rational question. On the contrary, the doubt in two of the cases was such as to divide the court 4−3.[12] Black concludes therefore:

> There is not the shadow of a ghost of a case for the proposition that it has been traditional practice for the Supreme Court to invalidate Acts of Congress only

where all rational men must necessarily agree that they are unconstitutional.[13] [. . .] In no case in which the Supreme Court has declared an Act of Congress unconstitutional has the question been one on which no rational man could have a contrary opinion.[14]

2. *Application of the presumption*

The application of the presumption depends upon the existence in the mind of the judge of a reasonable doubt concerning the validity or otherwise of the statute. If there is no such doubt, if the statute is obviously invalid, the presumption is inapplicable. Constitutional prohibitions are mandatory in their terms, imposing upon the Court, in cases of clear and patent transgression, a duty to declare thus, unfettered by any presumption. The presumption cannot be used to validate a patently unconstitutional statute.

The nature of the constitutional provision which a statute is alleged to transgress is an important factor affecting the operation of the presumption. Is the provision a grant of power or a prohibition of it? A constitutional provision granting power to the legislature allows quite ample scope for the operation of the presumption, since the only question would be whether the legislature acted within or in excess of its powers. If the legislature has power to legislate with respect to, say, commerce, any law relating to commerce must be presumed to be *prima facie* within its bounds. The grant of power invests the legislature with a discretion to decide what are the commercial needs of the community, and what regulations are necessary or desirable. It has a mandate, conferred upon it by the votes of the electorate, to make this decision on behalf of the nation, and its judgment, whether right or wrong, should be respected by the court. As a body elected by, and responsible to, the people, an intention to use its power irrationally is not lightly to be imputed to it.

These considerations are inapplicable when the legislature legislates on a matter withdrawn from it by the Constitution. By withdrawing a matter from the legislature, the Constitution not only denies it competence over such matter but also positively prohibits it from legislating on it. Thus, under the Nigerian federal system, any matter reserved exclusively to the states is outside the competence of the federal legislature, and consequently is prohibited to it. Also, the guarantee of fundamental rights by the Constitution is a constitutional prohibition against the making of any law which will deny, abridge or otherwise violate such rights.

However, the effect of a constitutional prohibition on the presumption of constitutionality depends on whether the prohibition is an absolute or a qualified one. Where a prohibition is absolute in the sense that it admits of no exceptions, as in the case of the prohibition of inhuman treatment, slavery and discrimination or in the case of residual matters which are reserved exclusively to the states and so prohibited absolutely to the national assembly, any legislation in violation of the prohibition is *ex facie* unconstitutional; in other words, the law is presumed invalid unless and until the contrary is proved.

A great deal of the confusion about the 'presumption of constitutionality' could be resolved if it were clearly understood that presumptions may shift as facts come to light, or as more aspects of a case are noted. There is no necessary inconsistency whatever in asserting that there is a general presumption of constitutionality, but that a statute of a certain sort is presumed unconstitutional. [. . .] The question is simply whether the added fact — the fact that the challenged statute is of a certain sort — is or ought to be sufficient to shift the presumption.[15]

A qualified prohibition has, however, a different effect. For example, most rights in the bill of rights of the Constitution are guaranteed by the same device of a positive prohibition of violation by state action, but this is qualified by an exception clause authorising violation by a law that is reasonably justifiable in a democratic society in the interests of defence, public safety, public order, public morality or public health either at all times (as regards freedom of conscience, expression, assembly, association and movement) or only during an emergency (as regards life, personal liberty and freedom from forced labour). The effect of this is that no presumption can be made either in favour of or against the constitutionality of the law until it is shown positively that a rational connection exists between the law and defence, public safety, public order, etc. The facts showing the existence of such a connection have now to be established positively by the state, and not by means of a presumption. However, once the necessary factual foundation has been laid by the adduction of facts which establish the rationality of the connection between the law and the prescribed interests, the court must infer that the statute is justifiable in those interests. The effect of the presumption here is to lighten the burden on the state; it need not prove beyond reasonable doubt that the statute is justifiable in the stipulated interests, but only that it is rationally related to them, and thereupon the onus shifts to those impugning the statute to establish that it is not reasonably justifiable. 'It seems to me reasonable,' writes Charles Black, 'to cast on the governmental agency that would introduce an exception the burden of establishing that it is a valid exception, and not to cast on the man whose speech is being abridged the burden of showing that the exception is *not* a valid exception.'[16]

The supreme court of India has adopted much the same position as here adumbrated.

There is undoubtedly a presumption in favour of the constitutionality of a legislation. But when the enactment on the face of it is found to violate a fundamental right guaranteed under Article 19(1) (g) of the Constitution, it must be held to be invalid unless those who support the legislation can bring it within the purview of the exception laid down in clause (6) of the article. If the respondents do not place any materials before the court to establish that the legislation comes within the permissible limits of clause (6), it is surely not for the appellants to prove negatively that the legislation was not reasonable and was not conducive to the welfare of the community.[17]

Speaking for the U.S. supreme court in 1938, Justice Stone stated that

There may be a narrower scope for operation of the presumption of constitutionality when legislation appears on its face to be within a specific prohibition of the Constitution, such as those of the first ten amendments, which are deemed equally specific when held to be embraced within the Fourteenth.[18]

Although this statement appeared only as a footnote in the judgment, it has been cited with approval in three later cases.[19] Actually, the U.S. supreme court draws a distinction between the economic rights — property and private enterprise — guaranteed by the Fifth Amendment and the democratic freedoms — religion, speech, press and peaceful assembly — guaranteed by the First Amendment. In regard to legislation alleged to violate a right of the former type, it has held that no presumption is to be made unless and until it is shown by factual evidence that the impugned law is rationally related to the public welfare. The effect of the prohibition is thus as stated above.

As regards the democratic freedoms guaranteed by the first Amendment, the court is divided on whether the prohibition is to be treated as absolute, with the consequence that any law violating it will be presumptively invalid, or whether it is to be regarded as a qualified prohibition. While the majority of the court has favoured the latter view, they have also accorded to rights in this class a 'preferred position'. The effect of the preferred position of these rights varies according as the law in question prohibits or otherwise restrains in advance the exercise of the freedom or merely imposes subsequent punishment for acts done in the exercise of the freedom. By a majority of 6−4 the court in 1971 held that 'any system of prior restraints of expression comes to the United States Supreme Court bearing a heavy presumption against its constitutional validity, and a party who seeks to have such a restraint upheld thus carries a heavy burden of showing justification for the imposition of such a restraint.'[20]

Where, however, a law imposes no prior restraint on expression, peaceable assembly or religion, but merely punishes an act after it is done, then the effect of the preferred position of these rights is not to make the law presumptively invalid; it only 'balances' out the presumption of constitutionality, thereby placing on the state the burden to adduce proof that such subsequent punishment is justified by clear and present danger. No doubt the test of 'clear and present danger' requires of the state more than merely to establish a rational connection between its laws and the public welfare. Yet it implies no presumption of invalidity; it simply balances out the presumption of constitutionality, without compelling a presumption the other way.

The Zambian high court has adopted a similar attitude. In a case in 1968,[21] it held that the application of the presumption of constitutionality in the ordinary way to a law alleged to contravene a guaranteed right would be contrary to the underlying policy of the guarantee which, as appears from the introductory section of the bill of rights in the Zambian Constitution,[22] is to *secure* those rights, the limitations on them in favour of the state being only secondary, designed merely to 'ensure that the enjoyment of the said rights and freedoms by the individual does not prejudice the rights and freedoms of others or the public interest'.[23] Accordingly, the court held that it is for the state to show positively, and not by presumption, that a derogation is reasonably required in an objective sense in the interests of defence, public safety, public order, etc.

In the light of the approach adopted in this matter by the courts of India, the United States and Zambia, it is unfortunate that in Nigeria the prohibitory nature of the bills of rights has been lost sight of, with the result that the presumption of constitutionality has been applied to laws derogating from guaranteed freedoms in the same way as to other laws. It has thus bestowed presumptive constitutionality upon a statute alleged to have violated the guarantee of freedom of movement under the 1963 Constitution[24] by authorising the removal of a deposed chief from his own area to another within the country.[25] Without proof by the state, the court presumed the statute and the removal order made thereunder to be reasonably justifiable in terms of the constitutional provision, which permits restriction of movement or residence by a law that is reasonably justifiable in a democratic society in the interest of defence, public safety or public order;[26] further, it held that the presumption had not been rebutted by the arguments advanced against the statute and the removal order.[27] In an earlier case[28] where a statutory prohibition of political activity by juveniles was challenged, the court said that the passage of the statute through the legislature was presumptive evidence that it was reasonably justifiable in a democratic society, because the judgment of the legislature was entitled to great weight.

These decisions, as has been said, are unfortunate. The rationale for the presumption that the judgment of the legislature is entitled to respect because it presents the people, is questionable in the context of a constitutional guarantee of rights. Particularly in Nigeria under the 1963 Constitution, the bill of rights was meant primarily as a protection for minorities against the majority that dominated the legislature. To allow the judgment of the legislature to prevail in this case would be to impair the efficacy of that protection. In relation to human rights therefore the presumption of constitutionality would appear to be repugnant to the primary purpose for which those rights were guaranteed in the constitution. Also questionable is the application of the presumption to subsidiary legislation by the executive. 'As a general rule the legality of [administrative] acts is always open to attack, and there is no presumption in their favour.'[29] There is no reason for treating executive legislation differently from other administrative acts.

3. *Presumption of the regularity of legislative process*

The general principle is that the provisions of the Constitution relating to the enactment of laws are justiciable, imposing upon the court a duty, 'from the performance of which it may not shrink',[30] to enforce them. Thus, whether a quorum was present, whether a majority, ordinary or special was obtained,[31] whether two-thirds of a house meant a two-thirds majority of a quorum or of all the members,[32] whether a bill was read the required number of times, etc., are all questions that may be inquired into and decided by the court. As the judicial committee of the privy council said, 'the minority are entitled under the Constitution of Ceylon to have no amendment of it which is not passed by a two-thirds majority.'[33] 'In view of the express requirements of the Constitution', said the U.S. supreme court, 'the correctness of this general principle cannot be doubted.'[34]

To affirm the justiciability of these provisions is, however, quite a different thing from their actual judicial enforcement. The problem here is one of proof — of the nature of the evidence upon which a court may act when an issue is made as to whether these provisions had in fact been observed. Could the court go behind an enrolled act, duly authenticated in the manner required by the Constitution, by other laws or by convention, to inquire whether it was in fact passed by the legislature in the prescribed manner and form, or whether it corresponds in all respects with the original bill? May the journals of the legislative houses, the reports of their committees, other legislative documents or oral evidence be used to contradict the authentication of an enrolled act? If the enrolment of an act and its authentication by the signatures of the presiding officers of the legislative houses and of the head of state are conclusive evidence of due passage, then the justiciability of the constitutional provisions prescribing the manner and form of legislation is reduced to a mere formality, since, however clear it may be upon such other evidence that an enrolled act had not in fact been duly and regularly passed, the court is bound to reject such evidence. Such in fact is the law in the United States. The enrolment of an act and its authentication by the signatures of the presiding officers and the head of state are conclusive of its having been passed in due form by the legislature, and no other evidence can be used to controvert them. In some Commonwealth independence constitutions the rule has been given constitutional recognition in the provision making the certificate of the speaker conclusive evidence of the observance of the manner and form prescribed for constitutional amendment. And the judicial committee of the privy council has held in an appeal from Sri Lanka that this provision precludes the court from looking beyond the speaker's certificate.[35]

The rule has been applied to preclude judicial inquiry into an allegation that a revenue legislation originated in the senate instead of in the house of representatives as required by the U.S. Constitution;[36] that an act omitted amendments proposed by the senate and agreed to by the house of representatives of Mississippi;[37] that an act omitted a section in the original bill as it was passed by the legislative houses;[38] that a quorum was not present or that a majority of the quorum was not obtained;[39] that certain members of a quorum were seated without having certificates of election;[40] that the majority which passed an act over the president's veto was a two-thirds majority of a quorum, and not of all the members;[41] that a private act was obtained without notice to a person affected by it, as required by standing orders;[42] and that an act was procured by fraud or other improper means.[43] (In most of the U.S. cases the court did in fact, 'for the sake of argument', inquire into the question raised, while at the same time emphasising that its action should not be taken to mean that the legislative journals and other evidence might be used to contradict a duly enrolled and authenticated act.[44])

The rationale for the rule is that the signing of an enrolled bill by the presiding officers is an official attestation by the legislative houses of such a bill having been duly passed by them. It is a declaration by them, through their presiding officers, to the head of state that the bill has received, in due form, the sanction of the legislative branch. And when, on the strength of that declaration, the bill is approved and signed by the head of state, his signature together with those of the presiding officers is a solemn assurance to the court and to the nation that all necessary formalities have been observed. The respect due to coequal and independent departments requires the court to accept and act upon that assurance. To go behind the assurance would involve the subordination of the legislative and the executive branches to the court. The possibility that acceptance of such an assurance as conclusive might enable the presiding officers to impose upon the country as law a bill that was never passed by the legislative houses, was dismissed as too remote, and as imputing a deliberate conspiracy on the part of the presiding officers, the committee on enrolled bills and the clerks of the legislative houses to defeat the expressed will of the legislative houses. Judicial action based on such a suggestion is forbidden by the respect due to a co-ordinate branch of the government.[45] Further, public policy requires that an enrolled act should not be put in question after the public has given faith in its validity and regulated its relations and dealings accordingly. Great uncertainty and instability in statute law would result if an enrolled and duly authenticated act were to be subjected to impeachment on the basis of some evidence of lack of due passage.

Apart from considerations of public policy and the respect due to co-equal departments, the authentication of an enrolled act by the signatures of the presiding officers and the head of state may be considered the best evidence of its due passage. Legislative journals are prepared out of loose and hasty memoranda made in the pressure of business and amid the distractions of a numerous assembly, and its editing by subordinate officials, without authentication by the presiding officers, creates a greater danger of intentional falsification by, for example, the interpolation of sentences or the substitution of one name for another.[46] This does not of course mean that the journals of the legislative houses may never be consulted by the court for purposes other than that of contradicting the certificate of the presiding officers and the approval of the head of state. Indeed, as has been noted, the U.S. supreme court has often, 'for the sake of argument', looked at the legislative journals to demonstrate that the allegation of irregularity was in fact unfounded. The endorsements made on the original bill by the clerks of the legislative houses are no more satisfactory as evidence, for they are 'usually so expressed as not to be intelligible to any one except those who made them, and their scope and effect . . . cannot in many cases be understood unless supplemented by the recollection of the clerks.'[47] Oral evidence has its own difficulty, since it may entail the examination and cross-examination in court of all participating legislators, whose recollections of the proceedings on the bill may prove, after the lapse of time, to be imperfect and unreliable. In a case where the speaker of the U.S. house of representatives testified that he was certain that a section alleged to have been omitted from an act was in the bill when it was passed by the house, the court commented: 'What made him so certain of, or how he was able to recall, that fact, is not stated.'[48]

In Nigeria, the general principle is usually reinforced by specific legislative provision. Thus the Laws Authentication Law 1979 of Lagos state provides in s. 8 as follows:

Every law which purports to be published by the authority and bears a number and reference to a year and a date of commencement or reference to a section shall be received in all courts and by all persons as sufficient evidence that it has been assented to by the Governor or otherwise passed by the House of Assembly as the Law required.

However, the conclusiveness of the authentication of an enrolled act presupposes that the act is 'fair on its face'.[49] If there is something to the 'contrary appearing upon its face',[50] the court will declare it unconstitutional and void. Thus, where a presiding officer of a legislative house is constitutionally required to certify on a constitutional amendment bill that it has been passed by a two-thirds majority, it was held that the certificate being an essential part of the process for enactment, its absence was conclusive against such a majority.[51] Under the U.S. Constitution, when a bill is presented to the president for his approval and signature, and he fails to return it within ten days (Sundays excepted), the bill becomes law thereafter without his signature, unless the return of the bill is prevented by the adjournment of congress.[52] It was held that an act passed by congress less than ten days before the expiry of the session and left unsigned by the president was no statute at all.[53] For the purpose of determining whether an act is fair on its face, the privy council has suggested that the court is not concluded by the published version, but may consult the original bearing the signature of the head of state, which is normally in duplicate; since by law one copy of it has to be filed in the court registry, its inspection by the court, the privy council thought, would not involve an invasion of parliamentary privilege.[54] Such a course was in fact adopted in a South African case to determine whether an act was passed by both houses of parliament sitting jointly as required by that country's Constitution.[55] The published copy of the act stated that it was enacted by the king, the senate and the house of assembly; the court inferred that the omission of a statement that it had been enacted in accordance with the constitutional requirement of a two-thirds majority at a joint sitting was *prima facie* evidence that both houses functioned separately. The court then referred to the copy of the original act as signed by the governor-general, and filed with the registrar of the court. The certificates of the presiding officer of the two houses on this copy indicated that it had been passed by both houses respectively, a fact which the court construed as conclusive that the act was not passed at a joint sitting.[56] In respect of another act before the court, a reference to the original disclosed an endorsement by the speaker to the effect that it had been passed at a joint sitting of both houses.[57]

It remains to be seen whether the supreme court of Nigeria will accept the rule laid down by the U.S. supreme court that the authentication and enrolment of a statute is conclusive evidence of its having been passed in the manner and form prescribed by the Constitution.

REFERENCES

1. Charles Black, *The People and the Court* (1960), 216.
2. *United States* v. *Carolene Products*, 304 U.S. 144, 152 (1938) per Justice Stone.
3. Black, op. cit., 216.
4. *Fletcher* v. *Peck* (1819) 6 Cranch, 87, 128; also *Trustee of Dartmouth College* v. *Woodward* (1819) 4 Wheat, 518, 625.
5. *British Imperial Oil Co. Ltd.,* v. *Fed. Com. of Taxation* (1926) 38 C.L.R. 153, 180.
6. *Ogden* v. *Saunder* (1827) 13 Wheat, 213, 270.
7. Thayer, 'The Origin and Scope of the American Doctrine of Constitutional Law', *Harv. L. Rev.* (1893) 7, 129, 143−4.
8. As Scharpf has rightly commented, a very clear violation will occur only as a deliberate violation of the Constitution, which, in an extreme case, might evince a design towards a revolutionary act. And he wonders whether, if the legislature and the President were really so inclined, it is likely 'they would be stopped by a judicial decision explaining what must have been obvious all the time': 'Judicial Review and the Political Question: a Functional Analysis', *Yale L.J.* (1966) 75, 517, 571, n. 195.
9. Thayer, op. cit., 149.
10. The rationale of judicial review is discussed in chapter 19.
11. Black, *The People and the Court* (1960), 212.
12. *Ogden* v. *Saunder*, ibid.; *Chicago M & St. P. Ry. Co.* v. *Minnesota* (1890) 134 U.S. 418.
13. Black, op. cit., 200.
14. op. cit., 201.
15. op. cit., 217.
16. op. cit., 218.
17. *Saghir Ahmad* v. *State of U.P.* (1955), 707, 726.
18. *United States* v. *Carolene Products*, ibid., 152, n. 4.
19. *Thornhill* v. *Alabama*, 310 U.S. 88, 95; *American Fedn. of Labour* v. *Swing*, 312 U.S. 321, 325; *Thomas* v. *Collins*, 323 U.S. 516, 530. In his protest against the 'preferred position' doctrine, Justice Frankfurter said that 'a footnote hardly seems to be an appropriate way of announcing a new constitutional doctrine': *Kovacs* v. *Cooper* (1949) 336 U.S. 77, 91.
20. *New York Times Co.* v. *United States* (1971) 403 U.S. 713; *Organisation for a Better Austin* v. *Keefe* (1971) 402 U.S. 415, 419; *Carroll* v. *Princess Anne*, 393 U.S. 175, 181 (1968); *Bantam Books, Inc.* v. *Sullivan*, 372 U.S. 58, 70.
21. *Patel* v. *Att.-Gen.* HP/CONST./REF. 1/1968 (unreported); contrast *Kachasu* v. *Att.-Gen.* 1967/HP/273 (unreported).
22. Constitution of Zambia 1973, art. 13.
23. ibid., art 13.

Presumption of Constitutionality of Legislation   293

24. Constitution of Nigeria 1963, s. 27.
25. *Arzika* v. *Governor, Northern Region* (1961) 1 All N.L.R. 379.
26. The removal or exclusion of a chief or ex-chief from his area is specifically authorised by the 1963 Constitution: s. 27(2)(iv).
27. (1961), 1 All N.L.R. 379, at 382.
28. *Cheranci* v. *Cheranci* (1960) N.R.N.B.R. 24 (High Court, N.R.).
29. Wade, *Administrative Law* (1971), 50—1; Bickel, *The Least Dangerous Branch* (1962), 214.
30. *Field* v. *Clark* (1892) 143 U.S. 649, 670.
31. *United States* v. *Ballin* (1892) 144 U.S. 1.
32. *Missouri Pac. Ry. Co.* v. *Kansas* (1919) 248 U.S. 276.
33. *The Bribery Commissioner* v. *Ranasinghe* [1965] A.C. 172.
34. *Field* v. *Clark*, ibid., 669.
35. *The Bribery Commissioner* v. *Ranasinghe*, ibid.
36. art. 1, s. 7; *Rainey* v. *United States* (1910) 232 U.S. 310; *Twin City National Bank* v. *Nebeker* (1897) 167 U.S. 196; *Flint* v. *Stone Tracy Co.* (1911) 220 U.S. 107.
37. *Ex parte Wren*, 63 Miss. 512.
38. *Field* v. *Clark*, ibid.; *Harwood* v. *Wentworth* (1896) 162 U.S. 547.
39. *United States* v. *Ballin*, ibid.
40. *Lyons* v. *Woods* (1894) 153 U.S. 649.
41. *Missouri Pac. Ry. Co.* v. *Kansas* (1919) 248 U.S. 276.
42. *Edinburgh and Dalkeith Ry. Co.* v. *Wauchope* (1842) 8 Cl. & Fin. 710; 1 Bell 252.
43. *Pickin* v. *British Railways Board* [1974] 2 W.L.R. 208 (H.L.); *Waterford, Wexford, Wicklaw and Dublin Ry. Co.* v. *Logan* (1850) 14 Q.B. 672; *Lee* v. *Bude and Torrington Junction Ry. Co.* (1871), L.R. 6 C.P. 576; *Hoani Te Heuheu Tukino* v. *Aotea District Maori Land Board* [1941] A.C. 308.
44. See particularly *Flint* v. *Stone Tracy Co.* ibid; and *Missouri Pac. Ry. Co.* v. *Kansas*, ibid.
45. *Field* v. *Clark*, ibid. at 673.
46. Wigmore thinks that there is no reason for trusting more to the realibility of the enrolment than to that of the journal, and that the one might be falsified as often and as easily as the other: 2 Wigmore, *Evidence* (2nd edn), s. 1350, cited by Finkelstein who explains the rule in terms of the political question doctrine: 'Judicial Self-Limitation', *Harv. L. Rev.* 37, 338, 356—9.
47. *Harwood* v. *Wentworth*, 162 U.S. 547, 562.
48. *Harwood* v. *Wentworth*, ibid., 561. The clerks of both houses also testified to the same effect.
49. *Field* v. *Clark*, ibid., 677.
50. *Field* v. *Clark*, ibid., 672; *United States* v. *Ballin*, 144 U.S. 1 at 3.
51. *The Bribery Commissioner* v. *Ranasinghe*, ibid., 197.
52. art. 1, s. 7, cl. 2.
53. *Okanogan Indians* v. *United States* (1929) 279 U.S. 655.
54. *The Bribery Commissioner* v. *Ranasinghe*, ibid.
55. *Harris* v. *Minister of the Interior* (1952[2]) S.A. 428.
56. ibid., 469.
57. ibid., 469—70.

16
THE JUDICATURE

1. *Organisation of judicial power and of courts*

It is proposed to discuss the way judicial power and the courts are organised by the 1979 Constitution under the following five different headings.

(i) *Extent of federal judicial power*

It hardly needs to be said that the division of powers implied in federalism applies not only to legislative and executive power, but to judicial power as well. But while the extent of federal legislative and executive powers (and state legislative and executive powers too) is clearly set out in the Constitution, no such clear and precise delimitation of federal (and state) judicial power is given. The provision that judicial power 'shall extend . . . to all inherent powers and sanctions of a court of law', and 'to all matters between persons, or between government or authority and any person in Nigeria, and to all actions and proceedings relating thereto, for the determination of any question as to the civil rights and obligations of that person' (s. 6[6][*a*] and [*b*]), is not a delimitation of the extent of federal or state judicial powers. It is rather a definition of the *nature* of judicial power, as a power for the determination of the civil rights and obligations of persons in cases or controversies brought before the courts by such regular proceedings as are established or recognised by law or custom. (The nature of judicial power is discussed more fully in chapter 17.) Even as a definition of judicial power, the provision (s. 6[6][*a*] and [*b*]) is defective in as much as it leaves out the determination of rights in disputes between the Federation and a State or between States (s. 212[1]).

Some indication of the extent of federal judicial power is, however, provided by the definition of 'federal causes' and 'federal offences' in relation to the jurisdiction conferred on state courts to administer federal laws. 'Federal causes' is defined to mean 'civil or criminal cause relating to any matter with respect to which the national assembly has power to make laws', while 'federal offence' means 'an offence contrary to the provisions of an act of the national assembly or any law having effect as if so enacted' (s. 250[3]). But it just cannot be the case that federal judicial power is confined to matters within the legislative competence of the national assembly. It must at least embrace additionally matters arising under the Constitution or those of its provisions that are of a federal character. In the United States, federal judicial power is not determined by federal legislative competence. It is, by express constitutional provision, extended

> to all cases, in Law and Equity, arising under this Constitution, the Laws of the United States, and Treaties made, or which shall be made, under their Authority; — to all Cases affecting Ambassadors, other public Ministers and Consuls; — to all Cases of admiralty and maritime Jurisdiction; — to Controversies to which the United States shall be a Party; — to Controversies between two or more States; — between a State and Citizens of another State; — between Citizens of different States; — between Citizens of the same State claiming Lands under the Grants of different States, and between a State, or the Citizens thereof, and foreign States, Citizens or Subjects.[1]

All such cases or controversies as are enumerated above are embraced in the federal judicial power, notwithstanding that the subject-matter of the case or controversy is within the exclusive legislative competence of a state. Within the boundary marked out by the Constitution, therefore, the judicial power of the United States embraces cases arising under both federal and state laws.

(ii) *Federal courts*
Whatever its extent, the federal judicial power is vested in courts referred to in s. 6(5) of the Constitution, 'being courts established for the Federation'. (The constitutional implications of the vesting of judicial power in the courts have already been discussed in chapter 14.) The words within quotation marks have the effect of restricting the vesting to courts established for the Federation. The significance of this lies in the fact that under s. 6(5)(g) a court which is not established for the federation may nevertheless be 'authorised by law to exercise jurisdiction on matters with respect to which the national assembly may make laws'. This means that the separation (which we have encountered elsewhere) between the vesting of power on the one hand and its exercise on the other is imported into the judicial field.

This arrangement is by no means peculiar to Nigeria. In the United States, while the federal judicial power is vested in the supreme court and such inferior courts as may be ordained and established by congress, it is declared that the Constitution and the laws of the United States shall be the supreme law of the land, and that 'the Judges in every State shall be bound thereby, any Thing in the Constitution or Laws of any State to the Contrary notwithstanding.'[2] This is taken as an implied authority, indeed direction, for the state courts to apply the Constitution and laws of the United States. The state courts are thus 'just as competent to try cases arising under federal law as are the federal courts'.[3] Indeed, because of the restrictions placed on the jurisdiction of the inferior federal courts by congress, many cases arising under federal laws can be tried only in the state courts. However, the whole of the United States is covered by a network of federal courts established by congress, the country being divided for this purpose into ninety districts. A district court is created for each district, and invested with original jurisdiction in all civil cases arising under the Constitution and laws of the United States where the value involved exceeds a prescribed amount or where, whatever the amount involved, the case relates to admiralty, bankruptcy, patents, copyrights, trade marks, revenue of the United States or to the United States as a party. The jurisdiction of the district courts is therefore for the most part concurrent with that of the state courts, except in the special cases mentioned above (i.e. admiralty, bankruptcy, etc.) and except for cases within the exclusive jurisdiction of the state courts. A federal court of appeal is established by an act of congress for each of the eleven judicial circuits into which the country is divided for the purpose of hearing appeals from the district courts.[4]

Only three courts are established for the federation by the Constitution, namely the supreme court of Nigeria, the federal court of appeal and the federal high court (s. 6). The federal capital territory is for this purpose treated as if it were a state, so that, like a state, there is established for it by the Constitution a high court and, if it so requires, a *sharia* court of appeal and/or a customary court of appeal (ss. 263 and 264).

A question that arises on the constitutional provisions is whether the federal judicature consists *only* of courts established for the Federation by the Constitution or whether the national assembly can establish other courts for the Federation additional to those established by the Constitution. It is to be noted, first, that no power to establish courts is specifically conferred on the national assembly (its powers in the federal capital territory are treated differently). In the case of a state house of assembly, there is specific provision authorising it to establish courts with jurisdiction subordinate to that of the high court (s. 6[4][a]). The absence of any provision conferring a like authority on the national assembly lends support to the view that there is no intention that it should have power to establish inferior federal courts in the states. The reference, in the clause vesting judicial power in the courts, to 'such other courts as may be authorised by law to exercise jurisdiction on matters' with respect to which the national assembly or a state house of assembly may make laws, confers no power to establish courts; it merely grants power to authorise a court, already established, to exercise jurisdiction arising under a federal law.

Secondly, it is significant that the authority for state courts to administer federal laws within the limits of their jurisdiction as prescribed in the relevant state law is now conferred directly by the Constitution, instead of being left to the federal legislature as hitherto.

While this authorisation is made subject to other provisions of the Constitution, it would seem logically to exclude a power in the national assembly to establish inferior federal courts to administer federal laws in the states, since the effect of that may be to enable the national assembly to exclude altogether the jurisdiction of the state courts in federal causes and offences, contrary to the explicit authority in that behalf conferred on them by the Constitution. The provision that the authorisation is subject to the Constitution can only reasonably refer to the original jurisdiction of the supreme court and the federal high court, which are courts established by the Constitution itself. With the fairly wide original jurisdiction vested in the federal high court, there cannot now be much need for inferior federal courts in the states anyway.

But while the national assembly may lack power to establish courts in the states, its power to do so in the federal capital territory is undoubted. It has the same power to establish inferior courts there as a state house of assembly has in relation to the state.

The power of a legislature, whether federal or state, to establish courts as part of the judicature invested with or authorised to exercise judicial power is qualified by the fact that only tribunals possessing the attributes of a court in the constitutional sense can be so established. These attributes are: (*a*) independence, impartiality, and the absence of bias; (*b*) openness, i.e. its proceedings must be in public, unless the interest of justice or other public interest dictates otherwise; (*c*) the presentation of their case by the parties to the dispute; (*d*) the ascertainment of facts in issue by means of evidence given on oath or affirmation by the parties, and other witnesses whose attendance upon the court's summons is compulsory; (*e*) the submission of argument on the facts and on the law by or on behalf of the parties; (*f*) a binding decision which disposes of the whole matter by a finding upon the facts and an application to the facts so found of the law as interpreted by the court. The point under discussion has been underscored by Chief Justice Griffith of Australia:

It is impossible under the constitution to confer such functions upon any body other than a court, nor can the difficulty be avoided by designating a body, which is not in its essential character a court, by that name, or by calling the function by another name. In short, any attempt to vest any part of the judicial power . . . in any body other than a court is entirely ineffective.[5]

The difference between courts established by the Constitution and those established by ordinary law is: first, a court established by the Constitution enjoys a constitutional status, which means that the legislature is thereby made incompetent to abolish it or to change its constitution and jurisdiction in any manner inconsistent with the provisions of the Constitution. This consequence is illustrated by two cases discussed in chapters 17 and 18 below.[6] (The legislature of a state which has a *sharia* court of appeal or a customary court of appeal is, however, specifically empowered by the Constitution to abolish them if it no longer wants them.) On the other hand, a court established by ordinary law can be abolished by the competent legislature or by the executive on an authority delegated to it by the legislature.

It is perhaps necessary to emphasise that the Constitution does not require that the establishment or abolition of inferior courts must be by law enacted directly by the assembly. There is nothing in the Constitution or in the nature of the function that precludes its being delegated to the executive, subject to the usual safeguards. The point is important because the practice, right from the early beginnings of customary or native courts in Nigeria, has been for the enabling law to authorise the governor or other public functionary to establish individual customary courts by warrant, and to suspend, vary or cancel such warrant as and when necessary or expedient. This practice has obvious advantages in its greater convenience and flexibility, since it enables the territorial area of each court, its jurisdiction, powers and quorum, as set out in its warrant, to be more easily amended than would have been the case if the court had been established directly by statute. Indeed, it is hardly possible to prescribe by statute the varying territorial jurisdiction of some of the courts, the extent of which has to be fixed in many cases after prior consultation with the communities concerned. In view of this, it can scarcely be right to say that 'by s. 6(4)(*b*) of the Constitution, only the house of assembly can abolish a customary court', and that the law authorising the governor of a state to abolish a customary court, through the cancellation of its warrant, is unconstitutional and void.[7] If this is right, it should follow by implication, that the establishment of a customary court by the governor by warrant, in pursuance of statutory authorisation, is also unconstitutional and void.

There is yet another difference between a court established by the Constitution and one established by the ordinary law. The former is by the Constitution declared a superior court of record and invested, save as otherwise prescribed by appropriate legislature, with the powers of such a court. The status of a superior court is made exclusive to courts established by the Constitution. Any court established by ordinary law must therefore necessarily be an inferior court. An inferior court is characterised by the fact that its jurisdiction is limited as regards both the types of cases it can try, the punishment it can award and its powers generally. It has no power, for example, to punish for contempt that is not committed in its face. A superior court, on the other hand, can punish for contempt of its authority whether committed in or out of court; and it can make any order or decree that it deems appropriate in a matter properly before it.

(iii) *Jurisdiction of state courts to exercise federal judicial power*
The Constitution establishes for each state a high court and, for a state that requires them, a *sharia* court of appeal and/or a customary court of appeal, and then authorises the legislature of the state to establish other courts with jurisdiction subordinate to the high court (s. 6). It seems that the state governor (or the president in the case of the federal capital territory) is the competent authority to decide for his state whether it requires a *sharia* court of appeal and/or a customary court of appeal (if the former does not already exist at the coming into operation of the Constitution). It is in these courts — those established by the Constitution and those established by ordinary law — that the judicial power of the state is vested.

With the exception of courts presided over by persons who are not or have not been qualified to practise as legal practitioners in Nigeria, state courts exercising jurisdiction under state law in civil or criminal matters, both at first instance and on appeal, are authorised by the Constitution to exercise a like jurisdiction to hear and determine 'federal causes' and 'federal offences' (s. 250).[8] Much of the jurisdiction in cases arising under federal law is thus exercised by state courts. However, the jurisdiction of state courts in such cases is limited in two ways. First, it is excluded by the jurisdiction vested in the supreme court in disputes between the federation and a state or between states.

Secondly, any matter within the jurisdiction of the federal high court cannot be tried by a state court on its own right. Except for the mere statement that the federal high court is to have jurisdiction in such matters connected with or pertaining to the revenue of the federal government as may be prescribed by the national assembly, the jurisdiction of the court is left to be prescribed by the national assembly (s. 230[1]). However, the former federal revenue court, established by decree in April 1973, is re-styled federal high court, with all the jurisdiction and powers conferred on it by any law (s. 230[2]). The jurisdiction of the court was not actually restricted to revenue matters, as the name revenue court suggests; it extended to admiralty cases, federal offences under the criminal code, and to cases, both civil and criminal, arising under enactments relating to companies, copyrights, patents, designs, trademarks and merchandise marks.[9] It has branches in every state of the federation.

The exclusion of the jurisdiction of state courts in federal matters within the jurisdiction of the federal high court is, however, not total. Under the statute governing the federal revenue court, a judge of the court may transfer a case pending before him to a magistrate's court of the state in which the cause of action arose, if the case is one which in his opinion will be more expeditiously dealt with in a magistrate's court. The transfer operates to vest jurisdiction in the case in the magistrate's court as if such jurisdiction had been conferred by the statute.[10] From a decision of a magistrate in a transferred case, appeal lies to the federal revenue court, now federal high court.[11]

(iv) *Jurisdiction of federal courts to exercise state judicial power*
As in the case of federal judicial power, the precise extent of state judicial power is not defined in the Constitution, but it may be assumed to embrace, subject to the exclusive original jurisdiction of the supreme court in disputes between the federation and a state or between states, cases arising under the Constitution as well as cases on matters within state legislative competence.

The jurisdiction of state courts in federal causes and offences is matched by the jurisdiction given to two federal courts, the supreme court and the federal court of appeal, in appeals from state courts within the judicial power of a state. Appeals in cases arising under the Constitution and those arising under federal and state laws alike go from the federal high court, the state high court, *sharia* court of appeal and customary court of appeal to the federal court of appeal and thence to the supreme court. The jurisdiction of the federal court of appeal in such appeals is exclusive (s. 219), and appeals from it to the supreme court are final (s. 215). The federal and state legislatures are thereby precluded from interposing another appeal court between state courts and the federal court of appeal, and from superimposing a further appeal from the supreme court. As courts of appeal for the whole country in cases arising under federal as well as state judicial power, the supreme court and the federal court of appeal are placed in a position quite unlike that of the supreme court of the United States, but analogous to that of the high court of Australia. While decisions by the state courts on issues of federal law may be appellable ultimately to it, the supreme court of the United States has no appellate jurisdiction whatever over their decisions on matters arising under state laws. No federal court in the United States indeed has jurisdiction to administer state laws. The vesting of the federal judicial power in the federal courts in the United States has the implication of marking out the limits of the jurisdiction that can be conferred on them.

(v) *Composition of the courts*
The supreme court consists of the chief justice of Nigeria, and such number of justices, not exceeding fifteen, as may be prescribed by an

act of the national assembly (s. 210[2]). The court is duly constituted by any five of its members, and so constituted it has full powers to exercise the jurisdiction vested in the court, except that it is required to sit with seven justices when exercising its original jurisdiction and on appeals involving questions as to the interpretation or application of the Constitution or involving allegations of contravention of constitutionally guaranteed rights (s. 214).

The federal court of appeal consists of a president, and whatever number of justices, not exceeding fifteen, as may be prescribed by the national assembly (s. 217[2]). Three judges constitute the court, provided that in appeals from a *sharia* court of appeal or customary court of appeal the three justices forming the court are justices of the court learned in Islamic personal law or customary law, as the case may be.

The composition of the federal or state high court is a chief judge and such number of judges as may be prescribed by federal or state law, as the case may be (ss. 228[2] and 234[2]). A court is formed by a single judge (ss. 232 and 238). A *sharia* court of appeal is composed of a grand *kadi* and such number of *kadis* as may be prescribed by the state house of assembly, with two *kadis* constituting a court (ss. 240 and 243). A customary court of appeal is composed of a president and whatever number of judges the state house of assembly may prescribe (s. 245), but the number of judges to constitute a court is to be prescribed by law (s. 248).

2. *Constitutional safeguards for the independence of the judiciary*

The structure of Nigerian society and politics has made constitutional safeguards for the independence of the judiciary a matter of utmost importance and concern since the days when political power began to shift from imperial to nationalist hands. The tribe was (and still is) a dominant element in the organisation of politics, resulting in the government being controlled by the major tribes. The small, minority tribes naturally viewed their position in this kind of set-up with considerable apprehension, and began therefore to demand constitutional protection of their rights as individuals. But it would not have been enough to guarantee rights in the constitution if there were no independent judiciary to enforce them impartially between the individual and the majority-controlled executive.

The Nigerian politician, uninhibited by the influence of tradition on which respect for the independence of the judiciary is based in Britain, is also exposed to far greater temptation to interfere with the judiciary, with judges having, unlike in Britain, to decide red-hot political questions concerning the constitutionality of legislative and executive acts. Without effective constitutional safeguards, a judiciary frequently giving decisions which have the effect of thwarting government policy is not likely to be tacitly suffered by politicians, especially politicians in a hurry to develop and modernise a society laid waste by years of colonial exploitation and neglect. It does not matter that the judge might have been perfectly honest and impartial. The danger is well illustrated by the reaction of some Nigerian politicians to the decision of the judicial committee of the privy council in the celebrated *Akintola* v. *Adegbenro* case.[12] The reaction can also be easily imagined, had the courts declared the federal government of Balewa invalid after the 1964 election.

These considerations seem to demonstrate clearly not only the necessity of guaranteeing the independence of the judiciary but also that something more than the simple English method of removing a judge for misbehaviour on an address by both houses of parliament is needed.[13] It is easy enough to devise, through the Constitution, some institutional mechanism for insulating the appointment and removal of judges from political control, but the problem is to balance such a device with the requirements of democratic government. The office of a judge is a strategic one in the machinery of government, and in a country that professes democracy it might be argued that judicial appointments should depend on the consent of the people just as those of the legislature and the executive do. That is indeed the position in some states of the United States, where judges are elected directly by the people. But the office of a judge requires special qualifications and ability, which cannot adequately be judged by the electorate. Given the unsuitability of the people as a body to appoint judges, it becomes important, if the requirements of democracy are to be adequately met, that the people's elected representatives in government should be actively associated in the process of appointment. The executive in particular has been chosen by the people and entrusted by them and by the Constitution with full responsibility for the government of the country. Its responsibility for government requires that, except for those elected directly by the people, it should have an effective say in the appointment of all important functionaries of the state.

The 1979 Constitution seems to strike a fair balance between the need for constitutional safeguards for the independence of the judiciary and the need for the executive to have an effective say in the appointment and removal of judges.

(i) *Appointment*

Three methods are instituted by the Constitution for the appointment of judges. The first method vests the appointment in the president in his discretion, subject to confirmation by the senate (s. 211[1]). This method applies only to the appointment of the chief justice of Nigeria. There is probably justification for the discretion given to the president, since the administrative functions of the chief justice as the head of the judiciary give the office political significance beyond that ordinarily associated with the office of a judge.

Under the second method, the appointment is vested in the president or governor, but acting on the advice of a judicial service commission established by the Constitution for the federation and for each state. Legally, when a power is made exercisable by someone on the advice of another, no discretion is imported; the power has to be exercised only as advised, the role of the repository of the power being the purely formal and nominal one of merely executing the advice. The real maker of the appointment under this method is thus the federal or state judicial service commission. Judges required to be appointed by this method are justices of the supreme court (s. 211[2]), the president of the federal court of appeal (s. 218[2]), the chief judge of a state high court (s. 235[1]), grand *kadi* of a *sharia* court of appeal (s. 241[1]) and the president of a customary court of appeal (s. 246[1]). The appointment in each case must additionally be confirmed by the senate or the state house of assembly, as the case may be.

Appointment under the third method is by the president or governor on the recommendation, instead of on the advice, of the federal or state judicial service commission. This method does not completely exclude a discretion in the president or governor. He cannot of course appoint a person who has not been recommended by the commission. The wording of the provision that 'the appointment of a person to the office of a judge . . . shall be made by the President (or Governor) on the recommendation of the Federal (or State) Judicial Service Commission' makes it clear that a person must be favourably recommended before he can be appointed. But the president or governor is not bound to appoint a person on whom a favourable recommendation has been made. A binding recommendation is a contradiction in terms. And if a recommendation is intended to be binding, the differentiation in the methods of appointment of judges, even of the same court, would have been unnecessary. Where, however, the president or governor turns down a person recommended by the commission, he cannot appoint someone else who has not been recommended at all. He must ask the commission to recommend another person. Appointment by this method applies to justices of the federal court of appeal (s. 218[2]), the chief judge and judges of the federal high court (s. 229[1]), judges of a state high court (s. 235[2]), *kadis* of a *sharia* court of appeal (s. 241[2]), and judges of a customary court of appeal (s. 246[2]). These appointments are, however, not subject to confirmation by the senate or state house of assembly.

The Constitution prescribes qualifications for judicial appointments which the president or governor and the federal or state judicial service commission have to respect. The qualification is that of a legal practitioner, but the person must have been qualified as such for a period of fifteen years, twelve years and ten years for appointment to the supreme court, the federal court of appeal and the high court respectively. Additionally, appointments to the supreme court and the federal court of appeal shall have regard to the need to ensure that there are among their members persons learned in islamic personal law and persons learned in customary law (s. 252[1]). In the case of the federal court of appeal the number is prescribed as three justices learned in islamic personal law and three justices learned in customary law (s. 217[2]). For this purpose a person is deemed to be learned in Islamic personal law or customary law if —

(a) he has attended and has obtained a recognised qualification in Islamic personal law from an institution approved by the federal judicial service commission and has held the qualification for a period of not less than fifteen years, and

(b) he has, in the opinion of the commission, considerable experience in the practice of Islamic personal law or is a distinguished scholar of Islamic personal law; and

(c) he has, in the opinion of the commission, considerable knowledge of and experience in the practice of customary law in addition to any other qualifications that may be prescribed by the national assembly.

Qualification as a legal practitioner is not required for appointments to the *sharia* court of appeal and the customary court of appeal. The only qualification required for appointment to the *sharia* court of appeal is possession of, a recognised qualification in Islamic personal law resulting from attendance at an institution approved by the state judicial service commission, and the possession of considerable experience in the practice of islamic law or being a distinguished scholar of islamic personal law (s. 241[3]). In the case of a customary court of appeal, considerable knowledge of and experience in the practice of customary law are the only qualifications for appointment, but the national assembly may prescribe additional qualifications (s. 246[3]).

The political acceptability or otherwise of the constitutional safeguards as institutionalised in the judicial service commission is determined partly by how it is composed. The role of the commission tends to excite political objection if it is composed predominantly of judges, with only one or two representatives or appointees of the executive, so that the judges are enabled to dominate and control judicial appointments, and to abuse them in order to favour their friends and ethnic relations and to keep out people of whom they disapprove for personal or other reasons. On the other hand, judicial representation on the commission should not be reduced to the point where the influence of judges in judicial appointments becomes almost completely ineffective. It must be accepted that judges are well placed to judge of the suitability of persons for judicial appointment, of their ability and competence as lawyers and of their independence and detachment of outlook. The years spent by a judge at the bar and on the bench give him an intimate knowledge of prospective judicial aspirants. It seems again that the provisions of the 1979 Constitution on the membership of the judicial service commission strike a fair balance.

The federal judicial service commission comprises the chief justice of Nigeria as chairman, and as members the president of the federal court of appeal, the federal attorney-general, two legal practitioners each with not less than fifteen years' standing appointed by the president from a list of not less than four such legal practitioners recommended by the Nigerian bar association, and two other persons (not legal practitioners) of unquestionable integrity appointed by the president (3rd Sch., para. 7). The membership of the state judicial service commission is the chief judge of the state high court as chairman, the state attorney-general, grand *kadi* of the *sharia* court of appeal if any, the president of the customary court of appeal if any, one legal practitioner with not less than ten years' standing appointed by the governor, and one other person (not a legal practitioner) of unquestionable integrity appointed by the governor (3rd Sch., part II, para. 7). A person cannot be a member of a judicial service commission while he is employed in the federal or state public service; he is deemed to have resigned the later office on his appointment as a member (ss. 143[2] and 181[2]).

The council of state must be consulted on the appointment of members of the federal judicial service commission, which must also be confirmed by the senate (s. 140). Appointment of members of a state judicial service commission must likewise be confirmed by the state house of assembly (s. 179).

The removal of members of a commission by the president or governor is circumscribed by the requirement that removal can only be on the ground of inability to discharge the functions of the office (whether arising from infirmity of mind or body or any other cause) or of misconduct, and must be requested by the senate or state house of assembly in an address supported by two-thirds of its members (ss. 144[1] and 182[1]).

A judicial service commission is guaranteed independence in other ways. The president or governor or any other person cannot direct or control it in the exercise of its functions in relation to the appointment and removal of judges (ss. 145[1] and 183). The salaries and allowances of its members are prescribed by the appropriate legislature, and constitute a charge on the consolidated revenue fund of the federation or state. And such salaries as well as conditions of service (other than allowances) cannot be altered to the detriment of members after their appointment (ss. 78 and 116).

(ii) *Removal*

The Constitution spells out the grounds and the procedure for removing judges. The only grounds allowed are inability to discharge the functions of the office (arising from infirmity of either mind or body but not from any other cause), misconduct or contravention of the code of conduct (s. 256[1]).

Two procedures are instituted. The first permits removal by the president or governor on an address by the senate or a state house of assembly, as the case may be, supported by a two-thirds majority of its members, praying removal on any of the grounds above. While the president or governor cannot remove without such an address, the presentation of an address does not oblige him to remove; he has a discretion to act or not to act on it. Although a judge who is removed for inability, misconduct or a breach of the code of conduct cannot complain that he has been treated unfairly, there is the danger that proceedings in the senate or state house of assembly, even when the judge is afforded a hearing and legal representation, are not likely to lend themselves to dispassionate assessment of the evidence, such as characterises the proceedings of a tribunal. Misconduct leaves a lot of room for political prejudice to creep in. In Britain, the United States, Canada, Australia and New Zealand, where this procedure is used, the security of tenure enjoyed by judges rests more, as previously noted, on the force of deeply-rooted tradition of respect for the independence of the judiciary. But it may be over-optimistic to expect that Nigerian politicians would be as restrained and impartial as their British and American counterparts, especially in the face of judicial decisions invalidating important legislative or executive acts or which are otherwise inimical to the interests of the majority. Happily, this procedure is restricted to the removal of judges exercising administrative duties as heads of the various courts, viz the chief justice of Nigeria, the chief judge of the high court of a state, grand *kadi* or a *sharia* court of appeal and the president of a customary court of appeal, but not the president of the federal court of appeal or chief judge of the federal high court (s. 256[1][*a*]).

The normal procedure, which applies in the case of the other judges, permits removal by the president or governor only if it is recommended by the federal or state judicial service commission, as the case may be, on any of the grounds above (s. 256[1][*b*]).

(iii) *Appointment, dismissal and disciplinary control of magistrates, judges and members of area courts and customary courts*
These are vested in the state judicial service commission (3rd Sch., part II, para. 9[*d*]). On the coming into operation of the Constitution on 1 October 1979, magistrates, judges and members of area courts and customary courts are deemed, by virtue of s. 275(4), to have been appointed by the state judicial service commission who alone can thereafter remove or exercise disciplinary control over them. An order of the governor of Bendel state revoking the appointments of all presidents and members of customary courts in the state was accordingly held to be unconstitutional and void.[14]

The state judicial service commission is also responsible for the appointment, dismissal and disciplinary control of the chief registrar and deputy chief registrar of the state high court and the chief registrars of the *sharia* court of appeal and of the customary court of appeal (3rd Sch., part II, para. 9[*d*]), while the federal judicial service commission exercises a like power in respect of the chief registrars and deputy chief registrars of the supreme court, the federal court of appeal and the federal high court (3rd Sch. part I, para. 8[*d*]).

(iv) *Other constitutional guarantees of judicial independence*
The salaries and allowances of judges, which must be prescribed by law, are removed from annual vote by the legislature by being made a permanent charge on the consolidated revenue fund of the federation or state; also judicial salaries as well as conditions of service (other than allowances) are protected against alteration prejudicial to a judge after he has taken office (ss. 78 and 116). The recurrent expenditure of judicial offices (in addition to judicial salaries and allowances) is similarly made a charge on the consolidated revenue fund of the federation or state (ss. 78[6] and 116[6]).

The voluntary and compulsory retiring ages for judges are fixed by the Constitution at sixty and sixty-five years respectively (s. 255[1]). At the age of 65 years after not less than fifteen years' service, a judge retires with a pension for life equal to his last annual salary in addition to any retirement benefits to which he may be entitled; if his period of service is less than fifteen years, he gets either a pension calculated on a *pro rata* basis or the pension and other retirement entitlements under his terms and conditions of service, if any, whichever is higher (s. 255[2]). If he is retiring before attaining the age of sixty-five, his pension and other retirement benefits will be as determined by the appropriate legislature. These constitutional provisions are not, however, to deprive a judge of the benefit of any law that provides for pensions, gratuities and other retirement benefits for persons in the public service (s. 255[3]).

REFERENCES

1. art. III, s. 2.
2. art. VI, s. 2.
3. Edward Barret Jr. *et al.* (ed.), *Constitutional Law, Cases and Materials*, 3rd edn. (1968), 41.
4. op. cit., 39–42.
5. *Waterside Workers' Fedn. of Australia* v. *J.W. Alexander Ltd.* (1918), 25 C.L.R. 434 at 442. See chapter 14 for a discussion of the constitutional implications of the vesting of judicial power in the courts.
6. *Olawoyin* v. *Police* (1961), 1 All N.L.R. 203; *Ngwenya* v. *Deputy Prime Minister* Civ. T.4/1973 of Jan. 1973 (Swaziland).
7. *Obayuwana* v. *The Governor of Bendel State & others*, Suit No. B/25/80 of 24 June 1980, High Court, Benin City.
8. The 1963 Constitution did not directly confer such authority; it derived rather from an act of parliament, see Interpretation Act, s. 44, cap. 89; the provisions of this act not repealed by the Interpretation Act, 1964, were redesignated the Law (Miscellaneous Provisions) Act. See also Regional Courts (Federal Jurisdiction) Act, 1958; Criminal Procedure (Northern Region) Act, 1960, s. 4.
9. Federal Revenue Court Decree 1973, s. 7(1).
10. s. 26.
11. s. 27(*b*)
12. [1963] A.C. 614.
13. de Smith, 'Judicial Independence in the Commonwealth', *The Listener*, 15 January 1959.
14. *Obayuwana* v. *Governor of Bendel State & Others*, op. cit.

17
JUDICIAL REVIEW OF THE CONSTITUTIONALITY OF LEGISLATIVE AND EXECUTIVE ACTS

1. *Dimensions of judicial review*

Judicial review is the power of the court, in appropriate proceedings before it, to declare a legislative or executive act either contrary to, or in accordance with, the Constitution, with the effect of rendering the act invalid or vindicating its validity and so putting it beyond challenge in future. The latter result is often spoken of as validating the act in question, implying that the act lacked validity before the court's decision in its favour. But that is not strictly so. An act of a competent governmental authority done in the exercise or purported exercise of its power under the Constitution has apparent validity until it is pronounced otherwise by the court. All a favourable court decision does is to vindicate or affirm its validity; it pronounces it *not* unconstitutional and thereby removes whatever doubt or cloud existed before concerning its validity. This is illustrated by cases where the court declines on jurisdictional or other grounds to review a governmental act on the merit, i.e. declines to rule for or against the act. The result is that the act continues in force with its efficacy unimpaired, and it does so by its initial authority without vindication by the court.

To recapitulate briefly the discussion in previous chapters, the court may declare a legislative or executive act unconstitutional and void on the following grounds:

(a) that it was not passed in the prescribed manner and form;

(b) that it exceeds the powers of the federal or state government under the federal scheme of division of powers;

(c) that it is an abdication or unauthorised delegation of power to another organ or authority of government contrary to the principle of separation of powers, e.g. the delegation of non-judicial functions to the courts;

(d) that it usurps or otherwise interferes with the constitutional powers of other organs of government contrary to the principle of separation of powers;

(e) that it contravenes a constitutionally guaranteed right;

(f) that it ousts the jurisdiction of the court;

(g) that it has retrospective effect in relation to any criminal offence;

(h) that it is otherwise inconsistent with, or contrary to, the Constitution.

The omnibus ground in (*h*) above is necessary to take care of any cases of unconstitutionality not covered by the specific grounds. Thus in *Olawoyin* v. *Police*,[1] the plaintiff claimed that the Northern region High Court (Amendment) Law 1960, which provided for a judge of the *sharia* court of appeal to sit in the high court on appeals from native courts, was contrary to the 1960 Constitution of Northern Nigeria which created the high court and prescribed its constitution. The Amendment Law had been enacted in pursuance of a provision in the pre-independence Constitution authorising such legislation. However, the Independence Constitution of 1960 contained no such provision, and the federal supreme court held that this omission constituted a withdrawal of the authority and amounted to an implied revocation of the High Court (Amendment) Law; by creating the high court and prescribing its constitution, it was the implied intention of the Independence Constitution that only the duly appointed judges of the court should exercise the jurisdiction vested in it. In *Olajire* v. *Superintendent of Local Government Police*,[2] it was contended that the provision of the Western region Local Government Police Law relating to the appointment of a superintendent of local government police with function to supervise, train and discipline all local government police forces in the region was contrary to the Independence Constitution, which authorised the establishment by the regions of local police forces on a provincial basis only. The high court, on a reference from the Ilesha customary court grade A, held that the provision in question was not contrary to the Constitution.

2. *Jurisdiction of the court to review the constitutionality of legislative and executive acts*

The power of the court to review the constitutionality of legislative and executive acts derives from various provisions and sources in the Constitution.

(*a*) The supreme court, though essentially an appellate court, is nevertheless invested with original jurisdiction to determine, to the exclusion of any other court, questions as to the existence or extent of a legal right arising in any dispute between the federation and a state or between states (s. 212[1]).

(*b*) Unlimited original jurisdiction is given to the high court of a state and to the high court of the federal capital territory 'to hear and determine any civil proceedings in which the existence or extent of a legal right, power, duty, liability, privilege, interest, obligation or claim is in issue or to hear and determine any criminal proceedings involving or relating to any penalty, forfeiture, punishment or other liability in respect of an offence committed by any person'. The jurisdiction of the high court of a state extends to proceedings arising under both federal and state laws (s. 250). Federal laws cover all matters in the federal capital territory (s. 263). The vesting in the high court of unlimited original jurisdiction in all matters, including by implication constitutional cases, is one of the significant innovations of the new Constitution.

(c) On the application of a person alleging that a right guaranteed by the Constitution has been, is being or is likely to be contravened, in relation to that person in any part of the country, the high court having jurisdiction in that part is to hear and determine the allegation (s. 42). The jurisdiction of the high court in respect of such an application does not of course exclude that of a lower court where allegation of contravention of a guaranteed right is raised in proceedings before it.

(d) The appropriate high court is vested with original jurisdiction to hear and determine, to the exclusion of any other court, questions concerning the validity of elections to the office of president, vice-president, governor, deputy-governor, member of a legislative house, or whether their term of office or seat has ceased or become vacant, as the case may be (s. 237). The appropriate high court is

> (i) the federal high court or the high court of the federal capital territory when constituted, where the case involves the office of president or vice-president;
> (ii) the high court of a state in the case of a state governor or deputy-governor;
> (iii) the high court of a state in which the constituency or senatorial district is located;
> (iv) the high court of the federal capital territory in the case of the one senatorial district located in that territory.

(e) Appeal is allowed as of right from decisions in both civil and criminal proceedings given by the high court, whether at first instance or on appeal, to the federal court of appeal, and thence to the supreme court, where the question concerns the interpretation or application of the Constitution or an allegation of the contravention of a guaranteed right or the validity of an election or tenure of office of the president, vice-president, governor, deputy-governor or member of a legislative house.

(f) Then there is the provision for the reference to the high court, federal court of appeal and the supreme court for authoritative rulings, of questions concerning the interpretation or application of the Constitution arising in other courts (including the *sharia* court of appeal and the customary court of appeal). If the court before which the question arose is of opinion that the question raises a substantial point of law, it may, and shall if any of the parties to the proceedings so requests, refer it to the high court having jurisdiction in that part of the country. The high court shall in turn refer the question to the federal court of appeal if it is itself of the opinion that it raises a substantial point of law, otherwise it will give its ruling or directions which will then be applied in the determination of the case by the court that made the reference (s. 259[1]). Where the question arises in proceedings in the high court or in the federal court of appeal, and the court is of the opinion that it raises a substantial point of law, then the high court may, and shall if so requested by a party, refer it to the federal court of appeal for a ruling; in the case of a question arising in the federal court of appeal reference is to the supreme court (s. 259[2] and [3]).

These provisions have a wider scope than the corresponding provisions in the 1963 Constitution which dealt only with the referral of questions concerning the interpretation of the Constitution, but not questions concerning its application. Strictly, interpretation is concerned with definition or ascertainment of meaning, not with the application of a provision as interpreted to particular situations or acts. In *Olawoyin* v. *Police*,[3] however, the supreme court expressed the view that 'when no doubt exists, or the law is well established by a final court of appeal or by an overwhelming consensus of judicial decisions, the mere application of it to a particular set of facts does not constitute a substantial question, however important the issue may be for the decision of that particular case.' If this is correct, the extension of the provision to questions concerning the application of the Constitution is useless. It is submitted that the application of the Constitution to particular situations or acts can raise substantial questions of law.

It is important to stress that the provision for referral applies only if the constitutional question involves, in the opinion of the court before whom it is raised, a substantial point of law. Even when the court is of that opinion, it still has a discretion whether or not to refer. The court is only under an obligation to refer a question where it involves a substantial point of law, and where a party to the proceedings so requests. There has been a tendency to regard every question of the interpretation or application of the Constitution as amounting to a substantial question of law, so as to enable a party to apply for reference to be made. In *Gamioba* v. *Esezi II*,[4] counsel for both parties, having agreed between themselves that the case involved a question as to the interpretation of the Constitution, requested the high court at Warri to refer it to the supreme court, which the court did without even seeing the pleadings, apparently believing that its jurisdiction had been ousted by the joint request for reference. (Actually what the judge did was to transfer the case to the supreme court for hearing and determination; this was held to be completely wrong as being outside the provision.) The supreme court held, in striking out the case, that no referal can properly be made unless the question to be referred is one which must necessarily be decided in the cause or matter.

Where, as in the present case, a case could be decided on two or more grounds, including the ground of constitutional invalidity, reference should not be made until the other grounds have been decided and rejected, since it is only then that the constitutional question will fall necessarily to be decided.[5] Even then, the question should not be referred unless it involves a substantial question of law, and to be substantial the question must be 'one on which arguments in favour of more than one interpretation might reasonably be adduced'.[6] The supreme court of India has laid it down that 'the proper test for determining whether a question of law raised in the case is substantial would, in our opinion, be whether it is of general public importance or whether it directly and substantially affects the rights of the parties and if so whether it is either an open question in the sense that it is not finally settled by [the highest] court . . . or is not free from difficulty or calls for discussion of alternative views.'[7]

A question for reference must be

one which is capable of being formulated with precision, and before a question is referred to this court it should be so formulated as to enable this court to deal with all points which fairly arise, and at the same time to confine itself to those points. [. . .] Any suggestion that a power conferred by law is inconsistent with the Constitution should specify the provision of the Constitution with which it is suggested that the power is inconsistent. . . .[8]

This statement was made in a case[9] in which s. 4 of the Western region Communal Land Rights (Vesting in Trustees) Law 1958 was alleged to be unconstitutional but without specifying the section of the Constitution alleged to have been so contravened.

(g) Finally, the power to review the constitutionality of legislative and executive acts may be implied from the inherent logic of the function of the court to declare and apply the law in the determination of disputes brought before it. The point, as propounded by Chief Justice Marshall of the U.S. supreme court in 1803, is that, given that the Constitution is law, where both the Constitution and an ordinary law are relevant to the decision of the case before the court, then, if the ordinary law is inconsistent with the Constitution, and since the Constitution is the superior of the two, the court is bound to apply the Constitution and disregard the ordinary law.[10] The argument is unanswerable.

3. Conditions for the exercise of the jurisdiction

(i) Lack of initiative

In government, the ability to initiate action has pre-eminent significance. The courts are denied this vital attribute of power, the power to initiate the process of review of legislative and executive acts.[11] Given a justiciable violation of the Constitution by the political organs of government, however flagrant, the court cannot intervene on its initiative. It must wait until it is moved by someone. It is eminently sensible and politic that the court should not intervene in disputes except at the instance of a complainant. A meddlesome judiciary poses the danger of abuse, and of conflict with the government, and is well calculated to undermine, if not destroy, the court's popular image of an impartial, disinterested arbiter between contestants in a dispute. It is this posture of impartiality and disinterestedness that makes a decision invalidating a governmental act tolerable to the government. Realising that the court is not the prime mover or instigator of its discomfiture, that its only role is to interpose its machinery between the government and its opponents, the government should have no reason to feel antagonised by an adverse decision. It might well feel some disappointment or embarrassment, but not antagonism. But if the court were itself to initiate action, it would at once appear in the posture of an interested contestant, of an opponent of government, and would thereby forfeit all claim to impartiality in the eyes of the government.

(ii) Adversary litigation between individual parties as the context of the court's role in government

The judicial character of the court's role does not consist merely in a lack of initiative. The statement that it must wait until moved by someone expresses only part of the judicial character of its role. The interest of that someone is of paramount importance in determining whether a judicial situation has arisen justifying the court's intervention. The court's role would be other than judicial if anyone, with or without individual interest in the governmental action under challenge, could ask for the court's intervention in the matter. The court would then be a general reviewing forum, a second or third legislative chamber, in which anyone defeated in the lower chamber could try to rally fresh support in an attempt to get the measure reversed. The U.S. supreme court has put the point classically thus:

> The theory upon which, apparently, this suit was brought is that parties have an appeal from the legislature to the courts; and that the latter are given an immediate and general supervision of the constitutionality of the acts of the former. Such is not true. . . . It never was the thought that, by means of a

friendly suit, a party beaten in the legislature could transfer to the courts an inquiry as to the constitutionality of the legislation.[12]

The court does not have a general kind of power to entertain, at the instance of anyone, any matter raising a constitutional issue. Its role is not that of 'standing as an ever-open forum for the ventilation of all grievances that draw upon the Constitution for support'.[13] As the U.S. supreme court said in another case: 'We have no power *per se* to review and annul Acts of Congress on the ground that they are unconstitutional. . . . [To intervene] would be not to decide a judicial controversy, but to assume a position of authority over the governmental acts of another and co-equal department. . . .'[14]

The interpretation of the constitution is *primarily* the function of the political organs. With respect to the legislature, for example, the interpretative function is necessarily implied in its power to make laws.[15] Every legislative act is an interpretative determination by the legislature that the act is within its powers under the Constitution. The Constitution provides no political process by means of which that determination may be reviewed and revised. The courts are not vested with that power, and it would be a manifest usurpation for them to assume it. For, being in its nature political, such a power would establish them as a supreme legislative chamber, with a primary power to receive, review and revise all acts of the legislature.

The role of the courts in the interpretation and application of the Constitution is purely judicial, and arises only as a *last* resort when impelled by the necessity of deciding ordinary adversary litigation between individual parties. 'The question of constitutionality is dealt with by the court simply because it arises as an issue in the case; the court has to decide it in order to decide the case.'[16] The court cannot pronounce any statute . . . void, because irreconcilable with the constitution, except as it is called upon to adjudge the legal rights of litigants in actual controversies.'[17]

Adversary litigation requires therefore (*a*) a dispute or controversy between two parties; (*b*) that the dispute or controversy must be real and concrete, not hypothetical, academic or moot; (*c*) that it must affect the legal relations or rights of the parties; (*d*) that the rights or interests of the parties must be adverse to one another; and (*e*) that the dispute or controversy must be brought before the court for determination by such regular proceedings as are established by law or custom.[18]

The rationale for this requirement is the same as for the exercise of ordinary judicial power. The pendency of adverse litigation between individuals in a real controversy guarantees the kind of stake in the proceedings that would induce the parties to prosecute a case with vigour and to undertake the expense in money, time and effort necessarily entailed in the effective conduct of a court case. It assures 'that concrete adverseness which sharpens the presentation of issues upon which the court so largely depends for illumination of difficult constitutional questions.'[19] The need for concrete adverseness is therefore to ensure a vigorous prosecution that would make available to the court all relevant information on facts and law, which in turn would enable the court to reach an informed and intelligent decision that takes into account all the aspects and dimensions of the case.

It follows from its judicial character that the scope of the court's role is very limited indeed. 'What it means in effect is that the political branches have pretty complete leeway until the rights of real people get involved. Then and only then can a court enter the scene, because it is only then that any identifiable litigant has any rights which he can assert as a party in court.' The result is 'that large areas of governmental action remain wholly outside its [the court's] reach. There are a vast number of things done by government which do not affect any identifiable persons in a manner sufficiently direct to form the subject matter of a legal claim.'[20] Even when they have a direct effect on an identifiable person, he may not have the resources, the time or the inclination to institute a court action. Thayer cites in illustration the question of the establishment of a United States bank. Although the question of its constitutionality provoked so much controversy throughout the country, dividing both Washington's cabinet and the political parties, it did not find its way into court until twenty-three years after the bank's establishment.[21]

(iii) *The nature of litigants' interest required for invocation of the court's intervention in constitutional cases*

Granted that a person seeking the court's intervention in a constitutional case must have a right in the subject-matter of the dispute, what is the nature of the right justifying the court's intervention, and in what way or to what degree should the right be affected?

In ordinary litigation, the parties are required to have antagonistic interests in a real, concrete dispute. They must be adversaries not just in the sense that they entertain opposing views on law relevant to their respective positions; in addition there must be between them a real dispute, involving actual, concrete facts, which injuriously affect their legitimate interests, whether business, pecuniary, personal or of any other kind recognised by law. The antagonistic interests of the parties and the passion and conflict which they evoke in them, make judicial resolution of the controversy a *practical necessity* as otherwise the parties might be tempted to take the law into their own hands. 'The adjudicatory process is most securely founded when it is exercised under the impact of lively conflict between antagonistic demands, actively pressed, which make resolution of the controverted issue a practical necessity.'[22] A suit lacking these features will be dismissed on the ground of lack of standing or because it is frivolous, vexatious or otherwise an abuse of the court's process. Only the parties to the dispute are entitled to invite the court's intervention. A third party with no legitimate interests of his own in the subject-matter of the dispute and not being a duly authorised representative of a disputant, cannot do so for the simple reason that, though there is a concrete factual situation, he is a mere busybody with no stake in the matter.

The question is whether the same intensity of interest is necessary to give a person standing to ask for an adjudication in constitutional cases. To begin with, a governmental measure, legislative or executive, alleged to violate the Constitution may be said to affect the interest of every citizen. A citizen is not a stranger in the affairs of the government of his country in the same way as C is a stranger to a dispute between A and B. He has a stake in seeing that the government is conducted lawfully according to the Constitution and the laws, but legitimate as his interest is, it is one that he shares with the generality of his fellow-citizens. A violation of the Constitution or other law by the government is a wrong to the whole country of which he is only one of several millions of members. If the violation does not also occasion an injury to him as an individual, does the injury to his general interest as a citizen constitute between him and the government such an adversary controversy as to give him standing to invoke the court's intervention? The injury to his general interest as a citizen undoubtedly has an element of adverseness but not a sufficient one; moreover the absence of injury to an individual interest deprives the controversy of concreteness.

The *locus classicus* on this point is the American case in which a woman alleged that a federal grant-in-aid programme aimed at reducing maternal and infant mortality was unconstitutional, because the expenditure under the programme — aggregating a maximum of $1,500,000 annually — would, by increasing her burden of future federal taxes, constitute a taking of property without due process of law.[23] However, because there was no showing that should the enabling act be declared unconstitutional, the federal tax burden and her own tax bill would be reduced, it was held she had no standing to invoke the court's intervention. A 'party who invokes the power', the court said, 'must be able to show, not only that the statute is invalid, but that he sustained or is immediately in danger of sustaining some direct injury as the result of its enforcement, and not merely that he suffers in some indefinite way in common with people generally.'[24] In another action by citizens of the United States, taxpayers and members of a voluntary association, for a declaration that the Nineteenth Amendment was unconstitutional the court dismissed the action, saying 'the plaintiffs had only the right possessed by every citizen "to require that the Government be administered according to law and that the public moneys be not wasted".'[25]

The matter may be further illustrated with a hypothetical but more striking example. Suppose that, contrary to the express guarantee of the Constitution, the legislature makes a law authorising the detention of persons without trial. The invalidity of the law appears clearly on its face, and it may be assumed that the government enacted it in open disregard of the Constitution in order to intimidate disaffected persons. The patent unconstitutionality of the statute will still not support an action by anyone who is not threatened with detention under it. The mere existence of the law in the statute book when no detentions have taken place or been threatened under it cannot involve anyone in a real dispute or controversy with the government over the law.[26] The law may remain in the statute book without ever being executed.

Now, a violation of the constitution or the laws by the government, such as the one in the example above, may, in addition to being an injury to the entire community or to a section of it, affect the individual interest of a person. The private interest affected, individual though it is, can hardly be said to be of the same intensity as that necessitating litigation in ordinary cases, nor is it so adverse and antagonistic to that of the government as to excite a passionate and lively conflict making resolution by the court a practical necessity. It has been held, however, that where a legislative apportionment act, in violation of the Constitution, assigns the same number of seats to vastly unequal constituencies in terms of population, thereby debasing the value and effectiveness of the votes in the more populous constituencies, a disadvantaged voter has a right to impugn the statute.[27] And in another case the court, by a majority of five to four, upheld the standing of members of a state legislature to compel a state legislative official to erase an endorsement on the senate resolution ratifying an amendment to the Constitution proposed by congress.[28] On the other hand, it is insisted in some cases that the individual's interest must be such as to create the 'strictest necessity' for the court's intervention.[29]

The definition of the interest necessary to confer standing in constitutional cases, in terms of injury or the immediate threat of it, calls for special comment in relation to four different factors.

(a) *Self-enforcing laws.* It is necessary to qualify the statement that 'the mere existence of a . . . statute would constitute insufficient grounds to support a . . . court's adjudication of its constitutionality . . . if real threat of enforcement is wanting.'[30] This must not be taken to mean that *under no circumstances* will the mere existence of a statute without an immediate threat of enforcement confer standing to challenge it. For a statute may be self-executing. Surely a law attainting a named person of treason and which also directs his imprisonment and the confiscation of his property or which bars him from government employment for life is largely self-enforcing. The attainder takes effect immediately by the force of the statute, and under the bill of rights in the 1979 Constitution it unequivocally contravenes the right to a fair hearing by an independent and impartial court in respect of a criminal charge. The bar from government employment is also self-enforcing. The confiscation of property needs to be executed but it carries with it an immediate threat of execution. The U.S. supreme court has held that the existence of a zoning legislation which, by prohibiting industrial and commercial uses of the plaintiff's land, greatly reduced its value and destroyed its marketability for those purposes, constituted 'a present invasion of appellee's property rights and a threat to continue it'.[31]

A statute which, on pain of punishment, required all parents to send their children to public schools thereby threatening a private and parochial school with closure through the diversion of its students to the public schools is yet another example of a self-enforcing statute. The action of the private and parochial school to prevent the enforcement of the statute was brought fifteen months before the statute was to become effective, so that there could have been no direct threat of enforcement at the time of the action.[32] Furthermore, the statute could not have been enforced against the plaintiffs, since its commands were directed to parents. However, because parents had, in anticipation of the enforcement of the statute, started withdrawing their children from the plaintiffs' school, an anticipatory invalidation was justified since otherwise the injury would have become irreparable by the operative date of the act.[33] Judicial review in advance of a threat of enforcement was also sought in a case where a West Virginia statute regulating the supply of natural gas accorded preference to the intrastate market in the event of supply not being sufficient to satisfy both intra- and inter-state demands. The purpose of withdrawing the interstate supply of natural gas was sufficiently manifest on the face of the statute to justify action before the preference provision could be put into practice.[34]

And according to Basu, citing a decision of the Indian supreme court,[35] 'where an enactment may immediately on its coming into force take away or abridge the fundamental rights of a person by its very terms, the aggrieved person may at once come to the court without waiting for the state to take some overt action threatening to infringe his fundamental right.'[36]

(*b*) *Criminal or penal laws*. If a statute prohibits the exercise of a right guaranteed by the Constitution, such as the right to form a political party other than the ruling party, everyone who wishes to form or belong to a rival political party may be said to have a real dispute with the government. The injury is as individual as the debasement of the vote of a voter in a grossly under-represented constituency. A controversy does not arise only when prosecution under the statute is brought or threatened. It exists by the fact of the prohibition, on pain of punishment, of what the Constitution permits. Yet is the injury to the individual's interest of such an intensity as to put him in a position of active antagonism and conflict with the government so great as to make resolution by the court a practical necessity? It has been said that, short of actual prosecution, only a threat of prosecution would create such a practical necessity.[37] In other words the court will entertain a challenge to a governmental measure only from 'one who is himself immediately harmed or immediately threatened with harm by the challenged action';[38] a right is not interfered with by the mere prohibition of its exercise but only by a prosecution under the prohibition or an immediate threat of it. But how direct and immediate must the threat be? Is it the directness and immediacy of an arrest on a criminal charge or information from reliable sources that prosecution is being contemplated? Is it enough that prosecution is probable, very likely, likely or only possible?

As already noted, the 1979 Constitution guarantees access to the high court to anyone who alleges that any of the constitutionally guaranteed rights 'has been, is being or *is likely* to be contravened in relation to him' (s. 42). (This is a marked advance from the phraseology in the 1963 Constitution, namely 'Any person who alleges that any of the provisions of this chapter has been contravened in any territory in relation to him may apply to the High Court.') The new form of the enforcement provision puts it beyond doubt that the mere likelihood of contravention of a guaranteed right confers a right of access to the court. For it is very likely, indeed more than likely, that a known violation or defiance of a criminal prohibition of the exercise of a guaranteed right will be prosecuted or otherwise dealt with. That is what the enforcement authorities of the state are there for. It is not reasonably to be expected that they will compound violations of the criminal law. A criminal prohibition exposes everyone subject to it to a strong likelihood of prosecution. Why should such a person wait until he is actually prosecuted or arrested or learns upon good authority that he is to be prosecuted? The words 'in relation to him' mean nothing more than that the contravention or likelihood of it must be individualised, but an injury or its likelihood can be individualised although it also affects other persons, even a large and indefinite number of them. All that is required before prosecution or other act of enforcement can be said to be likely in relation to a person is that he must be so placed by reason of his employment, profession, business or other circumstance as to become involved in conduct prohibited by the statute. Prosecution or enforcement cannot be likely in relation to a person to whom a criminal prohibition is not directed.

This interpretation of the new formulation adopted in the enforcement provision of the Constitution is in line with the decision of the U.S. supreme court in *Adler* v. *Board of Education*[39] where enforcement was more speculative than likely. A New York law authorised the dismissal from the state's public schools of any teacher who advocated or was knowingly a member of an organisation which advocated the overthrow of the government by force or violence. It directed the board of requests to list, after notice and hearing, organisations which it found to engage in these activities, and membership of which was to be *prima facie* ground for dismissal. Before any list had been drawn up, action was instituted by (among others) four teachers in the state's public school system, for a declaration of invalidity against the law, and for an injunction restraining the board from enforcing the statute. The teachers did not allege that they advocated the forcible overthrow of the government or that they were members of or intended to join any organisation advocating such views. Nor did they claim that they had been deterred from doing so by fear of dismissal under the law. They merely argued that by authorising dismissal on these grounds the law would have a deterrent effect on teachers as a group. The trial court held that they lacked standing to maintain the action. On appeal, eight of the nine judges of the U.S. supreme court ruled on the merits of the case without any discussion of the plaintiffs' standing, on the assumption of course that they had it.[40] Only Justice Frankfurter, dissenting, considered the issue of standing. He ruled that 'since we rightly refused in the *Mitchell* case[41] to hear government employees whose conduct was much more intimately affected by the law there attacked than are the claims of plaintiffs here, this suit is wanting in the necessary basis for our review.' He thought too that until the board of requests had drawn up a list of prohibited organisations, the claim of the plaintiffs was 'abstract or speculative'.[42]

The *Adler* decision affords therefore a clear authority that a person has standing to impugn a statute by way of a declaratory action upon a showing of likelihood of enforcement, and must be taken to have overruled a contrary decision given five years earlier[43] and also the *obiter dictum* in another earlier case.[44] The new form of the enforcement provision in the 1979 Constitution must likewise be taken as a repudiation of the decision of the supreme court of Nigeria in *Olawoyin* v. *Att.-Gen., Northern Region* that a person could not obtain standing 'by the mere enactment of a law with which he may in the future come in conflict'.[45] The statute under challenge in this case prohibited political activities by juveniles as well as the inducing of such activities by adults. The plaintiff alleged that the prohibition infringed the guarantee of private and family life, freedom of conscience and freedom of expression in the Constitution (1954). As the plaintiff had not induced any juveniles to engage in political activities, there could not have been any prosecution or direct threat of it against him. However the plaintiff's case was that he had children he wished to instruct politically, but was unable to do so for fear of violating the statute. He wanted also to allege that the prohibition affected him in his capacity as secretary of a political party, but as this capacity had not been raised or proved in the court below, the Appeal Court disallowed argument on it. Although this was not argued, the plaintiff might also have fallen foul of the statute if in the course of his activity as a politician he had addressed a political assembly of juveniles, solicited their membership of a political party or associated with them politically. These circumstances clearly placed the plaintiff in a position which made him likely to be prosecuted. If the circumstances had been that he had no children or had not been involved or associated in politics, then prosecution could not be said to have been likely in relation to him. Apart altogether from the consideration that he was likely to be prosecuted, the plaintiff also had a right in his children's welfare, which embraced every child's rights and freedoms; a child's standing thus enures to his parents.[46] And just as a qualified voter has an individual right to maintain the quality and effectiveness of his vote, so also has a child an individual right to participate in politics; a violation of either confers standing to impugn the contravening statute. A parent also has a right to direct his children's education, both secular and religious,[47] but the exercise of this right would have exposed him to conflict with the statutory prohibition.

The acceptance by the 1979 Constitution of the view, established in the *Adler* decision, that the likelihood of prosecution confers standing to challenge the constitutionality of a criminal or penal law must be applauded. It accords more with the wide jurisdiction of the court in declaratory actions. As Edwin Borchard writes, criticising the decision in *Liberty Warehouse Co.* v. *Grannis*,[48] which denied adjudication to warehousemen and auctioneers of leaf tobacco who impugned the validity of the penal provisions in Kentucky's Warehouse Act:

But even if he [the attorney-general] had prepared no indictments, the mere existence of the statute was a threat to the plaintiff's business and gave them a clear right to an injunction, had they sought it. A *fortiori*, they were entitled to the milder relief by declaration of rights, merely a judgment that the Act was unconstitutional.[49]

Secondly, the requirement of standing should not be used as a discretionary technique for avoiding decision of otherwise justiciable issues. Justiciability, in so far as it relates to standing, should not depend upon a discretionary balancing of the 'appropriateness of the issues for decision by courts and the hardship of denying judicial relief',[50] but it should rest squarely on constitutional principle. If there is an immediate risk or likelihood of injury to a legal right, a person affected thereby should be able to invoke the jurisdiction of the court, and it should not be in the discretion of the court to entertain or to decline the suit for lack of 'appropriate' standing in the particular complainant. To make justiciability (i.e. standing) depend upon such a discretionary evaluation is to say that justiciability should be regarded as 'an attitude rather than as a concept possessing determinable content'.[51]

Likelihood of enforcement is, however, the minimum condition required by the constitutional provision to confer standing, from which it follows that standing will be lacking where enforcement is *unlikely*. This position has also the support of the decision of the U.S. supreme court in *Poe* v. *Ullman*.[52] The facts and the decision are sufficiently interesting and important to merit discussion. What was at issue in the case was the validity of a Connecticut statute, which prohibited the use (but not the manufacture or sale) of contraceptives to prevent pregnancy, and the giving of medical advice as to their use. The statute was impugned by a registered doctor and three of his patients, a husband and wife and another married woman, on the grounds that it interfered with the patients' right to life and liberty under the Fourteenth Amendment and with the doctor's right to liberty and property under the same Amendment. The evidence before the court revealed that throughout the eighty years of the statute's existence there had been no prosecution of anyone for illegal use of contraceptives, although it was a notorious fact that contraceptives were openly sold in the state's drug stores. Only once had a prosecution taken place in respect of the giving of medical advice on the use of contraceptives, but even that concerned advice given not privately but in an open dissemination of contraceptive information in a birth control clinic by two doctors and a nurse. Nor was the purpose of that prosecution to enforce the prohibition by securing the conviction and punishment of the accused persons; it was rather to obtain a judicial pronouncement on the validity of the statute. This purpose having been accomplished in a ruling upon a preliminary objection to the validity of the statute (the statute was declared constitutional by the state's supreme court), the enforcement authority entered a *nolle prosequi* terminating the prosecution. Thereafter the clinic was closed down, as were seven other such clinics, a circumstance which led

Justice Brennan to comment that the true controversy over the statute related to birth control clinics on a large scale.[53]

From this consistent record of non-enforcement extending over eighty years, the U.S. supreme court concluded by a majority of 5–4 that prosecution was unlikely. The giving of private medical advice and the private use of contraceptives, the court said, were less likely to invite the attention of the authorities and to move them to action than the ubiquitous, open and public sale of the devices. There had been not merely a 'prosecutorial paralysis' but a deliberate policy, indeed a 'tacit agreement', not to enforce the statute, amounting to a virtual 'nullification of the law',[54] a fact which deprived 'these controversies of the immediacy which is an indispensable condition of constitutional adjudication',[55] and gave them a distinct 'unreality'. Insofar as the plaintiffs had been deterred from giving and receiving advice in the use of contraceptives, this resulted not from a realistic fear of threat of prosecution but from their moral outlook as law-abiding citizens. Although the patients/plaintiffs had suffered an impairment of their constitutional right to life and liberty by reason of the impossibility of obtaining medical advice on the use of contraceptives from their doctor, the statute was not self-enforcing for that reason. This conclusion has been criticised on the ground that 'the court's intuitive jump . . . from its conclusion that the doctor's alleged fear of enforcement was irrational to the conclusion that it was unreal suggests an absence of a clear analysis of the interests involved.'[56]

Academic opinion is critical of the denial of standing in a situation where enforcement is unlikely. It is argued that in actions for a declaration, exposure to jeopardy is the operative factor creating the condition of justiciability. A threat of enforcement is just one type of jeopardy; jeopardy is created by the very existence of a penal statute, and a threat of enforcement only adds weight to it. The point has been put by Edwin Borchard in an eloquent passage that perhaps deserves to be quoted *in extenso*:

In the twentieth century, with its kaleidoscopic changes and the resulting necessity of new legislation and regulation to maintain the social equilibrium, much of it carrying a criminal penalty, there has been a special need for speedy determination of the constitutionality and construction of legislation and regulations imposing burdens on the individual. . . . To make it . . . a condition of justiciability, that the affected group or individual await a *threat* of the District Attorney or the Attorney-General to *enforce* the statute or regulation before challenging the legality or applicability of the statutory burden, overlooks the fact that the injury is done, in most cases, by the *enactment* of the damaging statute or regulation, long before or even quite without any 'threat' of enforcement by an official. Justiciability or the right to initiate an action . . . is created by the jeopardy or restriction placed by the statute upon the plaintiffs' freedom of action. The statute or regulation now constitutes the cloud which the plaintiff has the right to challenge and, if successful, to remove. . . . It matters or should matter not in the slightest what the District Attorney thinks about the statute — whether he likes it or not, whether he intends to enforce it or not, whether he threatens or not. The fear, jeopardy, danger and insecurity are created by the statute, not by the District Attorney. . . . Law enforcement may by dereliction or hesitation become lax, with resulting responsibility to the government and the people as a whole; but the injured or jeopardized citizen should not be obliged to change his mode of life or livelihood in fear of criminal prosecution without opportunity to challenge the damaging statute until the District Attorney chooses to 'threaten' him with enforcement.[57]

(c) *Action by the federation or a state challenging the constitutionality of one another's act or of the act of another state.* It is an established principle of law that the state represents the public as a collection of individuals, and has therefore sufficient title to bring an action to assert a right belonging to the public, notwithstanding that no rights or powers of the state in its corporate capacity as a government are involved. This principle, it has been rightly held,[58] applies in a federal system so as to enable the attorney-general of a constituent state to institute proceedings against another constituent state or against private persons in order to assert the rights of the public of his state. Thus, an action by the state of Tasmania in the Commonwealth of Australia complaining that an act of another state of the Commonwealth, the state of Victoria, had violated the rights of the citizens of Tasmania was held to be competent, although no rights of the state itself in its corporate capacity as a government had been affected.[59] It seems that, in an action by a state to assert the rights of the public of the state, the mere enactment by another constituent state of a law adverse to such rights is enough, without proof of actual injury or threat of it.

However, the standing of a state in a federation to assert in a court action the rights of the public of the state, as distinct from its own rights, is subject to two qualifications. First, it does not avail against the federation; in other words a state cannot sue to enforce against the federation the rights of the public of that state. Federalism involves no dichotomy between the people of the federation and the people resident in each state; they are one, indivisible people. Accordingly, as against the federation, there can be no question of a state enforcing against it (the federation) the rights of the people resident within the territorial area of the state. There must be involved some right or power of the state in its corporate capacity as a government before it can maintain an action against the federation. Affirming this qualification, the U.S. supreme court has said: 'It cannot be conceded that a state, as *parens patriae*, may institute judicial proceedings to protect citizens of the United States from the operation of the statutes thereof. While the state, under some circumstances, may sue in that capacity for the protection of its citizens,[60] it is no part of its duty or power to enforce their rights in respect of their relations with the federal government. In that field it is the United States, and not the state, which represents them as *parens patriae* when such representation becomes appropriate; and to the former, and not to the latter, they must look for such protective measures as flow from that status.'[61] A state cannot therefore impugn a federal law if the only ground for the challenge is that, for example, it was not passed in the manner and form prescribed by the Constitution or that it contravenes rights guaranteed to individuals.

The second qualification relates to cases that are subject to the original jurisdiction of the supreme court. The 1979 Constitution vests in the supreme court, to the exclusion of any other court, original jurisdiction 'in any dispute between the Federation and a State or between States if and in so far as that dispute involves any question (whether of law or fact) on which the existence or extent of a legal right depends' (s. 212[1]). The phrase 'if and in so far as that dispute involves any question (whether of law or fact) on which the existence or extent of a legal right depends' is apt to give the impression that the original jurisdiction of the supreme court can be invoked by the federation or a state when none of its own rights but only those of the public or individual members of it are involved. But the primary requirement of the provision is that there must be a 'dispute between the federation and a state or between states'. It would be absurd to talk of a state having a dispute with the federation or with another state when no property or other rights or constitutional powers of the state in its corporate capacity as a government are involved.

The federation or a state invoking the original jurisdiction of the supreme court must therefore be able to show that it has a right which is or may be affected by the action complained of, and the court must determine, as a preliminary issue, the existence or extent of the right so claimed. Only if the right is found to exist can the court assume jurisdiction over the substantive claim. Thus, in *Attorney-General, Eastern Nigeria* v. *Attorney General of the Federation*,[62] the Government of Eastern Nigeria had brought an action in the original jurisdiction of the supreme court for a declaration that the Government of the Federation was not entitled to accept or act on the 1963 census, on the ground, *inter alia*, that the figures had been inflated, and were vitiated by irregularities. The plaintiff argued that acceptance of the figures could affect the demarcation of constituencies under s. 43 of the 1963 Constitution, and also the making of monetary grants under

s. 141 of the same Constitution. The supreme court held that Eastern Nigeria had no legal right to any particular number of constituencies or seats in the federal house of representatives, since the Constitution, unlike other federal constitutions, did not apportion constituencies among the constituent units. The rule that no constituency shall form part of more than one constituent unit, while it made for administrative convenience, conferred no legal right on a constituent unit to have any particular number of constituencies established within its boundaries. It was Nigeria, not the several constituent units, that was divided into constituencies for the purpose of elections to the house of representatives. Secondly, that Eastern Nigeria had no legal right to have the formula for the allocation of revenue under s. 141 of the Constitution maintained unaltered, since it was entirely within the discretion of parliament, acting with the votes of a two-thirds majority of its members and the consent of each legislative house of at least three regions, to alter it for any purpose including that of making it reflect the new population figures. The court then concluded that, as no legal right had been shown to exist in favour of Eastern Nigeria, it lacked jurisdiction to enquire into the substantive claim, i.e. whether the census figures had been inflated or vitiated by irregularities.

Where the federation or state as complainant has the right claimed, then it has under s. 212(1) of the Constitution sufficient title to pursue in the supreme court a claim in a substantive action without proof of actual injury or immediate threat of it as in the case of an action by a private person.

The point that deserves to be emphasised is that the right, the existence or extent of which is the criterion of the original jurisdiction of the supreme court under s. 212(1) of the Constitution, must be that of the federation or state as complainant. The original jurisdiction of the supreme court cannot be invoked unless there is a dispute between the federation and a state or between states, and there can be no dispute between the federation and a state or between states where the only rights involved are those of the public or of individual members of it, and where no question as to the existence or extent of the rights or constitutional powers of the federation or state in its corporate capacity as a government therefore arises. This is borne out by decisions of the U.S. supreme court based on the provision in the country's Constitution to the effect that 'in all cases . . . in which a State shall be a party, the Supreme Court shall have original jurisdiction.' (art. 3, s. 2[2]). In a case where a state brought an action in the original jurisdiction of the supreme court seeking to enforce, not its own rights, but those of depositors and creditors of an insolvent State bank against a shareholder of the bank, the supreme court declined jurisdiction; it held that under art. 3 s. 2(2) a state could invoke its original jurisdiction only where the matter directly affects the rights or interests of the state as a government.[63] In another case the court observed:

> We are of the opinion that the words, in the Constitution, conferring original jurisdiction on this court, in a suit 'in which a State shall be a party' are not to be interpreted as conferring such jurisdiction in every cause in which the State elects to make itself strictly a party plaintiff of record and seeks not to protect its own property, but only to vindicate the wrongs of some of its people or to enforce its own laws or public policy against wrongdoers, generally.[64]

Even more striking are the observations of Justice Harlan in a case where the state of Louisiana brought an action in the original jurisdiction of the U.S. supreme court complaining that an officer of the state of Texas had maladministered the laws of that state to the injury of its citizens. Said he:

> The case involves no property interest of that state.[. . .] When the Constitution gave this court jurisdiction of controversies between states, it did not thereby authorise a state to bring another state to the bar of this court for the purpose of testing the constitutionality of local statutes or regulations that do not affect the property or the powers of the complaining state in its sovereign or corporate capacity, but which at most affect only the rights of individual citizens or corporations engaged in interstate commerce. The word 'controversies' in the clause extending the judicial powers of the United States to controversies 'between two or more States' and to controversies 'between a state and citizens of another state' and the word party in the clause declaring that this court shall have original jurisdiction of all cases' in which a state shall be a party', refer to controversies or cases that are justiciable as between the parties thereto, and not to controversies or cases that do not involve either the property or powers of the state which complains.[. . .] The citizens of the complaining state may, in proper cases, invoke judicial protection of their property or rights when assailed by the laws and authorities of another state; but their state cannot, even with their consent, make their case its case and compel the offending state and its authorities to appear as defendants in an action brought in this court.[65]

In the light of these authorities, it is an over-statement to say that 'the attorney-general of a State has a sufficient title to invoke a provision of the Constitution for the purpose of challenging the validity of Commonwealth legislation which extends to, and operates within, the state whose interests he represents.'[66] A state attorney-general has no such title to challenge a federal legislation which neither affects the property rights of his state nor trenches upon its powers under the Constitution, but which merely infringes rights guaranteed to individuals or is alleged not to have been made according to the prescribed manner and form. The case in which the statement was made in fact concerned an allegation that a statute of the Australian parliament and the executive actions taken under it (the making and supplying of clothing by the federal government) had usurped the powers of the states. The high court rightly held the action to be competent in as much as the complaint involved the rights and powers of the state as a government. In the other Australian case on the point, the complaint again was that a federal statute had usurped a function reserved to the state by the Constitution.[67] (As stated earlier, where a state is asserting against another state the rights of the public of the state, then, since such a claim cannot constitute a dispute between states, the action should be brought in some other court than the supreme court.)

(d) *Constitutional policy based on the public interest in the enforcement of constitutional limitations.* There has in recent years been a noticeable shift in the U.S. supreme court away from a strict adherence to the *locus standi* rule. In place of that, 'the emphasis now is on the court's function as protector of a public interest in the enforcement of constitutional limitation.'[68] No longer would it allow an attack on a statute to be easily blocked on a mere plea of lack of *locus standi*, as was the case in the past. In the school prayer and Bible-reading cases, the court allowed any parent who had children in the schools to challenge the practice.[69] An owner of a barbecue in Alabama was allowed to challenge the Civil Rights Act of 1964 which desegregated places of public accommodation, although there was not so much as a contemplation of enforcement action against him, the government being unaware of the existence of his barbecue.[70] (The act was however held to be constitutional.) The disregard of the *locus standi* rule in this case is said to have been induced by the court's belief that 'a prompt constitutional decision [on the Act] would be in the public interest, even though not impelled by the necessities of litigation, whereas a postponement of decision might create uncertainty.' In a later decision,[71] enjoining criminal prosecutions under a state law alleged to interfere with political liberties, 'the opinion candidly stated that one of the reasons for interfering was that otherwise the existence of the statute and risks of prosecution might deter the exercise of constitutional rights by persons unwilling to risk prosecution.'[72]

The court has also allowed a litigant, none of whose own constitutional rights have been infringed but who has otherwise suffered or is in imminent danger of suffering injury, to avail himself of the rights of others, if the act cannot otherwise be challenged. Thus, a white person sued on a covenant forbidding the sale of land to negroes was allowed to enjoin the enforcement of the covenant, by setting up the right of negroes not to be denied the equal protection of the law.[73] The circumstances being such that it might have been impossible for negroes to challenge the enforcement of the covenant, a strict adherence to the *locus standi* rule would altogether have prevented the constitutional challenge to be raised. The court explained:

> Under the peculiar circumstances of this case, we believe the reasons which underlie our rule denying standing to raise another's rights, which is only a rule of practice, are outweighed by the need to protect the fundamental rights which would be denied by permitting the damages action to be maintained. In other unique situations which have arisen in the past *broad constitutional policy has led the Court to proceed* without regard to its usual rule.[74]

Such a case was that in which, in an action challenging a statute which required all parents to send their children to public schools, the plaintiff, a private and parochial school, was allowed to set up the constitutional right of parents to direct the education of their children.[75] The National Association for the Advancement of Coloured People was also allowed to use the right of its members to establish its standing to challenge a court decision requiring it to submit a list of its members within the state of Alabama.[76] It is worth emphasising the policy premise of the court's action in these cases; the departures from the rule were, as the court stated, in deference to 'broad constitutional policy'.

This broad constitutional policy, based on the public interest in the enforcement of constitutional limitations, was urged upon the federal court of appeal of Nigeria in a case in 1980 in which a senator complained that the appointment of a chairman of the federal electoral commission made by the president with the approval of the senate was unconstitutional and void, because the appointee was at the time of his appointment a judge of the high court of Bendel state.[77] It was contended in support of the senator's title to bring the action that there is implicit in certain provisions of the Constitution (ss. 6, 33[1], 236[1] and 4[8]) an indication that the courts should be open to every citizen for the enforcement of constitutional limitations, and that these provisions demand that people should not be prevented by the *locus standi* rule from invoking the judicial authority for the preservation of the Constitution. In this case the plaintiff had a greater concern for the preservation of the Constitution than the ordinary citizen in that, as a senator, he had subscribed to an oath to 'preserve, protect and defend the Constitution', and was interested in ensuring that the senate, of which he was a member, did not confirm the appointment of an unqualified person.[78]

The public interest in the observance of the Constitution was conceded by the attorney-general of the federation, but he argued that the interest being a public, and not a private one, the plaintiff lacked standing to assert it in a court action; his individual right must be involved or else he must show that the injury to the public right had inflicted upon him special damage over and above the injury to the public.

While accepting that as a general rule, as laid down in the English authorities,[79] standing to challenge the legality of the *administrative* action of public authorities requires actual or threatened interference with the plaintiff's private rights or special damage peculiar to himself where the right infringed is a public one, the federal court of appeal held that the point must be determined by reference to the relevant provisions of the 1979 Constitution, and that the general rule is incorporated into the Constitution in the provision that the judicial power vested in the courts 'shall extend to all matters between persons, or between government or authority and any person in Nigeria, and to all actions and proceedings relating thereto, for the determination of any question as to the civil rights and obligations of that person' (s. 6[6][*b*]). The appeal court then concluded as follows:

> The expression 'of that person' which is at the end of the 'determination of any question as to the civil rights and obligations' clearly delimits the person who has the right to bring the question as to the civil rights and obligations before the court. The question before the court must involve the determination of the civil rights and obligations of the person who has brought the issue for determination. In our view, it is therefore necessary for the plaintiff/respondent to show that the exercise by the 1st defendant/appellant of this power of appointment, and the exercise by the senate of their confirming power under s. 141 of the Constitution, injures him and therefore confers on him a right which he can enforce against the 1st defendant/appellant and 2nd defendant/appellant.

The appeal court further held that the invalidity of the impugned appointment affected no civil rights and obligations of the plaintiff in that, first, the confirmation of the appointment by the senate did not infringe any of his individual rights as a senator; and secondly, the oath taken by him as a senator to 'preserve, protect and defend the Constitution' confers no legal rights or powers on him. Accordingly he has no standing to question the appointment in court proceedings.

The argument of counsel for the plaintiff in this case does give the impression that he was urging the complete abandonment of the *locus standi* rule in constitutional cases. In so doing, he has clearly overstretched the point. Yet it is regrettable that s. 6(6)(*b*) of the Constitution has been interpreted to preclude the relaxation of the strict application of the *locus standi* rule so as to permit the courts, in deference to the public interest in the enforcement of constitutional limitations, to allow the constitutionality of the legislative and executive acts of public authorities to be challenged in cases where a broad constitutional policy makes it desirable, as in cases where a strict adherence to rule would altogether prevent the enforcement by the courts of constitutional limitations. This is so particularly in cases of unconstitutional appointments which can hardly ever affect anyone else's civil rights and obligations.

The decision of the federal court of appeal in this case has been affirmed by the supreme court, but, happily, the leading judgment delivered by the chief justice of Nigeria exhibits a very liberal attitude to the rule of *locus standi* in constitutional cases, though the reasoning is not altogether easy to follow, especially in the light of the final conclusion reached in the case. The learned chief justice seemed to distinguish three different categories of cases. First, in cases relating to a guaranteed right, the contravention alleged must relate to the person alleging it. Secondly, in other cases of alleged violation of the Constitution not involving any question as to the constitutionality of a law passed by the legislature, only a person whose civil rights and obligations are affected can sue; this second category embraces the present case as well as other cases of non-compliance by the president of the constitutional conditions governing the exercise of his executive powers. Thirdly, where a law is alleged to be inconsistent with the Constitution on grounds other than that it contravenes a guaranteed right, any one can sue. The right to sue, he says, derives from the provision of the Constitution declaring invalid any law inconsistent with its provisions. Any person resident in Nigeria has, by virtue of this, a civil right, indeed an obligation, 'to see to it that he is governed by a law which is consistent with the provisions of the Nigerian Constitution'.

In a developing country with a multi-ethnic society and a written federal constitution, where rumour-mongering is the pastime of the market places and the construction sites, to deny any member of such a society who is aware or believes, or is led to believe, that there has been an infraction of any of the provisions of our Constitution, or that any law passed by any of our legislative Houses, whether Federal or State, is unconstitutional, access to a court of law to air his grievance on the flimsy excuse of lack of sufficient interest is to provide a ready recipe for organised disenchantment with the judicial process. . . . In the Nigerian context, it is better to allow a party to go to court and to be heard than to refuse him access to our courts. Non-access, to my mind, will stimulate the *free-for-all in the media* as to which law is constitutional and which law is not! In any case, our courts have inherent powers to deal with vexatious litigants or frivolous claims.

4. *A policy of avoidance*

Behind many of the decisions on the interest which a person must have before he may invoke the court's intervention in constitutional cases lies a deliberate policy to avoid adjudication of such cases. Decisions denying standing to a plaintiff who had suffered an injury because he was thought not to be in a position to raise the ultimate issue in the clearest and most developed fashion[80] or because, notwithstanding his injury, the timing of the action was considered premature in the sense that the full impact of the operation of the governmental measure under challenge had not materialised, were certainly of this kind.[81] The limitation on judicial power resulting from these decisions is perhaps better regarded as self-imposed than inherent,[82] and as motivated by an attitude of self-restraint which finds practical expression in a policy of avoidance. Indeed, Justice Frankfurter of the U.S. supreme court, the arch-apostle of this policy, has said:

The most fundamental principle of constitutional adjudication is not to face constitutional questions but to avoid them, if at all possible. And so the 'court developed for its own governance in cases confessedly within its jurisdiction, a series of rules under which it has avoided passing upon a large part of all the constitutional questions pressed upon it for decision'.[83]

Apart from the *locus standi* rule and the so-called doctrine of the political question,[84] these rules, as catalogued by Justice Brandeis in *Ashwander* v. *TVA*,[85] are: there must arise upon the facts before the court a real necessity for deciding a point of constitutional law; the court will not 'anticipate a question of constitutional law in advance of the necessity of deciding it';[86] it will not 'declare, for the government of future cases, principles or rules of law which cannot affect the result as to the thing in issue in the case before it'.[87] Even where a point of constitutional law is properly raised in a case before the court, but the case can be disposed of on another ground, the court will decide it on this other ground and refrain from pronouncing upon the constitutional point.[88] Further, 'when the validity of an Act of the Congress is drawn in question; and even if a serious doubt of constitutionality is raised, it is a cardinal principle that this court will first ascertain whether a construction of the statute is fairly possible by which the question may be avoided.'[89] What this means is that the necessity for deciding a point of constitutional law must be an absolute one, in the sense that such determination is unavoidable.[90] It is important to note, however, as Gerald Gunther has pointed out,[91] that these rules do not result in an avoidance of all decision on merit.

Another facet of the principle is the rule that where administrative or statutory remedies are available, these must first be exhausted before a challenge to the constitutionality of legislation will be entertained. Thus where a statute provides that a milk dealer dissatisfied with an order made by a milk control board may be heard in opposition or may apply to the board to modify the order, it was held that this remedy should be utilised by the dealer before resorting to a suit to enjoin the enforcement of the order.[92] The principle was even applied to debar accused persons in a prosecution from raising the defence of statutory invalidity.[93] In yet another case where the civil service commission was authorised by statute to remove civil servants who engaged in political management but no provision was made for administrative or statutory review of the commission's dismissal order, it was held that, there being no question as to the exhaustion of administrative remedies, a challenge to the statute would lie.[94] The implication is that, had a review of the commission's decision been provided for, the statute would not have been allowed to be challenged before the remedy of review had been utilised.

What justification can there be for requiring a worker dismissed under an unconstitutional statute which provides for appeal to the dismissing or other authority, first to avail himself of that remedy before impugning the statute itself? If he resorted to the statutory remedy so provided, he would clearly have taken advantage of the statute, an implied acceptance of its authority, which, according to the decisions relating to waiver discussed below, would preclude him from thereafter questioning its constitutionality.[95] The aggrieved person thus finds himself on the horns of a dilemma. He is barred from challenging the unconstitutional statute until he has pursued the statutory remedy, and if his recourse to the latter remedy is unsuccessful he is deemed to be guilty of acquiescence and so barred from challenging the statute. The effect of course is to throw an impenetrable shield of protection on the statute, an intolerable position which seems to hold the rule of law as no more than a rhetorical flourish.[96]

The rule that a person who has voluntarily taken the benefit of a statute is deemed to have waived his right to challenge its validity is another aspect of the 'techniques of not doing'.[97] He 'cannot claim the benefit of statutes and afterwards assail their validity. There is no sanctity in such a claim of constitutional right as prevents its being waived as any other claim of right may be.'[98] Thus, where a plaintiff, after filing a claim for compensation in the court of claims for land compulsorily acquired, as provided for in an act of congress, brought another action in the ordinary court in which, among other things, he contended that the statutory provision for reference of claims for compensation to the court of claims was unconstitutional, the supreme court held that, by instituting a claim in the court of claims, the plaintiff had voluntarily accepted the provision of the act, and so precluded himself from thereafter questioning its constitutionality.[99] So also stockholders who had, pursuant to certain statutes, instituted proceedings for the valuation of their stock were held to have waived their right to assail the validity of those statutes.[100] A party who elected to have his damages assessed by a jury in the exercise of a power given by a statute was precluded from denying the validity of other provisions of the statute.[101]

The principle of law which underlies waiver and provides its rationale is that of estoppel. It is just that a person who agrees to waive his right should not be allowed afterwards to go back on it. But that presupposes his knowledge of the right which he is agreeing to waive. Knowledge lies at the root of all questions of waiver or acquiescence. For a person cannot agree to waive a right if he has no knowledge of it. The point is so well established by judicial decisions as to be beyond dispute. Now, a person may accept a benefit under a statute without knowledge of its unconstitutionality. The constitutionality of a statute is a legal question of considerable sophistication, which no layman can be expected to know without the advice of a specialist lawyer. And it is comparatively seldom that people seek legal advice before accepting a benefit under a statute. Moreover, the constitutionality of a statute may arise in relation to a completely different matter from that in relation to which the benefit was accepted. And a person may lodge a claim under a statute purely from an anxiety to comply with a stipulation as to time for the lodgement of claims. In a matter of constitutional rights, so fundamental to the individual, waiver would seem to be out of tune with the 'broad constitutional policy' which should inform and guide such questions. The supreme court of India has, gratifyingly, rejected the doctrine of waiver of a constitutional right, on the ground that it has no 'relevancy in construing the fundamental rights conferred by Part III of our Constitution.[. . .] These fundamental rights have not been put in the constitution merely for individual benefit. . . . They have been put there as a matter of policy, and the doctrine of waiver can have no application to provisions of law which have been enacted as a matter of constitutional policy.'[102]

Judicial self-restraint is undoubtedly the rationale behind the policy of avoidance. Restraint is said to be called for by the gravity and delicacy of judicial review of governmental measures; by 'the comparative finality of those consequences; the consideration due to the judgment of other repositories of constitutional power concerning the scope of their authority; the necessity, if government is to function constitutionally, for each to keep within its power, including the courts; the inherent limitations of the judicial process, arising especially from its largely negative character and limited resources of enforcement.'[103]

No one would dispute that the exercise of power, any power, calls for self-restraint, for self-restraint is, after all, a counsel of prudence. The need for such prudential restraint is perhaps greater in the case of an unelected body, like a court, exercising critical political power.

Prudence demands indeed that the court should never lose sight of the legal limits of its power or of the practical limitation upon it, and that it should approach its relations with the political organs with a 'high sense of strategy and tactics'[104] without however compromising its own powers. Yet this simple truth, the undoubted need for prudence, does not require the elevation of self-restraint into a doctrine, or a slogan of judicial action or rather inaction. For there is a certain incompatibility between the duty of the court to redress all justiciable violations of the law by government and the call for abstention from that duty implicit in the slogan of judicial self-restraint. The former demands courage, fearlessness and firmness tempered no doubt by prudence, while the latter partakes of an act of timidity — of 'buck-passing', one might almost say. The line between 'prudent restraint and courageous decisiveness'[105] may be thin, yet there is something of cowardice, timidity and opportunism in one who, rather than face the burden of responsibility, would evade it either by sweeping the problem under the carpet or by shifting it to others. In so far as it expresses the need for a broad construction of constitutional grants of power, judicial self-restraint is a truism if nonetheless a salutary principle of constitutional interpretation. In so far, however, as it aims to justify abstention from intervention for the protection of the individual against violations of the law, especially of the prohibitions of the constitution, restraint is a positive danger.

The prohibitions of the bill of rights impose upon the courts a positive duty for their enforcement, which cannot but be enfeebled by the notion, implicit in the idea of restraint, that judicial review is a usurpation, since 'it is natural to favour "restraint" in the exercise of a supposedly usurped function.'[106] It is not only the legitimate and proper function of the courts to enforce these prohibitions against the government; the efficacy of the guarantees is a paramount requirement of the rule of law, calling therefore, not for restraint but for a 'vigorous, vigilant, courageous activism on the part of the court'.[107] While it may be undesirable to encourage 'the professional litigant and the meddlesome interloper to invoke the jurisdiction of the courts in matters that do not concern him',[108] there is something paradoxical in the idea of a judge refusing, on the ground of lack of standing, to entertain a challenge to a law he himself knows to be unconstitutional because it makes criminal the exercise of a right granted by the constitution. The impression that this would leave on the ordinary man would be that the court was throwing a cloak of approval around the law, and thereby condoning oppression. The result in the public eye would be to bring the law and the courts into disrepute.

Certainly a constitutional grant of power needs to be given an interpretation broad and liberal enough to facilitate the attainment of purposes considered beneficial to society by government. By such an approach, an activist judiciary would be an ally to social progress, ready to interpret social and economic legislation in a manner conducive to the attainment of its social objectives. This does not of course require the court to abandon its responsibility to watch over the civil liberties of the individual or to compromise its ability and preparedness to act as a liberalising influence upon government. However, while championing civil liberties — life, personal liberty, and freedom of speech, assembly, association and religion — an activist judiciary should at the same time appreciate the need in a modern welfare state for subordinating the individual's economic freedoms — freedom of property, of contract, etc. — to needful programmes of economic development. The dual position of championing both civil liberties and social welfare legislation may appear to involve a contradiction, the so-called 'Holmesian dilemma'.[109] No such contradiction is in fact involved in this position. It only demands of the court adherence to the same broad approach in the interpretation of the constitutional guarantee of civil liberties as it adopts in the interpretation of constitutional grants of power. As the U.S. supreme court has observed, 'it would be a strange rule of construction that language granting powers is to be liberally construed and that language of restriction is to be narrowly and technically construed.'[110]

The mark of judicial activism adopted here is thus one of an active concern with public policy in its widest sense. In so far as the policy and social needs underlying social welfare legislation, rather than a literal legalistic outlook, informs judicial interpretation of such legislation, the judiciary may rightly be said to be playing an activist role. What an activist role demands of the judiciary is to get away from the notion, traditional in the Commonwealth, that policy is outside the concern of the courts.[111] Activism requires of the judiciary a preparedness to break free of excessive legalism and to interpret the law broadly, not according to its literal meaning but in the light of the dictates of public policy; an ability to reflect in its decisions the ideals of the nation, its needs and ethical sensibilities and the attitude of the public towards questions of the day.

REFERENCES

1. (1961), 1 All N.L.R. 203.
2. (1961), 1 All N.L.R. 826.
3. (1961), 1 All N.L.R. 622, at 625.
4. (1961), 1 All N.L.R. 584.
5. The supreme court relied on the English case of *Weed* v. *Ward* (1889) 40 Ch.D. 555 relating to the reference of questions under the Judicature Act, 1873, s. 56, to the Official or Special Referee.

6. ibid., at 588.
7. *Mehta & Sons Ltd.* v. *Century Spinning and Manufacturing Co. Ltd.* (1962) All India Rep. 1314. Contrast *Olajire* v. *Superintendent of Local Govt. Police* (1961) 1 All N.L.R. 588.
8. Per Brett F.J., delivering the judgment of the supreme court in *Gamioba* v. *Esezi II* (1961), 1 All N.L.R. at 588–9.
9. *Gamioba* v. *Esezi II* ibid.
10. *Marbury* v. *Madison* (1803), 1 Cranch, 137.
11. See *Mafindi* v. *Bauchi Native Authority* (1956) N.R.N.L.R. 41; also *Ogoja* v. *Adamawa N.A.* (1959) N.R.N.R. 151. There are a few exceptions, e.g. *The King* v. *Fed. Court of Bankruptcy, Ex parte Lowenstein* (1938), 59 C.L.R. 556 sustaining the validity of an act which authorised the court of bankruptcy in Australia to charge a bankrupt and try him summarily; also *Att.-Gen. for The Gambia* v. *N'Jie* [1961] A.C. 617 (P.C.) affirming the power of a judge to initiate disciplinary action against a lawyer for professional misconduct.
12. *Chicago & G.T.R. Co.* v. *Wellman*, 143 U.S. 339, 345; quoted with approval in *Poe* v. *Ullman*, 367 U.S. 497, 506 (1961).
13. Wechsler, 'Towards Neutral Principles of Constitutional Law', in *Selected Essays on Constitutional Law*, ed. Assn. of American Law Schools (1963), p. 466; reprinted from *Harv. L. Rev.*, 73 (1959), 1.
14. *Massachusetts (Frothington)* v. *Mellon*, 262 U.S. 447, 488–9.
15. See James Thayer, 'The Origin and Scope of the American Doctrine of Constitutional Law', *Harv. L. Rev.* (1893), 7, 129, 135 6.
16. C. L. Black, *The People and the Court* (1960), 28; see also Alexander Bickel, 'The Passive Virtues', in *Selected Essays on Constitutional Law*, op. cit., 26; reprinted from *Harv. L. Rev.*, 75, 40.
17. *Liverpool, N.Y. & P.S.S. Co.* v. *Emigration Comrs.*, 113 U.S. 33, 39 quoted with approval in *Baker* v. *Carr*, 369 U.S. 186, 204 (1962).
18. *In re Pacific Ry Comm* 32 F. 241, 255, per Chief Justice Marshall; *Aetna Life Insurance Co.* v. *Haworth*, 300 U.S. 229, 240–1 (1937), per Chief Justice Hughes; *Flast* v. *Cohen*, 392 U.S. 83, 94–5 (1968) per Chief Justice Warren.
19. Per Justice Brennan in *Baker* v. *Carr*, ibid., 204.
20. C. L. Black, op. cit., 28.
21. James Thayer, op. cit., 136.
22. Per Justice Frankfurter in *Poe* v. *Ullman*, 367 U.S. 497, 503.
23. *Massachusetts (Frothington)* v. *Mellon*, 262 U.S. 447.
24. ibid., p. 488 accepted as controlling in *Ex-Cell-o Corporation* v. *Chicago*, 115 F. 2d 627 (7th Cir. 1940).
25. *Fairchild* v. *Hughes*, 258 U.S. 126. See also the concurring judgment of Justice Brandeis in *Ashwander* v. *TVA*, 297 U.S. 288. 'We can only adjudicate an issue as to which there is a claimant before us who has a special, individualized stake in it. One who is merely the self-appointed spokesman of a constitutional point of view cannot ask us to pass on it' per Justice Frankfurter in *Coleman* v. *Miller* (1939), 307 U.S. 433, 467.
26. See *Adegbenro* v. *Att.-Gen. of Nigeria* (1962), 1 All N.L.R. 432, 437.
27. *Baker* v. *Carr*, ibid.
28. *Coleman* v. *Miller*, ibid. relying on *Koening* v. *Flynn* (1932), 285 U.S.

375; *Smiley* v. *Holm* (1932) 285 U.S. 355; and *Hawker* v. *Smith* (1920) 253 U.S. 221.
29. *Parker* v. *County of Los Angeles*, 338 U.S. 327, 333; quoted with approval in *Poe* v. *Ullman*, ibid., p. 503.
30. *Poe* v. *Ullman*, ibid., 507.
31. *Euclid* v. *Ambler Realty Co.* (1926) 272 U.S. 365, 386.
32. *Pierce* v. *Society of Sisters* (1925) 268 U.S. 510.
33. See *Colum. L. Rev.*, 62, 106, 115.
34. *Pennsylvania* v. *West Virginia* (1923) 262 U.S. 553. For other self-enforcement situations, see *Carter* v. *Carter Coal Co.* (1936) 298 U.S. 238; *AFL* v. *Watson* (1946) 327 U.S. 582; *Terrace* v. *Thompson* (1923) 263 U.S. 197; *Joint Anti-Fascist Refugee Comm.* v. *McGrath* (1951) 341 U.S. 123, 159.
35. *Lochunni* v. *State of Madras A*, 1959 S.C. 725, 731.
36. Basu, *Commentary on the Constitution of India*, vol. 1, 5th edn., 182–3.
37. See the cases discussed by Borchard, 'Challenging "Penal Statutes" by Declaratory Action', *Yale L.J.*, 52 (1943), 445.
38. Per Justice Frankfurter in *Poe* v. *Ullman*, 367 U.S. 497, 504. Cf. Justice Thompson in *Cherokee Nation* v. *Georgia*, 5 Pet 1, 75: 'A law must be brought into actual or threatened operation, upon rights properly falling under judicial cognisance, or remedy is not to be had here', quoted with approval in *Georgia* v. *Stanton*, 6 Wall. 50, 75, and in *New Jersey* v. *Sargent*, 269 U.S. 328, 331. For the factors responsible for the assumption that a threat of enforcement is a condition of justiciability, see Borchard, op. cit., *Yale L. J.* 52, 445, 459 ff.
39. (1952) 342 U.S. 485.
40. ibid., 504.
41. *United Public Workers* v. *Mitchell* (1947) 330 U.S. 75.
42. 342 U.S. 485, 498.
43. *United Public Workers* v. *Mitchell* (1947) 330 U.S. 75.
44. *Poe* v. *Ullman*, 367 U.S. 497.
45. (1961) 1 All N.L.R. 269; also *Adegbenro* v. *Att.-Gen. of Nigeria* (1962) 1 All N.L.R. 432.
46. *Adler* v. *Board of Education* (1952) 342 U.S. 485. Dissenting from the majority decision upholding a parent's standing in this case, Justice Frankfurter said that a parent's desire to have his child educated in a school system where teachers are not restrained by unconstitutional limitations on their freedom of speech and association is not a legal interest such as is required to give standing to evoke the Court's jurisdiction. 'The hurt to parents' sensibilities is too tenuous or the inroad upon rightful claims to public education too argumentative to serve as the earthy stuff required for a legal right judicially enforceable' (502–3).
47. *McCollum* v. *Board of Education*, 333 U.S. 203.
48. (1927) 273 U.S. 70.
49. Borchard, 'The Constitutionality of Declaratory Judgments', *Colum. L. Rev.*, 31, 561, 585–6.
50. Per Justice Frankfurter in *Joint Anti-Fascist Refugee Comm.* v. *McGrath*, 341 U.S. 123, 156.

51. Comments, *Colum. L. Rev.*, 62, 106, 132.
52. 367 U.S. 497.
53. ibid. at 509. But see Comment in *Colum. L. Rev.* 62, 106, 130, n. 146.
54. Cf. Alexander Bickel, *The Least Dangerous Branch* (1962), 148.
55. 367 U.S. 497 at 508.
56. Comments, *Colum. L. Rev.*, 62 pp. 106, 129–30; also Bickel, op. cit., p. 146.
57. Borchard, 'Challenging "Penal Statutes" by Declaratory Action' (1943) *Yale L.J.* 52, 445, 456–5.
58. *State of Tasmania* v. *State of Victoria* (1935), 52 C.L.R. 157, particularly 171.
59. *State of Tasmania* v. *State of Victoria*, ibid.
60. Citing *Missouri* v. *Illinois*, 180 U.S. 208, 241.
61. *Massachusetts* v. *Melon* (1923) 262 U.S. 447, 485–6.
62. (1964) 1 All N.L.R. 224.
63. *Oklahoma ex rel. Johnson* v. *Cook* (1938) 304 U.S. 387.
64. *Oklahoma* v. *Atchison, T & S.F. Ry. Co.* (1900) 220 U.S. 277, 289.
65. *Louisiana* v. *Texas*, 176 U.S. 1, 24–5.
66. *Att.-Gen. for Victoria* v. *Commonwealth*, ibid. at 556 per Gavan Duffy C.J.
67. *Att.-Gen. (N.S.W.)* v. *Brewery Employees Union of New South Wales* (1908), 6 C.L.R. 469.
68. Archibald Cox, *The Warren Court* (1968), 19.
69. ibid., 20.
70. *Katzanback* v. *McClung*, (1964) 379 U.S. 294.
71. *Dombrawski* v. *Pfister*, 380 U.S. 479 (1965).
72. Cox, op. cit, 18.
73. *Barrows* v. *Jackson*, (1953) 346 U.S. 349.
74. ibid., 257. Emphasis supplied.
75. *Pierce* v. *Society of Sisters*, 268 U.S. 510.
76. *NAACP* v. *Alabama*, 357 U.S. 449. See Sedler, 'Standing to Assert Constitutional Jus Tertii in the Supreme Court' (1962) *Yale L.J.*, 71, 599.
77. *President of the Fed. Republic of Nigeria & Another* v. *Adesanya*, FCA/L/93/80.
78. Compare *Coleman* v. *Miller* (1939) 307 U.S. 433; *Koening* v. *Flynn* (1932) 285 U.S. 375; *Smiley* v. *Holm* (1932) 285 U.S. 355; *Hawker* v. *Smith* (1920) 253 U.S. 221.
79. The appeal court reviewed the following English authorities: *L.P.T.S.* v. *Moscrop* [1942] 1 All E.R. 97; *Clark* v. *Epsom Rural District Council* [1929] 1 Ch. 287; *Boyce* v. *Paddington Borough Council* [1903] 1 Ch. 109 at 114; *Gouriet* v. *Union of Post Office Workers* [1977] 3 All E.R. 70; *Ex parte Island Record Ltd.* [1978] 3 All E.R. 824.
80. E.g. *Tennessee Electric Power Co.* v. *TVA*, 306 U.S. 118 (1939). Also see Justice Frankfurter in *Joint Anti-Fascist Refugee Comm.* v. *McGrath* (1951) 341 U.S. 123, 151.
81. Bickel, *The Least Dangerous Branch* (1962), 123–7.
82. Manley O. Hudson, 'Advisory Opinions of National and International Courts' (1923–4) *Harv. L. Rev.* 37, 970, 971; *Colum. L. Rev.* (1962) 62, 106, 110.

83. *United States* v. *Lovett*, 328 U.S. 303, 320 (concurring), quoting Justice Brandeis in *Ashwander* v. *TVA*, 297 U.S. 288, 346. Justice Frankfurter's judgment in Lovett reads like a sermon on judicial restraint. See also his judgment in *Poe* v. *Ullman* (1961) 367 U.S. 497, 503.
84. See Nwabueze, *Judicialism in Commonwealth Africa* (1977), chap. 2.
85. 297 U.S. 288.
86. *Liverpool, N.Y. & P.S.S. Co.* v. *Emigration Commrs.*, 113 U.S. 33; *Kariapper* v. *Wijesinha* [1967] 3 All E.R. 485 (P.C.).
87. *Tyler* v. *Judges of Court of Registration* (1900) 179 U.S. 405, 409.
88. *Siler* v. *Louisville & N.R. Co.*, 213 U.S. 175, 191, *Gamioba* v. *Esezi II* (1961), 1 All N.L.R. 584; *Ajayi* v. *Zaria N.A.* (1963), 1 All N.L.R. 169; *Umeze* v. *The State* (1973), 6 S.C. 221.
89. *Crowell* v. *Benson*, 295 U.S. 22, 62.
90. *Burton* v. *U.S.*, 196 U.S. 283, 295.
91. Gerald Gunther, 'The Subtle Vices of the "Passive Virtues" — a Comment on Principle and Expediency in Judicial Review' (1964) *Colum. L. Rev.*, 64, 1, 16–20.
92. *Hegeman Farm Corpn.* v. *Baldwin*, 293 U.S. 163, 172 (1934); also *Petersen Baking Co.* v. *Bryan*, 290 U.S. 570, 575.
93. *Yakus* v. *United States* (1944) 321 U.S. 414.
94. *United Public Workers* v. *Mitchell* (1947) 330 U.S. 75, 93.
95. *Great Falls Manufacturing Co.* v. *Garland* (1888), 124 U.S. 581; *Wall* v. *Parrot Silver & Copper Co.* (1917), 244 U.S. 407; *St. Louis Malleable Casting Company* v. *Prendergast Construction Co.* (1923) 260 U.S. 469.
96. It is submitted in chapter 18 that this rule is unconstitutional in so far as it allows an administrative or statutory remedy to override a constitutional one.
97. 'The techniques of not doing are the most important thing we do,' per Justice Brandeis in *Ashwander* v. *TVA*, ibid.
98. *Wall* v. *Parrot Silver & Copper Co.* (1917) 244 U.S. 407, 412.
99. *Gt. Falls Manufacturing Co.* v. *Garland* (1888), 124 U.S. 581.
100. *Wall* v. *Parrot Silver & Copper Co.*, ibid.
101. *Electric Co.* v. *Dow*, 166 U.S. 489; see also *St. Louis Malleable Casting Co.* v. *Prendergast Construction Co.* (1923) 260 U.S. 469.
102. *Pesikata* v. *State of Bombay*, 1955 1 S.C.R. 613, 654–5.
103. Per Justice Rutledge in *Rescue Army* v. *Municipal Court*, 331 U.S. 547, 571 (1947).
104. Rostow, *The Sovereign Prerogative* (1962), 34.
105. C.L. Black, *The People and the Court* (1960), 89.
106. Black, op. cit., 27.
107. ibid., 100.
108. de Smith, *Judicial Review of Administrative Action* (1968), 22.
109. Konefsky, *The legacy of Holmes and Brandeis* (1956); Grove, 'The "Sentinels" of liberty? The Nigerian Judiciary and Fundamental Rights', *J.A.L.* (1963), 52.
110. *Fairbank* v. *United States* (1901) 181 U.S. 283, 288–9.
111. Brett, 'The Role of the Judiciary in a Federal Constitution' in *Problems of Federalism in Nigeria* (1960), 21.

18
CONSTITUTIONAL REMEDIES FOR JUSTICIABLE VIOLATIONS OF THE CONSTITUTION

1. *The constitutional basis of the right to relief for justiciable violations of the Constitution*

Whether a violation of the constitution is justiciable depends not only upon the appropriateness of the violated provision for judicial adjudication, and the standing of the complainant, but also on the availability of a remedy for enforcing the violation. The court may be under a duty to adjudicate all justiciable violations of the Constitution, but the duty cannot be performed if the law provides no remedy for the particular violation. What this means is that the duty is dependent upon the law of remedies. The notion of a duty on the part of the court to decide all justiciable violations of the constitution would be negated or at least attenuated if remedies for such violations had no basis in the Constitution, and were entirely dependent upon the general law (statutory and decisional). For then the legislature could dispose of them as it pleased, either denying them or making the conditions for their award unduly restrictive or giving the courts a free or wide discretion. Such a situation can only be avoided if the constitution itself provides explicitly or by implication certain remedies for the violation of its justiciable provisions.

It is here that the classical theory of judicial review runs into a serious self-contradiction. It asserts that the courts are under an obligation to adjudicate all violations of the constitution that are properly brought before them and are suitable for judicial determination. At the same time, it acknowledges that this duty is entirely conditioned by, and dependent upon, the general law of remedies. Thus, in dealing with the plaintiff's claim in the parent case of *Marbury* v. *Madison* Chief Justice Marshall posed the questions for decision as follows:

1st. Has the applicant a right to the commission he demands?
2ndly. If he has a right, and that right has been violated, do the laws of his country afford him a remedy?
3rdly. If they do afford him a remedy, is it a *mandamus* issuing from this court?[1]

Professor Wechsler, the leading present-day classicist, has rationalised Marshall in a somewhat pontifical statement.

Only when the standing law, decisional or statutory, provides a remedy to vindicate the interest that demands protection against an infringement of the kind that is alleged, a law of remedies that ordinarily at least is framed in reference to rights and wrongs in general, do courts have any business asking what the Constitution may require or forbid, and only then when it is necessary for decision of the case that is at hand.[2]

A self-contradiction is obvious in this proposition. The court's obligation to adjudicate cases arising from the Constitution cannot depend upon a power to enforce which rests entirely on the general law and consequently on the will of the legislature. There can be no inescapable duty to decide if there is no inherent (i.e. constitutionally-based) right to appropriate judicial remedies for violations of the Constitution. Is there such a right? Does the Constitution provide, explicitly or by implication, any remedies for the violation of those of its provisions that are justiciable?

The contradiction may be said to result mainly from the limited original jurisdiction granted to the only court, the supreme court, established by the U.S. Constitution. By the terms of the Constitution, the supreme court has original jurisdiction in constitutional cases only where ambassadors, other public ministers and consuls are affected, and in those where a state is a party. The creation of other federal courts and the distribution to them of the residue of the federal judicial power not vested exclusively in the supreme court is left to congress. The limited original jurisdiction of the supreme court, and the plenary power of congress to establish or disestablish lower federal courts and to regulate their jurisdiction prompt the conclusion that congress has a pretty complete power over remedies since, in order to deny a remedy, all it needs to do is to deny jurisdiction to any court to give the remedy.[3] As the U.S. supreme court observed:

Courts created by statute must look to the statute as the warrant for their authority; certainly they cannot go beyond the statute, and assert an authority with which they may not be invested by it, or which may be clearly denied to them. This argument is in no wise impaired by admitting that judicial power shall extend to all cases arising under the Constitution and laws of the United States. Perfectly consistent with such an admission is the truth, that the organisation of the judicial power, the definition and distribution of the subjects of jurisdiction in the federal tribunals, and the modes of their action and authority have been, and of right must be, the work of the Legislature.[4]

The 1979 Nigerian Constitution differs from the American, first, in guaranteeing to every person, in explicit terms, the right of access to the courts for the determination of his civil rights and obligations (s. 33[1]); and secondly, in conferring on courts established by it unlimited jurisdiction, both original and appellate, to hear and determine all types of cases, including constitutional cases (see chapter 16 above).

Yet the explicit constitutional grant of jurisdiction in constitutional cases is not necessarily a grant of power to award any kind of remedy. What can indisputably be predicted upon it is that in a substantive, conventional action, e.g. action in tort or contract for damages between two private persons, or between the government as plaintiff and a private person or in a criminal proceeding against a person, the court has power to declare a legislative or executive act void for unconstitutionality in so far as the rights or liabilities of the parties depend upon that. That is the crux of the power of judicial review which must be taken to have been conclusively established in *Marbury* v. *Madison*. The limitation of an action for damages is that it presupposes actual violation of a right and actual injury too if other than nominal damages are to be awarded. For this reason therefore a conventional action for damages has a limited value in redressing violations of the Constitution by the legislature or the executive. Criminal proceedings presuppose that a person will first have to break the criminal law, but few people would be prepared to run the risk of a possible conviction and the attendant punishment, which may be a fine or imprisonment or both, just to create an opportunity to test the constitutionality of the law.

The question is whether there is a constitutional right to a preventive or anticipatory relief in the form of an injunction or declaratory judgment which would enable the question of constitutionality to be decided before violation of or injury to private right takes place or without the individual having first to break the criminal law. Writing on the U.S. Constitution, Henry Hart Jr asserts that 'the tradition of our law that preventive relief is the exception rather than the rule . . . naturally makes it hard to hold that anybody has a constitutional right to an injunction or a declaratory judgment.'[5] And there are decisions of the U.S. supreme court to the effect that a challenge to the constitutionality of legislation would not be entertained until available administrative remedies have been exhausted,[6] the implication being that there is no constitutional right to relief against unconstitutional legislation. For surely, if a right to a declaration or injunction exists under the Constitution, it cannot be overridden by the fact that an application for it is preventive or anticipatory in nature or by the availability of alternative administrative remedy.

(i) *Declaratory relief*

The jurisdiction granted to the high court under the 1979 Constitution is jurisdiction 'to hear and determine *any civil proceedings* in which the existence or extent of a legal right, power, duty, liability, privilege, interest, obligation or claim is in issue or to hear and determine any criminal proceedings involving or relating to any penalty, forfeiture, punishment or other liability in respect of an offence committed by any person' (s. 236[1]). The phrase 'any civil or criminal proceedings' is wide and apt enough to embrace a conventional form of action as well as proceedings in which the preventive or anticipatory relief of a declaratory judgment is sought. To interpret the phrase as limited to a conventional action for damages or criminal proceedings is to do violence to the clear intention of the Constitution as manifested in the words used.

The six courts established directly by the Constitution — the supreme court, the federal court of appeal, federal high court, high court of a state, state *sharia* court of appeal and the state customary court of appeal — are expressly declared to be superior courts of record and, save as may be otherwise prescribed by the appropriate legislature, are invested with the powers of such a court (s. 6[3]). The judicial power vested in the courts is further declared to 'extend, *notwithstanding anything to the contrary in this Constitution*, to all inherent powers and sanctions of a court of law' (s. 6[6]). Now, a superior court of record has an inherent power to make any order or decree that it deems appropriate in a matter properly within its jurisdiction, including a declaration of invalidity.

Furthermore, the Constitution itself contains an express declaration making void any law that is inconsistent with its provision (s. 1[3]). From the constitutional declaration of invalidity arises an obligation on the part of the court to echo and apply it in cases of justiciable violation brought before it by whatever form of action used, notwithstanding anything to the contrary in the general law of remedies, provided only that the court's intervention is sought by a person with an adverse interest in a real, concrete controversy. It cannot be for nothing that the Constitution, having imposed limitations and prohibitions on government, couples it with a declaration of invalidity against legislative and executive acts transgressing those limitations and prohibitions. The constitutional declaration of invalidity must have some significance. It is intended to confer — and, it is submitted, does confer — upon any person whose rights are violated or threatened with violation by an unconstitutional legislative or executive act, a right to apply to the court to administer and enforce the constitutional declaration. Upon such application the court is obliged to pronounce on the question of unconstitutionality, although the question is not brought before it by means of a substantive, conventional action for damages. The constitutional declaration may thus be regarded as a direction to the court to apply and enforce it upon the application, whether in an action for damages or by an originating notice of motion, of a person adversely affected by an unconstitutional legislation.

The modern declaratory judgment procedure is in effect merely a legislative recognition of the individual's constitutional right to apply to the court for the enforcement of the constitutional declaration of invalidity. It is surprising that the constitutional basis of this procedure should ever be doubted. The ground for this doubt is the now-exploded[7] one that 'the declaratory judgment imposes on the courts powers non-judicial in character and that it requires them to decide cases that are moot or to render advisory opinions, or, in some instances, even, that judgments that carry no execution are unconstitutional.'[8]

The legislature or the court through its rule-making power may regulate the procedure for making an application to the court, but in default of such regulation, a simple application by originating notice of motion is sufficient. It needs to be emphasised that the right to make an application exists by the Constitution, and is distinct from the power of the legislature (or the court) to regulate the procedure for making it. It cannot be taken away or overriden by the latter. As the U.S. supreme court has rightly held,[9] given a real, concrete controversy between parties with adverse interests, the form of the application, whether it be an action for damages or even by an originating notice of motion, is immaterial. Neither the procedure of damages nor the new declaratory judgment procedure is, constitutionally, a prerequisite for the enforcement by the court of the constitutional declaration of invalidity. Any appropriate way of bringing the question to the court would suffice. 'The judiciary clause of the Constitution', said the U.S. supreme court in 1937, '. . . did not crystalise into changeless form the procedure of 1789 as the only possible means for presenting a case or controversy otherwise cognisable by the federal courts.'[10]

Thus, the legislation establishing the declaratory judgment procedure has a 'procedural operation only',[11] and only provides a simplified method for the more convenient exercise of a right that exists independently of it, and which, being rooted in the Constitution, cannot be taken away by the legislature in exercise of its power to regulate the practice and procedure of the courts. The statement by the U.S. supreme court in upholding the (Federal) Declaratory Judgment Act of 1934 that 'in dealing with methods within its sphere of remedial action the congress may create and improve as well as abolish or restrict',[12] must be taken to refer to procedure, not to the constitutional right to apply for the enforcement by the court of the constitutional declaration of invalidity.

It has thus rightly been held that the Petitions of Right Act or Law, which requires that the consent of the attorney-general be obtained before an action in contract or tort can be instituted against the government, has no application in cases involving the Constitution as well as in cases in which a declaration is sought.[13] Neither are such cases barred by the period prescribed by the Public Officers Protection Act or Law for bringing action against public officers.[14]

While the declaratory judgment clearly has a constitutional basis, and provides a simple, cheap, effective[15] and fairly comprehensive remedy, which has made it 'the most ubiquitous [and] perhaps the most generally useful of the remedies' against public authorities,[16] its limitations need to be emphasised. First, the fact that it serves the purposes of anticipatory or preventive adjudication does not mean that it can be used to prevent the introduction or passage of legislative proposals on the ground that their enactment into law would be unconstitutional, The court of appeal in Zambia has accordingly held that the mere announcement by the government of an intention to introduce legislation cannot be a violation of the Constitution, castigating as 'absurd' any suggestion that 'the legislature intended the courts to be vested with the power to pronounce in advance that if the government pursued an expressed intention, legislation on the lines of that expressed intention would be *ultra vires* the Constitution. The consequences of such a construction would be truly chaotic.[17] Even when the intention has been formulated into a bill no question of law arises at that stage, for a bill is not law, and as such cannot be an unconstitutional exercise of the power of law-making inasmuch as it may be abandoned or amended before the processes of its translation into law are completed; it cannot therefore affect the rights of any person.

Secondly, its function is to declare legal relations as they exist, not to constitute new ones. Accordingly, a declaration is appropriate when it relates to a right, the liability or non-liability of a person, and the validity or invalidity of an act or decision. But where a decision or act is merely voidable, meaning that it is provisionally valid until quashed or set aside, then neither a declaration of validity nor one of invalidity can appropriately be made in respect of it. For, to make a declaration of invalidity in such a case is to give the declaratory judgment a constitutive rather than a declaratory effect.[18] If a declaration of invalidity does not have a constitutive effect where a voidable decision or act is concerned, and since the decision or act is valid and continues to be so until quashed or set aside by an appropriate legal procedure, a declaration of invalidity leaves the impugned decision or act still in existence, alongside the court's declaratory judgment, which means that there could exist on the matter two lawful but inconsistent decisions. And unless the authority which gave the impugned decision 'had power to rescind or vary its original determination or unless the declaration would effectively preclude the tribunal from acting upon it',[19] a declaration would be useless.

This limitation has reality, since an error of law by public authorities, whether patent or latent, only makes a decision voidable, and not void. (The House of Lords in Britain was divided 3−2 in favour of the view that failure to observe the procedural rules of natural justice has the latter effect.[20]) If the aggrieved person were to ask instead for a declaration that the decision in question is wrong in law, the position would still be the same. In *Punton* v. *Ministry of Pensions and National Insurance (No. 2)*,[21] the national insurance commissioner, acting within his power, had misconstrued the relevant provision of the National Insurance Act 1946, in refusing an award of unemployment benefit to the plaintiffs, who then asked for a declaration that they were entitled to the benefit. The declaration was refused because, although the commissioner's decision might have been wrong in law and so liable to be quashed by *certiorari*, yet while it remained unquashed it was a valid, binding decision, having been made within the commissioner's jurisdiction. And, since the commissioner had no power to rescind his decision or substitute a new one, and since only a favourable decision by him gave a right to a benefit under the act, no benefit could become payable in consequence of a declaration that the decision was wrong in law. Also in *Anisminic* v. *Foreign Compensation Commission*,[22] where it was alleged that the decision of the commission to refuse the plaintiffs compensation was wrong in law, the court of appeal (England) refused for the same reason to make a declaration to that effect.[23] The unavailability of a declaration to correct errors of law, both patent and latent, deprives it of whatever comprehensiveness it might otherwise have had.[24]

It has been doubted whether a declaration of invalidity or of right is appropriate in a situation calling for a positive action by the government to remedy the violation complained of, as in cases of malapportionment of constituencies and school segregation. In the view of Justice Frankfurter a declaration in that kind of situation is but an exercise in rhetoric if the court cannot couple it with a coercive order affirmatively directing either election at large or re-apportionment in a particular way, e.g. consolidation of certain constituencies or the splitting up of others. Justice Frankfurter observed:

We are soothingly told . . . that we need not worry about the kind of remedy a court could effectively fashion once the abstract constitutional right to have courts pass on a state-wide system of electoral districting is recognised as a matter of judicial rhetoric, because legislatures would heed the court's admonition. This is not only a euphoric hope. It implies a sorry confession of judicial impotence in place of a frank acknowledgement that there is not under our

Constitution a judicial remedy for every political mischief, for every undesirable exercise of legislative power.[25]

With courageous activism, the American courts have not allowed such considerations as this to stand in the way of judicial protection of constitutional rights, and the declaration has proved surprisingly effective in inducing the desired remedial action, even in legislative malapportionment.

But school segregation in the United States did present problems of a complexity and sensitivity that needed something more than a mere declaration of unconstitutionality. Given the explosive sentiment felt by many Southern whites on this matter, and given centuries-old attitudes and practices, and various problems of school administration,[26] would a declaration alone, unaccompanied by a positive decree, have been enough to induce the state authorities voluntarily to desegregate their public schools? Assuming a voluntary acceptance of the declaration by the state authorities, would that have guaranteed their good faith in actual implementation? No one could reasonably expect desegregation to be accomplished overnight, and since it is no part of the function of a declaration to set deadlines, the state authorities might seize upon that loophole to frustrate desegregation, resorting to delays or attempting only half-hearted or token implementation while in effect continuing to operate *de facto* segregation.

The history of desegregation following upon the court's outlawing of segregation in 1954[27] (particularly the refusal of the Arkansas government to accept the court's decision as manifested in an amendment of the state Constitution which flatly commanded the state legislature to oppose 'in every constitutional manner the unconstitutional desegregation decision . . . of the U.S. supreme court', and the action of the state governor in sealing off for three weeks a Little Rock school with a contingent of the state's national guard so as to prevent the admission of nine negro children whom the school authorities had agreed to admit as part of its desegregation plan[28]) shows that school segregation was not to be given up on a mere declaration of its unconstitutionality by the court, and that the deep-seated prejudices that sustained it could be broken down by nothing short of a coercive decree vigorously executed by the organised force of the national government. It needed an injunction at the instance of the federal government to prevail upon the Arkansas governor to withdraw his troops from the Little Rock school and otherwise to desist from further obstruction, and the use of federal troops despatched by the president to effect the eventual admission of the negro students.

The point, of course, is not that without a positive coercive decree a declaratory judgment is completely useless or ineffective in this type of case. As Professor Bickel has said of the decision declaring school segregation unconstitutional:

Like poetry, then, as a verse by Auden tells us, the great School Segregation decision of May 17, 1954, made nothing happen. But only like poetry. Only as it may sometimes seem that nothing but power, purposefully applied, can affect reality, only thus could it be said that the first decision had no consequences. And this is a species of romantic illusion. In fact, announcement of the principle was in itself an action of great moment, considering the source from which it came. Immediately, in the phrase Lincoln used about slavery, segregation was placed 'where the public mind shall rest in the belief that it is in course of ultimate extinction'; and very shortly, in many places, there was a palpable effect. By early 1955, although there had as yet been no decree and there was thus no command outstanding which bound anyone to act, more than five hundred school districts had abandoned policies of segregation. This did not represent a large percentage of all segregated districts, and the number of Negro pupils actually admitted to white schools was even less impressive. Still, some 250,000 Negro pupils were affected.[29]

But subsequent proceedings after the initial declaration revealed the matter to be beyond the competence and efficacy of a mere declaration. The plaintiffs in all five suits (consolidated into one for the purposes of the appeal in the supreme court) must have appreciated this, and so asked instead for an injunction to enjoin the enforcement of the laws requiring or permitting segregation in their various areas. Having declared school segregation unconstitutional, the court adjourned for further argument (with the participation of the attorneys-general of the United States and of the states requiring or permitting racial segregation in their public schools) on whether the admission of negro children into formerly all-white schools should follow 'forthwith'[30] or whether the court should exercise its equitable jurisdiction to permit integration on a gradual but effective basis and, if the latter, what should be the terms of the decree.

It emerged upon re-argument[31] that variations in local conditions, practices and intensity of racial prejudice added to the complexity of the problem of school integration, making it desirable that judicial oversight of the good faith of the implementation effort by the school authorities should be left to the courts of first instance who were in closer touch with the local conditions and could undertake further hearings when necessary. The enforcement action of those courts was however to be governed by the principle of practical flexibility and a facility for adjusting and reconciling public and private needs, that characterise equitable jurisdiction. While the plaintiffs were entitled by the constitutional principle to be admitted to the white schools 'as soon as practicable',[32] account had to be taken of the practical obstacles in the way of the transition to integration and of the time needed to eliminate them. The authorities had, as a first step, to make 'a prompt and reasonable start'[33] at implementation, and thereafter satisfy the courts as to what additional time, consistent with compliance in good faith at the earliest practicable date, was necessary in the public interest, having regard to the problems of administration arising from the physical condition of the school plant, the school transportation system, personnel, and the revision of school districts and the attendance areas into compact units.[34] With these guiding principles, the cases were accordingly remanded to the courts of first instance 'to take such proceedings and enter such orders and decree . . . as are necessary and proper to admit to public schools on a racially non-discriminatory basis *with all deliberate speed*[35] the parties to these cases'.[36]

Yet another factor limiting the practical scope of the declaratory judgment is the wide discretion which the court has to withhold it. It is sometimes said that a declaration will be granted 'sparingly', 'with great care and jealousy', or 'with extreme caution',[37] and in a recent case Viscount Simonds accepted the contention that 'where the administrative or the quasi-judicial powers of the Minister are concerned, declaratory judgments should not readily be given by the Court.'[38] Such a discretion in the court would be unconstitutional where the act challenged was done in violation of the Constitution. In practice, however, the court has usually granted a declaration, even against ministers,[39] where an illegality has been committed.[40] In the United States, the supreme court has used the discretion to withhold adjudication when the constitutionality of an impugned state statute has not authoritatively been pronounced upon by the state courts.[41] And Justice Frankfurter has suggested that the discretion could be invoked in aid of the policy of avoidance. 'The discretionary element characteristic of declaratory judgment', he said, 'offers a convenient instrument for making . . . effective' the policy against premature constitutional decisions.[42] The general consideration governing the exercise of the discretion is whether '(1) the judgment will serve a useful purpose in clarifying and settling the legal relations in issue, and (2) [whether] it will terminate and afford relief from the uncertainty, insecurity, and controversy giving rise to the proceeding. It follows that when neither of these results can be accomplished, the courts should decline to render the declaration prayed.'[43]

In contrast to a *certiorari* application, the refusal of a declaration on discretionary grounds operates as a *res judicata* to bar the party from raising the point in other proceedings.[44]

(ii) *Injunction*
There can be no doubt that injunction, like a declaration, has a basis in the 1979 Constitution. The jurisdiction vested in the high court to

'hear and determine any civil proceedings in which the existence or extent of a legal right, power, duty, liability, privilege, interest, obligation or claim is in issue' (s. 236[1]), must embrace an action for an injunction.

However, an injunction, partly because of its coercive nature, suffers from certain inherent limitations.[45] To begin with, an injunction, equally as a declaration, will not issue to restrain the introduction or passage of legislation on the ground that it would be unconstitutional if enacted into law. The high court of Australia thus rightly dismissed an application to prevent a bill passed by the federal legislature from being presented for the governor-general's assent, on the ground that the bill was beyond the powers of that legislature.[46] In his judgment in the case, Chief Justice Dixon criticised as incorrect a decision of the supreme court of the state of New South Wales which granted an injunction to restrain the presentation of a bill which had been passed by the state legislature but which was not submitted to a referendum as required by law.[47] Part of the rationale for this rule is that, since a bill is not law, its introduction or passage in the legislative assembly cannot be an unlawful exercise of the power of law-making inasmuch as it may be abandoned or amended before the processes of its translation into law are completed. And not being law, it cannot affect the rights of anyone anyway.

In the same way as the court cannot by injunction restrain the legislature from enacting a law on the ground that it would be contrary to the Constitution, it also cannot restrain the president from executing it after it has become law but before it has been pronounced unconstitutional in an appropriate proceeding. An action by the State of Mississippi seeking to restrain the president of the United States from executing certain acts of congress — the Reconstruction Acts — before their unconstitutionality had been decided was accordingly dismissed by the supreme court.[48] What this means is that a claim for injunction to restrain the execution or enforcement of a law is not appropriate for testing its constitutionality.

But a more fundamental question is whether an injunction lies at all against the state and its functionaries, especially the head of state. At common law it was never disputed that an injunction would never lie against the state, although whether it would lie against a government department or against a state functionary for a wrongful act done in his official capacity was uncertain. Various conflicting views are held on the point.[49] In the United States too there are conflicting lines of authority as to whether public officers can be restrained by injunction for acts done in their official capacity, but it seems that, as under the common law in England, the state or the government itself cannot be so restrained.[50] In Nigeria there is authority that an injunction lies against a state functionary,[51] but the common law rule forbidding an injunction against the state or government would appear to apply here too.

There is good reason for not allowing an injunction against the state or government. Injunction is a coercive relief, enforceable only by attachment and imprisonment. It being legally and physically impossible to arrest and imprison the state or government, an injunction against it is singularly inappropriate. It is also inappropriate in the case of the president under the Nigerian Constitution for precisely the same reason. An incumbent president enjoys constitutional immunity from arrest and imprisonment 'in pursuance of the process of any court or otherwise' for all acts done by him both in his private and official capacity (s. 267 of the Constitution). An injunction against him is therefore futile since it cannot be enforced by arrest and imprisonment, which is the only means available for its enforcement. The president of the United States enjoys no such immunity under the Constitution of that country, and may well be amenable to an injunction.[52]

2. *Constitutional remedies for the enforcement of the bill of rights*

The bill of rights contained in the 1979 Constitution is a significant advance on the American, in that it guarantees access to the court, by means of a simple application, for the enforcement of the rights it guarantees. Any person alleging that his constitutional right has been, is being or is likely to be contravened may simply apply to the high court for redress, and the court, after hearing and determination, may make such orders, issue such writs and give such directions as it may consider appropriate for enforcing the right in question (s. 42).

The practice and procedure of the court in the exercise of this jurisdiction is to be prescribed by rules made by the chief justice of Nigeria (s. 42[3]). The chief justice has since made some rules, the Fundamental Rights (Enforcement Procedure) Rules 1979 which came into force on 1 January 1980. Before the promulgation of the rules, the courts have adopted a liberal attitude in the matter, refusing to allow procedural technicality to impede the exercise of the jurisdiction. It allowed an application to be made simply by originating notice of motion.[53]

Confirming this practice, the Fundamental Rights (Enforcement) Rules 1979 permit application to be made by either notice of motion or originating summons. But they also require that, before an application is made, leave to make it be first obtained from the court or judge. The first step, therefore, is for the person aggrieved to apply *ex parte* for leave, which must be done within twelve months from the date of the matter or action complained about, unless the court or judge grants extension of time. It may be questioned whether leave of the court or judge can validly be attached as a condition for the exercise of a right (i.e. the right to apply to the court for the enforcement of a fundamental right) which the Constitution itself guarantees, unless leave is to be granted as a matter of course with no discretion in the court or judge to refuse it.

In an application *ex parte* for leave where wrongful or unlawful detention is alleged, the court or judge may either forthwith order the person detained to be released or direct that an originating summons be issued or adjourn the *ex parte* application so that notice thereof may be given to the person having the custody of the detainee.

The enforcement provisions in the Constitution make no reference to specific remedies, merely authorising the court to determine an application and to make such orders, issue such writs and give such directions as it may consider appropriate.[54] Despite the lack of express mention of specific orders or writs, it is believed that the court may continue to use the old-established remedies. One of the important innovations of these provisions, which deserves to be emphasised, is that they do away with the wall of demarcation that the common law erects between the ordinary remedies — damages, injunction and declaration — and the extraordinary ones — *certiorari*, prohibition and *mandamus* — the effect of which is to forbid the combination of both classes of remedies in the same action. The right of a person making an application under the provisions to ask for both classes of remedies together is in no way restricted by the impossibility of combining them in the same action at common law. The common law cannot operate to qualify the clear words of the constitution. The effect of this may indeed be considered of revolutionary proportions, as the following case of *Aoko* v. *Fagbemi*[55] illustrates.

A woman was convicted of adultery under customary (unwritten) law, sentenced to 5 Naira fine or one month's imprisonment, and ordered to pay 10 Naira compensation plus 2.70 Naira costs. The Constitution prohibits conviction and punishment for a criminal offence under an unwritten law (s. 33[12]). The woman applied to the high court under the enforcement provisions for an order to quash the conviction and for the refund of the money she paid as fine, compensation and costs. *Certiorari* was not asked for in terms. The application was simply in terms of the constitutional provisions. Affirming the procedure adopted, the court said that the whole purpose of this special procedure was to provide easy and speedy access to the courts, and that this would be defeated if the slow and sometimes cumbersome procedure required for an application for *certiorari* were adopted.[56] The court then quashed the conviction by a simple quashing order, and ordered the refund of the various sums.

It has also been held that a declaratory judgment was proper and competent under the provisions.[57] A declaration can thus be combined with a simple quashing order under these provisions, or with whatever other order, writ or direction the court may think appropriate for the enforcement of the right in question,[58] including the old remedies, particularly *habeas corpus*.

It should perhaps be emphasised that these provisions have just one purpose, namely the enforcement of the bill of rights. It has thus been argued that an application under them should not be used to impugn a law or administrative act alleged to violate other provisions of the Constitution; that an application must contain no other allegation than the infringement of a guaranteed right. While acceding to the validity of this argument as a general principle, the court nevertheless overruled it in a case where, in an application under the provisions, a statutory regulation was challenged both for violating a guaranteed right and for being in conflict with its enabling act; such a rigid approach, the court held, may be undesirably restrictive where questions concerning the validity, effect and application of legislation are mixed up with allegations of violation of a guaranteed right.[59]

The procedure for the old established remedies is bound to influence in some ways the exercise of the court's special jurisdiction under these provisions. In particular, the limitations on the remedy of *certiorari* may condition what quashing orders the court may be prepared to make under the provisions. The historical origin of *certiorari* as a remedy for the control of inferior courts of law has meant that, even after it (and prohibition as well) was extended to local government authorities, other statutory bodies, central government departments, ministers and other public officials, its scope continued to be delimited by reference to the functions of a court of law. Hence the rule that it lies to control only those functions of public officials that partake of a judicial character or spirit. A public authority has therefore to be under a duty to act judicially in order to be amenable to *certiorari*.[60] Indeed Lord Goddard posits an order or something in the nature of an order as the basis for the grant of *certiorari* because otherwise, he says, there would be nothing to be brought up to be quashed. Accordingly, he maintains, the ordinary administrative decision of an official, not being such an order, cannot be the subject of *certiorari*.[61]

However, a duty to act judicially is to be implied whenever power is given to a public authority to decide a question affecting the property or other vested rights of a person, or to penalise him for alleged misconduct — e.g., by dismissal from an office or expulsion from a professional association — unless by the express words or necessary intendment of a statute the authority is absolved from the duty.[62] Given such a power, and in the absence of anything to the contrary in the enabling statute, the duty follows necessarily from the power, and nothing more is required to impose it; in other words, a duty to act judicially is not a separate characteristic, but flows necessarily from a power to decide a question affecting rights or to penalise for alleged misconduct.

The consequence of this limitation is that an unlawful decision or act of a public authority which does not affect private rights or penalise for alleged misconduct, e.g. a purely ministerial act, is not controllable by *certiorari*. Nor are all such decisions that affect private rights remediable by *certiorari*. Preventive detention for security reasons is an obvious example.[63] Security ceases to be security if a detaining authority must act judicially before exercising the power to detain on security grounds. A duty to act judicially will also not be implied in the case of decisions affecting the rights of a large class of individuals, making a hearing impossible by reason of the number involved, or decisions involving no *lis* but based largely on policy or expediency. The most serious consequence of this limitation is the unamenability of legislative acts to prerogative remedies. An unconstitutional statute or a delegated legislation made contrary to its enabling act cannot be quashed by *certiorari*[64] nor can prohibition lie to restrain the exercise of legislative power. (Review by the U.S. supreme court of the decisions of lower courts is usually by way of a petition for *certiorari* under the Judiciary Act 1925, and such petitions account for the bulk of the court's docket, 1,600 out of 1,911 in the 1960 term. This does not mean that the court can quash a legislative act by *certiorari*, though an application to quash the decision of a lower court on the question of unconstitutionality does enable the court to pronounce upon that question.)

A quashing order under the enforcement provisions of the bill of rights in the 1979 Constitution is unlikely to be granted outside these limits. Nor is it desirable that a court should go beyond declaring legislation void to quash it positively. A cardinal advantage of the declaratory judgment is its amicable character and its avoidance of the language of compulsion and command of the coercive remedies. For this reason it is not calculated to excite the antagonism of the government.

3. *Constitutional remedies relating to elections and membership of legislative houses*

Yet another innovation of the 1979 Constitution is the special procedure which it has instituted whereby a person aggrieved may apply to the high court to have determined the validity of the election of the president or vice-president, governor or deputy governor, or a member of the national assembly or state house of assembly or whether their term of office or seat has ceased or become vacant, as the case may be (s. 237). The national assembly is empowered to make provision with respect to (*a*) the persons who may apply to the high court; (*b*) the circumstances and manner in which and the conditions upon which an application may be made; and (*c*) the powers, practice and procedure of the court in relation to an application (s. 73). The provision thus clearly contemplates a simple application to the high court similar to that under the enforcement provision of the bill of rights, which imparts to the procedure the cardinal merits of the latter, subject to the qualification that the conditions and manner for making the application are to be prescribed by the national assembly. It is significant that the court is not, as in the case of the bill of rights, specifically authorised to make such orders, issue such writs and give such directions as it may consider appropriate, but there can be doubt that a declaration and injunction are authorised by implication.

Reversing a decision of the high court, which dismissed an application on the ground that it was incompetent without an implementing legislation, the supreme court of Nigeria held that to make such legislation a prerequisite for an application would mean that the legislature could, by its own omission or inadvertence, disable the court from exercising the jurisdiction, thereby making the provision a dead letter; a member of a legislative house who has been excluded therefrom ought not to 'be driven from the judgment seat', merely because the legislature has omitted to make the necessary provision.[65] In the absence of such a provision, the plaintiff in this case had brought his case in the form of an action. As this is the ordinary way of approaching the court with a request to have a matter in difference decided and relief granted, the supreme court ordered the action to proceed to trial. The plaintiff had sought both a declaration and injunction.

The importance and value of the enforcement provisions is illustrated by the judicial invalidation of an attempt by the legislature of Swaziland to substitute a different remedy. On 25 May 1972, one Ngwenya, who earlier that month had been elected to parliament, was deported from the country as a prohibited immigrant on an order made by the deputy prime minister under the Immigration Act 1964. He challenged his deportation on the ground that, being a Swaziland citizen, he was not liable to deportation, since the act under which the order was made expressly excepted from the power a person who 'belongs to Swaziland'. The high court held the plaintiff to be a Swaziland citizen, and so declared his deportation invalid. From this decision the government appealed. While the appeal was pending, the government in November 1972 amended the Immigration Act. The amendment established a special tribunal to decide, upon a reference by the chief immigration officer or the permanent secretary of the office of the deputy prime minister, questions as to whether 'a person belongs to Swaziland' in terms of the principal act. The jurisdiction thus vested in the special tribunal was declared to be exclusive, and to be exercisable 'notwithstanding any judgment, decision or order previously made by any authority, tribunal or court'. There was however a right of appeal to the prime minister, whose decision was final. It was expressly provided that a decision of the special tribunal or of the prime minister should not be subject to appeal to any court, and should be deemed to supersede and nullify any previous decision or order given in the matter by any court or tribunal.

Despite the high court's declaration that Ngwenya was a Swaziland citizen, the question whether he belonged to Swaziland was nevertheless referred to the special tribunal by the chief immigration officer. Ngwenya challenged the validity of this reference on the ground that the enabling act was invalid or, alternatively, did not apply to him assuming it to be valid.[66] He alleged that the act infringed jurisdiction expressly vested in the high court by the Constitution, namely jurisdiction for the enforcement of guaranteed rights, and for the determination of the validity of elections. Among the rights protected by the Constitution was the right of a citizen not to be expelled from, or denied entry into, the country.[67] This right being dependent upon citizenship, its enforcement presupposed that the court should also have jurisdiction to determine the question of citizenship itself. Among the qualifications for election was the requirement that the person must be qualified for registration as a voter, which in turn required the person to be a citizen.[68]

The court of appeal for Swaziland held, reversing the trial judge, that the exclusive and final jurisdiction conferred on the special tribunal and the prime minister ousted completely the jurisdiction of the high court to determine questions of citizenship as a qualification for election to the national assembly; accordingly it declared the act *ultra vires* the Constitution and void.[69] Rejecting the argument that the jurisdiction of the special tribunal was for immigration purposes only and left unaffected the court's jurisdiction to determine citizenship rights for purposes of eligibility for election, the court pointed to the conflict that would arise if a person declared by the court to be a citizen for the latter purpose were later declared not to be so by the special tribunal for immigration purposes. On the argument based on the court's jurisdiction to enforce the protected rights, the court observed that, while that too could be supported, 'it is not necessary to examine the matter on these wider lines.'[70] The decision of the appeal court was handed down on 27 March, and on 12 April, following upon it, the king of Swaziland, on a petition by parliament, abrogated the separate existence of the judicial power in the country.[71]

REFERENCES

1. 5 U.S. (1 Cranch), 154.
2. Weehsler, 'Towards Neutral Principles in Constitutional Law' in *Selected Essays on Constitutional Law*, ed. Assn. of American Law Schools (1963), p. 466, reprinted from *Harv. L. Rev.* (1959), 73, 1.
3. Henry Hart Jr., 'The Power of Congress to Limit the Jurisdiction of Federal Courts: an Exercise in Dialectic' in *Selected Essays on Constitutional Law*, op. cit., 63, reprinted from *Harv. L. Rev.* (1953), 66, 1362.
4. *Cary* v. *Curtis* (1845), 3 How. 236.
5. Henry Hart Jr, loc. cit.
6. *Hegeman Farm Corpn.* v. *Baldwin* (1934), 293 U.S. 163, 172; *Petersen Banking Co.* v. *Bryan*, 290 U.S. 570, 575; *Yakus* v. *United States* (1944), 321 U.S. 414.
7. See *Aetna Life Insurance Co.* v. *Haworth* (1937), 300 U.S. 227; *Nashville Co. & St. L. Ry.* v. *Wallace* (1937), 288 U.S. 249.
8. Edwin Borchard, 'The Constitutionality of Declaratory Judgments', *Colum. L. Rev.* (1931), 31, 561, where the relevant American cases, both federal and state, are reviewed.
9. *Nashville Co. & St. L. Ry.* v. *Wallace*, ibid.; *Aetna Life Ins. Co.* v. *Haworth*, ibid.
10. *Nashville Co. & St. L. Ry.* v. *Wallace*, ibid., 264.
11. *Aetna Life Ins. Co.* v. *Haworth*, ibid., 240. Cf. Borchard, 'Constitutionality of Declaratory Judgments', *Colum. L. Rev.* (1931), 31, 561–607: 'The declaratory action involves a mere matter of practice and procedure.'
12. *Aetna Life Ins. Co.* v. *Haworth*, ibid., 240.
13. *Igbe* v. *Governor, Bendel State*, Suit no. B/303/79; *Obayuwana* v. *Governor, Bendel State*, Suit no. B/25/80; *Dyson* v. *Att.-Gen.*, [1911] 1 K.B. 410.
14. *Igbe* v. *Governor, Bendel State*, ibid; *Griffiths* v. *Smith* [1941] 1 All E.R. 66 (H.L.); *Adams* v. *Naylor* [1946] 2 All E. R. 241, 244 per Viscount Simon.
15. As Gordon Borrie observes: 'Normally a declaration of law is enough and no coercive backing is needed to compel officials to observe the law or to remain or be kept within the bounds of legality. Public bodies . . . would never blatantly disregard an authoritative declaration of law obtained against them' ('The Advantages of the Declaratory Judgment in Administrative Law', M.L.R. [1955], 18, 138. In view of the experience with the school segregation decision in the United States, this is perhaps too optimistic.
16. Friedmann, *Law in a Changing Society* (2nd edn., 1972), 427.
17. *Nkumbula* v. *Att.-Gen. for Zambia*, Appeal No. 6 of 1972, per Baron J.P.

18. de Smith, *Judicial Review of Administrative Action* (2nd edn., 1968) 539.
19. de Smith, op. cit., 539–40.
20. *Ridge* v. *Baldwin* [1964], A.C. 40, 80, 86, 119–20, 126, 135, 141–2 (H.L.)
21. [1964] 1 W.L.R. 226.
22. [1967] 3 W.L.R. 382.
23. Contrast, however, *Pyx Granite Co. Ltd.* v. *Ministry of Housing and Local Govt.* [1958], Q.B. 554 (C.A.); *Taylor* v. *National Assistance Board* (1956), 470 (first instance decision).
24. Note also the restrictive effect of the *locus standi* rule. Whereas anyone may apply for *certiorari* or prohibition without having to prove injury, actual or threatened (though in practice only a person aggrieved is likely to get it), only a person injuriously affected or threatened can in general secure a declaration.
25. *Baker* v. *Carr*, 369 U.S. 186, 269–70.
26. See Bickel, *The Least Dangerous Branch* (1962), 248, for an account of these problems.
27. *Brown* v. *Board of Education* (1954) 347 U.S. 483.
28. *Cooper* v. *Aaron* (1958), 358 U.S. 1, where the Arkansas opposition to the court's desegregation decision is fully described. For opposition from other quarters see Bickel, op. cit., 254ff.
29. Bickel, op. cit. 245–6. About 5,000 school districts, nearly 9 million white and nearly 3 million black children were involved, op. cit., 248.
30. The trial court in the case from Delaware had ordered admission 'forthwith'. The trial courts in the other four cases held, under the rule in *Plessy* v. *Ferguson* (1896), 163 U.S. 537, that school segregation was not unconstitutional provided the separate facilities were equal, and in three cases where inequality was proved in respect of certain facilities, equalisation measures were ordered.
31. *Brown* v. *Board of Education* (1955), 349 U.S. 294.
32. ibid., 300.
33. ibid., 300.
34. See Bickel, op. cit., 248, for an elaboration of these problems.
35. Italics supplied. 'A most elusive phrase' as Bickel describes it, adding that 'with all convenient speed' is the phrase familiar to English equity, op. cit., 253.
36. ibid., 301.
37. *Russian Commercial and Industrial Bank* v. *Br. Bank for Foreign Trade Ltd.* [1921] 2 A.C. 438; *Vine* v. *National Dock Labour Board* [1957] A.C. 488, 500.
38. *Pyx Granite Co. Ltd.* v. *Ministry of Housing and Local Govt.* [1960] A.C. 260, 287.
39. *Pyx Granite* case, ibid.
40. *Vine's* case, ibid.
41. *Poe* v. *Ullman* (1961), 367 U.S. 497; *Fedn. of Labour* v. *McAdory*, 325 U.S. 450.
42. *Poe* v. *Ullman*, ibid., 507. See 'Developments in the Law: Declaratory

Judgments — 1941–49', *Harv. L. Rev.*, 62, 787, 805–17. Cf. Stone C.J. in the *McAdory* case, ibid., 471; 'In the exercise of this Court's discretionary power to grant or withhold the discretionary remedy it is of controlling significance that it is in the public interest to avoid needless determination of constitutional questions. . . .'

43. Borchard, *Declaratory Judgments* (2nd edn, 1941), 299; cited with approval in several American cases.

44. Wade, *Administrative Law* (1971), 145.

45. See de Smith, *Judicial Review of Administrative Action* (2nd edn., 1968) 461–4; also Brett (ed.), *Constitutional Problems of Federalism in Nigeria* (1960), 18.

46. *Hughes and Vale Pty. Ltd.* v. *Grair* (1954), Argus L.R. 1094.

47. *Trethowan* v. *Peden* (1930), 31 S.R. (N.S.W.) 183. The decision was based on the peculiar provision of the Constitution which in terms prohibited presentation for royal assent before approval at a referendum. In *McDonald* v. *Cain* (1953), V.L.R. 411, which arose out of a similar provision in the Constitution of Victoria, two of the three judges of the State Supreme Court supported what was done in the *Trethowan* case. For a review, see Cowan, 71 L. Q.R., 376.

48. *Mississippi* v. *Johnson* (1867) 4 Wall 475.

49. As to which see H. Street, *Governmental Liability*, 140, n. 5; Glanville Williams, *Crown Proceedings*, 136, n. 26; also Strayer, 'Injunctions against Crown Officers' (1964), 42 *Can. Bar Rev.* 1.

50. See K.C. Davis, *Administrative Law Treatise*, iii, Chap. 27; R.S. Arnold, 'The Power of State Courts to Enjoin Federal Officers' (1964), 73 *Yale L.J.*, 1385.

51. *Williams* v. *Majekodunmi* (No. 3) (1962), 1 All N.L.R. 413; *Williams* v. *Majekodunmi* (No. 2) (1962), 1 All N.L.R. 328; *Williams* v. *Majekodunmi* (1962), 1 All N.L.R. 324. See also *Adegbenro* v. *Att.-Gen. of the Fedn.* (1962), 1 All N.L.R. 431; *Awolowo* v. *Minister of Internal Affairs*, High Court of Lagos Suit No. LD/595/62 — application for injunction dismissed on the merits.

52. See chapter 5 above.

53. *Cheranci* v. *Cheranci* (1960), N.R.N.L.R. 24; Cf. the Zambian case of *Kachasu* v. *Att.-Gen. of Zambia*, 1967/HP/273.

54. The Constitution of Ghana 1969 specifically spelt out that the orders and writs the court may issue include 'writs or orders in the nature of *habeas corpus*, *certiorari*, *mandamus*, prohibition and *quo warranto*': art. 28(2).

55. (1961), 1 All N.L.R. 400.

56. ibid., 403.

57. *Olawoyin* v. *Att.-Gen.* (1961), 1 All N.L.R. 269.

58. See *Nkumbula* v. *Att.-Gen. for Zambia*, Appeal No. 6 of 1972.

59. *Kachasu* v. *Att.-Gen. for Zambia*, 1967/HP/273.

60. *R* v. *Electricity Commissioners* [1924], 1 K.B. 17, 205 per Atken L.J., quoted with approval in *Nakkuda Ali* v. *Jayaratne* [1951], A.C. 66, 78 (P.C.); *R.* v. *Metropolitan Police Commr.* [1953], 2 All E.R. 717, 718–19; *Pyx Granite* case [1958], Q.B. 554, 571 (C.A.).

61. *R.V. Metropolitan Police Commr.*, ibid, 720–1.

62. *Ridge* v. *Baldwin* [1964], A.C. 40 (H.L.).
63. See *Arzika* v. *Governor, Northern Region* (1961), 1 All N.L.R. 371.
64. *R.* v. *Church Assembly Legislative Committee* [1928], 1 K.B. 411.
65. *Fajinmi* v. *The Speaker, Western House of Assembly* (1962), 1 All N.L.R. 205.
66. *Ngwenya* v. *Deputy Prime Minister* Civ. T. 4/1973 of Jan. 1973.
67. s. 5(1) (i).
68. ss. 56(1), 43, and 51.
69. *Ngwenya* v. *Deputy Prime Minister* Civ. A. 1/1973 of 27 March 1973.
70. ibid.
71. See *Rand Daily Mail*, 13 April 1973.

19
JUDICIAL REVIEW AND DEMOCRATIC GOVERNMENT

When the court invalidates a legislative or executive act for unconstitutionality or vindicates its validity, the primary implication for the political process and for democracy is to check the government or to confer legitimacy upon the act in question. The discussion of the role of judicial review in a democratic political process has been in these terms, i.e. in terms of its checking and legitimating effect.

1. *The checking function of judicial review*

When the court holds a legislative or executive act unconstitutional and void, it necessarily frustrates the will of the legislature or the executive. The legislation may have been supported by an overwhelming vote of the legislature or even by a unanimous vote. It is said to be antithetical to the democratic theory of majority rule that an unelected body should be able to frustrate the will of an elected legislature on matters of policy, and that, accordingly, the checking function, being a 'countermajoritarian force', is 'undemocratic'.[1]

This clearly misrepresents the meaning and processes of democratic government. Democracy is not just rule by an elected majority. The idea and processes implied in the concept are more complex and subtle than that. Essentially, it connotes self-government, that is to say, government conducted by the people as a collectivity and as individuals. The 'self' there refers not only to the people as a free and independent community but also to the attribute of personal participation by the several individuals comprising the community. Democracy is thus a form of government in which the highest premium is placed on the participation of the individual in government. The primary meaning of democracy, Arthur Lewis has said, is that all those affected by a decision should participate in making it.[2]

Majority rule is thus only one element in the processes of democratic government, dictated as it is by the inexpediency of unanimity in decision-making. It is the most practical expedient for reaching decisions in a society of individuals with differing interests and prejudices. But the majority referred to here is not a majority of the people. It is a majority of the legislature, to whom the people, by a majority, have delegated their power of self-government, the delegation being necessitated by the inexpediency of collective decision by the entire population of a large, complex community comprising millions of people spread over a wide territory. The act of delegation, which is effected through the mechanism of a constitution, is complemented by election at reasonably frequent intervals, whereby the people, again by a majority, choose those to represent and act for them in the legislative and executive organs of government. The democratic theory of self-government by the people is assured, however approximately, by these two processes of delegation and election.

But the ideal of individual participation has also to be assured in some form for the system of government to be fully democratic. Since they are determined by a majority, the processes of delegation and periodic elections do not effectively assure individual participation. It is in this connection that the terms of the delegation acquire vital importance in a democracy. Democracy presupposes that the delegation is not to be free and unencumbered, but should rather be subject to terms designed to safeguard the position of the individual, and to enable him to intervene where the safeguards are being transgressed. If the size and complexity of modern society make it inexpedient for every individual to participate personally in decisions which affect him, then his fundamental rights as an individual need to be protected against those elected to the governing bodies. This is the function of a constitutional guarantee of individual rights, otherwise known as a bill of rights. Such a guarantee or bill of rights becomes an essential feature of a modern democratic constitution. A government of the people by the people is not fully democratic unless the instrument constituting it also guarantees and protects the basic rights of the individual.

Yet the safeguard of a constitutional bill of rights would be rendered practically nugatory if an individual who alleges that his guaranteed right is being violated by the legislature or executive is not able to appeal to a body independent of these organs, whether the ordinary courts or some other kind of tribunal. Review of governmental acts by an independent body in the interest of maintaining the efficacy of the constitutional guarantee of individual rights is thus also an essential and important mechanism of democratic government. Being at the instance of an aggrieved individual, the democratic virtue of such a review is that it assures the individual's personal participation in government, thus imparting greater reality to the concept of self-government. As we have seen, it is not only subject to a bill of rights that the delegation of the people's power of government is made. The other limitations also serve the same democratic function of assuring to the individual the right of intervention to protect the terms of the delegation against infringement or abuse by the wielders of power.

The review of governmental acts, through the agency of an independent tribunal and in accordance with the limitations set out in the basic instrument of government, is the people's own device for the control of the power they have entrusted to their elected representatives. Judicial review, writes Charles Black, 'is the people's institutionalized means of self-control',[3] the 'self-restraint of democracy'.[4] Being a practical incident of the terms and conditions upon which the majority in the legislature and executive holds its powers, the review of governmental acts in terms of the constitutional limitations upon government is indeed a constituent element of majority rule; to regard it as antithetical to it is to misconceive the true basis of majority rule.

A court as the reviewing authority seems to be indicated by the nature of the limitations. If, as is clear, the intention is that the limitations should not be merely political or moral incantation but should be *legally* enforceable, then this would at once suggest a court as the appropriate reviewing body, a court being 'the place where law is to be sought'.[5] For 'where but in a court would the people look for the skilled reading and application of law?'[6] The words of Alexander Hamilton seem apt here. 'Constitutional limitations', he wrote, 'can be preserved in practice no other way than through the medium of courts of justice. [. . .] Without this, all the reservations of particular rights or privileges would amount to nothing.'[7]

The counter-majoritarian argument asserts, however, that the concept of the 'people' in relation to the limitations imposed on government by the constitution is a 'myth', an 'abstraction', and one that obscures 'the reality that when the Supreme Court declares unconstitutional a legislative act or the action of an elected executive, it thwarts the will of the representatives of the *actual people of the here and now*; it exercises control, not on behalf of the prevailing majority, but against it.'[8] This is a fallacy. The concept of the people, with its imperfections and limitations, has as much reality in relation to the two processes of delegation and periodic elections. Once adopted, a constitution binds not only the generation of the people who adopted it but also posterity, although the latter have a right to refuse to be ruled by their ancestors long deceased. They can exercise this right to change the constitution in its entirety or to amend only such parts of it as do not meet with their approval. It is their birthright, but non-exercise of it indicates approval of, or at least acquiescence in, what the people of the past have bequeathed to them. A constitution, though made 200 years before, has a continuing basis in current popular consent and approval. The suggestion that the U.S. Constitution has no democratic basis, that it is an imposition from a past age, is one from which most Americans would recoil.

It is further asserted that 'although democracy does not mean reconsideration of decisions once made, it does mean that a representative majority has the power to accomplish a reversal.'[9] If by this is meant that a representative majority has the power to reverse the limitations imposed upon it by the constitution, then this is the exact antithesis of a constitutional democracy. 'By definition', writes an eminent authority, Carl Friedrich, 'a constitutional democracy is one which does not grant all power to the majority.'[10] It is rule by the majority according to pre-determined rules. A representative majority that is not bound or limited by rules beyond its power to reverse is not a democratic body but an autocratic and arbitrary one.[11]

Granted that review of governmental acts by the court is a people's institution, it is said to be nonetheless undemocratic unless the personnel of the court are responsible to the people. Power, especially critical political power, is unsupportable without responsibility, which is attained only through the process of election. Three observations may be made upon this argument. First, the equation of responsibility with accountability through the process of election is much too narrow. While elections at reasonably frequent intervals are indispensable to democracy because they enable the people to give practical expression to their changing outlook and wishes on government, the concept of responsibility is wider than that. Responsibility demands not only the accountability of the government to the people through the electoral and other communication processes, but also that governmental actions should respond to the needs of the people as revealed in public opinion, which should therefore be among the factors informing policy.

So conceived, judges are unquestionably responsible, because they are responsive to the needs of the people, not so much to their immediate material needs, but to their need for principle in government, for those enduring values which are the ultimate end of government, and which serve to give lasting meaning and purpose to the life of the people. The legislature and executive, pre-occupied as they are with the expedient resolution of pressing problems, have failed all too often to take account of society's fundamental moral values in framing their measures. Insulated from the clash of interests and the pressures for expedient accommodation, the courts are well placed to distil principle out of society's fundamental presuppositions, establishing them as active principles of the constitutional system according to which the propriety (i.e. constitutionality) of actions of the legislature and executive are to be judged. In this way the court serves the ends of democratic government.

Judicial decisions are also responsive to the attitude of the public towards questions of the day. The changing positions adopted by the U.S. supreme court on race relations have reflected the attitudes prevalent in the society; the spirit of equality prevailing in the immediate aftermath of the civil war led to decisions unfavourable to segregation;[12] the swing in public attitude back to racial segregation produced the decision establishing the separate-but-equal formula,[13] while the desegregation decisions of the 1950s may be accounted, in part at least, as the court's response to the mood for unseparated equality dominant in the nation at the time.[14] Further, although considerations of what is good or desirable for society are primarily a matter for the political organs, the courts should not be unconcerned with them. Policy in its widest sense should be among the factors informing judicial decision.

Secondly, as Eugene Rostow says, 'the task of democracy is not to have the people vote directly on every issue, but to assure their ultimate responsibility for the acts of their representatives, elected or appointed.'[15] This ultimate responsibility or control is assured by the right of the people, or the legislature in most African countries, to reverse the judges' interpretation of the constitution through a constitutional amendment, as has happened not infrequently.[16] McWhinney has even asserted, citing the experience in the United States and South Africa in 1937 and 1956 respectively, that in a conflict that becomes an election issue the court will always pipe down if the government obtains a renewed mandate in the election.[17] This seems to take too cynical a view of the court's checking function in practice. Was it really, as Charles Black 'conjectured', the 'crushing decisiveness of the 1936 election and the high public emotion swirling around the Packing Plan'[18] that brought about the change in the court's earlier position over the New Deal in the United States? While, as Charles Black also admits, 'the decisive factor in producing the change will perhaps never be known',[19] it seems nearer the truth to say that the change was largely the result of a genuine and honest conviction on the part of two of the justices that their earlier position was wrong, and that there was sufficient warrant in the Constitution for many of the New Deal measures. Nor can it be said with certainty that in eventually affirming the Senate Act 1955, and the South Africa Act Amendment Act 1956, the South African supreme court merely bowed to the renewed mandate given to the government in the 1953 election at which the conflict with the court was the dominant issue.[20]

Thirdly, in democratic practice election is not an invariable requirement regardless of its unsuitability or undesirability for particular decision-making processes. 'Every democracy divides issues of policy into several categories, to be settled by different means'[21] as appropriate. It is just not appropriate or desirable that judges should be elected. The office of a judge requires special qualifications and ability, which cannot adequately be judged by the electorate, whose judgment must inevitably be swayed by other considerations. Moreover, the process of election, characterised as it is by party or group interests and by political campaigning, is likely to impair the image of a judge as an impartial and independent guardian of the limitations imposed upon the majority for the protection of the individual. In fact, the appointment and removal of judges are done in most countries by the method that approximates most nearly to the democratic ideal after election by the people, namely by the people's elected representatives in the executive and legislature.

No doubt, limitations upon government and their enforcement by the court imply a distrust by the people of their elected representatives. Such a distrust is said to have a tendency to weaken the democratic processes by causing laxity and irresponsibility in the legislature and apathy in the electorate. This criticism is best articulated by James Thayer in the following passage:

The legislatures are growing accustomed to this distrust and more and more readily inclined to justify it, and to shed the considerations of constitutional restraints, — certainly as concerning the exact extent of these restrictions — turning that subject over to the courts; and what is worse, they insensibly fall into a habit of assuming that whatever they could constitutionally do they may do — as if honour and fair dealing and common honesty were not relevant to their inquiries. [. . .] It should be remembered that the exercise of it [the power of judicial review], even when unavoidable, is always attended with a serious evil, namely that the correction of legislative mistakes comes from the outside, and the people thus lose the political experience, and the moral education and stimulus that comes from fighting the question out in the ordinary way, and correcting their own errors. The tendency of a common and easy resort to this great function, now lamentably too common, is to dwarf the political capacity of the people, and to deaden its sense of moral responsibility.[22]

Alexander Bickel has constructed from this a whole doctrine of judicial action, by the intriguing name of the 'passive virtues', which advocates that, as far as possible, the court should abstain from ruling for or against the constitutionality of governmental measures so as to allow society time to work out its own balance in the endless conflict between principle and expediency.[23]

Contrary to what Thayer says, the checking function of judicial review exercises a sobering influence on government by inducing in it a humane and tolerant attitude towards power. It has certainly not made government careless of the need for fair dealing and common honesty. Rather it has introduced into governmental processes standards of judicial behaviour, such as those of openness, good faith, fairness, reasonableness and the more specific requirements of natural justice. Constitutionalism, it has been truly said, 'is the application of judicial methods to basic problems of government; administrative justice, extending this application, attempts to extend the judicial methods to the wider sphere of activities which government is handling today.'[24] And it has sharpened, not deadened, the people's 'sense of moral responsibility', witness the court's desegregation decisions in the United States which have awakened many Americans to their moral responsibility towards the under-privileged negroes in their midst. It has also enhanced, not dwarfed, the people's political capacity — witness the lively interest in government which recent supreme court decisions have generated among Americans, an interest which cannot but increase their capacity to influence government, thus ensuring that 'legislative and executive policy would be formed out of free debate, democratic suffrage, untrammelled political effort, and full enquiry.'[25]

2. *The legitimating function of judicial review*

A court decision vindicating or affirming the validity of a governmental act frees it from doubts of impropriety on constitutional grounds. A court is society's final authority on questions of law, and its decision in favour of an impugned governmental act ought to satisfy a reasonable objector that the limitations imposed on government by law have not in fact been violated. To persist in the objection after that is to adopt a position that is not only indefensible but one that at once denies the established societal mechanism for resolving conflicts and disagreements within the community. The court's vindication of the governmental act may be right or wrong in point of law, but even when it seems wrong the individual ought to be satisfied that an opportunity, the best in the nature of fallible human institutions, has been afforded him for ventilating his grievances before a disinterested, impartial and independent reviewing body. The result, for the reasonable complainant at least, is that the governmental act in question is impressed with the stamp of legitimacy, that is to say, the court's vindication of the act generates public acceptance of it as authorised by the constitution.

Charles Black has illustrated the operation of this legitimating function by reference to the acute public controversy surrounding the New Deal programme of the F.D. Roosevelt administration in the United States in the 1930s. So deeply divided was the country by the question of the constitutionality of the programme that argument alone could not have resolved the controversy. 'The arguments in the affirmative', writes Black, 'seemed good to millions, but the arguments in the negative seemed good to other millions, and there is no reason for supposing that the first could have coerced the minds of the second. . . .'[26] Only a national arbiter accepted by both sides for its impartiality and its learning and authoritativeness in matters of law, and endowed in the eyes of all with a 'mystic spell' and significance as the symbol of constitutionalism, could have resolved the controversy. And so it was that when the supreme court eventually affirmed the constitutionality of most of the New Deal measures, the effect was to bestow upon them an 'affirmative stamp of legitimacy',[27] thus bringing to an end a bitter controversy that had threatened American society with chaos. Bickel has also illustrated the point with the legitimating effect which the court's decision has produced in the country in the hotly contested issue of racial segregation, especially in schools.[28]

However, the efficacy of the court's legitimating function depends on a number of factors. First, the legitimacy of governmental measures presupposes the legitimacy (i.e. the appropriateness) of the system of government and of governmental institutions established by the constitution. Secondly, the public's confidence in the integrity of the court is vital. To command public acceptance of its role as a national arbiter the integrity of the court must be above suspicion. Even an appearance of bias in favour of the government is calculated to undermine its acceptability and credibility. The experience of Nigeria from 1960 to 1966 illustrates this very well. The fact that, with one exception, all the constitutional cases went in favour of the government deprived the decisions of much of their legitimating effect. For the credibility of the court's legitimating function is an incident of the checking function. A court that validates everything that is brought before it can impart little legitimacy to impugned governmental measures by its decisions.[29]

The point here is not that every one of the decisions handed down by the Nigerian supreme court between 1960 and 1965 was necessarily wrong in law, but that they should all have gone in favour of the government was remarkable, and naturally created the impression of political bias. People began to feel, rightly or wrongly, that the justice administered in the courts was influenced by extra-legal considerations, by political or sectional interests; that it was intended not to uphold the law but to repress interests opposed to the government. The situation was all the more lamentable because most of the decisions concerned individual civil liberties. To what purpose, people were prompted to ask, were civil liberties guaranteed in the Constitution if every violation of them, however flagrant-seeming, received the sanction of the courts? It began to look as if the courts were actively aiding the politicians in the persecution of opponents and in the perversion of the Constitution. Confidence in their ability to decide political issues impartially was consequently undermined, and the position was eventually reached where there was a general disinclination to take political complaints to them. To go to court on such matters was felt to be a vain effort; from past experience, a decision in favour of the government was considered a foregone conclusion. Moreover, the over-confident way in which the ruling politicians sometimes challenged opponents to take their complaints to court, as if to say they had been assured that the courts would never decide against them, helped to sap public confidence in the courts still further.

This situation represented a real tragedy in Nigeria's experiment in constitutional government. For it is not enough that the judiciary, as the guardian of the constitution and of the people's rights, should be impartial; it is equally important that it should be seen to be so. Whatever the quality of its decisions in point of law, it can command no respect or acceptability if the public has no confidence in it, because of the known political involvement of its members or because of their sympathy or subservience to ruling politicians. And when things have come to such a pass that people with genuine grievances against the government are no longer willing to have recourse to the courts for redress, then that is the end of constitutional government, and the stage is set for anarchy. The experience of Western Nigeria in 1965 bears testimony to this. Convinced that they would get no justice from the courts for the assault on their right to choose who should govern them — Chief Adegbenro, leader of the Action Group and the legitimate winner of the election, had been forced by Chief Justice Morgan to renounce the executive council which he had formed, or go to prison[30] — the people of Western Nigeria naturally resorted to violence as the only remedy open to them in the circumstances. For them the law and its guardians had lost their title to obedience and must give way to the rule of the jungle in which right had to be vindicated by might in its crudest, most uninhibited form.

Lastly, a decision affirming the constitutionality of a governmental measure regardless of its wisdom, fairness or justice cannot persuade or satisfy those whose objection to the measure is based on these latter grounds, and who regard fairness and justice as a necessary condition of the legitimacy of a governmental act. For example, will a conscientious objector withdraw his objection if the court tells him that the constitution does not protect his right of conscience? In such a case, as Scharpf says, 'the objectors might see themselves impelled into civil disobedience against the constitutional order, rather than into acceptance.'[31] This raises the question whether in reviewing governmental acts the court should go beyond the confines of legal validity, which at present is its sole concern, in order to inquire into the wisdom, desirability, fairness or justice of impugned governmental measures.

REFERENCES

1. Bickel, *The Least Dangerous Branch* (1962), 16 and 17.
2. Arthur Lewis, *Politics in West Africa* (1965), 75.
3. Charles Black, *The People and the Court* (1960), 107.
4. ibid., 115.
5. ibid., 118.
6. ibid.
7. Alexander Hamilton, *The Federalist*, no. 78.
8. Bickel, op. cit., 16–17. Italics supplied.
9. Bickel, op. cit., 17.
10. Carl J. Friedrich, *Constitutional Government and Democracy* (1950), 123.
11. See Nwabueze, *Constitutionalism in the Emergent States* (1973), 1.
12. *Railroad Company* v. *Brown* (1873), 17 Wall. 445.
13. *Plessy* v. *Ferguson* (1896), 163 U.S. 537.
14. *Brown* v. *Board of Education* (1954), 347 U.S. 483.
15. Eugene Rostow, *The Sovereign Prerogative: The Supreme Court and the Quest for Law* (1962), 153.
16. E.g. the Eighteenth Amendment to the U.S. Constitution; the Constitution of Western Nigeria (Amendment) Law, 1963; and the South Africa Act Amendment Act, 1956.
17. McWhinney, *Judicial Review in the English-Speaking World* (1965), 190.
18. Black, op. cit., 60.
19. ibid., 60.
20. The South African constitutional crisis of 1952–7 is discussed in Nwabueze, *Judicialism* (1977), chapters 10 and 13.
21. Rostow, op. cit., 120.
22. James Thayer, *John Marshall* (1901), 103–4, 106–7; quoted in Bickel, op. cit., 21–2.
23. Bickel, op. cit., particularly chapter 4.
24. Carl J. Friedrich, *Constitutional Government and Democracy* (1950), 117.
25. Rostow, op. cit., 173.
26. Black, op. cit., 60.
27. ibid., 64.
28. Bickel, op. cit., 130.
29. Black, op. cit., 78; Bickel, op. cit., 29.
30. *Att.-Gen. Western Nigeria* v. *Adegbenro*, Suit No. 1/64C/65 of 1965. The renunciation in the form of a press statement read in part: 'Since His Excellency the Governor had appointed Chief S.L. Akintola as Premier of Western Nigeria on the 13th October, 1965, I did not form any rival government. All statements or representations attributed to me or to any of my colleagues purporting to set up a rival Premier or Cabinet for Western Nigeria are hereby withdrawn.' Thereupon the state entered a *nolle prosequi*, discontinuing the prosecution.
31. Scharpf, 'Judicial Review and the Political Question: a Functional

Analysis', *Yale L. J.* (1966), 75, 517, 535, n. 59; see also Black, 'The Problem of the Compatibility of Civil Disobedience with the American Institutions of Government', *Texas L. Rev.* (1965), 43, 492, and Keeton, 'The Morality of Civil Disobedience', *Texas L. Rev.* (1965), 43, 507.

20
PUBLIC SERVICE

1. *Public service defined*

A meaningful definition of public service must have regard to four things. First is the concept of 'public', and its true connotation in the context. It can refer to either of two things: the government of Nigeria or the people of Nigeria as a collection of individuals distinct from the government. The latter is untenable in the context. The idea of 'service' of the entire people is meaningless, from a legal point of view, since as a collection of individuals the people have no legal personality apart from its government. Thus when the United States supreme court holds that 'immunity in our courts should be granted only with respect to causes of action arising out of a foreign state's public or governmental actions',[1] 'public' is used as interchangeable or synonymous with 'government'. Accordingly, public service must be taken to mean government service.

The second factor in the definition of public service is the nature of the service. Taken together with the concept of 'public' as defined above, what does government service connote? Government service is traditionally conceived as of the nature of a welfare service, i.e. not based on considerations of economic gain, but aimed rather at providing for the needs of the society for law and order, defence, roads and such other traditional functions of government. But, as Lord Denning observed in 1977, while 'a century ago no sovereign state engaged in commercial activities', 'in the past fifty years there has been a complete transformation in the functions of a sovereign state. Nearly every country now engages in commercial activities.'[2] This has necessitated drawing a distinction between two types of activities undertaken by modern governments — between those of a governmental nature called *acta jure imperii* and those of a commercial nature, *acta jure gestionis*. From this development arises the question whether government service in the constitutional sense is apt to embrace both types of activities. The attitude of most countries today is to recognise only acts of the former type (*acta jure imperii*) for purposes of the grant of sovereign immunity.[3] Constitutionally, there is nothing to stop a state defining its public service to embrace both types of activity, but it does sound a little odd to designate as a 'public service' a commercial activity undertaken by a government for purely economic gain.

The third factor is the status of the institution or organisation employed by the state for carrying on a particular activity. A government may engage in commercial activity either directly through one of its departments or indirectly through some other distinct legal entity created by its own statute or incorporated as an ordinary trading company. The question prompted by this is whether government service does not imply an activity carried on through the instrumentality of a department or arm of government. Surely the status, as a department or arm of government, of the institution or organisation carrying on an activity on behalf of the government should be a constitutional requirement for designating the activity as a government service. Otherwise the whole concept of government service would have become meaningless.

It must be accepted as an incontrovertible principle of law that the mere fact of carrying on an activity on behalf of or as agent of the government does not stamp an organisation with the character or status of a department or arm of government. The point was in issue in a recent case before the English courts involving the central bank of Nigeria. The issue was whether the central bank, as a government bank and a prime bank, is to be regarded as a department or arm of the government of Nigeria, and whether its act in issuing a letter of credit to pay for cement ordered by the ministry of defence is to be regarded as being in the nature of a governmental act (*actus jure imperium*). The court of appeal in England held, reversing the judgment of the high court,[4] that the central bank is not an arm or department of the government, and that its act in issuing the letter of credit is not of the nature of a governmental act. The grounds for this decision are —

First, the law that created it, namely the Central Bank of Nigeria Act, 1958, with its various amendments, contains no indication and manifests no intention that the bank is to be an arm or department of the government. 'If', said Lord Justice Shaw, 'it was designed as a department of state, many titles indicative of that status come readily to mind. What was conferred on it was the title of a bank. Nowhere in the legislation is it called anything but a bank. . . . The fifty-two sections of the principal Act and the several amending orders and enactments contain no direct indication that the bank is a department of the government and there are many indications which deny it that status. The very name has a commercial ring.'[5]

Secondly, the powers and functions of the bank do not identify it with the government, and in some respects preclude identification with the government. For example, the provision in s. 4 of the act that the bank is 'to act as banker and financial adviser to the federal government' envisages the bank's function in this regard as independent of and external to the immediate realm of government. And, while the function of issuing legal tender and safeguarding the international value of the currency is undoubtedly of the nature of a governmental function, that does not confer on the bank a governmental status. The function is delegated to it merely as agent for the government; and in its capacity as agent the bank is subject to a very tight control.

The court then concluded that while 'it is clear that the bank was the subserving agent of the government in a variety of activities, . . . this is not adequate to constitute it as an organ or department of government. I cannot find in the constitution of the bank or in the functions it performs or in the activities it pursues or in all those matters looked at together, any compelling or indeed satisfactory basis for the conclusion that it is so related to the government of Nigeria as to form part of it.'[6]

The fourth factor involved in the definition of public service is the status of the individuals employed in it. Indeed, it may be said that the term 'public service' is often used to refer primarily to employment in the public service or rather to the persons employed in it. Now, if it is not a constitutional requirement that an organisation carrying on activity on behalf of government must be an arm or department of government before the activity can be regarded as a public or government service, then the constitutional status of the persons employed by that organisation for carrying on that activity becomes an important issue. If, notwithstanding that the organisation is not an arm or department of government, the activity may still be regarded as a public or government service, are the persons employed in it public or government officers? Can the question whether the employees are public or government officers be meaningfully divorced from the status of the employing organisation as an arm or department of government? It is submitted that the employees can only meaningfully be designated public or government officers if the organisation employing them is an arm or department of government; they must derive their constitutional status as public or government officers from the status of their employer as an arm or department of government. Any other view of the matter makes nonsense of the concept of public service. A public officer is a person holding or acting in an office under the state or government. If an organisation is not an arm or department of government, offices in it cannot be offices under the state or government, and those holding or acting in them cannot be public officers.

It is in the light of the foregoing analysis of the concept of public service that its definition in the Constitution is to be considered. Recognising the factors discussed above as constitutional requirements in any meaningful conception of public service, the 1963 constitution of Nigeria defined the public service of the federation as 'the service of the Republic in a civil capacity in respect of the government of the Federation' (s. 165). This makes it clear that it is government service carried on by departments of state. The 1979 Constitution extends the definition to include, *inter alia*, service as (*a*) staff of any statutory corporation established by an act of the national assembly; (*b*) staff of any educational institution established or financed principally by the government of the federation; and (*c*) staff of any company or enterprise in which the government of the federation or its agency owns controlling share or interest (s. 277). (The public service of a state is defined in similar terms.)

The inclusion in this definition of university staff and those of commercial concerns in which the government has a controlling share or interest introduces a complication and confusion in the concept of public service. If the central bank, according to the decision discussed above, is not an arm or department of government, then *a fortiori* the universities are not, while it would border on the absurd to suggest such status for the commercial concerns in which the government has a controlling share or interest. And if they are not an arm or department of government, offices in them are not offices under the state or government, so that their staff cannot be public or government officers.

Except for the purposes of the code of conduct, the Constitution does not say that they are. Neither does their inclusion in the definition of public service carry that implication. On the contrary, the Constitution seems to contemplate a distinction between an office under the state and one in a statutory corporation when it provides that the guarantee of freedom from discrimination shall not invalidate any law by reason only that the law imposes restrictions with respect to the appointment of any person to any office under the state or to an office in the service of a body corporate established directly by any law in force in Nigeria (s. 39[3]). The reference to an office in a statutory corporation suggests that it is not an office under the state or it would not have been mentioned separately.

The supreme court of Nigeria in a case in 1977, *Rufus Alli Momoh v. Afolabi Okewale and Lagos City Council*, has adopted an even narrower definition of a public officer based on how and by whom he was appointed. It held in that case that a bus driver of the Lagos city council is not a public officer for the purposes of the Public Officers Protection Act because he had not been appointed by the public service commission. In the view of the court, the implication of the provision in the 1963 constitution vesting in the public service commission, subject to certain exceptions, power to appoint persons to hold or act in offices in the public service is that a person cannot be a public officer unless he holds a public office by virtue of appointment by the public service commission.

Notwithstanding the extended meaning given to public service by the Constitution, an officer or member of the public service is not (except for the purposes of the code of conduct) a public officer if he is not the holder of an office under the state or government. The anomalous result is of course created of having in the public service a large number of officers or members who are not public officers (except again for the purposes of the code of conduct). The directive of the federal military government declaring university staff to be public officers, not just for the purposes of the code of conduct but generally, has thus no warrant in the Constitution.

2. *Structure of the public service*

The structure of the public service is indicated by its definition in the Constitution as 'the service of the federation in any [not just a civil] capacity in respect of the government of the federation', and by the stipulation that it shall include service as

(*a*) clerk or other staff of the national assembly or each house of the national assembly,
(*b*) member or staff of the supreme court, the federal court of appeal, the federal high court, the high court of the federal capital territory . . . or other courts established for the federation by this Constitution and by the national assembly,
(*c*) member or staff of any commission or authority established for the federation by this Constitution or by an act of the national assembly,
(*d*) staff of any statutory corporation established by an act of the national assembly,
(*e*) staff of any educational institution established or financed principally by the government of the federation,
(*f*) staff of any company or enterprise in which the government of the federation or its agency owns controlling share or interest, and
(*g*) members or officers of the armed forces of the federation or the Nigeria police force' (s. 277).

The public service of the federation consists therefore of the seven services enumerated above, each of which forms a distinct segment thereof. To the seven enumerated services must however be added the following —
(*a*) the civil service, which is defined as the 'service of the federation in a civil capacity as staff of the office of the president, the vice-president, a ministry or department of the government of the federation assigned with the responsibility for any business of the government' (s. 277);
(*b*) the political arm of the executive, i.e. the president, vice-president, ministers, special advisers and other members (as distinct from staff) of the government;

(c) members of the national assembly, though their position is not altogether clear. In their capacity as such members, they are unquestionably in the service of the federation, but whether their service is in respect of the government of the federation depends on the meaning of the term 'government of the federation' in the context. The context would appear to suggest government, not as the executive alone, but in its widest signification as embracing all three organs of government. It would be anomalous if non-official members of constitutional commissions are public servants while those of the national assembly are not.

(i) *Civil Service*
In its definition of the civil service quoted earlier, the Constitution implies that the civil service with its offices and staff is to be organised into ministries or departments, but exactly how this is to be done and by what form are left to the president. The president, the Constitution says, may assign to the vice-president or a minister responsibility for any business of government, including the administration of any department of government. In practice the establishment or disestablishment of ministries is done quite informally, in marked contrast to the practice in the United States where departments can only be created by statute.

In addition to the cabinet office, there are at the time of writing twenty-one federal ministries, namely agriculture and rural development, civil aviation, communications, defence, economic planning, education, establishments, external affairs, finance, health, industries, information, internal affairs, justice, labour, youth and sports, mines and power, trade, transport, and works and housing, science and technology, and steel development. Each ministry comprises divisions, departments and other agencies too numerous to mention. Quite a few of the agencies within the ministries are created by statute. Where an agency of an unquestionably public nature, such as the productivity, prices and incomes board, national youth corps directorate, is created by a statute but is not declared in the statute to be a corporate body, the implication is that it is to be part of either the cabinet office or the ministry with which its functions are most closely connected. In one case the establishing decree specifically declares that the agency, the Nigerian standards organisation, shall be an integral part of the ministry of industries.

Then there are the extra-ministerial departments or agencies like the department of customs and excise, or the inland revenue department. (The corrupt practices investigation bureau was specifically declared by its constituent statute, now repealed, to be a distinct department of the federal government.)

As for offices in the civil service, only a few are established or referred to specifically in the Constitution: namely the secretary to the government, the head of the civil service, ambassadors, high commissioners or other principal representatives of the country abroad, permanent secretaries or other chief executives in any ministry or department however designated and the director of audit.

The functions of the civil service are not defined by the Constitution, but they have been simply described, albeit in broad outline, by a former secretary to the federal government as follows: (a) the initiation of policy and advising government on the policy options open to it; (b) execution of policy after it has been decided by the government or by a particular minister; (c) administration of the laws enacted by the legislature; (d) to provide continuity and to serve as a store of knowledge of past government decisions and procedures; (e) to serve as a factor of unity and stability in the nation; (f) to serve as an embodiment of government in the day-to-day life of the people, and to help preserve the mystique and authority of the government through the daily contact of officials at all levels with the general public; and (g), as part of the élite, to play a leadership role both within the service and in the community as a whole.

(ii) *Constitutional commissions*

Eight federal commissions are established by the Constitution — the council of state, the federal civil service commission, the federal electoral commission, the federal judicial service commission, the national economic council, the national population commission, the national security council, the public complaints commission and the police service commission. Their membership and functions have already been discussed.

(iii) *The disciplined forces*

The disciplined forces comprise two wings distinguished by the fact that one is armed while the other is not.

The armed forces comprise three units — army, navy and air force. The organisation of each such unit into branches, etc., is left to the national assembly, but five offices are established — the commander-in-chief who is the president himself, the chief of defence staff and the heads of the three units. The Constitution contemplates compulsory military service for Nigerian citizens.

In contrast to its silence on the functions of the civil service and perhaps to remind them of the limits set on their role, the Constitution spells out the functions of the armed forces as (a) the defence of Nigeria from external aggression; (b) the maintenance of its territorial integrity and securing its borders from violation on land, sea or air; (c) the suppression of insurrection and acting in aid of the civil authorities to restore order when called upon to do so by the president, but subject to such conditions as may be prescribed by an act of the national assembly; and (*d*) performing such other functions as may be prescribed by an act of the national assembly. As commander-in-chief, the president determines the operational use of the armed forces, but regarding the defence of the sovereignty and territorial integrity of the country he is advised by a national defence council established by the Constitution.

The unarmed wing of the disciplined forces is the police, which is created as just one, single force for the whole country under the style of the Nigeria police force. How it is to be organised and administered, and what powers it is to have for the effective discharge of its functions, is left to the national assembly. Its basic function is stated to be the maintenance and securing of public safety and public order.

The Constitution does provide, however, that the force is to be commanded nationally by an inspector-general and at the state level by a commissioner subject to the inspector-general's control. In the operational use of the force for the maintenance and securing of public safety and public order, the inspector-general and the state commissioner are respectively subject to the lawful directions of the president and state governor, although before carrying out any directions by the governor, the commissioner may request that the matter be referred to the president for his directions.

(iv) *Statutory corporations*

Apart from including them in the definition of public service, the Constitution contains no provisions for the organisation and functions of statutory corporations and the appointment and removal of their staff. But these corporations have over the past few years increased immensely in number and importance in the machinery of government. Over sixty of them have been established since 1966 by the federal government, dealing with such varied services as industrial, agricultural, educational and medical research, arts and culture, insurance, steel development, establishment and maintenance of standards of industrial products, river basin development, electricity, financing of commerce and industry, housing, marketing of agricultural commodities, and so on.

In 1968 four of these corporations, while retaining their separate identities, were, for purposes of appointment, removal and disciplinary control of their staff, brought together under a common agency, the statutory corporations service commission, on much the same lines as the public service commission and with similar powers, functions and immunities.⁸ The salaries and allowances of their staff were made uniform, and it was provided that in future they would be subject to salaries and allowances fixed by the federal executive council for civil servants.⁹ The experiment was abandoned in 1978, the commission was dissolved and its constituent decree was repealed with effect from August 1975.¹⁰

3. Obligations and duties of public service

Public service imposes quite severe obligations on its members, particularly on civil servants. Four such obligations may be noted here:

(a) *Impartiality*. The public interest demands political impartiality in the civil service. It is important that the expert advice on policy provided by the civil service and its executive service should be impartial regardless of the political complexion and outlook of the party in power.

(b) *Fairness in the administration of law*. The civil service serves not only the government of the day, but also the public at large in the capacity of administrators of the law. Their interpretation and application of the law may adversely affect the interest of individuals — and to minimise this, impartiality, fairness and the absence of any kind of bias, whether based on political or personal interest, are required of the civil servant. He must grant an individual adversely affected by his decision the opportunity to be heard. These obligations are required in order that it may be seen by all that the administrator is impartial and fair, since only thus can public confidence in his impartiality and fairness be maintained.

(c) *Probity*. Honesty, integrity and incorruptibility are a cardinal requirement of public service. A public servant should not engage in any corrupt practices or other forms of abuse of office.

(d) *Public accountability*. Public accountability requires that the rulers should be accountable to the public for their actions. Accountability involves not just a periodic progress report by radio broadcast or during an election campaign. It presupposes also freedom on the part of the people at all times directly or through their elected representatives to question or criticise the action of government, a duty on the part of the government to explain and try to justify its conduct, and lastly the availability of sanctions for unsatisfactory or unjustifiable action. For the application of the requirement of public accountability, 'rulers' are mostly identified with those holding elective political offices. This identification is today considered too narrow, and is increasingly being abandoned in favour of exacting accountability from all public functionaries whose exercise of authority affect the interest of individuals. Upon the complaint of an individual adversely affected, a public servant should be required to explain and justify the fairness and propriety of his decision or action before an independent body.

4. *Restrictions, disqualifications and disabilities*

The Constitution establishes for public servants a code of conduct which imposes on them certain restrictions, disqualifications and disabilities. Although a public officer is defined for purposes of the code to include not only public officers properly so called, i.e. persons holding office under the government, but also the chairmen and board members of other governing bodies and the staff of statutory corporations and of companies in which the federal or state government has controlling interest as well as all staff of universities, colleges, and institutions owned and financed by the federal or state governments or local government councils, the application of the code to the various categories of public servant must vary according as he is an officer under the government or not. For the obligations of an officer under the state are different from those of an officer in a university or commercial concern. These restrictions, disqualifications and disabilities will now be considered. In the discussion that follows, the term 'public servant' will be used in preference to 'public officer', for two reasons: first, because a public servant need not hold an established office; and secondly because a person in the public service is not strictly a public officer if his office is not one under the state or government.

(i) *Political neutrality*

A public servant is forbidden to put himself in a position where his personal interest conflicts with his duties and responsibilities. More specifically, he is not to be a member of, belong to, or take part in any society the membership of which is incompatible with the functions or dignity of his office.

The thorny and burning question raised by this disability concerns its application to participation by a public servant in political activities. Strong arguments have been advanced for and against political neutrality as a general concept governing the public service. On the one side it is asserted that if public servants are

beneficiaries of political patronage rather than professional careerists, serious results might follow. . . . Public confidence in the objectivity and integrity of the civil service system might be so weakened as to jeopardise the effectiveness of the administrative government. Or it might founder on the rocks of incompetence, if every change in political fortunes turned out the incumbents, broke the continuity of administration, and thus interfered with the development of expert management at the technical levels. Or if the incumbents were political adventurers or party workers, partisanship might colour or corrupt the processes of administration of law with which most of the administrative agencies are entrusted.[11]

On the other hand, some of the African nationalist leaders who succeeded to the government on the departure of the British at independence were inclined to view the concept as a 'fiction', which, 'if carried to its logical conclusion, would in fact deprive the civil servant of his basic democratic right to vote. For in casting his vote, he exercises a choice in favour of one political party and thereby demonstrates a bias.'[12] They argued further that the need for dedication and loyalty far outweighs any advantages of maintaining the political neutrality of the civil service. And maximum dedication and loyalty in the civil service can only be ensured if civil servants share the government's outlook. For, although their training has conditioned them to be able to subordinate their own personal political views to their duty of loyalty to the government of the day, yet the pull of conscience may occasionally prove so strong as to override the civil servant's sense of loyalty.[13] Enthusiasm in the civil servant's application to his work, said Julius Nyerere of Tanzania, 'is a most important national asset. We cannot afford the luxury of administrators who are neutral.'[14]

The question also sharply divided the judges of the United States supreme court when it was called upon to decide the constitutionality of legislation enforcing the political neutrality of public servants as a general concept. An act of the congress prohibited all employees in the executive branch of the federal government, with certain exceptions — notably the president and vice-president, political heads of departments, political office-holders and part-time employees — from taking 'any part in political management or in political campaigns' both during and after office hours, and made dismissal and a permanent ban against re-employment in the same position the penalty for violation. Among the activities specifically prohibited were serving as an election officer; publicly expressing political views at a party caucus or political gathering for or against any candidate or cause identified with a party; soliciting votes for a party or candidate; participating in a political parade; writing for publication or publishing any letter or article in favour of or against any political party, candidate or faction; and initiating or canvassing for signatures on community petitions or petitions to congress. The prohibition was however without prejudice to the right of public employees to vote as they pleased and to express their opinion on all political subjects. It was reckoned that approximately 3 million federal employees were affected by the prohibition, and many thousands of state employees who worked for state agencies financed in whole or part by federal grants or loans were also affected.

The prohibition was attacked by a labour union of public employees and by individual employees as an unconstitutional deprivation of a public servant's freedom of speech, press and assembly and of the fundamental right of the people of the United States to engage in political activity.[15] By a majority of four to three the court held the prohibition to be constitutionally justified on the ground that, since no one has a constitutional right to be a public employee, government must be allowed power to adopt measures necessary to meet the obvious need to 'promote efficiency and integrity in the discharge of official duties, and to maintain proper discipline in the public service'.[16] Partisan political activity by public servants, the majority reasoned, has the inherent danger that service to a political party and political connections may replace official performance and merit as the criterion for advancement and for the grant of favours generally; they pointed to the further danger of coercion of subordinates by their superiors or of members of the public by government employees using their official position. In their view the effect of partisan political activity by public servants on efficiency and morale has to be viewed from the standpoint both of the public service as a whole and of individual public employees. For although such activity may not undermine the efficiency of a particular public servant, it may undermine morale in the service as a whole.

The minority felt, first, that the prohibition contradicted the very right conceded by the act to public employees to express opinions on all subjects. What it amounted to was that 'whatever opinions employees may dare to express, even secretly, must be at their peril. They cannot know what particular expressions may be reported to the commission and held by it to be a sufficient political activity to cost them their jobs.'[17] In the result, therefore, the constitutionally protected liberty of public employees was reduced to 'less than a shadow of its substance', and millions of people were thereby relegated to the 'role of mere spectators of events upon which hinge the safety and welfare of all the people'.[18] Secondly, 'legislation which muzzles several million citizens threatens popular government, not only because it injures the individuals muzzled, but also because of its harmful effect on the body politic in depriving it of the political participation and interest of such a large segment of our citizens.'[19] Thirdly, the danger of coercion, and of dismissals or promotions based on political consideration rather than on merit, could be dealt with by a law narrowly drawn to penalise those guilty of such practices instead of by a general prohibition of active political activity by all public employees.

Arguments for and against the political neutrality of public servants as a general concept are not conclusive on the interpretation and application of a specific constitutional prohibition. The question is not as to the general advantages or disadvantages of political neutrality as applied to the entire public service, but whether political activity by a particular public servant holding a particular position conflicts with his official duties and responsibilities or is otherwise incompatible with them. In this connection it is of great significance that, unlike its predecessor, the 1979 Constitution specifically mentions a political party as an association which the individual is guaranteed the right to form or belong to. It is also significant that freedom of association is no longer, as under the 1963 constitution, subject to a reasonably justifiable restriction imposed by law upon persons holding office under the state.

In the United States case discussed above, the point was actually raised that the decisive factor should be the nature of the duties of any particular public employee, and the bearing and influence which they have on policy and the administration of government. That case concerned in part an industrial worker, a roller in the mint, who also held an office in a political party as a ward executive committeeman. It was argued that the political neutrality of an industrial worker such as a roller in a mint, a lift operator, a bus conductor or a cleaner does not have the same significance as the political neutrality of an employee in the administrative category, and that 'no discussion of the problem which ignores the *differences between categories of employees* is anything but an academic consideration of the problem.'[20]

The majority of the court held that even if the work on which a particular public servant is employed has no bearing on policy or that his performance of it cannot be affected by his political activities, still his advancement may be affected thereby; and that 'whatever differences there may be between administrative employees of government and industrial workers under its employ are differences in detail so far as the constitutional power under review is concerned. Whether there are such differences, and what weight to attach to them, are all matters of detail for Congress.'[21]

Two of the judges in the minority took the other extreme that political neutrality, as a general principle, should not be enforced on any class of public employees, both administrative and industrial. But the third member conceded that the arguments urged in favour of it 'might well apply to the entire group of civil servants in the administrative category — whether they are those in the so-called expert classification or are clerks, stenographers and the like. They are the ones who have access to the files, who meet the public, who arrange appointments, who prepare the basic data on which policy decisions are made. Each may be a tributary, though perhaps a small one, to the main stream which we call policy-making or administrative action. If the element of partisanship enters into the official activities of any member of the group, it may have its repercussions or effect throughout the administrative service.'[22] In his view, however, an industrial worker like a roller in the mint is so remote from contact with the public or from policy-making or from the functioning of the administrative process that no harmful conflict or incompatibility can exist between his official duty and his political activity.

This is undoubtedly the right approach to the application of the stipulation in the code of conduct in the Nigerian Constitution forbidding a public servant to put himself in a position where his personal interest conflicts with his duties and responsibilities or to be a member of, belong to, or take part in any society the membership of which is incompatible with the functions or dignity of his office. Membership of a political party by a permanent secretary or other government administrative officer, or overt participation by him in political activities such as canvassing for votes for a candidate at an election, or contributing to the funds of a political party or to the election expenses of such a candidate, clearly creates a conflict with his ability to give impartial advice and executive service to a government of a different political persuasion. As applied to him, the government directive of 8 September 1978 that 'all holders of public offices who intend to take active part in partisan politics at the end of the present administration should be required to relinquish their public posts immediately' is entirely in consonance with the code of conduct. But the application of the directive to the category of industrial workers has no basis in the code of conduct.

The application of the directive to university staff has been the subject of much controversy. A member of staff of the university neither advises the government on policy — not officially at any rate — nor executes or administers its policies and laws. The function of a university staff is essentially that of teaching and research or, for the non-academic staff, organising teaching and research. There is no meaningful conflict between teaching or research and membership of a political party or participation in political activities such as to require political neutrality of a university staff member. If anything, they are or can be made complementary. For politics through the platform of a political party can provide a convenient medium for the conception and propagation of ideas, which is an essential function of teaching and research. The order of the federal government directing that 'university staff, of all categories, being public officers, shall not participate in partisan politics, collectively or individually, in any manner or form, including belonging to political parties, or taking part in political rallies or undertaking any form of political activities whatsoever' is clearly not warranted by the provision of the code of conduct on which apparently it purports to have been based.

No doubt, university staff cannot, as a body or association, 'canvass for votes for any candidate at election or contribute to the funds of any political party or to the election expenses of any candidate at an election', that being a function reserved by the Constitution exclusively to a political party (ss. 201 and 209). Yet the restriction of the Constitution in this regard does not go as far as to prohibit an association of university staff or of other workers from declaring support for a political party, so long as support is not expressed in the form of canvassing for votes or contributing to the funds of a political party or the election expenses of a candidate.

The federal government's directives also ban overt party political activities in the universities and the formation or operation of university wings or local branches of political parties. University students, as individuals, can only belong to political parties and take part in political rallies or any form of political activities outside the campus. This directive overlooks the character of the university as a distinct legal entity separate from and outside the government; it also overlooks the fact that the campus and other properties of the university are vested in it as such a distinct legal entity. It is true that the university is financed by the government, yet the law that separates it from, and puts it outside, the government deserves to be respected. The control of the university which its financial interest gives to the government should be exercised through the legally constituted authorities of the institution.

(ii) *Ban on private business or receipt of multiple emolument*

As a corollary to the requirement that a public servant should not put himself in a position where his personal interest conflicts with his duties and responsibilities, the code enjoins a public servant not to

(*a*) engage or participate in the management or running of any private business, profession or trade (part-time public servants excepted). Business is defined as 'any profession, vocation or trade and includes any adventure or concern in the nature of trade, and farming';

(*b*) receive or be paid the emoluments of any public office (i.e. office under the state) at the same time as he receives or is paid the emoluments of any other public office. Emoluments in the context of the code means 'any salary, wage, overtime or leave pay, commission, fee, bonus, gratuity, benefit, advantage (whether or not that advantage is capable of being turned into money or money's worth), allowance, pension or annuity paid, given or granted in respect of any employment';

(c) accept, after his retirement from public service and while receiving a pension from public funds, more than one remunerative position; or

(d) take employment in a foreign company or foreign enterprise after his retirement as president, vice-president, chief justice of Nigeria, governor or deputy governor.

A ban on private practice is imposed by statute on public servants who are professionals — architects, accountants, dentists, engineers, estate managers, lawyers, doctors, nurses, pharmacists, quantity surveyors, physiotherapists, radiographers, and teachers — see Regulated and other Professions (Miscellaneous Provisions) Decree, 1978. And 'public officer' for the purposes of the statute is as widely defined as under the code of conduct.

(iii) *Prohibition of corruption*

The code prohibits corruption and abuse of office by a public servant. It forbids him to take a bribe as an inducement for the discharge of his duties or to do any arbitrary act prejudicial to the rights of any other person knowing that such act is unlawful or contrary to government policy. To this end, he is specifically enjoined

(a) not to ask for or accept any property or benefits of any kind for himself or any other person on account of anything done or omitted to be done in discharge of his duties; receipt by him of any gifts or benefits from a commercial firm, business enterprise or a person who has a contract with the government is presumptive evidence of corruption unless the contrary is proved. Gifts or donations to him on public or ceremonial occasions are to be treated as gifts to the institution that he represents. The only gifts or benefits permitted are those from relatives or personal friends, but only to such extent and on such occasions as are recognised by custom;

(b) not to accept a loan (except from the government or its agencies or his employer, a bank, building society or other recognised financial institution) or any benefit of whatever nature from any company, contractor or businessman or the nominee or agent of such person — this is limited to the president, vice-president, governor, deputy governor, minister, permanent secretary or head of a public corporation, university or other parastatal organisation;

(c) not to maintain or operate a bank account in any country outside Nigeria — limited to the president, vice-president, governor, deputy governor, ministers, members of legislative houses and such other public officers as the national assembly may by law prescribe.

Corruption by public servants has come under very severe prohibition and punishment. The Corrupt Practices Decree of 1975 (since repealed) made it an offence for a public servant to accept or be offered gratification as an inducement for the discharge or non-discharge of his function, particularly in relation to the award of contracts.

(iv) *Declaration of assets*
A public servant is required to make a written declaration of all his properties, assets and liabilities and those of his spouse and unmarried children under the age of twenty-one years within three months of the coming into force of the code of conduct or immediately after taking office, and thereafter at the end of every four years, and at the end of his term of office. The declaration is to be submitted to a body, the code of conduct bureau, specially created for the purpose. It is a breach of the code to make a false declaration. The purpose of the declaration is to keep a check on the acquisitions of public servants with a view to detecting and checking any which are corrupt. To this end, any property acquired after a declaration and which is in excess of what might be fairly attributable to legitimate income, gift or loan is deemed to have been acquired in breach of the code unless the contrary is proved.

Declaration of assets by public servants is already an established regime since 1966, but it is arguable whether the declaration required by the code represents the limit of the imposition that may be made on a public servant in this regard. Under existing statutes of the military government, he may be required to make a declaration of assets at any time. The Investigation of Assets (Public Officers and other Persons) Decree 1968, which repeals an earlier decree of 1966 and edicts of the Western and Mid-Western states, authorises the head of state or state governor, if he considers it necessary in the public interest, to require a public servant to make a declaration of his assets in a prescribed form at any time. (The requirements of the Corrupt Practices Decree were repealed in 1979, shortly before the end of the military government.)

There is nothing in the code of conduct indicating an intention to preclude declaration of assets by public servants being required in the interval (which may be as long as four years) between the dates specified in the code for the making of a constitutional declaration. It may be concluded therefore that, apart from declarations required by the code, a public servant may additionally be required under a statute to make a declaration of his assets at any time. (The definition of public officer for the purposes of the Investigation of Assets (Public Officers and Other Persons) Decree includes university staff and a member of the board (but not the staff) of a company appointed by the government by virtue of its shareholding in the company.

(v) *Disqualification with respect to elective offices*
As previously stated, a public servant is disqualified for election as president, vice-president, governor, deputy governor or a member of a federal or state legislative house. The disqualification extends only to election, but not to mere candidature. In other words, subject to the political neutrality required of civil servants, a public servant who is not a civil servant can be a candidate for an elective office and can campaign for it, but must resign before the actual poll takes place.

The disqualification in the Electoral Decree 1977 applies to civil servants and employees of statutory corporations which include university staff (s. 73[1][*f*]). And it extends to a time four months before the election; this time requirement is inconsistent with the Constitution and is therefore invalid. Employees of a government-controlled company are however not affected by the disqualification in the Decree; a member of its board as well as a member of a statutory corporation or local government is not even required to resign, although his membership automatically ceases on his election.

5. *Sanctions and enforcement procedures*

(i) *Investigatory or inquisitorial proceedings*
The code of conduct is rather sketchy on this, merely stating that a declaration of assets by a public officer shall be received and examined by the code of conduct bureau, which is also to receive complaints about non-compliance with or breach of the code and to refer them, in the absence of an admission, to the code of conduct tribunal. It leaves it to the National Assembly to provide for the detailed powers needed to enable the bureau more effectively to discharge its functions. The bureau consists of not less than nine members appointed by the president with the approval of the senate, but it owes responsibility to the national assembly. Its members enjoy the same tenure as officers in the civil service.

A declaration of assets under the Investigation of Assets (Public Officers and Other Persons) Decree, 1968, is first investigated by a bank examiner or other qualified person with a view to verifying its accuracy. Thereafter a tribunal may be appointed to enquire whether, and if so to what extent the public servant concerned has corruptly or improperly enriched himself or any person by virtue of his office or by any means in abuse of his office. The tribunal operates under the Tribunals of Inquiry Decree, 1966, and has all the powers conferred by that decree. It can also prohibit the disposition of property under investigation.

The public service was the subject of a radical corrective treatment in the later half of 1975 following the coup of July that year. Among the things authorised by the enabling decree, the Public Officers (Special Provisions) Decree, 1976, (made on 23 February 1976 but backdated to 29 July 1975) was the investigation by a panel into the assets or performance of any public officer for the purpose of ascertaining whether he had been engaged in corrupt practices or had corruptly enriched himself or any other person. The panel functioned in much the same way and with much the same powers as a tribunal of enquiry under the Investigation of Assets (Public Officers and Other Persons) Decree, 1968.

In all these cases investigation has to be initiated by the government or one of its high-ranking functionaries, and they are mostly concerned with corruption by public officers. The Public Complaints Commission Decree, 1975, provides a procedure for investigation which may be initiated by a private person, and covers, with certain exceptions, all administrative actions of a public servant, including in particular administrative acts which are or appear to be (i) contrary to any law or regulation; (ii) mistaken in law or arbitrary in the ascertainment of fact; (iii) unreasonable, unfair, oppressive or inconsistent with the general functions of administrative organs; (iv) improper in motivation or based on irrelevant considerations; (v) unclear or inadequately explained; or (vi) otherwise objectionable. Investigation for purposes enumerated above is not limited to acts of individual officers or servants; it extends also to those of the employing organisation, both governmental and non-governmental, including a registered company, whether government-owned or not.

Certain matters are however exempted from investigation under this procedure, namely any matter pending before the supreme military council (*the power vested in the supreme military council by the decree now presumably belongs to the National Assembly*), the national council of states, the federal executive council or a court of law. These bodies are not of course exempted; only a matter still pending before them, but not one already completed, is exempted. However the decision of a court cannot be investigated, but its administrative procedures can. Also exempted is an act done in respect of a member of the armed forces and the police force under their respective constituent acts.

A serious limitation on the scope of investigation under this procedure is the requirement that a complainant must first exhaust all available legal or administrative procedure. If the requirement means what it says, then it defeats the reason for its being set up. It is viewed as a more convenient, accessible and effective method of investigating administrative lapses and abuses than the available legal procedure, with its long delays, technicality, injustice and inadequacy.

The procedure is under the control of a public complaints commission, made up of a chief commissioner and such number of commissioners as the supreme military council was to determine, all of whom are appointed and removed by the supreme military council, to whom also they are responsible. This is not to say that the supreme military council could direct them in the exercise of their functions. It is expressly declared that they shall not be subject to the direction or control of any person or authority (other than themselves) in the exercise of their powers.

The introduction of this procedure is a great advance in making public administration open, fair and accountable to the people. The interposition between the administration and the public of an independent and impartial body with power to investigate complaints of administrative abuses is something quite fundamental, deserving therefore to be incorporated in the basic law. The constitution drafting committee so recommended, but the constituent assembly surprisingly expunged it from the draft constitution prepared by the constitution drafting committee. The supreme military council in turn put it back by entrenching the Public Complaints Decree in the Constitution.

The fact that the commissioners owed their appointment and tenure and were responsible to the supreme military council shows that it is an instrument not of the head of state, but of that council. The commission is thus conceived in the character and role of an ombudsman. The provisions of the decree are yet to be adapted to bring them into conformity with the civilian, democratic government instituted by the 1979 Constitution. If the reference to the supreme military council is adapted to read national assembly, the character of commission as an ombudsman would have been confirmed. The backing of the authority of the national assembly is expected to impart more effectiveness to the work of the commission as a watchdog of the citizen's right against the administration. But the backing of the national assembly cannot be fully harnessed unless the findings and recommendations of the commission in each case are reported to it. An annual report containing a summary of the cases should also be laid before the assembly. Herein lies the shortcoming in the procedure in that the decree made no provision for any kind of reporting to the supreme military council, either in individual cases or by way of annual summaries.

Furthermore, the public should have access to the commission's report in individual cases, to the annual reports and to its proceedings. This is important if it is effectively to serve the role of making the administration accountable to the public. To leave it, as the decree does, in the 'absolute discretion' of a commissioner whether, and if so in what manner, he should notify the public of his action or intended action in any particular case is hardly calculated to promote public accountability.

(ii) *Trials*

Complaints of non-compliance with or breach of the code of conduct are to be tried by a code of conduct tribunal. The tribunal has a chairman and two other members. Its status is that of a superior court of record as regards appointment, removal and retirement of its members. The president appoints them acting in accordance with the recommendation of the judicial service commission. He may remove them only for inability or misconduct or for contravention of the code, and only on an address supported by two-thirds majority in each house of the national assembly. The jurisdiction of the tribunal is not exclusive of that of the courts where the conduct is also a criminal offence.

(iii) *Punishments, disciplinary penalties and remedial actions*

A public servant found guilty by the code of conduct tribunal of contravening the prohibitions of the code is liable to the following punishments or penalties —

(*a*) Vacation of office or seat in a legislative house. This provides a method of removal additional to the normal removal procedure provided in the Constitution or the statutes or regulations of the organisations concerned. It is unconstitutional to remove a civil servant or member of the police in any other way. The power given to the head of the federal military government or the state military governor by the Public Officers (Special Provisions) Decree 1976, to remove or retire compulsorily any public officer on the ground of his involvement in corruption, his inefficient or discreditable performance, or the need to facilitate improvements in the organisation of his department is inconsistent with the Constitution. Happily, the power expired on 31 December 1975 by the express terms of the decree itself.

The power of removal under the Public Officers (Special Provisions) Decree 1970, is conferred on the proper constitutional authorities, the public service commission, the police service commission and (in respect of the chief executives) the head of government, and accordingly is not unconstitutional. It enables the appropriate authority to remove or retire compulsorily a public officer found to have actively engaged or to have counselled, aided or abetted a hostile or subversive act or rebellion against any government in the federation between 15 January 1966 and 15 January 1970, or whose conduct during that period was such that his further or continued employment would not be in the public interest. Upon such removal or retirement the officer forfeits his right to pension, gratuity or compensation unless forfeiture is waived. There is however a right of appeal to the head of state.

(b) Disqualification from membership of a legislative house and from the holding of any public office for a period of not more than ten years.

(c) Forfeiture to the state of any property acquired in abuse or corruption of office. This constitutes an exception to the prohibition in s. 40(1) of the Constitution against the compulsory taking of movable or immovable property without prompt payment of compensation. The state cannot, therefore, on the ground of corruption or abuse of office, validly forfeit a public servant's movable or immovable property except on a finding, after due trial, by the code of conduct tribunal that he has committed a breach of the code. Forfeiture of such property on the order of the head of state or state governor following on the findings of a tribunal of enquiry under the Investigation of Assets (Public Officers and Other Persons) Decree, 1968, is now unconstitutional and void.

However, property other than what is movable or immovable, such as shares, bank accounts, negotiable securities and other choses in action, are not protected by the prohibition in s. 40(1), and accordingly may, without the order of the code of conduct tribunal, be forfeited by the government under the 1968 decree on the ground that they have been corruptly acquired.

Under the code of conduct, only property acquired in abuse or corruption of office may be forfeited. But the 1968 Decree enables other assets to be forfeited if those corruptly acquired are no longer subsisting either at all or in a form in which they could have been made the subject of a forfeiture order. It seems that this is within the spirit of the forfeiture authorised by the code. The decree also authorises the tracing of assets to the hands of third parties. Where the public servant concerned has no assets at all to be forfeited, and there are none to be traced to the hands of third parties, an order may nevertheless be made under the decree adjudging him liable to make reparations in such amount as may be specified. The order shall then be filed in the high court, and when so filed, it has the effect of a judgment of the court, and may be enforced in priority to all other debts of the public servant concerned.

None of the sanctions discussed above is available to the public complaints commission. All that the commission is authorised to do after its investigation into a complaint of administrative abuse is to make recommendations to the appropriate person or responsible administrative agency. It may recommend that the offending administrative or other act be reconsidered, modified or cancelled, that a regulation or ruling should be altered or that the complainant be furnished full reasons behind the act in question. It may also recommend disciplinary action or prosecution in appropriate cases. The commission ought to have been given power in appropriate cases to recommend also payment of compensation, restoration of property wrongfully taken or restoration in employment.

REFERENCES

1. *Alfred Dunhill of London Inc.* v. *Republic of Cuba* 24 May 1976, U.S. Supreme Court.
2. *Trendtex Trading Corpn. Ltd.* v. *Central Bank of Nigeria* [1977], 1 All E.R. 881; [1977] 1 Q.B. 529.
3. *Trendtex Trading Corpn. Ltd.* v. *Central Bank of Nigeria*, ibid., and the cases considered therein.
4. *Trendtex Trading Corpn. Ltd.* v. *Central Bank of Nigeria* [1976], 3 All E.R. 437.
5. [1977], 1 All E.R. 881 at 906.
6. *ibid.*, 907, per Shaw L.J.; see also the judgments of Stephenson L.J., 897−8; and Lord Denning M.R., 893−5.
7. See G.A.E. Longe, 'Preparing the Civil Servant for New Role', *Daily Times*, 27 & 29 January 1979.
8. See the Statutory Corporations Service Commission Decree 1968.
9. See the Statutory Corporations (Salaries & Allowances, etc.) Decree 1968.
10. See the Statutory Corporations Service Commission (Dissolution) Decree 1978.
11. Per Justice Douglas of the U.S. supreme court in *United Public Workers* v. *Mitchell* (1947), 330 U.S. 75 at 121−2.
12. Kwame Nkrumah, *Africa Must Unite* (1963), 89.
13. ibid., 89−90.
14. Julius Nyerere, 'How much Power for a Leader', *Africa Report* (1962), vol. 7, no. 7.
15. *United Public Workers* v. *Mitchell* (1947) 330 U.S. 75.
16. ibid., 96−7.
17. ibid., 108.
18. ibid., 115.
19. ibid., 111.
20. ibid., 125, n. 13.
21. ibid., 102.
22. ibid., 122.

21
CITIZENSHIP

Citizenship is derived from the concept of nationality. Every state has the right to define who its nationals are, for the purpose of according them protection and exacting obedience from them while they are in foreign countries. Nationality has thus primarily an international connotation. Citizenship, on the other hand, serves essentially a domestic purpose. A state may, in defining its nationals, distinguish for domestic purposes between different classes of them, extending to some the specific status of citizenship and denying it to others. International law does not, however, concern itself with the differentiations which any state deems it expedient to make between various classes of its nationals.

It follows from its primarily international character that nationality, together with citizenship, presupposes the status of a country as a state in international law. The state of Nigeria came into being on 1 October 1960, when the country achieved independence from Britain. Nigerian nationality is therefore a product of the birth of the Nigerian state. Previously, Nigeria was subsumed under the British state for the purposes of international relations, in consequence of which its natives bore the status of British nationals in international law, though under British domestic law they were either British citizens (if born in the former colony of Lagos) or British protected persons (if born in the former protectorate of Nigeria).[1]

The Nigerian Constitution of 1979 recognises only one class of nationals, namely citizens of Nigeria of whom there are three categories —

1. *The categories of citizenship*

(i) *Citizens by birth*

Citizenship by birth is used in the Constitution, not in its generally accepted sense of citizenship derived from the circumstance of birth in a country (jus soli), but rather in the special sense of citizenship acquired automatically at birth. Birth in Nigeria by itself alone confers no citizenship, as it does in many other countries, e.g. the United Kingdom. It needs to be combined with descent from a Nigerian citizen or indigene. More precisely, a person born in Nigeria is a citizen thereof only if (*a*) in the case of birth after the date of independence, any of his parents or grandparents is a citizen of Nigeria; and (*b*) in the case of birth before the date of independence, any of his parents or grandparents was born in Nigeria and belongs or belonged to a community indigenous to the country (s. 23). However, descent alone confers citizenship where a person is born outside Nigeria and either of his parents is a Nigerian citizen. Descent from a Nigerian parent carries therefore greater importance than birth within the country.

A parent or grandparent of a person is deemed to be a citizen of Nigeria if at the time of the birth of that person such parent or grandparent would have possessed that status by birth if he had been alive on the date of independence (s. 28).

These provisions assume a pre-existing status of a person as a Nigerian citizen; in other words, if, under the law as it stood immediately before 1 October 1979, a person is a citizen of Nigeria, whether by birth, descent, registration or naturalisation, his status as such is taken for granted as a criterion for his children or grandchildren being invested with Nigerian citizenship by birth under the new Constitution. To determine whether the parent or grandparent of a person is or was a citizen for the purposes of these provisions, therefore, the law as it stood immediately before 1 October 1979 may become relevant. This law is contained in the 1963 constitution and the Nigerian Citizenship Acts, 1960 and 1961, as amended. Under these enactments, every person born in Nigeria became a Nigerian citizen on 1 October 1960, provided that one of his parents or grandparents was also born in Nigeria and he was a citizen of the United Kingdom and Colonies or a British protected person on 30 September 1960.[2] A person born in Nigeria after 30 September 1960, also became a Nigerian citizen at birth unless (a) neither of his parents was a citizen of Nigeria and his father possessed such immunity from suit and legal process as is accorded to an envoy of a foreign sovereign power accredited to Nigeria; or (b) his father was an enemy alien and the birth occurred in a place then under occupation by the enemy.[3]

A person born outside Nigeria became a Nigerian citizen on 1 October 1960 if (a) he was a citizen of the United Kingdom and Colonies or a British protected person on 30 September 1960, and (b) his father was born in Nigeria and was a citizen of the United Kingdom and Colonies or a British protected person on 30 September 1960.[4] So also a person born outside Nigeria after 30 September 1960, became a Nigerian citizen at birth if his father is a citizen of Nigeria otherwise than by descent.[5]

As stated earlier, the provisions embraced any of the following if they had been duly registered as Nigerian citizens under the pre-existing law: (a) a person who was born in Nigeria and having the status of a citizen of the United Kingdom and Colonies or a British protected person on 30 September 1960, but who did not become a citizen of

Nigeria on 1 October 1960, because neither of his parents nor any of his grandparents was born in Nigeria, provided the application was made before 1 October 1962;[6] (b) a person born after 30 September 1960 outside Nigeria of a father who is a Nigerian citizen by descent only;[7] (c) a woman who is or has been married to a person who is a Nigerian citizen by birth or descent, or who would have become such but for his death before 1 October 1960, but the woman must herself be a citizen of the United Kingdom and Colonies or a British protected person;[8] (d) a woman who is a citizen of the United Kingdom and colonies or a British protected person and is or was married to a Nigerian citizen by registration under (a) above, or who, but for his death before 1 October 1960, would have been entitled to be so registered under (a) above, if in the first case application is made within twelve months (or such extended period as the minister might allow) after her husband's registration and in the latter case before 1 October 1962;[9] (e) any person who on 30 September 1960 became a citizen of the United Kingdom and Colonies by naturalisation or registration in Nigeria under the provisions of the British Nationality Act, 1948, provided the application for registration was made before 1 October 1962;[10] (f) citizens of the United Kingdom and Colonies, Canada, Australia, New Zealand, India, Pakistan, the Federation of Rhodesia and Nyasaland, Ceylon, Ghana, the Federation of Malaya, the State of Singapore, the Republic of Cyprus, Sierra Leone, Tanganyika, Jamaica, Trinidad and Tobago, and Uganda (all of whom were accorded the status of Commonwealth citizens);[11] citizens of the Republic of Ireland, and British protected persons.[12] A person in this category was not however entitled to be registered unless he satisfied the minister (i) that he was of good character; (ii) that he had a sufficient knowledge of a language in current use in Nigeria; and (iii) that he was ordinarily resident in Nigeria and had been so resident throughout the period of five years, or such shorter period as the minister might in special circumstances of a case accept, immediately preceding his application.

Also embraced in the provisions were any persons who had been granted certificate of naturalisation in accordance with the law as it existed immediately before 1 October 1979.[13]

(ii) *Citizens by registration*
The president is empowered to grant Nigerian citizenship by registration to two classes of persons, namely (a) a person of full age and capacity born outside Nigeria any of whose grandparents is a Nigerian citizen; and (b) a woman who is or has been married to a Nigerian citizen (s. 24). The grant can only be made on the president being satisfied as to the good character of the person and that he has shown a

clear intention of his desire to be domiciled in Nigeria and has taken the oath of allegiance.

(iii) *Citizens by naturalisation*

The president is also empowered on application made to him to grant Nigerian citizenship by naturalisation to any person who satisfies him that (*a*) he is a person of full age and capacity and of good character; (*b*) he has shown a clear intention of his desire to be domiciled in Nigeria; (*c*) he is, in the opinion of the governor of state where he is or proposes to be resident, acceptable to the local community in which he is to live permanently, and has been assimilated into the way of life of Nigerians in that part of the country; (*d*) he is a person who has made or is capable of making a useful contribution to the advancement, progress and wellbeing of Nigeria; (*e*) he has taken the oath of allegiance; and (*f*) he has, immediately preceding the date of his application, either (i) resided in Nigeria for a continuous period of fifteen years, or (ii) resided in Nigeria continuously for a period of twelve months, and during the period of twenty years immediately preceding that period of twelve months has resided in Nigeria for periods amounting in the aggregate to not less than fifteen years (s. 25).

2. *Loss of citizenship*

Citizenship of Nigeria may be lost either by operation of law or by deprivation by the president, depending on the class of citizenship. Citizenship by birth is regarded by the Constitution as an inalienable right beyond the power of the president to take away. A person cannot be deprived of it under any circumstances. It can only be lost by operation of law in the event of a person acquiring the citizenship of another country. This operates to forfeit the citizenship forthwith; even so, forfeiture takes place, not automatically in every case, but only if the person concerned failed to renounce the foreign citizenship within twelve months from 1 October 1979 (i.e. the date the new Constitution came into force) or twelve months from the date he attains the age of twenty-one years, whichever is later (s. 26[3]). It is thus only in the case of an adult becoming a foreign citizen after the twelve months' period from 1 October 1979 that forfeiture would take place automatically.

Citizenship both by registration and by naturalisation is conditional upon (*a*) effective renunciation, within twelve months of their grant, of the citizenship or nationality of any other country which the person concerned may have at the time of the grant; if the foreign citizenship is acquired after registration or naturalisation as a Nigerian citizen, the Nigerian citizenship is forfeited forthwith; (*b*) continued loyalty to Nigeria, with the consequence that they are liable to deprivation by the president if satisfied, from the records of proceedings of a court or other tribunal, or after due enquiry in accordance with regulations made by him, that the person concerned (i) has shown himself by act or speech to be disloyal towards the country; or (ii) has, during any war in which Nigeria was engaged, unlawfully traded with the enemy or been engaged in or associated with any business that was in the opinion of the president carried on in such a manner as to assist the enemy of Nigeria in that war, or unlawfully communicated with such enemy to the detriment of or with intent to cause damage to the interest of Nigeria.

Citizenship by naturalisation is also conditional upon good behaviour, with the further consequence that it may be revoked by the president if satisfied that the person concerned has within a period of seven years after becoming naturalised been sentenced to imprisonment for not less than three years.

3. *Status of citizens and aliens distinguished*

In general a citizen of Nigeria enjoys full legal capacity, which entitles him to all the rights and privileges bestowed by the law. (Disabilities or special privileges may however be imposed or conferred on the grounds of infancy, sex, insanity, bankruptcy etc.) He is entitled to the protection of the state both within and without its territory. Correlative to his right of protection is his duty of allegiance to the state. Allegiance obliges a citizen to be obedient and faithful to the commands and authority of the state under whose protection he is. And since the protection accorded by a state to its nationals is extra-territorial, the citizen's duty of obedience and fidelity to the criminal law of his state, particularly the duty imposed by the law of treason, is also extraterritorial. In other words, a Nigerian citizen who, while in a foreign country, commits an offence against the criminal law of Nigeria is liable to be prosecuted for it in the Nigerian courts. A non-citizen, on the other hand, is entitled to protection only while he is within the country but not outside it, and his duty of obedience is also correspondingly limited. While in Nigeria therefore he is fully amenable to its criminal law to the same extent as a citizen, but he ceases to be so amenable for acts or omissions committed by him outside Nigeria.

Apart from protection, a non-citizen does not have within Nigeria the full rights of a citizen. He is subject to disability in various respects. He can neither exercise the franchise nor be a candidate for any elective office. He may be employed in the service of the government, though the government's Nigerianisation policy requires that a noncitizen should not be employed when there are Nigerians qualified and competent to be so employed. Certain business enterprises are completely barred to him, while he needs the partnership or association of Nigerians in order to engage in other businesses, but even so his participation is limited to a prescribed percentage of the capital of the business. He is also subject to disability in regard to entry into Nigeria, residence, movement, occupation and other activities, and deportation.

(i) *Entry*
While a citizen has a right to enter Nigeria at any time (s. 38), a non-citizen cannot do so as of right, but only under a permit issued by an immigration officer.[14] If the purpose of the entry is for residence, a special residence permit must be obtained from the chief immigration officer who may decline to issue it if he is not satisfied, on information supplied by the immigrant, that it is expedient so to do.[15] An alien entering Nigeria for the purpose of residence must also give security in such amount as the appropriate federal minister may prescribe.[16] Before accepting any employment (other than employment with the federal government or a state government), he must obtain the consent in writing of the chief immigration officer, nor can he, on his own account or in partnership with any other person, practise a profession or establish or take over any trade or business (including business carried on by a limited company) without the consent of the minister given on such conditions as to the locality of operation and persons to be employed in the business as the minister may prescribe.[17]

Immigration officers may prohibit an immigrant (who is not a Nigerian citizen) from entering Nigeria on the ground, *inter alia*, that he is a prohibited immigrant, or has no current visa (where one is required), or where a medical officer so advises for medical reasons. The categories of persons designated as prohibited immigrants include a person who is without visible means of support, or who is likely to become a public charge; an idiot or insane person; a person convicted in any country of an extraditable offence within the meaning of the Extradition Act; and a person whose admission would in the opinion of a minister of state be contrary to the interest of national security.[18] The federal minister in charge of immigration is given power to add to the categories of prohibited immigrants, and may absolutely prohibit the entry into Nigeria of any person or class of persons, whether falling within the categories of prohibited immigrants or not, if he deems it conducive to the public good.[19]

(ii) *Restriction on residence, movement etc.*
The Immigration (Control of Aliens) Regulations 1963[20] made under the Immigration Act 1963 provide for the appointment of a chief aliens officer for the whole country and an aliens officer for each

province in the federation. They also provide for both a central register of aliens, to be maintained by the chief aliens officer, and a provincial register under the charge of the aliens officer of each province. When an alien arrives in Nigeria for a visit lasting twenty-eight days or more, the immigration officer must report the fact of the arrival to the chief aliens officer (departure must likewise be reported). An alien arriving in Nigeria must immediately register himself with the aliens officer of the province in which he is staying, and for this purpose must furnish particulars as to his full names and sex; present nationality; profession or occupation; date, place and mode of arrival in Nigeria; photograph; particulars of passport or other document establishing nationality or identity; signature; and fingerprints if required. After registration, the alien is given a registration certificate which he must produce whenever required to do so. A copy of the particulars so registered will then be forwarded by the provincial aliens officer to the chief aliens officer together with such other information as may be required for the alien's identification, registration and control. The owner or manager of an hotel or other premises where lodging or sleeping accommodation is provided for payment must keep a register of aliens staying there and may be required to make a daily return of these registered particulars to the aliens officer of the province.

Before changing his address, an alien must give at least seven days' notice of his intention to do so to the aliens officer of his province, and if the change involves moving to another province, the alien must on arrival there report himself to the aliens officer of the new province and submit to him for examination his passport, residence permit, certificate of registration and full particulars of his residential and postal addresses. An alien cannot travel away from his home for a period of seven days or more unless prior information of the intended destination is given to the aliens officer of his province. Furthermore, the chief aliens officer may, by notice in writing addressed to any particular alien, require him to report his movements to an aliens officer or a police officer, and to notify the aliens officer of his province of his intention to be absent from home for more than twenty-four hours; the notice may also require him to obtain a permit before undertaking a journey of more than 30 miles and to report his arrival at his destination to an aliens officer.

An alien found committing an offence or reasonably suspected of having committed one against the regulations may be arrested without warrant by any aliens officer, customs officer, immigration officer or police officer; and premises in which it is reasonably believed the offence is being committed may be searched without warrant by an aliens officer or by a police officer authorised by an aliens officer or by a superior police officer.

(iii) Deportation

A citizen of Nigeria cannot be deported out of the country, but there are wide powers vested in the minister to order the deportation of non-citizens. There are three circumstances in which a non-citizen may become liable to deportation. First, if the minister is satisfied that the public interest so requires, he may order any non-citizen to be deported as a prohibited immigrant. It is not a condition of the exercise of the minister's power in this respect that the deportee should have been prosecuted for an offence, and the minister's order cannot be challenged on any ground whatever.[21] Secondly, the minister may from time to time by notice direct that persons within any category specified in the notice entering Nigeria otherwise than by sea or air shall be liable to deportation as prohibited immigrants without the intervention of any court.[22] The minister has directed that all immigrants entering Nigeria by inland water or overland (i.e. otherwise than by sea or air) and who fail to report to an immigration officer at the nearest port shall be liable to deportation as prohibited immigrants.[23] And thirdly, the minister may make an order of deportation against a non-citizen who, on conviction for a criminal offence punishable by imprisonment without the option of a fine, is recommended for deportation by the court convicting or sentencing him, but an order of deportation is not to be made until after the abandonment or determination of any appeal that may properly have been lodged.[24] A non-citizen against whom a deportation order has been made may, instead of being actually sent out of the country, be detained in custody if the minister considers his deportation to be impracticable or prejudicial to the efficient prosecution of any war in which Nigeria may be engaged and that the detention is necessary or expedient for securing public safety, the defence of the realm or maintenance of public order.[25] The employer of a person subject to a deportation order is liable to indemnify the government against the expenses incurred in the transportation and maintenance of the deportee.[26]

(iv) Extradition

It is necessary to distinguish deportation from extradition, to which both a citizen and an alien may be subject, depending on the terms of the extradition arrangement between Nigeria and any particular foreign country. Extradition is a practice whereby a person who has fled to a country after committing a crime or being convicted in another country may be sent back to the latter country to stand his trial or to serve his sentence. Because, in the absence of grant, no state is able to exercise any kind of jurisdiction within the territory of another state, a fugitive criminal is placed beyond the reach of the state on whose territory the crime was committed once he has escaped from it, hence the need for the re-capture of such an offender to have the consent of the country of refuge, expressed in the form of a treaty or other agreement. But the 'need for extradition is recognised by practically all civilised states as a matter both of morality and expediency; of morality since mankind deprecates escape from the consequences of, at all events, serious crimes; of expediency in that no state desires to become a haven of refuge for the underworld'.[27]

The extradition of fugitive criminals from Nigeria to foreign countries is governed by the Extradition Decree 1966. The authority of the decree can be invoked only in respect of countries with which Nigeria has subsisting extradition arrangements, and to which the provisions of the decree have been applied by order in the gazette. The decree applies by its own force to every country in the Commonwealth and no extradition agreement or order is necessary for the purpose, but its application to any Commonwealth country may be modified if the law of that country no longer contains substantially equivalent provisions. The direct application of the decree to Commonwealth countries does not preclude the conclusion of an extradition agreement with any of them; in that case, the decree will no longer apply to that country by its own force but by virtue of and in accordance with the agreement and the order applying it.

(v) *Diplomatic immunity*

There is a class of aliens whom the law treats with special favour, namely those entitled to diplomatic immunity. Not only are they not subject to some of the disabilities attaching to aliens, but they enjoy special privileges and immunities not possessed by citizens. Diplomatic immunity is governed partly by the common law, which accepts and acts upon the principle of international law that a state and its head and accredited foreign representative ought not to be impleaded in the courts of another country.[28] This common law rule has been confirmed by statute, the Diplomatic Immunities and Privileges Act 1962[29] which has also extended the classes of persons covered by the immunity. The persons entitled to immunity are (*a*) a foreign envoy and a foreign consular officer, the members of their families (i.e. wife and children), the members of their official or domestic staff and their families;[30] (*b*) the chief representative of a Commonwealth country and his family, members of his official and domestic staff and their families;[31] (*c*) representatives of the governments of Commonwealth countries attending conferences in Nigeria and members of their staff;[32] (*d*) organisations declared by the minister for external affairs to be international organisations; persons representing any organ of such organisation, and such high officials of the organisation as may be specified, together with the families of such representatives and high officials; persons employed on mission on behalf of the organisation as are specified, and junior officers;[33] (e) Section 12 enables the minister from time to time by order to confer on the judges and registrars of the international court of justice established by the charter of the United Nations, and on suitors to that court and their agents, counsel, and advocates, such immunities, privileges, and facilities as may be required to give effect to any resolution of, or convention approved by the General Assembly of the United Nations. The minister may also by notice in the gazette confer immunity on representatives of foreign governments attending a conference in Nigeria.[34] It should be mentioned that a Nigerian member of the staffs of the persons enumerated above are not entitled to immunity.[35]

The immunity accorded to these classes of non-citizens is immunity from suit and legal process and inviolability of residence and official archives, but its extent is not the same between all persons entitled to it. To begin with, the exact effect of this immunity is not clear. On one view, it might be said that the mere issue of a writ for the commencement of an action against a person enjoying immunity is void.[36] The better view seems to be, however, that the mere issue of a writ is only voidable by the person covered by the immunity who may either avoid it by pleading his immunity or submit to jurisdiction by waiving his immunity.[37] However, the issue of any process for the arrest or imprisonment of a person enjoying immunity or for the seizure or attachment of his goods is declared to be absolutely void,[38] but a member of the official or domestic staff of a foreign envoy or consular officer or the chief representative of a Commonwealth country is not immune from arrest unless his name was, before the arrest, recorded with the minister.[39] Another difference in the extent of the immunity enjoyed by the different classes of persons is that while an envoy, consular officer or chief representative of a Commonwealth country is immune from liability and from the law relating to bankruptcy or insolvency for his trading activities, members of his official and domestic staff are not.[40] The immunity of the junior officer of an international organisation extends only to immunity from suit and legal process in respect of things done or omitted to be done in the course of the performance of their official duties.[41]

As regards privileges, the minister of finance is empowered to grant exemption from taxation, including stamp duties, death duty, customs and excise duty, etc., to persons enjoying immunity. There are other concessions that may be made to international organisation.[42] Again, a junior officer of an international organisation is entitled to exemption only from taxes in respect of emolument received as an officer or servant of the organisation and from taxes on the importation of furniture and effects imported at the time he first took up his post in Nigeria.[43]

REFERENCES

1. This is only a generalisation. For details, see ss. 4, 5 and 32, British Nationality Act 1948; also the British Protectorates, Protectoral States Order in Council 1934.
2. s. 7(1), Constitution of the Federation (1963), s. 7(1).
3. ibid., s. 11.
4. ibid., s. 7(2).
5. ibid., s. 12.
6. ibid., s. 8(1); also Nigerian Citizenship Act 1960, s. 3A.
7. Nigerian Citizenship Act 1960, s. 3(2).
8. Constitution of the Federation (1963), s. 8(2), Nigerian Citizenship Act 1961, s. 3B.
9. Constitution of the Federation (1963), s. 8(3) and (4); Nigerian Citizenship Act 1961, ss. 3C and 3D.
10. Constitution of the Federation (1963), s. 9; Nigerian Citizenship Act 1961, s. 3E.
11. Constitution of the Federation (1963), s. 14.
12. Nigerian Citizenship Act 1960 s. 3(5)(a). Power was given to the president to add to the list of countries enumerated.
13. Nigerian Citizenship Act 1960, s. 6, and Second Schedule.
14. Immigration Act 1963, s. 1(2), which repeals the Immigration Act, Cap. 84, 1958 Laws; Aliens Restriction Act, Cap. 10 and the Aliens (Deportation) Act, Cap. 9. The provisions of the 1963 Act as to entry, residence and Immigration (Special Provisions) Decree 1969.
15. ibid., s. 9.
16. ibid.
17. ibid., s. 8(1).
18. ibid., s. 17.
19. ibid., s. 17(2).
20. See also Aliens Restriction Regs. made under the Aliens Restriction Law (W.R.), Cap. 4.
21. s. 18(2) Immigration Act 1963, s. 18(2).
22. ibid., s. 24(1).
23. L.N. 92 of 1963.
24. ibid., s. 20(1) s. 233A of the Criminal Code, Cap. 42 and s. 476 of the Penal Code (N. Region) Federal Provisions Act, 1960, prescribe deportation as the punishment for certain offences; in those cases no recommendation by the court is necessary after conviction.
25. ibid., s. 44.
26. ibid., s. 20(3).
27. Wade and Phillip, *Constitutional Law*, 6th edn, 245.
28. See Lord Atkin in *The Cristina* [1938] A.C. 485; also Brett L.J. in *The Parlement Belge* (1880), 5 P.D. 197.

29. Replacing the Diplomatic Immunities and Privileges (Commonwealth countries and Republic of Ireland) Act, Cap. 58, Laws 1958; the Diplomatic Privileges (Extension) Act, Cap. 53, Laws 1958. It appears that the Diplomatic Privileges Act 1708, is also in force in Nigeria as a statute of general application, but the act, which is very limited in scope, is merely declaratory of the common law; see D.C. Holland, *Diplomatic Immunity in English Law* (1951), 'Current Legal Problem', 81.

30. Diplomatic Immunities and Privileges Act 1962, s. 1(1).
31. ibid., ss. 3 and 4.
32. ibid., s. 6.
33. ibid., s. 11. As Holland remarked the use of the word "diplomatic" in relation to international organisations is perhaps inapt since they are not concerned with diplomatic purposes, op. cit., 90−1.
34. ibid., s. 13.
35. ibid., s. 10.
36. *Musurus Bey* v. *Gadban* [1894], 2 Q.B. 352.
37. Holland, op. cit., 94. An ambassador or the chief representative of a Commonwealth country cannot waive his immunity without the consent of his government, but he can waive the immunity of a member of his family, and members of his official and domestic staff and their families, without the like consent: ibid., s. 2.
38. ibid., s. 1(2); waiver of immunity down to judgment will not enable execution to be levied unless immunity from execution is also waived.
39. ibid., s. 1(3)(*a*).
40. Ibid., s. 1(3)(*b*).
41. ibid., s. 11.
42. As to which see Schedule to the Act.
43. ibid., s. 11.

22
RIGHT TO LIFE AND DIGNITY OF THE HUMAN PERSON

1. *The constitutional guarantee*

The Constitution declares that 'every person has a right to life', and then goes on to secure the right by prohibiting intentional (as distinct from accidental) deprivation of life, 'save in execution of the sentence of a court in respect of a criminal offence of which [a person] has been found guilty in Nigeria' (s. 30[1]). Any law authorising intentional killing in violation of the Constitution, whether by the agents of the government or by private individuals, is therefore void. The Constitution, however, recognises that intentional killing might be justified in certain circumstances, and so provides that a person is not to be regarded as having been deprived of his life in violation of the guarantee 'if he dies as a result of the use, to such extent and in such circumstances as are permitted by law, of such force as is reasonably necessary

(*a*) for the defence of any person from unlawful violence or for the defence of property;

(*b*) in order to effect a lawful arrest or to prevent the escape of a person lawfully detained; or

(*c*) for the purpose of suppressing a riot, insurrection or mutiny' (s. 30[2]).

It is important to emphasise that the Constitution sanctions intentional killing for the specified purposes only where the killing results from the use of force in circumstances and to an extent permitted by the ordinary law. The scope permitted by law of self-defence as a justification for intentional killing varies between the Southern and Northern states. The Criminal Code applicable in the South requires that in the case of death inflicted in self-defence against assault, the assault must be reasonably apprehended to cause death or grievous harm and that such death or grievous harm cannot be prevented in any other way.[1] Killing in defence of property is restricted to the defence of a dwelling-house against thieves by a person in peaceable occupation of it and persons lawfully assisting him, provided that no more force is used than is reasonably necessary.[2]

The Penal Code in force in the Northern states permits killing if it occurred in the course of private defence of the body against an attack which causes reasonable apprehension of death or grievous hurt, against the commission of rape or of an assault with the intention of gratifying unnatural lust or abduction or kidnapping; or in the course of private defence of property against robbery, house-breaking by night, mischief by fire committed on any building, tent or vessel used for dwelling or as a place for the custody of property, or theft, mischief or house-trespass in such circumstances as may reasonably cause apprehension that, if such right of private defence is not exercised, death or grievous hurt will be the consequence — provided in every case than the force used is not more than is necessary.[3]

Killing for the purpose of effecting a lawful arrest is limited to cases where a person who has committed a felony punishable with death or imprisonment for at least seven years, takes to flight in order to avoid a peace officer (i.e. a magistrate or any police officer of or above the rank of assistant superintendent) or police officer coming to arrest him, but it has to be shown that the arrest could not be otherwise effected, and that the offence is one for which the victim could have been arrested without warrant.[4] It is a condition for the legality of killing for the purpose of preventing the escape of a person lawfully detained that the force used is reasonably necessary, and that the offence which he is alleged to have committed is one for which he could be arrested without warrant.[5]

The circumstances in which killing is permitted by law for the purpose of suppressing a riot or insurrection are that a proclamation has first to be made by a peace officer (as defined above) commanding the rioters to disperse peaceably;[6] if after a reasonable time there are still twelve or more people riotously assembled together, he may take action to disperse them and, if resistance is offered, he and any persons assisting him may use force as reasonably necessary for overcoming it; any death resulting from the use of such force is justified.[7]

Finally, the master of a ship or any person acting by his order may justifiably kill anyone involved in a mutiny on board the ship if the safety of the ship or of persons therein cannot be otherwise secured.[8]

Dignity of the human person is guaranteed by an affirmation of the right to it and by the prohibition of torture and of inhuman or degrading treatment (s. 31[1]). The wider import of the word 'treatment' needs to be emphasised. It is not restricted to punishment imposed by a court following upon a conviction for a criminal offence. Also embraced within its meaning is treatment meted out to people in police custody and those serving prison terms. Imprisonment pursuant to a court order does not deprive the convict of his constitutional right not to be subjected to torture or other inhuman or degrading treatment while in prison.

Dignity of the human person is further protected by the prohibition of slavery, servitude and forced labour (s. 31[1]), except where such labour (a) is required in consequence of the sentence or order of a court; or (*b*) is reasonably necessary in the event of any emergency or calamity threatening the life or wellbeing of the community; or (*c*) forms part of normal communal or other civic obligations for the wellbeing of the community.

Except to the extent just indicated, the guarantee of the dignity of the human person is not subject to abridgement at all by the state in the interest of defence, public safety or public order, either in normal times or during an emergency; the guarantee of the right to life is also not so subject except for killing resulting from an act of war.

2. *Constitutionality of the death penalty*

The exceptions to the guarantee of the right to life which have been considered above present no problem, since the purposes which provide justification for them are specifically set out in the Constitution, leaving only the extent of permissible force and the circumstances for its application to be prescribed by ordinary law. But the power of the state to prescribe death as a punishment for a criminal offence needs to be considered in the light of the constitutional right to the dignity of the human person which is sanctioned by a prohibition against torture and inhuman or degrading treatment (s. 31[1][*d*]). In view of this, is it constitutionally permissible for the state to prescribe death for any criminal offence that it likes? And is death a permissible punishment at all for any criminal offence?

Admittedly, the constitutional guarantee of the right to life is subject to an express saving in favour of a death sentence ordered by a court as punishment following on a conviction for a criminal offence. Yet this fact does not foreclose the questions posed above. The power of a court to impose a death sentence depends on the constitutional validity of the law authorising killing as a punishment for crime, which in turn depends on whether or in what circumstances the death penalty may be an inhuman or degrading punishment. The U.S. Supreme Court has accepted, quite rightly, that the power of the legislature to authorise the death penalty for crime is not exempted from the constitutional prohibition against cruel and unusual punishments merely because the Constitution provides elsewhere that 'no person shall be held to answer for a capital . . . crime, unless on a presentment or indictment of a Grand Jury; nor shall any person be subject for the same offence to be twice put in jeopardy of *life* . . .; nor be deprived of *life* . . . without due process of law.'[8]

The Court also refused to infer that the framers of the Constitution intended to exempt the death penalty from the prohibition against cruel and unusual punishments because the death penalty was common and recognised by law at the time the prohibition was adopted. In the Nigerian situation, it is significant that the 1979 Constitution omitted the provision in the 1963 Constitution which expressly exempted any punishment that was lawful and customary in any part of Nigeria on 1 November 1959, and recognised as reasonably justifiable any amount of force authorised by law as at that date. It may be concluded therefore that a law authorising killing as a punishment for crime following on conviction and sentence by a court is unconstitutional and void if the death penalty is an inhuman or degrading punishment in all cases or for a particular offence or because of the method by which it is inflicted.

While it is recognised that what is inhuman or degrading punishment is difficult to define precisely, certain guiding principles are discernible from decisions of the U.S. supreme court on the matter.[9] These principles take into account both the inherent nature of a particular punishment, its length or severity, and the method used to carry it out. Taking these elements into account, the general principle is that a punishment that denies a person status as a human being or which degrades his personality as a human being is inhuman. All the other principles are derived from this basic one.

First, any punishment involving torture, such as the rack, the thumbscrew, the iron boot, the stretching of limbs, burning alive or at the stake, crucifixion, breaking on the wheel, embowelling alive, beheading, public dissection and the like, or involving mutilation or a lingering death, or the infliction of acute pain and suffering, either physical or mental, is inherently inhuman and degrading. Such punishments are constitutionally prohibited regardless of whether public sentiment favours them or not. Thus, to deprive a natural-born citizen of his citizenship by reason of a conviction by court-martial for wartime desertion has been held to involve such acute mental suffering as makes it 'more cruel and more primitive than torture' in that it renders the person concerned stateless, which entails 'the total destruction of the individual's status in organised society'.[10] Corporal punishment by flogging or caning is degrading because of the acute physical pain it inflicts, and has for this reason been held to be constitutionally impermissible.[11] Particularly so is the type of corporal punishment known as *haddi* or symbolic lashing which is in use in the Northern states of Nigeria: the difference between it and caning is that while the object of caning is the infliction of physical pain on the offender, the purpose of *haddi* lashing is to expose to disgrace. Also, not more than twelve strokes could be awarded in the case of caning, but there is theoretically no limit to the number of symbolic lashings that might be ordered, and the ordering of as many as 100 or more has been known. With the omission from the 1979 Constitution of the provision in the 1963 Constitution sanctioning any punishment that was lawful and customary in any part of Nigeria on 1 November 1959, both caning and *haddi* lashing as punishments for crime stand invalidated by the constitutional prohibition against inhuman or degrading treatment.

Secondly, notwithstanding that a punishment is not inhuman or degrading by its very nature or by its mode of execution, and notwithstanding that popular sentiment may favour it, a punishment must not be excessive in the sense of being, by its length or severity, disproportionate or unnecessarily harsh in relation to the offence for which it is prescribed. The entire thrust of the constitutional guarantee, it has been said, is against 'that which is excessive'.[12] The infliction of a punishment for the offence of falsifying official records of fifteen years' imprisonment with hard labour under shackles, followed by perpetual surveillance, loss of voting rights, loss of the right to hold public office, and loss of the right to change domicile freely was held to be unnecessarily severe.[13] A punishment is also unnecessary and therefore excessive if it does not serve more effectively than a less severe one any of the permissible purposes of punishment, such as deterrence, isolation, and rehabilitation.[14] A punishment may also be unnecessary simply because it is a punishment. A person is not to be punished for being 'mentally ill, or a leper, or . . . afflicted with a venereal disease'; the imposition of imprisonment for ninety days following upon a conviction for being addicted to narcotics was thus held to be unconstitutional and void.[15] Punishment in these circumstances is degrading because 'to inflict punishment for having a disease is to treat the individual as a diseased thing rather than as a sick human being. That the punishment is not severe "in the abstract" is irrelevant.'[16] For, 'even one day in prison would be a cruel and unusual punishment for the "crime" of having a common cold.'[17]

Thirdly, a punishment may be regarded as not comporting with human dignity if it is unacceptable to contemporary society. Acceptability may be inferred from the fact that the punishment has been widely used in the past and at the present time, although past usage is not conclusive of present acceptance. If there are objective indicators from which it may be concluded that society considers a punishment unacceptable because of its severity, then that may be a basis for regarding it as not comporting with human dignity. This principle implies a concept of an inhuman or degrading treatment as a changing rather than a static one. It is a concept which, in the words of the U.S. supreme court, 'must draw its meaning from the evolving standards of decency that mark the progress of a maturing society.'[18] What was morally acceptable in the past may therefore be abhorrent to the moral values of today's society. Thus the acceptability of a punishment needs to be continually re-examined in the light of society's changing moral outlook; a judicial decision that a particular punishment is not inhuman or degrading is accordingly not binding as precedent, as otherwise the meaning of the phrase will have become fixed and immutable for all times.[19]

Lastly, a severe punishment implies a denial of a person's status as a human being if, instead of being applied generally across the board, it is selectively or discriminately inflicted against a class or group to which he belongs. 'It is cruel and unusual', said Justice Douglas, 'to apply the death penalty — or any other penalty — selectively to minorities whose numbers are few, who are outcasts of society, and who are unpopular, but whom society is willing to see suffer though it would not countenance general application of the same penalty across the board.'[20] It was on this ground that the U.S. supreme court, by a majority of 5−4, held unconstitutional and void a death sentence imposed on three negroes, one for murder and the two others for rape, under a law that left it in the discretion of the judge or jury whether to impose the death sentence or a lesser punishment in any particular case. The evidence showed that the discretion had been exercised in a discriminatory manner against blacks, the poor and the ignorant and in favour of the wealthy. The majority therefore held that, because of the discretion given to the jury to select death or another penalty as they liked, and because the selection had been done in a discriminatory manner against blacks, the imposition of the death sentence against these three black defendants constituted cruel and unusual punishment in violation of the Eighth and Fourteenth Amendments to the U.S. Constitution.[21]

It is of course to be expected, as the court recognised, that a decision that a particular punishment is degrading or inhuman may involve the application of more than one of these principles. For it is seldom that a democratically-elected legislature operating under a democratic constitution will prescribe a punishment of which it can conclusively be said that it is fatally offensive even under one of the principles.

It is in the light of these principles that the constitutionality of the death penalty has to be determined. The question has been before the supreme court of the United States four times — in 1879, 1890, 1947 and 1972.[22] On the three earlier occasions, the constitutionality of the death sentence was taken for granted, the only issue for decision being whether the methods used to carry it out were constitutionally permissible. But although the point did not arise for decision, some of the judgments contained affirmations of the constitutionality of the death penalty. In the first case, the court unanimously upheld a sentence of public execution by the firing squad imposed pursuant to a conviction for premeditated murder.[23] The second case upheld electrocution as a permissible mode of inflicting the death penalty.[24] In the third case, a second attempt at electrocution was upheld after the first had proved unsuccessful owing to mechanical failure which resulted in the defendant not dying when the current first passed through him.[25]

Only in the last of the cases was the constitutionality of the death penalty itself, as opposed to the mode of its execution, squarely and explicitly raised and dealt with in a judgment covering nearly 250 pages.[26] As already noted, the case was decided on the narrow ground that the death penalty as applied in this case violated the prohibition against cruel and unusual punishments, and was therefore void. Of the five justices in the majority, three found it unnecessary to reach the ultimate question whether the death penalty is constitutionally impermissible *in all circumstances*, though at the same time acknowledging that a strong case has been made out against the death penalty.[27] The two remaining majority justices held the death penalty to be *per se* unconstitutional as a violation of the prohibition against cruel and unusual punishments, and went to great lengths to demonstrate the point by reference to the principles stated above. Death, they asserted, necessarily involves the infliction of severe physical pain and suffering, and there appears to be no method available that guarantees an immediate and painless death. But more important even than the physical pain is the mental suffering. The process of carrying out a death sentence, with the inevitable long wait between the imposition of sentence and the actual infliction of death, is 'often so degrading and brutalising to the human spirit as to constitute psychological torture',[28] and in many cases to lead to insanity.[29]

Reviewing the history of the death penalty in the United States and a mass of statistics and other data on the subject, the judgment noted the changes that have taken place in the modes of execution from the gallows and the firing squad to the more humane methods of electrocution and the gas chamber; the drastic decline in the crimes punishable with death from about sixty to four for all practical purposes — murder, treason, kidnapping and rape (as late as 1800 in England, capital offences numbered more than 200); the decline in death sentences actually carried out, the national average being about fifty a year in a population of 200 million people (the figures were as low as twenty-one in 1963, fifteen in 1964, seven in 1965 and one in 1966); the unwillingness of juries to convict for capital offences, which led to the legislatures making its imposition discretionary rather than mandatory as before; and the partial or complete abolition of the punishment in as many as thirteen States in the country (the punishment was abolished but later restored in eight other States, and a bill to abolish it for all federal offences was killed in committee). These changes, they concluded, provide strong enough objective indication that the death penalty is today unacceptable to contemporary American society. It is noteworthy, too, that the death penalty has been abolished in seventy other jurisdictions outside the United States.

On the question whether the death sentence serves any penal purpose more effectively than imprisonment, the two justices noted that the controversy in the nation over the punishment has been waged largely on the basis of two different moral approaches to punishment — the 'ancient and deeply rooted beliefs in retribution, atonement or vengeance on the one hand, and, on the other, beliefs in the personal value and dignity of the common man that were born of the democratic movement of the eighteenth century, as well as beliefs in the scientific approach to an understanding of the motive forces of human conduct, which are the result of the growth of the sciences of behaviour during the nineteenth and twentieth centuries.'[30] The data indicate that American jurisprudence has always accepted deterrence, . . . isolation of dangerous persons and rehabilitation as proper goals of punishment. Retaliation, vengeance and retribution have been roundly condemned as intolerable aspirations for a government in a free society. Punishment as retribution has been condemned by scholars for centuries, and the Eighth Amendment itself was adopted to prevent punishment from becoming synonymous with vengeance.'[31]

In their judgment the evidence is clear and convincing that capital punishment is not necessary as a deterrent to crime in the country, nor does it serve any other permissible penal purpose more effectively than life imprisonment. On the contrary, the finality of death rules out rehabilitation completely. Death destroys a person's very existence, with all the rights inherent in human existence, including the right to relief where conviction and sentence have been wrongly imposed. By its very nature, therefore, the calculated killing of a human being by the state involves a denial of the person's humanity.

While expressing abhorrence of the death penalty and a desire for its abolition, the four dissenting justices maintained that the punishment is not barred by the constitutional prohibition against cruel and unusual punishments, and that, accordingly, abolition can constitutionally be accomplished, not by judicial action but by legislation, which 'in a democracy is presumed to embody the basic standards of decency prevailing in the society. This presumption can only be negated by unambiguous and compelling evidence of legislative default. There are no obvious indications that capital punishment offends the conscience of society to such a degree that our traditional deference to the legislative judgment must be abandoned.'[32]

In their view death only becomes a cruel punishment when inflicted by torture or other methods involving extreme cruelty; the cruelty has to be extreme to make death constitutionally impermissible as a punishment for crime. But in the absence of extreme cruelty, the mere extinguishing of life is not cruel in the constitutional sense. An extreme cruelty is defined as something of the same order as torture, something so inhumane as to be abhorrent to society's standards of decency. However intractable it may be to articulate, the standard of extreme cruelty, they maintained, is what the Eighth Amendment requires. They rejected the principle that there is cruelty if the punishment is disproportionate to the offence or is unnecessary in the sense of serving no legitimate penal purpose that cannot be served equally effectively by a less severe punishment, arguing that the purposes of punishment do not lend themselves to precise measurement, and that in prescribing a penalty, a legislature is not required by the Eighth Amendment to make it proportionate to the offence; nor is the Amendment intended to purge the penal law of its retributive elements.

It seems that the analysis of principles and the conclusions arrived at by the two justices in the majority are more relevant to the Nigerian constitutional provision than those of the four dissenting justices. The U.S. Constitution makes no such explicit affirmation of the right to respect for the dignity of the human person as is contained in the Nigerian Constitution, and a cruel punishment would appear to have a narrower reference than inhuman or degrading treatment. The Nigerian provision speaks, not of *inhumane* punishment but of inhuman treatment, by which must be meant treatment which, even if not necessarily cruel, does not accord with human dignity. And even assuming that the word 'inhuman' can be equated with cruel in the sense of the American Constitution, the word 'degrading' is unquestionably more far-reaching in its connotation. Flogging, for example, is today universally admitted to be degrading, yet as a punishment for robbery or murder it cannot be said to be cruel, especially if a cruel punishment is construed to be something of the same order as torture. The death penalty, viewed as retribution for murder, may well not be cruel in the constitutional sense, but it is inhuman to terminate human existence by killing, and the fact that it is inflicted as a punishment for crime does not make it any less so. If it is not inhuman, and even if some method of making it completely painless could be devised, it is still degrading, and therefore a violation of the constitutional prohibition against degrading treatment.

Aside from the constitutionality or otherwise of the death penalty, the modes by which it is executed in Nigeria, namely hanging and the firing squad, are questionable on constitutional grounds. Although public execution by shooting was upheld by the U.S. supreme court in 1879,[33] it is today viewed with such abhorrence by American society that it has had to be abandoned. As was said in the 1972 case, 'no longer does our society countenance the spectacle of public executions, once thought desirable as a deterrent to criminal behaviour by others. Today we reject public executions as debasing and brutalizing to us all.'[34] Being so clearly degrading, public executions are outlawed under the Nigerian Constitution. In the United States, even executions in private by shooting and hanging have also virtually ceased since the development of the supposedly more humane methods of electrocution late in the nineteenth century and lethal gas in the twentieth century.[35]

It is sad that in an age when the trend in most countries has been towards a reduction in the number of capital offences and a partial or complete abolition of the death penalty, the military government of Nigeria should have extended capital punishment to offences relating to armed robbery, kidnapping, counterfeiting of the currency, disruption of the production and distribution of petroleum products and offences against public order — in addition to the existing capital offences of murder, treason and treachery.

REFERENCES

1. Criminal Code, ss. 286 and 287.
2. ibid., s. 202.
3. Penal Code 1959, ss. 60, 65 and 66.
4. Criminal Code, s. 271.
5. ibid., s. 273.
6. ibid. s. 72.; Criminal Procedure Code (Northern States), s. 101.
7. s. 73, Criminal Code, s. 73; and Criminal Procedure Code, ss. 102 and 103.
8. *Furman* v. *Georgia*, 408 U.S. 238, at 283 (1972).
9. See particularly *Furman* v. *Georgia*, ibid.; *Trop* v. *Dulles*, 356 U.S. 86 (1958); *Louisiana ex rel. Francis* v. *Resweber*, 329 U.S. 459 (1947); *Weems* v. *United States*, 217 U.S. 349 (1910); *Howard* v. *Fleming*, 191 U.S. 126 (1903); *O'Neil* v. *Vermont*, 144 U.S. 323 (1892); *In re Kemmler*, 136 U.S. 436 (1890); *Wilkerson* v. *Utah*, 99 U.S. 130 (1879); and *Pervear* v. *Commonwealth*, 5 Wall 475 (1867).
10. *Trop* v. *Dulles*, ibid.
11. *Jackson* v. *Bishop*, 404 F2d 571 (CA8 1968).
12. *O'Neil* v. *Vermont*, ibid. at 340; *Furman* v. *Georgia*, ibid. at 332.
13. *Weems* v. *United States*, ibid.
14. *Rudolph* v. *Alabama*, 375 U.S. 889 (1963); *Furman* v. *Georgia*, ibid.
15. *Robinson* v. *California*, 370 U.S. 660 (1962). Punishment for being drunk in a public place was however sustained in *Powell* v. *Texas*, 392 U.S. 514 (1968), where it was emphasised that even if a person was a chronic alcoholic, punishing him for public drunkenness could clearly be justified in terms of deterrence, isolation and treatment.

16. *Furman* v. *Georgia*, ibid. at 273.
17. *Robinson* v. *California*, ibid. at 667.
18. *Trop* v. *Dulles*, ibid. at 100−1.
19. *Furman* v. *Georgia*, ibid. 329−30.
20. *Furman* v. *Georgia*, ibid. at 244−5; also at 242.
21. *Furman* v. *Georgia*, ibid.
22. *Wilkerson* v. *Utah*, 99 U.S. 130 (1879); *In re Kemmler*, 136 U.S. 436 (1890); *Louisiana ex rel. Francis* v. *Resweber*, 329 U.S. 459 (1947); and *Furman* v. *Georgia*, 408 U.S. 238 (1972).
23. *Wilkerson* v. *Utah*, ibid.
24. *In re Kemmler*, ibid.
25. *Louisiana ex. rel. Francis* v. *Resweber*, ibid.
26. *Furman* v. *Georgia*, ibid.
27. ibid. at 306 and 311.
28. ibid. at 288, quoting the California supreme court in *People* v. *Anderson*, 6 Cal 3d 628, 649 (1972).
29. ibid at 288, referring to the judgment of Justice Frankfurter in *Solesbee* v. *Balkcom*, 339 U.S. 9, 14 (1950).
30. ibid at 296, quoting T. Sellin, *The Death Penalty*, a Report for the Model Penal Code Project of the American Law Institute 15 (1959).
31. At 343.
32. At 384−5.
33. *Wilkerson* v. *Utah*, 99 U.S. 130 (1879).
34. *Furman* v. *Georgia*, ibid. at 297.
35. loc. cit. Eight states in the United States still employ hanging, and one, Utah, also employs shooting in private, but the nine states have accounted for less than 3 per cent of the executions in the country since 1930.

23
PERSONAL LIBERTY

1. *The constitutional guarantee*

As with life and the dignity of the human person, personal liberty is guaranteed by a constitutional declaration and affirmation of the right followed by a prohibition of its deprivation except in the cases specified, and provided that deprivation in the specified cases is carried out in accordance with a procedure permitted by law (s. 32[1]). The Constitution itself sets out in some detail the basic procedure and conditions for a lawful deprivation which, subject to the constitutional stipulations, may be supplemented by the legislature.

The main part of the guarantee (i.e. minus the procedural safeguards) raises some interpretative difficulty, and for this reason it may be necessary to set it out here in its precise terms:

'Every person shall be entitled to his personal liberty and no person shall be deprived of such liberty save in the following cases and in accordance with a procedure permitted by law —
(*a*) in execution of the sentence or order of a court in respect of a criminal offence of which he has been found guilty;
(*b*) by reason of his failure to comply with the order of a court or in order to secure the fulfilment of any obligation imposed upon him by law;
(*c*) for the purpose of bringing him before a court in execution of the order of a court or upon reasonable suspicion of having committed a criminal offence, or to such extent as may be reasonably necessary to prevent his committing a criminal offence;
(*d*) in the case of a person who has not attained the age of eighteen years, for the purpose of his education or welfare;
(*e*) in the case of person suffering from infectious or contagious disease, persons of unsound mind, persons addicted to drugs or alcohol or vagrants, for the purpose of their care or treatment or the protection of the community; or
(*f*) for the purpose of preventing the unlawful entry of any person into Nigeria or of effecting the expulsion, extradition or other lawful removal from Nigeria of any person or the taking of proceedings relating thereto.'

Two interpretative questions arise upon this provision. First, are the two legs of the provision — the one giving to every person the right to personal liberty and the one setting out the circumstances and manner in which 'such liberty' may be taken away — independent of each other? Mr. Justice Omololu Thomas has suggested that the two legs of the provision are to be read conjuctively, and that the scope of personal liberty is not cut down by the fact that all the circumstances enumerated in the second leg relate to freedom from physical restraint of the person by arrest or detention.[1] In this view, personal liberty embraces all rights of a personal nature, including freedom of contract, private enterprise and right of property.

This interpretation is clearly not tenable. There is a clear indication in the provision that its two legs are not independent of one another, and that the second is intended to delineate the scope of the first. If the first leg is construed independently of the second so as to guarantee freedom of contract, private enterprise and other personal rights, the result will be that, since all the circumstances specified in the second leg relate exclusively to freedom from physical restraint of the person by arrest or detention, freedom of contract, private enterprise and other personal rights are guaranteed free of any qualification in favour of the state's regulatory authority. This is especially so because the provision is not among those made subject to regulation by the state in normal times in the interest of defence, public safety, public order, public health, public morality or the protection of the rights and freedom of others (s. 41). It is unthinkable that the Constitution should guarantee freedom of contract and private enterprise free of such qualification.

The second question raised is whether, subject to procedural safeguards prescribed in the Constitution or other laws, the provision is in itself an authority for the executive to deprive a person physically of his liberty in any of the circumstances specified, without an authority specifically conferred by statute or the common law. Without such authorisation, can the executive by compulsion and coercion confine a person of less than eighteen years of age for the purpose of his education or welfare, or confine a person suffering from infectious or contagious disease, a person of unsound mind or a person addicted to drugs or alcohol for the purpose of his care or treatment or the protection of the community, or detain any person on a reasonable suspicion of his having committed a criminal offence or to prevent him from committing a criminal offence? What is the meaning of the phrase 'save . . . in accordance with a procedure permitted by law'? It is submitted that the phrase implies that deprivation of personal liberty in the specified cases must be specifically authorised by law, the statute law or the common law. It seems more in consonance with the spirit of the guarantee of rights in the Constitution and with the fundamental presupposition of our constitutional system as discussed in chapter 6 above to say that deprivation of personal liberty is unlawful except in the specified cases, and that even in the specified cases it is still unlawful unless it is specifically authorised by law. The Constitution authorises no direct action by the executive in violation of a person's personal liberty, even in the specified cases.

Personal liberty is reinforced by the guarantee of the freedom of movement. The Constitution declares and affirms the right of *every citizen* of Nigeria . . . to move freely throughout Nigeria and to reside in any part thereof', and forbids his expulsion from the country or refusing him entry into or exit from it (s. 38[1]).

Except in the specified cases and subject to the procedural safeguards prescribed in the Constitution or other law, personal liberty is not, as already noted, subject to regulation or curtailment by the state in normal times in the interest of defence, public safety, public order, public health, public morality or the protection of the rights and freedom of other persons. Derogation is permitted only during a period of emergency duly proclaimed in accordance with the Constitution, but any derogation during such a period must be authorised by an act of the national assembly (not a law of a state house of assembly), and must be reasonably justifiable for the purpose of dealing with the situation created by the emergency (s. 41[2]).

Freedom of movement may however be regulated by law (federal and state) that is reasonably justifiable in a democratic society, both in normal times and during a period of emergency, in the interest of defence, public safety, public order, public morality, public health or for the purpose of protecting the rights and freedom of other persons (s. 41[1]). The test for the reasonable justifiability of a regulatory law is that of rational connection discussed in chapter 14. The guarantee of freedom of movement also specifically excepts any reasonably justifiable law which

(*a*) imposes restrictions on the residence or movement of any person who has committed or is reasonably suspected to have committed a criminal offence in order to prevent him from leaving Nigeria; or

(*b*) provides for the removal of any person from Nigeria to any other country for the purpose of his trial there for a criminal offence or to undergo imprisonment in execution of the sentence of a court in respect of a criminal offence of which he has been found guilty, provided that there is reciprocal agreement between Nigeria and such other country in relation to such matter (s. 38[2]).

We shall now proceed to consider the procedure and conditions for the deprivation of personal liberty by means of arrest or detention under the Constitution.

2. *Arrest*

The cases in which a person may constitutionally be deprived of his personal liberty by means of an arrest have been set out above, but as stated earlier, the specification of these cases in the Constitution provides no legal authority for an arrest in the absence of some law (statute or common law) specifically authorising it in each particular case. In the main, with the authority of such a law, a person may constitutionally be arrested only for the purpose of bringing him before a court in execution of the order of a court or upon reasonable suspicion of having committed a criminal offence or to prevent him committing a criminal offence. The method of effecting an arrest, i.e. whether it should be by warrant or without warrant, is not stated in the Constitution, this being left to the ordinary law the requirements of which must be complied with in order for the arrest to be lawful under the Constitution. A warrant is thus not a constitutional pre-requisite for a lawful arrest as in the United States.

The law on the matter, which derives both from the common law and from statute, is that, generally speaking, an arrest is unlawful if it is not effected on the authority of a warrant issued by a magistrate (or sometimes by a judge) on a sworn information of the commission of a criminal offence, the person to be arrested and the offence alleged to have been committed by him being specified in the warrant. A person swearing to the information or affidavit must of course have reasonable grounds for the belief that an offence has been committed. This rule originated from the decisions in the general warrant cases in the eighteenth century where the English courts declared illegal a practice, which had been going on for some 100 years, of issuing general warrants of indefinite duration, directed against no particular individual or specific article.[2] The requirement that the person to be arrested and the offence alleged against him should be specified in the warrant limits the opportunities for arbitrary arrests, while the interposition of a neutral judicial officer who must bring his independent judgment to bear upon an application for a warrant and to satisfy himself as to the existence of a probable cause for the arrest is supposed to limit still further arbitrariness by the executive.

An arrest without a warrant is not however unlawful if it is made not arbitrarily but for a good or probable cause, as where the person arrested had committed a breach of the peace or a felony. An arrest without a warrant is permitted by law in the following cases if it is by a policeman:[3]

(a) anyone who commits any offence in his presence or whom he reasonably suspects of having committed or being about to commit any felony, misdemeanour or breach of the peace or whom any other person suspects of having committed a felony or misdemeanour, or charges with having committed a simple offence if such other person is willing to accompany the police officer to the police station and to enter into a recognisance to prosecute the charge;[4]

(b) any person whom any other person charges with having committed a felony or misdemeanour;[5]

(c) any person who obstructs a police officer while in the execution of his duty, or who has escaped or attempts to escape from lawful custody;

(*d*) any person in whose possession anything is found which may reasonably be suspected to be stolen property or who may reasonably be suspected of having committed an offence with respect to such thing;

(*e*) any person having in his possession without lawful excuse any implement of house breaking;

(*f*) any person for whom he has reasonable cause to believe a warrant of arrest has been issued by a court of competent jurisdiction;

(*g*) any person who has no ostensible means of subsistence and who cannot give a satisfactory account of himself; and

(*h*) any person found taking precautions to conceal in circumstances which afford reason to believe that he is doing so with a view to committing an offence which is a felony or a misdemeanour.

The power of a private person to arrest without warrant extends only to the arrest of a person committing in his view an indictable offence (i.e. an offence punishable with more than two years' imprisonment or 400 Naira fine, or which is not defined by the law creating it to be punishable on summary conviction) or whom he reasonably suspects of having committed a misdemeanour by night or a felony;[6] he may also arrest anyone committing an offence involving injury to his property.[7]

Whether it is made with or without a warrant an arrest is unlawful unless within twenty-four hours of the arrest, the person arrested is informed in writing and in a language that he understands of the facts and grounds for the arrest (1979 Constitution, s. 32[3]). What this requires in the case of an arrest with a warrant is that the warrant should be shown or read to the person arrested either at the time of the arrest or within twenty-four hours. In a case where a police constable arrested a person suspected of being a receiver of stolen goods, without informing him of the reason for his arrest, the arrest was held to be unlawful, Lord Simon observing: 'A person is, *prima facie*, entitled to his freedom and is only required to submit to restraints on his freedom if he knows in substance the reason why it is claimed that this restraint should be imposed.'[8] The person arrested need not, however, be told at the time of the precise charge which it may be decided to bring against him, but the charge when eventually framed must be supported by the facts disclosed to him at the time of his arrest; it is wrongful to arrest for a crime which is completely different from the one subsequently charged.[9]

3. Detention

With the sanction of a law enacted by the legislature, five types of detention are permitted under the constitutional guarantee of personal liberty, namely protective or corrective custody, detention ordered by a court for non-compliance with a court order, detention in connection with the commission of a criminal offence, preventive detention, and detention pursuant to conviction and sentence by a court for a criminal offence. The first two types call for no special comment. The discussion which follows will therefore be confined to the last three.

(i) *Detention in connection with the commission of a criminal offence*

Detention is constitutionally permitted if it is authorised by law in the case of a person reasonably suspected of having committed a criminal offence. But a person so detained must be brought before a court of law within a reasonable time (s. 32[4]), which is defined as a period of one day where there is a court of competent jurisdiction within a radius of 40 kilometres of the place of detention — or, where there is no such court within that radius, a period of two days or 'such longer period as in the circumstances may be considered by the court to be reasonable' (s. 32[5]). The latter situation presupposes that detention will have been suffered for longer than two days before its reasonableness or otherwise shall have been determined by the court. If the court should decide that the person detained ought to have been brought before it within two days, then the period spent in detention in excess of two days is unlawful.

The purpose of requiring a person under detention to be brought before a court within a day or two, as the case may be, is to enable the court to decide whether or not to order his release (s. 32[4]). Entitlement to bail and the conditions for it are however not provided for in the Constitution beyond the stipulation commanding the release, either unconditional or upon conditions necessary to secure his appearance at his trial, of a detainee whose trial does not take place within two months from the date of his arrest or detention (s. 32[4]). A person in detention on a reasonable suspicion of having committed a capital offence is not entitled to the benefit of this provision (s. 32[7][a]). Under the ordinary law, a person charged with a misdemeanour is entitled to be admitted to bail, unless the court sees good reason to the contrary, but in cases of felony bail is at the discretion of the court (of a judge of the high court alone in capital cases). In exercising its discretion, the court (or judge) must consider the nature of the charge, the severity of the punishment and the character of the evidence.[10] The general law stipulates that bail must not be excessive;[11] and it seems that the discretion of the court in the matter of bail is further controlled by the constitutional provision which requires that a detainee who is not tried within two months is to be released either 'unconditionally or upon such conditions as are reasonably necessary to ensure that he appears for trial at a later date'. This suggests that bail should not exceed what is reasonably necessary to secure appearance at the trial.

Detention which does not comply with the conditions stated above is unlawful, and the person thus unlawfully detained is entitled to compensation and public apology from the appropriate authority or person as may be specified by law (s. 32[6]).

(ii) *Preventive detention*

Detention may be authorised by law to 'such extent as may be reasonably necessary to prevent [a person] from committing a criminal offence' (s. 32[1][c]). Detention simply to prevent a person from committing a criminal offence when it is not alleged that he has done so, and when there is not even a reasonable suspicion of his having done so, is nothing but preventive detention. No doubt its scope is limited by the fact that detention must be shown to be reasonably necessary to prevent the person detained from committing a criminal offence. The provision does not permit the detention of a person simply because his activities are considered socially undesirable or prejudicial to the economy, public order or public security; the prevention of the commission of acts which may endanger public order and the security of the state, which is the usual ground for preventive detention, is not enough unless the act to be prevented is a criminal offence.

It is not often realised that the bill of rights in the Nigerian Constitution permits the legislature to authorise the detention of persons against whom no reasonable suspicion of involvement in any criminal conduct exists, and whose only offence may be that they oppose the government and are for that reason considered a danger to the political security of the ruling group. This is the cardinal danger of any system of preventive detention even when limited to the prevention of the commission of a criminal offence; anything that threatens the personal political fortunes of those in control of the government tends to be equated with a criminal threat to the security of the state and its institutions. Political opponents of government thus face the risk of being clapped into detention, ostensibly to prevent them from committing subversion or other criminal offences against the state although no shred of evidence exists that they ever contemplate anything of the kind.

The constitutional safeguard whereby every person detained must be brought before a court within a day or two for the purpose of enabling the court to decide whether or not to release him on bail is, unfortunately, unavailing to a person in preventive detention, because the jurisdiction of a court to order bail is limited to the cases of persons in custody on an accusation of crime. Where a person is lawfully detained for reasons unconnected with his involvement in criminal conduct, no court has power to order his release on bail. The constitutional safeguard of trial within a reasonable time is equally unavailing, since there is no criminal charge for which he can be tried. However, he cannot be held in custody longer than two months. He is entitled to the benefit of the constitutional provision which requires that a detainee who is not tried within two months should be released either unconditionally or upon such conditions as are reasonably necessary to ensure that he appears for trial at a later date. Since no question of appearance at a trial arises in the case of a detainee who is not alleged to have committed a criminal offence, he is entitled to be released unconditionally after two months. This entitlement, however, is but a cold comfort to a person in preventive detention. For someone who has committed no criminal offence, even one day in police or prison custody is an unjustified incarceration likely to outrage his feelings and depress his spirit. But the fact that a person in preventive detention is entitled to be released unconditionally after two months may indeed be no comfort at all, for he can be re-arrested and re-detained for successive periods of two months at a time, just as he is leaving his place of detention. This is not forbidden by the Constitution; its command would have been satisfied once a detainee is allowed to regain his freedom for some period of time, no matter that the freedom is so short-lived as to be utterly illusory.

A person held in detention for the purpose of preventing him from committing a criminal offence is, like someone held on a reasonable suspicion of having committed a criminal offence, entitled to be informed of the facts and grounds for his detention; failure to do so invalidates the detention.

The provision making it possible for the legislature to authorise the detention of persons to 'such extent as may be reasonably necessary to prevent his committing a criminal offence' was reproduced, apparently without a full appreciation of its import, from the 1963 Constitution (s. 21[1] [c]), which in turn copied it from the original, independence Constitution of 1960 (s. 20[1] [c]). In the absence of an implementing legislation, the provision is apt to escape notice because of the way it is tucked in among other provisions that are in no way objectionable. There had been a plan to sponsor an implementing legislation in 1963; the prime minister and the regional premiers had agreed among themselves that a preventive detention law was necessary to deal with the increasing threat of subversion in the country.

The public was first alerted of this plan in the issue for 20 July 1963 of one of the national daily newspapers.[12] Questioned on the matter on their arrival in Lagos a few days later for the all-party conference on a republican Constitution, the three regional premiers all spoke warmly in support of the plan. Public opinion, however, was immediately whipped up against it by a relentless press attack. Both the Bar Association and the opposition party, the Action Group, condemned it. Sensing the public indignation and the ruinous consequences for their parties if the proposal were carried through in spite of it, the premiers and their lieutenants promptly announced that the proposal had been shelved. It was a great victory for public opinion, but the storm of public indignation still continued with almost unmitigated fury after the announcement, and soon threw the premiers into some disarray. On 2 August the Northern Peoples Congress (N.P.C.), in an attempt to clear its leader, Sir Ahmadu Bello, of responsibility for the origination of the proposal, issued a statement in which it alleged (as it said, reluctantly) that Dr. Okpara, the premier of Eastern Nigeria, was the 'originator and brain' behind the proposal, and as such the person against whom public censure should properly be directed; 'it was Dr. Okpara who first suggested the idea to the meeting of Premiers and lobbied other Premiers to support his suggestion.'[13] This allegation was promptly denied by Dr. Okpara who sought to exculpate himself by the revelation that the proposal originated from the federal prime minister, Sir Abubakar Tafawa Balewa, during a meeting of the premiers summoned by him in Lagos to consider the threat of subversion in the country. The seriousness with which the Eastern premier regarded the attempt to fix responsibility on him is reflected in the language of his denial: 'How can any fair-minded and responsible citizen wish to pin the idea of the preventive detention law on me alone? I didn't summon the meeting of the Prime Minister and Premiers. I certainly lobbied no one to support it. What indeed was the purpose of the meeting summoned by the Prime Minister? Was it just to talk about subversion and disperse, with no action taken? Who after all was going to apply the law? Was it I? I can only say that on a matter [about which] we all reached complete unanimity, it would be childish and cowardly to give the impression that I was the only person interested in the preventive detention law.'[14] In his characteristically statesman-like way, Sir Abubakar took responsibility for the introduction of the proposal.[15]

Not surprisingly, preventive detention laws became part of the arsenal of the military government that ruled Nigeria from 1966 to 1979. There were some twenty decrees authorising the detention of named individuals in the interest of public security. And there was the Armed Forces and Police (Special Powers) Decree 1967 which empowered the inspector-general of police or the chief of staff of the armed forces to detain any person for any length of time on his own subjective satisfaction that the person was or recently had been concerned in acts prejudicial to public order or in the preparation or instigation of such acts. Under the Trade Disputes (Essential Services) Decree 1976, in a case where a trade union had been proscribed, the inspector-general of police or the chief of staff, supreme headquarters, was empowered to order the detention of any official or member of the union if he was satisfied that such official or member had since the proscription been concerned in acts prejudicial to industrial peace or in acts calculated to obstruct or disrupt the smooth running of any essential services, and that it was necessary to exercise control over him. The scope of detention authorised by these decrees was clearly not limited to what might be reasonably necessary to prevent a person detained from committing a criminal offence. They went far beyond that, and consequently constituted a violation of the constitutional guarantee of personal liberty. Happily, all the decrees, except the Trade Disputes (Essential Services) Decree (now Act) were repealed in 1978 to pave the way for the return to democratic government.[16]

(iii) *Detention pursuant to conviction and sentence by a court for a criminal offence*

Deprivation of personal liberty 'in execution of the sentence or order of a court in respect of a criminal offence of which [a person] has been found guilty' (s. 32[1][*a*]) is indisputably justifiable in a democratic society. The justification is predicated on the position of a court as a neutral and impartial arbiter between the individual and the government.

Conviction and sentence for a criminal offence by a court strictly so-called is still not a lawful justification for imprisonment (or any other punishment) unless certain conditions and safeguards prescribed by the Constitution (and other laws) are met. These constitutional safeguards will be considered in the next chapter.

REFERENCES

1. *Adewole & Others* v. *Jakande & Others*, Suit No. M/120/80 of 22 August 1980.
2. *Leach* v. *Money* (1765), 19 St. Tr. 1002; *Wilkes* v. *Wood* (1763), 19 St. Tr. 1153; *Entick* v. *Carrington* (1765), 19 St. Tr. 1029.
3. See Criminal Procedure Act, s. 10, and Police Act, s. 20. There are various other statutes authorising police officers and others to arrest without warrant. The power of arrest without warrant was very limited at common law.

See also Criminal Procedure Code, ss. 26–30, applicable in the Western States.
4. Criminal Procedure Act, s. 12.
5. ibid., s. 13.
6. Criminal Procedure Act, s. 12; Criminal Procedure Act 1960 (Northern States), s. 28.
7. Criminal Procedure Act, s. 13.
8. *Christie* v. *Leachinsky* [1947] A.C. 573, at pp. 587–8.
9. ibid., particularly the judgment of Lord Simonds.
10. On bail generally see Criminal Procedure Act, ss. 118–143; on the power of the police to release on bail a person arrested without warrant see Police Act, s. 23; Criminal Procedure Act, ss. 17–20.
11. Criminal Procedure Act, s. 120.
12. *West African Pilot*.
13. ibid, 3 August 1963.
14. ibid.
15. House of Representatives Debates, 7 August 1963.
16. See Federal Republic of Nigeria (Certain Consequential Repeals, etc.) Act 1979.

24
CONSTITUTIONAL SAFEGUARDS FOR TRIAL IN CRIMINAL CASES

These safeguards are an attempt to give constitutional sanctity to the rules evolved by the common law as the fundamental pre-requisites for a fair trial. They apply in all criminal trials whether the offence is one punishable by death, imprisonment, fine or any other kind of penalty.

It is perhaps necessary to state that only a court in the strict constitutional sense as provided in section 6 of the Constitution can convict and sentence for a criminal offence. It must be a court that forms part of the established and regular courts invested by the Constitution with the judicial power of the Federation or a State. This is because conviction for a criminal offence and the imposition of sentence therefor pertain exclusively to judicial power,[1] so that only a court qualified under section 6 of the Constitution to exercise judicial power can convict and sentence for a criminal offence. A tribunal which is not a court in the sense of section 6 of the Constitution cannot competently convict and sentence for a criminal offence, no matter how independent and impartial it may be. The reference to 'a court or tribunal' in the provision that a person charged with a criminal offence is 'entitled to a fair hearing in public within a reasonable time by a court or tribunal' (s. 33[4]) must therefore be read with this qualification.

This point has far-reaching significance, which is reinforced by the fact that, except to the extent indicated later in this chapter, the constitutional safeguards for a fair trial in criminal cases cannot be abridged or denied in the interest of public safety, public order, public health or public morality, in normal times equally as in periods of emergency. It means that, so long as the courts are still in a position to function, and so long as they have not been completely incapacitated by actual military operations resulting from a foreign invasion or civil war, which make it impossible for them to administer criminal justice according to law, martial law or the trial of civilians by military tribunals, whether authorised by law or by mere executive order, is constitutionally prohibited. 'Martial law can never exist where the courts are open, and in the proper and unobstructed exercise of their jurisdiction.'[2] (The point is discussed fully in chapters 6 and 14 above.)

1. *Trial must be for an existing offence defined in a written law*

Conviction is unconstitutional unless the 'offence is defined and the penalty therefor is prescribed in a written law'. A written law for this purpose means an act of the national assembly or law made by a State house of assembly, or any subsidiary legislation under the provisions of such act or law (s. 33[12]). It seems probable that this requirement is aimed at preventing trumped-up charges by the executive against its opponents for offences which are nowhere defined by law.[3] But the prohibition has been used by the high court in the former Western Nigeria to quash the conviction by a customary court of a woman for the customary (unwritten) offence of adultery.[4]

The prohibition also reflects something of the principle that crimes must be defined with sufficient explicitness to inform those subject to them what conduct on their part will render them liable to penalties. Unless a crime is defined in a written law, there may arise some uncertainty as to its exact ingredients, or as to the exact conduct proscribed by it. On the wider principle, a statute creating a criminal offence is void if its terms are 'so vague that men of common intelligence must necessarily guess at its meaning and differ' as to the conduct it proscribes.[5]

The prohibition as contained in the 1979 Constitution omits the proviso which appears in the 1963 Constitution to the effect that it shall not 'prevent a court of record from punishing any person for contempt of itself notwithstanding that the act or omission constituting the contempt is not defined in a written law and the penalty therefor is not so prescribed' (s. 22[10]). It does not, however, follow from this that a court of record can no longer punish for contempt of itself unless the offence of contempt is defined in a written law. The provision in the 1979 Constitution is expressed to be 'subject as otherwise provided by this Constitution' (s. 33[12]). The judicial power vested in the court in section 6 of the Constitution is defined as extending, 'notwithstanding anything to the contrary in this Constitution, to all inherent powers and sanctions of a court of law' (s. 6[6][a]). A court of record retains thus constitutional competence to punish for contempt of itself as part of the 'inherent powers and sanctions of a court of law', notwithstanding that contempt may not be defined in a written law. (It is in fact so defined in most of the States in the country.)

Not only must the offence be defined in a written law which is sufficiently explicit in its terms, but it must also exist at the time of the act or omission charged. The Constitution expressly enjoins that 'no person shall be held to be guilty of a criminal offence on account of any act or omission that did not, at the time it took place, constitute such an offence; and no penalty shall be imposed for any criminal offence heavier than the penalty in force at the time the offence was committed' (s. 33[8]). Also the national assembly and the state legislatures are denied power to make a law which shall have retrospective effect in relation to any criminal offence (s. 4[9]). The scope of these two provisions has already been considered in chapter 14 above.

2. Prompt notification of charge

Just as a person arrested on suspicion of having committed a criminal offence must be informed of the facts and grounds for his arrest, so must he, after having been formally charged, be 'informed promptly in the language that he understands and in detail of the nature of the offence' (s. 33[6] [a]). The information must be prompt and must give details of the offence. The detail required must be such as would be adequate to enable the accused to meet the charges against him. Insufficiency of detail, like failure to furnish grounds for an arrest, is not a mere matter of procedure, which can be cured by appropriate remedy; its effect may be to invalidate the trial and any conviction resulting from it.[6] It is also a violation of the right of a fair trial to convict a person of an offence of which he is not charged.[7]

3. An accused person must be given adequate time and facilities for the preparation of his defence

A person charged with a criminal offence is 'entitled . . . to be given adequate time and facilities for the preparation of his defence' (s. 33[6][b]). The question of adequate time has arisen mainly in connection with an accused person's request for an adjournment to enable him brief counsel or call a witness. In one case an accused person, who had been brought before a magistrate by a bench warrant, apparently ignorant that his case was coming up for trial on that date, asked for adjournment to enable him to arrange for counsel. But the magistrate would only adjourn until the afternoon of the same day, even though the nearest place where counsel could be found was 23 miles away. When the trial was resumed that afternoon the accused, in the absence of counsel to defend him, refused to take any more part in the proceedings, which ended in his conviction. Holding that the accused had not been given adequate time for the preparation of his defence, and that this amounted to denial of fair trial, the high court on appeal quashed the conviction and ordered a new trial.[8]

But while the court must ensure that the accused is given adequate time to prepare his defence, other demands of a fair trial, like the need for a quick dispensation of justice, have also to be considered in deciding whether or not to grant an accused person's application for adjournment. Provided, therefore, that the court exercises its discretion judiciously, refusal to grant an application for an adjournment is not a denial of fair trial such as to invalidate the trial and any conviction based on it.[9]

It is not altogether clear with what facilities an accused person is entitled to be provided in accordance with the constitutional requirement. It has been suggested that the 'facilities' to which he is so entitled include all the evidence in the possession of the prosecution, including statements made by prosecution witnesses as well as those made by the accused, the record of any previous conviction of the prosecution witnesses, and other relevant documents; in other words the accused has, by virtue of the constitutional provision, a right to be furnished with all such evidence.[10]

But do 'facilities' also include assistance of counsel provided by the state at its own expense? This must depend on whether at the stage of preparation assistance of counsel is a pre-requisite for a fair trial. The U.S. supreme court has held that it is; it held the period from the framing of a formal charge until the beginning of trial as the most 'critical stage' in the process of criminal prosecution when consultation with counsel is 'vitally important', and indeed indispensable to a fair trial.[11] Overruling an earlier ruling to the effect that the provision of counsel by the state is not a 'fundamental right, essential to a fair trial',[12] the court emphasised that under the adversary system of criminal justice, a person charged with a criminal offence, 'who is too poor to hire a lawyer, cannot be assured a fair trial unless counsel is provided for him'.[13] The indispensability of counsel's assistance to an effective preparation of the defence means therefore that it is a facility which the accused is entitled to be given under the constitutional provision.

The right to legal aid provided by the state at its own expense is of course not absolute. Yet the only permissible considerations limiting its application are the ability of a defendant to retain counsel of his own choice, and whether the offence charged carries a penalty of imprisonment, i.e. whether loss of personal liberty might result from conviction. If the accused is not able to retain counsel of his own choice and the offence is punishable with imprisonment, he is entitled to have counsel provided for him by the state, without regard to the existence or otherwise of any special circumstances, such as the personal characteristics of the accused not related to his ability to pay for counsel of his choice (e.g. youth, immaturity, inexperience, limited education, insanity or mental abnormality), the nature of the offence, the technicality or complexity of the defence, and developments during the trial tending to prejudice its fairness. As the court held in 1972, no person may be sentenced to jail who was convicted in the absence of counsel, unless he validly waived his right.[14] But the court reserved decision on the right to counsel in criminal cases in which loss of personal liberty is not involved.

In the light of the constitutional right of an accused person to legal aid to enable him to prepare his defence, the provision of the Legal Aid Act 1976 limiting entitlement to legal aid to persons earning not more than 720 Naira per annum, who are charged before specified types of court with certain types of offences specified in the act (murder, manslaughter, malicious or wilful infliction of bodily harm and assault occasioning actual bodily harm) and such others as may be specified by the federal executive council, is open to attack for unconstitutionality, insofar as it relates to the preparation of the defence. The act empowers the federal executive council to provide by regulations for the giving of legal aid, on a contributory basis, to persons whose income exceeds 720 Naira per annum, but in view of the requirement that legal aid, where there is a constitutional entitlement to it, has to be adequate, compulsory contribution by the accused is also constitutionally questionable — insofar, again, as it relates to the preparation of the defence.

When the case comes to trial after the preparation, the accused is entitled to 'defend himself in person or by legal practitioners of his own choice' (s. 33[6][c]). The necessity for legal representation at the trial stage was given eloquent expression by the U.S. supreme court as follows:

> The right to be heard would be, in many cases, of little avail if it did not comprehend the right to be heard by counsel. Even the intelligent and educated layman has small and sometimes no skill in the science of law. If charged with crimes, he is incapable, generally, of determining for himself whether the indictment is good or bad. He is unfamiliar with the rules of evidence. Left without the aid of counsel he may be put on trial without a proper charge, and convicted upon incompetent evidence, or evidence irrelevant to the issue or otherwise inadmissible. [. . .] He requires the guiding hand of counsel at every step in the proceedings against him. Without it, though he be not guilty, he faces the danger of conviction because he does not know how to establish his innocence.[15]

But an accused person under the Nigerian Constitution is not entitled to have counsel provided by the state at the stage of trial. His only right is to be defended by counsel of his own choice. Counsel of one's choice clearly implies that the representation is to be paid for by the accused; he cannot have the right of choice of counsel at someone else's expense. A 'legal practitioner of his choice' means one retained by the accused on terms privately and mutually agreed between him and the counsel. He cannot choose a counsel on agreed terms and expect the state to honour those terms on his behalf.

The right to counsel retained by the accused at his own expense is absolute, and cannot be denied by statute barring the appearance of lawyers in a court exercising jurisdiction in criminal matters. The right is not made subject to the qualification that appeared in the 1963

Constitution in favour of statutes barring legal representation in native or customary courts (1963 Constitution, s. 22[5]). As was said by the U.S. supreme court, 'regardless of whether petitioner would have been entitled to the appointment of counsel, his right to be heard through his own counsel was unqualified. [. . .] A necessary corollary is that a defendant must be given a reasonable opportunity to employ and consult with counsel.'[16]

It has been held however that counsel of one's own choice within the meaning of the constitutional provision means counsel who has the right of audience in the Nigerian courts, and who, if outside Nigeria, has the right to enter it. The facts of the case were that an accused person had briefed a British counsel, who was then an enrolled legal practitioner of Nigeria, to defend him against a charge of treasonable felony and conspiracy. On the order of the minister of internal affairs given under the Immigration Act, cap. 84, counsel on arrival was refused permission to enter the country for the purpose of undertaking the defence of the accused.[17] The correctness of the decision upholding the validity of the minister's order may be questioned on the ground that, since the right is not expressly or by necessary implication made subject to the condition that counsel must be a person entitled to enter Nigeria as of right, the conflict between the freedom of the individual and the right of the government to exclude non-citizens ought to have been resolved in favour of individual freedom, except possibly where the overriding interests of the state, for example security, are involved, which was not the case here.

An accused person who cannot afford to retain his own counsel at the trial stage may have one provided for him by the state, but since he is not entitled to this as a matter of constitutional right, the state may by law regulate the terms on which such legal aid may be given. The provisions of the Legal Aid Act 1976 will then be fully applicable.

4. *A person charged with a criminal offence must be tried within a reasonable time*

The Constitution guarantees to every person charged with a criminal offence the right to be tried within 'a reasonable time' (s. 33[4]). Trial within a reasonable time, or speedy trial in the words of the U.S. Constitution (Sixth Amendment), is fundamental to a fair trial, because delay impairs the ability of an accused person to defend himself through the fact that a vital witness may have died in the interval or the recollection of the facts by other witnesses may have become blurred.[18] There is also the danger of the trial judge losing his impressions of the demeanour of the witnesses after the lapse of a long time during which he has also to watch the demeanour of witnesses in a variety of other cases.[19] Undue delay is thus fraught with the danger of a miscarriage of justice, and for that reason is frowned upon by the courts.[20] Furthermore, a public accusation of crime arising from a police arrest exposes the person involved to anxiety and concern, which it is unfair to prolong unduly.[21]

The rationale underlying the provision suggests that the word 'charged' appearing in it should be interpreted broadly and in the context of the provision requiring that a person arrested on a reasonable suspicion of having committed a criminal offence should be charged to court within one or two days, as the case may be (s. 32[4] and [5]). For the purposes of the guarantee of trial within a reasonable time, time should be calculated from when the person concerned should have been charged in accordance with the constitutional provision, not from when he was actually charged; he should be deemed to have been charged on the day when he was supposed to be taken to court on the charge. An accused person should not have his right to speedy trial postponed indefinitely because of the failure of the law enforcement authorities to charge him within the time required by the constitution. It follows from this that 'charged' in the context of this provision refers, not to a formal charge on information or indictment, but to a police charge. Indeed, in the United States the rule is that the right need not await a formal charge but begins from the moment of arrest if that precedes the preferring of a formal charge.[22]

What is reasonable time is, however, relative to the circumstances of each case, the relevant factors to be taken into account being, *inter alia*, the length of delay, the reasons for it, the amount of prejudice to the fairness of the trial occasioned by the delay, and the accused person's assertion of his right.[23] In a case,[24] described by the federal court of appeal as a classic one of unreasonable delay, an interval of over six years had elapsed from the arrest of the accused persons in December 1973 to the delivery of judgment in April 1980. The information formally charging the accused persons was laid in March 1976, more than two years after the arrest. The accused were brought to court for the first time nine months later, and thereafter 'the case went asleep to surface before another judge one and half years later.' Further delays were caused mostly by adjournments at the request of the prosecution and by lapses on the part of the court itself. In the absence of substantial and satisfactory reason for these delays, the federal court of appeal held that they amounted to a denial of the constitutional right of the accused to a trial within a reasonable time; and that as a retrial would be hardly fair in the circumstances, the accused were entitled to be acquitted and discharged, which it accordingly ordered.

Another significant feature of the case, as appeared from the judgment of the federal court of appeal, is that the records did not show that bail was granted to the accused after their arrest in December 1973 until 13 June 1978 when they were released on bail. In other words, the accused had been in detention for four and half years while awaiting trial. Unless the crime of arson with which they were charged carries a longer term of imprisonment than four and half years, their detention for that length of time is a violation of the provision of the Constitution prohibiting the detention of an accused person awaiting trial, for a period longer than the maximum period of imprisonment prescribed for the offence (s. 32[1] proviso). The constitutional right of the accused to be brought before a court within a reasonable time was also violated by the failure to do so until December 1976 after their arrest in December 1973.

Trial within a reasonable time must also be regarded in the context of the provision which requires every court established under the Constitution to 'deliver its decision in writing not later than three months after the conclusion of evidence and final addresses' (s. 258[1]). Indeed the provision that 'an accused person or any person authorised by him in that behalf shall be entitled to obtain copies of the judgment in the case within seven days of the conclusion of the case' (s. 33[7]) is open to the argument that judgment must be delivered within seven days of the conclusion of the case for both the prosecution and the defence (the point is pursued further on page 444 below).

5. *Trial must be in public*

The requirement of a public trial is designed as a safeguard against the dangers of manipulation and perversion to which a secret trial exposes the courts. It ensures that the courts would not be employed as an instrument to convict an accused person unjustly and unfairly or to persecute him in any other way.[25] The presence of the public at a criminal trial, especially the press, cannot but restrain any tendency on the part of the executive to employ intimidation or other oppressive tactics to obtain the conviction of an accused person.

What determines the public character of a trial is not so much the place where it is held, whether it is a regular place for holding a court or not, as the public's right of access to the trial. The constitutional requirement is satisfied if the public has access to the trial, notwithstanding that it was held in a place, such as the chambers of a judge, which is not strictly a regular court place.[26] A trial in a private room to which the public has no access is a nullity.[27]

The right to a public trial is subject to two qualifications expressly recognised in the Constitution itself. First, the court is permitted to exclude persons other than the parties or their counsel in the interest of defence, public safety, public order, public morality, the welfare of persons who have not attained the age of eighteen years, the protection of the private lives of the parties or to such extent as it may consider necessary by reason of special circumstances in which publicity would be contrary to the interests of justice (s. 33[4] [a]). The court has thus wide powers to exclude the public.

The constitutionality of exclusion of the public by the court has arisen mainly in relation to the press. While the press cannot be barred altogether, it has been held that excessive press publicity, such as the live televising of a trial, may be barred by the court because of its tendency to prejudice a fair trial.[28] A conviction following a televised trial was accordingly quashed.[29] Where the press is allowed to be present at a trial, it is unconstitutional for the court to bar them from reporting any aspect of the proceedings taking place in public, and not in camera; the court should rather use other means to protect the rights of an accused person to a fair trial — such as isolating the jury from news reports, moving the trial to another location or postponing the trial.[30]

The second qualification relates to matters as to which the court is satisfied, on the evidence of a federal minister or a state commissioner, that it would not be in the public interest to disclose publicly. The court is then to make arrangement for evidence relating to such matters to be heard in private, and shall take such other action as may be necessary or expedient to prevent disclosure (s. 33[4] [b]).

6. *Accused is presumed innocent until proved guilty*

By prohibiting a presumption of guilt, the provision that a person charged with a criminal offence is presumed innocent until he is proved guilty (s. 33[5]), has the effect that the guilt or innocence of the accused is made to depend solely on evidence of facts produced in court. The burden is on the prosecution to prove, by affirmative evidence, the guilt of the accused, who is thus saved the ordeal of having to establish his innocence. It seems not to be fully appreciated how difficult and embarrassing it can be to have to establish one's innocence, until one is actually put in the position of having to do so. The presumption of innocence has thus rightly been described as the bedrock of our system of criminal justice.[31]

But the provision stops short of prescribing specifically the standard of proof required to establish the guilt of an accused person. It seems, however, that this is implied in the words 'until he is proved guilty'. The words clearly imply that guilt has to be proved conclusively, and it cannot be said to have been conclusively established if it is still open to a reasonable doubt. The U.S. supreme court has rightly held, against the dissent of a minority of its members, that proof beyond reasonable doubt, being the concrete substance of the presumption of innocence, is incorporated in the Constitution as part of the presumption.[32]

The presumption would seem clearly to be violated by a section (s. 156) of the Criminal Procedure Code (applicable in the Northern States) which provides that 'when the accused appears or is brought before the court, the particulars of the offence of which he is accused shall be stated to him and he shall be asked if he has any cause to show why he should not be convicted.' The constitutionality of other sections of the Code (ss. 158, 159 and 160[1]) had also been challenged on this ground.[33] They provide that a magistrate before whom an accused person is brought may, without any charge being framed, proceed to hear the complaint and the prosecution witnesses, who may be cross-examined by the accused; further the magistrate may examine the accused with a view to obtaining his explanation of any circumstances appearing in the prosecution evidence. If, from the evidence so given and the accused's explanation, the magistrate is of the opinion that there is ground for presuming that the accused has committed an offence, then the magistrate shall frame a charge against the accused at that stage. It was contended before both the high court of the former Northern Nigeria and the supreme court that the framing of a charge after the magistrate has heard the prosecution case meant that the magistrate has already made up his mind about the accused's guilt at the time when the charge is framed, and that being the case, the presumption of innocence has been violated. The appeal was dismissed by the supreme court on the ground that the framing of a charge by the magistrate after he has heard the prosecution case does not mean that he has made up his mind to convict; all that could be implied from it is that the magistrate is satisfied that a *prima facie* case has been established against the accused. It is submitted with respect that the supreme court has misconceived the appellant's submission, which was not that the magistrate had made up his mind to convict but that the implied acceptance by him that a *prima facie* case has been made out places an onus on the accused to throw doubt by means of evidence upon the prosecution case or else be convicted. This means that at the time of framing the charge the presumption (rebuttable by the accused) was one of guilt and not of innocence. This is admittedly a difficult case. It seems clear that the provisions of the Code relevant to this case and the procedure adopted conformed to the spirit of the constitutional requirement, but in strict logic they constitute a violation of it.

A point of considerable interest is whether the presumption of innocence requires all the facts forming an element of a crime to be proved affirmatively by evidence, or whether it permits a fact to be presumed from the proof of another fact. For example, can a statute which prohibits the possession of marijuana which has been illegally imported authorise the fact of illegal importation to be presumed from the fact of possession? While the requirement of proof beyond reasonable doubt does not completely bar a statutory presumption of this kind, a rational connection must be shown to exist between the fact proved and the one to be presumed from it. The presumption of innocence is violated if 'the inference of one fact from the proof of another is arbitrary because of a lack of rational connection between the two in common experience.'[34] The test of rational connection for this purpose is that it must 'at least be said with substantial assurance that the presumed fact is more likely than not to flow from the proved fact on which it is made to depend.'[35] Thus a statutory provision giving authority for the knowledge of illegal importation of marijuana to be inferred from the fact of possession was voided, on its being shown that, while the greater part of marijuana consumed in the country was of foreign origin, a considerable amount was produced domestically, so that there was no way of being sure that the majority of those possessing marijuana had any reason to know that theirs was imported.[36] A statutory presumption from the possession of a firearm that it had been transported in inter-state commerce was similarly voided.[37]

The proviso that the presumption of innocence shall not invalidate any law by reason only that it imposes on an accused person the burden of proving particular facts is not intended to authorise shifting to the accused the burden of proving facts forming part of the offence charged except to the extent indicated above. For otherwise the presumption of innocence would be seriously eroded. The kind of particular facts in relation to which the burden of proof may be shifted to the accused are, for example, those relating to the defence of insanity, provocation or self-defence[38] or the defence of alibi.[39] The limits of the power of the legislature to shift the burden of proof to the accused are illustrated by a case which involved an act of the congress of the United States which prohibited abortion unless it was performed by a physician as being 'necessary for the preservation of the mother's life or health'. Reversing the district court, the U.S. supreme court held that the onus of proving that abortion was necessary for the preservation of the mother's life or health could not, consistently with the presumption of innocence, be shifted from the prosecution to the accused, and that, in any case, the statute, properly interpreted, did not have the effect of shifting the onus to the accused.[40]

7. *Accused must be given a fair hearing at the trial*

Fair hearing in this context implies that an accused person must be heard in his own defence, either in person or through counsel, that he must be allowed 'to examine in person or by his legal practitioners the witnesses called by the prosecution before any court and to obtain the attendance and carry out the examination of witnesses to testify on his behalf before the court on the same conditions as those applying to witnesses called by the prosecution'; and that he is 'to have without payment the assistance of an interpreter if he cannot understand the language used at the trial of the offence' (s. 33[6][c], [d] and [e]). (Fair hearing in the context of the provision giving to an accused person the right to 'a fair hearing in public within a reasonable time' is rightly regarded as interchangeable or synonymous with a fair trial.[41])

The right to cross-examine prosecution witnesses is essential to a fair trial because it provides an opportunity to test their veracity. An accused person under the Nigerian Constitution does not have the right, guaranteed to an accused person under the U.S. Constitution, 'to be confronted with the witnesses against him'.[42] The right of confrontation implies that the prosecution cannot use the evidence of a witness who, because he is not present in court, cannot be confronted by the accused; the use of depositions or *ex parte* affidavits in criminal cases is thus barred,[43] even when they are admissible under any of the recognised exceptions to the hearsay rule.[44] The Nigerian provision, on the other hand, does not extend to all prosecution witnesses but only to those actually called before the court, so that depositions of witnesses not called are not barred unless they are inadmissible under the hearsay rule.

The conviction of an accused person is unconstitutional and will be quashed on appeal where he has been denied the right to call witnesses[45] or to cross-examine prosecution witnesses.[46]

An accused person cannot be said to have been heard if the language spoken by him or his witnesses is not understood by the court; nor can he present his defence effectively if, owing to language difficulties, he does not understand the proceedings. In such circumstances the trial is a nullity if a facility for full and accurate interpretation is not provided by the court.[47]

8. *Accused must not be compelled to give evidence at the trial*

The presumption of innocence is reinforced by the provision that a person under trial for a 'criminal offence shall not be compelled to give evidence at the trial' (s. 33[11]). The two rules together provide the pillars upon which the accusatorial system of criminal justice is founded.

The prohibition against compulsory evidence by the accused is both narrower and wider than the corresponding provision in the U.S.

Constitution, which says that 'no person . . . shall be compelled in any criminal case to be a witness against himself.'[48] Whereas the protection of the American provision is available in any criminal case to every person, irrespective of whether he is the accused or not, the Nigerian provision prohibits only compelled evidence by an accused person at his trial. As so limited to an accused person, however, the Nigerian provision bars compelled evidence of any kind, whether incriminating or exculpatory or altogether neutral. On the other hand, the American provision, by its terms, bars only compelled evidence which is against the person concerned, but not exculpatory or other non-prejudicial evidence. Judicial interpretation has limited the American provision still further to evidence which is incriminating, in the sense that it might lead to the person concerned being convicted of a criminal offence. Protesting against this restrictive interpretation, a justice of the U.S. supreme court has said that 'wisely or not the Fifth Amendment protects against the compulsory self-accusation of crime without exception or qualification', limiting it only to cases where criminal conviction might result.[49]

While compulsory oral evidence by the accused comes more readily to mind, documentary evidence is not outside the pale of the provision. An accused person cannot be compelled to produce at his trial a document written or made by him, even though it had been written or made voluntarily and without compulsion.

Equally a document made by an accused person cannot be tendered in evidence at his trial by the prosecution if it has been made under compulsion, notwithstanding that there is no compulsion on the prosecution to tender it. This has especial relevance to statements made to the police by the accused. Such statement cannot be tendered at the trial by the prosecution if it had been made, not voluntarily, but by compulsion or coercion. The rationale for excluding such evidence is not that a statement obtained by coercion or compulsion is unlikely to be true or trustworthy, but simply because, whether true or false, the fact that coercion or compulsion has been employed in extracting it makes it unfair to use it as evidence. 'The prosecution', said the U.S. supreme court in a leading case, 'may not use statements . . . stemming from custodial interrogation of the defendant unless it demonstrates the use of procedural safeguards effective to secure the privilege against self-incrimination.'[50] There seems to be implicit in the court's conclusion the feeling that 'police interrogation as conceived and practised was inherently coercive and that this compulsion . . . was contrary to the protection assured by the self-incrimination clause, the protection afforded in a system of criminal justice which convicted a defendant on the basis of evidence independently secured and not out of his own mouth.'[51]

The Nigerian Constitution enshrines part of these procedural safeguards in the provision that 'any person who is arrested or detained shall have the right to remain silent or avoid answering any question until after consultation with a legal practitioner or any other person of his own choice' (s. 32[2]).

The refusal of an accused person to give evidence at his trial should not be the subject of adverse comment by the judge or prosecution. This is because such comment might make it appear that the accused is being penalised for exercising his constitutional right; 'it cuts down on the privilege by making its assertion costly.'[52]

9. *Court must keep record of proceedings and furnish a copy of judgment to accused*

A court trying a person for a criminal offence is enjoined to keep a record of the proceedings (s. 33[7]), and to furnish all parties with duly authenticated copies of its decision on the date it is delivered (s. 258[1]). The latter part of the duty imposed on the court seems to be in conflict with the provision that 'an accused person or any person authorised by him in that behalf shall be entitled to obtain copies of the judgment in the case within 7 days of the conclusion of the case' (s. 33[7]). The duty of the court to furnish the accused with an authenticated copy of its judgment on the date it is delivered gives him a correlative right to obtain a copy on that date. The conflict can be removed only if the words 'conclusion of the case' in s. 33(7) are interpreted to mean, not the date of the judgment, but the date on which both the case for the prosecution and that for the defence are concluded, which will mean that the court is allowed only seven days from that date to deliver its judgment. But this interpretation seems hardly reasonable in view of the specific provision prescribing three months as the period within which a decision must be rendered after the conclusion of evidence and final addresses (s. 258[1]).

In a criminal appeal before the federal court of appeal or the supreme court, each member of the court must deliver a separate written opinion, even if it be only to say that he adopts the written opinion of another member (s. 258[2]).

10. *A person convicted or acquitted of or pardoned for an offence shall not be tried again for the same offence*

The Constitution enjoins that 'no person who shows that he has been tried by any court of competent jurisdiction for a criminal offence and either convicted or acquitted shall again be tried for that offence or for a criminal offence having the same ingredients as that offence save upon the order of a superior court' (s. 33[9]); a pardon also confers an immunity from trial for the same offence (s. 33[10]). The provision in s. 33(9) incorporates in the Constitution what is commonly referred to as the doctrine of double jeopardy which takes its name from the provision in the U.S. Constitution as adapted from the common law, that no person shall be 'subject for the same offence to be twice put in jeopardy of life or limb' (Fifth Amendment).

The formulation of the doctrine in the Nigerian Constitution raises the question as to what constitutes jeopardy. Is it the ordeal, the anxiety, embarrassment, expense and fear of possible conviction which a criminal trial causes to an accused person? Or the taint, ignominy and the disabilities resulting from actual conviction? Or the punishment actually suffered consequent upon sentence after conviction? An acquittal by itself involves no jeopardy; indeed it terminates the jeopardy. But the fact that jeopardy is created for an accused person although his trial ends in an acquittal means that it is the trial itself, and not its result, whether acquittal or conviction, and whether the sentence is a fine or imprisonment or has actually been suffered, that constitutes jeopardy. It follows that, although conviction carries some taint and disabilities, it is as irrelevant as is an acquittal to the jeopardy that provides the rationale for the doctrine. A sentence based on it is also, *ipso facto*, irrelevant. The conclusion thus clearly emerges that it is the hazards of a criminal trial — the ordeal, anxiety, embarrassment and expense of prosecution together with the fear of possible conviction — which constitute jeopardy. 'The underlying idea,' said the U.S. supreme court, 'is that the state with all its resources and power should not be allowed to make repeated attempts to convict an individual for an alleged offence, thereby subjecting him to embarrassment, expense and ordeal and compelling him to live in a continuing state of anxiety and insecurity, as well as enhancing the possibility that even though innocent he may be found guilty.'[53]

But if this is the rationale of the doctrine, the insistence that the trial must have ended in a conviction or acquittal is difficult to justify. Jeopardy would have been fully suffered if, after the trial has been completed but before judgment is delivered, the trial is terminated at the instance of the prosecution and without the consent or over the protests of the accused, or if the case ends in a finding of not guilty without a formal order of acquittal. It is more consistent with the underlying rationale that an accused person should have the benefit of the doctrine from the point in time when it can be said that he has suffered substantially the hazards of a criminal prosecution and trial. This is the position in the United States. Jeopardy is there accepted as attaching before the completion of the trial — in jury trials when the jury is sworn and in trials before a judge without a jury when the first evidence is presented.[54] But an accused person is not put in jeopardy by a preliminary examination and discharge by a magistrate,[55] by an indictment which is quashed,[56] or by arraignment and pleading to the indictment.[57]

A much agitated question is whether proceedings on appeal from a conviction or acquittal constitute a trial a second time or a trial all over again. The question is relevant only in the case of an appeal by the prosecution against acquittal. An appeal by the accused, whether or not it amounts to a second trial, is not a double jeopardy for him, since it is he who asks for it. If the appeal results in the conviction being set aside, then, since this amounts to an acquittal, the prosecution cannot be begun again save on the order of the appeal court for a fresh trial. A court order for a fresh trial is an exception to the rule specifically recognised by the Constitution. The exception is justified because it involves no double jeopardy for the accused. For, by appealing against his conviction the accused is voluntarily taking the chance that the appeal court may order a new trial, and he does so in the hope that a new trial offers him a chance of escaping the original conviction.

In the United States a fresh prosecution, after a conviction is set aside on an appeal at the instance of the accused, is permitted even without its being ordered by the court, on the ground that by challenging his conviction through an appeal, the accused has 'waived' his right to object to further prosecution.[58] The waiver theory has been characterised as 'totally unsound and indefensible',[59] but the court has not only maintained the practice but has also been reluctant to find a new rationalisation for it.[60]

As to whether a criminal appeal is a trial a second time, the U.S. supreme court has taken the position that it is, and further that it amounts to a second jeopardy which operates to bar an appeal against an acquittal by the prosecution.[61] Dissenting from this view, a minority of three held that, while a criminal appeal is a separate trial from the trial at first instance, it does not constitute a second jeopardy for the accused, but one continuing jeopardy; it is the one, original jeopardy that continues until the case is brought to final conclusion by the judgment of the final court of appeal. 'It seems to me', wrote Mr. Justice Holmes, one of the dissenters, 'that logically and rationally a man cannot be said to be more than once in jeopardy in the same cause, however often he may be tried. The jeopardy is one continuing jeopardy from its beginning to the end of the cause. Everybody agrees that the principle in its origin was a rule forbidding a trial in a new and independent case where a man already had been tried once. But there is no rule that a man may not be tried twice in the same case.'[62] The majority view was re-affirmed fifty-three years later, though the court was more divided this time than before, with four out of the total bench of nine dissenting.[63]

It may be doubted whether in Nigeria a criminal appeal is a trial at all. For a criminal appeal, unlike a civil one, is not by way of rehearing, but rather a limited appeal which precludes the court from reviewing the evidence and making its own evaluation of it.[64] It follows that if a criminal appeal is not by way of a rehearing, it cannot be a trial within the meaning of s. 33(9) of the Nigerian Constitution 1979. But even if a criminal appeal, whether by way of rehearing or not, can properly be regarded as a trial, it is still not such a trial as is prohibited by s. 33(9) of the Constitution. The words 'shall again be tried' as used in the subsection seem clearly to indicate a separate and independent trial at first instance. The word 'again' is defined in the *Concise Oxford Dictionary* as 'another time'. A criminal appeal is not a trial at another time or occasion or a trial all over again; it is merely a continuation of the one and only trial. While it may be a double jeopardy to continue a trial after it has terminated in an acquittal, such continued trial does not mean that the accused is being tried 'again' within the meaning of s. 33(9) of the Nigerian Constitution. Indeed, if an appeal is such a trial as is referred to in the subsection, then on a strict, literal reading of the provision, an appeal by an accused against conviction would be precluded as well.

Secondly, the words 'save upon the order of a superior court' make it clear that 'shall again be tried' refers to a new, independent trial or a retrial. The order of a superior court referred to in the subsection can only be an order for a retrial; it cannot be an order for an appeal. This makes it clear that an appeal is not the concern of the subsection, and is therefore not within its prohibition, even if it is a trial. Its concern is with a new, independent trial in a completely different case or a retrial in the same case. But if the subsection allows a retrial on the order of a superior court, it cannot consistently forbid a rehearing by a superior court on appeal. Moreover, if an appeal is a trial within the meaning of the subsection, then an order of an appeal court granting leave to appeal comes within the phrase 'save upon the order of a superior court'. In any case, an order of a superior court for a retrial can only be made on an appeal. It cannot be made if an appeal, whether by the accused or prosecution, is altogether precluded.

The argument that an appeal by the prosecution against an acquittal is barred by s. 33(9) of the Nigerian Constitution was thus rightly rejected by the supreme court. While agreeing that the common law rule against double jeopardy is part of the law of Nigeria, it held that its application is restricted by the formulation of it in s. 33(9), which makes it clear that an appeal is 'but one and the *same trial* and not — as learned counsel for the appellant contends — another or second trial', quoting with approval the minority view of Mr. Justice Holmes above.[65] In a separate concurring judgment, Mr. Justice Udo Udoma frowned on the attempt to import the American doctrine of double jeopardy which, 'unless carefully and critically examined, might turn out to be a gloss on, and a pollution of the pure and sparkling stream of our new Constitution'.

There are other restrictions on the doctrine. It does not bar successive trials for different offences based on the same act. 'The test is not whether the defendant has already been tried for the same act but whether he has been put in jeopardy for the same offence.'[66] Thus, one act of sexual intercourse could be the basis of consecutive prosecutions for rape and incest.[67] The charging in one trial of multiple counts based on different offences arising from one act or transaction raises a different kind of question, which hardly involves double jeopardy, since all the counts are tried together. But the U.S. supreme court has held that the test to be applied in determining whether the offences are to be treated as one offence or as separate ones is whether each offence requires 'proof of an additional fact which the other does not'.[68]

The doctrine does not also bar separate, consecutive trials where an act constitutes the same offence under different jurisdictions within a federal system. Although the offences are the same in nature in the sense that they have the same ingredients, yet the violation of the penal laws of one government in a federation is not excused from prosecution by the authorities of that government merely because the offender has been tried and convicted or acquitted for the 'same' offence under the laws of another government.[69]

REFERENCES

1. See *Waterside Workers' Fedn. of Australia* v. *J.W. Alexander Ltd.* (1918), 25 C.L.R. 434, 444 — per Griffith C.J.
2. See *Ex parte Milligan*, (1864) 2 Wall 2; also *Duncan* v. *Kahanamoku* (1945), 327 U.S. 304.
3. See Denning, *Freedom under the Law* (1949), 42.
4. *Aoko* v. *Fagbemi* (1961), 1 All N.L.R. 400.
5. *Connally* v. *General Construction Co.* (1926), 269 U.S. 385, 391; *Jordan* v. *De George* (1951), 341 U.S. 223, 230; *United States* v. *National Dairy Prod. Corp.* (1963), 372 U.S. 29, 32–3.
6. *Att.-Gen. for Zambia* v. *Chipango* (1970), S.J.Z. 1979; but contrast *Uganda* v. *Commissioner of Prisons, ex parte Matovu* (1966) E.A. 514; *Greene* v. *Home Secretary* [1941], 3 All E.R. 388 (H.L.).
7. *Oyediran* v. *The Republic* (1967), N.M.L.R. 123.
8. *Gokpa* v. *Inspector-General of Police* (1962), 1 All N.L.R. 423 (High Court of the former Eastern Nigeria). Consider *Shempfe* v. *Commissioner of Police* (1962), N.N.L.R. 87, where the High Court of the former Northern

Nigeria came to a different conclusion on somewhat similar facts. See also *Olawoyin* v. *Commissioner of Police* (1962), N.N.L.R. 29 (High Court N. Nigeria).

9. *Police* v. *Okafor* (1964), 2 All N.L.R. 166.

10. See Niki Tobi, 'Essentials of Fair Trial' — paper read at the Sixth Commonwealth Law Conference, Lagos, August 1980; citing *Note*: 'The Prosecutor's Constitutional Duty to Reveal Evidence to the Defendant', 74 *Yale L.J.* (1964), 136–40; *Note*: 'The Duty of the Prosecution to Disclose Exculpatory Evidence', 60 *Colum. L. Rev.* (1960), 858; Louisell, 'Criminal Discovery: Dilemma, Real or Apparent?', 49 *Calif. L.R.* (1961), 56, 64–7. On the question whether there is a reciprocal obligation on the part of the accused to disclose evidence to the prosecution, see *Note*: 'Discovery and Disclosure: Dual Aspects of the Prosecutor's Role in Criminal Procedure', 34 *Geo. Wash. L. Rev.* (1964), 92, 101–4.

11. *Powell* v. *Alabama* (1932), 287 U.S. 45; *Escobedo* v. *Illinois* (1964), 378 U.S. 478; *Massiah* v. *United States* (1964), 377 U.S. 201; *Spano* v. *New York* (1959), 360 U.S. 315; *United States* v. *Wade* (1967), 388 U.S. 218, 226.

12. *Betts* v. *Brady* (1942), 316 U.S. 455.

13. *Gideon* v. *Wainwright* (1963), 372 U.S. 335, at 344.

14. *Argersinger* v. *Hamlin* (1972), 407 U.S. 25, which must be regarded as severely modifying the earlier decision making the application of the right dependent on the existence or otherwise of special circumstances: *Hamilton* v. *Alabama* (1961), 368 U.S. 52.

15. *Powell* v. *Alabama* (1932), 287 U.S. 45 at pp. 68–9.

16. *Chandler* v. *Fretag* (1954), 348 U.S. 3 at p. 9, 10; also *House* v. *Mayo* (1945) 324 U.S. 42; *Hawk* v. *Olson*, 326 U.S. 271 (1945); *Reynolds* v. *Cochran* (1961), 365 U.S. 525.

17. *Awolowo* v. *The Federal Minister of Internal Affairs*, High Court of Lagos, Suit No. LD/595/62.

18. See *United States* v. *Ewell* (1966), 383 U.S. 116, 120; also *Smith* v. *Hooey* (1969), 393 U.S. 374, 377–9; *Dickey* v. *Florida* (1970), 398 U.S. 30, 37–8; *Barker* v. *Wingo* (1972), 407 U.S. 514, 519.

19. Per Idigbe JSC in *Akpor* v. *Iguoriguo* (1978), 1 L.R.N.; quoted in *Oluka Obaze Ozulonye and Others* v. *The State* FCA/E/79/80 of 22/1/81.

20. See *Kakara & Another* v. *Imonikhe and Another* (1974), 1 All N.L.R. 383, 384; *Onosiaherhonwe Ekeri & Others* v. *Edo Kimisede & Others* (1976), 1 N.M.L.R., 194; *Awobiyi* v. *Igbalaiye Brother* (1965), 1 All N.L.R. 163.

21. *United States* v. *Ewell*, ibid.

22. *United States* v. *Marion* (1971), 404 U.S. 307, 313, 320, 322.

23. *Barker* v. *Wingo*, ibid.

24. *Oluka Obaze Ozulonye & Others* v. *The State*, ibid.

25. *In re Oliver* (1948), 333 U.S. 257, 266–70; *Estes* v. *Texas* (1965), 381 U.S. 532, 538–9.

26. *Willy John* v. *R.* (1956), 23 E.A.C.A. 509.

27. *Biffo* v. *R.* (1960), E.A. 965.

28. See *Sheppard* v. *Maxwell* (1966), 384 U.S. 333; *Irvin* v. *Dowd* (1961), 336 U.S. 717.

29. *Estes* v. *Texas*, ibid.

30. *Nebraska Press Assn.* v. *Stuart* (1976), 427 U.S. 539.
31. *In re Winship* (1970), 397 U.S. 358, 363.
32. ibid.
33. *Ibeziako* v. *Commissioner of Police* (1963), N.R.N.L.R. 88.
34. *Tot* v. *United States* (1943), 319 U.S. 463, 467.
35. *Leary* v. *United States* (1969), 395 U.S. 36.
36. ibid.
37. *Tot* v. *United States,* ibid.
38. *Davis* v. *United States* (1895), 160 U.S. 469, 486−7; *Leland* v. *Oregon* (1952), 343 U.S. 790; *Johnson* v. *The Queen* (1962), 46 C.A.R. 55; *Oluka Obaze Ozulonye & Others* v. *The State,* ibid.
39. *Stump* v. *Bennett* (1968), 398 F. 2d. 111 (c. A.8) Cert. den. 393 U.S. 1001. Alibi being a common law, and not a statutory, defence in Nigeria, the burden is not on the accused to prove it, see *Yanor* v. *The State* (1965), N.M.L.R., 337; *Adedeji* v. *The State* (1971), 1 All N.L.R., 75, 78; *Oluka Obaze Ozulonye & Others* v. *The State,* ibid.
40. *United States* v. *Vuitch* (1971), 402 U.S. 62.
41. *Isiyaku Mohammed* v. *Kano N.A.* (1968), 1 All N.L.R. 424; *Whyte* v. *Commissioner of Police* (1968), 1 All N.L.R. 424.
42. Sixth Amendment.
43. *Mattox* v. *United States* (1895), 156 U.S. 237, 242−3; *Kirby* v. *United States* (1899), 174 U.S. 47, 55, 56; *Pointer* v. *Texas* (1965), 380 U.S. 400; *Douglas* v. *Alabama* (1965), 380 U.S. 415; *Bruton* v. *United States* (1968), 391 U.S. 123.
44. *California* v. *Green* (1970), 399 U.S. 149, 155−6; *Dutton* v. *Evans* (1970), 400 U.S. 74, 80−6.
45. *Sadua of Kunya* v. *Abdul Kadir of Fagge* (1956), 1 F.S.C. 39.
46. *Tulu* v. *Bauchi N.A.* (1965), N.M.L.R. 343.
47. *Buraimoh Ajayi & another* v. *Zaria N.A.* (1963), 1 All N.L.R. 169.
48. Fifth Amendment.
49. *Ullmann* v. *United States,* 350 U.S. 422, 443 — per Justice Douglas.
50. *Miranda* v. *Arizona* (1966), 384 U.S. 436, 444−5.
51. See *The Constitution of the United States of America: Analysis and Interpretation* (1973), 1133.
52. *Griffin* v. *California* (1965), 380 U.S. 609, 614.
53. *Green* v. *United States* (1957), 355 U.S. 184, 187−8.
54. *Downum* v. *United States* (1963), 372 U.S. 734.
55. *Collins* v. *Loisel* (1923), 262 U.S. 426.
56. *Taylor* v. *United States* (1907), 207 U.S. 120, 127.
57. *Bassing* v. *Cady* (1908), 208 U.S. 386, 391−2.
58. *United States* v. *Ball* (1896), 163 U.S. 662.
59. *Green* v. *United States* (1957), 355 U.S. 184, 197.
60. *United States* v. *Tateo* (1964), 377 U.S. 463, 466; *United States* v. *Ewell* (1961), 383 U.S. 116, 121.
61. *Kepner* v. *United States* (1904), 195 U.S. 100.
62. ibid. at 130.
63. *Green* v. *United States* (1957), 355 U.S. 184.
64. *Aladesuru* v. *R.* [1955], 3 W.L.R. 517 (P.C.).

65. *Nafiu Rabiu* v. *The State*, SC.49/80 delivered on 21/11/80 in a separate judgment.
66. *Morey* v. *Commonwealth* (1871), 108 Mass. 433, 434.
67. *Morey* v. *Commonwealth*, ibid.; *Gore* v. *United States* (1958), 357 U.S. 386, 392–3. Compare *In re Nielsen* (1889), 131 U.S. 176; *Ashe* v. *Swenson* (1970), 397 U.S. 436.
68. *Blockburger* v. *United States* (1932), 284 U.S. 299, 304.
69. See *United States* v. *Lanza* (1922), 260 U.S. 377; reaffirmed over strong dissent in *Abbate* v. *United States* (1959), 359 U.S. 187, 195. Also *Bartkus* v. *Illinois*, 359 U.S. 121; *Herbert* v. *Louisiana* (1924), 272 U.S. 312; *Screws* v. *United States* (1945), 325 U.S. 91, 108; *Jerome* v. *United States* (1943), 318 U.S. 101.

25
FREEDOM FROM DISCRIMINATION

1. *The constitutional guarantee*

Discrimination against a citizen of Nigeria, based on certain specified grounds or classifications, is absolutely prohibited by the Constitution. The absolute character of the prohibition results partly from its rigid and precise wording and partly from the fact that the provision is completely withdrawn from the power of the state to regulate fundamental rights in the interest of defence, public safety, public order, public morality, public health or the protection of the rights and freedom of others, both in normal times and during an emergency. The terms of the prohibition are therefore very material for a proper understanding of its nature and scope. They enjoin (s. 39):

(1) A citizen of Nigeria of a particular community, ethnic group, place of origin, sex, religion or political opinion shall not, by reason only that he is such a person —
    (*a*) be subjected either expressly by, or in the practical application of, any law in force in Nigeria or any executive or administrative action of the government to disabilities or restrictions to which citizens of Nigeria of other communities, ethnic groups, places of origin, sex, religious or political opinions are not made subject, or
    (*b*) be accorded either expressly by, or in the practical application of, any law in force in Nigeria or any such executive or administrative action, any privilege or advantage that is not accorded to citizens of Nigeria of other communities, ethnic groups, places of origin, sex, religious or political opinions.

(2) No citizen of Nigeria shall be subjected to any disability or deprivation merely by reason of the circumstances of his birth.

It is to be noted that the protection against discrimination is restricted to Nigerian citizens only, and, secondly, that discrimination is prohibited only when it is based on the grounds of ethnicity, place of origin, sex, religion or political opinion. The inclusion of sex among the prohibited grounds for discrimination is an innovation from the previous Constitutions. It was not even in the draft prepared by the constitution drafting committee. It got into the Constitution by way of an amendment introduced by a female member of the constituent assembly. A further point which it is necessary to note is that the reference to 'any law in force in Nigeria' covers customary law, Islamic law and common law as well as the statute law. It follows that a rule of any of these systems of law in Nigeria which imposes special disabilities or restrictions or accords special privileges or advantages based on any of the specified grounds or classifications is unconstitutional and void. The point is particularly significant because of the inferior position accorded to women under both customary and Islamic law.

The words 'restrictions' and 'advantage' appearing in the provision also deserve special notice. They are words of the widest import, and carry the scope of the provision far beyond what is implied by the words 'disabilities' and 'privilege'. The latter are essentially words of art. Disability indicates 'an incapacity for the full enjoyment of ordinary legal rights', while privilege implies something approximating to a legal right, such, for instance, as the non-liability of members of the national assembly for words spoken during the proceedings of the assembly.[1] The words 'restrictions' and 'advantage', on the other hand, are not so limited in their ambit.

What this means is that any restriction whatever imposed upon, or any advantage accorded to, women by any law or any executive or administrative action of the government is unconstitutional and void if the restriction or advantage is not applied equally to men. Certainly, a democratic Constitution founded on the worth of the individual as an autonomous legal entity should not tolerate class discrimination, whereby people are treated differently by the state in the distribution of restrictions or advantages, not because of any real and substantial differences between them, but simply because they belong to different social classes, whether the classification is based on sex, race, ethnicity, religion or political opinion. Fairness or justice demands that people who are similarly circumstanced should be treated equally by the state. Yet there is no discrimination where special restrictions imposed upon a class, or special advantages accorded to it, are reasonably designed to reflect real and substantial differences between it and other classes or groups. It is indeed unfair and unjust to treat unequal things equally.

The inescapable truth and logic of this proposition is indeed recognised by the courts in the United States in interpreting the provision of the Constitution guaranteeing to all persons 'the equal protection of the laws'.[2] In succinct but pungent words, Mr. Justice Frankfurter has said that 'the Constitution does not require things which are different in fact or opinion to be treated in law as though they were the same';[3] it does not intend to create 'a fictitious equality where there is a real difference'.[4] Protection is not unequal merely because real and substantial differences between classes or groups are recognised by law for purposes of special protection or treatment reasonably related to such differences. Provided therefore that such special protection or treatment is reasonable, and not arbitrary, oppressive or capricious, there is no denial of equal protection.[5] A class, e.g. a religious or political group, may be isolated for special treatment if it constitutes a danger to public order, public security, public health or public morality, or if it is so vulnerable by reason of its peculiar circumstances as to require special protection.[6] 'The mere production of inequality', said the U.S. supreme court,[7] 'is not enough. Every selection of persons for regulation so results, in some degree. The inequality produced, in order to encounter the challenge of the Constitution, must be "actually and palpably unreasonable and arbitrary"[8]. Thus classifications have been sustained which are based upon differences between fire insurance and other kinds of insurance;[9] between railroads and other corporations;[10] between barber shop employment and other kinds of labour. . . . .'[11]

However, special treatment based on race is regarded as 'suspect' and *prima facie* arbitrary and capricious, requiring 'a far heavier burden of justification'.[12] While classification based on sex is also subjected to 'close scrutiny',[13] the court recognises that there are real and substantial differences between men and women, saying: 'The civil law, as well as nature itself, has always recognised a wide difference in the respective spheres and destinies of man and woman. . . . The natural and proper timidity and delicacy which belongs to the female sex evidently unfits it for many of the occupations of civil life.'[14] It cannot be denied that there are emotional as well as physical differences between men and women. In the words of Mr. Justice Frankfurter in a case in which the court upheld a law virtually prohibiting all women from being bar-tenders, 'the fact that women may now have achieved the virtues that men have long claimed as their prerogatives and now indulge in vices that men have long practised, does not preclude the States from drawing a sharp line between the sexes, certainly in such matters as the regulation of the liquor traffic.'[15]

The approach of the U.S. supreme court as exemplified in these cases is, unfortunately, not open to Nigerian courts because of the rigid and precise wording of the provision in the Nigerian Constitution, and because the prohibition is not amenable to the state's police power. The consequences are indeed far-reaching, for there are numerous instances of special restrictions imposed upon, or special privileges accorded to, women by the law in Nigeria. The Labour Act 1974, for example, provides that a woman employed in any industrial, commercial or agricultural undertaking 'shall not be permitted to work during the six weeks following her confinement'; that she is entitled to be paid not less than 50 per cent of her wages during any period of absence on maternity leave; that, while nursing a child, she shall be allowed half an hour twice a day during her working hours for that purpose; and that she shall not be employed on night work or on underground work in a mine.[16] Clearly these are either restrictions or advantages imposed or conferred by law on women, but which are not applied to men. They cannot stand in the face of the constitutional guarantee.

The right of a wife to be maintained by her husband, to pledge his credit, and to be paid alimony on divorce not caused by any fault on her part is also constitutionally invalid as an advantage or privilege which is not accorded to the husband. So also are the numerous restrictions imposed on women under customary law, Islamic law and the common law as well as under the statute law.

The 1963 Constitution had a provision which exempted from the prohibition against discrimination any law imposing disability or restriction or according privilege or advantage that, 'having regard to its nature and to the special circumstances pertaining to the persons to whom it applies, is reasonably justifiable in a democratic society.' (s. 28[2][d]). This exemption, which incorporates the American decisions discussed above, is, strangely, omitted from the 1979 Constitution. Also omitted, but rightly so, is the exemption of a law which 'imposes restrictions with respect to the acquisition or use by any person of land or other property' (1963 Constitution, s. 28[2][c]). The only exception allowed in the 1979 Constitution is that relating to restrictions on the appointment of any person to an office under the state or as a member of the armed forces or of the Nigerian police force or to an office in the service of a body corporate established directly by law (s. 39[3]).

The complete emancipation of women by the 1979 Constitution is also reflected in the right which it gives them, on an equal footing with men, to vote and be voted for at elections to a local government council, state house of assembly, house of representatives, senate, the office of governor of a state and the presidency of Nigeria; the right to form or belong to a political party, trade union or other association for the protection of common interest; the right to participate in the discussion of public affairs, to criticise the actions of government, to campaign freely for public causes, and to agitate for change. And Nigerian citizenship can now be acquired equally through a male and a female parent.

2. *Equality as a fundamental objective and principle of state policy*

The notion of equality as an ideal to which the state should aspire is affirmed both in the preamble and in the substantive part of the Constitution. Equality, together with freedom and justice, is proclaimed as the ideal of the social order established by the Constitution, while the eradication of discrimination on the grounds of place of origin, sex, religion, status, and ethnic or linguistic association is prohibited as part of the nation's political objectives (s. 15[2]). The state is enjoined to ensure, in furtherance of the ideal of equality, that 'every citizen shall have equality of rights, obligations and opportunities before the law'; that 'all citizens without discrimination on any ground whatsoever have the opportunity for securing adequate means of livelihood as well as adequate opportunities to secure suitable employment'; that 'there is equal pay for equal work without discrimination on account of sex'; and that 'there are equal and adequate educational opportunities at all levels'.

These are worthy declarations of objectives. But it is necessary that their nature as declarations of objectives and directive principles of state policy, and not as declarations of justiciable rights, should be appreciated. The state is enjoined, as a matter of constitutional duty, to conform to, observe and apply the objectives and directives — although this confers upon the individual no right to go to court to enforce their observance.

REFERENCES

1. See Mozley and Whiteley's *Law Dictionary*, 9th edn (Butterworth).
2. Fourteenth Amendment.
3. *Tigner* v. *Texas* (1940), 310 U.S. 141, 147.
4. *Quong Wing* v. *Kirkendull* (1912), 223 U.S. 59, 63.
5. *Ferguson* v. *Skrup* (1963), 372 U.S. 726, 732; *Lindsley* v. *Natural Carbolic Gas Co.* (1911), 220 U.S. 61, 78−9.
6. See *New York ex rel. Bryant* v. *Zimmerman* (1928), 278 U.S. 63, where many of the cases are collected.
7. *Radice* v. *New York*, 264 U.S. 292, 296.
8. Quoting *Arkansas Natural Gas Co.* v. *Arkansas R. Commission*, 261 U.S. 379, 384.
9. *Orient Ins. Co.* v. *Daggs*, 172 U.S. 557, 562.
10. *Tullis* v. *Lake Erie & W.R. Co.*, 175 U.S. 348, 351.
11. *Petit* v. *Minnesota*, 177 U.S. 104, 168.
12. See particularly *Mchaughlin* v. *Florida* (1964), 379 U.S. 184, 192, 194.
13. *Reed* v. *Reed* (1971), 404 U.S. 71.
14. *Bradwell* v. *Illinois* (1873), 16 Wall (83 U.S.) 130, 141.
15. *Goesaert* v. *Cleary* (1948), 335 U.S. 464, 466.
16. ss. 53−5.

26
FREEDOM OF SPEECH AND THE PRESS

1. *The preferred position of speech and the press*

It is an established doctrine of the law of the Constitution in the United States that freedom of speech and the press have a preferred status over all other rights, including indeed the right to life and personal liberty. What this priority means is that those rights — to freedom of speech and the press — are more jealously guarded against governmental interference than other rights.

It may seem rather strange that speech or press should be accorded greater importance than life itself. One would have thought that life is more basic and valuable, since without it there can be no speech and no press. The latter are mere incidents of life, manifestations of man's existence as a living being. This is unquestionably true, but it is true only from the standpoint of the lone individual. From the perspective of the community, however, the evaluation is reversed. Freedom of speech and the press are indeed the very life of the political community. Life in the sense of physical existence is not really at stake for the community, since government itself cannot exist without a society to govern. What is at stake for the community is its right to self-government; that is its life.

Speech concerning public affairs has rightly been said to be 'more than self-expression; it is the essence of self-government.'[1] Given the impossibility of government by all the members of a modern, complex society comprising millions of people spread over a large territory, free speech and free press are the means by which the society as a collection of individuals can participate in government; they are the very definition of democracy, the ultimate values of all democratic living. The primary meaning of democracy, Professor Sir Arthur Lewis has said, is that all those affected by a decision should participate in making it.[2]

Free speech and a free press are instruments of self-government by the people because they enable the people to be informed and educated about affairs of government, thereby also enabling them to form and express intelligent opinions on such matters. Free dissemination and discussion of ideas and opinions is thus indispensable to democratic government. Political responsibility as a concept of democratic government requires that public opinion should be one of the factors informing the actions of government. Indeed, an extreme view of political responsibility postulates public opinion as the determinant of policy, since, as it is said, a responsible person is one whose 'conduct responds to an outside determinant'.³ On this view, government should do nothing of which public opinion disapproves.

The priority accorded to freedom of speech and of the press is predicated further on the belief that free discussion is indispensable to the discovery of political truth. 'When ideas compete in the market, [. . .] full and free discussion exposes the false. . . . Full and free discussion even of ideas we hate encourages the testing of our own prejudices and preconceptions.'⁴ Furthermore, it conduces to wise policies by ensuring that decisions are taken only after various policy options have been publicly debated.

More important, by allowing free discussion, ideas held by the government and those advocated by its opponents have the opportunity to compete for acceptance by the public. If after full and free discussion the opposing ideas are rejected by the public as unworthy of support, their advocates cannot in justice be aggrieved or moved to adopt unlawful methods, knowing that rejection has come about not through government suppression but by the democratic choice of the people. Having had a fair chance to offer their ideas and urge them upon the public for acceptance, they should be sportsmen enough to respect the people's right of choice. But where the ideas opposed to the government's emerge from the competition as the ones favoured by the people, their acceptance by the people would thus enable change to be effected by peaceful means instead of by force. It is, as was remarked by the U.S. supreme court,⁵ in a peaceful change based on the worthiness and appeal of opposing programmes and ideas presented to the public by the competitors for power, that the security of constitutional government lies.

Free speech and a free press also enable corruption, abuse of office and other official wrongdoing by public servants to be publicly exposed. The fact that their conduct and character are open to public debate in the mass media may be accounted the greatest check on official misconduct. As the U.S. supreme court observed in 1931, 'the administration of government has become more complex, the opportunities for malfeasance and corruption have multiplied, crime has grown to most serious proportions, and the danger of its protection by unfaithful officials and of the impairment of the fundamental security of life and property by criminal alliances and official neglect, emphasise the primary need of a vigilant and courageous press.'⁶ The exposure of President Nixon's involvement in the Watergate affair through the efforts of the press in the United States bears out eloquently the primacy of the need for free speech and a free press in the maintenance of constitutional government.

The administration of government is not of course the only thing on which it is important for the public to be informed and educated. The necessity also exists in connection with all other matters of public concern. In our modern industrial economy the management of the affairs of working people is indeed of great concern to the public as a whole. Free speech and a free press enable the conditions in industry to be publicly discussed, and the oppression of workers, sub-standard wages and objectionable working conditions, where they occur, to be exposed. 'Free discussion concerning the conditions in industry and the causes of labour disputes appears to us indispensable to the effective and intelligent use of the processes of popular government to shape the destiny of modern industrial society.'[7]

And just as free speech and a free press are indispensable in assisting the public to make an intelligent and informed choice of those who are to conduct the government of the nation, so are they in the choice of trade union representatives. Industrial democracy is today as vital to public peace and harmony as representative democracy in national government. In the words of Justice Jackson of the U.S. supreme court in a case involving the right of a trade union leader to address a mass meeting of workers in a particular industry and to solicit them to join his union, 'the necessity for choosing collective bargaining representatives brings the same nature of problem to groups of organising workmen that our representative democratic processes bring to the nation. Their smaller society, too, must choose between rival leaders and competing policies. This should not be an underground process. [. . .] If free speech anywhere serves a useful social purpose, to be jealously guarded, I should think it would be in such a relationship.'[8]

With politics and industrial relations, religion is a fundamental factor in the life of any society, and freedom to preach or disseminate religious views is therefore essential to its harmony and wellbeing. Only in the context of free speech and a free press does freedom of thought and conscience have practical meaning. It is not much use for a man to be free to think, feel and believe what he likes if he is not able to express his thought, feeling and belief on religious to the same extent as on political matters. Freedom to propagate and disseminate religious views must co-exist with freedom to advocate political views if peace and harmony are to be achieved in society.

Freedom of peaceable assembly and of association is yet another right which cannot be meaningfully enjoyed without freedom of speech. Discussion of matters of common concern with a view to the redress of grievances and the protection of legitimate common interests is the sole purpose for which law-abiding people associate and assemble together. These rights are therefore founded upon, and are inseparable from, freedom of speech and the press, and derive their vitality from it.

2. Press freedom defined

Few issues in the Constitution at the time it was drafted provoked so much public controversy as the freedom of the press, and this is appropriate to the importance of the subject. Unfortunately much of the discussion is confused and unedifying.

The confusion stems from three main sources. There is, first, the erroneous assumption that press freedom requires special protection for the press as an institution. In the context of that concept, the press is not an institution comprising special members; it is simply a vehicle, an organ, for the dissemination of ideas or opinions to the public through the medium of the printed word. A newspaper, magazine or other periodical is operated as a business and has to be manned by workers, but its use for the dissemination of ideas or opinions is open to the public at large. The protection needed is not for the workers as such, but for access to the medium by any person for the dissemination of information and ideas. Nor, as the U.S. supreme court has emphasised, is the press of a country 'confined to newspapers and periodicals. It necessarily embraces pamphlets and leaflets. These indeed have been historic weapons in the defence of liberty, as the pamphlets of Thomas Paine and others in our own history abundantly attest. The press in its historic connotation comprehends every sort of publication which affords a vehicle of information and opinion.'[9] Books and handbills have thus been held to be included,[10] so have motion pictures which indeed are today a significant medium for the communication of ideas and information.[11]

The second source of confusion in the controversy is the failure to appreciate the difference between freedom of speech and press freedom. It lies not just in the difference between the spoken and the printed word, and the wider range of the latter. Speech is an irrepressible attribute of a man's being. So long as he lives, he cannot be prevented from speaking if he wants to do so. You can punish him for what he says, but that is after he has said it. Gagging apart, it is physically impossible to prevent a living person from speaking what he pleases. His audience may be restricted by government regulation banning assemblages of persons in public places, but he remains free to speak his mind privately if he has the courage to damn the consequences. A constitutional guarantee of freedom of speech is thus concerned to provide protection not so much against suppression as against unreasonable punishment or other consequences.

With press freedom on the other hand, the protection needed is essentially against suppression or prior restraint in the technical language of the law on the subject. Unlike speech, expression through the medium of the press can be prevented by a system of licensing or by the proscription of a publication already in circulation. It can also be stifled by the imposition of unreasonable punishment for what is published. But punishment subsequent to publication is a far less danger to press freedom than complete inability to publish at all; as with speech, courage can overcome the former, but it is impotent against the power of the censor.

It is for this reason that press freedom has come to mean essentially freedom from all prior restraints whether in the form of a licence refusal of which prevents publication from inception or a ban or proscription of further publication or distribution. It connotes therefore the right of every person to own a printing press, to publish what information or ideas he pleases, to decide the editorial policy of the publication and to enforce it upon his staff, and to distribute or circulate it freely, without having to obtain a licence from the authorities or to face suppression or proscription.

While this is the principal meaning and concern of press freedom, freedom from unreasonable punishment for what is published is by no means irrelevant to the concept. For, press freedom would be made largely nugatory if the state can punish for any publication that it considers harmful or offensive. Provided, however, that punishment is reasonably justifiable in the interest of the public welfare, the concept of press freedom in this secondary sense implies no special protection for publications in a newspaper; their authors and publishers are amenable to the general law just like other members of the community.

It is this principle of freedom from all prior restraints complemented by that of freedom from unreasonable punishment for what is published that lies at the basis of all legal definitions of press freedom. Writing in the eighteenth century, Sir William Blackstone defines it as consisting in 'laying no *previous* restraint upon publication, and not in freedom from censure for criminal matter when published. Every free man has an undoubted right to lay what sentiments he pleases before the public; to forbid this, is to destroy the freedom of the press; but if he publishes what is improper, mischievous or illegal, he must take the consequences of his own temerity.'[12] Blackstone has been rightly criticised for excluding freedom from unreasonable punishment for what is published. The U.S. supreme court has also defined press freedom as meaning principally the prevention of 'all such *previous restraints* upon publications as had been practised by other governments,' adding that it does not 'prevent the subsequent punishment of such as may be deemed contrary to the public welfare'.[13] 'Liberty of the press', it said in another case, 'has meant, principally although not exclusively, immunity from previous restraints or censorship.'[14] With great passion it observed in yet another case:

The struggle for the freedom of the press was primarily directed against the power of the licensor. It was against that power that John Milton directed his assault by his 'Appeal for the Liberty of Unlicensed Printing'. And the liberty of the press became initially a right to publish *without* a licence what formerly could be published only *with* one.' While this freedom from previous restraint upon publication cannot be regarded as exhausting the guaranty of liberty, the prevention of that restraint was a leading purpose in the adoption of the constitutional provision. . . . [15]

But it is claimed that press freedom embraces not only the right to report news without prior restraint or unreasonable punishment for what is published, but also an unrestrained right of newsmen to gather information and the right not to be compelled to disclose its source. As regards the right to gather information, the U.S. supreme court has held that no 'constitutional right of special access to information not available to the public generally' is guaranteed to the press.[16] 'The right to speak and publish', said the court, 'does not carry with it the unrestrained right to gather information.'[17] There is neither a 'constitutional right to have access to particular government information or to require openness from the bureaucracy' nor a constitutional duty on the part of the government to furnish to newsmen information that is not available to members of the general public.[18] (In the United States, journalists and others do have a limited right to obtain government information which does not impinge on national security or personnel matters, but the right is not a constitutional one; it derives entirely from congressional legislation, the Freedom of Information Act 1966 as amended in 1974.)[19]

A more hotly contested point is whether the press has a constitutional right not to be compelled to disclose the source of the information it publishes.[20] The argument that the press under the U.S. Constitution has such a special immunity was first raised before the country's supreme court in 1958.[21] The claim was again urged in 1972 in three cases which came together before the court, involving some newsmen who had refused to testify before a grand jury or to disclose the identity of participants in criminal activity reported by them or to disclose the source of information in another report.[22]

The premise of the claim is that the Constitution guarantees a free flow of information to the public, and that to compel newsmen to disclose their source of information would drive a wedge of distrust between the news media and informants which, in turn, might deter such informants from confiding information to the news media in future; on the part of newsmen themselves it is claimed that compelled disclosure would cause them to censor their report of information in an effort to avoid being subpoenaed. On this premise, it is contended that a newsman should not be compelled either to appear or to testify before a court or other tribunal until and unless sufficient grounds are shown that he possesses information relevant to the matter under investigation, that the information is unavailable from other sources, and that the need for the information is sufficiently compelling to override the newsman's immunity against compelled disclosure which is secured by the constitutional guarantee of a free flow of information to the public. The privilege claimed is thus not absolute, but a qualified one.

But even as qualified, it was rejected by the U.S. supreme court by a majority of 5–4. It held that the press has no immunity from the general law which is not available to other members of the general public;[23] accordingly, as no immunity from disclosure is accorded to the ordinary citizen before a court, none can be claimed by the press. As the court observed:

A number of States have provided newsmen a *statutory* privilege of varying breadth,[24] but the majority have not done so, and none has been provided by federal statute. Until now the only testimonial privilege for unofficial witnesses that is rooted in the Federal Constitution is the Fifth Amendment privilege against compelled self-incrimination. We are asked to create another by interpreting the First Amendment to grant newsmen a testimonial privilege that other citizens do not enjoy. This we decline to do.[25]

On the argument that refusal to grant the immunity would undermine the freedom of the press to collect and disseminate news, the court observed that 'this is not the lesson history teaches us. As noted previously, the common law recognised no such privilege, and the constitutional argument was not even asserted until 1958. From the beginning of our country the press has operated without constitutional protection for press informants, and the press has flourished. The existing constitutional rules have not been a serious obstacle to either the development or retention of confidential news sources by the press.'[26] Furthermore, it said:

The administration of a constitutional newsman's privilege would present practical and conceptual difficulties of a high order. Sooner or later, it would be necessary to define those categories of newsmen who qualified for the privilege, a questionable procedure in light of the traditional doctrine that liberty of the press is the right of the lonely pamphleteer who uses carbon paper or a mimeograph just as much as of the large metropolitan publisher who utilizes the latest photo composition methods. . . . The informative function asserted by representatives of the organised press in the present cases is also performed by lecturers, political pollsters, novelists, academic researchers, and dramatists. Almost any author may quite accurately assert that he is contributing to the flow of information to the public, that he relies on confidential sources of information, and that these sources will be silenced if he is forced to make disclosures.[27]

A minority of the court maintained that the right to gather news is a corollary of the right to publish, since otherwise news might be cut off at source; that the right to gather news implies, in turn, a right to a confidential relationship between a newsman and his source. For 'confidentiality may be a necessary prerequisite to a productive relationship between a newsman and his informants.'[28] They maintained that the reporter himself was bound to be deterred by the fear that contact with a controversial source or publication of controversial material might lead to a subpoena. In the event of a subpoena, then, without a constitutional immunity, the reporter would have to choose between being punished for contempt if he refuses to testify or violating his profession's ethics and impairing his resourcefulness as a reporter if he discloses confidential information. They asserted that the existence of deterrent effect through fear and self-censorship was well attested by the individual reporters and by surveys.[29]

Six years later (in 1978) — in another case involving a *New York Times* reporter who refused to turn over certain investigative evidence to a New Jersey court, relying on the state's 'shield' law which allowed a reporter to protect his source of information — the state supreme court held the law invalid, on the ground that it violated the guarantee of a fair trial in the federal Constitution.[30] The U.S. supreme court refused to grant leave for an appeal.

The point arose before a Lagos state high court in 1980. The editor of the *Daily Times* of Nigeria had been invited to appear before the senate to substantiate a story published in the paper which alleged that senators spent their time playing cards in the house and hunting for contracts in government offices.[31] The court held that to compel a journalist to disclose the source of information published by him in a newspaper is an 'interference' within the meaning of the guarantee in the Nigerian Constitution of the right to 'impart ideas and information without *interference*' (s. 36[1]). According to the court,

It is a matter of common knowledge that those who express their opinions, or impart ideas and information through the medium of a newspaper or any other medium for the dissemination of information enjoy by customary law and convention a degree of confidentiality. How else is a disseminator of information to operate if those who supply him with such information are not assured of protection from identification and/or disclosure?

Defining 'interference' as meaning to hinder or prevent, he said there could be no doubt in 'anybody's mind that the 49 wise men who formulated the Constitution of the country were conscious of the unsavoury consequences attendant in any attempt to deafen the public by preventing or hindering the free flow of information, news and/or ideas from them.' But surely, if compelling a person to disclose his source of information is an interference with his freedom of expression, it must be so whether the person concerned is a journalist or not. And while compelled disclosure may hinder the gathering of information, it is difficult to see how it can deter anyone of average courage from publishing information after it has been gathered. The law should not be solicitous for the chicken-hearted.

The point did not actually arise for decision in the case in which the court made these pronouncements, since the circumstances in which the senate can compel people to appear or testify before it did not exist in this case. The power is limited to cases where such attendance and testimony is necessary to enable the assembly to make new laws, to correct defects in existing law or to expose corruption, inefficiency or waste in the execution or administration of laws and in the disbursement or administration of funds appropriated by it (s. 82). Having held the invitation to the plaintiff to be incompetent, the observations of the court concerning the constitutional right of a newsman not to be compelled to disclose his source of information is *obiter*.

3. Guarantee of freedom of speech and press in the Constitution

Regrettably, the confused thinking that characterised much of the controversy about press freedom has obscured the important innovation introduced by the 1979 Constitution in this regard. The 1963 Constitution provided that 'every person shall be entitled to freedom of expression, including freedom to hold opinions and to receive and impart ideas and information without interference' (s. 25[1]). Although the press is not specifically mentioned, it is unquestionably comprehended in freedom of expression: ideas and information are imparted by speech, by the printed word in a newspaper or other publication, by means of a motion picture etc. Except for emphasis, specification of the various media of expression really adds nothing to the guarantee, while on the other hand it may raise the inference of an intention to exclude any medium of communication not so specifically mentioned. The wording of the guarantee has therefore the advantage of elasticity and brevity without really losing anything by a lack of emphasis. Not only are all media of expression covered, but the explicit stipulation about non-interference with the communication of ideas and information also imparts unequivocal immunity from both previous restraint and subsequent punishment.

The 1979 Constitution reproduces the 1963 provision in its exact terms, and then goes further to say that without prejudice to its generality, 'every person shall be entitled to own, establish and operate any medium for the dissemination of information, ideas and opinions' (s. 36). Freedom from state licensing of newspapers, magazines or other publications and from proscription or ban on account of what is published is thus differentiated from speech and accorded a separate and more emphatic constitutional protection. The provision says that every person has a right not only to own or establish any medium of communication but also to *operate* it. The operation of a medium of communication — say, a newspaper — carries with it the right of the operator to publish in it what information, ideas and opinions that he pleases, to decide its editorial policy, and to distribute or circulate it freely, without licence and without censorship by the authorities. That is the kind of emphasis that can appropriately be included in a constitution, not an emphasis directed to a newspaper as a medium.[32] Press freedom cannot be better guaranteed than in these words.

In point of fact, the innovation in the 1979 Constitution is prompted, not by any peculiar need of the press for special protection over and above that provided in the 1963 Constitution, but by the threat of government monopoly of the mass media. The government had — in 1976, when the new Constitution was being drafted — just taken over the two most influential newspapers in the country, the *Daily Times* and the *New Nigerian*, leaving in private hands only three of the twelve or so newspapers in the country. In this context of government monopoly of the newspaper industry, a constitutional guarantee of freedom of the press has hardly any meaning, since a newspaper or other news medium owned or controlled by the government can have no freedom to publish what it pleases.

How to deal with this threat posed to the constitution drafting committee a question of considerable perplexity. Its sub-committee on Fundamental Objectives had recommended inclusion in the Constitution a stipulation that 'government shall not be involved in the ownership and operation of the newspaper industry.'[33] The main committee turned this down on the ground that government is as much entitled as the individual to put across its own point of view on any issue, and that it can only do so effectively through its own medium; secondly, that, judging by the performance of the privately-owned newspapers in the country, exclusion of government completely from the newspaper industry might leave the nation without any newspaper worthy of the name. The solution adopted by the committee and now embodied in s. 36(2) is to stipulate expressly in the Constitution that the individual is not to be excluded by government from owning or operating a newspaper or other medium of communication, with the exception of television or wireless broadcasting which is reserved exclusively to government, both federal and state, or any other person or body authorised by the president.

The solution prescribed by the Constitution may or may not be the right one, but it has undoubtedly improved and reinforced the constitutional guarantee of press freedom secured by its 1963 formulation. It has, without over-burdening the Constitution, written into it the main principle of the concept of press freedom, which is immunity from prior restraint.

4. Freedom of expression and the state's regulatory authority

Admittedly, the scope and efficacy of the freedom should be determined by reference both to the terms of its guarantee in the Constitution and the qualifications made upon it by that instrument. It is inevitable that freedom of speech and the press must be balanced with the security of the state, orderly government, public morality and the preservation of the reputation of individual members of the community. The preferred status accorded to these freedoms implies no absolute protection. In spite of the sweeping language of the guarantee in the Constitution of the United States, its supreme court has held that 'the protection even as to previous restraint is not absolutely unlimited.'[34] 'Civil liberties . . . imply the existence of an organised society maintaining public order without which liberty itself would be lost in the excesses of unrestrained abuses.'[35]

The Nigerian Constitution fixes the necessary balance in rather broad language. It is provided that the constitutional protection accorded to these rights shall not invalidate any law that is reasonably justifiable in a democratic society (*a*) in the interest of defence, public safety, public order, public morality or public health; (*b*) for the purpose of preventing the disclosure of information received in confidence, maintaining the authority and independence of courts or regulating telephones, wireless broadcasting, television or the exhibition of cinematograph films; (*c*) which imposes restrictions upon persons holding office under the government, members of the armed forces or members of the police force; or (*d*) for the purpose of protecting the rights and freedoms of other persons.

The main exception is the one permitting restriction by law in the interest of defence, public safety, public order, public morality or public health. Unfortunately it is in the formulation of this exception that specificity is sadly lacking. The formulation does little more than re-state the general principle that freedom must be balanced with public welfare. While it is arguable how far a constitution can go in detailed specification, a certain amount of specificity would certainly have been useful in marking out the scope of permissible interference. As it is, the task of working out a precise balance between freedom and state authority falls on the courts. In this, Nigeria's courts are in the same position as the courts under the Constitution of the United States. Both have to grapple with precisely the same problem with no real assistance from the Constitution. (The phrase, reasonably justifiable in a democratic society in the Nigerian Constitution, affords hardly any guidance for the judicial determination of the problem presented.) But this puts our court in good company by making available to them, as a relevant and persuasive precedent, the vast learning and insight of American decisions over the years.

The general principle established in these decisions is that liberty is the rule, and restriction an exception, the tradition is to allow 'the widest room for discussion, the narrowest range for its restriction'.[36] In a metaphor employed by the U.S. supreme court in 1957, 'the door barring federal and state intrusion ... must be kept closed and opened only the slightest crack necessary to prevent encroachment upon more important interests.'[37]

As to when the security of the state, orderly government and public morality become a more important interest than freedom of speech and of the press, the following principles are discernible from the cases.

(i) *Freedom from initial censorship*

Censorship of the making of a speech or the establishment of a printing press is absolutely prohibited by the constitutional guarantee. The absolute prohibition is perfectly justified, since the mere establishment of a press, when no publication has taken place, or the mere announcement of an intention to make a speech can have no harmful impact on the security of the state, orderly government or public morality.

Censorship usually takes two forms. It may be by way of prohibition of the establishment of a press or the making of a speech. Or it may be by a system of state licensing whereby before making a speech or establishing a press a person is required to apply for and obtain a permit or licence which may be granted or refused as the appropriate state functionary may — in his discretion based on his appraisal of the character of the applicant, the propriety or advisability of granting it or other relevant facts — decide, subject or not to such conditions as he may impose. Licensing is objectionable not because a licence might, in abuse of power, be refused in particular cases, but because the threat or risk of refusal pervades every case, including a case where a licence might be had for the asking. The pervasiveness of the threat inherent in a licensing system makes it as repugnant to freedom of speech and the press as an absolute prohibition.[39]

A licensing system is exemplified by a city ordinance which prohibited the distribution anywhere within the city of pamphlets, magazines and periodicals without the permission of the city manager and which authorised their suppression by the city police.[40] Another example of censorship through licensing is provided by a municipal ordinance which required any person wishing to solicit orders for or to sell books within the residential portion of a city first to obtain a permit, which was to be issued only if, after investigation, the mayor deemed it proper or advisable to do so; the conviction of a Jehovah's Witness for making a house to house distribution of religious books and soliciting contributions towards the cost of the publication contrary to the requirement of the ordinance was accordingly nullified together with the ordinance.[41] In another case where three Jehovah's Witnesses (a man and his two sons) were convicted under a statute which made solicitation of money, subscriptions or any valuable thing for a religious cause conditional upon the certificate of a state official approving the cause as a genuine religious one, the statute was declared invalid as a form of censorship, and the convictions were quashed.[42]

A town ordinance which required an application to be made to the chief of police and the obtaining of his written permit before any form of canvassing or solicitation or the distribution of circulars could be made within the town, and which empowered him to refuse a permit if, on the basis of particulars furnished in the application or from other sources, he was of the opinion that the applicant was not of good character or that the project he proposed to promote or the literature he intended to distribute was not free from fraud, was likewise held unconstitutional.[43] A statute which required a permit for the exhibition of motion pictures and authorised the banning of any considered sacrilegious was likewise invalidated.[44] While not expressing any concluded opinion on the matter, the court thought that the licensing of motion pictures might be permissible under a clearly-drawn statute designed to prevent the showing of obscene films. In other words, recognising motion pictures as part of the press of the country does not necessarily entitle it to the same absolute immunity from censorship as is accorded to speech and publications.

Where a statute does not go as far as to require a permit or licence, as where it merely requires the filing of particulars of a newspaper or other publication that will enable it to be identified, the question has arisen whether such an identification or registration requirement carries the taint of licensing forbidden by the constitutional guarantee. Registration or identification undoubtedly differs from licensing in that it is granted as a matter of course on the furnishing of the requisite information. No discretion to withhold a registration or identification card is given to the authorities, since no conditions as to qualifications or content of publication are required. The role of the state under such a requirement is purely ministerial, involving no exercise of discretion to allow or disallow speech or publication according to an appraisal of the facts to be made by a state functionary.

The U.S. supreme court has held by a majority of five to four that speech at a public meeting organised for the discussion of political, religious, economic or social questions poses no inherent danger to public order, safety etc., such as to warrant previous identification of the speakers; and that so long as no more is involved than the exercise of the rights of free speech and free assembly, a registration or identification requirement is incompatible with it, and thus invalid.[45] And a person is not necessarily doing more than exercising the right of free speech because he at the same time solicits membership of a political party, trade union or religious association. Solicitation of membership cannot be restricted by a registration or identification requirement without depriving free speech of the protection of the constitutional guarantee. The line between solicitation and discussion is too fine to be drawn surely or securely. 'The effort to observe it could not be free speech, free press or free assembly in any sense of free advocacy of principles or causes.'[46]

However, it seems to be conceded that solicitation of subscriptions at a public meeting,[47] or the collection of them[48] is more than mere speech, and may be regulated by a registration or identification requirement. The rationale for upholding such a requirement in cases involving solicitation or collection of money from the public lies in the fact that the modern state has a duty to protect the public from the untrustworthiness, dishonesty or irresponsibility of those who seek for one purpose or another to obtain its money.[49]

But the information called for must not be more than is reasonably necessary to enable the person concerned to be identified. It is arguable whether requiring information not only as to name, address, citizenship, credentials, party or trade union affiliations, but also as to any previous convictions and the nature of the offences for which they were imposed is not more than is reasonably necessary to enable a person to be identified. (The point was left open in *Thomas* v. *Collins*.[50])

Since ownership of a press for the publication of a newspaper or periodical is a business, a registration or identification requirement in respect of it is constitutionally justified. For example, the Newspaper Act[42] requires a person wishing to set up a press for the publication of a newspaper to swear before a magistrate or a commissioner for oaths an affidavit declaring his name, the title or name of the newspaper and a description of the house or building where the newspaper is to be printed, and to deposit 500 Naira or otherwise execute a bond in that amount with one or more sureties, to guarantee the payment of any penalty or damages and costs that may be awarded against him in connection with the publication of the paper. Under the Printing Presses Regulation Act,[51] the owner of a printing press is required to declare before a magistrate, a description of the place where the press is situated, subject to a penalty of six months' imprisonment or 100 Naira fine or both in case of default. The requirements in both statutes may be said to be constitutionally justified. While the deposit requirement in the Newspaper Act can have no bearing on the identification of an owner, and while its amount has been criticised as excessive,[52] it seems that it can be justified as being necessary for the protection of the rights and freedoms of other persons in terms of the constitutional provision.

(ii) *Freedom from subsequent proscription or ban of publication or distribution*
While prohibition and licensing aim at stopping a speech from being made or a press from coming into existence at all, proscription or a ban presupposes the existence of a press and that its publication has been in circulation for some time, from which it can be judged whether what is published is harmful or detrimental to the public interest. The record of its past publication provides a basis, lacking in the case of initial censorship, for testing the reasonableness of the decision to ban it. But although it comes after initial publication, proscription is a form of prior restraint.

The principle seems clearly established in the American decisions that proscription or ban of a newspaper, magazine or other publication forming part of the press of the country is permitted only in 'exceptional cases',[53] as where the publication is inimical to the effective prosecution of a war in which the nation is engaged,[54] or is clearly obscene, lewd or lascivious, or in cases of incitement to acts of violence and the overthrow by force of orderly government. It is not such an 'exceptional case' merely that a newspaper, magazine or other publication regularly published defamatory scandal by maliciously accusing public functionaries of gross neglect of duty, inefficiency, illicit relations with criminal gangsters, and corruption. It is therefore unconstitutional to proscribe or suppress the publication as a public nuisance for this reason or to make resumption of publication in future dependent upon the authorities being satisfied as to the character of the new publication. As the U.S. supreme court said, 'the fact that liberty of the press may be abused by miscreant purveyors of scandal does not make any the less necessary the immunity of the press from previous restraint in dealing with official misconduct. Subsequent punishment for such abuses as may exist is the appropriate remedy, consistent with the constitutional privilege.'[55]

So also where the government of the United States sought by means of an injunction to suppress the publication by two newspapers (the *New York Times* and the *Washington Post*) of the contents of a classified government document bearing on its policy in Vietnam, the U.S. supreme court held that the government had not discharged the burden of showing that the danger to national security posed by the publication was an exceptional one. 'Any system of prior restraints of expression,' the court said, 'comes to the United States Supreme Court bearing a heavy presumption against its constitutional validity, and a party who seeks to have such a restraint upheld thus carries a heavy burden of showing justification for the imposition of such a restraint.'[56] The justification must prove that publication will inevitably, directly and immediately endanger national security or orderly government. Mere surmise or conjecture of such consequences is not enough.[57]

After publication has taken place, it is a debatable question whether its distribution should be subject to censorship, aimed at protecting the public interest in defence, safety, order and morality. The U.S. supreme court has however held that, save in exceptional cases, distribution, equally with publication, is immune from censorship, on the ground that 'liberty of circulating is as essential to that freedom as liberty of publishing; indeed, without the circulation, the publication would be of little value.'[58]

Censorship of distribution is exemplified by enactments forbidding knocking on doors or ringing the doorbells of residences in order to deliver a handbill,[59] or the distribution of a handbill which does not bear on its face the name and address of the author, publisher and distributor.[60] The court felt that the public interests the protection of which was being sought in these enactments, e.g. prevention of crime and assuring privacy in an industrial community where many worked on night shifts and had to obtain their sleep during the day, were insufficient to justify the prohibition.

Prohibition of distribution is no less an unconstitutional censorship because it is restricted to a limited number of places, such as streets, sidewalks, alleys, wharfs, boat landings, docks and parks. 'The streets', the court observed, 'are natural and proper places for the dissemination of information and opinion; and one is not to have the exercise of his liberty of expression in appropriate places abridged on the plea that it may be exercised in some other place.'[61] The prohibition by a company of the distribution of handbills on a sidewalk in a company-owned town was also invalidated, against vehement dissent by a minority of the court who characterised the extension of the principle to private premises as a 'novel constitutional doctrine'.[62] The Illegal Markets and Street Trading (Prohibition) Edict 1978 of Lagos state which prohibited, on pain of a fine or imprisonment, the sale or distribution of newspapers, among other things, in public streets, car parks, bus stops, squares or other public places or within the vicinity of a public building is thus clearly an unconstitutional prior restraint on press freedom.

Nor does prohibition of distribution in streets and other public places become constitutionally permissible because its purpose is to prevent the littering of such places. The fact that the throwing of leaflets or other papers on the ground, which is admitted to be within the power of the state to prohibit, may be encouraged by, or may actually result from, the distribution of leaflets and handbills in the street is not enough to justify prohibition of their distribution as opposed to the prohibition of the actual littering of the street with them.

Suppression otherwise than in appropriate exceptional cases is constitutionally forbidden even when it is indirect and limited in form, as by the imposition of a special tax on newspapers. A tax of such a kind is viewed as 'a deliberate and calculated device . . . to limit the circulation of information to which the public is entitled in virtue of the constitutional guarantee'.[63] Statutes exacting a fee for the privilege of distributing tracts or other publications in public streets have been held invalid on this ground.[64] (Likewise solicitation of membership of a political party, religious association or trade union could not be restricted by the imposition of tax on those engaged in it.[65])

(iii) *Freedom from unreasonable punishment for what is said or published*

It is not disputed that the state may inflict punishment for what is said or published, but the question is whether punishment is constitutionally justified if detriment to public security, public order, public morality or public health is merely likely or even probable. Or should detriment be imminent? The U.S. supreme court has laid it down emphatically as a principle of the law of the Constitution that a man may not be punished for what he says or publishes merely because of the likelihood or even probability of detriment resulting from it to the public interest in the maintenance of public security or order. (Public morality raises a different consideration which is discussed later.) Only the imminence of detriment justifies punishment. In the language popularised by the decisions of the court, the utterance or publication in question must create a *clear and present* danger of disorder or insecurity. Expatiating on this test in 1927, a famous member of the court, Justice Brandeis, said:

Those who won our independence by revolution . . . did not exalt order at the cost of liberty. To courageous, self-reliant men, with confidence in the power of free and fearless reasoning applied through the processes of popular government, no danger flowing from speech can be deemed clear and present, unless the incidence of evil apprehended is so imminent that it may befall before there is opportunity for full discussion. If there be time to expose through discussion the falsehood and fallacies, to avert the evil by the process of education, the remedy to be applied is more speech, not enforced silence.[66]

Thus the test of substantial and rational connection which is applied to determine the constitutionality of governmental interference with other rights and freedoms, is not enough when freedom of speech and the press is concerned. In the words of the court in a subsequent case in 1945:

> Any attempt to restrict these liberties must be justified by clear public interest, threatened not doubtfully or remotely, but by clear and present danger. The rational connection between the remedy provided and the evil to be curbed, which in other contexts might support legislation against attack on due process grounds, will not suffice. These rights rest on firmer foundation. Accordingly, whatever occasion would restrain orderly discussion and persuasion, at appropriate time and application, must have clear support in public danger, actual or impending. Only the gravest abuses, endangering paramount interests, give occasion for permissible limitation.[67]

Of course, whether a speech or publication creates an imminent danger to public security or public order will depend, not alone on the words uttered or published, but on all the circumstances. The circumstances, such as the speaker's enthusiasm for the result, may give words, otherwise innocuous, the character of an incitement. 'Eloquence', said the great Justice Holmes, 'may set fire to reason.'[68] Furthermore, opinions may naturally differ as to whether words taken in the circumstances and manner in which they were uttered or published create imminent danger of disorder or insecurity. Bearing that in mind, the following have been held to create such imminent danger in their particular circumstances: impassioned condemnation of conscription and incitement to resist it during war-time;[69] the advocacy, by a member of the left-wing section of the socialist party, of action for the overthrow of organised government by force or violence and the establishment of the dictatorship of the proletariat;[70] the advocacy by a member of the communist labour party of action for the overthrow by sabotage, violence or terrorism of capitalism and the establishment of working class government,[71] or incitement to violence or disorder. In most of these cases the court was sharply divided, not on the principle but on the question of fact whether there existed in the particular circumstances of each case a clear and present danger of the destruction of the system of government or of disorder.

Whatever divergent opinions may be entertained by individual judges on the application of the clear and present danger test, it is important to bear in mind the wide difference between advocacy and incitement. Publication of abstract doctrine or academic discussion having no quality of incitement to any concrete action cannot constitutionally be punished. Neither can advocacy, unrelated to any effort to instigate action, be punished, even when, with evil intent, it urges the forcible overthrow of the government by violence; it has to be wilful advocacy *of action* for the attainment of that end by language reasonably calculated to incite persons to such action. 'Throughout our decisions', the U.S. supreme court observed, 'there has recurred a distinction between the statement of an idea which may prompt its hearers to take unlawful action, and advocacy that such action be taken.'[72] No doubt, as the court recognised, the distinction is a subtle one and difficult to grasp, for in a sense every idea is an incitement. Yet the distinction is so fundamental as to require that it should be consistently maintained.

Advocacy, not of immediate action, but of action in the future has been held sufficient to justify punishment since advocacy of future action creates a present danger. So long as those to whom the advocacy is addressed are 'urged to do something, now or in the future, rather than merely to *believe* in something',[73] punishment is justified. Where the advocacy is for action at some future date, government need not wait until such future date arrives before taking action to stop the plan. As the court rightly said, a plan to overthrow the government by force at some future date, 'even though doomed from the outset because of inadequate numbers or power of the revolutionists, is a sufficient evil for [the Government] to prevent. The damage which such attempts create both physically and politically to a nation makes it impossible to measure the validity in terms' of the immediacy of the violent action advocated.[74]

However, where the advocacy is of violence directed, not at the overthrow of government itself, but at a particular group or towards the redress of a particular grievance, then, to support a finding of clear and present danger, it must be shown that the advocacy makes violence imminent; in other words, the advocacy must have the quality of an incitement to violence.

State regulation under penalty of defamation, particularly criminal defamation, requires special notice. Should the libel of individual officials of government, or indeed of private persons, be criminally punishable, consistently with the constitutional protection of free expression? Is libellous publication not sufficiently redressed by the law of civil defamation? The danger that the individual defamed might be provoked to violent retaliatory action, while it passed as a justification for the criminal punishment of defamation in the old, more violent days, seems rather outworn in modern times, conditioned by more civilised ideas about the redress of grievance through the established process of the law. For this reason, prosecutions for defamation have virtually fallen into disuse in many countries. Yet while criminal defamation remains part of the law, the question is whether it can be squared with the constitutional protection of freedom of expression.

The governing rule was finally settled by two epoch-making decisions of the U.S. supreme court in 1964, both of which involved the criticism of the official conduct of certain public officials.[75] In one of them[76] a district attorney, at a press conference, attributed a large backlog of pending criminal cases to the inefficiency, laziness and excessive vacations of the judges, and accused them of hampering his enforcement of the vice laws by refusing to authorise the expenses for the necessary investigations. He also alluded to certain 'racketeer influences on our eight vacation-minded judges'. He was tried and convicted of criminal defamation. The U.S. supreme court reversed the conviction. It also affirmed the constitutionality of criminal defamation while at the same time greatly narrowing its scope and that of civil defamation as well in order to minimise the conflict with the constitutional guarantee of freedom of speech and press.

First, in criminal as well as civil defamation of a public official in respect of his official conduct, truth is a complete defence, notwithstanding that the utterance or publication had been motivated by ill-will, hatred, enmity or a desire to injure. This is because the interest in private reputation is overborne by the larger public interest, secured by the Constitution, in the dissemination of truth concerning public officials and their official conduct. It is therefore unconstitutional to require that the publication of a true statement should also be for good motives and for justifiable ends.

Secondly, to justify interference with the constitutional protection of free speech and the press, it is not enough that the publication be false, since erroneous statement is inevitable in free debate of public affairs and needs to be protected if such debate is to be pursued with vigour, and free from the deterrent effect of civil damages or criminal punishment. False statement is to be penalised only if made with *actual* malice, i.e. with knowledge of its falsity or in reckless disregard of whether it was true or false. This is because utterances honestly believed contribute to the free interchange of ideas and the ascertainment of truth. To presume malice from the mere falsity of the publication or from the fact of ill-will, hatred or desire to inflict harm would make it unduly hazardous to speak out against a popular politician, with the result that the dishonest and incompetent will be shielded; besides criticism of popular political figure is seldom free of ill-will or selfish political motives. In the dissemination of information and comments on public affairs, the court asserted emphatically:

Only those false statements made with the high degree of awareness of their probable falsity . . . may be the subject of either civil or criminal sanctions. For speech concerning public affairs is more than self-expression; it is the essence of self-government. The First and Fourteenth Amendments embody our 'profound national commitment to the principle that debate on public issues should be uninhibited, robust, and wide-open, and that it may well include vehement, caustic, and sometimes unpleasantly sharp attacks on government and public officials'.[77]

Thirdly, given that a statement concerning the official conduct of a public official is false and is published with knowledge of its falsity or in reckless disregard of whether it was true or false, criminal punishment is still not constitutionally justified unless the publication is calculated or has an imminent tendency to cause a breach of the peace, in the sense not merely of provoking the individual defamed to violent retaliation, but of provoking public disorder, which may happen only in the case of a popular political figure with large following among the population. The court disapproved of statements in its earlier decisions,[78] which suggested that the Constitution does not protect libellous publication or that the clear and present danger test is inapplicable in criminal defamation cases. 'Libel', it declared, 'can claim no talismanic immunity from constitutional limitations.'[79] Rejecting the assertion that criminal libel can be punished without a showing of clear and present danger, it said that 'whether the libel law be civil or criminal, it must satisfy relevant constitutional standards.'[80] The decision in this case may be said to have inflicted a death-blow on criminal defamation. Indeed, one member of the court, Justice Goldberg, took the position that libel on the official conduct of government officials 'has no place in our Constitution'.

The principles established in these two cases would — if adopted by Nigerian courts, as they ought to be — operate to invalidate much of the country's civil and criminal defamation laws, to the extent that they make truth a defence in criminal defamation only if the publication of the defamatory statement is also for the public benefit, and to the extent also that the privilege conferred on a defamatory statement made concerning public officials and their conduct of public affairs is conditional upon good faith. The same fate would also befall the Newspaper Amendment Act of 1964 which made it an offence for anyone to publish in any newspaper any false statement, rumour or report. Knowledge of the falsity of the statement was to be presumed against the publisher unless he proved that, prior to publication, he took reasonable measures to verify its accuracy; this is in direct conflict with the principle that the constitutional guarantee of freedom of the press requires that knowledge of the falsity of the statement should be proved as a fact by the state, and not presumed. In more blatant violation of the constitutional guarantee is the Public Officers (Protection Against False Accusation) Act 1976, which punishes with two years' imprisonment, without the option of a fine, any false statement alleging corruption against a public officer, regardless of whether or not the author of the statement has knowledge of the falsity of the statement.

The punishment of speech or publication which is injurious to public morality raises a peculiar problem because, while the test of clear and present danger rests on objective standards, morality is a subjective concept, which is largely determined by the moral feeling or conscience of the community. An utterance or publication may be morally reprehensible or offensive to the moral feeling or conscience of the community although it does not immediately excite immoral conduct or any other observable anti-social act. This makes the clear and present danger test inappropriate in determining what utterances or publications may be prohibited in the interest of public morality. Obscenity, for example, is considered immoral, although it tends to excite merely lustful *thoughts or desires*, which need not be manifested in actual anti-social conduct; that is to say, such lustful thoughts or desires need not create an imminent danger of anti-social conduct.

Without the objective standard of overt conduct, the question is posed of how a court is to determine what utterances or publications offend against the moral feelings or conscience of the community. It seems that it simply has to assume the role of interpreter of the moral feeling or conscience of the community.

In the view of the U.S. supreme court, the moral feeling or conscience of the community in that country abhors obscenity as something 'utterly without redeeming social importance',[81] or if it has social value at all, such value is so slight as to be outweighed by the social interest in order and morality.[82] But whether a particular utterance or publication is obscene depends, not on the effect of isolated passages on a particularly susceptible person, but rather on whether, applying contemporary community standards, its dominant theme, taken as a whole, excites a lustful thought or desire in an average person.

5. *Nigerian courts and the enforcement of the constitutional guarantee of freedom of speech and the press*

From the foregoing analysis, the conclusion may safely be made that the guarantee of freedom of speech and of the press in the 1979 Nigerian Constitution is adequate. If it turns out not to be effective in practice, the fault would not be that of the Constitution but of the courts in which is reposed the responsibility for their interpretation and enforcement. They have all the learning and insight of the U.S. supreme court to draw from. What they need in order to be able to rise to the challenge is courage. Unfortunately, their performance in the past by this criterion is distinctly uncomfortable. In a judgment devoid of insight or appreciation of the problem of balancing posed to it, the Nigerian supreme court sustained the sedition law which makes it an offence merely to publish words with the intention to excite hatred, contempt or disaffection against the head of state or the government or the Constitution, regardless of whether the words are calculated to incite to immediate violence. The reasoning behind the decision is the sweeping statement that 'it must be justifiable in a democratic society to take reasonable precautions to preserve public order, and this may involve the prohibition of acts which, if unchecked and unrestrained, might lead to disorder, even though those acts would not themselves do so directly.'[83] Judged by the constitutional standards discussed above, the law is clearly unconstitutional and invalid.

It is interesting to note that the law is almost identical to the Sedition Act 1798 of the United States, which became the subject of one of the fiercest constitutional controversies ever to take place in that country, with Thomas Jefferson, James Madison and others vigorously condemning it as unconstitutional. One hundred and sixty three years after the act expired by its own terms, the U.S. supreme court pronounced on it as follows:

Although the Sedition Act was never tested in this Court, the attack upon its validity has carried the day in the court of history. Fines levied in its prosecution were repaid by Act of Congress on the ground that it was unconstitutional. . . . Calhoun, reporting to the Senate on February 4, 1836, assumed that its invalidity was a matter 'which no one now doubts'. Jefferson, as President, pardoned those who had been convicted and sentenced under the Act and remitted their fines, stating: '. . . .I considered, and now consider, that law to be a nullity.' [. . .] The invalidity of the Act has also been assumed by Justices of this Court.[84] [. . .] These views reflect a broad consensus that the Act, because of the restraint it imposed upon criticism of government and public officials, was inconsistent with the First Amendment.[85]

REFERENCES

1. *Garrison* v. *Louisiana* (1964), 379 U.S. 64, 74–5.
2. Arthur Lewis, *Politics in West Africa* (1965), 75.
3. Carl J. Friedrich, *Man and His Government* (1963), 310.
4. Per Justice Douglas in *Dennis* v. *United States* (1951), 341 U.S. 494.
5. *De Jonge* v. *Oregon* (1936), 299 U.S. 353, 365.
6. *Near* v. *Minnesota* (1931), 283 U.S. 697.
7. *Thornhill* v. *Alabama* (1939), 310 U.S. 88, 102–3.
8. *Thomas* v. *Collins* (1945), 323 U.S. 516, 546.
9. *Lovell* v. *Griffin* (1938), 303 U.S. 444.
10. *Largent* v. *Texas* (1942), 318 U.S. 418; *Cantwell* v. *Connecticut* (1939),

310 U.S. 296 — books; *Jamison* v. *Texas*, 318 U.S. 413; *Talley* v. *California* (1960), 362 U.S. 60 — handbills.
11. *Burstyn* v. *Wilson* (1952), 343 U.S. 495.
12. Sir William Blackstone, 4 BL. Com. 151, 152.
13. *Patterson* v. *Colorado*, 205 U.S. 454, 462.
14. *Near* v. *Minnesota*, ibid.
15. *Lovell* v. *Griffin* (1938), 303 U.S. 444.
16. *Branzburg* v. *Hayes* (1972), 408 U.S. 665, at 684; see also *New York Times Co.* v. *United States* (1971), 403 U.S. 713.
17. *Zemel* v. *Rusk* (1965), 381 U.S. 1, at 17.
18. See Potter Stewart, 'Or of the Press', *Hastings Law Journal*, 26: 633–4. Also Note, 'The Right of the Press to Gather Information', 71 *Col. L. Rev.* (1971), 838.
19. See Fred R. Harris, *America's Democracy* (1980), 72.
20. See, e.g., Guest and Stanzler, 'The Constitutional Argument for Newsmen Concealing Their Sources' (1969), 64 *N.U.L. Rev.* 18; Note, 'Reporters and their Sources: The Constitutional Right to a Confidential Relationship' (1970), 80 *Yale L.J.*, 317; Comment, 'The Newsmen's Privilege: Government Investigations, Criminal Prosecutions and Private Litigation', 58 *Calif. L. Rev.* (1970), 1198; Nelson, 'The Newsman's Privilege Against Disclosure of Confidential Sources and Information', 24 *Vand. L. Rev.* (1971), 667.
21. See *Garland* v. *Torre*, 259 F2d 545 (CA2), cert. denied 358 U.S. 910 (1958).
22. *Branzburg* v. *Hayes* (1972), 408 U.S. 665.
23. See *Associated Press* v. *N.L.R.B.* (1937), 301 U.S. 103, 132–3; *Oklahoma Press Publishing Co.* v. *Walling* (1946), 327 U.S. 186, 192–3; *Mabee* v. *White Plains Publishing Co.* (1946), 327 U.S. 178; *Associated Press* v. *United States* (1945), 326 U.S. 1.
24. Seventeen as at the date of the judgment.
25. *Branzburg* v. *Hayes*, ibid. at 689–90.
26. ibid. at 698–9.
27. ibid. at 704–5.
28. ibid. at 729.
29. ibid. at 731–3.
30. Discussed in Harris, op. cit., 75.
31. *Momoh* v. *Senate of the National Assembly & others*, Suit No. M/27/80 of 15/4/80.
32. See Abdulai in *The Great Debate*, 123.
33. Report of the Constitution Drafting Committee (1976), vol. II, 36.
34. *Near* v. *Minnesota*, ibid.
35. Per Chief Justice Hughes in *Cox* v. *New Hampshire* (1941), 312 U.S. 569, 574.
36. *Thomas* v. *Collins* (1945), 323 U.S. 516, 530.
37. *Roth* v. *United States*; *Alberta* v. *California* (1957), 354 U.S. 476.
38. *Lovell* v. *Griffin* (1938), 303 U.S. 444.
39. See *Thornhill* v. *Alabama* (1939), 310 U.S. 88, 97.
40. *Lovell* v. *Griffin*, ibid.

41. *Largent* v. *Texas* (1942), 316 U.S. 416.
42. *Cantwell* v. *Connecticut* (1939), 310 U.S. 296.
43. *Schneider* v. *Irvington* (1939), 308 U.S. 147.
44. *Burstyn* v. *Wilson* (1952), 343 U.S. 495.
45. *Thomas* v. *Collins*, ibid.
46. ibid. at 536; see also *Jamison* v. *Texas*, 318 U.S. 413; *Marsh* v. *Alabama*, 326 U.S. 501; *Tucker* v. *Texas*, 326 U.S. 517.
47. *Cantwell* v. *Connecticut*, ibid.
48. *Thomas* v. *Collins*, ibid.
49. ibid. at 545.
50. (1945) 323 U.S. 516.
51. Cap. 129, 1958 Laws of Nigeria, s. 3.
52. See *Constitutional Problems of Federalism in Nigeria*, 65.
53. *Near* v. *Minnesota*, ibid.
54. *Schenck* v. *United States* (1919), 249 U.S. 47.
55. *Near* v. *Minnesota*, ibid.
56. *New York Times Co.* v. *United States* (1971), 403 U.S. 713; see also *Organisation for a Better Austin* v. *Keefe* (1971), 402 U.S. 415; *Carroll* v. *Princess Anne* (1968), 393 U.S. 175, 181; *Bantam Books, Inc.* v. *Sullivan* (1963), 372 U.S. 58, 70.
57. See particularly the judgment of Justice Brennan at 725–7.
58. *Lovell* v. *Griffin* (1938), 303 U.S. 444.
59. *Martin* v. *Struthers*, 319 U.S. 141.
60. *Talley* v. *California* (1960), 362 U.S. 60.
61. *Schneider* v. *Irvington* (1939), 308 U.S. 147 at 163.
62. *Marsh* v. *Alabama*, 326 U.S. 501.
63. *Grosjean* v. *American Press Co.*, 297 U.S. 233.
64. *Murdock* v. *Pennsylvania* (1943), 319 U.S. 105; *Follett* v. *McCormick*, 321 U.S. 573.
65. *Jones* v. *Opelika*, 319 U.S. 103; *Murdock* v. *Pennsylvania* ibid; *Follett* v. *McCormick*, ibid.
66. *Whitney* v. *California* (1927), 274 U.S. 357.
67. *Thomas* v. *Collins* (1945), 323 U.S. 516.
68. *Gitlow* v. *New York* (1925), 268 U.S. 652.
69. *Schenck* v. *United States* (1919), 249 U.S. 47.
70. *Gitlow* v. *New York*, ibid.
71. *Whitney* v. *California* (1927), 274 U.S. 357; *De Jonge* v. *Oregon* (1937), 299 U.S. 353; *Dennis* v. *United States* (1951), 341 U.S. 494.
72. *Yates* v. *United States* (1957), 354 U.S. 298 — quoting from a concurring judgment in *Dennis* v. *United States*, ibid.
73. *Yates* v. *United States*, ibid. at 324–5.
74. *Dennis* v. *United States*, ibid.
75. *New York Times Co.* v. *Sullivan* (1964), 376 U.S. 254; and *Garrison* v. *Louisiana* (1964), 379 U.S. 64.
76. *Garrison* v. *Louisiana*, ibid.
77. ibid. at 74–5.
78. *Roth* v. *United States*, 354 U.S. 476; *Beauharnais* v. *Illinois*, 343 U.S. 250.

79. *New York Times Co.* v. *Sullivan*, ibid., 269.
80. *Garrison* v. *Louisiana*, ibid., 67.
81. *Roth* v. *United States* (1957), 354 U.S. 476.
82. *Chapliniky* v. *New Hampshire*, 315 U.S. 568. For more recent cases, see *Memoirs* v. *Massachusetts* (1966), 383 U.S. 413; *Miller* v. *California* (1973), 413 U.S. 15; *Jenkins* v. *Georgia* (1974), 418 U.S. 153; *South Western Promotions Ltd.* v. *Conrad* (1975), 420 U.S. 546.
83. *D.P.P.* v. *Obi* (1961), 1 All N.L.R. 186, 196; also *The Queen* v. *The Amalgamated Press (of Nigeria) Ltd.* (1961), 1 All N.L.R. 199.
84. Citing Justices Holmes and Brandeis in *Abrams* v. *United States*, 250 U.S. 616, 630; Justice Jackson in *Beauharnais* v. *Illinois*, 343 U.S. 250, 288−9.
85. *New York Times Co.* v. *Sullivan*, ibid. at 276.

27
FREEDOM OF ASSOCIATION

1. *The constitutional guarantee*

The Constitution provides that 'every person shall be entitled to assemble freely and associate with other persons, and in particular he may form or belong to any political party, trade union or any other association for the protection of his interests' (s. 37).

Freedom to form or belong to a political party or a trade union is singled out for special mention because of the great importance of these two forms of associations relative to the other forms. Freedom of political association is important to democratic government because, while free discussion assures to the community information and participation in public affairs, freedom to form a political party enables those who are politically inclined and share common ideas about government to associate and organise together in order to make their advocacy of their ideas more effective, and to seek, ultimately, an opportunity to implement them by persuading people to vote them into power on the basis of those ideas. Political parties are the traditional platform for organising and carrying on political activity;[1] politics in our modern complex society would be impossible to conduct effectively without them. And democracy has little meaning without a free competition for power between associations of persons with opposing ideas about government.

Without an organised party in opposition, government may tend to take the people for granted, and may become unresponsive to their feelings. The political responsibility of the government to the governed can only be realised in the context of an organised opposition party alert to expose to the public the weaknesses and failures of the government, and capable of accepting the mantle of office should the people be inclined to bestow that upon it. 'All change', said the U.S. supreme court, 'is, to a certain extent, achieved by the opposition of the new to the old, and in so far as it is within the law, such peaceful opposition . . . is recognised as a symbol of independent thought containing the promise of progress.'[2]

Organised labour or workers' associations otherwise called trade unions have become a potent force in modern industrial society, also with far-reaching impact in politics and government. In the machinery of collective bargaining, which is their underlying purpose, they serve as a pillar to which industrial peace and progress are anchored.

2. Rights secured by the constitutional guarantee

With the exception of political parties and religious associations, the constitutional guarantee of the right to associate with others for the protection of common interests secures to no one a constitutional right to pursue the objects of association. It is not a guarantee of freedom to engage in any particular activity. No limitation is therefore implied by it on the power of the state to regulate, subject to the Fundamental Objectives and Directive Principles, what activities individuals and associations may engage in, and the conditions for doing so. What this means in effect is that the freedom of individuals to form associations for the protection of their interest is conditioned by the fact that an association, or an individual for that matter, can undertake only such activities as are permitted by law, and subject to such restrictions as may be imposed by the state.

Subject to this, the constitutional guarantee secures to everyone the right to join with others to form an association; to join an association already formed; to remain a member; to participate in the affairs of the association, to contest offices and to share in other benefits of membership, and the right to privacy as to one's associational ties. Declaring invalid a statute which made it a condition of employment in any state-supported school or college that every teacher must file annually an affidavit listing without limitation every organisation to which he has belonged or regularly contributed money within the preceding five years, the U.S. supreme court, by a majority of 5–4, held that 'to compel a teacher to disclose his every associational tie is to impair the teacher's right of free association.'[3]

While the right to associate is an individual right, the formation of an association gives rise to collective rights in favour of the association as such — for example the right to adopt a constitution and the right, in accordance with such a constitution, to take whatever appropriate and lawful measures may be necessary to maintain itself in existence. These include the right to organise itself — to elect officers, to establish other organisational support like setting up a secretariat or headquarters and branch offices, to assemble in order to choose its officers, to discuss and inform people of the advantages of the association with a view to persuading them to join and generally to solicit membership, to take subscriptions and manage the funds of the organisation and its affairs generally; the right to federate or amalgamate with other associations; and finally the right to continued existence and not to be dissolved. These rights are guaranteed to every association by the Constitution. But though they belong to the association itself, any interference with them is simultaneously an interference with the rights of the individual members.[4]

It is pertinent to point out that, strictly speaking, there can be no such thing as a right to associate with others if by that is implied a correlative duty on the part of those others to accept the association. The so-called freedom of association presupposes and is conditional upon the willingness of others for association. Thus while a worker has a constitutional right to join a trade union, the U.S. supreme court has held that the trade union, being a voluntary association of working people, has an inherent constitutional right to deny membership to any worker on terms stipulated in its constitution[5] or to expel a member, subject however to the power of the court to nullify an expulsion on such grounds as lack of a hearing or lack of notice of it, a faulty charge, procedural irregularities, denial of the opportunity for defence, bad faith, expulsion in violation of the regulations of the association or invalidity of the regulation relating to expulsion or expulsion motivated by racial or religious discrimination.[6] Equally too a political party has an inherent constitutional right to stipulate in its constitution or other regulations, the conditions for membership, such as agreement with its aims and objectives, observance of its rules as to discipline etc., and payment of subscriptions, and to deny membership to any one who does not satisfy these conditions. It also has the right to suspend or expel any member in accordance with its rules. What it cannot do is to deny membership to any citizen of Nigeria on the ground merely of his place of origin, sex, religion or ethnic affiliation (s. 202[*b*]).

Where an individual has a choice of political parties to belong to, the right of a political party to grant or refuse membership or to expel a member is perhaps not such a serious qualification on the individual's freedom of association. Where only one party exists, either *de jure* or *de facto*, then there is brought into sharp conflict the right of an interested individual not to be excluded from participation in politics within the single party, and the inherent right of any organisation to determine who to admit as a member and the conditions of such membership. Even in such a case, it seems unjustified to grant a right of automatic membership in the constitution. For an organisation which is open to all and sundry, notwithstanding that they may be disloyal or hostile to the aims and objectives of the association, or which has no power to expel those guilty of flagrant breaches of its rules or other serious misconduct, can hardly be expected to be able to maintain its authority. It is arguable too that if membership of the party in a one-party state is automatic by right of citizenship alone and with no commitment to its beliefs, aims and objectives, then the party would have become co-extensive with the nation, and thereby cease to function as a party in any serious sense. Since Nigeria is not a one-party state, it is unnecessary to pursue the argument further.

It is important to emphasise the supremacy of an association over its dealings with its members. The court may only intervene to ensure that the association keeps within its constitution and the rules of natural justice. Within these limits any decisions taken by an association affecting a member is an internal concern of the association, and the court will not substitute its own will for that of the association. This has ample justification in the fact that membership in an association by anyone is a matter of voluntary choice on his part, by which he binds himself to abide by the constitution and decisions of the association. Even when the constitution or decisions limit his rights or fetter his freedom of action, he cannot complain, provided he joined the association voluntarily, for he is perfectly at liberty to agree to forgo his rights or to accept a limitation on them. He does not of course thereby become a slave to his association. His freedom of choice is preserved by his right to resign from the association, but if he chooses not to resign, then he is liable to expulsion or other disciplinary action in accordance with the constitution of the association should he refuse to comply with its decisions.

Thus in a case where a registered political party in the country, the People's Redemption Party (P.R.P.), directed that the two state governors elected on its platform should no longer attend the institutionalised or regular meetings of the nine so-called progressive governors, the high court of Lagos state held that the direction was within the power of the party to give, and that the two governors, by their voluntary membership in the party, were bound by it; whatever effect the direction had on their freedom of action resulted from their own voluntary agreement, as members, to be bound by the decisions of the party, and they could not remain in the party and refuse to obey its decisions.[7] The course open to them was to resign.

Other rights secured by the constitutional guarantee are peculiar to political parties and religious associations. The right to engage in lawful political activity, to field candidates for an election and to canvass votes for them is constitutionally guaranteed to a political party. An association which is not a political party is prohibited to canvass for votes at presidential, gubernatorial, legislative or local government elections or to contribute to the election expenses of a candidate (s. 201). This prohibition gives to political parties a pre-eminent position in political activity.

A religious association like an individual is guaranteed the right to manifest and propagate its religion or belief in worship, teaching, practice and observance, and to that end is entitled to establish a church or school, these being the traditional and most effective forum for propagating religion by the four means enumerated above. The Constitution explicitly ordains that 'no religious community or denomination shall be prevented from providing religious instruction for pupils of that community or denomination in any place of education maintained wholly by that community or denomination' (s. 35[3]). It seems to be clearly implied in this constitutional injunction that a school established by a religious body need not devote its teaching entirely to religious subjects; it is entitled to combine it with secular education.[8] Its right to acquire and own property for the purposes of a school, to choose pupils and patrons, to appoint teachers, and generally to manage the school is part of the freedom secured to it by the constitutional guarantee.[9]

In the case of trade unions, apart from the right to form them, the Constitution does not specify what objects they can pursue. It is argued, however, that the right to form a trade union implies the right to bargain collectively with respect to the betterment of wages, hours of work and other terms and conditions of employment, that being the underlying purpose, the *raison d'être*, of a trade union. Further, that because the strike weapon is the ultimate sanction in the hands of workers for making collective bargaining effective, the right of collective bargaining necessarily also implies the right to strike.

These arguments were rejected by the judicial committee of the privy council in an appeal from Trinidad and Tobago based on the guarantee of freedom of association in that country's Constitution.[10] It held, agreeing with the local courts, that freedom of association implies no constitutional right to pursue the objects of association; that, while the improvement of wages and conditions of employment is the main purpose of most trade unions, it is not an object inherent in, or inseparable from, a trade union nor is it the only purpose which trade unions pursue. Their objects may be any among a large number — religious, social, political, economic, educational, cultural, sporting or charitable. Accordingly, it held — again affirming the local courts — that a statute which abridged the freedom of workers to bargain collectively and to strike is not an abridgement of the constitutional guarantee of freedom of association as to be unconstitutional and void. (The Constitution of Trinidad and Tobago guarantees 'liberty', which in the United States has been interpreted as embracing freedom to bargain collectively and to strike; the judgments both in the privy council and the local courts never considered the matter from this standpoint.)

The reasoning seems to be correct. Yet it is not conclusive on the status of collective bargaining and the strike under the Nigerian Constitution. As the privy council rightly pointed out, under the law of Trinidad and Tobago, as under those of Great Britain and Nigeria, a trade union is not a legal person but simply an unincorporated association, with no separate existence from the several individuals who make it up. That being the case, the constitutional guarantee of freedom of association confers upon an individual a right to exercise in combination or association with others any rights guaranteed to him by the Constitution. To that extent, it alters the ordinary law relating to combinations. Freedom of association does not of itself imply the right to pursue the objects of association, but it does unquestionably confer upon the individual the constitutional right to pursue in combination or in common with others any object or right guaranteed to him by some other provision of the Constitution.

One such constitutional right is the freedom of expression and assembly. When a person bargains with an employer or prospective employer over wages and conditions of employment, he is doing no more than exercising his constitutional right to discuss, to express himself on a matter of great personal and legitimate interest.[11] By the constitutional guarantee of freedom of association, he is entitled to associate with others in order to exercise the right of discussion or negotiation. Bargaining, whether individually or collectively, obliges neither the workers nor the employer to make an agreement. The right of workers in association to picket in an orderly and peaceable way in order to disseminate information concerning the facts of a trade dispute is also included in the guarantee.[12]

The Constitution also guarantees to every individual freedom from servitude and from forced or compulsory labour (s. 31). This imports freedom to decide whether to be self-employed or to work for an employer, to bargain with an employer about terms and conditions of employment, to quit work either permanently or temporarily, and to choose another employer. (This point and the decisions bearing on it are discussed in chapter 26 below.) As with freedom of expression, the constitutional right to bargain with an employer and to quit work temporarily, which is all a strike means, can be exercised in combination with others under the guarantee of freedom of association. The right to strike does not, however, embrace the sit-down or slow-down strike.[13]

Undoubtedly the exercise, in combination with others, of the individual's right to bargain freely and to quit work temporarily, while it is sanctioned by the Constitution, creates a situation which the state is entitled to regulate in the interest of public order, public safety, defence or public health, or for the purpose of protecting the rights and freedom of other persons (s. 41). Freedom to combine or associate with others to bargain or to strike is thus not absolute. As the U.S. supreme court has said: 'The right to strike, "the unquestional right to quit work",[14] because of its more serious impact upon the public interest, is more vulnerable to regulation than the right to organise and elect representatives for lawful purposes of collective bargaining which this court has characterised as a "fundamental right" and which, as the court has pointed out, was recognised as such in its decisions long before it was given protection by the Labour Relations Act.'[15] This means that, while the temporary quitting of work by the lone worker cannot be regulated by the state in the public interest except during an emergency (s. 31), the exercise of the right in combination with others can be so regulated.

3. *State control of freedom of association and assembly*

As with freedom of speech and the press, the constitutional guarantee of freedom of association is subject to any law that is reasonably justifiable in a democratic society in the interest of defence, public safety, public order, public morality or public health, or for the purpose of protecting the rights and freedom of other persons (s. 41[1]). The test of validity of any restriction is not the clear and present danger test applied in the case of freedom of expression but the less exacting one of rational connection. A restriction, to be valid, must have a rational connection with defence, public safety, public order, public morality or public health, or with the protection of the rights and freedom of other persons. To be rational, the connection must suggest itself to a reasonably intelligent mind; the bearing which the restriction has on the stipulated interests must therefore be a proximate one; i.e. it must be reasonably close and not too remote or far-fetched.

It may perhaps be noted that the power of the state to restrict guaranteed rights is narrower in Nigeria than in the United States, where the state's police power embraces the whole field of the public welfare or public interest. In Nigeria, the public interests for the protection of which a right may be restricted are limited to defence, public safety, public order, public morality or public health or the protection of the rights and freedom of other persons. It follows that the Constitution does not authorise the restriction of a guaranteed right in the interest of economic wellbeing, or economic development, national unity or any other public interest outside those mentioned in the Constitution.

It is also pertinent to note that labour, including trade unions, industrial relations, conditions, safety and welfare of labour, industrial disputes, national minimum wage, industrial arbitration (item 33, exclusive legislative list) and the regulation of political parties (item 55) come under the exclusive legislative authority of the federal government, while religion is a residual matter exclusive to the states.

In discussing the extent of the authority which the state (federal or state government) can by law exercise to regulate political parties, trade unions and religious organisations in the specified public interests, it is proposed for convenience to consider each type of organisation separately, but certain general principles, applicable equally to all three of them, will first be noted.

(i) Membership and participation

Three main questions are raised here. First, can the state, in the interest of defence, public safety, public order, public morality, public health or the protection of the rights and freedom of other persons, bar from membership of, or participation in, a lawful political party, trade union, religious or other association, certain classes of persons, e.g. persons below a certain age (children and young persons), civil servants, members of the police force, the prison service, the armed forces and other public servants? A statute which prohibits children of fifteen years of age or under from joining the membership of any political party, attending its meeting or taking part in any political activity whatever[16] was held by the high court of Northern Nigeria to be reasonably justifiable in the interest of public morality on the ground that

if juveniles are allowed to take part in politics, their receptive and uncritical minds make them easy victims to thoughtless or unscrupulous people who wish to take advantage of their youth to indoctrinate them with a particular ideology before they are old enough to think the matter out for themselves. Juveniles may be attracted to any idea which is presented in an interesting form; they have neither the experience nor the standards of comparison to enable them to discriminate. This seems particularly likely to be the case in an area such as the Northern Region where education is still at its infancy and even adults may be bewildered by the recent inrush of new ideas.[17]

The learned judge also held that participation of juveniles in politics constitutes a special threat to public order, because

they have not had time to acquire that sense of restraint and responsibility which it is hoped the years have brought to their elders. Their enthusiasms are easily aroused and their natural high spirits lead them to thoughtless excesses. It is not difficult to anticipate the exciting effect on youthful minds of political activity, of meetings, and speeches, flags and slogans, or of the danger to the public of mobs of excited juveniles half controlled by political organisations.[18]

The arguments used by the learned judge are pretty convincing, and it is difficult not to agree with his conclusions. But, in spite of this, a second attempt was made to get the law nullified; this second attempt failed *in limine* because the plaintiff lacked sufficient interest in the subject-matter of the action to entitle him to maintain it.[19]

In the United States a similar question has arisen under a statute which in effect prohibited, as part of comprehensive child labour legislation, the sale or distribution in public streets of religious literature by girls under eighteen and boys under twelve, sanctioned by a criminal penalty for any parent or guardian who compelled or permitted such activity.[20] It was argued that a person distributing or even selling religious literature in the streets is engaged, not in a commercial activity, but in an act of genuine religious evangelism which can be restricted only on a showing of grave and immediate danger to public order, health or morals. The U.S. supreme court held by a majority that, while the restriction of the statute might be invalid in the case of adults, it was justified with regard to children, because street activity exposes them to the diverse influences of the street which are harmful to their morals, and because the zealous exercise of the right to propagandise the community, whether in religious, political or other matters, may and at times does create violent or disorderly situations difficult enough for adults to cope with and wholly inappropriate for children to face; also, there are other harmful possibilities of emotional excitement and psychological or physical injury. 'A democratic society', the majority asserts, 'rests, for its continuance, upon the healthy, well-rounded growth of young people into full maturity as citizens, with all that implies.'[21]

A minority of one maintained that, while these evils might justify prohibition of ordinary commercial activity in the street by children, they pose no grave and immediate danger to public order, morals or health in the case of the religious activity involved in the distribution or sale of religious literature, since children engaged in serious religious evangelism are imbued with such high moral character as shields them from the harmful influences of the street.

The participation by public employees in partisan politics and trade union activities does certainly have an impact on the administration of government, but its impact is on efficiency, discipline and integrity rather than on defence, public safety, public order etc. Whether it can justifiably be forbidden must therefore rest on these other considerations. The 1963 Constitution in terms empowered the state to restrict by law the freedom of association of persons holding office under the state, members of the armed forces and members of the police force.[22] The omission of this qualification from the 1979 Constitution means that the guarantee of freedom of association is not subject to it, although something of it still survives in another form in a different provision already considered in chapter 20 above.

The second question concerns the solicitation of membership or of subscriptions or the actual collection of subscriptions. A member (not being a paid organiser) cannot be required to register himself as a condition for soliciting members for a political party, trade union or religious association (as distinct from soliciting subscriptions or actually collecting them).[23] That would be an unconstitutional restriction on his right of participation. The position of a paid organiser with respect to a registration or identification requirement is disputed. The argument is that a paid organiser, i.e. a person paid to solicit members for a political party, trade union or religious association, is engaged in a calling, a business, and like all other practitioners of a calling or vocation — e.g. doctors, nurses, lawyers, notaries, bankers, accountants and insurance agents — should be subject to a reasonable registration or identification requirement. The contention on the other side is that the solicitation of members for a political party, trade union or religious association is not a business in the same sense as the practice of medicine, law and so on, but an exercise of a constitutionally guaranteed right to form or belong to such organisations and to persuade others to join, and that the fact that a person is paid to do the solicitation does not change the character of the right from a *civil* to a *business* right.

In a celebrated case involving a trade union, the supreme court of the United States, by a majority of 5—4, endorsed the latter view of the matter.[24] The facts of the case were that the president of a labour union had in the course of a speech solicited members for his union at a mass meeting of workers arranged as part of a campaign to organise workers in a particular oil refinery into a local branch of his union. The solicitation was made in defiance of a restraining order issued, in anticipation of the speech which had been scheduled and advertised in advance, by a district court at the instance of the attorney-general under a statute which, under penalty of fine or imprisonment, required every paid labour union organiser, before soliciting members for his union, to apply to the secretary of state for an organiser's card, stating his name in full, his labour union affiliations and his credentials. The statute made it mandatory for the secretary of state to issue the card on receipt of an application. The majority of the court held, reversing the courts below, that in the circumstances of the case it was an unconstitutional prior restraint of the freedom of speech, the press, assembly and association to require a paid organiser of a labour union first to identify himself before soliciting members for his union. In the opinion of the majority, to require such identification would necessarily deprive freedom of speech, assembly and association of the protection of the constitutional guarantee, because it cannot be determined with certainty where the line should be drawn between discussion and solicitation.

Solicitation of subscriptions or the actual collection of them is of course another matter which, it is conceded, the state can, in order to protect the public from the dishonesty or irresponsibility of those seeking to obtain its money, regulate by requiring the persons concerned in it to identify themselves.[25]

Thirdly, there is the question whether the state can constitutionally prohibit mere membership of an association that is formed for a criminal purpose or which, while not formed for a criminal purpose, actually engages in criminal activity or conduct, and whether it can punish attendance at a meeting held under the auspices of such an association or any other kind of participation in the affairs of the association or compel a member to disclose the fact of his membership. It has been held that the state is constitutionally permitted to prohibit membership of, and participation in, such an association, since the constitutional guarantee of freedom of association might otherwise be turned into a licence for crime. The U.S. supreme court has thus sustained the validity of statutes under which members of the Communist Party, part of whose object was to advocate action for the forcible overthrow of the government by violence, were convicted for wilfully and deliberately assisting in the formation of the party;[26] for their membership of it;[27] and for preparing and distributing a manifesto advocating action for the overthrow of the government by violence and other unlawful means.[28] (By a subsequent statute of 1950, congress removed the sanction of criminality for membership of or the holding of office in any Communist organisation.[29]) But to sustain a conviction it must be shown beyond reasonable doubt that the association is formed for a criminal purpose or actually engages in criminal conduct or activity.[30] The state is not entitled to compel a person to disclose the fact of his membership of a criminal association merely because it has the power to prohibit such membership.[31]

Furthermore, it does not follow from the fact that an association is formed for a criminal purpose or engages in criminal conduct or activity that every meeting held under its auspices can be prohibited and all those participating in it or assisting in its conduct punished as criminals, regardless of whether they are members and whether what was said or done at the meeting was unlawful or not. The conviction of a person for assisting in conducting a meeting held under the auspices of the Communist Party, which was admitted to advocate criminal syndicalism, was quashed by the U.S. supreme court, where it was admitted that criminal syndicalism was not in fact advocated at the meeting and that nothing else unlawful was said or done; the statute which made it an offence to assist in the conduct of a meeting merely because it was held under such auspices was declared unconstitutional.[32] The court pertinently observed:

> The holding of meetings for peaceable political action cannot be proscribed. Those who assist in the conduct of such meetings cannot be branded as criminals on that score. The question, if the right of free speech and peaceable assembly are to be preserved, is not as to the auspices under which the meeting is held but as to its purpose; not as to the relations of the speakers, but whether their utterances transcend the bounds of the freedom of speech which the

Constitution protects. If the persons assembling have committed crimes elsewhere, if they have formed or are engaged in a conspiracy against the public peace and order, they may be prosecuted for their conspiracy or other violation of valid laws. But it is a different matter when the State, instead of prosecuting them for such offences, seizes upon mere participation in a peaceable assembly and a lawful public discussion as the basis for a criminal charge.[33]

Membership or participation in a secret oath-bound association may also be restricted, even though it is not formed for a criminal purpose and does not engage in criminal conduct. Thus, the U.S. supreme court sustained a statute which made it an offence for a person to become a member or to remain a member or to attend a meeting of such an association, with knowledge that it has not filed with the secretary of state, as required by the statute, a sworn copy of its constitution, by-laws, rules, regulations and oath of membership, together with a roster of its members and a list of its officers for the current year. As the court observed:

> There can be no doubt that under the [police] power the state may prescribe and apply to associations having an oath-bound membership any reasonable regulation calculated to confine their purposes and activities within limits which are consistent with the rights of others and the public welfare. The requirement in s. 53 that each association shall file with the secretary of state a sworn copy of its constitution, oath of membership, etc., with a list of members and officers, is such a regulation. It proceeds on the twofold theory that the state within whose territory and under whose protection the association exists is entitled to be informed of its nature and purpose, of whom it is composed and by whom its activities are conducted, and that requiring this information to be supplied for the public files will operate as an effective or substantial deterrent from the violations of public and private right to which the association might be tempted if such a disclosure were not required. The requirement is not arbitrary or oppressive, but reasonable and likely to be of real effect.[34]

Part of the reason for the decision was of course that the organisation concerned in this case, the Ku Klux Klan, was engaged in acts of unlawful intimidation and violence.

A secret society in fact enjoys no constitutional protection under the Nigerian Constitution of 1979. For it is expressly declared that the guarantee of freedom of thought, conscience and religion shall not 'entitle any person to form, take part in the activity or be a member of a secret society', which is defined as 'a society or association, not being a solely cultural or religious body, that uses secret signs, oaths, rites or symbols (*a*) whose meetings or other activities are held in secret; and (*b*) whose members are under oath, obligation or other threat to promote the interest of its members or to aid one another under all circumstances without due regard to merit, fair play or justice, to the detriment of the legitimate expectation of those who are not members'

(s. 35[4]). It seems that the exemption of a cultural or religious body from this definition applies only if it does not operate in the manner described, since only then can its objects or activities be said to be 'solely' cultural or religious.

(ii) *Licensing and registration of associations*

As stated in connection with freedom of speech and press, it is, in the absence of specific constitutional provision, unconstitutional to restrain in advance by means of prohibition, licensing or proscription, the formation of political parties, trade unions and religious associations. The U.S. supreme court has put the point quite emphatically thus:

> It is settled by a long line of recent decisions of this court that an ordinance which, like this one, makes the peaceful enjoyment of freedom which the Constitution guarantees contingent upon the uncontrolled will of an official as by requiring a permit or licence which may be granted or withheld in the discretion of such official — is an unconstitutional censorship or prior restraint upon the enjoyment of those freedoms.[35]

A political party, trade union, religious or other association may, however, justifiably be required to file certain information about itself which will enable it to be identified, provided that the information required is not more than is reasonably necessary for identification purposes. Thus, an order of a state court, issued in pursuance of a statute, compelling the National Association for the Advancement of Coloured People to produce a list of its members in the state was held unconstitutional and void, on the Association showing that on past occasions revelation of the identity of its rank-and-file members had exposed those members to economic reprisals, loss of employment, the calling-in or denial of bank loans, foreclosure of mortgages, threat of physical coercion, and other manifestations of public hostility.[36] The court affirmed that disclosure in the circumstances would abridge the right of the members to engage in lawful association in support of their common beliefs, that effective advocacy of both public and private points of view, particularly controversial ones, is undeniably enhanced by group association, and that inviolability of privacy in group association may in many circumstances be indispensable to preservation of freedom of association, particularly where a group aspouses dissident beliefs. It is not decisive therefore that no action had been taken by the state directly to restrict the ability of members of the Association to associate freely; indirect governmental actions such as that involved here could also have a highly restrictive effect on membership. The character of the Association as a lawful organisation engaged in the promotion of constitutional rights for all races on the basis of equality is of course an underlying premise of the decision. This decision was subsequently re-affirmed even against a city ordinance which required any organisation operating within the city to give certain information, including the names of all who paid dues, assessments or contributions. In the view of the court there is no 'relevant correlation' between the city's power to impose occupation licence taxes and the compulsory disclosure and publication of membership lists.[37]

Compulsory disclosure of membership may be constitutionally justified in the case of an association which is formed for criminal purposes or engages in criminal conduct[38] or which is a secret oath-bound society.[39]

(iii) *Public meetings and processions in streets or other public places*
The use of streets and other public places for meetings or processions by political parties, trade unions, religious or other associations is subject to a wider power of control, although opinion differs as to its exact extent. The position of the U.S. supreme court on the matter was initially that the state had an absolute power of control;[40] the reasoning was that as the state can always put an end to the dedication of streets and other public places to public uses, it can take the lesser step of limiting the public use to certain purposes only; accordingly the prohibition of their use for public speaking, meetings and processions would be 'no more an infringement of the rights of a member of the public than for the owner of a private house to forbid it in his house';[41] also that the right absolutely to prohibit must necessarlly include authority to determine under what circumstances use may be permitted. Applying this principle, the court sustained a city ordinance which prohibited public speaking on public grounds without a permit from the mayor, and affirmed a conviction for speaking on the city common without the necessary permit.[42]

In 1938 by a majority of five out of the seven participating justices, the court changed to a more liberal position, which rests on the premise that streets and other public places are held by the state in trust for the public and that, so long as they remain dedicated to public use, their use for public speaking, meetings and processions cannot be absolutely denied by the state.[43] 'Uncontrolled official suppression', said the majority, 'cannot be made a substitute for the duty to maintain order in connection with the exercise of the right.'[44] Accordingly, it declared unconstitutional and void a city ordinance which, under penalty of a fine or imprisonment, required persons wanting to use the public streets, highways, public parks or public buildings for public parades or assemblies to apply for a permit from the director of public safety, who might refuse it if he thought refusal proper in order to prevent riots, disturbances or disorderly assemblage. In this case, the state authorities had, as a deliberate policy, repeatedly refused permission to a particular labour organisation to hold meetings in the city although the meetings were for the lawful purpose of organising workers in the city into labour unions with a view to collective bargaining, and had enforced this policy by physically removing the organisation's agents from the city and by other acts of harrassment.

Reaffirming this position in a unanimous decision in 1951, which arose out of a refusal of a licence to hold bible talks in a public park, the court emphasised that a discretion to grant or refuse a licence is invalid where there are 'no narrowly drawn limitations; no circumscribing of this absolute power; no substantial interest of the community to be served.'[45] The conviction of a baptist minister for holding a religious meeting on a public street without a permit contrary to a city ordinance which vested a similarly uncontrolled discretion in an official to refuse it, was also quashed together with the ordinance; an application for a permit had been refused twice merely on the ground that the applicant had at a previous meeting ridiculed and denounced other religious beliefs.[46]

Judged in the light of this later, more liberal approach, the law in some parts of Nigeria authorising public authorities to refuse a permit to hold a public meeting or procession if, in their opinion, a breach of the peace is likely,[47] must be considered unconstitutional, because of its potentiality for becoming an instrument for arbitrary suppression of the political opponents of the government, as indeed it did become in the period before the military intervention in 1966. If an unfettered discretion to refuse a licence is unconstitutional, so, *a fiortiori*, must an unlimited discretion to ban it altogether for periods ranging from fourteen days to three months whenever, in the opinion of the official, a ban is necessary to prevent serious disorder.[48] The incompatibility of an uncontrolled discretion to ban with the right to hold public meetings and processions is again demonstrated by the extent to which the discretion was abused in many parts of the country in the days of the First Republic.

In considering the validity of statutes restricting public meetings and processions in public places, the question in each case is whether the restriction is designed to secure or promote the convenience or safety of the public as a whole in the use of such places. Provided there is no unfair discrimination in the treatment of applications, a licensing requirement is justified where it confers only a limited discretion to refuse a permit if the time, place and manner of a public meeting or procession involves the risk of overlap with other meetings or processions or the risk of serious obstruction of the primary use of streets for passage and traffic since by it the state is enabled to prevent the confusion of overlapping meetings or processions, to secure convenient use of the streets by other members of the public, and to minimise the risk of disorder generally.[49] In a subsequent case involving an identical licensing requirement as applied to the holding of religious services and instruction in parks and other public open spaces, the court described the requirement as conferring no real discretion, being merely a 'ministerial, police routine for adjusting . . . the unrestrained exercise of religions with the reasonable comfort and convenience of the whole city'.[50] (It is something of an over-statement to describe the licensing requirement in this case as a mere ministerial routine.)[51]

Yet a licensing requirement of this kind may still in its practical operation result in the arbitrary denial of the right by the official invested with the discretion wrongfully refusing to grant a licence, as indeed happened in this case. And the court has ruled that while a person may act in defiance of an unconstitutional law, a wrongful refusal of a licence is not a bar to a conviction for acting without the requisite licence, and that the right thing to do is not to defy the refusal (defiance is justified where the refusal is not only arbitrary but discriminatory as well[52]), but to go to court to compel the issue of the licence. To the argument that the enjoyment of the right may be postponed for many years pending the final determination of the court action, the court said that, while 'delay is unfortunate . . . the expense and annoyance of litigation is a price citizens must pay for life in an orderly society where the rights of the First Amendment have a real and abiding meaning.'[53] There is clearly something in the argument that this makes the constitutional protection illusory. As a minority of the court (a minority of two) observed, 'defiance of a statute is hardly less harmful to an orderly society than defiance of an administrative order. The vice of a statute, which exacts a licence for the right to make a speech, is that it adds a burden to the right. The burden is the same when the officials administering the licensing system withhold the licence and require the applicant to spend months or years in the courts in order to win a right which the Constitution says no government shall deny.'[54]

Given a valid licensing requirement, such as is described above, a fee may lawfully be charged for granting it if the amount is reasonable and is intended to meet the expenses of policing the meeting or procession.[55]

It is also justified, in order to afford opportunity for proper policing, to require prior notice of a public meeting or procession to be given to the authorities, specifying the time and place of the meeting or the time and route of a procession.[56]

It appears that the use at meetings in public places of sound amplification devices which emit 'loud and raucous' noises may be banned in the interest of public peace and convenience.[57] But the requirement of a licence to use a sound amplification device of any kind, irrespective of the amount and nature of the noise produced, is unconstitutional.[58]

But while the constitutional right of the individual to hold public meetings and processions in a public street or other public place cannot be restrained by a licensing system that gives to the state an unfettered discretion to refuse a licence, it must be balanced with the undoubted duty of the state to control the tendency of such meetings and processions to provoke a breach of the public peace. The conflict involved in this situation between private right and state power raises perhaps the most delicate problem of balancing.

The judicial approach to the problem makes the conduct and words used by the organisers of a meeting or the speakers at it the determining factor. If they conduct themselves in an orderly manner and avoid the use of language that is calculated to incite others to break the peace, then they are entitled to the protection of the police and the law against the hostility of any members of the audience to whom their views may be unwelcome. The duty of the police is not to break up the meeting but to remove those seeking to disturb it, unless the situation develops into a riotous one beyond the power of the police to control. The police may then disperse the meeting, but the law should be made to take its course against the disturbers.

The protection of the law may be lost, however, where the organisers of a public meeting conduct themselves in a disorderly manner or use inciting words. 'No one', said the U.S. supreme court, 'would have the hardihood to suggest that the principle of freedom of speech sanctions incitement to riot or that religious liberty connotes the privilege to exhort others to physical attack upon those belonging to another sect.'[59] But the mere use of offensive, abusive or insulting language would not in itself justify the police in breaking up a meeting. For in commenting on public affairs, a speaker at a public meeting may lawfully make derogatory remarks concerning the character and conduct of those involved in them. The fighting speech is a lawful method of criticism. 'In the realm of religious faith and in that of political belief, sharp differences arise. In both fields, the tenets of one man may seem the rankest error to his neighbour. To persuade others to his own point of view, the pleader, as we know, at times, resorts to exaggeration, to vilification of men who have been, or are, prominent in church or state, and even to false statement. But the people of this nation have ordained in the light of history that, in spite of the probability of excesses and abuses, these liberties are, in the long view, essential to enlightened opinion and right conduct on the part of the citizens of a democracy.'[60] It is therefore only when offensive, abusive or insulting language is uttered with the deliberate intention of provoking a breach of the peace or when in the circumstances of a particular case its effect is to provoke the listeners to break the peace, that the restraining hand of the law may be laid on a speaker, and the meeting dispersed.

The governing principles as stated above seem to represent a fair balance, but, as a case before the U.S. supreme court shows, their application in given situations may still leave the police with a lot of arbitrary power to disperse public meetings and to prosecute speakers in the name of the preservation of public peace and tranquility. The facts of the case[61] were that a student addressed a mixed crowd of whites and negroes numbering about eighty, through a loud-speaker system from a box at the corner of a sidewalk and a highway. In the course of the speech he made derogatory remarks about some public officials, and called upon the negroes to rise up in arms and fight for equal rights. His speech stirred up some excited feeling among the audience; there was tension between supporters and opponents which manifested itself in some pushing and shoving. A member of the audience threatened to throw the speaker off the box if the police would not act, whereupon the police twice asked the speaker to stop speaking and then arrested him when he refused to do so. His conviction for disorderly conduct was affirmed by the U.S. supreme court by a majority of five, on the ground that the restlessness produced in the audience by his speech, particularly his call on negroes to rise up in arms, justified police intervention to prevent the meeting from resulting in a fight, and that in the light of the excited state of the audience the speaker's refusal to stop speaking on the order of the police amounted to conduct likely to cause a breach of the peace.

In the view of the majority, 'the possible danger of giving over-zealous police officials complete discretion to break up otherwise lawful public meetings' should not be a reason for denying them power to prevent a breach of the peace when, as here, 'the speaker passes the bounds of argument or persuasion and undertakes incitement to riot.'[62]

A minority of the court took the position that there had been no incitement to violence; that the reaction of the audience was by no means unusual on occasions when controversial topics were aired in public; that the situation created by the reaction of the audience was not so critical as to warrant the police intervening to halt the speech; that a man making a lawful public speech is not obliged to be silent merely because a police officer directs it; that the first duty of the police in the circumstances of the case should have been to protect the speaker by discouraging the man threatening assault and by arresting him if he persisted; that in shirking that duty and instead halting the speech, the police acted as agents of suppression; and that the decision of the majority allows the police a dangerous discretion to silence the public expression of unpopular views as soon as the audience begins to show the customary hostility.

4. State control of political parties

It is now proposed to consider what powers the Constitution grants for the licensing of political parties and the control of their activities over and above those authorised by the general principles discussed above.

There is a provision, slipped in at the last minute by the supreme military council, that the guarantee of freedom of association 'shall not derogate from the powers conferred by this Constitution on the Federal Electoral Commission with respect to political parties to which that Commission does not accord recognition' (s. 37). It is to be noted that only powers conferred by the Constitution for the recognition of political parties are relevant; powers conferred by any other law are irrelevant; furthermore the provision itself grants no power to accord or not to accord recognition. The power has to be looked for in other provisions of the Constitution. The only provision relevant to this point is that (s. 202) which states that 'no association by whatever name called shall function as a political party, unless

(a) the names and addresses of its national officers are registered with the Federal Electoral Commission;

(b) the membership of the association is open to every citizen of Nigeria irrespective of his place of origin, sex, religion or ethnic grouping;

(c) a copy of its constitution is registered in the principal office of the Commission in such form as may be prescribed by the Commission;

(d) any alteration in its registered constitution is also registered in the principal office of the Commission within 30 days of the making of such alteration;

(e) the name of the association, its emblem or motto does not contain any ethnic or religious connotation or give the appearance that the activities of the association are confined to a part only of the geographical area of Nigeria; and

(f) the headquarters of the association is situated in the capital of the Federation.'

Three comments may be made on this provision. First, it does not prohibit the formation of a political party in the first instance. The conditions which it prescribes relate, not to the initial formation of a political party or to its formal or nominal existence thereafter, but to its operation as a political party. The distinction between incorporation of a company and commencement of business is familiar enough. Under the provision therefore the formation of a political party is a purely private act, but before it can begin to function and in particular to canvass for votes for any candidate at an election, it must satisfy the six conditions stipulated in the constitutional provision.

Secondly, and more important, the provision gives no power to the federal electoral commission to recognise or not to recognise an association as a political party. Apart from the power granted to the commission to prescribe the form of the party constitution, e.g. whether it should be typed or printed and whether it should be in bound form, the provision grants no power at all to the electoral commission. Its concern is to impose obligations on an association regarding the conditions it must satisfy before beginning to function as a political party. Only three of such obligations have any relation to the commission (the other three make no reference at all to it), but they relate to it in the sense, not of conferring power, but rather of requiring identification particulars to be furnished to it. The requirement that the constitution of an association (and any amendments of it) as well as the names and addresses of its national officers should be 'registered' with the commission merely casts an obligation on the association to furnish the prescribed information and document to the commission for identification purposes; no power is thereby created in favour of the commission to grant or withhold recognition. The commission's role in the matter is the purely formal one of taking the party constitution into its custody and recording the names and addresses of the party officers in its books.

Of course the commission can refuse to accept a party's constitution for custody or registration if it is not in the form prescribed by the commission or if it does not contain the provisions prescribed by the Constitution. By the constitutional prescription (s. 203[1]) 'the constitution and rules of a political party shall provide
(a) for the periodical election on a democratic basis of the principal officers and members of the executive committee or other governing body of the political party; and
(b) ensure that the members of the executive committee or other governing body of the political party reflect the federal character of Nigeria.'
(Periodical election is defined as election held at regular intervals not exceeding four years while federal character in this context means that members must be drawn from at least two-thirds of all the states in the federation (s. 203[2]). Also 'the programme as well as the aims and objects of a political party shall conform' with the Fundamental Objectives and Directive Principles of State Policy set out in the Constitution (s. 204). Now, the function conferred on the commission by these provisions is merely clerical: to verify that the contents of a party's constitution are as prescribed by the Constitution. Once a

party's constitution and rules are found to contain the provisions specified by the Constitution, the commission must accept and register them. Whether these stipulations are being complied with in actual practice is another matter with which the constitutional provisions quoted above are not concerned. (It may be observed that the reference to a political party in the provisions implies that an association can be a political party before its constitution is registered with the electoral commission.)

The third comment concerns the question of how to ensure that an association complies with the constitutional requirements and how to enforce them should it begin to function as a political party without complying with them. Although the provision is couched in the form of a prohibition, no criminal offence is thereby created. At worst, the acts done in contravention of the prohibition may be unconstitutional and void. It is significant however, that, even given the unconstitutionality of such acts, the electoral commission is granted no power directly by the Constitution to ensure compliance — for example, by withholding recognition — or to enforce contraventions. Significantly, too, the prohibition is not among the provisions for the contravention of which the national assembly is empowered to prescribe punishment. However, it can legislate sanctions for contravention of the prohibition through its authority to confer power on the electoral commission to enable it 'more effectively to ensure that political parties observe the provisions of this Part of this Chapter' (s. 208[d]), and through its general power to regulate political parties.

But it cannot, in the exercise of its general power to regulate political parties, authorise the denial of recognition to any political party. That would amount to licensing which, as was stated earlier, is unconstitutional. Any law, whether an existing or a future one, which purports to do so is void. It follows that the power conferred on the federal electoral commission by the Federal Electoral Commission Decree 1977 to 'register political parties and determine their eligibility to sponsor candidates for elections' is unconstitutional and void. In any case, the decree expired by its own terms on 1 October 1979. The Lagos State high court is clearly wrong in holding that, notwithstanding that an express expiry date is prescribed, the decree is still in force by virtue of the provision in s. 271(1) of the Constitution to the effect that 'the electoral commission established for the Federation under any law in force immediately before the date when this section comes into force shall be responsible for performing the functions conferred on the Federal Electoral Commission established by the provisions of this Constitution.'[63] The effect of this provision is not to continue the decree in force, but merely to authorise the members and staff of the commission established under it to exercise the functions conferred on the federal electoral commission by the Constitution.

It is for a good reason that the Constitution grants no power for the licensing of political parties. Such a power would enable the authority vested with it to turn the country into a one-party or even a no-party state, since it would be a perfectly lawful exercise of its uncontrolled discretion to rule that only one association or none at all qualified for licensing as a political party. Such a result would be both antithetical to and subversive of the Constitution, which clearly envisages competition for power among various parties.

The function of the federal electoral commission in regard to political parties relates essentially to the control of their finances. Every political party must, annually and in a form approved by the commission, submit to it a detailed statement and analysis of its sources of funds and other assets and of its expenditure (s. 205[2]). In addition to the annual statement, the commission may also require a statement of assets and liabilities to be submitted to it and published at such times and in such a way as it may specify (s. 205[1]). And it may direct political parties as to the books or records of financial transactions to be kept by them (s. 205[4]). The commission is empowered to examine the accounts of political parties, and to carry out investigations that will enable it to form an opinion as to whether proper books of accounts and proper records have been kept (ss. 205[4] and 206[2]). For this purpose, the commission and its members or duly authorised agents have a right of access at all times to the books and accounts and vouchers of political parties, and are entitled to require from party officials any information and explanations. The commission is to report to the national assembly once a year on its examination and investigation, spotlighting particularly any cases where in its opinion accounts have not been properly kept or where there has been a failure or inability to obtain necessary information.

Political parties are constitutionally forbidden to hold or possess funds or other assets outside Nigeria or to retain funds or assets sent to them from abroad. Any funds or assets received from abroad must be paid over or transferred to the electoral commission within twenty-one days of its receipt with such information as the commission may require (s. 205[3]). The national assembly may prescribe punishment for persons involved in the management or control of a political party found after due inquiry to have contravened this prohibition (s. 208[a]).

Apart from their finances, the Constitution controls another aspect of the activities of political parties by prohibiting the organising, training and equipping of strong-arm units to be used for the purposes of coercion in promoting political objectives (s. 207). The electoral commission has no function in respect of this, but any contravention of this prohibition may earn for those involved in the management or control of the political party such punishment as may be prescribed by the national assembly.

Subject to the specific constitutional provisions just considered and to the limitations implied in the general principles discussed earlier, the national assembly, as has been previously noted, is vested with power to regulate by law the activities of political parties (item 55, exclusive legislative list). The extent of the power that it can exercise for this purpose depends on the nature of the activity, whether it is a political or business activity. An issue of considerable interest which has been widely agitated in the United States is whether the legislature can constitutionally bar from the ballot a political party that advocates the overthrow of government by violent and unlawful means. On this the courts in the United States are divided.[64] But if the activity is a purely business one, then the right of a political party to engage in it can be controlled in much the same way as in the case of an individual or an ordinary business association.

5. *State control of trade unions*

Trade unions, it has been said, are essentially 'business associations; their object is generally business dealings and relationships as is manifest from the financial statements of some of the national unions. Men are persuaded to join them for business reasons as employers are persuaded to join trade associations for like reasons.'[65] Yet the state cannot control the main object of a trade union — collective bargaining, with its sanctioning weapon of a strike action — as completely as it controls the objects of other business associations. This is because, as noted earlier, the right to form or belong to a trade union, to bargain collectively about conditions of employment and to strike in aid of it is secured by the Constitution through the guarantee of freedom of association, freedom of expression and freedom from forced or compulsory labour. A denial or restriction of them is constitutionally permitted only if it is sanctioned by a law that is reasonably justifiable in a democratic society in the interest of defence, public safety, public order, public morality or public health or for the protection of the rights and freedom of other persons, in the sense of being closely, proximately and rationally related to these specific interests. It is not a justification for a denial or restriction of these rights that the law imposing it is reasonably justifiable in some other interest not specified in the relevant constitutional provision, such as economic wellbeing, economic development or national unity. But trade unions, being business associations, are more vulnerable to state regulation than political or religious associations; in other words, less is required to establish the necessary connection between a regulatory statute and the specified interests in the case of trade unions than in the case of political or religious associations.

It is in the light of this that the existing law relating to trade unions and industrial disputes is to be considered. Under the Trade Unions Decree 1973,[66] trade unions may be freely formed, but a trade union cannot, after it has been so formed, function as such until it is registered, and upon its ceasing to be registered, it shall also cease to function.[67] Application for registration must be signed by at least two members[68] but there is no real discretion to refuse registration. There is perhaps nothing exceptionable in this requirement. Indeed a statutory prescription of a minimum number of persons necessary to form a trade union or a political party is not necessarily a restriction of the right to form them, and has been held valid in the United States.[69] However, under the reorganisation introduced by a decree of 1978,[70] all existing trade unions were dissolved and their certificates cancelled, and they were formed into just seventy unions. The registrar of trade unions was directed to register them without any conditions whatsoever. The registration of new unions is made dependent on 'the approval of the minister on his being satisfied that it is expedient to register the union either by regrouping existing trade unions, registering a new trade union or otherwise howsoever, but no trade union shall be registered to represent workers or employers in a place where there already exists a trade union.'[71] The compulsory merger of trade unions and the discretion vested in the minister to grant or refuse permission to form new unions have no rational or substantial connection with the preservation of public safety, public order, public morality or public health; they are therefore an unjustified denial of the right guaranteed by the Constitution to form trade unions, and are accordingly unconstitutional and void. The decree also established the Nigeria Labour Congress and made it the only permitted central labour organisation to which all trade unions, other than associations of senior staff or employers, are deemed to be affiliated. This is also unconstitutional as a denial of a constitutionally-guaranteed right.

Power to proscribe a trade union the members of which are employed in essential services was taken under a decree of 1976, the Trade Disputes (Essential Services) Decree as amended in 1977. If the head of state is satisfied that such a union is or has been engaged in acts calculated to disrupt the economy or acts calculated to obstruct or disrupt the smooth running of any essential service, or has wilfully failed to comply with the procedure for the settlement of trade disputes, he may proscribe the union, which shall then cease to exist. Essential services are the public services — services relating to electricity, water or fuel, broadcasting, posts and telecommunications, ports, harbour, docks, aerodromes, transportation by road, rail, river or air, banking, hospitals etc. Several unions have been proscribed under this power. The decree also prohibits the formation or registration within six months of the proscription of another trade union having the same or similar objectives, and consisting of the same or substantially the same members as those of the proscribed union.

The power of the state to control the activities of those in its service is governed by different considerations, and it may be conceded that it can prohibit or proscribe trade unions in the civil service. Insofar, therefore, as the essential services designated in the act are part of the civil service, the ban is constitutionally unexceptionable.

Outside the civil service, the constitutionality of proscription would depend on the connection between the activities of the trade unions concerned and defence, public safety, public order, public morality or public health. While the activities of unions engaged in the services enumerated in the decree may well have a direct impact on the economy to the extent of causing a disruption of it, the constitutionality of proscription depends, not on that but on the impact of such activities on defence, public safety and public order. There can be no doubt that acts calculated to disrupt the economy have a bearing on the public interests stipulated in the Constitution, but the question is whether such bearing is sufficiently proximate and rational to make proscription reasonably justifiable in a democratic society in those interests. Clearly the connection between the activities of the unions and defence, public safety and public order is an ultimate, not a proximate, one. We may here recall again the decision of Justice Magnus of the Zambian high court in a 1968 case, where he said:

> It could conceivably happen that complete financial anarchy might so weaken the economy that internal disaffection might be caused, leading to rioting and civil disturbance. So might widespread unemployment caused, say, by overpopulation. So might prolonged drought which disrupted agricultural production. One might think of many things which could, ultimately, affect the public safety. None of them would, however, have the quality of proximateness which would justify involving this exception.[72]

The compelling logic of his reasoning exposes the fallacy of an earlier decision by Chief Justice Blagden of the same court in a case in 1967 concerning the constitutionality of a statutory regulation which required children in government or government-aided schools to sing the national anthem and to salute the national flag on certain occasions.[73] The constitutional validity of the regulation depended on whether it was reasonably required in the interests of public safety and public order. The chief justice held that it was. His reasoning was that the singing of the national anthem and the saluting of the national flag were necessary to inculcate among the people, especially among children in their formative stages, a love of nation, and a consciousness of common belonging. He further reasoned that national unity is the basis of national security, and then concluded that whatever was reasonably required in the interests of national unity must also be reasonably required in the interest of national security.

But surely the connection between the singing of the national anthem or the saluting of the flag and national security is an ultimate and not a proximate one. The danger to national security in school children not being made to sing the national anthem or to salute the flag is rather remote. Indeed, the U.S. supreme court has held that it was not permissible under the U.S. Constitution to use compulsion to try to achieve national unity. 'To believe that patriotism will not flourish if patriotic ceremonies are voluntary and spontaneous instead of a compulsory routine is to make an unflattering estimate of the appeal of our institutions to free minds.'[74] Accordingly it held, reversing its earlier decision,[75] that the compulsory flag salute and singing of the national anthem were unconstitutional.

It may therefore be concluded that, however much the activities of a trade union may be calculated to disrupt the economy, proscription for that reason alone is not reasonably justifiable in the interest of defence, public safety, public order, public morality or public health, and that the act authorising it is unconstitutional and void to the extent that it affects services outside the civil service.

The unconstitutionality of proscription (except insofar as it relates to the civil service) renders invalid all the other provisions of the decree based on it. Such are the provisions forfeiting to the state the property of a proscribed trade union or barring its officials from thereafter holding an office in a trade union any members of which are employed in any essential services. There is also the provision authorising the detention of an official or member of a trade union believed to have been concerned in acts prejudicial to industrial peace or calculated to disrupt the smooth running of any essential services. The act also ousts the jurisdiction of the courts to enquire into anything done under it. But even if proscription under the decree is not unconstitutional, detention without trial, forfeiture of movable or immovable property and ouster of the court's jurisdiction are contrary to other specific prohibitions of the Constitution, and therefore invalid.

Trade disputes generally have been a subject of close government control, no doubt because of their potentially disruptive impact on the economy. The relevant law is the Trade Disputes Act 1976, as amended in 1977. The constitutionality of the act depends on whether it unjustifiably takes away the constitutional right of workers to try to settle a trade dispute by collective bargaining with the employer, and their constitutional right to use the strike weapon to back up their bargaining power.

The Trade Disputes Act 1976 institutes a compulsory procedure for the settlement of trade disputes by arbitration, but under the original act before the 1977 amendment, the procedure could be invoked only in the event of a failure by the parties to the dispute to settle it amicably between themselves by an agreed in-house method for settling such disputes or through the mediation of an outside mediator appointed by them with mutual agreement. The parties are specifically required by the act first to try to settle the dispute amicably in this way. In default of amicable settlement by these methods, the parties must then report the dispute to the minister for labour in order to enable him to set in motion the compulsory procedure instituted by the act. Even after the dispute is reported to him, if the minister is not satisfied that the two avenues of amicable settlement have been substantially utilised, he is not to invoke the compulsory procedure, but is to direct the parties what steps to take to achieve an amicable settlement. Only where the dispute remains unsettled after the steps directed by him have been taken, or where either party refuses to take those steps, may he then invoke the compulsory procedure.

The first procedure in the statutory process — the appointment of a conciliator by the minister — actually involves no compulsion. Apart from the fact that his appointment is by the minister and not by the parties, the conciliator is like a mediator in that his role is simply to try to settle the dispute by negotiation with the parties. He cannot impose a settlement. Where settlement by conciliation fails, the matter is then to be referred by the minister to the industrial arbitration panel also appointed by the minister and from which an arbitration tribunal is constituted to try to settle the dispute. Where either party objects to an award made by the tribunal, a further reference is made to the national industrial court, whose decision is final and binding on the parties, without a right of appeal. Except when an objection is made, an award made by an arbitration tribunal and confirmed by the minister also binds the parties. Failure to comply with a binding award is made a criminal offence. The national industrial court is also given power to determine questions as to the interpretation of an award made by an arbitration tribunal or by itself. Disputes involving workers employed in essential services as well as those where reference to an arbitration tribunal would not be appropriate go straight to the national industrial court. Both an arbitration tribunal and the national industrial court have power to compel the attendance of witnesses, to compel answers to questions and the production of books, papers, documents and other things. The jurisdiction of the national industrial court in the settlement of trade disputes is to the exclusion of any other court.

It seems that no interference with the right of collective bargaining is implied in the settlement of trade disputes by a compulsory procedure which is designed, not to override collective bargaining, but merely as a supporting machinery to be employed in default of amicable settlement by mutual agreement. The state intervenes only because the parties themselves have failed to settle the dispute by agreement. It cannot be suggested that, with the parties unable to agree, the dispute should be left to remain in a state of indefinite stalemate.

However, a new element was introduced into the matter by the amending act of 1977. First, it empowers the minister, where a trade dispute, though not yet formally declared, is apprehended by him, to take the initiative by appointing a conciliator to try to negotiate a settlement or to refer the dispute to the industrial arbitration panel or to set up a board of inquiry without waiting until the parties have first tried and failed to settle it amicably. The imposition of a compulsory procedure before the parties have tried and failed to settle their dispute by agreement is unquestionably an interference with the freedom of collective bargaining.

The amendment act also limits freedom of collective bargaining by prohibiting, under penalty of fine or imprisonment, a general or percentage wage increase without the approval of the minister.

As the connection between these restrictions on freedom and public order and public safety can hardly be described as proximate or rational, they are unconstitutional and void. Admittedly, in the United States congress and the state legislatures have been held to have power to fix by law wages, hours of work and other conditions of services. Statutes fixing minimum wages and maximum hours of employment have thus been sustained.[76] By these decisions the court reversed its earlier holding which invalidated statutes prescribing maximum hours[77] or minimum wages,[78] and also statutes outlawing the practice whereby workers were required by employers to sign an agreement not to become union members.[79]

In reversing itself and upholding the validity of a statutory minimum wage or maximum hours of work, the supreme court of the United States said that congress and the state legislatures are not to be 'put in a straitjacket when they attempt to suppress business and industrial conditions which they regard as offensive to the public welfare'.[80] This statement underlines the wider scope of the state's police power in the United States which, as earlier noted, is measured by reference to public welfare generally, unlike in Nigeria where any interference with a guaranteed right is required to be justified by the specific and narrower interests of defence, public safety, public order, public health, public morality or the protection of the rights and freedom of others.

It is not suggested however that in Nigeria a statutory regulation of conditions of employment is necessarily invalid. Its constitutionality depends on whether it infringes the rights of workers. *Prima facie*, a statutory minimum wage or maximum hours of work is designed for the benefit of workers as against the employer, and cannot be an infringement of their right. The constitutional prohibition of servitude and forced or compulsory labour, from which the right of the workers derives, confers upon the employer no constitutional right which will enable him to challenge a statutory minimum wage or maximum hours. The Nigerian Constitution does not guarantee a generalised liberty, which is the basis of the right of an employer in the United States to be free to agree with his workers on terms and conditions of employment, including wages and hours of work. It follows that the national assembly in Nigeria can fix by law minimum wages or maximum hours of work. What it cannot do is to fix maximum wages or minimum hours.

The restrictions on the right to strike are perhaps more direct and serious. The act makes it an offence punishable by a fine or imprisonment for any worker to take part in a strike in connection with any trade dispute where (*a*) no attempt has been made to settle the dispute by agreement; (*b*) a conciliator has been appointed by the minister or the dispute has been referred to the industrial arbitration panel or to the national industrial court; and (*c*) an award made by an arbitration tribunal has become binding or the national industrial court has made an award. A strike is defined as the cessation of work, or a refusal to continue to work in consequence of a dispute, by a body of employees acting in combination, and done as a means of compelling an employer to accept or not to accept terms of employment and physical conditions of work; cessation of work includes deliberately working at less than usual speed or with less than usual efficiency.

Whether in connection with a trade dispute or not, a worker employed in an essential service commits a criminal offence, similarly punishable, if, with knowledge that quitting his work will result in the community or any part of it being deprived of any essential service, he nevertheless quits work, either alone or in combination with others, without giving to his employer at least fifteen days' notice. 'Essential services' is given substantially the same meaning as under the Trade Disputes (Essential Services) Act 1976. Fifteen days' notice (similarly sanctioned by fine or imprisonment in case of default) is also required of any other worker who, either alone or in combination with others, wants to quit work knowing that the probable consequence of that will be (*a*) to endanger human life; (*b*) seriously to endanger public health or the health of the inmates of any hospital or similar institution; (*c*) to cause serious bodily injury to any person or persons; or (*d*) to expose any valuable property to destruction or serious injury.

It is clearly established in the decisions of the U.S. supreme court that to make it a criminal offence for a worker to quit work temporarily or permanently or unless he gives a prescribed period of notice is forced labour or servitude.[81] The statutory prohibition of a strike thus violates the constitutional guarantee of freedom from forced or compulsory labour which, in the case of a worker acting alone, and not in combination with others, is not subject to state regulation at all, except in an emergency or calamity threatening the life or wellbeing of the community (s. 31).

Where a worker is acting in combination with others, then it has to be conceded that the state is competent to regulate his right to quit work provided that the regulatory statute is reasonably justifiable as being rationally or proximately related to defence, public safety, public order, public morality or public health. There is no such rational or proximate connection between the specified interests and the prohibition of a strike in aid of a trade dispute in the circumstances specified in the act or its prohibition in the case of workers employed in an essential service where fifteen days' notice is not given. The prohibition in cases where the quitting of work without fifteen days' notice will endanger life, public health or the safety of persons or property seems to be reasonably justifiable in the specified interests, and therefore valid.

A final question concerning the constitutionality of the Trade Disputes Act is whether the power it vests in an arbitration tribunal or the national industrial court for the compulsory settlement of trade disputes trenches on the judicial power of the courts under the Constitution. If the power for the compulsory settlement of trade disputes under the act is part of the judicial power vested in the courts and the two tribunals are not a court in the sense of the Constitution, then the provisions are unconstitutional and void.

The principle is settled on the highest judicial authority that the power to compel the attendance of witnesses, answers to questions and the production of documents is not exclusive to judicial power, so that its exercise by an administrative agency or tribunal is not an interference with judicial power.[82]

It is also settled law that the settlement of trade disputes by conciliation and arbitration through an administrative tribunal does not by itself interfere with judicial power, since it is concerned not with the determination of rights and liabilities as they *at present exist*, but with settling what in the opinion of the arbitrator or tribunal *ought to be* the conditions of employment.[83] It is a peculiar attribute of judicial power that it is concerned with existing rights, i.e. those which the parties actually have at the inception of the suit, and not those which it may be thought they ought to have. On the other hand, industrial arbitration, as provided for under the Trade Disputes Decree, is concerned with settling conditions of employment as they should be in the future. Even more decisive is the fact that, under the decree, the enforcement of an award given by the arbitration tribunal or the national industrial court is outside the power of both tribunals. Not being part of the judicial power vested in the courts by the Constitution, the functions of the arbitration tribunal and the national industrial court for the settlement of trade disputes are not an interference with that power of such a nature as to be unconstitutional.

Perhaps a comparison with the Australian Commonwealth court of conciliation and arbitration, and the decision[84] on its constitutionality, might be illuminating. The court was established by an act of the Australian parliament as a court of record, with a president appointed by the governor-general during good behaviour for seven years. Its primary function was the settlement of industrial disputes by conciliation and arbitration, terminating in an award. In the exercise of its conciliation and arbitration functions, it was given power to alter the standard hours of work in an industry, the basic wage for workers, and to make provision for long service leave with pay. These were clearly functions of an administrative, arbitral and executive character. Powers of a judicial character were also given to it, namely (*a*) to impose penalties for breach or non-observance of an award; (*b*) to order compliance with its order or award; and (*c*) to grant *mandamuses* and injunctions against committing or continuing a contravention of the act.

It was contended that the 'court' was not a court in terms of the Constitution, as its president was appointed, not for life, as required by the Constitution, but for seven years, and that the vesting of judicial functions in it was a usurpation. The high court held that the power conferred upon the court to enforce the rights or liabilities created by an award made by it was judicial; therefore it could only be conferred on a court strictly so called; that the court of conciliation and arbitration was not such a court because its president was appointed for seven years and not for life; accordingly the provisions of the act conferring upon it power to enforce its awards were invalid.

In accordance with the decision of the high court the act was subsequently amended altering the membership of the 'court' to a chief judge and such other judges as might be appointed, and their appointment, tenure and remuneration were put on the same footing as those of judges of the high court under the Constitution. In spite of this, the judicial committee of the privy council held, affirming a majority of the high court, that by its primary functions the 'court' still remained an administrative body, and that notwithstanding that its members were now appointed for life the vesting of judicial functions in it was invalid.[85] Thus it was the power given to it to enforce its decision, and not its power to determine trade disputes by arbitration, that invalidated the court.

REFERENCES

1. See *Sweezy* v. *New Hampshire* (1957), 354 U.S. 234.
2. *Stromberg* v. *California* (1931), 283 U.S. 283 U.S. 359.
3. *Shelton* v. *Tucker* (1960), 364 U.S. 479, 485–6.
4. *Sweezy* v. *New Hampshire*, ibid. at 250.
5. *Coppage* v. *Kansas* (1915), 236 U.S. 1.
6. See Fellman, *The Constitutional Right of Association* (1963), 37.
7. *Rimi* v. *People's Redemption Party*, Suit No. M/133/80 of 23 December 80; See also *Rimi & Another* v. *People's Redemption Party & others*, Suit No. LD/1556/80 of 12/12/80.
8. *Prince* v. *Massachusetts* (1944), 321 U.S. 158, 166.
9. *Pierce* v. *Society of Sisters* (1925), 268 U.S. 510.
10. *Collymore* v. *Attorney-General* (1969), 2 All E.R. 1207; [1969] 2 W.L.R. 233; [1970] A.C. 538.
11. *Thornhill* v. *Alabama* (1939), 310 U.S. 88.
12. ibid.
13. *National Labour Relations Board* v. *Fansteel Metallurgical Corpn.*, 306 U.S. 240, 256.
14. So described in *National Labour Relations Board* v. *Fansteel Metallurgical Corpn.*, ibid.
15. *International Union* v. *Wisconsin Employment Relations Board* (1949), 336 U.S. 245; citing *National Labour Relations Board* v. *Jones & Laughlin Steel Corpn.*, 301 U.S. 1, 33.
16. Children and Young Persons Law 1958 (Part VIII).
17. *Cheranci* v. *Cheranci* (1960), N.R.N.L.R. 24 at 31.
18. ibid. at 32.
19. *Olawoyin* v. *Commissioner of Police* (1962), N.R.N.L.R. 29.
20. *Prince* v. *Massachusetts* (1944), 321 U.S. 158.
21. ibid. at 168.
22. s. 26(2).
23. *Thomas* v. *Collins* (1945), 323 U.S. 546.
24. ibid.
25. *Cantwell* v. *Connecticut* (1939), 310 U.S. 296.
26. *Whitney* v. *California*, 274 U.S. 357; also *Burns* v. *United States*, 274 U.S. 328; *United States* v. *Socony-Vacuum Oil Co.*, 310 U.S. 150.
27. *Dennis* v. *United States* (1951), 341 U.S. 494; *Scales* v. *United States* (1961), 357 U.S. 203.
28. *Gitlow* v. *New York*, 268 U.S. 652.
29. See *Yates* v. *United States* (1957), 354 U.S. 298, 330.
30. *Fiske* v. *Kansas*, 274 U.S. 380; *Stromberg* v. *California*, 280 U.S. 359.
31. *Barenblatt* v. *United States* (1959), 360 U.S. 109; *Uphaus* v. *Wyman*

(1959), 360 U.S. 72.
32. *De Jonge* v. *Oregon* (1936), 299 U.S. 353.
33. ibid. at 365.
34. *New York ex rel. Bryant* v. *Zimmerman* (1928), 278 U.S. 63, 72.
35. *Staub* v. *Baxley* (1958), 355 U.S. 313.
36. *National Ass'n for the Advancement of Coloured People* v. *Alabama* (1958), 357 U.S. 449; re-affirmed in *Bates* v. *Little Rock* (1960), 361 U.S. 516.
37. *Bates* v. *Little Rock*, ibid.; see also *Louisiana ex rel. Gremillion* v. *N.A.A.C.P.* (1961), 366 U.S. 293.
38. *Viereck* v. *United States* (1943), 318 U.S. 236; *Communist Party* v. *Subversive Activities Control Board* (1956), 351 U.S. 115; *Communist Party* v. *Subversive Activities Control Board* (1961), 361 U.S. 1; *Konigsberg* v. *State Bar of California* (1961), 366 U.S. 36.
39. *New York ex rel. Bryant* v. *Zimmerman* (1928), 278 U.S. 63.
40. *Davis* v. *Massachusetts* (1897), 167 U.S. 43; endorsed in *Wilson* v. *Eureka City* (1898), 173 U.S. 32.
41. *Davis* v. *Massachusetts*, ibid. at 47.
42. ibid.
43. *Hague* v. *Committee for Industrial Organisation* (1939), 307 U.S. 496.
44. ibid.
45. *Niemotko* v. *Maryland* (1951), 340 U.S. 268, 272.
46. *Kunz* v. *New York* (1951), 340 U.S. 290.
47. See Public Order Law 1957, s. 9 as amended in 1964, Northern Region.
48. Public Order Act (Lagos), s. 5(2), and corresponding provisions in the Public Order Laws of the other states.
49. *Cox* v. *New Hampshire* (1941), 312 U.S. 569.
50. *Poulos* v. *New Hampshire* (1953), 345 U.S. 395, 403–5.
51. See the dissenting judgment of Justice Douglas at 425–6.
52. See *Niemotka* v. *Maryland* (1951), 340 U.S. 268.
53. *Poulos* v. *New Hampshire*, ibid. at 409.
54. ibid. at 424.
55. *Cox* v. *New Hampshire*, ibid.
56. See Public Order Act (Lagos), s. 4(1), and corresponding provisions in the Laws of other states.
57. *Kovacs* v. *Cooper*, 336 U.S. 77.
58. *Saia* v. *New York*, 334 U.S. 558.
59. *Feiner* v. *New York* (1951), 340 U.S. 315, 320.
60. *Cantwell* v. *Connecticut*, 310 U.S. 296, 310.
61. *Feiner* v. *New York*, ibid.
62. ibid at 320–1.
63. *Lawal* v. *The Lagos State Electoral Commission*, Suit No. ID/73/80 of 24 March 1980, High Court, Ikeja.
64. See Fellman, *The Constitutional Right of Association* (1963), 40–2.
65. *Thomas* v. *Collins*, 323 U.S. 516, 556 (1945).
66. Repealing the Trade Union Act, cap. 200, Trade Unions (Amendment) Decree 1970, and the Trade Unions (Amendment) Decree 1971.
67. s. 2(1).

68. Substituted by Trade Unions (Amendment) Decree 1978.
69. *State ex rel. McGrael* v. *Phelps*, 144 Wis. 1.
70. Trade Unions (Amendment) Decree 1978.
71. s. 3(2).
72. *Patel* v. *Att.-Gen. of Zambia*, 1968 S.J.Z. 1.
73. *Kachasu* v. *Att.-Gen. of Zambia*, 1967/HP/273.
74. *West Virginia State Board of Education* v. *Barnette* (1943), 319 U.S. 624.
75. *Minersville School District* v. *Gobitis* (1940), 310 U.S. 586.
76. *United States* v. *Darby* (1941), 312 U.S. 100, 125.
77. *Lochner* v. *New York*, 198 U.S. 45.
78. *Olsen* v. *Nebraska*, 313 U.S. 236, 244–6; *Osborn* v. *Ozlin*, 310 U.S. 53, 66, 67; Chas *Wolff Packing Co.* v. *Court of Industrial Relations of State of Kansas*, 262 U.S. 522.
79. *Coppage* v. *Kansas*, 236 U.S. 1.
80. *Lincoln Federal Labour Union* v. *Northwestern*, 1 & M Co 69 S. Ct Reporter 251.
81. *Clyatt* v. *United States* (1905), 197 U.S. 207; *United States* v. *Reynolds & United States* v. *Broughton*, 235 U.S. 133; *Taylor* v. *Georgia*, 315 U.S. 25; *Bailey* v. *Alabama* (1908), 211 U.S. 452; *Pollock* v. *Williams* (1944), 322 U.S. 4.
82. See *Rola Co. (Australia) Ltd.* v. *The Commonwealth* (1944), 69 C.L.R. 185; *Shell Co. of Australia Ltd.* v. *Fed. Com. of Taxation* [1931], A.C. 275 (P.C.); sub. nom. *British Imperial Oil Co. Ltd.* v. *Fed. Com. of Taxation* (1926), 38 C.L.R. 153.
83. *Waterside Workers' Fedn. of Australia* v. *Alexander (J.W.) Ltd.* (1918) 25 C.L.R. 434; also *United Engineering Workers' Union* v. *Devanayagam* [1967], 3 W.L.R. 46 (P.C.).
84. *Waterside Workers' Fedn. of Australia* v. *Alexander (J.W.) Ltd.*, ibid.
85. *Attorney-General for Australia* v. *R. & Boilermakers' Society of Australia* [1957], A.C. 288 (P.C.).

28
FREEDOM OF PRIVATE ENTERPRISE

1. *Freedom of private enterprise defined*

Freedom of private enterprise is used here in the sense of the liberty of a person to pursue any lawful business, profession or vocation. It implies that, while the state may enter into business in competition with private persons and may regulate private enterprise in the interest of the public welfare, it cannot by law assume a monopoly of business enterprise so as altogether to prevent or exclude private initiative, nor can it impose unwarranted restrictions on it. Freedom of private enterprise therefore connotes absence of state monopoly of business activity with an exclusiveness conferred by law, as well as absence of unwarranted state regulation of private enterprise. An economy under which the means of production and distribution are publicly owned and managed to the exclusion of private persons, or which may be regulated by the state as it likes, is the antithesis of economic freedom.

Freedom of private enterprise does not however connote absolute immunity from any state regulation of economic activity. It is conceded that the state must be able to regulate private economic activities in order to ensure that the public welfare is adequately protected and promoted, since an unregulated freedom of private enterprise is nothing but social anarchy. As the United States supreme court observed, 'government cannot exist if the citizen may at will use his property to the detriment of his fellows or exercise his freedom of contract to work them harm.'[1]

But the crucial point here is as to the limits, rather than the existence, of the state's power to regulate private economic activities. When is state regulation of economic activities unwarranted, and therefore an encroachment upon freedom?

First, a regulation that makes the pursuit of an enterprise conditional upon a licence which may be granted or refused by the state in its uncontrolled discretion is, in general, unwarranted. The general principle, as settled by a long line of decisions of the supreme court of the United States, is that a law which 'makes the peaceful enjoyment of freedom which the Constitution guarantees contingent upon the uncontrolled will of an official — as by requiring a permit or licence which may be granted or withheld in the discretion of such official — is an unconstitutional censorship or prior restraint upon the enjoyment of those freedoms.'[2] It follows that where freedom of private enterprise is guaranteed in the constitution, the requirement of a licence from the state for carrying on any business is, in general, a denial of the right.

Secondly, apart from a licence requirement, a regulation of private enterprise is permissible only if uncontrolled private enterprise poses a real and substantial danger to the public welfare, and the regulatory measure is not otherwise unreasonable, arbitrary or discriminatory. A state regulation of economic activities which does not satisfy those conditions is an unwarranted interference with liberty. Thus, under the Constitution of the United States, statutes regulating working hours, wages, professional and service fees, workmen's compensation, prices and labour organisation, and a host of other regulatory measures, have been declared invalid because they did not bear a real and substantial relation to any likely danger to the public welfare, or were otherwise unreasonable, arbitrary or discriminatory. The limitation which these requirements impose on governmental regulation of economic activities is all the more far-reaching because the 'reasonableness of each regulation depends upon the relevant facts', with the result that 'a regulation valid for one sort of business, or in given circumstances, may be invalid for another sort, or for the same business under other circumstances'.[3] In upholding a building zone law which excluded from residential districts apartment houses, business houses, retail stores and shops, and other like establishments, the U.S. supreme court observed that 'regulations, the wisdom, necessity and validity of which, as applied to existing conditions, are so apparent that they are now uniformly sustained, a century ago or even half a century ago, probably would have been rejected as arbitrary and oppressive. Such regulations are sustained, under the complex conditions of our day, for reasons analogous to those which justify traffic regulations, which, before the advent of automobiles and rapid transit street railways, would have been condemned as fatally arbitrary and unreasonable. . . . A regulatory zoning ordinance, which would be clearly valid as applied to the great cities, might be clearly invalid as applied to rural communities.'[4]

The attitude of the U.S. supreme court in this matter has indeed undergone considerable change since 1934, culminating in 1949 in the overruling of the line of decisions which invalidated laws fixing minimum wages and maximum working hours or prices, and laws regulating business activities.[5]

2. *Extent of freedom of private enterprise under the Constitution*

The extent of freedom of private enterprise under the 1979 Constitution has to be determined by reference to two different chapters of that

Constitution, namely the bill of rights in chapter IV and the Fundamental Objectives and Directive Principles of state policy in chapter II.

(i) *Freedom of private enterprise under the bill of rights*
The Nigerian Constitution differs markedly from the American in the extent of freedom of private enterprise which they guarantee as a legally enforceable right. In this particular, their respective bills of rights are of quite different character. By prohibiting deprivation of 'life, liberty or property, without due process of law', the taking of private property for public use without just compensation, the impairment of the obligation of contract, or the abridgment of the privileges or immunities of citizens, the U.S. bill of rights entrenches an economic philosophy based on private enterprise and private property. The effect of these constitutional prohibitions is to forbid *exclusive* state ownership of the means of production and distribution; the question of the government assuming powers of management over the economy is thereby ruled out. The state can enter into business in competition with private persons, but it cannot by law assume a monopoly of economic activities or any aspects of them, and exclude private persons therefrom. It cannot also impose unwarranted restriction on economic activity by private persons. To do either of these would infringe the constitutional guarantee of 'liberty', which has been interpreted by the U.S. supreme court as embracing liberty to engage in any business of one's choice, to enter into contract and to acquire rights and property in connection with that business 'The liberty mentioned in that amendment', said the U.S. supreme court, while invalidating a statute that regulated marine insurance contracts, 'means not only the right of the citizen to be free from the mere physical restraint of his person, as by incarceration, but the term is deemed to embrace the right of the citizen to be free in the enjoyment of all his faculties; to be free to use them in all lawful ways; to live and work where he will; to earn his livelihood by any lawful calling; to pursue any livelihood or a vocation, and for that purpose to enter into all contracts which may be proper, necessary or essential to his carrying out to a successful conclusion the purposes above mentioned.[6]

But whereas the U.S. Constitution guarantees liberty in a generalised sense as defined above, the Nigerian bill of rights guarantees only personal liberty. In the context of the Nigerian guarantee, personal liberty means simply the right of the citizen to be free from physical restraint of his person, or more specifically freedom from arrest or detention save as authorised therein.

However, in a recent case involving the plan of the Lagos State Government to abolish private primary schools in the state, Mr. Justice

Omololu Thomas held that the guarantee of personal liberty in the Nigerian bill of rights embraces all privileges, immunities and rights of a personal nature, and that the word 'and' which begins the second leg of the guarantee is to be read conjuctively.[7] Now, if 'personal liberty' has the same meaning and scope as 'liberty', then the word 'personal' which seems clearly intended to qualify 'liberty' would have been made completely otiose. Furthermore, as has already been said, the context seems to negate the interpretation adumbrated by the learned judge. The second leg of the guarantee is intended to amplify its scope, and makes it clear that it is limited to freedom from physical restraint of the person by means of arrest or detention.

Even the *right to family life*, guaranteed in the 1963 Constitution and repeated in the draft submitted by the constitution drafting committee, disappeared for an unknown reason from the 1979 Constitution as finally enacted, and with it the right of a parent as an incident of family life to direct the upbringing of his children and how or where they should be educated — what subjects they are to study,[8] and what school, private or public, they should attend — and the right of the children to receive such education. Affirming the constitutional guarantee of these rights under the U.S. Constitution, the supreme court of that country has observed that 'the fundamental theory of liberty upon which all governments in this Union repose excludes any general power of the state to standardise its children by forcing them to accept instruction from public teachers only. The child is not the mere creature of the state; those who nurture him and direct his destiny have the right, coupled with the high duty, to recognise and prepare him for additional obligations.'[9] It also held that the patronage which children attending their schools confer on the owners and operators of private schools is a legitimate business interest equally protected by the Constitution against legislation arbitrarily or unreasonably interfering with it. (These rights still exist under the Constitution, but only as an incident of the freedom of expression — see below.)

While the right to associate with others for the protection of common interests is guaranteed (s. 37), yet, apart from an association formed for the purpose of party politics, trade unionism or religion, the purposes and objects for which people may associate together are not guaranteed. What businesses people can engage in, and the organisational form for doing so, are thus left very much in the control of the state.

The right of property, its acquisition, holding and use, is also not guaranteed. Not even the taking of property for public use without just compensation is prohibited. All the Constitution says is that 'no movable property or any interest in an immovable property shall be acquired compulsorily in any part of Nigeria except in the manner and for the purposes prescribed by a law that, among other things (a) requires the prompt payment of compensation therefor; and (b) gives to any person claiming such compensation a right of access for the determination of his interest in the property and the amount of compensation to a court of law or tribunal or body having jurisdiction in that part of Nigeria.'

It is to be noted, first, that the provision speaks only of movable or immovable property, which has a much more restricted meaning than property generally. In economic affairs, movable and immovable property is a small part of property. What is overwhelmingly of great importance economically is the intangible, incorporeal rights conferred by corporate shareholding, bank accounts, various commercial instruments like bills of exchange, and contracts generally. It is these that form the real essence of property in the present world of commerce and industry. All these may be expropriated as the government pleases without compensation.

Secondly, what the provision prohibits is not taking in a general sense but the taking of possession and acquisition. The reference to possession and acquisition excludes the kind of constructive taking held to be prohibited by the U.S. bill of rights, as where right in property is destroyed by restriction on its use, although the owner remains in possession of it and the state does not appropriate it or make any use of it. Thus the continuous flying of army bombers directly above a person's land at a height of 83 feet where the light and noise from these planes caused him to loose sleep and his chickens to be killed was held to be a 'taking' of property for public use.[10] A statute which forbids the mining of coal in such a way that the mining causes the subsidence of any structure used as a human habitation was held invalid on the ground that 'to make it commercially impracticable to mine certain coal has very nearly the same effect for constitutional purposes as destroying it' without just compensation, and this notwithstanding that the restriction was in the public interest and that the property so restricted remained in the possession of its owner, and that the state did not appropriate it or make any use of it.[11]

Thirdly, there is no constitutional requirement that the compulsory taking of possession or acquisition must be for public purpose. Any purpose prescribed by the enabling law is permitted, whether it is for the public welfare or not; the purpose may even be to enable the property to be transferred to another private person. This is a serious departure from the 1963 Constitution which incorporated by reference the statutory definition of public purpose as at 31 March 1958.

Fourthly, there is no such requirement as was contained in the 1963 Constitution that compensation should be adequate. Compulsory acquisition is either compulsory purchase or it is confiscation. The idea underlying compulsory purchase is that the owner receives for the property so acquired its equivalent in money, so that the property is not diminished in amount, but is only compulsorily changed in form. The word 'adequate' emphasises the nature of the acquisition as a purchase, albeit a compulsory one. It entitles the owner to be paid the full market value of the property; that is to say, the price he would have bargained for if he had been a willing seller in the open market.[12] Thus, where a compulsory acquisition act provides for the payment of compensation on the basis of a *fair* market value, its constitutionality was questioned on the ground that a fair market value is something less than adequate compensation.[13] It cannot be disputed that a fair market value may be, and often is, less than a full market value. Happily, however, the court in this case refused to allow the statute to be voided on this ground, because, as the court reasoned, a willing seller in the market does not always get the full market value. If he gets a fair market value — and he usually does get it — he is happy and contented; accordingly, compensation based on a fair market value is adequate compensation within the meaning of the constitutional provision (1963), for though not an exact or full equivalent in money, it is a *just* equivalent.

By not stipulating that compensation for compulsory acquisition should be adequate, the 1979 Constitution thus enables the legislature to prescribe any compensation that it likes, whether or not it represents a fair market value or a just monetary equivalent of the property compulsorily acquired. Where compensation bears no relation to the fair market value or to a just monetary equivalent, then the acquisition is a form of confiscation, in that the amount by which the fair market value exceeds the amount of compensation is confiscated by the government.

It is pertinent to mention that in certain circumstances no obligation to provide for payment of any compensation is cast on the legislature at all. Such circumstances relate, *inter alia*, to cases where under a *general* law property is taken (a) in satisfaction of a tax, rate or duty; (b) in execution of a judgment; (c) by way of penalty for breach of some law; (d) as an incident of a lease, mortgage or charge; (e) in circumstances where it is reasonably necessary to do so because the property is in a dangerous state or injurious to the health of human beings, animals or plants; (f) in consequence of any law with respect to the limitation of actions; or (g) for so long as may be necessary for the purposes of any examination, investigation, trial or inquiry or, in the case of land, for the purpose of carrying out on it work of conservation of soil or other natural resources (s. 40[2]).

It can be said that none of these situations amounts strictly to confiscation. The deprivation involved in a statute of limitation, for example, results, not from a positive act of confiscation, but from the failure of the owner to assert his right in time; it is, as the judicial committee of the privy council has observed, thanks to his own inaction.[14] When property is taken in execution of a court judgment or as an incident of a lease, mortgage or charge, it is again thanks to the failure of the owner to honour obligations freely entered into; there is nothing at all of confiscation about that. The same might be said of a deprivation resulting from failure to pay taxes or rates, or from the breach of some law.

Fifthly, the Constitution incorporates the existing law[15] which vests in the federal government the entire property in and control of all minerals, mineral oils and natural gas in, under or upon any land in Nigeria, including its territorial waters and exclusive economic zone. It empowers the national assembly to prescribe by law how these assets are to be managed (s. 40[3]).

Finally, the determination of entitlement to compensation and the amount of it may be made by any authorised tribunal or body, not necessarily a court of law. If, as seems clearly to be the case, the intention is to make final and conclusive the determination of such questions by a tribunal or body which is not a court of law or which is not constituted in such a way as to secure its independence and impartiality, then the provision is in conflict with another provision of the bill of rights, to the effect that the determination of a person's civil rights and obligations by an administrative tribunal or body which is not constituted in such a way as to secure its independence and impartiality shall not be final and conclusive (s. 33[1]). In such a conflict, the latter provision certainly prevails. However, the provision of the Land Use Act 1978 divesting the courts of jurisdiction to enquire into any question concerning or pertaining to the amount or adequacy of compensation for compulsory taking of possession or acquisition under the act is saved by its entrenchment in the Constitution. It is provided that nothing in the Constitution shall invalidate the act, and that its provisions 'shall continue to apply and have full effect in accordance with their tenor and to the like extent as any other provisions forming part of this Constitution' (s. 274[5]).

It is of interest also to note that the provision relating to the compulsory acquisition or the taking of possession of movable or immovable property is not what was approved by the constituent assembly. Both the constitution drafting committee's draft and that of the constituent assembly provide:

> Every person shall be entitled to own or hold property, and accordingly, no property, movable or immovable, shall be taken possession of compulsorily and no right over or interest in any such property shall be acquired compulsorily in

any part of Nigeria except for public purposes and by the provisions of a law that —
(a) requires the prompt payment of adequate compensation therefor; and
(b) gives to any person claiming such compensation a right of access for the determination of his interest in the property and the amount of compensation, to the High Court having jurisdiction in that part of the Federation.

Thus the Constitution as finally enacted by the supreme military council omits the guarantee of the right to own or hold property and the requirement that private property can be compulsorily acquired only for public purposes, that compensation for property compulsorily acquired must be adequate, and that only the high court can determine entitlement to compensation and its amount. It is remarkable that the address of the head of state, announcing the amendments made to the constituent assembly draft by the supreme military council, made no mention of these particular changes, which clearly are the most far-reaching of all the amendments.

The omission of a requirement that compensation for compulsory acquisition of movable or immovable property must be adequate obviously has to do with the entrenchment in the Constitution of the Land Use Act 1978, which abolished all private ownership of land and transferred it to the state, free of any obligation to pay compensation. All that is now recognised in a former private owner is a right of occupancy, and even this is divested to the extent that the land, being undeveloped land in an urban area, exceeds half hectare. The excess of occupancy right in undeveloped land in the urban area over half hectare is also transferred to the state again free of any payment of compensation.

The state is empowered by the act to revoke a right of occupancy if the land is required for public purposes, mining or oil pipeline purposes or for the extraction of building materials, but subject to payment of compensation. The amount of compensation is governed by the Mineral Act or the Mineral Oils Act where revocation is for purposes of mining or oil pipeline. Where it is for public purposes or the extraction of building materials, compensation is as follows:
(a) as respects the land itself — an amount equal to the rent, if any, paid by the occupier during the year in which the right of occupancy was revoked;
(b) as respects buildings, installation or other improvements — the amount of the replacement cost of the building, installation or improvement. The assessment of replacement cost is to be done by the chief lands officer of the State (or the chief federal lands officer in the case of the Federal Capital Territory) according to the prescribed method, which is not specified. In respect of improvement in the nature of reclamation works, the cost of such works is recoverable to

the extent that it can be substantiated by documentary evidence and proof to the satisfaction of the chief lands officer. Simple interest at the prevailing bank rate is payable for delayed payment of compensation;

(c) as regards crops on land — an amount equal to the value as determined by the chief lands officer.

The determination of disputes as to the amount of compensation is the responsibility of the Land Use and Allocation Committee exclusively of the courts. Disputes as to the persons entitled to compensation and all questions concerning occupancy titles and their incidents (other than one concerning the right of the governor or local government to grant occupancy rights under the Act) remain a matter for the courts.

The act seems to have been intended as a socialist measure, as a charter for the common man, a charter of egalitarianism and of social justice. It is said that because land is the primary means of production in an agricultural community, its ownership should be vested in the state to enable it to be controlled for the common benefit of all. With the control conferred by ownership, the state can try to achieve certain socialist objectives with respect to land — greater social justice in the distribution of the land itself and the income from it, control of land speculation and absentee landlordism with all its exploitative tendencies, and a more productive use of land. It is easy to see also that to require compensation to be adequate would greatly inhibit any socialist programme of nationalisation of the means of production and distribution. Without the requirement that compensation must be adequate, the government is left free to prescribe by law how compensation is to be assessed, and the law cannot be impeached on the ground that the assessment results in a compensation that is inadequate or unfair.

But while freedom of contract generally is not guaranteed, the Constitution does guarantee freedom from servitude and from forced or compulsory labour (s. 31[1]). What this means is that, subject to exceptions which we shall mention, no one in Nigeria can be compelled by law or by force to work for the government or for any other employer. There is guaranteed to every person freedom to decide whether to be self-employed or to work for an employer.

In the United States, the prohibition of involuntary servitude in the Constitution (Thirteenth Amendment) has been applied by the supreme court of the country to invalidate statutes which made it a criminal offence for a person, without making restitution, to leave the services of an employer from whom he had obtained money or property upon a promise to work for him.[16] It was emphasised that the constitutional prohibition of servitude means that a 'crime to be punished by imprisonment cannot lawfully be predicated upon the breach of a promise to perform labour or services.'[17] A person may of course borrow money and undertake to repay it by labour or services, but while, like any other contractor, he is liable to an action for damages for breach of that contract, he is free to elect to break it at any time, and no law or force can lawfully compel performance or continuance of the service. As the U.S. supreme court observed:

> The undoubted aim of the Thirteenth Amendment . . . was not merely to end slavery but to maintain a system of completely free and voluntary labour throughout the United States. Forced labour in some special circumstances may be consistent with the general basic system of free labour. For example, forced labour has been sustained as a means of punishing crime, and there are duties such as work on highways which society may compel. But in general the defence against opresive hours, pay, working conditions or treatment is the right to change employers. When the master can compel and the labourer cannot escape the obligation to go on, there is no power below to redress and no incentive above to relieve a harsh overlordship or unwholesome conditions of work.[18]

Flowing from the constitutional prohibition of servitude and forced or compulsory labour is the right of an individual to withdraw his labour or services from a particular employer, either permanently or temporarily. The right to strike — the 'unquestioned right to quit work', as it has been described by the U.S. supreme court[19] — is thus constitutionally guaranteed to the individual. No law can therefore 'make the quitting of work any component of a crime or make criminal sanctions available for holding unwilling persons to labour'.[20] The right of the individual to bargain freely as to the terms and conditions on which to sell his labour or services flows also from the constitutional prohibition of servitude and forced or compulsory labour as well as from the constitutional guarantee of freedom of speech. Freedom of speech is not limited to political discussion; the discussion by an employee and employer of the terms and conditions of employment is clearly embraced within its ambit,[21] although the discussion need not necessarily result in agreement nor is the employer necessarily prevented from determining unilaterally what terms he is prepared to offer, leaving it to the worker to accept or reject them.[22]

The constitutional prohibition of servitude and forced or compulsory labour is not of course without some qualifications. The exceptions relate to (a) labour or service required in consequence of the sentence or order of a court or which is reasonably necessary in an emergency or calamity threatening the life or wellbeing of the community; (b) labour or service required of members of the Nigerian armed forces or the Nigeria police force as part of their duty, as well as labour or service required of conscientious objectors in lieu of service in the armed forces; (*c*) any labour or service that forms part of normal communal or other civic obligations for the wellbeing of the community; and (*d*) compulsory national service required by an act of the national assembly to be performed in the armed forces or as part of the citizen's education and training (s. 31[2]). Significantly, this prohibition is not among those which the state under s. 41(1) of the Constitution is authorised to police or regulate in the interest of defence, public safety, public order, public morality or public health or for the purpose of protecting the rights and freedom of other persons. It follows therefore that, except during an emergency such as is mentioned above, the state's regulatory power does not apply to the individual's right to bargain freely over the terms and conditions of his employment or to quit work either permanently or temporarily. However, when he combines with others to exercise the rights to bargain and to strike, a different situation is created, which the state may regulate in the exercise of its police power (this is discussed in chapter 27 above).

The right positively to engage in business activity or enterprise is guaranteed in respect of the following four types of business activity: (*a*) The right to engage in political activity is guaranteed by the freedom to hold opinions and to impart ideas and information without interference (s. 36[1]); to move about freely (s. 38[1]); to assemble and associate with others, and in particular to form or belong to a political party (s. 37); and to vote and be voted for (ss. 71[2], 61, 123). A free competition in politics is thus guaranteed by the Constitution. And while the Constitution contemplates that political activity should be organised on the platform of a political party, the Constitution establishes no single political party as the only one to which people may belong nor does it restrict the number that may be formed. In the realm of politics a free trade in ideas and in organisational patterns is guaranteed. However, certain kinds of political activity can only be carried on by a registered political party, namely the fielding of candidates for an election and the canvassing of votes for them. An association which is not a political party is prohibited from canvassing for votes at presidential, gubernatorial, legislative or local government elections and from contributing to the election expenses of a candidate (s. 201).

(*b*) Freedom of religious activity is also guaranteed (s. 35[1]). The guarantee confers the right not only to believe what one likes but also to indulge the belief — alone or in community with others, in public or in private — by means of worship, teaching, practice or observance. It need hardly be said that religious activity is today carried on as a business, often big business.

(c) There is the guarantee of the right to own, establish and operate any medium for the dissemination of information, ideas and opinions (s. 36[2]). The ownership of a printing press and the business of printing and distributing newspapers, magazines, books etc. are thus guaranteed to the individual by the Constitution. The guarantee does not, however, extend to the ownership or operation of a television or wireless broadcasting station, which is reserved exclusively to the government or persons whom it has authorised.

(d) There is finally the right to establish, own and operate a school as a business which is secured by implication from two different provisions in the bill of rights. The guarantee of the right (either alone or in community with others) to manifest and propagate one's religion or belief in the forms of worship, teaching, practice and observance (s. 35[1]) implies a right to establish a church as well as a school, these being traditionally the most effective media for these purposes in the country. But a school cannot be used effectively and conveniently for this purpose unless it is owned and maintained wholly by a religious body wishing so to use it. The practice of using schools as a medium for religious instruction and practice is given constitutional recognition in the provision that 'no religious community or denomination shall be prevented from providing religious instruction for pupils of that community or denomination in any place of education maintained wholly by that community or denomination' (s. 35[3]).

The guarantee of the right to receive and impart ideas (s. 36[1]) — the word 'ideas' is apt to cover the whole field of knowledge — clearly contemplates that all means appropriate for the purpose of imparting ideas should be open to the individual. This seems to imply the right to establish, own and operate a school or other institution for the purpose, the right of teachers employed in such a school or other institution to impart ideas, and the right of children to attend and receive the ideas being imparted there. The constitutional basis of these rights, as well as the right of a parent to choose a school for his children, has been affirmed by the high court of Lagos state and the federal court of appeal in a decision which holds as unconstitutional a purported attempt by the state government to abolish, by executive action, private primary and secondary schools.[23] The court also held that the guarantee of the right 'to own, establish and operate any medium for the dissemination of information, ideas and opinions' (s. 36[2]) is not restricted to the mass media, but extends to any intermediate agency for the dissemination of information, ideas and opinions, and that a school or other educational institutions are clearly included.

The failure of the bill of rights to guarantee freedom of private enterprise (except to the very limited extent indicated above) has the constitutional implication that

(a) The take-over by the state, with appropriate statutory backing, of all or most business activities and the prohibition of private enterprise will not be a violation of anyone's constitutional rights (except again for the guaranteed right to engage in the few business activities mentioned earlier) — the extent of the power of the state to do this has of course to be judged by reference also to the provisions of the fundamental objectives and directive principles of state policy in chapter II of the Constitution.

(b) The state has full power (subject as aforesaid) to regulate by law business activities, as it sees fit, and in particular the acquisition and use of property and the making of contracts, whether or not such regulation has a real and substantial relation to the protection and promotion of the public welfare, and whether or not it is reasonable, arbitrary or discriminatory. Its regulatory power is thus not a mere police power, as in the United States. The idea of a police power implies that the government's power of control over a particular field is not general and unlimited, but is restricted to the making of only such regulations as are necessary for the protection and promotion of the public health, safety, morality, general convenience, prosperity and welfare.

The Nigerian statute book is littered with laws regulating various aspects of the economic life of the country in a manner which no American government would dare to attempt: laws fixing minimum wages, prohibiting general wage increases, pegging income from dividends, fixing prices for various commodities, controlling fees and fares chargeable respectively by certain professionals and operators, controlling rent and the use and disposition of land, requiring a licence for or otherwise restricting the carrying on of certain professions, trades or industrial activities, etc. However unreasonable or arbitrary, and however unrelated to the public interest such regulations may be, no court in Nigeria can interfere. The Constitution recognises no such theory as is applied in the U.S. supreme court, e.g. that prices may not normally be regulated, because 'the public interest and private right are both adequately protected when there is "free" competition among buyers and sellers', and that state regulation is constitutionally permitted only when there exists 'a situation or combination of circumstances materially restricting the regulative force of competition, so that buyers or sellers are placed at such a disadvantage in the bargaining struggle that serious economic consequences result to a very large number of members of the community.'[24] These observations were made in a case holding invalid a statute which limited the resale price of theatre tickets, and were repeated in another case invalidating a statute which regulated fees charged by employment agencies.[25]

One of the most remarkable of these regulations is the indigenisation of business enterprises whereby certain types of enterprises are reserved exclusively to Nigerian citizens or associations, while the participation of non-citizens in all other types of enterprise is limited to a prescribed proportion with a mandatory injunction on non-citizen business proprietors to sell their excess shares to Nigerian citizens within a stipulated time. The law also regulates the quantum of shares which a Nigerian citizen can acquire in any business compulsorily indigenised. No doubt the law discriminates against non-Nigerians, but the Constitution does not prohibit that.

Whether the use made of the state's regulatory power is adequate and purposeful enough, whether it is directed sufficiently towards the re-distribution of the nation's wealth, to social justice, the minimisation of the exploitation of man by man, and to other goals aimed at maximising the public welfare, is another question.

(ii) *Freedom of private enterprise and the directive principles of state policy*

While the extent of freedom of private enterprise guaranteed by the bill of rights is thus very limited, it does not follow that the state is left with unfettered freedom to pursue either capitalism or socialism as it pleases. The Constitution sets out principles of economic policy to be followed by government. First, it empowers the national assembly by resolution to declare what areas of the economy are to be 'major sectors' to be managed and operated exclusively by the federal government, and directs that until a resolution to the contrary is made by the national assembly all economic activities being operated exclusively by the federal government on the date immediately preceding the coming into force of the Constitution shall be deemed to be major sectors. Secondly, it directs that, within the context of the ideals and objectives which it ordains for the nation, the state shall

'(*a*) control the national economy in such manner as to secure the maximum welfare, freedom and happiness of every citizen on the basis of social justice and equality of status and opportunity;

(*b*) without prejudice to its right to operate or participate in areas of the economy other than the major sectors of the economy, manage and operate the major sectors of the economy;

(*c*) without prejudice to the right of any person to participate in areas of the economy within the major sector of the economy, protect the right of every citizen to engage in any economic activities outside the major sectors of the economy' (s. 16[1]).

Perhaps the first point to notice about these directives concerns the constitutional protection which they bestow upon freedom of private enterprise as well as upon exclusive state monopoly. It is not clear however whether pending a resolution of the national assembly, the exclusiveness of the government's operation of any economic activity needs to exist *de jure* or merely *de facto* in order to constitute the activity a major sector of the economy. For example, the railways are an exclusive monopoly of the federal government, but the monopoly merely exists *de facto* and does not rest upon a legal prohibition of private enterprise as in the case of postal, telegraphic and wireless communications. It seems that once an economic activity is being operated exclusively by the federal government, whether *de facto* or *de jure*, it is deemed a major sector by virtue of this provision.

A further doubt is as to whether the government operation of an economic activity needs to be *completely* exclusive. Electricity is a case in point. Not only is private enterprise not legally prohibited, but the federal government does not have, through the national electric power authority, a complete *de facto* exclusive monopoly over the generation, distribution and supply of electricity. It may be that the constitutional provision envisages a state monopoly that does not completely exclude a measure of private enterprise. This seems to derive some support from the provision that the duty of the state to protect private enterprise outside the major sectors is 'without prejudice to the right of any person to participate in areas of the economy within the major sector of the economy'. The clear implication of this provision is that private persons are not completely excluded from the major sectors of the economy. On this view, exclusiveness has a special meaning under the constitutional provision. While a majority of the federal court of appeal in the private school case from Lagos state preferred to leave the point open, Mr. Justice Nnameka-Agu expressed the view that the phrase 'without prejudice to the right of any person to participate in areas of the economy within the major sector of the economy' is a contradiction of the idea of exclusiveness and is therefore meaningless and ineffective.[26]

But a far more important point for consideration is the extent of the power of the national assembly to declare areas of the economy to be major sectors. The assumption, which is widely shared, is that the assembly has an unfettered discretion in the matter. This is not correct. The national assembly cannot by its declaration exclude a person from an area of economic activity which he has a right to pursue under the bill of rights. The directive principles from which the national assembly derives its power to declare areas of the economy to be major sectors are meant to define the duties of the state towards the individual, not to curtail the rights guaranteed to him by the bill of rights. As the federal court of appeal rightly observed in the private school case,[27] relying on a decision of the supreme court of India[28] and affirming the judge of first instance, 'the Directive Principles of State

Policy have to conform to and run subsidiary to the chapter on Fundamental Rights.'

Furthermore, any declaration by the national assembly has to be made within the context of the ideals and objectives ordained for the nation by the Constitution. It must therefore conform with the declared *ideals* of freedom, equality, social justice and democracy; and with the declared *objectives* of a planned and balanced economic development; avoidance of concentration of wealth or the means of production and exchange in the hands of few individuals or of a group; provision of adequate means of livelihood and employment opportunities; suitable and adequate shelter; suitable and adequate food; a reasonable national minimum living wage; old age care and pensions; and unemployment and sick benefits for all citizens.

The *objectives* of preventing exploitation and the concentration of wealth, on the one hand, and the *ideals* of equality and social justice on the other hand, manifest a stand against capitalism in its pure, undiluted form, since 'unlimited private enterprise generates inequality, concentration of wealth (through survival of the fittest in the cutthroat competition of capitalism), exploitation (because wealth accumulation involves private appropriation of profit which defines exploitation of labour) and is, therefore, inherently unegalitarian.'[29] Equally, the ideals of freedom and participatory democracy point against thoroughbeing socialism. There would seem thus to be implied by the declared ideals and objectives a kind of half-way house between capitalism and socialism, a mixed kind of system that will permit of individual freedom of participation in the economy as well as optimum state participation and control, aimed at promoting social justice, the public welfare, and the minimisation of exploitation, inequality and concentration of wealth.

Granted this mixture of capitalist and socialist elements, the really crucial question is to determine the proportions in which the Constitution has directed that these elements should be mixed, and whether the one or the other should predominate in the mixture. While the ideal of freedom of economic participation by the individual is matched against that of equality and social justice, all the declared objectives have a socialist orientation. Effective national planning, for example, has quite aptly been said to be incompatible with private enterprise having a dominant position. Taking the ideals and the objectives together, therefore, the emphasis is perhaps more on the side of socialism, but it is not socialism in the sense that the state should own and manage all or most of the means of production and distribution. While the state may own and operate a limited number of business enterprises, the directives in chapter II of the Constitution seem to contemplate more the use of the state's virtually unlimited regulatory power in a purposeful manner to bring about a socialist-oriented economy; that is to say, an economy that strives, by means of appropriate regulations, for the minimisation of exploitation and the concentration of wealth in a few hands; the securing of adequate means of livelihood and employment opportunities, suitable and adequate shelter, a reasonable minimum living wage, old age care and pensions, unemployment and sick benefits etc. These objectives do not necessarily dictate state ownership and management of all or most of the means of production and distribution, since they can, without going to that extreme, be quite effectively pursued through purposeful regulation, as the indigenisation programme of the military government illustrates. The law which authorises the indigenisation of foreign enterprises operating in the country lays it down as a guideline that:

(a) Beneficial ownership of the affected enterprises should be as widespread as the circumstances of each case would justify, and deliberate efforts must be made to prevent the concentration of ownership in a few hands.

(b) Except in the case of owner-managers, no enterprise should be sold or transferred to a single individual and in no case is a single individual to be allowed to have control of more than one enterprise.

(c) As far as appropriate, the appropriate authorities must ensure that no individual is to have in any enterprise more than 5 per cent of the equity or more than 50,000 Naira nominal value of the equity whichever is the higher.[30]

As earlier stated, the state's power to regulate private business activities is not a mere police power, being unrestricted by any constitutional guarantee of freedom of private enterprise, which will make it necessary for a regulation, in order to be constitutionally valid, to have a real and substantial relation to the protection and promotion of the public welfare, and not to be otherwise unreasonable, arbitrary or discriminatory. The directive principles in chapter II *require* the state, as a matter not of discretion but of constitutional duty, to exercise this power to regulate the economy in a socialist-oriented direction to bring about greater social justice through a redistribution of the nation's wealth, the minimisation of exploitation and of the concentration of wealth. It is in this sense more than in the sense of a mere coexistence of public and private sectors that the Constitution may be said to envisage a mixed economy. In the words of one commentator:

A mixed economy combines the individual's enterprise and initiative which permit the best use of one's talents for a productive advantage with a state regulatory and redistributive interest. It contrasts with a capitalist system by the simple fact that the state regulations and guidelines are an important feature of the economy in order to direct the economy towards a particular pattern of behaviour and a social goal. It also contrasts with a socialist system because the individual initiative which is given a little consideration in the socialist system is encouraged and maximised in the ideal economy.[31]

It seems a little too doctrinaire to say that a modern industrial economy must be 'either essentially capitalist or essentially socialist'.[32] There should be no logical inconsistency in an economy being socialist-oriented without being 'essentially' socialist. Admittedly, the socialist-oriented economy contemplated by the Constitution may be 'partly exploitative, partly unfree, partly undemocratic, partly unequal, partly unjust',[33] but there has to be only that amount of freedom of private enterprise that can acceptably be combined with the minimum of exploitation, inequality and social injustice.[34]

Some judicial light has recently been shed on the mixed economy concept of the Constitution. In the private school case already referred to, Justice Agoro of the Lagos state high court observed that 'the state is enjoined to protect the right of every citizen to engage in any economic activities outside the major sectors of the economy as may from time to time be declared by a resolution of each house of the national assembly.' On the argument that the directive of equal and adequate educational opportunities, being a specific provision, overrides the general protection of the right to engage in any economic activities outside the major sectors of the economy, he observed:

> While it is true that fundamental objectives are ideals towards which the Nation is expected to strive whilst directive principles lay down the policies which are expected to be pursued in the efforts of the Nation to realize the national ideals, it seems to me that the provision of "equal and adequate educational opportunities" under section 18 of the Constitution only means that the Government should make provision for educational facilities throughout the administrative divisions or local government areas in the State. The requirement to provide equal and adequate educational opportunities could not be interpreted, in my view, to mean that only schools established and operated by the Government or its agencies could exist in the State. The free education programme of the Government could be implemented, in my view, without destroying the private primary or elementary schools which had been and are still regarded as useful and meritorious. The fundamental objectives and directive principles enunciated in Section 18 of the Constitution are, in my view, objectives required to be carried out by any Government in the Federation without necessarily restricting the right of other persons or organisations to provide similar or different educational facilities at their own expense.[35]

This view of the meaning and effect of the provisions was affirmed by the federal court of appeal.[36]

(iii) *The non-justiciability of the fundamental objectives and directive principles*

It is necessary to state that the recognition and protection conferred on freedom of private enterprise under the fundamental objectives and directive principles of state policy in chapter II of the Constitution cannot be enforced in a court of law. Unquestionably, the state is legally bound and under obligation to respect it. In the words of the Constitution itself, 'it shall be the duty and responsibility of all organs of government, and of all authorities and persons exercising legislative, executive or judicial powers to conform to, observe and apply the provisions of this Chapter' (s. 13). Yet the obligation of the state 'to conform to, observe and apply' the fundamental objectives and directive principles is not amenable to judicial inquiry or enforcement (s. 6[6] [c]).

But does the non-justiciability of the chapter mean that judicial inquiry on the meaning of the provisions is also excluded? If the national assembly were by resolution to declare all economic activities to be within the major sectors, thereby making them exclusive to the state, is the private industrialist or businessman adversely affected by the resolution denied access to the courts for an authoritative ruling on the true meaning of the relevant constitutional provisions? The non-justiciability of the objectives and directives is one of the most hotly-debated issues in the new Constitution, and the criticisms of it would be unanswerable if it went so far as to preclude the courts, as the authoritative interpreters of the law, from saying what the provisions mean.

The exclusionary clause therefore needs to be looked at closely to see if it extends to questions of interpretation. It states that the judicial power vested in the courts 'shall not, *except as otherwise provided by this Constitution*, extend to any issue or question as to whether any act or omission by any authority or person or as to whether any law or any judicial decision is in conformity with the Fundamental Objectives and Directive Principles of State Policy set out in Chapter II of this Constitution' (s. 6[6] [c]). The phrase 'except as otherwise provided by this Constitution' seems to exempt from the exclusion the provision of s. 259 of the Constitution for the reference from a lower to a higher court of questions arising in proceedings before it as to the interpretation of the Constitution. It may be concluded that the interpretation of the objectives and directives with a view to determining their true meaning is, like the interpretation of the other provisions of the Constitution, within the jurisdiction of the courts. The exclusion relates to questions concerning the implementation or non-implementation by government of the directives about provision of free education, adequate medical and health facilities, suitable and adequate shelter etc.

Happily, there is judicial support for this view. Among the points referred for interpretation to the federal court of appeal by Justice

Agoro in the private schools case in Lagos state are the questions whether the ownership or operation of a school is not an economic activity outside the major sectors of the economy which an individual is entitled to engage in and to have protected by the state under s. 16(1) (c); and whether the obligation of the state to provide equal and adequate educational facilities under s. 18(1) precludes the right of private persons to provide similar or different educational facilities at their own expense. Accepting jurisdiction in the matter, the federal court of appeal answered both questions in the affirmative. It explained that the duty of the judiciary, in common with other organs and functionaries of government, 'to conform to, observe and apply' the fundamental objectives and directive principles obliges it to interpret their provisions and to have regard to them, as so construed, in the interpretation of other provisions of the Constitution as well as in the interpretation of statutes, so long as it limits itself to mere interpretation and no more.

The court's jurisdiction in this matter ought indeed to extend to the rendering of declaratory judgments generally but unaccompanied by any coercive orders. That was what the appropriate sub-committee of the constitution drafting committee had recommended. The argument that the courts should not be involved in matters of policy is not convincing when the supreme law of the land gives definite directives on policy. The danger to the existence and integrity of the courts, which it is feared such involvement might engender, tends to be exaggerated. Constitutional adjudication, if it is sufficiently dynamic and activist, involves considerable risk to the court in any case, but should we abolish judicial review altogether because of that? A coercive order by a court directing the government to provide, say, free education would be palpably imprudent as being fraught with the danger of destructive confrontation, but a mere declaration that, given the resources available to it, the government should be able to provide free education does no more than reinforce the provisions of the objectives and directives and so brings the matter more forcefully upon the attention of the government.

Furthermore, the line between interpretation and a declaration of right is never clear-cut. Clearly the decision of both the high court and the federal court of appeal that the ownership or operation of a school is an economic activity outside the major sectors of the economy which a private person is entitled to engage in and to have protected by the state under s. 16(1) (c), and that the obligation of the state to provide equal and adequate educational facilities under s. 18(1) does not preclude the right of private persons to provide similar or different educational facilities at their own expenses is, for all practicable purposes, indistinguishable from a declaration of right. It amounts in effect to a declaration that the purported abolition of private primary schools by the Lagos state government is a violation of the right protected by s. 16(1)(c). The caveat by the federal court of appeal that, 'as chapter II is not justiciable the above discussion (i.e. its pronouncement on the meaning and effect of s. 16[1] [c]) is only intended to assist in the correct interpretation of chapter IV', makes no difference to this conclusion.

REFERENCES

1. *Nebbia* v. *New York* (1934), 291 U.S. 502.
2. *Staub* v. *Baxley* (1956), 355 U.S. 313.
3. Per Justice Roberts in *Nebbia* v. *New York*, ibid. at 524.
4. *Village of Euclid* v. *Ambler Realty Co.*, 272 U.S. 365.
5. See *Lincoln Federal Labour Union* v. *North-Western Iron and Metal Co.* (1949), 335 U.S. 525.
6. *Allgeyer* v. *Louisiana* (1897), 165 U.S. 578.
7. *Adewole & others* v. *Jakande & others*, Suit No. M/120/80 of 22 August 1980.
8. *Meyer* v. *Nebraska*, 262 U.S. 390.
9. *Pierce* v. *Society of Sisters* (1925), 268 U.S. 510 at 535; see also *Prince* v. *Massachusetts* (1944), 321 U.S. 158, 166.
10. *United States* v. *Causby* (1946), 326 U.S. 256.
11. *Pennsylvania Coal Co.* v. *Mahon* (1922), 260 U.S. 393.
12. *U.S.* v. *Miller* (1942), 317 U.S. 369.
13. *Esi* v. *Warri Divisional Council Planning Authority*, Suit No. M/2/1966 of 20 June 1969, High Court, Warri (Nigeria).
14. *Ajakaiye* v. *Lieut-Governor* (1929), 9 N.L.R. 1, at 5 (P.C.)
15. Mineral Act; Mineral Oils Act.
16. See *Clyatt* v. *United States* (1905), 197 U.S. 207; *United States* v. *Reynolds & United States* v. *Broughton*, 235 U.S. 133; *Taylor* v. *Georgia*, 315 U.S. 25; *Bailey* v. *Alabama* (1908), 211 U.S. 452; *Pollock* v. *Williams* (1944), 322 U.S. 4.
17. Per the supreme court of Florida, quoted in *Clyatt* v. *United States*, ibid.
18. *Pollock* v. *Williams*, ibid at 17–18.
19. *National Labour Relations Board* v. *Fansteel Metallurgical Corpn.*, 306 U.S. 240, 256.
20. *Pollock* v. *Williams*, ibid., 18.
21. *Thornhill* v. *Alabama*, 310 U.S. 88.
22. *National Labour Relations Board* v. *Jones & Laughlin Steel Corpn.*, 301 U.S. 1.
23. *Archbishop Okogie & others* v. *Att.-Gen. of Lagos State*, Suit No. ID/17M/80 of 18 July 1980 decided by Agoro J.
24. *Tyson & Bro.* v. *Banton*, 273 U.S. 418.
25. *Ribnik* v. *McBride*, 277 U.S. 350; see also *Nebbia* v. *New York*, ibid.
26. *Archbishop Okogie* v. *Att.-Gen. of Lagos State*, Suit No.

FCA/L/74/80 of 30/9/80.

27. *Archbishop Okogie & others* v. *Att.-Gen. of Lagos State*, ibid.

28. *State of Madras* v. *Champakam* (1951), S.C.R. 252.

29. B. Onimode and E. Osagie, 'Economic Aspect of the Draft Constitution' in *The Great Debate*, a *Daily Times* publication, 424.

30. See Nigerian Enterprises Promotion Act 1977, which repeals the Nigerian Enterprises Promotion Act 1972 and its amending Acts of 1973, 1974 and 1976.

31. E.C. Ndukwu, 'Mixed Economy' in *The Great Debate*, op. cit., 413.

32. Eskor Toyo, 'Mixed Economy: is it a solution to Modern Socio-Economic Problems?' in *The Great Debate*, op. cit., 452.

33. Eskor Toyo, op. cit., 453.

34. Cf. Nwosu, 'Issues in the Nigerian Draft Constitution', in *The Great Debate*, ibid., 25−6, 27.

35. *Archbishop Okogie & others* v. *Att.-Gen. of Lagos State*, Suit No. ID/17M/80 of 18 July 1980.

36. *Archbishop Okogie & others* v. *Att.-Gen. of Lagos State*, Suit No. FCA/L/74/80 of 30/9/80.

29
PROSPECTS FOR THE FUTURE: A NATIONAL ETHIC

A national ethic raises the question of our attitude, as Nigerians, to the state and its Constitution. It involves essentially the following —
1. A sense of commitment to the Constitution as an inviolable law. A Constitution cannot be adequately sanctioned by organised force alone. More important is the sanction of a *national attitude* that regards the Constitution as something inviolable, something so fundamental in the life of the nation that respect for it should be regarded as almost a kind of religion, and any violation of it as a sacrilege. In short, a Constitution should enjoy sacrosanctity. It is no blasphemy to say this, since the Constitution of the United States does in fact enjoy something of this status. Among Americans it is worshipped and venerated almost as an object of religious faith. That is part of the explanation for its longevity. It has now endured for over 190 years, and its endurance for a long time to come seems assured.

Respect for the Constitution does mean that it should be treated as above the game of politics, and not tampered with in order to buttress the political fortunes of the rulers. The use of the Constitution as an instrument in the struggle for political power, as in the numerous cases of constitutional amendments rushed through for the sole purpose of safeguarding the interests of the ruling party or impeding those of the opposition, is perhaps one of the saddest reflections on African governments. Its effect has been to rob the Constitution of any claim to respect and devotion. That is not what the amending power is meant for. To guard against this kind of abuse, the more fundamental provisions of Nigeria's 1979 Constitution should have been more rigidly entrenched by requiring a referendum for their amendment.
2. The second thing which a national ethic requires of the rulers is a democratic spirit, by which is meant a spirit of fair play and of tolerance of other people's interests and opinions. It also demands of the rulers a willingness to accept that the power they exercise belongs to the people, that the people have a right to choose who should govern them, and that their choice should be free and be respected. It is the absence of a democratic spirit that accounted for much of the perversion of the democratic processes of government during Nigeria's First Republic as manifested in political coercion, electoral malpractices and the undermining of the freedom of the press and of assembly. Legal sanctions alone cannot guarantee observance of the rules of the

political game. Their observance is more a matter of the spirit, of a mind disciplined to accept that fair play and tolerance are indispensable for the success of government.

3. A tradition against abuse of office or power. A democratic spirit should be complemented by a willingness on the part of the rulers to observe the limits upon governmental powers, a habit of restraint and moderation even when an action is within the limit of their power, and a statesmanlike acceptance that the integrity of the whole governmental framework and the regularity of its procedures should transcend personal aggrandisement. It is of course important, in order that such a tradition should become established and be effective, that the people themselves should be alive to cry out against any case of abuse. The force of public censure is perhaps the best guarantee against abuse of power. No matter what checks and restrictions are embodied in a Constitution against tyranny and abuse of power, there can be no constitutional government unless the wielders of power as well as the governed are adequately imbued with such an ethic. In the words of Julius Nyerere quoted in an earlier chapter, 'when the nation does not have the ethic which will enable the government to say: "We cannot do this, that is un-Tanganyikan" — or the people to say: "That we cannot tolerate, that is un-Tanganyikan" — if the people do not have that kind of ethic, it does not matter what kind of constitution you frame. They can always be victims of tyranny.'

4. A feeling of patriotism and respect for the national interest. The origin of the modern Nigerian state as an instrument of colonialism has meant that for us Nigerians, rulers and the ruled alike, its interests do not arouse in us a strong enough feeling of identity and attachment, especially when they happen to be — as they frequently are — in conflict or competition with our selfish interests. We seem all too willing to subordinate and even sacrifice the interest of the state to our own. Every abuse of public office, whether it be in the form of a kick-back, an appointment or the siting of development project based on selfish or sectional consideration, involves the sacrifice of the national interest. Nationalism is not enough if it is not infused by a patriotic feeling, strong enough to subordinate the selfish or sectional interest to that of the nation. With us Nigerians the state is treated as an object of plunder to satisfy the interests of the rulers and their friends and relations. Patriotism demands more. It requires of everybody a commitment to the survival of the state as a united, stable nation, a nation in which the effective maintenance of law and order as the basis of orderly social life is accepted as the common concern of all.

5. A habit or tradition of probity in public affairs. Independently of an ethic that enjoins patriotism and respect for the national interest, we need to cultivate and nurture a habit of public probity, a tradition

that condemns, on purely moral and ethical grounds, the practice of bribery and corruption which is so rampant in our society. The origins and causes of this practice are not really relevant here, but its wide prevalence is of such concern as to give urgency to efforts aimed at its eradication. The ineffectiveness of legal sanctions to curb this practice again shows the problem to be more a matter of social attitude, infused by a high sense of social discipline.

6. A habit or tradition of respect for the liberty of the individual. A great American jurist, Judge Learned Hand, has said that civil liberties lie in 'habits, customs — conventions if you will — that tolerate dissent, and can live without irrefragable certainties; that are ready to overhaul existing assumptions. . . . If such a habit and such a temper pervade a society, it will not need institutions to protect its "civil liberties and human rights"; so far as they do not, I venture to doubt how far anything else can protect them: whether it be Bills of Rights, or courts that must in the name of interpretation read their meaning into them.' The emphasis again is on *habit* and *tradition*, not legal prescription. The liberty of the individual can have meaning and reality not so much by constitutional declarations and guarantees as by a libertarian tradition and temper infusing the society. In so far as such a tradition and temperament is yet to infuse our society, it can be said that civil liberties do not exist in Nigeria, notwithstanding the fact that a bill of rights has existed in our Constitution for nearly twenty years now.

7. A habit of obedience to the laws. It would not be exactly right or fair to say that Nigerians are a lawless people, prone to disorder and violence, to flagrant flouting of the laws or to civil disobedience. We do have respect for constituted authority, and we are, in a sense, law-abiding. It remains true nonetheless to say that our capacity to circumvent the law, to act outside and against it, is surpassed, if at all, only by a few countries. The image of us created by this is that we are unwilling to be governed by laws and to conduct our affairs according to the regulations of the state. This particular predilection is being carried to such a point as to suggest that we may even be ungovernable. State control of prices, rents, foreign exchange dealings, traffic, taxi fares, land transactions, to mention only a few instances, has been reduced to ineffectiveness because of this. It hardly needs to be said that an unrestricted freedom of individual action in all things is nothing but a state of chaos and anarchy. An ethic that would inculcate in us a habit of obedience to the law is thus a dire necessity in Nigeria if ordered progress is to be achieved.

Of course, one is by no means advocating passive submission to a totalitarian regimentation of our lives by the state. Totalitarian control by the state is the other extreme of unrestricted freedom of individual action. As earlier suggested, a tradition of public protest against abuse of power or office and against unwarranted governmental action is indispensable to an effective national ethic.

The civic responsibilities of the citizen go beyond refraining from breaking the law. They call in some cases for positive action, as, for example, to vote at national, state or local government elections in order to ensure that only people of the right calibre get elected into government offices and assemblies; to prevent the commission of an offence or to report it to the law enforcement agencies after it has been committed; to pay tax; to keep the streets free of litter and rubbish, and so on. Again this involves disciplined social habits.

8. A habit of self-reliance. Among the crises facing Nigeria today is that of self-confidence and self-reliance. As a people, we are yet to discover ourselves, to develop faith in ourselves and in our ability to do things for ourselves. It is this lack of faith in ourselves that lies at the root of our preference for imported goods and expatriate expertise. It is a pity that our emergence as a state post-dated the development of modern technology and industrialisation and that the accessibility of its products and expertise has made it convenient for us to import them rather than rely on our own devices. The spirit of creativity born of necessity is thus killed. Had these things not been accessible to us, we would have had somehow to create them ourselves by a process of trial and error and gradual improvement.

We may now re-state our conception of a national ethic. It is that kind of tradition or habit which will enable us to say that it is *un-Nigerian* to violate the Constitution, either in its letter or in its spirit, to circumvent or act outside the laws, to pervert the democratic processes, to abuse an office or power entrusted to us, to accept a bribe or indulge in other forms of corruption, to act arbitrarily or tyrannically towards others, to allow selfish or sectional interests to override the national interest or to refuse to patronise local products and expertise.

It is conceived that a democratic constitution should have some such habits or traditions as its fundamental presuppositions if it is to work smoothly and if government is to function effectively. Being presuppositions they are necessarily extra-constitutional. What this means is that the question of a national ethic is essentially not one to be solved by constitutional prescriptions. Habit, tradition and a moral sense are not automatically created by stipulations in a constitution; they are formed from actual social behaviour over a period of time.

How, then, is the behaviour of Nigerians to be changed to conform to the requirements of the national ethic? The change called for has to be of a revolutionary character. Change in social behaviour is primarily a function of political leadership. It calls for a leadership that is at once dedicated, single-minded, selfless, disciplined, patriotic and highly motivated in the national interest. It must be a leadership with a sincerity of purpose so transparent as to induce people to abandon their old ways, and with a dedication to the cause sufficiently total and selfless to inspire public confidence, a leadership that can persuade and convert people by example rather than precept. Far from inspiring public confidence, a leadership that is not seen to be practising what it preaches creates disillusionment among the people. It has also to be a leadership capable of mobilising the nation behind itself in a concerted march towards the objective.

Obviously a leadership of this kind is difficult to come by. We have lost two opportunities of achieving it, first, in January 1966 by the failure to canalise the favourable mood created by the coup of that month, and then in 1976 by the assassination of General Murtala Muhammed. The coup of January 1966 had put Nigerians in a mood to be led into new ways if only a leader with the right motivation had been available, while General Murtala Muhammed had by his sincerity of purpose and his selfless and single-minded leadership set the tone for change. It is to be hoped that the opportunities thus lost may come again.

Revolutionary change, such as our situation demands, is hardly possible without the active support of an enlightened and upright press. Its instrumentality is indeed crucial in attuning people's minds and in rallying the nation behind the leadership.

But the change demanded by our situation is not the function of the political leadership alone. The judiciary too is in a unique position to mould public attitudes towards the Constitution. It should indeed be in the vanguard of a national effort towards the development of a tradition of respect for the Constitution. The attitude of the people, both rulers and the ruled alike, towards the Constitution is conditioned to a large extent by the way it is interpreted and applied by the courts. Whether its prescriptions are to become active principles for restraining governmental actions depends upon what the courts make of them. A liberal, purposive interpretation coupled with a courageous, dynamic application might be expected to impart vitality and reality to the provisions of the Constitution, and to infuse in the rulers a consciousness of the peremptoriness of its commands, and the futility of disregarding them. It is hoped that a government, faced with such imminent risk of having its acts invalidated by an ever-watchful judiciary, might make respect for the Constitution a touchstone of all its actions. On the part of the governed, the effect would be to create a willingness, indeed eagerness, to seek the intervention of the court against any transgression of constitutional prescriptions by the government.

That has been the unique contribution of the judiciary in the United States in the development of a tradition of reverence for the Constitution, which is one of the factors responsible for its sacrosanctity and longevity. From the early beginnings of the Union, the supreme court, under the energetic leadership of its head, Chief Justice John Marshall, made the Constitution the controlling force in the government of the country, and so generated a feeling of reverence for its commands, which over the years has acquired the force of a tradition.

It seems that the introduction in Nigeria of the new presidential Constitution, based on the American, has imbued our courts with something of the 'vigorous, vigilant, courageous activism' of their American counterpart. Viewed against the background of their past performance, it is refreshing that our courts have, from the record so far, shown themselves willing and determined to live up to such a leadership role. Within a short period of ten months after the 1979 Constitution came into force, more than a dozen rulings were made against the government (both federal and state) in suits challenging, on constitutional grounds, the appointment of an attorney-general in the Cross River state; the deportation by the federal government of the majority leader in the Borno state house of assembly on the ground that he is not a Nigerian; an order summoning a newspaper editor to appear before the senate to substantiate a statement published in his newspaper; an executive directive of the Lagos state government purporting to abolish private schools in the state; an order by the governor of Bendel state which suspended local government councils in the state, removed their members and replaced them by committees of management; a planned election into local government councils in Lagos state on the basis of the register of voters compiled in 1978 for the purposes of the presidential, gubernatorial and legislative elections.[1] In one of the suits, the Lagos State Local Government Law 1980 was declared unconstitutional and void in its entirety on the ground, *inter alia*, that it violated a cardinal principle of the Constitution, the separation of powers, by delegating to the governor, without any guiding standards, power to delimit the areas of authority of the local government councils.[2]

Particularly remarkable is the determination shown by the courts in these cases to get to the merits unhindered by the technicalities of pleading and procedure. They have shown themselves prepared to break away from a rigid application of the *locus standi* rule, such as characterised constitutional adjudication in Nigeria in the past, resulting in many otherwise meritorious suits being frustrated *in limine*. Witness, for example, the ruling that a legislator has, by his oath to preserve, protect and defend the Constitution, sufficient interest to challenge in court any violation of the Constitution by the executive;[3] that an executive directive announcing the abolition of private schools as from a specified date was not a mere declaration of government intention, but contained a threat of interference with guaranteed rights sufficiently likely and immediate to justify a suit by parents and school proprietors affected by it;[4] and that the use for a local government election of a voters register compiled two years earlier (1978), with the consequent disenfranchisement of voters who had in the meantime attained voting age, constituted special and peculiar damage to a prospective candidate at the election to entitle him to sue.[5] Witness also the commendable readiness with which the court, in its determination to reach and determine the substantive merits in one of the cases, amended the pleading to reflect the true capacity in which, from the evidence before it, the defendant was sued.[6] In doing so, the court boldly affirmed it to be its duty, notwithstanding that a case may have been conducted in a slipshod or cavalier manner, to see to it that, in the interest of justice, the real issue in controversy between the parties is reached and determined. Not the least commendable is the promptitude with which they acted in all these cases.

The effect of the activist posture adopted by the courts in these cases has been a most desirable one. It has bestowed upon the Constitution an enhanced standing in the public estimation as the truly controlling force in the government of the country. There is an eagerness to draw upon it for support in all kinds of controversy. There seems to be taking root a healthy national attitude of viewing governmental acts scrupulously in terms of their conformance or otherwise with the Constitution, and of immediately taking to the courts for adjudication all such as are considered to violate its provisions. Witness again the suit in 1980 against the president of the Republic challenging his appointment of chairmen for the federal electoral commission and the code of conduct bureau, and the order of the court stopping the swearing-in of the appointees pending the determination of the case.[7] All this is healthy. It is from such beginnings that the American habit of reverence for the Constitution developed.

But the American reverence for the Constitution owes its existence in part too to indoctrination. Sentiment is generated and inculcated by teaching and by practice. Among children in their formative years, a belief in the Constitution can easily be inspired and nurtured by teaching. Hence the practice in some states in the United States of requiring by law instruction in the Constitution as part of the school curriculum. The aim, as declared in the relevant statutes, is to foster and perpetuate 'the ideals, principles and spirit of Americanism'.[8] We need too to foster and perpetuate among our youth the ideals, principles and spirit of Nigerianism by requiring the teaching of our

Constitution in all schools. Our Constitution embodies in its letter and spirit the ideals and principles that should form our national ethic, and what is needed is to popularise them into a concept of Nigerianism.

The use of symbols is another method by which people, especially children, in the United States have been indoctrinated in the ideals, principles and spirit of Americanism. The flag in particular has been accorded the greatest symbolic value in evoking among the people the spirit of Americanism. It is regarded as signifying 'government resting on the consent of the governed; liberty regulated by law; the protection of the weak against the strong; security against the exercise of arbitrary power; and absolute safety for free institutions against foreign aggression'.[9] Conscious of the value of symbols in fostering a national ethic, congress has, by a joint resolution, required that a pledge of allegiance to the American flag should be rendered, on appropriate occasions, by standing with the right hand over the heart, and reciting: 'I pledge allegiance to the flag of the United States of America and to the Republic for which it stands, one Nation indivisible, with liberty and justice for all.' Compliance is optional as no penalty is imposed for nonconformity.

But some states have gone farther to make the flag-salute a compulsory ceremony in their public schools, and to punish non-compliance by expulsion and by denial of readmission until compliance, thus arousing conscientious objection by members of the Jehovah's Witness sect. While the latter are prepared publicly to proclaim their respect for the nation's flag and to acknowledge it as a symbol of freedom and justice to all, they refused to salute it, on the ground that that would amount to worshiping an 'image', contrary to the tenets of their religion. In an action challenging the constitutionality of flag-salute as a compulsory, instead of a voluntary, ceremony in public schools, the supreme court at first sustained it.[10] It held that the flag being a symbol of national unity which in turn is the basis of national security, it should be within the power of the state to try to evoke in children through such a compulsory ceremony a love of nation and an appreciation of its hopes and ideals. In the words of the court:

> The ultimate foundation of a free society is the binding tie of cohesive sentiment. Such a sentiment is fostered by all those agencies of the mind and spirit which may serve to gather up the traditions of a people, transmit them from generation to generation, and thereby create that continuity of a treasured common life which constitutes a civilisation. We live by symbols.[11]

That expresses eloquently the important role of symbols in the life of a people. Although the decision was overruled in a subsequent case three years later,[12] on the ground that 'to believe that patriotism will not flourish if patriotic ceremonies are voluntary and spontaneous instead of a compulsory routine is to make an unflattering estimate of the appeal of our institutions to free minds',[13] the court still acknowledged symbols as an effective, if primitive, way of communicating ideals. It observed:

'The use of an emblem or flag to symbolise some system, idea, institution, or personality, is a short cut from mind to mind. Causes and nations, political parties, lodges and ecclesiastical groups seek to knit the loyalty of their followings to a flag or banner, a colour or design. The State announces rank, function, and authority through crowns and maces, uniforms and black robes; the church speaks through the Cross, the Crucifix, the altar and shrine, and clerical raiment. Symbols of State often convey political ideas just as religious symbols come to convey theological ones. Associated with many of these symbols are appropriate gestures of acceptance or respect: a salute, a bowed or bared head, a bended knee.'[14]

Nigeria does have a flag, like every other state, but its symbolism is hardly appreciated by Nigerians. It is necessary therefore to indoctrinate the people about the flag's significance, and to create appropriate gestures of acceptance or respect for it. Like Americans and, even more, like our former colonial masters, we must learn to live by symbols if a national ethic is to evolve in the country as an effective instrument of thought and social behaviour.

The Constitution is of course by no means irrelevant in evolving a national ethic. It may prescribe standards or principles of conduct with or without the backing of coercive sanction. It is by means of legal regulations backed by coercive sanction that behaviour is generally controlled. Depending of course on the nature of the sanction, the fear of it may often be effective in inducing the desired behaviour. The sanctions prescribed in the Constitution are generally not of a nature to create such a degree of fear as would induce the desired behaviour, being mostly in the form of judicial orders quashing or prohibiting a governmental act or declaring it invalid, or ordering the payment of compensation or release from imprisonment. However, the 1979 Constitution does, in respect of certain forms of misconduct by public officers, prescribe sanctions of a more coercive type — vacation of office, forfeiture of assets and disqualification from holding public office for a stipulated length of time. It is expected that such sanctions may be effective to some extent in inducing the desired behaviour among public officers.

Even when it is not backed by a coercive sanction, constitutional prescription of standards or principles of conduct still has value in emphasising the importance of the behaviour prescribed. The mere fact of the prescription being contained in the Constitution may conceivably induce an initial predisposition to comply, which may eventually be canalised into a habit on the part of the leadership.

The 1979 Constitution combines both types of prescription. By means of non-justiciable stipulations, it affirms the sovereignty of the people and their right to choose those who will govern them, directs that all corrupt practices and abuse of power should be eradicated, proclaims discipline, self-reliance and patriotism as the national ethic, and enjoins upon the mass media the obligation to uphold the fundamental objectives of the nation and the responsibility and accountability of government to the people.

It guarantees the rights and liberties of the individual — life, the dignity of the human person, personal liberty, fair hearing, private and family life, freedom of thought, conscience and religion, freedom of expression and the press, freedom of assembly and association, freedom of movement, and freedom from discrimination. These guarantees are in the form of constitutional prohibitions enforceable in the courts by means of declaratory orders, monetary compensation, release from imprisonment, or orders quashing or prohibiting an interfering act. A justiciable code of conduct is also prescribed for public officers.

There is yet another provision which seeks to secure the inviolability of the Constitution: 'The federal republic of Nigeria shall not be governed, nor shall any person or group of persons take control of the government of Nigeria or any part thereof, except in accordance with the provisions of this Constitution.' This provision says nothing that would be of any practical value in a situation where a coup has succeeded. Nor can it prevent attempts at a violent overthrow of the Constitution. Also, to say that the federal republic of Nigeria shall not be governed except in accordance with the provisions of *'this'* Constitution contemplates the legal immutability of the Constitution, which is nonsense. Yet the inclusion of the provision indicates something of the desperateness of the question of a national ethic. In its application to the armed forces, this national ethic is one and the same as a professional ethic that requires of their members a tradition of non-interference in the politics and government of the country and an acceptance that their rôle should, in terms of the Constitution (s. 197[1]), be strictly confined to the defence of Nigeria from external aggression, the preservation of its territorial integrity, the suppression of insurrection, and the maintenance of order only when called upon to do so in aid of the civil authorities.

REFERENCES

1. *Shugaba* v. *Att.-Gen. of the Fedn.*, High Court Maiduguri (1980); *Lawal* v. *The Lagos State Electoral Commission*, Suit No. ID/93/80 of 24 March 1980; *Jideonwo* v. *Urhobo*, Suit No. B/292/79 of 28 February 1980, High Court Benin; *Ajayi* v. *Att.-Gen. of Lagos State*, Suit No. ID/118/80 of 20 March 1980, High Court Ikeja; *Akanro* v. *Lagos State Electoral Commission*, Suit No. ID/96/80 of 18 March 1980, High Court Ikeja; *Momoh* v. *Senate of the National Assembly*, Suit No. M/27/80 of 15 April 1980, High Court Lagos; *Okogie* v. *Att.-Gen. of Lagos State*, Suit No. ID/17M/80 of 18 July 1980, High Court Ikeja.
2. *Balogun* v. *Att.-Gen. of Lagos State*, Suit No. ID/114/80 of 17 March 1980, High Court Ikeja.
3. *Jideonwo* v. *Urhobo*, ibid.
4. *Okogie* v. *Att.-Gen. of Lagos State*, ibid.
5. *Lawal* v. *Lagos State Electoral Commission*, ibid.
6. *Lawal* v. *Lagos State Electoral Commission*, ibid.
7. *Adesanya* v. *The President of the Republic* (1980).
8. See, e.g., s. 1734 West Virginia Code, quoted in *West Virginia State Board of Education* v. *Barnette* (1943), 319 U.S. 624.
9. *Halter* v. *Nebraska*, 205 U.S. 34; also *United States* v. *Gettysburg Electric R. Co.*, 160 U.S. 668.
10. *Minersville School District* v. *Gobitis* (1940), 310 U.S. 586.
11. ibid. at 596 per Frankfurter J. delivering the judgment of the court.
12. *West Virginia State Board of Education* v. *Barnette* (1943), 319 U.S. 624.
13. Ibid., 641.
14. Ibid., 632.

INDEX

In this Index there is no reference to the United States of America, because there are comparisons between the Nigerian and U.S. Constitutions throughout the text.

accessibility of the courts, 19, 320, 332, 343
adaptive legislation, 55-6, 171-3, 249, 276-7
Ademola, Justice, 119
adjournment of sittings of national assembly, 213
adoption of Constitution, 1-4; by the people, 1, 4-7
Agoro, Justice, 536
aliens: status, 401-2, 404
amendments to Constitution, 13-16
amendments to draft constitution made by supreme military government, 3
Anderson, William, 85-6
Appropriation Acts, annual, 240, 242
armed forces: 57, 86, 91, 128-9, 380-1; composition: representation of all states, 26; deployment outside the country, 138, 234; president as commander-in-chief, 128, 381
arrest, 421, 422-4
association, freedom of, 250, 386, 483-514, 520, 527
Atta, Ofori, 83
attorney-general, 86, 114, 116, 127, 152-3, 228, 347; of states, 328
audit, 241-2
auditor-general, 86, 122, 125, 130, 138-9, 222
Australia, 14-15, 49, 72-3, 264-8, 513
authority of Constitution, 1-7

bail, 425, 427
Balewa, Sir Abubakar Tafawa, 428
Balogun, Justice, 177

Bartley, Chief Justice, 81
Bello, Sir Ahmadu, 428
bicameral legislature, 205
Bickel, Alexander, 349-50, 368
Black, Charles, 276, 281, 283-4, 285, 367, 369
Blackstone, Sir William, 28, 260, 461
Blagden, Chief Justice, 251, 507
Borchard, Edwin, 324-5
Botswana, 10, 13
Brandeis, Justice, 156, 333, 473-4
Brennan, Justice, 324
broadcasting and television: state ownership, 64, 106, 528
Bryce, Lord, 78, 80

Canada, 49
candidates: for election to national assembly, 207-8, 210-11; for presidency, 190, 193-201
capital punishment, *see* death penalty
Cardozo, Justice, 176
censorship, 468-72
censure motions of national assembly, 157-8
census, 129-31, 136-7, 145
ceremony, 78-81, 103
change of constitution, 6-7
Chase, Chief Justice, 273
checks and balances, 31, 136-44, 156
chief justice, 138-9
citizenship: 30, 170-1, 397-407; categories, 397-401; status of aliens, 401-2, 404
civil service, 120-5, 132, 165, 379-80; *see also* public servants
civil service commission, 122-3, 132, 138-9, 215, 334, 380

551

clerk of national assembly, 215–16, 221
code of conduct for public servants, 23–4, 377–8, 383, 387–92, 395–6
code of conduct bureau, 123–4, 138
code of conduct tribunal, 124, 137, 153–4, 203–4, 394
Coker, Justice, 119, 160–1
Cole, Professor, 64
commissions of inquiry, 71–3
Committee system in national assembly, 221–3
common law, 56, 452–3
Commonwealth African states, 9–11, 185
concurrent legislative list, 53–4
confederacy of states, 38
consolidated revenue fund, 240–3
constituencies: for members of national assembly, 208–9, 234; for president: the nation as a whole, 157
constituent assembly, 1–6
Constitution: amendments, 13–16; entrenchment of fundamental provisions, 13–14; justiciability, 1, 7–11; law enforceable by courts, 7–11; objectives, 7, 18–20; political character, 7–8; single constitution for federal and state governments, 50–1; source of authority, 1–7; supremacy over legislature, 12, 16
contempt, 226–9, 266
contingencies fund, 242–3
contract, freedom of, 421, 525, 529
Cooley, T.M., 247
corporal punishment, 412–13
corruption by public servants, 153, 389–90, 392
Corwin, Edward S., 203
council of state, 112–13, 130–1, 139, 144–9, 305, 380
courts of law: accessibility, 19, 320, 332, 343; composition, 300–1; impartiality, 19, 256; ouster of the court's jurisdiction, 273–7; powers and procedures, 33–5, 73–4, 256; powers of federal and state courts, 294–301; trials: constitutional safeguards, 431–48
criminal code, 58, 271–2
customary courts of appeal: in states, 255–6, 298–9, 301, 304, 311, 345; in federal capital territory, 296
customary law, 56, 452–3
Cyprus, 14, 22, 97

death penalty, 253–4, 263, 411–18
declaration of assets by public servants, 24, 123, 390–1
declaration of war, 137, 233–4
declaratory judgment by courts, 344–51, 355
delegated legislation, 173–9
Denning, Lord, 374
deputy president of senate, 214–15
deputy speaker of house of representatives, 214–15
detention, 421, 425–6
Devlin, Lord, 74
diplomatic immunity, 405–7
discrimination, 250, 253, 414, 452–6
dissolution of national assembly, 212–13
Dixon, Chief Justice, 352
Douglas, Justice, 179

economic policy: 29–30, 42, 61–4, 131, 233, 530–7; state ownership, 19–20, 64, 106, 466, 523, 528
economic principles of Constitution, 19–20, 22–3
elections: 30–1; contesting of results, 212, 356–9; local government councils, 60–1; members of national assembly, 11, 206, 208–11; president, 26, 111, 157, 190–201; state governors, 26–7; vice-president, 111
electoral commission, 60, 129–31, 138–9, 145, 196, 199, 208–10, 234, 380, 501–4
Electoral Decree 1977, 391
electoral procedures, 60, 67,

129−30, 209
electoral roll, 60, 129−30, 209
Eleko, Eshugbayi, 93
Emerson, Rupert, 276
emergency situations: 107, 253; abrogation of fundamental rights, 69−70, 95−102, 180−3, 250−4, 284−8, 319−21, 336−7, 422, 527; proclamation, 68−70, 95, 138, 151−2, 233−4
entrenchment of provisions, 14
equality before the law, 19−20, 250, 253, 414, 452−6
Eso, Justice, 195−6
exclusive legislative list, 53−4
executive: and judiciary, 31−5, 156, 163−7, 309−37, 363'−71; and legislature, 90, 137−44, 156−67, 232−4, 239, 243−5, 247−77; constitutional limitations, 30; need for effective government, 27−9; organisation of government under Constitution, 20−35
executive council, 86, 113, 117−20, 145−8, 160−1
extradiction of fugitive criminals, 404−5

Fatayi-Williams, Chief Justice, 193−4
federal capital territory, 56−7, 61, 296−7, 299, 310−11
federal commissions, 26
federal court of appeal, 119, 124, 136−9, 145, 255−6, 296, 301, 311−12, 345
federal high court, 145, 256, 296, 299, 310−12, 345, 357
federal nature of Constitution, 15, 25−7, 37−51
Federation Account, 65
finance procedure, 186−7, 205−6, 217−20, 240−3
flag, 507−8, 546−7
forced or compulsory labour, 410−11, 486, 512, 525−6
foreign policy, 91, 164−5
France, 7, 14, 170, 180

Frankfurter, Justice, 11, 209, 333, 348−9, 453
Friedrich, Carl, 28
fugitive criminals: extradition, 404−5
fundamental objectives of Constitution, 18−20
fundamental rights: 19−25, 30, 250−4, 336, 353−6, 364; abrogation in emergencies, 69−70, 95−102, 180−3, 250−4, 284−8, 319−21, 336−7, 422, 527; equality before the law, 19−20, 250, 253, 414, 452−6; freedom *from* discrimination, 250, 253, 414, 452−6; − forced or compulsory labour, 410−11, 486, 512, 525−6; − servitude or slavery, 410, 488, 512; freedom *of* association, 250, 386, 483−514, 520, 527; − contract, 421, 525, 529; − movement, 250, 421−2, 527; − press, 250, 457−79, 528; − private enterprise, 19−20, 421, 517−37; − religion, 250, 484−514, 527; − speech, 250, 457−79; life and dignity of the human person, 19, 253, 409−29; property rights, 3, 421, 520−5, 529
Fundamental Rights (Enforcement Procedure) Rules 1979, 353

Gambia, The, 13
Germany, Federal Republic of, 13−14, 180
Ghana, 11, 13, 83−4, 153, 270−1
Goddard, Lord, 355
grants-in-aid, 67−8
grants of pardon, 127, 131, 136−7, 144−6
Greece, 97, 180
Griffith, Chief Justice, 256, 297
Gunther, Gerald, 333

Hamilton, Alexander, 27−8, 139−40, 202, 365
Hand, Judge Learned, 541
Harlan, Justice, 328

Hart, Henry, Jr, 344
head of state, 76–84
Higgins, Justice, 265
high court: federal, 145, 256, 296, 299, 310–12, 345, 357; in federal capital territory, 296; in states, 299, 301
Hirschfield, R.S., 104, 107–8
Holmes, Justice, 163, 446, 448, 474
honours, 131, 145–6
house of representatives, see national assembly
human rights, see fundamental rights

impeachment, 82, 112, 141–4, 153, 157, 160, 203
India, 10, 22, 285–7, 313, 319
inhuman or degrading treatment, 253, 409, 412–18
injunction by courts, 344, 351–3
inspector-general of police, 125–7, 381
Investigation of Assets (Public Officers and Other Persons) Decree 1968, 390–1
Isaacs, Justice, 282
Islamic law, 56, 452–3
Italy, 97, 180

Jackson, Justice, 96–7, 108, 164, 459
Jefferson, Thomas, 80–1, 202, 479
Johnson, Andrew, 143, 160
joint committees of national assembly, 222
joint finance committee of national assembly, 205–6, 217–19, 222
judges: appointment and removal, 3, 302–8, 366–8
justiciability of Constitution, 1, 7–11
judicial appointments and removals, 304–8
judicial service commission, 131, 138–9, 145, 303, 305, 380
judiciary: and executive, 31–5, 156, 163–7, 309–37, 363–71; and legislature, 255–62, 288–92, 309–37, 363–71; avoidance of constitutional questions, 332–7; constitutionality of legislative and executive acts, 309–37; initiative for judicial action, 314; legitimating function, 369–71; powers and procedures of courts of justice, 73–4, 256, 294–301

Kaunda, President Kenneth, 84, 151
Kenya, 13, 45, 84, 185, 244

land, 3, 74, 524–5, 529
Land Use Act 1978, 523–4
land use and allocation committee, 525
language of national assembly, 216
Latham, Chief Justice, 265
law and order, 25, 57–8, 69–70, 90–1, 97, 125–8, 145, 250–3
Laws Authentication Law 1979, 291
legal aid to defendants, 434–6
legislation: adaption of existing laws, 55–6, 171–3, 249, 276–7; authority for governmental action, 161–2, 239–43; constitutionality, 281–93; directed against named persons or associations, 253, 256–62; initiation, 183–7, 205, 217; procedure, 187, 205, 217–21, 289–92; regulated by justiciary, 288–92; retrospective, 32, 271–2; role of national assembly, 159–63, 217–21, 232, 235–43, 247–9; role of president, 89–90, 159–63, 168–87, 218–21, 289
legislature: amendment to Constitution, 13–16; and executive, 90, 137–44, 156–67, 232–4, 239, 243–5, 247–77; and judiciary, 255–62, 288–92, 309–37, 363–71; supremacy of the Constitution, 12–13, 16
Lewis, Sir Arthur, 48, 363, 457
libel, 475–7
licensing and registration of associations, 495–500
Lincoln, Abraham, 97, 107, 119–20, 151

local government: 26, 30, 58–61, 66, 171–2; creation of areas, 60–1

McConnell, Grant, 186
McIlwain, Professor, 140
Madison, James, 479
Magnus, Justice, 251–2
Marshall, Chief Justice, 39, 81, 281, 313, 342, 544
martial law, 99–102, 254, 264, 431
members of the national assembly: 207–8; change of political party, 212; elections, 206, 208–11, 212; oath of allegiance, 210, 214–16; privileges and immunities, 223–9; qualifications, 207–8, 210–11; suspension, 225, 229; tenure of office, 211–12, vacancies of seats, 211–12, 225–6
military government: validity of decrees, 276–7
Mill, John Stuart, 44
Mineral Act, 524
Mineral Oils Act, 524
ministers of government: 86, 91, 114–25; debarred from membership of national assembly, 158, 210–11; tenure of office, 115
minutes of proceedings of national assembly, 216
movement, freedom of, 250, 421–2, 527
Munir, Chief Justice, 182

Nasir, Justice, 119
national anthem, 507–8
national assembly: 205–29; adjournment, 213; approval for presidential action, 137–41; censure motions, 157–8; clerk, 215–16, 221; committee system, 221–3; enforcement of directive principles of Constitution, 23; freedom of speech in debates, 223, 244–5; functions, 111–12, 123–5, 128, 232–45; house of representatives: speaker, 214–15, 226, 233;

impeachment of president or vice-president, 82, 112, 141–4, 153, 157, 160, 203; legislation, 159–63, 217–21, 232, 235–43, 247–9; legislation on public revenue, 64–7; limits of legislative power, 247–77; matters determined by resolution, 232–3; matters determined by simple approval, 233–4; membership, 206–12, 233–5; no-confidence motions, 157; ouster of the jurisdiction of the courts, 273–7; precluded from taking over legislative power, 158; proceedings, 214–23; relations between the two houses, 205–7; scrutiny of the executive, 141–54, 232–4, 239, 243–5, 247–77; *senate*: equal representation of states, 206–7; president of the senate, 207, 214–15, 233; primacy over house of representatives, 206–7; size of membership, 207; staff, 215–16
national defence council, 112–13, 129, 145
national economic council, 112–13, 131, 145, 183, 380
national flag, 507–8, 546–7
national honours, 131, 145–6
national population commission, 129–31, 138–9, 145, 380
national security council, 112–13, 127–8, 380
national security organisation, 3, 125, 127–8
national service, 527
national unity, 19–20, 25–7, 37–9, 45–7
natural resources vested in federal government, 523
nature of the Constitution, 1–16
New Zealand, 12
Nixon, President Richard M., 81, 458
Nkrumah, President Kwame, 80, 103, 115–16
Nnameka-Agu, Justice, 531

no-confidence motions in national assembly, 157
non-judicial functions vested in individual judges, 269–71
non-judicial functions vested in the courts, 264–71
Nyerere, President Julius, 102–3, 136, 384, 540

oath of allegiance, by: members of national assembly, 210, 214–16; president, 78, 154, 215–16; public servants, 78
official gazette, 114, 220–1

Pakistan, 10, 22, 44, 97, 102, 171, 180–3
parliamentary system of government, 3, 28
patronage, 21, 106, 114, 133–4
Petitions of Right Act, 346–7
points of order of national assembly, 214
police force: 57, 86, 91 125–7, 381; inspector-general, 125–7, 381
police service commission, 126–7, 138–9, 144–5, 380
political parties: 23, 108, 236–9, 483–514, 527; ethnic or religious connotation, 27; registration, 129; state control, 501–5
president: allegation of incapacity or misconduct, 112, 114, 157, 203–4, 207, 233; chief executive, 76, 84–6; commander-in-chief of armed forces, 128, 381; constitutional bases of executive power, 76, 84–6, 88–109, 111–135, 158–66; constitutional restraints, 30–5, 136–54, 163–6; criticism and abuse, 83–4; debarred from membership of national assembly, 158, 210–11; election and removal, 26, 111–12, 157, 190–201, 203, 207, 233; execution and maintenance of Constitution, 90–1; head of state, 76–84; immunity from court action, 80–3; leadership role, 103–8; oath of allegiance, 78, 154, 215–16; obligation to consult various bodies, 144–51; personal staff, 132–4; proclamation of emergency, 68–70, 95, 138, 151–2, 233–4; qualifications, 190, 198; right to attend national assembly, 211; role in legislation, 89–90, 159–63, 168–87, 218–21, 289; singleness of authority, 84–6; tenure of office, 31, 111–12, 157–8, 201–4, 233; territorial acceptability, 26, 193–201; vacancy of seat, 114
presidential liaison officers, 133–4
president of senate, 205–7, 214–15, 233
press, 106
press freedom, 250, 457–79, 528; disclosure of source of information, 462–5
preventive detention, 426–9
prime minister, 28, 84
private enterprise, 19–20, 421, 517–37; regulated by state, 517–18, 529, 533
privileges and immunities of members of national assembly, 223–9
probity in government, 20–24
proceedings of national assembly, 214–23
property rights, 3, 421, 520–5, 529
public accounts committee, 222
public complaints commission, 124, 380, 393, 395–6
Public Complaints Commission Decree 1975, 392
public expenditure, 67–8, 240–3
public meetings and processions, 496–501
Public Officers Protection Act, 347
Public Officers (Special Provisions) Decree 1976, 392
public offices outside the civil service, 131–4
public order and safety, *see* law and order
public revenue: 64–8, 217–21,

240–3; allocation, 30, 65–7, 219–20; allocation of loans or grants to state governments, 67–8; expenditure, 67–8, 240–3; responsibility of federal government, 64–7; sources of revenue, 64, 240

public servants: 138–41, 374–96, 540; appointment and removal, 120–5, 138–41, 152–3; code of conduct, 23–4, 391–6; debarred from membership of elective offices, 210–11, 391; declaration of assets, 24, 123, 390–1; oath of allegiance, 78; obligations and duties, 23–4, 382–3; —, enforcement of, 391–6; participation in politics and trade unions, 383–8, 491, 506–8; *see also* civil service

public service commission, 377–8

quorum of national assembly, 205, 214, 216

radio and television: state ownership, 64, 106, 528
rationale of Constitution, 18–35
register of births and deaths, 129
registrar of trade unions, 506
religion, freedom of, 250, 484–514, 527
retrospective legislation, 32, 271–2
Rhodesia, 97
Roosevelt, Franklin D., 104, 107, 202–3, 369
Roosevelt, Theodore, 91, 202
Rostow, Eugene, 367

Schwartz, Bernard, 62
secret societies, 494–5
select committees in national assembly, 222–3
senate, *see* national assembly
separation of powers between federal and state governments, 25–7, 29–35, 37–51, 53–74
separation of powers in government, 30–5, 137–44, 156–67, 294

servitude, 410, 488, 512, 525–6
sessions of national assembly, 213
sharia courts of appeal, *in* federal capital territory, 296; states, 255–6, 298–9, 301, 304, 310–11, 345
Simon, Lord, 424
sittings of national assembly, 213, 220
slavery, 410
social principles of Constitution, 19–20, 22–3
sovereignty of the people, 77–8, 168, 539
Soviet Union, 7–8, 22
Soyinka, Wole, 19
Speaker of house of representatives, 214–15, 226, 233
special advisers to president, 133–4, 137, 233
speech, freedom of, 250, 457–79
Sri Lanka, 12–14, 255, 260–1, 288–9
staff of national assembly, 215–16
standing committees of national assembly, 222
standing orders of national assembly, 214, 220, 222, 244
state ownership: major sectors of the economy, 19–20; natural resources, 523; newspaper industry, 466; radio and television, 64, 106, 528
states: boundaries, 234; courts of justice, 255–6, 298–9, 301, 304, 310–11, 345; creation of states, 29–30, 233; deputy governor, 81–2; division of powers, 25–7, 29–35, 37–51, 53–74; economic development, 29–30; equality of status, 41–4; governor, 26, 81–2; houses of assembly, 235; judicial service commission, 303, 305; number of states, 25, 29–30, 44–5, 47; reasonable balance in area and population, 43–4; representation in government and agencies, 25–7; secession or insurrection,

38–9; single constitution for federal and state governments 15–16, 25–7, 50–1; territorial area, 61
statutory corporations, 381–2
statutory instruments, 179
Stone, Justice, 286
strikes: right to strike, 487–8, 505, 508, 526–7
superior courts of record, 298–9, 345
supremacy of Constitution, 5–7, 12–13, 16
supreme court, 136–8, 145, 255, 296, 300–1, 310–13, 326–7, 345, 357
Swaziland, 357–9

Taft, William, 88–9
Tanzania, 10
taxation, 240
Taylor, Justice, 266
Technical Committee on Revenue Allocation, 30
tenure: of national assembly, 211–13, 233; of office of president, 31, 111–12, 137–8, 201–4, 233; of office of vice-president, 111–12
Thayer, James, 282–3, 316, 368
Thomas, Justice Omololu, 420, 520
torture, 410, 412
trade unions: 63, 483–514; registration, 506; state control, 505–14
transport and communications, 64
treaties, international, 164
trials: constitutional safeguards, 431–48

Tribunals of Inquiry Decree 1966, 391
Trinidad and Tobago, 487

Udoji, Chief Jerome, 134
Udoma, Justice Udo, 448
Uganda, 43–4
United Kingdom, 12–13, 77, 184–5, 225, 270
university staff, 377–8, 383, 387–8, 390
Uwaifo, Justice, 247

Vassiliades, Justice, 14
vice-president: 86, 111–14, 137; election and removal, 111–14, 207, 233; immunity from court action, 81–2; tenure of office, 111–12
Vile, M.J.C., 32
Vinson, Chief Justice, 90
voting in national assembly, 216–17

Washington, Justice, 282
Washington, George, 80, 150, 202
Wayas, Senator, 244
Wechsler, Herbert, 342–3
Wheare, Sir Kenneth, 44
Williams, Justice, 266–7
Wilson, President, 107
women: prohibition of discrimination, 453–5

Zambia, 10, 13, 83–4, 133, 244–5, 250–1, 287, 347